CAUSES

OF

UNEMPLOYMENT

EDITED BY

C. A. GREENHALGH, P. R. G. LAYARD
AND A. J. OSWALD

CLARENDON PRESS · OXFORD
1983

Oxford University Press, Walton Street, Oxford OX2 6DP

London Glasgow New York Toronto
Delhi Bombay Calcutta Madras Karachi
Kuala Lumpur Singapore Hong Kong Tokyo
Nairobi Dar es Salaam Cape Town
Melbourne Auckland
and associate companies in
Beirut Berlin Ibadan Mexico City

Published in the United States
by Oxford University Press, New York

OXFORD is a trade mark of Oxford University Press

British Library Cataloguing in Publication Data

The Causes of unemployment.
1. Unemployment
I. Greenhalgh, C. A.   II. Layard, Richard
III. Oswald, A. J.   IV. Review of economic
studies   V. Oxford economic papers
331.13'7   HD5707.5

ISBN 0-19-828484-5

Printed in Northern Ireland
at The Universities Press (Belfast) Ltd.

CONTENTS

THE CAUSES OF UNEMPLOYMENT

By C. A. GREENHALGH, P. R. G. LAYARD and A. J. OSWALD

SINCE 1973 unemployment has risen sharply, with bigger rises in Europe than in America. In many European countries there has been no year since 1973 in which unemployment fell to any significant degree. This has led more economists than before to focus on explaining the medium-term level of unemployment. At the same time, the search has continued for a convincing explanation of short-term fluctuations. Because of the importance of these problems, two journals, *The Review of Economic Studies* and *Oxford Economic Papers*, decided independently to publish Special Issues on the topic of unemployment.[1] This volume brings these issues together as Parts I and II respectively. Part I is written by a group of mainly British and American economists and looks at unemployment both in Europe and America; Part II is by British economists, writing about Britain.

The central starting point for most of the papers is the idea of the natural rate of unemployment (sometimes called the NAIRU, or non-accelerating inflation rate of unemployment). This is probably best defined as the long-run rate of unemployment: it is the unemployment that prevails if price expectations are fulfilled. The concept does not require that the world be perfectly competitive, as is still occasionally believed: the natural rate *could* be the product of some non-market-clearing process in which wages are determined for example by trades unions.

It is clearly vitally important to explain the determinants of this natural rate, and some of the papers in both Parts I and II try to do just this, using a number of different frameworks. The natural rate, it transpires, is affected among other things by unemployment benefits, taxes, trade union activity, and structural change. In addition it increases in the medium term if the rate of productivity growth falls or if the terms of trade change unfavourably—both of which happened in the 1970s.

Once the natural rate has been explained, the second key issue is what determines how unemployment fluctuates around its natural rate. Here there are two main approaches. One of these starts from the market-clearing approach to the natural rate and then maintains that, even when we are away from the natural rate, the market clears, and workers are on their supply curves. What drives the business cycle on the supply side is that in booms wages are higher than average so that workers are more willing to work; the reverse is true in slumps. This is the 'inter-temporal substitution hypothesis' made famous by Lucas and Rapping (1970); it corresponds to an equilibrium view of the cycle. The alternative approach to the cycle is to maintain what (whatever the nature of the natural rate) markets do not clear at all points in the business cycle. Instead there is a wage-determining

---

[1] *Review of Economic Studies*, Vol. 49 (5), 1982, and *Oxford Economic Papers*, Vol. 35 (4), 1983.

process (Phillips curve) and it is this rather than a supply function which interacts with demand in order to determine employment.

Part I

In Part I the first two papers apply the disequilibrium approach to the cycle to European economies, as well as trying to explain more medium-term movements in the natural rate. The next two papers compare the inter-temporal substitution approach with the disequilibrium approach, for Britain and the U.S.; while the next two are tests for the U.S. of the inter-temporal substitution hypothesis. In general the inter-temporal substitution hypothesis does not fare well. Let us look at the papers one by one.

The first paper by Bruno and Sachs is one of a series in which they have attempted to explain stagflation in Western economies by the rise in the prices of raw materials (relative to the price of output). If raw material prices rise, then real wages have to fall if employment is to be maintained. But real wages only adjust downwards after unemployment has emerged. At the same time, the real return on capital falls and this reduces investment, which in turn requires further falls in real wages before full employment can be restored. Bruno and Sachs estimate the parameters of this model for U.K. manufacturing and then use the model to simulate the response of the economy to a rise in relative raw material prices—both under sticky and flexible real wages.

The approach of Grubb, Jackman and Layard is in the same spirit, but they focus more heavily on the process of wage-setting. Their aim is to explain not the level of unemployment as such, but the fact that it now takes much more unemployment to stop inflation increasing (i.e. that the NAIRU—the non-accelerating inflation rate of unemployment—has risen). In their model the wage equation involves some nominal inertia and does not shift when the feasible growth of real wages changes. Hence, if the feasible growth falls, either inflation or unemployment (or both) must increase. They estimate wage and price equations for 19 OECD countries, and use these to show how changes in materials prices and lower productivity growth explain in roughly equal measure why the NAIRU has risen since 1973. In a final section the authors estimate a model in which the wage equation does adjust to changes in growth, but they find the adjustment to be slow. This delay may reflect delayed perceptions of trade-unionists or long-term implicit contracts, but is not well understood.

Andrews and Nickell attempt to explain the growth of unemployment since the War in Britain, comparing the results of the equilibrium and disequilibrium approach. Their equilibrium model has labour supply varying due to inter-temporal substitution (as in the pioneering study by Lucas and Rapping). But they find that the inter-temporal labour supply response to transitory wages is neither stable nor plausible. They prefer the disequilibrium estimates of wage and price equations. In both types of model the authors try to explain the long-term (cycle-free) level of unemployment not by a time trend alone (like so many authors) but by behavioural variables. In explaining a growth of $3\frac{1}{2}$ percentage points of unemployment between 1950s and 1970s they give roughly equal weight to the rate of change of industrial structure, the benefits/income ratio, the trade-union mark-up, trade union membership and a time trend.

Ashenfelter and Card also investigate the inter-temporal substitution hypothesis in a model with sticky wages. But their approach is quite different. Instead of estimating structural equations, they estimate dynamic final form equations for wages, prices, interest rates and unemployment (for the U.S.A.). They then compare these estimates with what would be implied by specified versions of the alternative models. As regards the inter-temporal substitution hypothesis, they find too much autocorrelation in unemployment to be consistent with it, unless there is serial correlation in individual labour supply. As regards the overlapping-contracts model of wage stickiness, they find an absence of moving average error which ought to be present in the wage equation if the hypothesis is true.

Altonji investigates the inter-temporal substitution hypothesis by focussing largely on the structural labour supply equation, using U.S. data. He uses three different approaches, all of which yield results unfavourable to the hypothesis. In the first he uses rational expectations forecasts of long-run wage levels, rather than adaptive expectations as used in Lucas and Rapping's study. In the second, he used perfect foresight, while in the third he does not include future wage expectations as such but uses consumption as a variable that must reflect them. In nearly all these estimates the wage and price and interest rate terms cither have the wrong sign or are insignificant. But unanticipated money, when included, has the right sign.

Clark and Summers also investigate the inter-temporal substitution hypothesis in the U.S.A., but using the labour force participation rate rather than the employment rate as the variable to be explained. According to the inter-temporal substitution hypothesis, past employment will tend to lower present participation. The authors contrast this 'timing' hypothesis with the 'persistence' hypothesis, according to which past employment will tend to raise present participation. They argue that 'persistence' dominates. First they show how after the Second World War female participation stayed higher than would otherwise have been expected. Then they run time series regressions which fail to show wage effects consistent with the inter-temporal substitution hypothesis. Finally they run interstate cross-section regressions which suggest that the long-run employment rate has a positive effect on labour supply, while the short-run transitory employment rate is rarely positive and significant.

The final paper by Bruno and Sachs is addressed to the question of whether unemployment will result when oil prices rise or when a country discovers oil. To investigate this they develop a more ambitious dynamic model than previous writers, which allows for short-run capital specificity and long-run capital mobility, international capital flows, and far-sighted optimising behaviour by firms and households. The model is solved by numerical simulation. It confirms many earlier results and shows in particular the importance of the government's budgetary policy. But above all it underlines the adjustment problems which result if wages are sluggish.

Part II

Turning to Part II, the papers concentrate on three possible reasons for a rise in equilibrium unemployment.
(i) An increase in trade union strength.
(ii) A rise in real unemployment benefit.
(iii) An increase in the level of taxes on employment.
What is the mechanism by which the equilibrium rate of unemployment might be raised by unions, unemployment benefit and labour taxes? One way to capture the argument is shown in Fig. 1. Imagine a two-sector economy where good X is produced using unionised labour, n, and good Y is produced using non-union labour, l. Assume that the working population is fixed at P, that capital is immobile, that the two goods are traded on world markets, and that the government pays unemployment benefit b to those without a job. Assume that the non-union sector has a competitive labour market and that the union in the other sector can influence wages by controlling entry. These assumptions—each of which is rather extreme—give a picture like that below. The demand curve for union labour is $n(w^u)$, that for non-union labour (read right to left) is $l(w^n)$. Union indifference curves

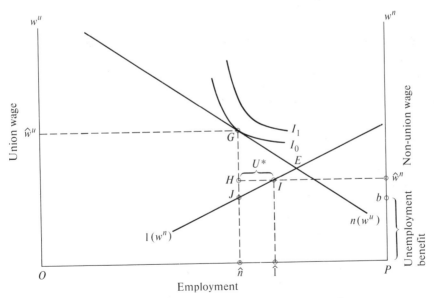

FIG. 1. The effects of unions and unemployment benefit.

(much like those assumed in the second paper by Nickell and Andrews, by Minford, and the theoretical article by Snower) are drawn in as I_0 and I_1. The union is assumed to like high wages and high employment, and to have a quasi-concave utility function. It takes the firms' labour demand curve as outside its control, treating it rather like a consumer would his budget constraint, and picks its target real wage. Then, if the union can enforce this, the equilibrium amount of employment in the union sector is $\hat{n}$.

In a world without unemployment benefits (so $b = 0$) the wage in the non-union sector would have to fall to point J, to ensure that the number of jobs in the non-union sector became $\hat{n}P$. If the government pays unemployment benefit of b, the reservation wage is likely to be something above this—leisure may have value, despite the social stigma of unemployment— at, say, level $\hat{w}^n$. Then the equilibrium rate of unemployment, denoted U^*, is given by the line HI. Two things here cause it to be positive. First, the union rations jobs in its sector, and hence there bids up the wage and the marginal product of labour. Second, the existence of state unemployment benefit prevents the non-union wage from falling to clear that labour market. Taxes on labour are reasonably easy to introduce into this model. They tend to lower the demand curves for labour and thus to increase the gap between H and I. The model can also be altered and extended in various ways. Nickell, for example, thinks of the union bargaining with the firm to fix a wage rate somewhere between G and E. Minford assumes that the union maximises the discounted wage bill subject to a partial adjustment labour demand function and so introduces dynamics. Snower has an explicit macroeconomic framework tied in with a neo-classical foundation. Nevertheless, the diagram does seem to capture the main ideas on how trade unions, unemployment benefit and taxes on employment might raise the equilibrium rate of unemployment.

In the empirical implementation of this type of model the paper by Nickell and Andrews has a certain amount in common with that by Minford. Both assume that trade union behaviour can be treated as if it were based on utility-maximising axioms, and both set up estimating equations for real wages and either employment or unemployment derived from a larger structural model of demand and supply in the labour market. Nevertheless, some of their precise answers differ rather radically. In particular, Minford finds much larger unemployment effects from unions and unemployment benefit. However, both analyses agree that labour taxes have had a significant effect on unemployment. The empirical findings of Nickell/Andrews and Minford thus confirm the directions of effect of these variables but disagree as to their magnitudes. However, since policies to reduce unemployment via these effects have welfare implications (lower wages in union jobs, lower benefits when unemployed, smaller public expenditure or alternative forms of taxation) we need to narrow the range of estimates before existing government policies are modified in response. Nevertheless, these two analyses of the distortions produced by monopoly elements and by taxes and subsidies in the labour market are contributions to our understanding of what determines the equilibrium rate of unemployment.

Further evidence concerning the impact of employment taxes is provided by Sumner and Ward. Their estimates of an expectations-augmented Phillips curve, which includes these taxes as determinants of money wages, suggest that National Insurance contributions and income tax significantly influenced wages in the last decade. Furthermore, they find that the long-run Phillips curve has become vertical, although there still appears to be a trade-off between unemployment and inflation in the short-run. They estimate that the 'natural' rate of unemployment averaged around 4% in the 1970s and attribute the change which they detect in the wage equation at the beginning of that decade to a change in the formation of expectations. Sumner and Ward make a further contribution in response to our initial set of questions, by investigating the impact of incomes policies in the post-war period. They report that, with one exception, incomes policies failed to make any detectable impact and even in the exceptional case the reduction in wage inflation was followed by 'catching up' which largely nullified its effects. These findings confirm earlier studies (see Fallick and Elliot, 1981), indicating that temporary incomes policies which fail to change the underlying wage determination process are unlikely to have any lasting impact.

The three papers by Dilnot and Morris, Lynch and McCormick differ from the other articles in this volume in that they examine micro-economic models and cross-section data. Even so, they link in with the main themes identified so far. Dilnot and Morris use the Family Expenditure Survey to provide some important figures, namely the distribution of income replacement rates which would be faced by U.K. families if the main earner were to become or remain unemployed. They show that in the decade up to 1978 the average replacement rate followed a steady upward path. However, the removal of Earnings Related Supplement and the taxation of unemployment benefits have combined to reduce short-run replacement rates. The 1982 mean rate, under assumptions discussed in the paper, was 0.61 for the 13 week period; in 1968 the figure was 0.66. Long run replacement rates are little different from in the late nineteen sixties. Relatively few individuals face replacement rates above 0.90, with the exception of families with three or more children, of whom nearly a third have incomes in work which hardly exceed benefits when unemployed. Unless work-related expenses are a very high proportion of earnings; these findings show that the majority would incur significant financial losses as a result of becoming or remaining unemployed.

Lynch focuses on unemployment among young people, using hypotheses drawn from the theory of job search. Lynch's methodology is not of the form used by Nickell and Andrews and by Minford: it follows the approach of Lancaster and Chesher (1984) in which an analytical model of job search is used to deduce the effects of changes in unemployment benefits and demand conditions on the probability of re-employment. When applied to data for 1980, this model suggests that demand factors are at least as important as supply factors—or, in other words, young people are not simply unemployed because they receive attractive unemployment benefits.

McCormick asks whether U.K. policy towards council and private rental housing has influenced unemployment either by affecting geographical mobility and thus the location of excess-supply unemployment; or by unreasonably increasing the natural rate of unemployment for tenants. These influences might arise from the location-specific nature of housing subsidies in the rental sector, which inhibit migration, or from the effects of housing policy on replacement ratios and household wealth. Using logit models of unemployment incidence, he finds that the equilibrium rate of unemployment is dependent on the mix of housing tenure. Outright owners have the highest unemployment probability, followed by council tenants and tenants in private rented accommodation, with mortgagees having by far the lowest probability. But over the life cycle the mean probability for tenants is about the same as that for those in the owner-occupied sector. The evidence suggests that council housing has affected the geographical pattern of unemployment by influencing the equilibrium rates of unemployment between tenure groups more than by influencing the geographical pattern of excess supply unemployment.

Conclusion

We believe that the essays in this book throw considerable light on the causes of unemployment. But there are still major mysteries. Few, if any, of the authors would claim that they completely understood the huge rises in unemployment which have occurred in the last ten years. We hope this book will stimulate much more work on this topic, which is so important to our society.

Review of Economic Studies (1982) XLIX, 679–705
0034-6527/82/00540679$00.50

Input Price Shocks and the Slowdown in Economic Growth: The Case of U.K. Manufacturing

MICHAEL BRUNO
Hebrew University and NBER

and

JEFFREY SACHS
Harvard University and NBER

This paper provides a theoretical and empirical analysis of the effects of input price shocks on economic growth, with a focus on United Kingdom manufacturing in the 1970s. The theoretical model predicts a discrete decline in output and productivity after an input price rise, and a longer-run slowdown in productivity growth, real wage growth, and capital accumulation. These features characterize the United Kingdom and most other OECD economies after 1973. The empirical results confirm the important role of input prices in recent U.K. adjustment, but also point to an important role for other supply and demand factors.

Two types of explanations have been offered for the sharp deterioration in U.K. economic performance in the past decade, focusing respectively on demand and supply factors. A standard Keynesian view holds that macroeconomic demand management has been either too expansionary or too contractionary, and that rising unemployment and falling output reflect the burden of anti-inflationary policies. An alternative view holds that various supply shocks are the main source of the poor output performance. In this interpretation, higher raw material prices (particularly oil), competition from the newly-industrializing countries (NICs), and perhaps an independent decline in productivity growth, all have lowered output growth and raised unemployment.

There is little doubt that both supply and demand shocks played their roles in the recent experience, and that their relative importance has varied over time. Buiter and Miller (1981) have argued persuasively, for example, that the sharp rise in unemployment during the Thatcher experiment (since 1979) is largely the result of demand restraint. In general, however, there is no settled macroeconomic framework for disentangling which factors are at work in particular cyclical episodes. The theoretical analyses in Malinvaud (1977, 1980) and related studies offer a promising advance in this direction, though they remain far from empirical implementation.

In this study, we focus our attention on the supply shocks, particularly raw material price increases, to see if they alone can take us far in understanding the recent experience. Qualitatively, the answer is "yes", since a model of input price shocks predicts a short-run decline in output and productivity after such a disturbance, and a longer-run slowdown in productivity growth, capital accumulation, and real wage growth. All of these features characterize Britain, and most other OECD economies, since 1973. Quantitatively, the answer is mixed. The evidence suggests that raw material price increases have had significant output, employment, and productivity effects, and that these effects have worked mainly through profitability and the incentive to produce and invest, rather than through aggregate demand. But there is also evidence that: (1) the raw material price increases alone do not explain Britain's recent productivity debacle; and (2) demand explanations are needed to account for deep recessionary episodes (such as 1975 and 1980–1981).

Table I highlights the decline in performance of U.K. manufacturing since 1973, and Table II depicts the severe squeeze in profitability that has accompanied that decline.

TABLE I

Output, inputs, and productivity in U.K. manufacturing[1]

	Output	Capital input	Labour input	Labour productivity	Apparent intermediate input	Total factor productivity
1960–1973	3·0	3·7	−0·9	3·9	2·5	0·8
1973–1975	−3·9	2·2	−2·6	−1·3	−4·6	−1·9
1975–1978	1·3	1·8	0·0	1·8	2·5	−1·5
1973–1978	−0·8	2·0	−1·0	0·2	−0·4	−1·7

Notes:
1. Percentage changes, at annual rate.
2. *Source:* Dicks-Mireaux data.

TABLE II

Profitability in U.K. manufacturing

	Product[1] wage	Product price of intermediate inputs	Labour share of value-added (average)	Pre-tax profit rate (average)	Net valuation ratio (average)
1960–1972	4·4	−0·5	0·72	9·5	0·69
1972–1975	3·7	5·3	0·77	5·5	0·37
1975–1978	−0·2	−1·4	0·78	4·0	0·27
1972	6·8	−0·4	0·73	7·8	0·64
1973	3·4	14·3	0·72	7·6	0·48
1974	1·5	11·0	0·81	3·3	0·27
1975	6·3	−8·0	0·81	3·1	0·11
1976	0·7	5·3	0·80	3·2	0·33
1977	−8·0	−3·2	0·77	4·7	0·27
1978	7·1	6·1	0·77	5·0	0·37

Notes:
1. Percentage change per year.
2. *Source:* Columns 1–3, Dicks-Mireaux data. Column 4, from W. E. Martin and M. O'Connor, Table B2, p. 23. Column 5, from Summers and Poterba (1981), Table 1, p. 30.

From the first table note that the slowdown in growth of gross output reflects a growth slowdown in capital and labour inputs, as well as an apparent decline in total factor productivity (TFP) growth. Unfortunately, there is no published volume index of intermediate inputs, so that we were forced to create our own variable. For a number of reasons (see Data Appendix) we regard our constructed index and thus our estimates of TFP, as subject to fairly large error. It must be emphasized that a TFP slowdown cannot easily be accounted for by an input price shock (aside from appeal to various measurement errors that such a shock might induce); to the extent that such a slowdown has occurred, it will require an explanation outside of our framework below.

Table II provides some basis for the supply shock view of U.K. performance. On a variety of measures, we see evidence for a deep and sustained squeeze on profitability in U.K. production that goes far beyond short-run cyclical fluctuations in labour's share of value. In the 1960s, the wage relative to product prices (henceforth the "product wage", denoted $W_P = W/P$) grew at about the rate of productivity increase. Labour's share of value in manufacturing, and the rate of return to capital remained fairly stable. Between 1969 and 1975, product wage growth accelerated substantially, squeezing profits sharply. Moreover, when intermediate input prices rose in 1973, and TFP growth declined, real wages failed to decelerate, further intensifying the profit squeeze. Product wage growth slowed sharply under the Labour Government incomes policies during 1976–1977, but then rebounded during 1978–1980. The final column, denoted "valuation ratio", records the valuation of corporate capital (in "industrial and commercial companies") relative to the replacement cost of corporate capital. This ratio, often denoted "Tobin's q", is an indicator of market expectations of future profitability of the existing capital stock. Under specific conditions, described below, it is also a good measure of the incentive to invest. Clearly, it has fallen very sharply in the 1970s.

The essence of the supply-side argument is that low output growth in the 1970s reflects poor incentives to supply output, rather than insufficient demand. Low investment rates, similarly, are deemed to reflect low expectations of future profitability. On a purely statistical basis, there is a strong link between profitability and output (Morley (1979) has also examined this link). The following regressions attest to this correlation; the theoretical models below provide a structural basis for such relationships:[1]

$$\log(Q_t) = 5 \cdot 8 + 0 \cdot 033 \text{ Time} + 0 \cdot 35 \text{ (Profit Share)}_{t-1} \qquad R^2 = 0 \cdot 97$$
$$\quad\;\; (46 \cdot 1)\; (20 \cdot 1) \qquad\qquad (5 \cdot 6) \qquad\qquad\qquad d.w. = 1 \cdot 39$$

$$\log(Q_t) = 7 \cdot 2 + \;\; 0 \cdot 036 \text{ Time} + 0 \cdot 33 \text{ (Profit Rate)}_{t-1} \qquad R^2 = 0 \cdot 97$$
$$\quad\;\; (21 \cdot 1)\; (19 \cdot 3) \qquad\qquad (6 \cdot 2) \qquad\qquad\qquad d.w. = 1 \cdot 67$$

The preceding evidence is of course circumstantial, and must be bolstered by more formal analysis. Our first step is to build a model of dynamic output supply for a competitive firm using capital, labour, and an intermediate input. Using that model, we depict the time path of adjustment to a rise in the product price of intermediate inputs. This adjustment is studied under alternative assumptions of real wage stickiness and full labour market clearing. In the succeeding section, the various equations of the model are estimated. The econometric estimates provide strong support for the view that wage and raw material price shocks were major determinants of declining profitability in the 1970s, and that output and employment fluctuations are linked to those shocks. While the equations clearly suffer from our maintained hypothesis of continuous output market clearing, the supply model still performs rather well. The short-run and long-run effects of a supply shock are measured, and various numerical simulations are undertaken. Possible extensions are considered in a concluding section.

1. THEORY OF AN INPUT PRICE SHOCK

(a) The value-maximizing competitive firm

Our analysis of input price shocks begins with the supply behaviour of a value-maximizing competitive firm. The firm produces gross output Q according to the well-behaved constant returns to scale production function $Q = Q(L, K, N)$ using labour, L, capital, K, and a raw material, N. The price of output is P, and that of the raw material is P_N. For the time being assume that the relative price $\Pi_n = P_n/P$ is given (as is the case if both N and Q are tradeable goods in a small open economy). We denote the product price of labour as $W_P = W/P$, the nominal cost of capital as r, and the real cost of capital as $R(=r - \dot{P}/P)$, where the dot signifies rate of change.

As a basic model, assume that the firm can costlessly and instantaneously adjust the inputs of L and N, while it can adjust K only subject to convex costs of adjustment.

The treatment of K as a quasi-fixed factor and L as a pure variable factor is admittedly extreme, and is relaxed in some of the empirical work later on. Denote the rate of gross capital formation as J, and the rate of depreciation as d, so the $\dot{K} = J - dK$. Total investment expenditure, I, includes payments on J, as well as adjustment costs. Let P_J be the cost of a unit of physical capital, and $\Pi_J \ (= P_J/P)$ its real price. Following Hayashi (1982), adjustment costs per unit of J are assumed to rise as a function of J/K, so that $I = \pi_J J + \phi(J/K)J$, where $\phi(\cdot)$ is the per-unit adjustment cost.

Under conditions of perfect foresight, the real market value of the firm is simply the discounted value of cash flow:

$$V = \int_0^\infty e^{-\Delta}[Q - W_P L - \Pi_n N - I]\,dt \tag{1}$$

where $\Delta = \int_0^t R(\tau)\,d\tau$.

The goal of the firm is to maximize V subject to the production technology, and the costs of adjustment in capital accumulation. By assumption, the firm is never demand-constrained in the output or factor markets.[2] The results of this maximization are straightforward: for a given K, the firm should short-run profit maximize, hiring L and N to the point where marginal productivities equal current factor costs. Investment should be undertaken as a function of the entire future profit stream, which depends on the entire future path of factor costs. The dependence of L and N on *current* costs, and I on expected *future* costs, results of course from the assumption about costs of adjustment.

The specific conditions for optimization are:[3]

$$Q_L = W_P \tag{2c}$$
$$Q_N = \Pi_N \tag{2b}$$
$$J = \phi(\tau)\cdot K \tag{2c}$$
$$\tau = \int_0^\infty e^{-\tilde{\Delta}}[Q_K + (J/K)^2\phi'(J/K)]dt, \quad \text{where } \tilde{\Delta} = \int_0^t [R(s)+d]ds \tag{2d}$$
$$V = \tau K \tag{2e}$$
$$\dot{K} = J - dK. \tag{2f}$$

(2a) and (2b) define short-run factor demands. (2c) is the investment equation, with J/K a rising function of Tobin's q, denoted as τ, the real equity value of a unit of the firm's capital. The value of τ may be written as in (2d), as the discounted value of the marginal productivity of capital. Notice that this marginal product is the sum of Q_K and $(J/K)^2\phi'(J/K)$, where the latter term is the contribution of an increment of K to a reduction in adjustment costs. (2e) shows that the value of the firm is simply τK.

In the specific case of linear adjustment costs, with

$$\phi = \frac{\phi_0}{2}\cdot\frac{J}{K},$$

the investment function is given by $J/K = (\tau - \Pi_J)/\phi_0$. In the steady state, $(\bar{J}/\bar{K}) = d$, so $\bar{\tau} = \Pi_J + \phi_0 d$. (The notation $\bar{x}$ will signify the steady state value of x.) From (2d), we may therefore derive that $\bar{Q}_K$ must equal $(R+d)\Pi_J + dR\phi_0 + \phi_0 d^2/2$ (note that $Q_K = R\Pi_J$ for $d = 0$). We will denote this critical long-run value of Q_K by $\bar{R}$. Clearly, τ and therefore investment will tend to be high if Q_K is expected to exceed $\bar{R}$ for an extended period.

In the simulations later we will modify the investment function to allow for certain features of the (post-1973) U.K. tax provisions on corporate earnings, depreciation, and

investment. Specifically, for corporate tax rate t_C, full expensing of new capital investment, and full equity financing, the investment equation is changed slightly to be

$$J/K = (\tau + t_c - \Pi_J)/[\phi_0(1 - t_c)]$$

Summers and Poterba [1981] provide a detailed account of how U.K. tax provisions
affect the form of the J/K function.

(b) The factor price frontier

The effects on supply of a shift in Π_n are governed by (2), which can best be understood
by appeal to the factor price frontier (FPF).[4] The FPF summarizes the information about
the gross output technology in terms of the maximal combinations of the three marginal
factor products, $F(Q_L, Q_K, Q_N) = 0$, which by substitution of (2a) and (2b) may be written
as $F(W_P, Q_K, \Pi_n) = 0$. The curve F_0, drawn in $W_P - Q_K$ space (see Figure 1) for a given
relative raw-material price Π_{n_0} is downward sloping and convex to the origin. The slope

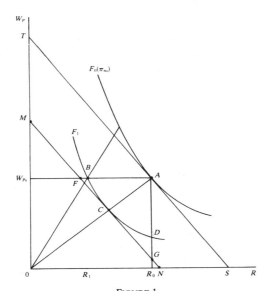

FIGURE 1

The factor price frontier

of the tangent at the point A measures the capital/labour ratio that corresponds to the
pair of factor returns (Q_K, W_{P_0}). Its intercept on the W_P axis (OT) measures Y/L, where
Y is $Q - \Pi_n N$ (i.e. value added in units of the final good). Likewise, the intercept on
the Q_K axis (OS) measures Y/K. The elasticity of FPF at the point $A = SA/TA$ measures
the relative shares of capital and labour in Y.

   Weak separability of the production function $\{Q = Q[V(L, K), N]\}$ implies weak
separability of the dual FPF, i.e. F_0 takes the form $F[f(W_P, Q_K), \Pi_n] = 0$. A raw-material
price increase, like Hicks-neutral technical regress, is thus represented by a homothetic
inward shift of F_0 to F_1. At the point C on the new FPF, on the ray OA, the capital/labour
ratio is the same as at A. Thus, for $K = K_0$ and $L = L_0$, a rise in Π_n shifts the factor
returns from A to C. We will call C the point of short-run adjustment (when $K = K_0$,
$L = L_0$). Following a rise in Π_n marginal factor products at C are reduced by the same

ratio from their original level at A. Total real income per unit of labour (Y/L) falls by the same proportion from OT to OM (and Y/K from OS to ON). Since $Q_K < \bar{R}$, there will tend to be disinvestment at A. The case of real wage rigidity at W_{P_0}, which may be termed the *very short run*, is represented by the point B where Q_K and Y/K must of necessity fall by more than at C and the capital/labour ratio is higher than at C. At the given capital stock, K_0, L will fall and unemployment will emerge.[5]

The polar case to the very short run $(W_P = W_{P_0})$ is that of an externally imposed long-run real rate of return $(Q_K = \bar{R})$. This is represented by the point D, to be termed the *long run*, at which the real wage and the capital/labour ratio are below their levels at C. In contrast to C, the point D represents an equilibrium steady-state level after capital has adjusted downward to the given real rate of return, $\bar{R}$. With full employment of labour, capital and output (gross and net) at D are both lower than at the initial point A.

Of course, the designations of very short run, short run, and long run responses to a change in Π_N are stylizations that must be flushed-out in a fully dynamic model. To get such a model, we must append a wage equation to (2a)–(2e), as we do in Section 1e below. We will consider two types of wage equations: continuous market clearing, and a Phillips curve mechanism.

First, however, the graphical representation can be given full analytical content. Consider any m-factor constant returns production function whose output (in logs) is q. Let the (log) quantity and product price of factor i be denoted by a_i and w_i $(i = 1, 2, \ldots, m)$, respectively.[6] Next, denote the cost share of the ith factor by s_i and let the Hicks-Allen elasticity of substitution be σ_{ij} where $\sigma_{ij} s_i = (w_j/a_i)(\partial a_i/\partial w_j)$. Using dots for rates of change, the unit factor demand functions are:

$$\dot{a}_i - \dot{q} = \sum_{j=1}^{m} \sigma_{ij} s_j \dot{w}_j \tag{3}$$

and

$$\sum_{j=1}^{m} \sigma_{ij} \dot{w}_j = 0 \quad \text{for all } i = 1, 2, \ldots, m.$$

Next we write down the factor-price-frontier in rate of change form:

$$\sum_{j=1}^{m-1} s_j \dot{w}_j = 0. \tag{4}$$

Equation (4) can be substituted into equation (3) to solve out for the case in which one of the factor (say, the mth) is fixed (in our case: capital is fixed in the short run). Thus, equation (3) can be rewritten:

$$\dot{a}_i - \dot{q} = \sum_{j=1}^{m} (\sigma_{ij} - \sigma_{im}) s_j \dot{w}_j \qquad (i = 1, 2, \ldots, m). \tag{3'}$$

Applying equation (3') to the three factor case (L, N, K), we get

$$\dot{l} - \dot{q} = s_l(\sigma_{ll} - \sigma_{lk})\dot{w}_p + s_n(\sigma_{ln} - \sigma_{lk})\dot{\pi}_n \tag{5}$$

$$\dot{n} - \dot{q} = s_l(\sigma_{nl} - \sigma_{nk})\dot{w}_p + s_n(\sigma_{nn} - \sigma_{nk})\dot{\pi}_n \tag{6}$$

$$\dot{k} - \dot{q} = s_l(\sigma_{kl} - \sigma_{kk})\dot{w}_p + s_n(\sigma_{kn} - \sigma_{kk})\dot{\pi}_n. \tag{7}$$

Equation (7), when reversed in sign $(\dot{q} - \dot{k})$, is the short-run supply function. Since $\sigma_{kk} < 0$, this readily shows that output (per unit of capital) is a negative function of the raw material price (π_n) when capital and raw materials are co-operant factors $(\sigma_{kn} > 0)$. Also, it is a negative function of the real wage (W_P) if capital and labour are co-operant factors $(\sigma_{kl} > 0)$.

By subtracting equation (5) from equation (7), we get an expression for the labour/capital ratio and likewise find that L/K is negatively related to w_p (for a given π_n) if $\sigma_{lk} > 0$, and is negatively related to π_n (at given w_p) as long as $\sigma_{kn} + \sigma_{lk} \geq \sigma_{ln} + \sigma_{kk}$. The latter condition is automatically satisfied in the case of raw material separability $(\sigma_{ln} = \sigma_{kn})$ to which we now turn.[7]

When separability $Q[V(L, K), N]$ is assumed, these equations can be further simplified. Since now $\sigma_{nl} = \sigma_{nk}$, equation (6) now becomes:

$$\dot{n} - \dot{q} = -\sigma \dot{\pi}_n \qquad (6')$$

where $\sigma = s_n(\sigma_{nk} - \sigma_{nn}) = \sigma_{nl} = \sigma_{nk}$ is the elasticity of substitution between V and N in Q. Similarly, it is easy to show that $s_l(\sigma_{kl} - \sigma_{ll}) = s_k(\sigma_{kl} - \sigma_{kk}) = \sigma_1$, is the elasticity of substitution between L and K in V. We can now write down the output supply per unit of capital and labour demand per unit of capital in the following simplified form:

$$\dot{q} - \dot{k} = -\sigma_1 s_l s_k^{-1} \dot{w}_p - s_k^{-1} s_n \sigma_1 \eta \dot{\pi}_n \qquad (7')$$

$$\dot{l} - \dot{k} = -\sigma_1 (1 + s_k^{-1} s_l) \dot{w}_p - s_k^{-1} s_n \sigma_1 \dot{\pi}_n \qquad (8)$$

where $\eta = (1 - s_n)^{-1}(s_l + \sigma_1^{-1} \sigma s_k) \lessgtr 1$, if $\sigma_1 \gtrless \sigma$. These equations can also be obtained more directly (see below).

Let us now reconsider the implications of a raw material price increase under the various time specifications. In the very short run, if the real wage is rigid and the capital stock is held constant, we move from the point A to B in Figure 1. One gets an output and employment reduction, respectively, of

$$\dot{q} = -(s_k^{-1} s_n \sigma_1 \eta) \dot{\pi}_n,$$

$$\dot{l} = -(s_k^{-1} s_n \sigma_1) \dot{\pi}_n.$$

When the real wage is allowed to adjust downwards, so as to maintain full employment at a given capital stock (this was termed the "short-run": $\dot{l} = \dot{k} = 0$), the economy moves to the point C in Figure 1. From the equation for $\dot{l} - \dot{k}$ we get $\dot{w}_p = -(1 - s_n)^{-1} s_n \dot{\pi}_n$ and therefore the output reduction is mitigated by the amount $(1 - s_n)^{-1} s_n s_l s_k^{-1} \dot{\pi}_n$.[8]

Finally, as we move to the long run at point D in Figure 1, we have $Q_K = \bar{R}$, $L = \bar{L}$, i.e. $\dot{\rho} = \dot{l} = 0$, (where $\rho = \log(Q_K)$). A constant rate of return implies, by (4) that $\dot{w}_p = -s_l^{-1} s_n \dot{\pi}_n$. Therefore, the drop in $\dot{q} - \dot{k}$ of the very short run is now recovered by the larger amount $s_k^{-1} s_n \sigma_1 \dot{\pi}_n > (1 - s_n)^{-1} s_n \sigma_1 s_l s_k^{-1} \dot{\pi}_n$, i.e. Q/K at D must be higher than at C, but it is most probably still lower than that at the starting point A.

Since K now falls, total output never rebounds to the level at A. The total long-run change in output from A to D can be written down directly by observing the symmetry with the case of the very short run with capital now replacing the role of labour. Exchanging the subscripts in the coefficient of π_n in equation (7) or (7') we have for the total output drop:

$$\dot{q} = -s_n(\sigma_{ln} - \sigma_{ll}) \dot{\pi}_n = [-(1 - s_n)^{-1}(s_k s_l^{-1} \sigma_1 + \sigma)] s_n \dot{\pi}_n$$

while the output drop in the very short run can be written as

$$[-s_k^{-1} s_n \sigma_1 \eta] \dot{\pi}_n = [-(1 - s_n)^{-1}(s_l s_k^{-1} \sigma_1 + \sigma)] s_n \dot{\pi}_n.$$

There is partial output recovery in the long run from the very short run as long as $s_l/s_k > s_k/s_l$, a condition on the relative labour share which empirically usually holds.

(c) A two-level CES production function

A logical sequel to the production framework discussed in the previous section is the nested (or two-level) CES production function for which the elasticites of substitution σ and σ_1 (but not necessarily the factor shares) are assumed constant. Thus we assume $Q = Q[V(K, L), N]$, where the intermediate input (N) is separable from real value added (V) and consider Q to be a CES function in V, N, with constant elasticity of substitution σ, and V to be CES in K, L with constant elasticity σ_1. As before, we use the convention of applying small letters (where capital letters also appear) to denote the natural logarithms and use dots for the time derivatives (e.g. $l = \ln L$, $\dot{l} = L^{-1} \partial L / \partial t$). We now denote the output elasticity of labour (s_l, etc.), the intermediate input, and capital by α, β, and γ, respectively, and again assume constant returns to scale ($\alpha + \beta + \gamma = 1$).

For any production function we have (ignoring technical progress) the rate of change of output:

$$\dot{q} = \alpha \dot{l} + \beta \dot{n} + \gamma \dot{k} \tag{9}$$

and for the dual price structure (letting $\rho = \ln (Q_K)$):[9]

$$0 = \alpha \dot{w}_p + \beta \dot{\pi}_n + \gamma \dot{\rho} \tag{10}$$

which leads to the factor-price-frontier in rate-of-change form:

$$\dot{\rho} = -\gamma^{-1} (\alpha \dot{w}_p + \beta \dot{\pi}_n) \tag{11}$$

In the discussion that follows we shall introduce technical progress in labour-augmenting form (at the rate λ). This implies that instead of L, we write $L' = Le^{\lambda t}$ and $\dot{l}' = \dot{l} + \lambda$ and similarly write $W'_p = W_{pe}^{-\lambda t}$ (and $\dot{w}_p' = \dot{w}_p - \lambda$) instead of W_P. Thus, equation (11) will take the form:

$$\dot{\rho} = -\gamma^{-1} [\alpha (\dot{w}_p - \lambda) + \beta \dot{\pi}_n]. \tag{11'}$$

We rewrite the rate of change of output supply (equation (7')) and labour demand (equation (8)) in the following revised form:

$$\dot{q} = -\gamma^{-1} \sigma_1 [\alpha (\dot{w}_p - \lambda) + \beta \eta \dot{\pi}_n] + \dot{k} \tag{12}$$

$$\dot{l} = -\gamma^{-1} \sigma_1 [(1 - \beta)(\dot{w}_p - \lambda) + \beta \dot{\pi}_n] + \dot{k} - \lambda \tag{13}$$

where $\eta = (1 - \beta)^{-1} [\alpha + \sigma_1^{-1} \sigma \gamma]$ and $\eta \leq 1$ for $\sigma_1 \geq \sigma$.

These equations reveal the danger of measuring total factor productivity by subtracting weighted inputs of labour and capital, but *not* intermediate goods, from a measure of output. The "conventional" measure yields:

$$\dot{q} - (1 - \beta)^{-1} (\alpha \dot{l} + \gamma \dot{k}) = (1 - \beta)^{-1} (\alpha \lambda - \beta \sigma \dot{\pi}_n). \tag{14}$$

Thus, the measure confounds the normal technical progress term, $\alpha \lambda$, with technical regress due to the rise in raw material input prices, $-\beta \sigma \dot{\pi}_n$. We suspect that some of the apparent slowdown in TFP growth in manufacturing in the industrial countries in the 1970s can be ascribed to this term.

(d) *The Dynamic Adjustment Process*

The last step in the theoretical analysis is to describe the explicit adjustment paths of factor prices, employment, output, and the capital stock, between the very short run and the long run. We will work with the case of weak separability of N in the gross output function; it is straightforward to extend the analysis to the general case. We have seen that output and employment can be written as functions of K, π_n, and w_p, while $\dot{K}$ is a function, through Tobin's q, of the future paths of π_n and w_p. We will continue to take π_n as exogenous, but will now specify the wage dynamics in order to close the model. At many points in the following discussion we will drop inessential constant terms that arise from linearization.

The alternative assumptions are:

$$l = l^f \qquad \text{Continuous full employment} \tag{15a}$$

or

$$\dot{w}_p = \theta (l - l^f) \qquad \text{Phillips curve} \tag{15b}$$

In case (15b), we assume that firms' demand for labour at the posted wage is always satisfied, so that l may exceed l_f in the short term. (15a) or (15b), together with (2) defines a complete dynamic model.

In the full employment case, $\dot{l} = 0$, so according to (8) we see that:

$$\dot{w}_p = [\dot{k} + s_k^{-1} s_n \sigma_1 \dot{\pi}_n] / [\sigma_1 (1 + s_k^{-1} s_l)].$$

By integrating this expression, we can write (with w_p^f the full-employment wage):

$$w_p^f = w_{po} + [(k - k_0) + s_k^{-1} s_n \sigma_1 (\pi_n - \pi_{no})] / [\sigma_1 (1 + s_k^{-1} s_l)]. \tag{16}$$

Weak separability is sufficient to ensure that w_p^f is an increasing function of k, and a decreasing function of π_n. As a first-order approximation, the FPF can be written as:

$$\rho - \rho_0 = -(s_n / s_k)(\pi_n - \pi_{no}) - (s_l / s_k)(w_p - w_{po}) \tag{17}$$

Next, use (16) and (17) to write:

$$\rho = \rho_0 - (s_n / s_k)(\pi_n - \pi_{no}) - (s_l / s_k)[(k - k_0)$$
$$+ s_k^{-1} s_n \sigma_1 (\pi_n - \pi_{no})] / [\sigma_1 (1 + s_k^{-1} s_l)] \tag{18}$$

Therefore, with continuous market clearing, ρ is a decreasing function of k and π_n, which we will write as $\rho = -ak - b\pi_n$.

From the firm's valuation equation,

$$\dot{\tau} = R\tau - [Q_K - (\tau - 1)^2 / (2\phi_0)]$$

which can be linearized around $\bar{\tau} = 1 + \phi_0 d$ (see page 9) as

$$\dot{\tau} = (R + \zeta)\tau - Q_K$$

with ζ a positive constant. Since

$$\rho = \ln(Q_k) = ak - b\pi_n,$$

we can approximate Q_k by linear function in k and π_n as well. Ignoring constants, and linearizing around $Q_k = \bar{R}$, we have

$$Q_k \simeq -a\bar{R}k + b\bar{R}\pi_n = -\bar{a}k - \bar{b}\pi_n \quad (\bar{a} = a\bar{R}, \bar{b} = b\bar{R})$$

Substituting into the equation for τ, we have

$$\dot{\tau} = (R + \zeta)\tau + \bar{a}k + b\Pi_n.$$

Together with (2f) we have a 2×2 linear differential equation system in τ and k:

$$\begin{bmatrix} \dot{k} \\ \dot{\tau} \end{bmatrix} = \begin{bmatrix} 0 & 1/\phi_0 \\ \bar{a} & R + \zeta \end{bmatrix} \begin{bmatrix} k \\ \tau \end{bmatrix} + \begin{bmatrix} 0 \\ \bar{b} \end{bmatrix} \pi_n + \text{constants}. \tag{19}$$

The system is shown graphically in Figure 2. Adding the phase plane arrows to the figure, we see immediately that the system is saddlepoint stable, with the trajectory given by the dashed line. The equation for τ as an integral of future profitability, (2d), is *equivalent* to the condition that the stock market price τ always adjusts to keep the economy on the stable trajectory after an unanticipated shift in π_n.[10]

Figure 3 examines such a shift in π_n. The figure depicts an unanticipated, once-and-for-all jump in π_n, under the assumption that K, L, and N are all co-operant factors, so that $dk/d\pi_n < 0$. The $\dot{\tau} = 0$ locus shifts to the left, moving the long-run equilibrium from E_0 to E_1. At the time of the change in π_n, the equity price falls from $\bar{\tau}$ to $\tau(0)$, giving the signal to firms to reduce gross fixed capital formation. Over time, k_0 falls to reach a new lower level at E_1, as τ rises back to $\bar{\tau}$. What about real wages? On impact,

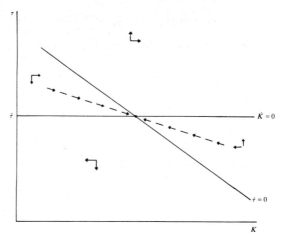

FIGURE 2

Dynamic path of K and τ.

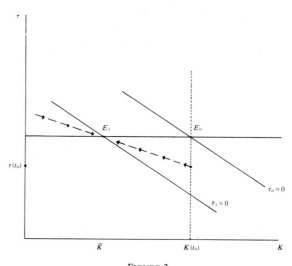

FIGURE 3

Dynamic response to a rise in Π_N.

we have a shift in w_p and ρ as shown from A to C in the FPF, Figure 1. Over time, w_p moves as in (16), and so $\dot{w}_p < 0$ along the entire path to E_1.

When the model is extended to include sluggish wage adjustment, both its realism and analytical complexity increase. First, we use the labour demand schedule in (8) to write employment as a function of k and τ:

$$l = l_0 + (k - k_0) - \sigma_1(1 + s_k^{-1} s_l)(w_p - w_{p_0}) - s_k^{-1} s_n \sigma_1(\pi_n - \pi_{n_0}). \tag{20}$$

Substituting this equation into the Phillips curve relationship (15b) we have

$$\dot{w}_p = \theta(k - k_0) - \theta\sigma_1(1 + s_k^{-1}s_l)(w_p - w_{po}) - \theta s_k^{-1}s_n\sigma_1(\pi_n - \pi_{no}). \tag{21}$$

Also, from the FPF,

$$\rho - \rho_0 = -(s_n/s_k)(\pi_n - \pi_{no}) - (s_l/s_k)(w_p - w_{po}).$$

Since $\dot{\tau}$ is $(R + \zeta)\tau - Q_k$, and $Q_k \simeq \bar{R}\rho$ (see above), we can write

$$\dot{\tau} = (R + \zeta)\tau + \bar{R}(s_n/s_k)(\pi_n - \pi_{no}) + \bar{R}(s_l/s_k)(w_p - w_{po}). \tag{22}$$

Equations (21) and (22), together with the capital accumulation equation describe a 3×3 differential equation system in τ, w_p, and k:

$$\begin{bmatrix} \dot{\tau} \\ \dot{k} \\ \dot{w}_p \end{bmatrix} = \begin{bmatrix} R+\zeta & 0 & (s_l/s_k)\bar{R} \\ 1/\phi_0 & 0 & 0 \\ 0 & \theta & -\theta\sigma_1(1+s_k^{-1}s_l) \end{bmatrix} \begin{bmatrix} \tau \\ k \\ w_p \end{bmatrix} + \begin{bmatrix} \bar{R}(s_n/s_k) \\ 0 \\ -s_k^{-1}s_n\sigma_1 \end{bmatrix} \pi_n + \text{constants}. \tag{23}$$

Once again, the dynamic system is saddlepoint stable,[11] so that τ always jumps after an unanticipated shock to keep the economy on a unique trajectory to long-run equilibrium. Because the system is 3×3, a graphical solution for the unique trajectory is not available.

For one-time, once-and-for-all jumps in π_n, we can determine τ according to a method suggested by Dixit (1981). He shows that $\tau - \bar{\tau}$ is a linear combination of $k - \bar{k}$ and $w_p - \bar{w}_p$, where the weights are the elements of the eigenvector corresponding to the positive characteristic root in (23). Thus

$$\tau - \bar{\tau} = a_1(k - \bar{k}) + a_2(w_p - \bar{w}_p) \tag{24}$$

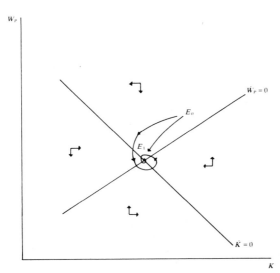

FIGURE 4

Direct and oscillatory approaches to equilibrium

where a_1 and a_2 are equal to

$$a_1 = a_2\theta/\lambda < 0$$

$$a_2 = -(s_l/s_k)\bar{R}[\theta\sigma_1(1+s_l/s_k)+\lambda] < 0$$

λ is the positive eigenvalue in the matrix in (23).

Notice that $\tau - \bar{\tau}$ is a negative function of $k - \bar{k}$ and $w_p - \bar{w}_p$. When π_n rises, both of these latter terms are positive under our assumptions, so that $\tau - \bar{\tau}$ correspondingly becomes negative. On impact, therefore, $\dot{k}$ must be less than zero. At time zero, with k and w_p as yet unchanged, the disturbance in π_n is exactly the *very short run* shock that was formally analyzed earlier.

To trace out the longer-run dynamic implications of the π_n increase, we may substitute (24) back into (23) to get

$$\begin{bmatrix} \dot{k} \\ \dot{w}_p \end{bmatrix} = \begin{bmatrix} (1/\phi_0)a_1 & (1/\phi_0)a_2 \\ \theta & -\theta\sigma_1(1+s_k^{-1}s_l) \end{bmatrix} \begin{bmatrix} k - \bar{k} \\ w_p - \bar{w}_p \end{bmatrix}. \tag{25}$$

Observe that (25) is globally stable, as confirmed by the phase diagram in Figure 4. Depending on ϕ_0 and ρ, the approach to equilibrium, say from E_0 to E_1, may be direct or oscillating. The traverse for these two cases is illustrated in the figure.

2. EMPIRICAL EVIDENCE ON INPUT PRICE SHOCKS: THE CASE OF U.K. MANUFACTURING

The goal of this section is to give a quantitative assessment of the dynamic responses in U.K. manufacturing to higher input prices in the 1970s. An investment equation, wage equation, and short-run production block are estimated using the framework of the previous section. The gross output technology is specialized to the CES case, and an output supply, labour demand, and FPF equation are jointly estimated with the appropriate cross-equation restrictions. A fully efficient estimation procedure would include the wage and investment equations in the jointly estimated block, but given the complexity of the resulting restrictions we did not pursue joint estimation of the complete model. The simplification is at the cost of some efficiency, but not consistency of the parameter estimates. One basic problem with the model as it now stands is the fact that while (11')–(13) are correct as written in rate-of-change form, the coefficients (i.e. elasticities) derived from output elasticities (α, β, γ) may vary (unless we are in a Cobb–Douglas world). One simplified approach, which we pursue here, is to consider a linear approximation of each equation around some fixed elasticities, which amounts to estimation of the equations in level form, and adding an intercept.[12] We shall consider both single equations and jointly estimated equations done on this basis.

To recapitulate, we estimate the following three equations for the gross output function:

$$\rho = \gamma_0 - (\alpha/\gamma)(w_P - \lambda t) - (\beta/\gamma)\pi_n \qquad \text{(factor-price frontier)} \tag{26}$$

$$q = \gamma_1 - (\alpha\sigma_1/\gamma)(w_P - \lambda t) - (\beta\eta\sigma_1/\gamma)\pi_n + k \qquad \text{(output supply)} \tag{27}$$

$$l = \gamma_2 - [(1-\beta)\sigma_1/\gamma](w_P - \lambda t) - (\beta\sigma_1/\gamma)\pi_n + k - \lambda t \quad \text{(labour demand)} \tag{28}$$

The γ_0, γ_1, γ_2 parameters are inessential constants. These equations are simply the level forms of (11'), (12), (13). Regression 1 in Table III shows a single-equation estimate of (26), reported earlier in Bruno (1981b). Regressions 2 and 3 show related estimates for Germany, and Japan. The estimates for the labour-augmenting productivity factor, λ, the share of profits in value-added, $\phi = \gamma/(1-\beta)$, and the share of intermediate goods in total costs, β, all have the right orders of magnitude. Figure 5 gives a graphic

TABLE III

Single-equation estimation of factor-price frontier, output supply, and labour demand schedules, 1956–1978

Dependent variable	$\log(w_P)_{-1}$	$\log(\pi_n)_{-1}$	$\log(K)$	time	$(S/Q)_{-1}$	Implied parameters λ	$\gamma/(1-\beta)$	β	$\bar{R}^2$	d.w.
1. ρ, United Kingdom	−4·994 (2·8)	−2·364 (3·8)	—	0·168 (2·3)	—	0·034	0·167	0·283	0·78	2·29
2. ρ, Germany	−3·698 (3·6)	−2·902 (3·4)	—	0·220 (3·1)	—	0·059	0·213	0·382	0·88	1·80
3. ρ, Japan	−1·426 (2·3)	−1·686 (3·3)	—	0·134 (1·8)	—	0·094	0·407	0·410	0·78	1·5
4. $\log(Q)$	0·1 (0·5)	−0·19 (1·1)	0·98 (2·2)	−0·01 (0·5)	—				0·97	1·5
5. $\log(Q)$	−0·1 (0·7)	−0·4 (3·1)	0·93 (3·0)	0·006 (0·55)	−0·25 (4·5)				0·99	2·16
6. $\log(L)$	−0·3 (2·0)	−0·01 (0·1)	0·5 (1·9)	−0·1 (1·7)	—				0·91	1·88
7. $\log(L)$	−0·3 (2·0)	−0·03 (0·3)	0·5 (1·9)	−0·01 (1·3)	0·0 (0·4)				0·91	1·8

Notes:
1. Numbers in parenthesis are t-statistics.
2. *Source*: Equations 1–3 are reproduced from Bruno (1981), Table II, p. 36. Equations 4–7 are for the United Kingdom, using Dicks-Mireaux data.

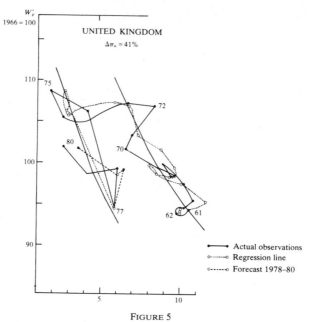

FIGURE 5

The factor-price-frontier for the U.K.

representation of the estimated factor price profile for the U.K. The chart is drawn in terms of the actual profit rate (Q_K) and the detrended product wage ($W'_P = W_{pe}^{-\lambda t}$), using the estimated λ. There is a clear upward movement in W'_P (at the expense of R) more or less along a given FPF before 1972, and a clear shift, to a new FPF after 1972. The U.K. evidences short-run real wage rigidity after the shift, during 1973–1976, and then a steep decline in W'_P in 1977. Data for 1978–1980 suggest that the product wage has more than recovered, and that R has continued to fall.

Notice that the estimated equation assumes a constant trend growth of TFP during 1961–1977. All shifts in labour-productivity after 1973 are therefore attributed to the higher level of π_n or a lower growth in (K/L), rather than to other productivity-reducing factors. While such a procedure yields plausible estimates, there is some worry that the method might attribute an independent decline in TFP to π_n. Since the apparent decline in TFP growth is so closely timed to the material price shock, we were not able to separate the two effects in our econometric estimates. We attempted to allow for a shift in λ after 1973, but the high multicollinearity of the time shift and Π_n led to unstable parameter estimates and high standard errors.

Regressions 5–6 show two versions of the single-equation estimation of the output supply function, and regressions 7–8 show analogous regressions for the labour demand schedule. These are annual ordinary-least-squares regressions for 1956–1978. After some experimentation with OLS and TSLS versions of the equations, we determined that *lagged* rather than current factor prices were more decisive for output supply and labour input. The importance of these lags probably reflects costs of adjustment in altering the variable factor inputs and/or a lead time in production planning. The simple equations do not perform particularly well, as the wage is insignificant in the output equation and the intermediate input is insignificant in the labour demand equation. The

TABLE IV

Linearized CES model for U.K. manufacturing[1]

	Factor price frontier			Model version and equation output equation			Labour equation		
	A	B	C	A	B	C	A	B	C
Coefficient Estimates									
Constant	-9.163	-9.215	-6.685	-5.247	-4.268	-3.753	-6.029	-4.648	-4.583
	(0.318)	(0.395)	(0.879)	(0.084)	(0.121)	(0.222)	(0.085)	0.186	
w_P	-2.714	-2.617	-1.941	-0.841	-0.437	-0.227	-1.50	-0.605	-0.345
	(0.359)	(0.438)	(0.597)	(0.091)	(0.065)	(0.115)	(0.104)	(0.080)	(0.161)
π_N	-1.044	-1.453	-2.098	-0.318	-0.337	-0.417	-0.323	-0.243	-0.246
	(0.233)	(0.225)	(0.371)	(0.104)	(0.058)	(0.099)	(0.077)	(0.048)	(0.092)
$\dotplus$	0.0796	0.0785	0.0683	0.0247	0.0131	0.0080	0.0044	-0.0119	-0.0231
	(0.0132)	(0.0167)	(0.0231)	(0.0034)	(0.0023)	(0.0037)	(0.0031)	(0.0025)	(0.0072)
V_{-1}	—	—	-0.837	—	-0.246	-0.388	—	-0.341	-0.274
			(0.281)		(0.036)	(0.060)		(0.053)	(0.083)
Statistics									
SE	0.1162	0.1122	0.0945	0.0399	0.0231	0.0290	0.0366	0.0233	0.0266
DW	1.3037	1.3714	1.9262	0.8430	1.3188	1.7352	0.9980	1.1342	1.1651
Mean of Dependent Variables	-6.82493	-6.82493	-6.82493	-4.52453	-4.52453	-4.52453	-5.47869	-4.47869	-4.47869
Estimated Parameters									
α	0.5704	0.5162	0.3852						
	(0.0424)	(0.0470)	(0.0752)						
β	0.2194	0.2866	0.4164						
	(0.0415)	(0.0395)	(0.0618)						
γ	0.2102	0.1973	0.1984						
	(0.0191)	(0.0194)	(0.290)						
λ							0.0293	0.0300	0.0352
							(0.0015)	(0.0018)	(0.0031)
σ							0.2895	0.4010	0.3572
							(0.2393)	(0.1559)	(0.1449)
σ_I							0.3098	0.1672	0.1172
							(0.0323)	(0.0262)	(0.0529)

Note:
1. Numbers in parentheses are standard errors.

REVIEW OF ECONOMIC STUDIES

capital stock is significant or nearly significant (at $p = 0.05$) in all of the equations. Our estimates with cross-equation restrictions improve upon these results markedly.

In regressions 5 and 7, we add the lagged inventory-output ratio (S/Q) as a regressor, and find a strongly significant effect in the output equation. Inventories have been cited in a number of recent studies as the channel through which demand shocks lead to serially correlated output fluctuations. An initial demand disturbance causes a large unexpected accumulation of inventory stocks. Part of the response to these shocks is de-stocking, and part is a reduction in output, until inventory levels are back to normal. In this case, the variable may proxy for the effects of demand disturbances on output. Note that it is highly significant, and that it raises the coefficient and significance on π_n, in the output equation. It also markedly improves the Durbin–Watson statistic, suggesting that it helps to explain the serially correlated fluctuations in Q.

Table IV presents estimates of the FPF, output supply, and labour demand, in which the cross equation restrictions are imposed. A variety of models are estimated: model A is as shown in earlier; model B adds the lagged inventory–output ratio to each of the regressions; and model C adds the inventory variable to the labour and output variables alone. When the system is estimated as a whole, the parameter estimates are almost all highly significant, and almost always are in the reasonable range for factor shares (α, β, γ) and labour productivity growth (λ). The estimated substitutability of value-added and the intermediate input (σ) is between 0.28 and 0.41, a plausible range that is in line with earlier estimates of Bruno (1981). More surprising are the exceedingly low estimates of σ_1, the elasticity of substitution between K and L in value added. The estimate in model A is the highest, at a mere 0.31; and they fall to only 0.12 in model C. While these estimates are indeed far from the standard Cobb–Douglas assumption, they of course do no more than reflect the sharp rise in labour's share of value added, which is contrary to the Cobb–Douglas assumption. Note that labour's share rose from an average of 0.72 during 1960–1972 to 0.77 during 1972–1975, and up to 0.78 during 1975–1978.

We can use the regression estimates in order to compute the components of change in $q - k$ in terms of the underlying explanatory variables. The first panel in Table V gives the component breakdown by sub-period for model C.

TABLE V

Components of change in output and labour input: U.K. manufacturing, 1956–1978 (annual percentages)[1]

	1956–1964	1964–1973	1973–1976	1976–1978	1973–1978
Gross output (Δq)	3·4	2·9	−2·2	1·2	−0·8
Capital stock (Δk)	4·2	3·5	2·0	2·0	2·0
Manhours (Δl)	−0·2	−1·0	−2·3	0·8	−1·0
Output per unit of capital $(\Delta q - \Delta k)$	−0·7	−0·5	−4·1	−0·7	−2·7
of which:					
Real wage $(\Delta w_p - \lambda)$	−0·1	−0·2	0·0	1·7	0·7
Material prices $(\Delta \pi_n)$	0·7	0·1	−2·2	−0·4	−1·5
Inventory-output ratios $(\Delta(v - q))$	−1·8	−0·3	−1·4	−1·0	−1·2
Unexplained residual	−0·5	−0·1	−0·4	−0·9	−0·7
Employment per unit of capital $(\Delta l - \Delta k)$	−4·2	−4·3	−4·1	−1·1	−2·9
of which:					
Real wage[2]	−2·5	−2·7	−2·4	0·2	−1·3
Material prices $(\Delta \pi_n)$	0·4	0·1	−1·3	−0·2	−0·9
Inventory-output ratio	−1·2	−0·2	−1·0	−0·7	−0·9
Unexplained residual	−0·9	−1·5	0·6	−0·4	−0·2

Notes:
1. The numbers are calculated on the basis of model C.
2. This incorporates a constant employment-reducing effect of technical progress of 1·2% per annum.

These estimates suggest that during the period 1973–1978, raw material prices directly explain over half of the 15% fall in output per unit of capital. The "demand" variable accounts (inventories) for another 45%. Real wages, relative to the productivity trend, were fairly rigid during 1973–1976 (especially when compared to the contemporaneous developments in some other industrial countries, like Japan and the U.S.; see Bruno and Sachs (1981)). Only in the latter part of the period, 1976–1978, did they mitigate the output-depressing effect of raw materials somewhat.[13] For the period 1973–1978 as a whole, the average contribution was slightly positive (0·7 relative to --2·7). There is an unexplained residual component of about 25% which may be due to productivity slowdown or other deflationary elements that are unaccounted for in this model.

The second part of Table V provides a similar breakdown for manhours per unit of capital. Real wages and technical progress account for most of the fall in the labour/capital ratio throughout the period 1956–1978, with raw material prices taking up about $\frac{1}{3}$ after 1973. The model *over-explains* the relative employment slowdown in 1973–1976, which may be evidence of labour hoarding, constituting the other side of the unexplained productivity residual.

It should be stressed that the direct attribution of one half of the change in $q - k$ to raw material prices at best represents only the direct short-term effect from the supply side. To this one should add the indirect effect of the profit squeeze on investment and capital stock, as we do in the simulations that follow. This point is best illustrated by appealing to the distinction made in Section I between the various time horizons. Using model C parameters the elasticity of response of output to a 1% increase in π_n is 0·42 in the very short run ($\dot{w}_p = \dot{k} = 0$), −0·26 in the short run ($\dot{l} = \dot{k} = 0$), and −0·29 in the long run ($\dot{l} = \dot{\rho} = 0$). The short run and long run differ so little because we have a small value for σ_1, the elasticity of substitution between k and l in v. There is little long-run reduction in k for $\sigma_1 = 0·1172$.[14] Finally, one may add the depressing effect of rising

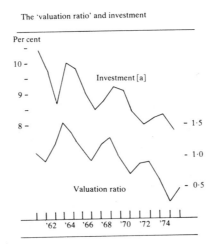

The 'valuation ratio' and investment

FIGURE 6

Investment and Tobin's q: (1960–1976), from Flemming (1976b)

[a] Industrial and commercial companies' gross fixed-capital formation as a percentage of capital stock (at replacement cost).

relative import prices on real incomes as well as on initiating contractionary macropolicies, which play their role here (if at all) through the inventory variable.

Next, we need numerical estimates of the investment and wage functions. There is now a growing literature that confirms the link between Tobin's q and investment in the United Kingdom (see especially Flemming (1976a,b) for pioneering estimates of τ; Oulton (1978); Jenkinson (1981); and Poterba and Summers (1981)). The potential for a strong econometric relationship is clearly evident in Figure 6, which is reproduced from Flemming (1976b). The investment rate is closely tied to fluctuations in τ, which seems to lead by about a year.

Some simple regressions between J/K and τ are shown in Table VI. The regressions are reproduced from Poterba and Summers (1981). These authors make various adjustments to the valuation ratio (the market value of the firm relative to the replacement cost of capital) to take account of U.K. tax laws. While the theory presented earlier argues for a contemporaneous relationship of investment and τ, the regression estimates clearly point to a lagged effect of τ on J/K as well. Tobin's q is shown to have a highly significant effect, though the low Durbin–Watson statistics suggest some misspecification in the basic equation. When the equations are re-estimated with corrections for first-order and second-order serial correlation, the estimated effect of τ diminishes somewhat, but still remains significant.

A surprising feature of the regression is the extremely small magnitude of the coefficients on τ. A drop of τ from $1{\cdot}0$ to $0{\cdot}5$ is calculated to result in a fall in J/K from about $0{\cdot}09$ to $0{\cdot}075$ (using regression 1). Such small effects of τ have also been reported for U.S. data (in Summers (1981), for example). The coefficient (or sum of coefficients) on τ measures the inverse of the adjustment cost parameter, according to the linear-adjustment cost model. Thus, the estimates of $\beta_1 + \beta_2 = 0{\cdot}02$ suggest a ϕ_0 of 50, which seems very high.

There is little doubt that data problems in part account for a downward bias on the τ coefficient, but theoretical problems also play a role. In the investment model we use, the observed firm value (subject to some important tax adjustments) is always the appropriate indicator of marginal investment decisions. In a world of vintage or putty-clay capital, however, it is possible for stock market movements to signal changes in the value of quasi-rents on old capital that do not affect investment decisions on new capital. In the jargon of the investment literature, "marginal Tobin's q" does not equal "average Tobin's q" (i.e. observed values of τ). Unfortunately, we remain a long way off from a convincing and empirically tractable vintage model of production with intermediate inputs.

Next, we turn to the wage equation. As thoroughly explained in Grubb, Jackman and Layard (1982), the form of the wage equation is both unresolved and enormously important to the questions at hand! Most importantly we must know: (1) whether the degree of labour market slack affects the rate of real wage increase; and (2) whether real wage growth responds to the difference of actual real wages and some "target" or "aspiration" level of real wages (the so-called Sargen effect). And if the target-wage model is correct, do target wages themselves respond adaptively to the history of actual wage growth? These questions remain subject to enormous dispute in the U.K. literature, with opposite answers reached by numerous authors on each of the issues.

For us the relevant question is whether temporary labour market slack is necessary and sufficient to reduce the path of real wages following an input price shock. Under what circumstances can real wage targets be reduced by a bout of unemployment? Some very simple, and imprecise evidence is gathered in the final three regressions of Table VI. Labour market slack is measured by the deviation of (log) manhours in manufacturing from a linear trend. Because lagged real wages are insignificant in regression 5, the equation implies that labour market slack leads to a reduction of real wages but not to a steady decline in real wages growth. If the model $\ln (W_P) = \alpha + \beta \ln (L)$ is correct, as is

TABLE VI

Investment and real wage equations

Investment equations	q	q_{-1}	Second-order serial correlation ρ_1	ρ_2	$\bar{R}^2$	d.w.
1. J/K, Annual 1950–1980	0·0133 (3·5)	0·010 (2·7)	—	—	0·66	0·46
2. J/K, Annual 1950–1980	0·0094 (4·9)	0·0054 (2·8)	1·28 (7·5)	-0·50 (2·9)	0·91	1·70
3. J/K, Annual 1950–1972	0·0102 (5·1)	0·0053 (2·5)	1·33 (6·7)	-0·55 (2·9)	0·93	1·65
4. J/K, Annual 1950–1980	0·0110 (5·0)	0·0069 (3·5)	0·63 (1·9)	-0·51 (1·6)	0·79	1·83

Wage equation	$\log(L)_{-1}$	$\log(L)_{-2}$	$\log(W/CP1)_{-1}$	Time	First-order serial correlation ρ	R^2	d.w.
5. $\log(W/CPI)$	0·46 (1·8)		6·05 (0·14)		0·42 (1·1)	0·99	1·87
6. $\log(W/CPI)$	0·61 (2·3)	-0·47 (1·8)	0·53 (1·5)	0·017 (1·3)	-0·09 (0·2)	0·99	1·99
7. $\log(W/CPI)$	0·79 (2·9)	-0·69 (2·9)	1·0 (constrained)	0·002 (0·67)	-0·25 (1·0)	0·25¹	2·04

Notes:
1. LHS variable is $\log(W/CPI) - \log(W/CPI)_{-1}$.
2. *Source*: Equations 1–4 are reproduced from Summers and Poterba, Table 2, p. 34. For Equations 5–7, W is the rate of hourly compensation and L is manhours, both for manufacturing from the U.S. Bureau of Labor Statistics (1981). The CPI is from the International Financial Statistics of the International Monetary Fund. Numbers in parentheses are *t*-statistics.

implied, then an input price shock *permanently* lowers the employment level in U.K. manufacturing. In the next regression, there is a modest effect of slack on real wage change. According to the equation, a one percent decline in manhours (relative to trend), sustrained for five years, results in a fall in w_P of only 0·33% relative to trend. Finally, in regression 7 we see again that changes in U.K. real wages are basically tied to changes in employment, but not closely to the employment level itself.

These results are suggestive but rather crude, as sophisticated wage equations must better account for: the difference of the real consumption wage and producer's labour costs; the timing of contract negotiations; pre-tax versus post-tax labour earnings; inflation expectations; incomes policies; and problems in measurement of labour market slack. Still, there is a strong feeling that downward real wage adjustment is not likely to be a smooth, costless process in the U.K. economy.

The complete supply-side model is now simulated, using (approximately) the parameters that we have estimated. The method for including various tax paramaters in the model is described in Summers and Poterba (1982). Model C of the joint estimates is selected for the gross output block. The simulation model is shown in full in Table VII. Two labour market equations are used, representing the alternatives of instantaneous market clearing and sluggish real wage adjustment. Three simulations are undertaken from an initial steady state: (1) a 10%, unanticipated permanent rise in Π_n in 1980, with

TABLE VII

Simulation model

Equations	
1.	$V = \tau \cdot K$
2.	$J/K = (1/\beta_0)(\tau - 1 + t_c)/(1 - t_c) + (d + n)$
3.	$\phi = 0 \cdot 5 \beta_0 (J/K - d - n)^2/(J/K)$
4.	$Q = (\mu_v Va^{\rho_2} + \mu_N N^{\rho_2})^{1/\rho_2}$
5.	$Va = (\mu_L L^{\rho_1} + \mu_K K^{\rho_1})^{1/\rho_1}$
6.	$P = (\mu_v^{\sigma_2} P_v^{(1-\sigma_2)} + \mu_N^{\sigma_2} P_N^{(1-\sigma_2)}]^{1/(1-\sigma_2)}$
7.	$W = W_p \cdot P$
8.	$L = (1 - \mu_L)^{1/\rho_1} K \cdot [(W/\mu_L \cdot P_v)^{\rho_1/(1-\rho_1)} - \mu_L]^{-1/\rho_1}$
9.	$N = Va \cdot (\mu_N/\mu_v)^{\sigma_2} (P_V/P_N)^{\sigma_2}$
10.	$\text{Div} = \gamma \cdot (1 - t_c) \cdot (Q - w_p L - \Pi_n N - dK)$
11.	$S = \text{Div} + J \cdot (1 - t_c + (1 - t_c)\phi) - (1 - t_c)(Q - W_p \cdot L - \Pi_n N)$
12.	$V_{t+1} = [V_t + S + (RV, -(1 - c)\text{Div})/(1 - c)]/(1 + n)$
13.	$K_{t+1}(1 + n) = J + (1 - d) \cdot K$
14.(a)	$L = 1$
14.(b)	$W_P = (L_{t-1})^{0 \cdot 8} (L_{t-2})^{-0 \cdot 6} (W_p)_{t-1}$

Notes:

1. Variable definitions

S	New equity issues
Div	Total divident payments
c	Capital gains tax rate
Va	Real value added
V	Value of the firm
n	Growth rate of efficiency labour
R	Required rate of return on corporate equity
d	Rate of depreciation
ϕ	Per unit cost of adjustment
γ	Dividend payout ratio
P	Price of gross output
P_v	Value added deflator
t_c	Corporate tax rate

2. Parameter values. $\beta_0 = 50 \cdot 0$, $c = 0 \cdot 15$, $s = 0 \cdot 06$, $\gamma = 0 \cdot 5$, $n = 0 \cdot 02$, $R = 0 \cdot 06$, $\rho_1 = -8$, $\rho_2 = -1 \cdot 8$, $\sigma_2 = 0 \cdot 4$, $t_c = 0 \cdot 5$, $\mu_L = 0 \cdot 7$, $\mu_K = 0 \cdot 7$, $\mu_N = 0 \cdot 4$ and $\mu_V = 0 \cdot 6$.

full employment of labour assumed; (2) the same increase in Π_n, but with slow real wage adjustment; and (3) a 10% rise in Π_n, announced in 1980 and commencing in 1983. The simulations yield the time paths of output, employment, investment, equity prices and wages following the given shock. They will be reported as percentage deviations from an initial full-employment steady-state growth path.

As pointed out above, the complete model exhibits saddlepoint stability, and the tricky part of the simulation exercise involves finding the particular initial value for Tobin's q that drives the system to a new steady state (all other values of τ lead to an explosive divergence from steady state). We use the method of multiple shooting, described in Lipton, Poterba, Sachs and Summers (1980), to find the saddlepoint-stable trajectory.

The results of the simulations are shown in Table VIII. In the full-employment case, the rise in π_n causes an immediate fall in real wages of 6·9%, and in productivity of 2·5%. Since Q_k is reduced below its long-run value, the stock market price falls, in

TABLE VIII

Simulation results[1]

	Simulation		
	1	2	3
1980			
Q	−2·5	−4·2	0·0
Q/L	−2·5	−1·7	0·0
W_P	−6·9	0·0	0·0
L	0·0	−2·6	0·0
K	0·0	0·0	0·0
Tobin's q	−2·7	−13·0	−8·2
1985			
Q	−2·6	−4·4	−4·7
Q/L	−2·6	1·0	−4·7
W_P	7·5	−2·1	−2·0
L	0·0	−3·4	−2·5
K	−0·2	−1·0	−1·0
Tobin's q	−1·7	−7·3	−8·8
1990			
Q	−2·6	−4·5	−4·8
Q/L	−2·6	−2·3	−2·3
W_P	−7·9	−5·3	−4·7
L	0·0	−2·1	−2·4
K	0·0	−1·6	−1·6
Tobin's q	−1·0	−3·2	−4·0
Steady-state			
Q	−2·6	−2·6	−2·6
Q/L	−2·6	−2·6	−2·6
W_P	−8·4	−8·4	−8·4
L	0·0	0·0	0·0
K	−0·6	−0·6	−0·6
Tobin's q	0·0	0·0	0·0

Notes:
1. All variables are measured as a percentage deviation from the initial steady-state growth path.
2. *Source*: Simulation 1: Ten-percent permanent rise in π_n in 1980; flexible w_P. Simulation 2: Ten-percent permanent rise in π_n in 1980; Phillips curve adjustment of w_P. Simulation 3: Ten-percent permanent rise in π_n in 1983; anticipated in 1980; Phillips curve adjustment of w_P.

this case a modest 2·7%. Far-sighted investors know that the marginal productivity of capital will rise in the future, so that they do not place to much weight on the immediate sharp deterioration of profitability. Over time, K continues to fall, pushing the real wage and productivity even further below the initial trend. Q_k rises, on the other hand, and Tobin's q approaches its initial value. In the long run, the real wage falls by 8·4%; productivity, Q/L, by 2·7%; and the capital stock, K, by 0·6%. The very modest long-run decline in K reflects the low value of σ_{KL} in the value-added function (set at 0·11 for the exercise). Since K must remain in almost fixed proportion to full-employment L, it changes little over the course of time.

Simulation 2 dramatically indicates the depressing effect of real wage resistance on the adjustment to a supply shock. Most directly, 1980 output falls more than in the first simulation (4·2% rather than 2·5%), and the unemployment rate rises to 2·6%. Since the higher real wage reduces profitability *and* since forward-looking investors correctly perceive a very slow decline in future wages, the 1980 level of Tobin's q falls more sharply than in the market-clearing case (down 13% rather than 2·7%). As a consequence, the real-wage rigidity leads to a steep process of capital decumulation. In the first simulation, K falls slowly to 0·6% below the baseline. With wage rigidity, K falls steeply to $-1·8\%$ below trend, and then slowly recovers as real wages fall. The model exhibits a strongly damped oscillation of the sort demonstrated in Figure 4. Since real wages decline so slowly, K falls below its long-run level; in turn, w_P is pulled below $\bar{w}_P$, which eventually pushes K above $\bar{K}$, etc. (The oscillation is in fact so damped that there is almost direct convergence to equilibrium.)

In the third simulation, the increase in π_n is anticipated (in 1980) three years before it actually occurs (in 1983). The stock market immediately capitalizes the decline in future profitability, as Tobin's q declines 8·2%. Since equity prices drive the investment process, the decumulation of capital starts in 1981, two years before the price increase. Of course, as K falls, employment is also reduced in the rigid real-wage case. In 1972, the unemployment rate stands at 0·3%. When the shock finally hits, the unemployment rate jumps and productivity falls, while the stock market hardly responds. The remaining adjustment profile is very similar to that of simulation 2.

These numerical simulations demonstrate the feasibility of specifying, estimating, and solving a dynamic non-linear supply model with forward-looking agents. In our papers, Bruno and Sachs (1982) and Sachs (1982) the approach is extended to a complete macromodel of the economy, with optimizing households as well as firms.

3. CONCLUSIONS

This paper develops a theoretical model of the effects of input price shocks, and applies the model to the case of U.K. manufacturing. With the theoretical model we trace out the dynamic adjustments to the price shock, and show that the paths of output, employment, and capital stock depend crucially on the responsiveness of real wages to labour market slack. Even with full labour-market clearing, an input price shock causes a fall in output, productivity, real wages and real equity prices on impact, and leads to a continued decline in the capital stock and output over time. When real wages are sticky, these effects are greatly magnified, and unemployment as well as reduced output becomes a major effect of the shock. With greater real wage stickiness, profitability is more sharply affected by the rise in input prices, and investment tends to be more sharply squeezed.

There is abundant evidence that higher input prices have played a significant role in the slowdown in economic growth since 1973 throughout the OECD. Most major economies have experienced a serious squeeze in profits and investment that dates from around the first oil shock (see Sachs (1979) and Bruno (1981b) for details). We develop this case in some detail for the U.K. by estimating a gross output function, investment equation, and real wage equation for the manufacturing sector, based on the theoretical model. Estimates of the factor-price frontier show a sharp shift in the frontier after 1973, in line with the observed drop in profitability from about 9·5% return on capital during 1960–1972 to under 5·0% during 1973–1978 (see Table II). Estimates of output supply also confirm the large role for input prices. We estimate that over half of the growth slowdown in output per unit capital (Q/K) after 1972 can be attributed to higher input prices. Moreover, the slowdown in K itself can be traced in large part to the higher input prices via reduced profitability. To show the complete dynamic effects, we simulate a small non-linear model based on the econometric estimates, and once again we find large effects of the input shock, particularly in the case of real wage resistance.

These are major shortcomings that remain at the conclusion of this work, involving: (1) lags in factor adjustment; (2) the productivity puzzle; and (3) the integration of demand factors into the supply-side framework. We touch on these in turn. With respect to factor adjustments, there is widespread evidence and a long tradition holding that labour, like capital, is adjusted only slowly over time in response to an exogenous shock. Indeed in our empirical work, we found it necesary to relate current employment and output to lagged factor prices. In his excellent study of labour demand in U.K. manufacturing, Symons (1982) also finds a lagged adjustment pattern. Conceptually, this slow adjustment is readily handled, by supposing convex costs of adjustment to labour, as in Sargent (1978), as well as capital. Empirically, though, the problem is trickier, as now labour demand depends on expectations of future real factor prices, and not just their current level.

An even more central empirical problem is our treatment of productivity developments since 1973. That labour productivity growth has deteriorated there is not doubt, but the allocation of that slowdown to various factors is still very much in doubt. On our limited post-1973 data we could make little progress in evaluating whether reduced capital and intermediate input utilization can explain the slowdown, or whether an exogenous slowdown in total factor productivity (TFP) growth had occurred. The implications of an input shock or exogenous TFP slowdown for output, unemployment, real wage growth, and investment are actually very similar, since an input price shock is analogous to technical regress. But for quantitative assessments it is important to know the sources and size of the productivity slowdown. Our Table I, and regressions in Bruno (1981) suggest that K and π_n *cannot* fully explain the U.K. productivity experience. In future empirical work, the TFP developments must be better integrated with the input price shock.

The greatest conceptual problem lies in the proper integration of supply and demand factors in the study of the macroeconomic adjustment process. Our model assumes that profit-maximizing firms are *always* on their supply schedules, so that fluctuations in output can always be attributed to shifts in the capital stock or factor prices. Pure demand disturbances, in which firms are rationed in the output market and hence not on their supply schedules, are not allowed. This treatment is extreme, though no more so than the typical Keynesian position which treats all fluctuations as pure demand disturbances. A more sensible position, no doubt, would allow for both supply and demand shocks to play distinct roles, whose importance varies over time. We would surmise that the deep recessions of 1975 and 1980 represent cases in which firms were pushed off their supply schedules by tight demand, while the rest of 1973-onward basically reflects the type of supply squeeze that we depict in the paper. We are now attempting to formulate a dynamic model that will allow for that possibility.

DATA APPENDIX[15]

For source abbreviations, see glossary at the end of this appendix.

Input–Output Accounts for U.K. Manufacturing, 1954–1978

The manufacturing sector is defined as Orders III, V–XIX of the Standard Industrial Classification. Order IV, "Coal and Petroleum Products", was excluded. Inputs were divided into four categories: labour, capital, energy, and non-energy intermediate inputs. Definitions of the constructed variables are as follows.

Gross Output $(P_Q Q)$

Price and quantity indices for output were constructed and then normalized to equal the value ($ million) of gross output, exluding stock appreciation (source: Table 21, DAE1), in 1968. Before normalization, P_Q = Wholesale Price Index of Home Sales, all manufactured products, 1975 = 100; ETAS 1980. Exclusion of the contribution of SIC Order IV was not possible with available data.

Q = Index of Industrial Production, Manufacturing, 1975 = 100; ETAS 1980. Using the Index for Coal and Petroleum Products (MDS, various) and appropriate weights the contribution of SIC Order IV was subtracted from Q.

Before normalization it was observed that the ratio of $P_Q Q$ to gross output (DAE1) for 1954–1968 was stable taking on values of 7·3 to 7·6.

Labour $(P_L L)$

Before normalization, P_L = Index of hourly compensation, manufacturing, 1967 = 100; USBLS. L = Index of total hours worked in manufacturing, 1967 = 100; USBLS. These were then normalized to equal the 1968 value of wages and salaries in manufacturing less that accruing in SIC Order IV (BB), plus employers' national insurance contributions (BB). An estimate for these contributions in SIC Order IV was estimated by a proportion of the total equal to the ratio of "employees in employment" in Order IV to total manufacturing. The ratio $P_L L$ to the constructed labour compensation series for 1954–1978 varied from 0·77 to 0·80.

Capital $(P_K K)$

Define:

$P_K K$ – BB: Profits in total manufacturing after stock appreciation, before depreciation; (BB various); no exclusion of SIC Order IV; 1954–1978.

$P_K K$ – DAE: As above excluding SIC Order IV (Table 25, DAE1). Only available for 1954–1968.

$P_K K$ – BD: $(P_K K$ – BB) (Average value of 1954–1968 of $(P_K K$ – DAE)/$(P_K K$ – BB)). $P_K K$ was constructed as $P_K K$ – DAE (1954–1968) and $P_K K$ – BD (1969–1978).

To construct K, define:

NK70:   Net capital stock all manufacturing, 1970 prices. (STUDOS).

PNK70:   Price index defined as ratio of current and constant (1970 as base year) price series for gross domestic fixed capital formation (BB).

ADJUST: NK70*0·0347, where 0·0347 equals the average value for 1954–1968 (period for which data was available) of the ratio of gross capital stocks in "mineral oil refining and coke ovens" to all manufacturing, Table 34–37, DAE1.

Giving us K defined as the nominal net capital stock equal to K = (NK70 – ADJUST)*PNK70, and P_K as an internal rate of return: $P_K = P_K K / K$.

Energy $(P_E E)$

E: Energy consumption (millions of therms) by final user all industries (excluding fuel producing ones). The available data for "all industry" includes "construction", "water", "other manufacturing and quarrying" for which disaggregate numbers are not available. Source, UKESD.

P_E was constructed as $P_E E/E$ where $P_E E$ was derived as follows. $P_E E$ by final users is only available post 1968 (see UKESD, 1980), and so a series was calculated by multiplying several disaggregate quantity and price series. Quantity series, as in E, were from UKESD. Price series were taken from: for 1954–1963, "Purchasers average prices of fuel in U.K." (p. 115, DAE2); for 1963–1979, "Prices of fuels used by manufacturing industry" (UKESD, 1977, 1980). In calculating expenditure the following assumptions were made: the price of coal, coke and breeze, other solid fuel was taken to be that of coal; the price of all types of gas was taken to be the published price; the price of petroleum and creosote-pitch mixture taken to be that of heavy fuel oil. This constructed series was used as an estimate of $P_E E$.

Non-Energy Intermediate Inputs $(P_M M)$

$P_M M$ was derived as the residual from $P_Q Q - P_L L - P_K K - P_E E$, and M as $P_M M/P_M$. P_M is defined as $P_M M = W_{NM}*P_{NM} + W_M *P_Q$, a weighted average of intermediate purchase from outside and from within the manufacturing sector, where

P_Q = as above, wholesale price index of home sales.

W_M = share of manufacturing non-energy purchases in manufacturing gross output in 1973. Calculated from 1973 Input–Output Tables (ET, June 1978). W_M = 0·3547.

W_{NM} = same as W_M for nonmanufacturing non-energy purchases. $W_{NM} = 0·6453$.

$P_{NM} = (P_{BM} - W_E *P_{IE})/(1 - W_E)$, where

P_{BM} = Wholesale Price Index of Materials purchased by manufacturing industry, average of monthly figures, 1970 = 100; MDS.

P_{IE} = Unit Value Index of Fuel Imports, U.K., average of quarterly figures, 1970 = 100; MDS.

W_E = Share of purchases of coal and crude petroleum (considered as materials not fuels in P_{BM}) by the mineral oil refining and coke oven industries is total non-energy intermediate input purchases by manufacturing, for 1973. W_E = 0·03696.

P_{NM} is therefore the material input price index for manufacturing excluding SIC Order IV.

Intermediate Inputs, Total (Energy and Non-Energy) $(P_N N)$

When the accounting framework is reduced to three inputs, aggregating energy and non-energy intermediate inputs, a price index (P_N) was calculated as,

$$P_N = 0·06076*P_{NM} + 0·0684*P_E + 0·3340*P_Q$$

where the coefficients are the shares, calculated from the 1973 Input–Output Tables (ET, June 1978), of non-manufacturing, energy, and manufacturing inputs respectively, in gross output. N is then calculated as $(P_E E + P_M M)/P_N$. (When a division index was used to create N, the change was trivial.)

Glossary of Source Abbreviations

BB: National Income and Expenditure, C.S.O.
DAE1:   "Structural Change in the British Economy, 1948–68," A Programme for Growth No. 12, Department of Applied Economics, University of Cambridge; Chapman and Hall, May 1974.
DAE2:   "The Demand for Fuel, 1948–1975," A Programme for Growth No. 8, Department of Applied Economics, University of Cambridge; Chapman and Hall, 1968.
ET: Economic Trends, monthly, CSO.
ETAS: Economic Trends Annual Supplement, CSO.

MDS: Monthly Digest of Statics, CSO.
STUDOS: New Contributions to Economic Statistics, Ninth Series. Studies in Official
           Statistics No. 33, 1977, CSO. Appendix II updated with more recent BB
           figures.
UKBLS: British Labour Statistics Year Book (1975); Appendix H "New estimates of
           employment on a continuous basis: United Kingdom," Department of
           Employment.
UKESD: U.K. Energy Statistical Digest, Department of Energy. Early issues were
           Ministry of Power Statistical Digest, Ministry of Power.
USBLS: Unpublished data prepared by the U.S. Department of Labor, Bureau of
           Labor Statistics, Office of Productivity and Technology.

We have benefited enormously from discussions with David Grubb, Richard Jackman, Richard Layard, and James Symons, and from our opportunities to present this work at seminars at the London School of Economics and Warwick University. The paper is part of a joint study of the authors on the macroeconomic effects of supply shocks. We thank Mr. Louis Dicks-Mireaux for very able research assistance. Support from the National Science Foundation is gratefully acknowledged.

NOTES

1. Profit share is the ratio of gross trading profits in manufacturing to gross output. The profit rate is the ratio of gross trading profits to the nominal value of the manufacturing capital stock. Both series are from the Dicks-Mireaux data. The regressions are based on annual data, for 1961–1978.

2. For a model with value-maximizing firms subject to quantity constraints in the output and factor markets, see Blanchard and Sachs (1982).

3. See Sachs (1980) for details. The derivation is a straightforward application of the optimum conditions for the Hamiltonian H:

$$H = e^{-\Delta}[(Q - W_P L - \Pi_n N - I) + \lambda (J - dK)].$$

4. A more detailed analysis for the single sector case and alternative technological assumptions is given in Bruno (1981).

5. In the putty-clay case in which the capital/labour ratio cannot immediately adjust to the new factor prices, the various solutions are given along the line FGC, i.e. in the rigid real wage, rigid capital/labour case the economy will be at F and not at B, the rate of profit falling by more and L by less than at B.

6. Here and elsewhere we shall adopt the convention of using lower-case letters for the natural log of a capital-lettered variable (e.g. $q = \ln Q$, etc.).

7. While the case of weak separability of intermediate inputs may be relevant for most industrial raw materials, it is most probably not applicable to the case of energy inputs, E, for which separability may take the alternative form $Q[L, G(K, E)]$ (see Bernt and Wood (1979)). Here energy combines with capital to form a composite from which labour (and other raw materials, here left out) are separable. By analogy, the resulting factor price frontier in the $Q_E - R$ space will now contract along the R axis at a rate which will be independent of the real wage. While the short-run implications may be different (e.g. L/K need not fall with a rise in energy prices), the long-run implications are qualitatively the same.

8. As will be seen, for realistic orders of magnitude of the parameters this is unlikely to reverse the output drop from the initial pre-shock level.

9. The full symmetry of the two dual expressions can be seen by writing (9) in the form:

$$0 = \alpha(\dot{l} - \dot{q}) + \beta(\dot{n} - \dot{q}) + \gamma(\dot{k} - \dot{q}).$$

10. The *two* conditions

$$\dot{\tau} = r\tau - [Q_k + (J/K)^2 \phi'(J/K)]$$

and

$$\lim_{t \to \infty} e^{-Rt}\tau(t) = 0$$

are equivalent to equation 2(d).

11. Saddlepoint stability in (23) requires that the matrix have two negative and one positive eigenvalue.

12. E.g. an equation like $\dot{z} = a\dot{x} + b\dot{y}$ is transformed into $z = c + ax + by$, where $\dot{x} = x - \bar{x}$, etc., and $c = \bar{z} - a\bar{x} - b\bar{y}$.

13. Note that during the earlier growth periods 1954–1964 and 1964–1973, capital deepening was accompanied by an increase in real wages (net of productivity), a point which is also apparent from direct inspection of the factor price profile (Figure 2). See also Sargent (1979); Glynn and Sutcliffe (1972).

14. With a higher value of σ_1, say $\sigma_1 = 0.30$, (all other parameters the same), the values become: -0.67 in the very short run, -0.26 in the short run, and -0.365 in the long run. The difference between short run and long run is magnified, since there is greater long-run substitution away from k.

15. Data construction and data appendix prepared by Mr. Louis-David Dicks-Mireaux.

REFERENCES

BERNDT, E. R. and WOOD, D. O. (1979), "Engineering and Econometric Interpretation of Energy-Capital Complementarity", *American Economic Review*, **69**, 342–354.

BLANCHARD, O. J. and SACHS, J. (1982), "Anticipations, Recessions, and Policy; An Intertemporal Disequilibrium Model", presented at the Conference on "International Aspects of Macroeconomics in France," INSEAD, Fountainbleau.

BRUNO, M. (1981a), "Price and Output Adjustment: Micro Foundations and Aggregation", *Journal of Monetary Economics*, **5**, 187–211.

BRUNO, M. (1981b), "Raw Materials, Profits and the Productivity Slowdown." (Discussion Paper No. 812, Jerusalem: Falk Institute).

BRUNO, M. and SACHS, J. (1981), "Supply Versus Demand Approaches to the Problem of Stagflation", *Macroeconomic Policies for Growth and Stability* (Institute fur Weltwittschaft, Kiel).

BRUNO, M. and SACHS, J. (1982), "Energy and Resource Allocation: A Dynamic Model of the 'Dutch Disease'", *Review of Economic Studies* (forthcoming).

BUITER, W. and MILLER, M. (1982), "The Thatcher Experiment: What Went Wrong?", *Brookings Papers on Economic Activity* (forthcoming).

DIXIT, A. (1980), "A Solution Technique for Rational Expectations Models with Applications to Exchange Rate and Interest Rate Determination" (mimeo, University of Warwick).

FLEMMING, J. (1976a), (with PRICE, L. and BYERS, S.) "Trends in Company Profitability", *Bank of England Quarterly Bulletin*.

FLEMMING, J. (1976b), (with PRICE, L. and BYERS, S.) "The Cost of Capital, Finance and Investment", *Bank of England Quarterly Bulletin*.

GLYN, A. and SUTCLIFFE, B (1972) *Capitalism in Crisis* (New York: Random House).

GRUBB, D., JACKMAN, R. and LAYARD, R. (1982), "Causes of the Current Stagflation", *Review of Economic Studies*, **49**.

HAYASHI, F. (1982), "The q Theory of Investment: A Neoclassical Interpretation", *Econometrica*.

JENKINSON, N. (1981), "Investment, Profitability, and the Valuation Ratio" (Bank of England Discussion Paper).

MALINVAUD, E. (1977) *Theory of Unemployment Reconsidered* (Oxford: Basil Blackwell).

MALINVAUD, E. (1980) *Profitability and Unemployment* (Cambridge University Press).

MARTIN, W. E. and O'CONNOR, M. (1981), "Profitability: A Background Paper", in Martin, W. E. (ed.) *The Economics of the Profits Crisis* (London: Department of Industry).

MORLEY, R. (1979), "Profit, Relative Prices, and Unemployment", *The Economic Journal*, **89**, 582–600.

OULTON, N. (1978), "Explaining Aggregate Investment in Britain: the Importance of Tobin's Q", *Economics Letters*, **1**.

OULTON, N. (1979), "Aggregate Investment and Tobin's q: Evidence from Britain." (Discussion Paper 5, University of Lancaster).

SACHS, J. D. (1979), "Wages, Profits and Macroeconomic Adjustment: A Comparative Study" *Brookings Papers on Economic Activity*, **2**, 269–332.

SACHS, J. (1982), "Energy and Growth under Flexible Exchange Rates", forthcoming in Bhandard and Putnam (eds.) *The International Transmission of Economic Disturbances under Flexible Exchange Rates* (MIT Press).

SARGENT, J. R. "Productivity and Profits in UK Manufacturing", *Midland Bank Review*.

SARGENT, T. (1978), "Estimation of Dynamic Labor Demand Schedules under Rational Expectations", *Journal of Political Economy*, **86**, (6).

SUMMERS, L. H. (1981), "Taxation and Corporate Investment: a q-Theory Approach", *Brookings Paper on Economic Activity*, **1**, 67–140.

SUMMERS, L. H. and POTERBA, J. (1982), "Dividend Taxes, Corporate Investment, and 'Q'." (mimeo, NBER).

SYMONS, J. S. V. (1982), "The Demand for Labour in British Manufacturing" (unpublished paper).

TOBIN, J. (1981), "Comment on Bruno and Sachs, 'Supply Versus Demand Approaches to the Problem of Stagflation'." Policies for Growth and Stability (Institute fur Weltwittschaft, Kiel).

Review of Economic Studies (1982) XLIX, 707–730
0034-6527/82/00550707$00.50

Causes of the Current Stagflation

D. GRUBB, R. JACKMAN and R. LAYARD

Centre for Labour Economics, London School of Economics

Since 1975 labour slack has been unusually high in the OECD countries, and yet inflation
has not diminished. The less favourable mix of unemployment and rate of change of inflation
(which we call stagflation) is explained by a fall in the feasible rate of growth of real wages
unmatched by a reduction in the constant term in Phillips curve. To investigate this mechanism,
conventional wage and price equations are estimated for 19 countries and then used for simulation.
Stagflation has been caused in roughly equal amounts by rising relative import prices and by
the fall in the rate of productivity growth. In the basic model the Phillips curve is assumed not
to adapt to falls in feasible real wage growth, but in a final section an adaptive wage equation
is estimated, which confirms that the process of adaptation is slow.

1. INTRODUCTION AND SUMMARY

Since 1975, labour markets in most advanced countries have been much slacker than
over any period of similar length since the Second World War. Yet OECD inflation is
still much the same as it was at the end of 1975. So why has the level of slack necessary
to control inflation increased?

One might of course question whether the slack has in fact increased. After all, a
rise in unemployment could reflect only changes in willingness to work or in demographic
structure. However, in Europe at least, there is clear evidence that vacancies have been
much lower since 1975 than in previous periods (see Figure 1), and capacity utilization
has also been down.[1] So something has happened to change the balance in the labour
market consistent with stable inflation.

Our explanation is as follows.

(i) In the demand function for labour, the feasible growth rate of real wages
consistent with given employment has fallen.

(ii) In the Phillips curve, there has not been a corresponding downwards adjustment
in the target growth rate of wages at given employment.

(iii) Hence lower real wage growth has had to be brought about either by a rise in
unemployment or, since there is some nominal inertia in the system, by a rise in inflation,
or by a mixture of the two.

Thus the fall in feasible real wage growth has worsened the mixes of unemployment
and the rate of change of inflation that are available. The exact mix of the two which
has come about depends of course on how far governments have accommodated the
shocks which have occurred. But the basic point is that the level of unemployment
consistent with stable inflation (NAIRU) has risen. This is what we mean by stagflation.
This approach can be compared with the approach which identifies stagflation simply
with high unemployment due to excessive real wages. That approach only explains
"stag", but not "flation". It fails to explain why inflation has not been falling, given the
high level of unemployment. In our approach the prime source of difficulty is that people
are *trying* to achieve too high real wages. It is this that raises the NAIRU, and the fact
that real wages become too high is a consequence rather than a prime cause of the
difficulty.

In recent years the feasible growth of real wages has fallen for two reasons. First there has been the increase in the relative prices of raw materials, which has been much stressed by Bruno and Sachs, in this volume and elsewhere. This reduced the real wage consistent with full-employment in the average OECD country by over 2% in 1973/74 and again in 1979/80. In addition there has been a sharp fall in the rate of productivity growth. Comparing 1974–1980 with 1960–1973, the average rate of growth of value-added per man was 2 percentage points *a year* lower in the average OECD country. While the facts of slower productivity growth have been bemoaned and their causes debated, there has, to our knowledge, been surprisingly little discussion of their bearing on the problems of inflation and labour slack.

To investigate these issues, the paper begins with a short section developing our basic model of stagflation. It consists of a wage and price equation, which are sufficient for analysing the determination of the NAIRU. We then estimate the wage and price equations for 19 OECD countries using annual data for 1957–1980. The effect of unemployment on inflation is negative in all countries, and significantly so in a high proportion.

Next we use these estimates to interpret the economic history of the period since 1973. For each country we simulate the effect on inflation of (i) the unfavourable trends in relative import prices and productivity growth (both tending to increase inflation) and of (ii) the higher level of unemployment (tending to decrease it). It turns out that in the average EEC country relative import prices made inflation in 1980 5% higher than it would have been if import prices had continued their pre-1973 trend. Lower productivity growth had an equal effect in boosting inflation. But these extra pressures were almost exactly offset by the effect of higher unemployment (net of trend). In total inflation rose somewhat, in line with its earlier trend rate of growth.

The wage equations used up to this point have the drawback that they would not, even in the very long run, lead to a restoration of full employment after a fall in productivity growth. In the last section, we attempt to remedy this defect by estimating a model whose NAIRU is in the long run invariant with respect to productivity growth. This work is somewhat experimental, and we have therefore not used it in our simulations. But the broad conclusion is that adaptation is slow, and that our earlier model captures quite well the influence of a productivity growth fall over the first six years or so. It is not clear why adaptation should be so slow, though there must be problems of distinguishing between temporary and permanent shocks (Brunner, Cukierman and Meltzer (1980)). But if we cannot altogether explain why adaptation is slow, this does not mean we can ignore the fact. This is especially so if it throws light on the sources of our current difficulties.

2. A SIMPLE MODEL

We can begin with an expectations-augmented Phillips curve:

$$\dot{w} = \dot{p}^e - \beta(U - U_0) + \dot{x}^e. \tag{1}$$

Throughout the paper small letters denote logarithms. w is hourly wages, with $\dot{w} = w - w_{-1}$; $\dot{p}^e$ is the expected rate of price inflation ($p^e - p_{-1}$); $U - U_0$ is labour slack;[2] and $\dot{x}^e$ is the target rate of growth of real wages embodied in settlements when there is zero slack.

Turning to the price equation, this can be obtained by first writing down the labour demand function with prices on the left hand side and employment on the right (see Annex 1):

$$p = w - x + \mu p_m - \gamma U + \text{const.} \tag{2}$$

Here x is the trend level of value-added per worker and p_m is import prices relative to domestic prices. Taking differences gives us an equation for price change

$$\dot{p} = \dot{w} - \dot{x} + \mu\dot{p}_m - \gamma\dot{U}. \qquad (2')$$

If prices are correctly foreseen ($\dot{p} = \dot{p}^e$), (1) and (2') imply

$$U = U_0 + \frac{1}{\beta}(\dot{x}^e - \dot{x} + \mu\dot{p}_m) - \frac{\gamma}{\beta}\dot{U}. \qquad (3)$$

This gives us the value of unemployment consistent with correctly foreseen prices in any particular year. If unemployment is stable, we can ignore the last term in equation (3). Hence unemployment in the medium term is given by

$$U = U_0 + \frac{1}{\beta}(\dot{x}^e - \dot{x} + \mu\dot{p}_m) \qquad (3')$$

It will be higher, the lower the productivity growth and the higher the growth of relative import prices. Thus medium term unemployment does not depend only on the parameters of the wage equation (as is often assumed), but also on variables (like productivity growth) entering the price equation. If productivity growth falls by 1%, and there is no change in the constant term in the wage equation, then unemployment must rise by $(1/\beta)\%$.[3]

If there is no nominal inertia in the system, there is no trade-off between unemployment and changes in the inflation rate. But most economies seem to be characterized by nominal inertia arising from adaptive expectations, long-term contracts or other sources. For simplicity we can investigate the implications of nominal inertia by assuming adaptive expectations in the first derivative of prices. This would not be a sensible forecasting device if inflation were continually increasing, but may not be too unrealistic in a world where governments have acted to keep inflation fairly steady.

Suppose $\dot{p}^e = \dot{p}_{-1}$ (though in our empirical work we use a more general form). Using this and substituting (1) into (2') we find that

$$\dot{p} - \dot{p}_{-1} = -\beta(U - U_0) + (\dot{x}^e - \dot{x} + \mu\dot{p}_m) - \gamma\dot{U}. \qquad (4)$$

If we set $\dot{p} - \dot{p}_{-1}$ equal to zero, we get back to equation (3). Thus equation (3') can now be interpreted as describing the NAIRU.

The NAIRU is useful as an explanatory construct because governments have tended to hold inflation down (see Figure 1). Given this, an economy that has adjusted to a permanent fall in feasible real wage growth must have experienced an increase in unemployment. In the process real wages will have risen relative to productivity, and this is the proximate cause of the unemployment. But the originating cause is the excess of $\dot{x}^e$ over $\dot{x}$. To see this point one only has to note that the system can be solved recursively. Equation (3') gives the level of U as a function of $(\dot{x}^e - \dot{x})$, and equation (2) gives the level of the excess real wage $(w - p - x)$ as a function of U. The elasticity of demand for labour $(1/\gamma)$ plays no part in the fundamental equation (3') determining medium term unemployment.

In any particular year, of course, unemployment need not be at the NAIRU and the problem of stagflation is therefore best analysed in terms of equation (4). This shows quite simply how increases in $(\dot{x}^e - \dot{x})$ will worsen the available combinations of unemployment and the rate of change of inflation.

REVIEW OF ECONOMIC STUDIES

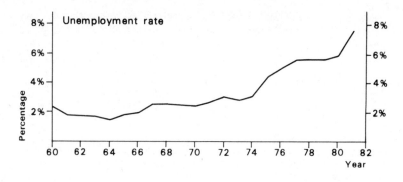

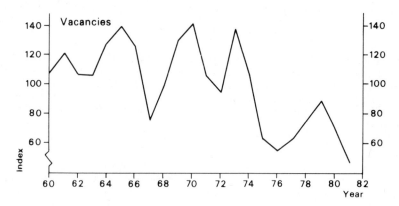

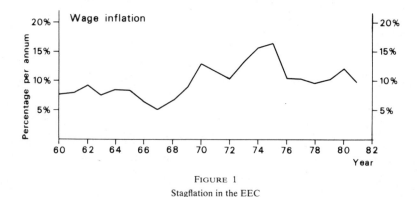

FIGURE 1

Stagflation in the EEC

Notes:
(1) Unemployment rate: average of unemployment rate of all EEC countries except Luxembourg and Greece. Weighted by 1975 labour force.
(2) Vacancies: geometric weighted average index of vacancies in Belgium, Germany, Netherlands and U.K. only. Weights are labour force. 1960–1981=100.
(3) Wage inflation: average of wage inflation rates in same countries as in (1). Weighted by 1975 GDP.
See Data Appendix for sources.

3. ESTIMATED WAGE AND PRICE EQUATIONS

Wage equation

We can now turn to estimation. The basic wage function which we estimate allows for nominal inertia in wages as well as prices, and is homogeneous of degree one in nominal variables:[4]

$$\dot{w} = \alpha \dot{p}_{-1} + (1-\alpha)\dot{w}_{-1} - \beta(U - U_0) + \dot{x}^e + \varepsilon \tag{5}$$

$(\beta U_0 + \dot{x}^e)$ is treated as a constant. For obvious reasons we are not happy with unemployment as a measure of labour slack. In many countries it has risen sharply relative to vacancies and capacity utilisation. Ideally one might have used vacancies as a (negative) measure of slack, but meaningful series were not available for enough countries.[5] We therefore used the unemployment series, but in those countries for which unemployment had a significant trend between 1960 and 1972 ($t > 2$) we used "adjusted unemployment" defined as the 1960–1972 average plus deviation from trend.[6] Wages are measured by average hourly earnings in manufacturing (in most countries) and prices by the consumers' expenditure price deflator. Detailed sources are in the Data Appendix.

Equation (5) was estimated for 19 countries on annual data for 1957–1980. The results are shown in Table I. The most striking feature of them is the consistency with which unemployment emerges as a restraining influence on inflation. In Table I all but four of the countries had t-statistics on $\hat{\beta}$ of above 1. This result is the more impressive because, by using the same specification in each country, we have avoided biases due to data mining. Also, up to a point the countries can be regarded as independent observations of the economic process. If the countries' data *were* independently generated and

TABLE I

Wage equation (equation 5)

Country	Constant/100	$\dot{p}_{-1}$	U	S.E. 100	R^2	DW
Belgium	3·61 (2·3)	0·28 (1·4)	−0·66 (2·3)	2·60	0·22	1·33
Denmark	5·23 (3·4)	0·78 (3·2)	−0·61 (2·4)	2·46	0·37	1·98
France	0·28 (0·2)	−0·22 (0·8)	−0·39 (0·6)	2·31	0·05	2·32
Germany	5·66 (3·2)	0·76 (3·2)	−1·24 (2·6)	2·71	0·36	1·88
Ireland	8·97 (2·3)	0·92 (2·6)	−0·79 (1·6)	4·30	0·27	2·09
Italy	12·02 (2·6)	0·98 (3·4)	−1·15 (1·7)	4·45	0·37	1·77
Netherlands	8·56 (3·6)	0·83 (3·2)	−2·49 (3·4)	3·20	0·41	1·87
U.K.	7·69 (3·0)	0·92 (2·9)	−2·01 (2·3)	3·75	0·33	1·49
Finland	1·81 (0·8)	0·01 (0·1)	−0·69 (1·0)	3·02	0·08	1·95
Norway	3·34 (1·1)	0·58 (2·2)	−0·70 (0·5)	3·08	0·19	1·71
Sweden	3·68 (1·7)	0·79 (3·5)	−0·63 (0·5)	3·73	0·38	1·79
Austria	1·33 (4·3)	1·02 (4·8)	−3·84 (3·3)	2·31	0·54	1·52
Spain	5·53 (2·3)	0·63 (2·8)	−0·43 (0·9)	5·54	0·28	2·31
Switzerland	1·86 (1·7)	0·34 (1·1)	−6·90 (2·6)	1·89	0·26	1·11
Australia	3·28 (2·7)	0·95 (3·3)	−0·66 (1·8)	3·09	0·41	1·33
New Zealand	1·68 (2·2)	0·45 (2·1)	−1·75 (1·8)	2·59	0·24	2·01
Japan	10·40 (1·8)	0·34 (1·1)	−5·31 (1·8)	4·21	0·14	1·71
Canada	5·17 (4·2)	0·49 (3·0)	−0·61 (3·2)	1·21	0·47	1·31
U.S.	2·64 (2·3)	0·40 (2·0)	−0·36 (2·0)	0·98	0·21	2·45
EEC Average	6·50 (2·6)	0·66 (2·4)	−1·17 (2·1)	3·22	0·30	1·84
OECD Average	5·51 (2·4)	0·59 (2·4)	−1·64 (1·9)	3·02	0·29	1·79

Notes:
1. t-statistics are in brackets (absolute values).
2. The coefficient on $\dot{w}_{-1}$ is 1 minus the coefficient on $\dot{p}_{-1}$. The equation was estimated in the form $\dot{w} - \dot{w}_{-1} = \alpha(\dot{p}_{-1} - \dot{w}_{-1}) - \beta U + \text{constant}$. Hence R^2 measures the proportion of Var $(\dot{w} - \dot{w}_{-1})$ explained.

REVIEW OF ECONOMIC STUDIES

TABLE II

Wage equation—Average statistics for eight EEC countries

	Constant /100	$\dot{p}$	$\dot{p}_{-1}$	U	$(w-p)_{-1}$	$t/100$	S.E. 100	R^2	DW
a. OLS to 1980	6·50 (2·57)		0·66 (2·39)	−1·17 (2·13)			3·22	0·30	1·84
b. 2SLS to 1980	6·43 (2·46)		0·65 (2·35)	−1·12 (2·01)			3·23	0·30	1·86
c. OLS to 1973	8·21 (2·44)		0·75 (2·38)	−1·74 (1·70)			3·11	0·36	1·87
d. OLS to 1980	5·97 (3·82)	0·90 (5·31)		−0·84 (2·16)			2·42	0·59	1·76
e. 2SLS to 1980	5·94 (3·61)	0·88 (4·88)		−0·80 (2·04)			2·43	0·58	1·79
f. OLS to 1973	7·72 (3·14)	0·98 (4·28)		−1·33 (1·44)			2·45	0·58	1·74
g. OLS to 1980	192·84 (1·27)		0·04 (2·07)	−1·59 (2·24)	−0·25 (1·22)	1·26 (1·37)	3·04	0·43	1·88
h. 2SLS to 1980	185·82 (1·22)		0·64 (2·04)	−1·54 (2·09)	−0·24 (1·16)	1·20 (1·31)	3·04	0·43	1·90
i. OLS to 1973	352·30 (1·35)		0·61 (1·84)	−1·29 (1·28)	−0·49 (1·32)	2·44 (1·41)	2·82	0·53	2·13
j. OLS to 1980	184·2 (1·51)	0·88 (5·23)		−1·13 (2·25)	−0·23 (1·43)	1·08 (1·60)	2·20	0·70	1·91
k. 2SLS to 1980	174·1 (1·38)	0·88 (4·78)		−1·08 (2·10)	−0·22 (1·31)	1·01 (1·47)	2·21	0·70	1·95
l. OLS to 1973	325·0 (1·91)	0·89 (4·13)		−0·74 (0·95)	−0·44 (1·86)	2·16 (1·98)	2·08	0·73	1·95

Note: See note to Table I.

a coefficient was truly zero in every country, then the sampling distribution of the average t-statistic for the 19 countries would have a standard deviation of $1/\sqrt{19}$. Hence one would only find an average absolute t-statistic greater than 0·45 in 5% of cases. In fact our average t for the unemployment coefficient in Table I is 1·9.[7]

Clearly a key feature of our model is the assumption that changes in productivity growth have not, within the period studied, affected the "constant term" in the wage equation. We tested for the presence of trend productivity growth (as defined below) in the wage equations and obtained an insignificant result, with the average OECD t-statistic equal to 0·09.

We performed various other wage equation estimates. The average results for the EEC countries are given in Table II—we shall in this paper concentrate more on results for the EEC than for the OECD as a whole, since the problem of labour slack appears to be most acute for the EEC countries.

After estimating equation (5) by OLS (row a), we reestimated it using 2-stage least squares,[8] with very similar results (row b). Then we estimated it with OLS to 1973 (row c). The average unemployment effect estimated to 1973 was somewhat higher, but its average t-statistic somewhat lower. To investigate the stability of equation (5), estimated with OLS, we report the Chow test in Table III. This is satisfied on average, especially for the EEC countries, where it only fails for Belgium and the U.K.

We next investigated the effect in equation (5) of replacing lagged price inflation ($\dot{p}_{-1}$) by current price inflation ($\dot{p}$). The results are shown in (d)–(f) of Table II.[9] The unemployment coefficients are somewhat reduced, as is the effect of lagged wages. We prefer the equations with $\dot{p}_{-1}$ to those with $\dot{p}$ because they make us worry less about

TABLE III

Chow test for stability of wage and price equations
Statistics based upon comparison of equations estimated 1957–1973 and 1957–80

	Wage equations				Price equation
Equations compared	a, c	d, f	g, i	j, l	
Variables used	$\dot{p}_{-1}$	$\dot{p}$	$\dot{p}_{-1}$ $(w-p)_{-1} / t$	$\dot{p}$ $(w-p)_{-1} / t$	
Degrees of freedom for F-statistic	(7, 14)	(7, 14)	(7, 12)	(7, 12)	(7, 10)
5% critical point	2·76	2·76	2·91	2·91	3·14
EEC Average F-statistic	1·73	1·11	1·78	1·56	3·13
OECD Average F-statistic	2·53	1·70	2·11	1·96	2·93
Countries rejected	Belgium U.K. Norway Sweden Australia Japan Canada	Norway Sweden Australia Canada	Belgium U.K. Sweden Austria Australia Japan	Denmark Norway Austria Australia	Ireland Italy Sweden Australia Canada U.S.A.

Note: $F = ([SSR(T+t)-SSR(T)]/t)/(SSR(T)/(T-K))$ where $T+t$ is the length of the longer estimation period, T the length of the shorter period, and K coefficients are independently estimated.

simultaneity and identification (a subject we return to later). It is interesting to note that, even when prices are included with a lag, the role of lagged wages is relatively small in EEC countries. We shall return later to the lower half of Table II.

Price equation

We estimate the price equation (2), in level form with an autoregressive error, and included additional terms for indirect tax rates (s), and lagged wages and import prices.[10] It then becomes

$$p - s = \delta_0 + \delta_1 w + (1-\delta_1-\delta_2-\delta_3)w_{-1} + \delta_2(p+p_m)$$
$$+ \delta_3(p+p_m)_{-1} + \delta_4 x - \gamma U + \varepsilon. \qquad (6)$$

In this equation, x represents the trend value of gross domestic product (y) per man (l). To find the trend value we must purge the year-by-year figures of cyclical influence. In the long-run

$$l = y - x$$

but in the short-run labour adjusts with a lag to changes in GDP and we may assume that, for annual data,

$$l = \psi l_{-1} + (1-\psi)y - (1-\psi)x$$
$$= \psi l_{-1} + (1-\psi)y - f(t).$$

We estimate this function for 19 countries using data from 1951–1980.[11] The function of time consists of a set of linear segments (i.e. a spline) with changes in slope occurring at the peak of each cycle in each country. A key feature of this approach is the imposed long-run constant returns to scale. This is at variance with much common practice and with the cross-sectional "findings" of Verdoorn's Law. One would, however, generally expect to find a statistical correlation between productivity growth and output growth, even if the true employment-output elasticity (holding productivity constant) is unity.[12] The results of this exercise are given in Table VI (below) and are discussed later.

TABLE IV

Price equation (equation 6)

Country	w	$(p+p_m)$	$(p+p_m)_{-1}$	x	U	ρ	S.E.100	DW
Belgium	-0.10 (0.9)	0.14 (1.9)	0.13 (1.8)	-0.72 (4.7)	-2.94 (12.3)	-0.12	1.08	1.99
Denmark	0.49 (3.0)	0.30 (4.3)	0.10 (1.4)	-0.62 (2.4)	-2.44 (13.7)	0.13	1.22	1.87
France	0.61 (3.6)	0.09 (1.5)	0.16 (2.7)	-0.51 (4.5)	-2.83 (2.5)	0.89	1.59	1.36
Germany	0.19 (1.6)	0.18 (3.6)	0.18 (2.3)	-0.52 (3.8)	-0.61 (1.0)	0.67	1.13	1.71
Ireland	0.52 (5.3)	0.07 (1.3)	0.15 (1.8)	-0.65 (4.5)	-0.60 (1.3)	0.33	1.25	1.96
Italy	0.36 (2.3)	0.12 (1.4)	0.13 (1.3)	-0.57 (2.5)	-1.85 (1.9)	0.94	3.09	1.19
Netherlands	0.34 (1.6)	0.22 (2.7)	0.18 (1.2)	-0.53 (1.4)	-0.71 (0.4)	0.55	2.11	1.56
U.K.	0.41 (4.7)	0.09 (2.4)	0.16 (2.8)	-0.77 (10.0)	-0.83 (2.0)	0.30	1.15	1.77
Finland	-0.66 (3.6)	0.16 (2.7)	0.06 (1.1)	-0.67 (7.6)	0.75 (1.6)	0.93	1.73	0.77
Norway	0.36 (2.2)	0.22 (2.3)	0.20 (1.6)	-0.40 (2.0)	0.44 (0.4)	0.91	1.82	1.27
Sweden	0.37 (3.4)	0.18 (2.6)	0.12 (1.6)	-0.85 (4.2)	0.55 (0.5)	0.86	1.81	1.65
Austria	0.14 (1.0)	0.37 (5.4)	0.16 (1.5)	-0.38 (2.0)	0.21 (0.2)	0.93	1.17	1.36
Spain	0.26 (1.7)	0.21 (2.0)	0.23 (2.0)	-0.47 (1.9)	0.55 (0.7)	0.60	3.38	1.43
Switzerland	-0.03 (0.3)	0.27 (6.0)	0.12 (3.0)	-0.32 (4.8)	-3.72 (2.0)	-0.07	0.82	2.01
Australia	0.41 (3.7)	0.05 (0.6)	0.07 (0.8)	-0.27 (2.4)	-3.27 (9.9)	0.31	1.23	1.70
New Zealand	0.47 (3.3)	0.08 (1.5)	0.13 (2.4)	-0.59 (3.3)	0.52 (0.5)	0.91	1.74	1.27
Japan	0.58 (2.5)	-0.07 (1.0)	0.10 (1.2)	-0.78 (5.9)	-11.50 (2.8)	0.89	2.87	1.35
Canada	0.86 (3.3)	0.24 (2.7)	0.12 (1.4)	-0.95 (4.4)	0.07 (0.2)	0.95	1.40	0.83
U.S.A.	0.64 (2.5)	0.09 (2.9)	-0.03 (0.6)	-0.77 (7.4)	0.19 (0.7)	0.92	0.99	0.88
EEC Average	0.35 (2.6)	0.15 (2.4)	0.15 (1.9)	-0.61 (4.2)	-1.60 (4.4)	0.46	1.58	1.68
OECD Average	0.40 (2.5)	0.16 (2.5)	0.13 (1.6)	-0.60 (4.2)	-1.53 (2.4)	0.62	1.66	1.47

Note: Constant term is not shown. The coefficient on w_1 is 1 minus the first three coefficients. R^2 is always 0.997 or more. The error structure is $\epsilon_t = \rho t_{t-1} + v_t$ (v i.i.d.), t-statistics are in brackets (absolute values).

There is an obvious problem of identifying the price equation. Whereas the wage equation excludes productivity and import prices, the price equation includes in some form all the main variables in the model. However, there is one key difference: unemployment affects the *level* of prices as compared with the *rate of change* of wages. Thus, if we difference the price equation for comparison with the wage equation, it contains $\dot{U}$ and excludes U. Moreover, we expect (and find) that a rise in $\dot{U}$ in the price equation will raise $(\dot{w} - \dot{p})$, whereas a rise in U in the wage equation will lower $(\dot{w} - \dot{p})$. In addition, since we use $\dot{p}_{-1}$ rather than $\dot{p}$ in the wage equation, we have further identification.

The results for the price equation are shown in Table IV. The coefficient on unemployment is negative in all EEC countries and the OECD average t-statistic for it is 2·4.

The results in Table IV were obtained by OLS. Two stage least squares estimates gave very similar results to OLS for the average EEC country.[13] We have preferred the OLS estimates for the individual countries, since in a few countries ill-determined 2SLS estimates gave curious simulation properties.[14]

4. EXPLAINING STAGFLATION 1973–1980

The aim of all we have done so far has been to help us understand the stagflation of the later 1970s. According to our theory stagflation has been caused by adverse shocks to relative import prices and productivity growth. The effects of these are already implied in the estimates of the previous section, but it is interesting first to document the shocks and then to draw out their consequences, using our previous estimates.

Relative import prices

Table V shows the course of relative import prices weighted by their shares in GDP. For the EEC countries the feasible real wage was improving on this account by nearly one half a per cent a year up to 1970–1973.[15] In 1974–1980 it worsened by about one third a per cent per year. The individual country figures of course reflect movements not only in the real prices of oil and other materials, but also in real exchange rates.

Productivity growth

Table VI shows our estimates of trend productivity growth. There was a fairly steady growth in most countries up to 1973 with a drop in growth in almost every country after that, averaging 2 percentage points.

Clearly an important issue is how far the fall in productivity growth can be considered exogenous and thus an independent source of stagflation rather than a consequence of higher unemployment. Since nobody has a satisfactory explanation of the fall in productivity growth, we cannot hope to fully resolve this issue but we can make a number of points.[16]

The first issue is whether our productivity measurements have properly allowed for short-term movements in output. It is sometimes argued that the fall in productivity growth since 1973 is simply the result of the low level of activity. A first reply to this is that productivity growth between 1977–1980 (when unemployment was roughly constant) was even lower than for 1974–1976—whether we use the trend estimates in Table VI or the simple unadjusted figures. Thus there has indeed been a substantial fall in productivity growth comparing points at the same level of capacity utilisation.

However it might then be argued that trend productivity growth is affected by the long-term level of capacity utilisation (Bruno (1982*b*)). The most obvious mechanism would be a fall in the level of investment.[17] It is certainly the case that the rate of growth of capital relative to labour force has been much slower since 1973 than before. If we multiply the change in the annual rate of growth of the capital/labour ratio by the share

REVIEW OF ECONOMIC STUDIES

TABLE V

Import price relative to consumption deflator, multiplied by import share
(Divisia index of log values ×100, 1970–1973=0)

Country	1955–1959	1960–1964	1965–1969	1970–1973	1974–1980	1974	1975	1976	1977	1978	1979	1980
Belgium	7·76	4·69	1·27	0·00	1·91	5·94	2·27	1·85	-0·24	-1·86	0·71	4·73
Denmark	13·55	7·73	2·65	0·00	1·48	4·08	2·25	1·76	1·35	-1·46	-0·39	2·74
France	3·55	2·69	1·07	0·00	0·63	3·29	0·80	0·59	0·92	-0·59	-0·57	-0·03
Germany	5·85	3·29	2·00	0·00	0·84	2·10	0·88	0·95	0·39	-0·71	0·46	1·83
Ireland	13·04	9·13	3·70	0·00	9·12	9·34	8·50	8·55	10·57	9·00	8·93	8·96
Italy	5·18	2·18	0·33	0·00	4·50	6·68	3·98	5·10	4·86	2·98	3·47	4·40
Netherlands	22·57	14·37	5·90	0·00	1·26	5·26	2·21	1·20	-0·05	-2·82	-0·19	3·22
U.K.	3·68	1·52	0·12	0·00	3·84	6·62	3·87	5·33	5·08	3·36	2·11	0·51
Finland	0·66	-0·40	-2·38	0·00	3·35	4·51	2·55	0·88	2·00	2·86	4·61	6·00
Norway	15·64	8·36	2·92	0·00	2·65	5·03	2·35	1·43	1·28	0·45	3·16	4·87
Sweden	6·74	3·47	0·91	0·00	3·49	5·38	3·50	2·33	2·45	2·12	4·06	4·56
Austria	6·08	2·80	0·64	0·00	1·29	0·94	-0·33	-1·50	-1·91	-2·75	-2·31	-1·20
Spain	4·77	3·73	0·98	0·00	-0·15	2·31	0·83	0·47	0·16	-1·57	-2·84	-0·42
Switzerland	8·73	5·56	2·22	0·00	-4·18	0·28	-2·91	-5·00	-3·65	-7·50	-6·57	-3·90
Australia	4·05	2·19	0·64	0·00	1·48	0·91	0·25	0·82	1·42	1·51	2·71	2·71
New Zealand	5·76	2·18	-0·01	0·00	7·06	3·39	7·20	9·07	7·14	5·33	7·77	9·53
Japan	7·03	4·14	1·71	0·00	1·15	2·76	2·37	1·97	0·47	-2·05	-0·08	2·64
Canada	0·96	1·28	0·87	0·00	2·98	1·56	2·46	0·99	2·04	3·45	4·58	5·78
U.S.A.	0·53	0·04	-0·21	0·00	2·96	2·54	2·71	2·49	2·73	2·63	3·34	4·27
EEC Average	6·18	3·58	1·45	0·00	1·94	4·26	2·02	2·30	1·96	0·38	0·90	1·79
OECD Average	3·90	2·19	0·77	0·00	2·15	3·11	2·23	2·07	1·92	0·96	1·80	2·99

Note: To allow for changes in the share of imports in GDP (μ_t) we construct a Divisia index (I) such that in year t, $\dot{I}_t = \mu_{t-1}\dot{p}_{mt} \times 100$. The index is obtained by summation, setting 1970–1973=0.

TABLE VI

Trend productivity growth (100ẋ)

Country	1951–1956	1957–1960	1961–1965	1966–1970	1971–1973	1974–1976	1977–1980	1960–1973	1974–1980	1974–1980 minus 1960–1973
Belgium	2·65	2·47	4·39	8·91	4·30	3·30	1·76	3·96	2·38	−1·58
Denmark	2·19	1·13	3·38	3·12	2·88	1·77	0·46	3·05	0·93	−2·12
France	3·73	5·31	4·82	4·21	5·01	3·19	2·61	4·72	2·82	−1·90
Germany	5·53	4·96	4·60	4·33	4·36	4·16	1·83	4·45	2·66	−1·79
Ireland	2·82	2·37	2·89	4·29	5·25	3·18	1·69	4·16	2·22	−1·94
Italy	3·09	6·56	6·16	5·75	3·56	−0·76	2·53	5·52	1·66	−3·86
Netherlands	3·70	2·71	3·63	4·60	5·01	2·23	1·69	4·15	2·08	−2·07
U.K.	2·07	2·10	2·28	3·47	2·77	1·42	1·79	2·76	1·66	−1·09
Finland	4·39	3·45	4·10	4·98	4·24	3·60	1·75	4·35	2·41	−1·94
Norway	1·98	4·94	3·57	3·81	2·05	3·33	2·04	3·43	2·50	−0·93
Sweden	3·71	2·06	3·64	3·52	2·22	−0·20	0·54	3·24	0·45	−2·79
Austria	5·67	4·80	4·04	5·42	5·28	3·00	1·85	5·02	2·42	−2·60
Spain	2·31	6·30	5·82	5·07	5·18	7·24	6·43	5·57	6·57	1·00
Switzerland	3·48	1·73	2·29	3·78	3·01	1·42	0·31	3·09	0·82	−2·27
Australia	2·68	2·00	1·82	2·50	2·93	2·17	0·91	2·42	1·36	−1·06
New Zealand	1·14	2·15	1·81	1·63	1·84	1·05	0·34	1·78	0·65	−1·12
Japan	3·03	8·28	8·54	8·60	7·85	2·34	3·15	8·17	2·86	−5·31
Canada	3·54	1·80	2·17	2·92	1·95	2·05	−0·37	2·20	0·49	−1·71
U.S.A.	2·35	0·83	2·43	1·64	1·56	0·57	0·74	1·94	0·68	−1·26
EEC Average	3·81	4·42	4·37	4·32	4·14	2·55	2·06	4·30	2·29	−2·01
OECD Average	3·07	3·33	3·98	3·73	3·47	1·81	1·62	3·75	1·71	−2·04

Note: For source see the price equation subsection of Section 3.

of capital in GDP we should, on growth-accounting assumptions, have a measure of the contribution of changes in capital-deepening to changes in labour productivity growth. Our estimates are in line with other studies in suggesting a relatively small contribution from this source. Of the 2 points fall in OECD trend productivity growth, only 0·3 points are on this reading due to the lower investment rate.[18]

Next there is the question of whether the fall in the value-added productivity growth is a statistical artifact due to rising raw material prices (Bruno (1982b)). As is explained in another paper (Grubb (1982)), we do not find this argument very convincing.[19] However the oil shock may well have had genuine effects on productivity growth, unrelated to questions of measurement. This might be so if parts of the capital stock were rendered obsolete in ways not captured in the standard measurement of capital (Baily (1981)). In addition there may have been a spontaneous drying up of invention in the U.S.A. plus some exhaustion of the scope for catching-up in other countries, (especially Japan) (Gomulka (1979), and Jorgensen and Nishimizu (1978)). Thus we believe that a substantial part of the productivity slowdown can be regarded as an exogenous cause of stagflation rather than a reflection of it. But whether or not the productivity fall is exogenous does not affect the validity of our simulations.

Simulations

We use our system to throw light on the changes in EEC inflation and unemployment between 1972 and 1980, focussing first on inflation and then on unemployment. The change in inflation between 1972 and 1980 can be attributed to:[20]

1. The excess of actual relative import prices above their 1960/62–1970/72 trend (Δp_m).

2. The shortfall of actual productivity below its 1960–1972 trend ($-\Delta x$).

3. The underlying rate of increase of inflation in 1972 (measured by its annual rate of increase from 1969 to 1972) cumulated over 8 years.

4. The excess of actual unemployment over its 1970/72 level (ΔU).

Table VII shows these four items in its first four columns. Adding these changes to $\dot{p}_{72}$ (shown in Column 5) gives $\hat{p}_{80}$ (shown in Column 6). This can be compared with the actual $\dot{p}_{80}$ (shown in Column 7).

Focussing on the results for the EEC (at the foot of the table), the actual net increase in inflation between 1972 and 1980 was 4·5%. According to our estimates this was due to:

Higher relative import prices	+ 5·2%
Lower productivity growth	+ 5·3%
Trend increase in inflation	+ 4·7%
Higher adjusted unemployment	− 11·0%
	4·2%

Another way of looking at the same information is to "account for" the changes in unemployment. We can define the amount of inflation that must have been suppressed by the rise in unemployment as

Inflation suppressed = Inflation generated − Inflation permitted = $1 + 2 + 3 - (7 - 5)$.

To get the unemployment cost of this suppression, we should divide the unemployment suppressed by the effect on inflation of a percent-year of unemployment ($d\dot{p}/dU$). This latter statistic ($d\dot{p}/dU$) is one of the most interesting magnitudes in macroeconomics, since its reciprocal tells us the unemployment cost of reducing inflation. In the EEC the average cost of reducing inflation by 1 percentage point is 1·25 point-years of unemployment.[21] Thus in Column 10 we can estimate the unemployment cost of inflation that

TABLE VII

Simulation of changes in inflation between 1972 and 1980

	1	2	3	4	5	6	7	8	9	10	11
	Effects on inflation of					1980 inflation rate		Suppressed inflation			Unemployment increase (point-years)	
Country	Rise in relative import prices (Δp_m)	Productivity fall ($-\Delta x$)	Trend increase in $\hat p$	Increase in unemployment (ΔU)	1972 inflation rate ($\hat p_{72}$)	Predicted (5+1+2+3+4)	Actual ($\hat p_{80}$)	$1+2+3-(7-5)$	$d\hat p/dU$	Predicted (8÷9)	Actual
Belgium	2·6	3·6	6·7	−16·4	5·3	1·7	6·3	11·8	0·61	19·4	27·0
Denmark	15·4	10·8	8·7	−30·3	7·9	12·5	11·2	31·5	0·95	33·1	31·8
France	−0·5	−0·2	−3·3	−2·7	5·6	−1·1	12·0	−10·4	0·31	−34·0	8·7
Germany	7·0	5·1	9·3	−14·4	5·4	12·4	5·2	21·6	0·72	29·8	19·9
Ireland	6·9	7·9	5·6	−13·4	9·2	16·1	16·7	12·8	0·61	20·8	21·9
Italy	9·0	13·6	9·0	−7·6	6·2	30·2	16·6	21·3	0·96	22·1	7·9
Netherlands	12·4	7·0	6·8	−25·1	8·4	9·5	6·6	28·0	1·60	17·5	15·7
U.K.	3·7	5·6	2·7	−10·3	6·4	8·1	14·8	3·5	1·42	2·5	7·3
Finland	1·5	2·5	15·6	−8·6	8·3	19·3	10·4	17·5	0·80	22·0	10·8
Norway	10·5	1·9	7·7	−1·0	6·4	25·5	9·7	16·8	0·48	34·7	2·1
Sweden	8·2	14·3	8·1	1·9	6·4	38·9	10·9	26·1	0·33	79·2	−5·8
Austria	3·1	7·5	8·0	−10·7	6·3	14·2	6·0	18·8	1·70	11·1	6·3
Spain	7·0	−2·5	12·2	−2·5	7·9	22·1	14·4	10·2	0·08	124·4	30·8
Switzerland	2·7	2·8	12·3	−11·0	7·3	14·2	4·4	20·8	4·45	4·7	2·5
Australia	2·5	1·6	5·4	−19·1	6·1	−3·6	8·5	7·0	0·81	8·6	23·5
New Zealand	4·5	2·5	4·1	−5·8	6·1	11·5	16·0	1·3	1·33	1·0	4·3
Japan	0·6	12·5	1·7	−22·8	5·2	−2·7	6·8	13·3	4·73	2·8	4·8
Canada	8·9	11·5	0·6	−5·7	4·0	19·2	10·0	14·9	0·66	22·7	8·7
U.S.A.	1·9	3·5	−2·9	−2·4	3·5	3·5	9·7	−3·8	0·27	−14·1	8·9
EEC Average	5·2	5·3	4·7	−11·0	6·0	10·2	10·5	10·8	0·80	13·4	13·8
OECD Average	3·5	5·6	1·8	−8·6	5·0	7·2	9·7	6·1	0·82	7·5	10·5

has been suppressed as

$$\text{Unemployment cost} = \frac{\text{Inflation suppressed}}{d\ddot{p}/dU} = \frac{\text{Col. 8}}{\text{Col. 9}}.$$

For the average EEC country, 10·8 points of inflation have been suppressed at a cost of 13·4 point-years of unemployment. This compares with 13·8 extra years of unemployment actually experienced.

Needless to say, the individual country comparison is generally less good than the average EEC comparison, where the errors on the individual country parameter estimates will tend to average out. In another paper we examine how far our present line of thought helps to explain inter-country differences in the growth of unemployment, and we also show how the concept of nominal wage flexibility ($d\ddot{p}/dU$) is related to the concept of real wage flexibility (Grubb, Jackman and Layard (1983)).

5. A FULLY ADAPTIVE WAGE EQUATION

The wage equation we have been using so far is not wholly satisfactory, since it assumes a constant target growth rate of real wages. However this target must in the long run adjust to the actual growth rate experienced. The most obvious evidence for this proposition is that, as between countries, unemployment is not systematically higher or faster-growing in countries with slower productivity growth. Yet in our wage equation the growth rate of target real wages is independent of actual real wage growth, and thus a fall in productivity growth leads to a permanent rise in unemployment. To give the model more realistic long-term properties, the target real wage must be allowed to respond to developments in the economy.

Model

A general model of wage-determination might assume that in each particular year settlements aim at a real wage which consists of a target real wage (ω^*), based on past experience, modified by the current level of labour slack. Hence, assuming that price expectations are correct apart from white noise error, we can describe the actual level of real wages (ω) in any year by

$$\omega = \omega^* - \beta(U - U_0) + \varepsilon. \tag{7}$$

If the target real wage is a linear function of past real wages this implies

$$\omega = \sum a_i \omega_{-i} - \beta(U - U_0) + \varepsilon. \tag{8}$$

Since unemployment depends on $\omega - \sum a_i\omega_{-i}$, we need to impose some restrictions on the parameters a_i. In particular we need to ensure that the parameters are such that $(U - U_0)$ is in the long run independent of the rate of growth of real wages ($\dot{\omega}$). This requires that equation (8) can be written entirely in terms of second differences, without specific reference to the levels of ω or $\dot{\omega}$ (see Annex 2). Hence equation (8) would have the form

$$\ddot{\omega} = \sum c_i \ddot{\omega}_{-i} - \beta(U - U_0). \tag{9}$$

Given this, we can imagine a situation in which wage growth was steady until t periods ago, then fell to a new lower rate. Thus $\ddot{\omega}_{-t}$ is negative, but all other $\ddot{\omega}_{-i}$ are zero. So (in the absence of errors),

$$U - U_0 = \left(\frac{c_t \ddot{\omega}_{-t}}{\beta}\right).$$

We expect c_t to be negative, since if $\ddot{\omega}_{-t}$ is negative we expect $U - U_0$ to be positive. Hence $(-c_t/\beta)$ tells us how much unemployment is created by a unit fall in real wage growth t periods ago.

To estimate the pattern of the c_is some further structure has to be imposed since the lag pattern may be very long. A reasonable approach is to assume a two-stage adaptive scheme for the real wage target (ω^*).[22] First, the target *level* of real wages is formed on the basis of levels observed in the past, updated by target growth:

$$\omega^* = \theta\omega^*_{-1} + (1-\theta)\omega_{-1} + \dot{x}^e. \tag{10}$$

Second, the target growth rate $(\dot{x}^e)$ is itself formed by a process of adaptation to actual real wage growth:

$$\dot{x}^e = \lambda\dot{x}^e_{-1} + (1-\lambda)\dot{\omega}_{-1}. \tag{11}$$

Using the lag operator, L, we can substitute out $\dot{x}^e$, $\dot{x}^e_{-1}$ and ω^*_{-1} from (10) and (11) to obtain an expression for ω^* in terms of lagged ωs. Substituting this into (7) gives (see Annex 2):

$$\ddot{\omega} = \left(\frac{-(\theta+\lambda)+\theta\lambda L}{(1-\theta L)(1-\lambda L)}\right)\ddot{\omega}_{-1} - \beta(U - U_0) + \varepsilon. \tag{12}$$

This equation includes three interesting special cases. If $\lambda = 1$ and $\theta = 0$, one can see from equations (10) and (11) that we obtain our original basic equation (1):

$$\omega = \omega_{-1} - \beta(U - U_0) + \dot{x}^e. \tag{13}$$

This implies immediate adaptation in levels but none in growth rates.

By contrast if $\lambda = \theta = 1$, so that there is no adaptation, we get a wage equation

$$\omega = \dot{x}^e t - \beta(U - U_0). \tag{14}$$

This equation is obviously unsatisfactory since if $\dot{x}^e$ happens to differ from the long-run growth of real wages, unemployment must rise indefinitely. A less extreme approach, though still subject to the same objection in terms of its long-run properties, is to take a weighted average of (13) and (14):

$$\omega = \zeta\dot{x}^e t + (1-\zeta)\omega_{-1} - \beta(U - U_0) + (1-\zeta)\dot{x}^e.$$

This equation is sometimes known as the Sargan (1964) equation. We report estimated versions of this equation in Table II, but have not used them for simulation due to the lowish t-statistics on ω_{-1}.

A final special case assumes immediate adjustment in levels and growth rates $(\lambda = \theta = 0)$, giving

$$\omega = \omega_{-1} + \dot{\omega}_{-1} - \beta(U - U_0). \tag{15}$$

More generally, for θ and λ between 0 and 1, if productivity growth falls permanently, unemployment will rise initially and then fall back towards U_0. At $\theta = \lambda = 0\cdot8$, for example, unemployment peaks after 3–4 years.

Estimation

To obtain estimates of wage adaptation in practice, we need to estimate (12). Initially we constructed numerical series for $\ddot{\omega}_{-1}(-(\theta+\lambda)+\theta\lambda L)/(1-\theta L)(1-\lambda L)$ assuming particular values for θ and λ, and used these series in the wage equation. However, a search over θ and λ indicated (for a variety of data sets) that the residual sum of squares was minimized at values of θ and λ greater than one. This result is behaviourally implausible, and arises because such estimation is subject to severe small-sample bias, which biases downwards the coefficients on lagged dependent variables, the more so the longer the

REVIEW OF ECONOMIC STUDIES

lag (see Annex 3). A complementary explanation is given by noting that (12) can be rewritten, by multiplying through by $(1 - \theta L)(1 - \lambda L)$, as a moving average error process for $\ddot{\omega}$. It has been shown for the first-order MA process (Davidson (1981) and references) that the residual sum of squares falls indefinitely (towards zero) as the assumed MA parameter (corresponding to θ and λ) is increased, regardless of the true value of the MA parameter.

To tackle these problems, we corrected for biases in the estimation of θ and λ by means of Monte Carlo simulations. To facilitate estimation, the model was respecified in the following form (the results will later be related to the form of (12)):

$$\ddot{\omega} = \frac{(\alpha_1 + \alpha_2 L)}{(1 - \phi L)} \ddot{\omega}_{-1} - \beta_1 U - \beta_2 \dot{U} + \varepsilon. \tag{16}$$

For different values of ϕ we then constructed the variable $z = \ddot{\omega} + \phi \ddot{\omega}_{-1} + \phi^2 \ddot{\omega}_{-2} \ldots$, ignoring terms in $\ddot{\omega}$ before 1952, for which no data were available. $\ddot{\omega}$ was then regressed on $z_{-1}, z_{-2}, U, \dot{U}$, and ϕ'. (This last term proxies for the effect of $\ddot{\omega}$ in years prior to 1952, which depreciates by the factor ϕ each year). For each value of ϕ assumed, this led to OLS estimates of $\hat{\alpha}_1, \hat{\alpha}_2, \hat{\beta}_1, \hat{\beta}_2$, for each country, which were then averaged for the OECD as a whole. Another statistic, $\partial \log RSS / \partial \phi$, was also recorded: this is the gradient relating the change in residual sum of squares to a marginal increase in the assumed value of ϕ.

In parallel with the estimates using real world data, Monte Carlo data were generated using the same value of ϕ, and specified values of c_1, α_2, β_1, and β_2 in equation (16), with pseudo-normal random numbers representing the errors ε. Exactly the same OLS estimation procedure was used with these Monte Carlo data.

The values of $\alpha_1, \alpha_2, \beta_1, \beta_2$, and ϕ used to generate the Monte Carlo data were adjusted until the Monte Carlo data gave the same results in OLS estimation (in terms of $\hat{\alpha}_1, \hat{\alpha}_2, \hat{\beta}_1, \hat{\beta}_2$ and $\partial \log RSS / \partial \phi$) as the real world data for the same ϕ. We were then able to conclude that the process generating the real world data was observationally equivalent to the process generating the Monte Carlo data.[23] Knowing this process, we had obtained an estimate of the parameters which corrected for the bias in OLS estimation.

The final estimates presented below are based on 21 Monte Carlo replications for each country, assuming the same parameter values for each country. Given the number of replications, any errors due to random factors in the Monte Carlo data must be negligible in relation to errors due to random factors in the real world data.

The variation of results from one Monte Carlo replication to another provides a basis for computation of standard errors of parameter estimates; the detailed methodology is available on request. The estimate of (16), with t-statistics in brackets, was

$$\ddot{\omega} = \frac{\left(\begin{array}{c}-0.63 \\ (10.2)\end{array} + \begin{array}{c}0.045L \\ (1.1)\end{array}\right)}{\left(\begin{array}{c}1 - 0.88L \\ (30.1)\end{array}\right)} \ddot{\omega}_{-1} - \frac{0.70U}{(4.4)} - \frac{11.06\dot{U}}{(3.6)} + \text{constant} + \varepsilon. \tag{17}$$

The t-statistics here are t-statistics for the common OECD parameter estimates: the 18 country data sets together allow relatively precise estimates to be made. The hypothesis that the adaptive parameter (ϕ) is 1 can easily be rejected ($t = 4.3$).

We can now relate these equation estimates to the earlier model of equation (12) by rewriting (17) as

$$\ddot{\omega} = \frac{(-1.24 + 0.57L)}{(1 - 0.60L)(1 - 0.88L)} \ddot{\omega}_{-1} - 1.76U + \text{constant} + \frac{\varepsilon}{(1 - 0.60L)}. \tag{18}$$

This rewritten form of the estimated equation comes fairly close to embodying the constraints in theoretical form (12), except for the presence of an autoregressive error. It is not possible to identify θ and λ individually, since (12) is symmetric in θ and λ. But both parameters seem to imply some lags in the adaptive process. This is illustrated by the weights on $\ddot{\omega}_{-1}$ in (9) which can easily be computed, and imply that the unemployment generated in year t by a 1% fall in the growth rate of real wages that has occurred in year zero is:

t	$100(U - U_0)$
0	0·569
1	0·703
2	0·714
3	0·685
4	0·635
5	0·578
7	0·463
10	0·319
15	0·167
20	0·086

The total percentage point-years of unemployment generated is 8·2, half of which is generated in the first 7 years. This result provides some evidence that real wage targets are, albeit slowly, falling into line with the slower growth rates experienced since 1973. But in the first 7 years or so the unemployment effect of a once-for-all fall in productivity growth is fairly flat, as it is in the basic model in the earlier part of this paper. This gives us some confidence in thinking that the basic model captures important aspects of the medium-term effects of a fall in the feasible growth of real wages. Thus the simple wage equation with which we are familiar seems to embody many of the main medium-term features of real wage resistance.

ANNEX 1

Deriving the price equation

Suppose the production function is separable of the form

$$Q = f[AK^{\gamma}L^{1-\gamma}, M]$$

where Q is gross output, K capital (taken as given), L labour and M imports. The factor-price frontier can as a first order approximation be written as[24]

$$(1-\gamma)(w-p) + \gamma r + \mu p_m = a + \text{constant}$$

where r is the real return on capital, p_m is the price of imports relative to final output and μ is the share of imports relative to the share of value-added and $a = \log A$. Since $l - k = r - (w-p) + \text{constant}$,

$$(w-p) = \gamma(k-l) - \mu p_m + \text{constant}.$$

At this point we can note that log value-added per worker is $a + \gamma(k-l)$. However, we are interested in the relation between $(w-p)$, unemployment (U) and value-added per worker net of cyclical effects (x). This relation is found by substituting $U = l^* - l$ where l^* is labour force, which gives

$$w - p = a + \gamma(k - l^*) - \mu p_m + \gamma U + \text{constant}$$

$$= x - \mu p_m + \gamma U + \text{constant}.$$

REVIEW OF ECONOMIC STUDIES

It is natural to ask whether these conclusions, which follow in part from the separability assumption, are reasonable. Work by Berndt and Wood on long-run production functions for manufacturing using energy, raw materials, capital and labour implies that the separability assumption does not hold. If one uses their results to compute the relevant elasticities of complementarity,[25] it turns out that holding constant K, L and materials, a 10% fall in energy use lowers the marginal product of labour by 1% and of capital by 10%. If the share of labour in value-added was initially 85% it would rise to 86·3%. A 10% fall in materials use (holding constant K, L and energy) lowers the marginal product of labour by 10% and of capital by 15%, with the share of labour rising to 85·7%. However, both these responses could only apply in the long-run. In the short-run one might suppose that materials, energy and labour (the variable factors) were strongly complementary to each other, in which case labour would (at full employment) bear the main burden of the reduction in energy use.[26] We are therefore reasonably happy to approximate the warranted real wage over the period we are studying by the preceding equation.

ANNEX 2

Forms of the fully adaptive wage equation

Proof of generality for the second differencing restriction on ω. If we have a general lag function of real wages in the wage equation

$$\omega = \sum_{i=1}^{T} a_i \omega_{-i} - \beta(U - U_0) \tag{A1}$$

this can be rewritten, without loss of generality, as

$$\ddot{\omega} = \sum_{i=1}^{T-2} c_i \ddot{\omega}_{-i} + c_{T-1} \omega_{-(T-1)} + c_T \omega_{-T} - \beta(U - U_0) \tag{A2}$$

since the coefficients $c_1 - c_T$ can be chosen to give the same weights on the ω_t as in (A1). Steady state growth is defined by the fact that $\dot{\omega}_t = \dot{\omega}_{t-1}$, i.e. $\ddot{\omega}_t = 0$ for all t. This is consistent with $U = U_0$ in (A2) only if the terms $c_{T-1}\omega_{-(T-1)} + c_T\omega_{-T}$ are zero. But these terms can only generally be zero—for a variety of levels and growth rates of ω—if $c_{T-1} = c_T = 0$. This proves that when desired real wages are made a linear lag function of past real wages, with the property that the NAIRU is in the long run invariant to the growth rate, it will in general be possible to write the wage equation in terms of second differences of real wages.

Derivation of adaptive expectations equation (12). Taking the negative of (11) and adding $\dot{\omega}$ to both sides, we have

$$\dot{\omega} - \dot{x}^e = \lambda(\dot{\omega} - \dot{x}^e)_{-1} + \ddot{\omega}$$

i.e.

$$\dot{\omega} - \dot{x}^e = \frac{\ddot{\omega}}{(1 - \lambda L)}, \quad \text{using the lag operator } L.$$

Similarly taking the negative of (10) and adding ω to both sides, we have

$$\omega - \omega^* = \theta(\omega - \omega^*)_{-1} + \dot{\omega} - \dot{x}^e.$$

So

$$\omega - \omega^* = \frac{\dot{\omega} - \dot{x}^e}{(1-\theta L)} = \frac{\ddot{\omega}}{(1-\theta L)(1-\lambda L)}$$

$$= \left(1 + \frac{(\theta + \lambda)L - \theta \lambda L^2}{(1-\theta L)(1-\lambda L)}\right)\ddot{\omega}$$

$$= \ddot{\omega} - \left(\frac{-(\theta + \lambda) + \theta \lambda L}{(1-\theta L)(1-\lambda L)}\right)\ddot{\omega}_{-1}$$

Substituting for $\omega - \omega^*$ into (7), we have (12).

ANNEX 3

Small sample bias with lagged dependent variables

It is known that estimated coefficients on lagged dependent variables are generally biased downwards in small samples (e.g. see Johnston (1963) p. 305). Marriott and Pope (1954) give a formula for the bias in the k-th order serial correlation coefficient.

$$E(\hat{\rho}_k) = \rho_k - \frac{1}{N}\left(\frac{(1+\rho)(1-\rho^k)}{(1-\rho)} + 2k\rho^k\right) \tag{A3}$$

where N = number of observations, ρ = true autoregressive parameter, k = order of lag.

As ρ tends to 1 the bias tends to $-4k/N$, i.e. it increases approximately linearly with k. It seems likely that a similar pattern of bias increasing with lag length could account for the implausible lag structure on $\ddot{\omega}$ estimated by least-squares methods. It is difficult to say more than this because little theoretical or empirical work on estimation of general multiple-lagged autoregressive structures has been reported. Our assumed data generating process is more complicated than that examined by Marriott and Pope, which means that their work can only be suggestive for our problem.

It would be possible to multiply (16) throughout by $(1-\phi L)$ to create a finite lag structure. This would require estimation with a moving average error and restrictions among error-process and other parameters. With the restrictions imposed, least squares estimation of the moving average version of (16) would produce the same problems of bias. Maximum likelihood estimation should be more satisfactory but might be difficult to carry out in practice.

It would be possible to estimate the model with quarterly data, in order to increase the sample size. However, according to the Marriott and Pope formula (A3) (with ρ near 1), the bias decreases proportionately to the number of observations (N), but it increases proportionately to the order of lag (K). Hence in estimating the coefficients on terms lagged by a given number of years (rather than a given number of estimation periods), moving to quarterly data does not reduce the bias.

DATA APPENDIX

The main data sources are as follows, supplemented by some individual country statistics. For OECD sources we use the following abbreviations: Main Economic Indicators (MEI); National Accounts (NA); Labour Force Statistics (LFS). For earlier years see the corresponding OEEC volumes.

1. Wages
Definition: Average hourly earnings in manufacturing (most countries).

Source: Most countries: MEI 1960–1979 and MEI 1955–1970. France, Italy and Netherlands: ILO Yearbooks chained. U.K.: British Labour Statistics Historical Abstract, Economic Trends Annual Supplement and ILO Yearbooks.

2. Prices
Definition: Ratio of consumers' expenditure to constant price consumers' expenditure (1975 prices).
Source: NA.

3. Unemployment rate
Definition: Unemployed as % of employed and unemployed (unemployed is based on country definitions, and employed includes self-employed).
Source: LFS (most countries).

4. Adjusted unemployment rate (as used in regressions)
Definition: We estimate for 1960–1972 the regression $U_t = a + bt$. For those countries for which the time trend fitted to 1960–1972 data have a t-value exceeding 2, unemployment is set at $\bar{U}_{60-72} + U_t - a - bt$. The countries affected are Austria, Denmark, France, Ireland, Netherlands, New Zealand, Spain, Sweden, Switzerland, U.K.
Source: As above.

5. Import prices relative to consumption deflator, and import share
Definition: Import price is value of imports divided by value of imports at 1975 prices.
Source: NA.

6. Trend productivity growth
Definition: See text.
Source: Employment: LFS (most countries).
        GDP at 1975 prices: NA.

7. Rate of indirect taxation
Definition: log (GDP including indirect taxes and subsidies/GDP excluding indirect taxes and subsidies).
Source: NA.

8. Unit value of world manufacturing exports ($)
Source: UN Yearbook of International Trade Statistics (various issues): Tables for world exports of market economies by commodity classes.

9. Sterling/dollar exchange rate
Source: IMF International Financial Statistics.

10. Growth rate of capital intensity
Definition: Growth in ratio of capital stock to trend man-hours. Capital stock is measured as initial capital plus accumulated gross investment (excluding increases in stocks) all depreciated annually at a rate of 6·8% (see Jorgensen and Griliches (1972) p. 69, Table 5). Initial capital stock (K_0) was chosen so as to ensure a roughly constant capital/GDP ratio from the intial date to 1970. Sensitivity analysis in which K_0 was replaced by $1·33K_0$ and by $0·66K_0$ showed that the change in the growth rate from 1960–1973 to 1974–1978 is little affected. The growth rate of trend man-hours is calculated as

$$\log\left[(L_t + L_{t-1})/(L_{t-1} + L_{t-2})\right]$$

where L is man-hours. The capital stock in year t is measured at the beginning of period t by including only investment up to and including that in $(t-1)$.
Source: NA.

11. Vacancies
Definition: Numbers of vacancies registered with the public employment service.
Source: MEI.

We are extremely grateful to Tayo Casas-Bedos for computing assistance, to O. Ashenfelter, M. Bruno, J. S. Flemming, M. A. King, S. J. Nickell, C. A. Pissarides and the referees for suggestions, to OECD for help with data and to the SSRC and the Esmee Fairbairn Charitable Trust for supporting the project.

NOTES
    1. Evidence on this point, together with country statistics on all our main variables, is provided in an earlier and fuller version of this paper, Centre for Labour Economics Discussion Paper No. 96.
    2. For a more exact definition of U_0 see footnote (3).
    3. This approach makes clear the meaning of the term U_0 in the wage equation. It is the level of unemployment which would prevail if wage-setting behaviour had fully adjusted to the feasible growth of real wages. Some people might like to call U_0 equilibrium unemployment (or the natural rate), but this may not be very helpful since U_0 may itself reflect union wage-setting and other disequilibrium phenomena not arising from incorrect expectations or slow adjustment (Jackman and Layard (1982)).
    4. We tested for homogeneity by estimating the equation in the following form: $\dot{w} - \dot{w}_{-1} = \alpha(\dot{p}_{-1} - \dot{w}_{-1}) + \xi \dot{w}_{-1} - \beta U + \text{const}$. The OECD average t-statistic on ξ was 0.8. In 5 countries ξ was significantly negative (Finland, France, Japan, Sweden and Switzerland) and in 2 significantly positive (Australia and Canada).
    5. Where the series were available, we did estimate equation (5) using vacancies and then capacity utilization, with broadly similar overall results to those reported for our "adjusted unemployment" measure.
    6. The countries affected are listed in the Data Appendix.
    7. When we did a time-series cross-section pooled regression, we found the t-statistic on unemployment was close to $\sqrt{19}$ times the average of the t-statistics on unemployment in the individual countries when these were each allowed to have their own coefficient. Other results from the pooled time-series cross-section estimates were as follows:
        (i) The t-statistic when unemployment was entered linearly (i.e. as U) was substantially higher than when it was entered as $1/U$ and somewhat higher than when entered as log U.
        (ii) The t-statistic when unemployment was entered as current U was substantially higher than when it was entered with a one year lag. When both U and U_{-1} were entered the coefficient on U_{-1} was positive and one third as large as the (negative) coefficient on U.
        (iii) In one analysis separate dummies were included for each date, so that the coefficient on unemployment only reflected the effect of differences of variables from their means across countries. The unemployment coefficient estimate was reduced by one third but was still highly significant. The pattern of the coefficients on the date dummies suggested support for the idea of wage push in 1970–1975 inclusive. Further details are available on request.
    8. In the 2SLS estimates, the instruments were p_{-1}, p_{-2}, w_{-1}, w_{-2}, $(p+p_m)_{-1}$, x, U_{-1}, y_{-1} and an instrument for current import prices equal to $(p+p_m-p^*)$, where p^* is the world price of manufactured exports (in £) and y is real GDP.
    9. The 2SLS version can be thought of as approximately including the effect of price expectations, since $\dot{p}$ is instrumented on the variables listed in the previous footnote. In fact the instruments include two current variables which would have to be excluded to permit this interpretation in full.
    10. We have not allowed for employers' social security contributions for which data were not available for all countries.
    11. For Spain the starting date was 1955.
    12. Suppose

$$\dot{y} = \dot{x} + \dot{l}.$$

If $\dot{l}$ and $\dot{x}$ are independent, as is often found, then in the regression

$$\dot{l} = \alpha + \beta \dot{y}$$

the coefficient β is $\text{Var}\, \dot{l}/(\text{Var}\, \dot{x} + \text{Var}\, \dot{l})$, which is less than unity. For discussion of this issue in the cross-sectional context see Kaldor (1966), Rowthorn (1975) and Kaldor (1975). In a time-series context the argument given earlier in this footnote relates to the case where all variables are measured net of trend.

13. The comparison is as follows (t-statistics in brackets)

	δ_1	δ_2	δ_3	δ_4	γ	ρ	DW
OLS	0·35 (2·6)	0·15 (2·4)	0·15 (1·9)	−0·61 (4·2)	−1·60 (4·4)	0·46	1·68
2SLS	0·42 (1·4)	0·14 (1·6)	0·13 (1·3)	−0·69 (2·8)	−1·85 (3·8)	0·36	1·78

14. We experimented with other versions of the price equation in order to test the robustness of the productivity effect. When we added a simple time trend to equation (6), the productivity effect became small. A similar result was found when (6) was estimated in first differences, and including a constant term. The same happened again when we estimated a reduced form of the system in which equation (6) was differenced and substituted into (5) to yield an equation from which prices were excluded. This gave a goodish explanation of $\dot{w}$ in terms of $\dot{p}_m$, $\dot{p}_{m,-1}$, $\dot{w}_{-1}$, U, $\dot{U}$ and $\dot{x}$. But the coefficient on $\dot{x}$ was generally insignificant. These disappointing results are not altogether surprising when productivity growth has altered so little over the period except for the last six years; and we maintain our belief that productivity affects prices.

15. The table shows import prices relative to the consumption deflator. This is only a proper measure of the impact on the feasible real wage if the consumption deflator equals the deflator for gross expenditure (T.F.E.) as a whole.

16. For discussion of the causes of the slowdown see Norsworthy *et al.* (1979), Denison (1979), Jorgensen (1981), Baily (1981) and Nordhaus (1982).

17. Other mechanisms that have been suggested include a fall in labour mobility but the evidence here is unconvincing (Jackman (1982)).

18. This calculation corresponds to $\gamma[(\dot{k}-\dot{l})_{74-78}-(\dot{k}-\dot{l})_{60-73}]$ where l is man-hours. Capital is measured as accumulated past investment subjected to a fixed proportional replacement rate as shown in Jorgensen and Griliches (1972) p. 69. Table 5. (See Data Appendix). This rate may be too high, in which case the fall in capital-intensity growth is less than we are saying. The share of capital is its share in GDP (not NDP), since capital produces the earnings that pay for depreciation.

19. The issue is whether the double-deflation method (with separate price indices for gross output and materials) causes bias in the measurement of real value-added. Clearly it matters which year's relative input price is used as base. If the year chosen as base precedes a rise in relative input prices, this will produce an artificial fall in measured value-added. For if Q is gross output, M materials, and P_M material prices (relative to output prices), then marginal productivity theory implies that approximately, if real value-added is constant, $\Delta Q = [(P_M^0 + P_M)/2]\Delta M$. But the measured change in value added is $\Delta Q - P_M^0 \Delta M$. Thus if base year prices are used, value added is measured as changing by $\frac{1}{2}\Delta P_M \Delta M$. As a fraction of value-added (V) this is $\frac{1}{2}(MP_M/V)(\Delta P_M/P_M)(\Delta M/M)$. So if material prices rise by 40% and their quantity falls by 10%, and materials cost $\frac{1}{2}$ of value-added, then value-added is estimated to fall by 1% when in fact it is constant. However this is not a large once-for-all effect. Moreover if one uses value-added at 1975 prices, one imparts a slight *upward* bias to the measured growth of value-added. Yet even on this basis the available data show roughly the same falls in productivity growth as when value-added is measured at 1970 prices.

20. (i) The theoretical basis for the comparisons made can be seen from equation (4). This shows that the cumulative change in $\dot{p}$ will depend on the path of $\dot{x}$, $\dot{p}_m$ and U. Thus the proper experiment is to simulate changes in each of these from some previous level. We also have to allow for the fact that when these variables were at their previous level inflation was increasing and would have continued doing so.

(ii) The simulation of each effect is done by first running the model with the exogenous variables taking the values they actually did, and then running it with one variable (z) at a time held to its former level. The resulting difference in $\dot{p}$ is the effect of z having its actual value as opposed to its former value.

21. The figures in Column (9) are obtained by dividing the inflation effect of ΔU (shown in Column (4)) by the actual extra unemployment (ΔU) shown in Column (11).

22. For a procedure with some common factors, see Jacob and Jones (1980).

23. First, for each ϕ, OLS estimates of the parameters were obtained for the real world data. Call these α_1^R, α_2^R, β_1^R and β_2^R. In addition the statistic $(\partial \log RSS/\partial\phi)^R$ was computed.

Next, for each value of ϕ, α_1, α_2, β_1 and β_2, 7 sets of Monte Carlo wage data were generated using each country's unemployment series plus the random number errors. OLS estimates were done on these Monte Carlo data with the same ϕ imposed to obtain the parameter estimates. Call these α_1^M, α_2^M, β_1^M and β_2^M. $(\partial \log RSS/\partial\phi)^M$ was also calculated.

The values of ϕ, α_1, α_2, β_1 and β_2 used to generate the Monte Carlo data were varied until, in the average OECD statistics, $\alpha_1^M = \alpha_1^R$, $\alpha_2^M = \alpha_2^R$, $\beta_1^M = \beta_1^R$, $\beta_2^M = \beta_2^R$, and $(\partial \log RSS/\partial\phi)^M = (\partial \log RSS/\partial\phi)^R$. The estimates shown in equation (17) are the ϕ, α_1, α_2, β_1 and β_2 used to generate the Monte Carlo data, which on average over the 7 replications satisfied these requirements. (In fact final convergence was done using 21 replications.)

Our analysis was done for 18 countries (our 19 excluding Spain). In generating the Monte Carlo data, some steps were taken to ensure that the data generating process accurately mimicked the real world. The most important of these concerned the variance of the equation error. The variance of the error relative to the variance of the exogeneous variables affects the size of the small sample bias. Given that the Monte Carlo data were generated using $N(0, 1)$ random numbers to represent the errors, the procedure was modified from that described in the main text in the following ways:

(i) The data on U were normalised by a linear transformation to zero mean and unit standard deviation for estimation with real world data, and for generating and estimating with Monte Carlo data.

(ii) The statistics recorded from the OLS regressions were not β_1 and $\hat{\beta}_2$ but $\hat{\beta}_1/\sqrt{RSS}$ and $\hat{\beta}_2/\sqrt{RSS}$ where RSS is the residual sum of squares.

(iii) When convergence had been achieved, the β_1, β_2 used to generate the Monte Carlo data were divided by $\sqrt{RSS^M/RSS^R}$ where RSS^M is the RSS in the equation estimated on Monte Carlo data and RSS^R is the RSS in the equation estimated on real world data.

(iv) In addition to (iii), the estimates of β_1 and β_2 were divided by the average standard deviation of U: this renormalises the coefficients to the natural scale of the U data (cf. (i)).

Another feature of the Monte Carlo data generating process was that the series was started up, taking the unemployment data as $N(0, 1)$ random deviates, for 40 periods. Only the Monte Carlo data for later periods, where the normalized real world unemployment data were used, were retained for estimation.

24. If $Q = f(X_1, \ldots, X_n)$, constant returns imply $Q = \sum X_i f_i$. Hence $dQ = \sum f_i dX_i + \sum X_i df_i$. But $dQ = \sum f_i dX_i$, so $\sum X_i df_i = 0$. Hence $\sum (f_i X_i/Q) d \log f_i = 0$. Integrating all the $d \log f_i$s yields $\sum v_i \log f_i = $ constant where v_i is the factor share. For a useful application of the factor-price frontier to the topics discussed here, see Bruno (1982a).

25. By inverting their substitution matrix.

26. Suppose a vintage model with a fixed capital stock, no short-run substitution between labour and materials, and perfect competition. Then suppose the price of materials rises, but output and employment are maintained via a rise in the output price, so that the price of an input bundle of labour and materials remains constant relative to the output price. It follows that the price of labour has fallen relative to the output price. But profit has remained constant in terms of output.

REFERENCES

BAILY, M. N. (1981), "Productivity and the Services of Capital and Labour", *Brookings Papers on Economic Activity*, **1**, 1–50.

BERNDT, E. R. and WOOD, D. O. (1975), "Technology, prices and the derived demand for energy", *Review of Economics and Statistics*, **57** (3), 259–268.

BRUNNER, K., CUKIERMAN, A. and MELTZER, A. H. (1980), "Stagflation, persistent unemployment and the permanence of economic shocks", *Journal of Monetary Economics*, **6**, 467–492.

BRUNO, M. (1982a), "Raw materials, profits and the productivity slowdown", *Quarterly Journal of Economics* (forthcoming).

BRUNO, M. (1982b), "World shocks, macroeconomic response and the productivity puzzle" (paper presented to the National Institute for Economic and Social Research Conference on Slow Growth in the Western World, London).

DAVIDSON, J. E. H. (1981), "Problems with the estimation of moving average processes", *Journal of Econometrics*, **19**, 295–310.

DENISON, E. F. (1979), "Explanations of Productivity Growth", U.S. Department of Commerce, *Survey of Current Business*, **59** (8).

GOMULKA, S. (1979), "Britain's slow industrial growth—increasing inefficiency versus low rate of technical change", in Beckerman, W. (ed.) *Slow Growth in Britain: Causes and Consequences* (Oxford).

GRUBB, D. (1982), "Raw material prices and the productivity slowdown: some doubts" Discussion Paper No. 133, London School of Economics Centre for Labour Economics.

GRUBB, D., JACKMAN, R. A. and LAYARD, P. R. G. (1983), "Wage rigidity and unemployment in OECD countries", *European Economic Review* (forthcoming).

JACKMAN, R. A. (1982), Comments on Bruno (1982b).

JACKMAN, R. A. and LAYARD, P. R. G. (1982), "Trade Unions, the NAIRU and a wage-inflation tax", *Economica*, **49**(3), 232–239.

JACOBS, R. L. and JONES, R. A. (1980), "Price expectations in the U.S., 1947–75", *American Economic Review*, **70** (3), 269–278.

JOHNSTON, J. (1963) *Econometric Methods* (McGraw Hill).

JORGENSEN, D. W. (1981), "Energy prices and productivity growth" (mimeo, *Harvard University*).

JORGENSEN, D. W. and GRILICHES, Z. (1972), "Issues in growth accounting: a reply to E. F. Denison", U.S. Department of Commerce *Survey of Current Business*, **52** (5).

JORGENSEN, D. W. and NISHIMIZU, M. (1978), "U.S. and Japanese economic growth 1952–74, an international comparison", *Economic Journal*, **88** (352), 707–727.

KALDOR, N. (1966) *Causes of the slow rate of growth of the U.K.* (Cambridge University Press).

KALDOR, N. (1975), "Economic growth and the Verdoorn Law: A comment on Mr. Rowthorn's article", *Economic Journal*, **85**, 891–896.

MARRIOTT, F. H. C. and POPE, J. A. (1954), "Bias in the estimation of autocorrelations". *Biometrika*, **41**, 390–402.
NORDHAUS, W. D. (1982), "Economic policy in the face of declining productivity growth", *European Economic Review*, **18**, 131–157.
NORSWORTHY, J. R., HARPER, M. J. and KUNZE, K. (1979), "The slowdown in productivity growth: analysis of some contributing factors", *Brookings Papers on Economic Activity*, **2**.
ROWTHORN, R. E. (1975), "What remains of Kaldor's Law", *Economic Journal*, **85**, 10–19.
SARGAN, J. D. (1964), "Wages and prices in the U.K.", in Hart, P. E., Mills G. and Whittaker, J. K. (eds.) *Econometric Analysis for National Economic Planning* (New York: Macmillan).

Review of Economic Studies (1982) XLIX, 731–759

0034–6527/82/00560731$00.50

Unemployment in the United Kingdom Since the War

MARTYN ANDREWS

and

STEPHEN NICKELL

London School of Economics

In this paper, we first present a competitive macroeconomic model of an open economy which is suitable for estimation and contrast this with a non-competitive model. We then derive unemployment equations from the various models and estimate them over annual data from 1948–1979. We draw the following conclusions. (i) The competitive model of the labour market does not fit the facts. (ii) The non-competitive model generates an equation for the constant inflation rate of unemployment which reveals how, at certain times such as the mid 1970s, a combination of factors conspired to raise this level forcing the government into a deflationary stance to prevent inflation rising drastically. (iii) A number of factors have raised the level of unemployment in a secular fashion since the war, in particular the increase in the variation of relative prices, the increase in the benefit to income ratio, the introduction of employment protection legislation and the rise in the intersectoral shifts of the labour force.

INTRODUCTION

The years from the end of the second world war until the mid 1960s have been remarkable in the context of Britain's economic history for their low levels of unemployment. Since then unemployment has pushed remorselessly upwards until, at the present time, we have reached a level which is reminiscent of the pre- rather than the post-war era. In this paper we attempt to illuminate this phenomenon by considering it in the context of a simple classical macro-economic model. Thus, although we also consider an alternative, our main aim is to examine the plausibility of the extreme classical model of unemployment. Such a model has not been rigorously tested in the British context and although it seems, *a priori*, implausible, it is essential to discover whether or not it is in fact consistent with the data. The remainder of the paper is set out as follows. In the first section we consider various types of classical model along with an alternative non-classical model and show how these lead to both structural and reduced form equations determining the level of unemployment. We then proceed to estimate these equations and consider what light the results shed both on the processes generating unemployment and on the workings of the aggregate economy. We finish with a brief summary and some general conclusions.

1. A FULL INFORMATION CLASSICAL MODEL

It is commonplace in the investigation of a "labour market" phenomenon such as unemployment to consider the market for labour in isolation from the rest of the economy. For example, in the seminal classical model of Lucas and Rapping (1970), some care is devoted to the analysis of the demand and supply of labour but it is explicitly assumed that the price level and the level of output are determined elsewhere. Thus the resulting levels of employment and unemployment are determined conditional on the values of these "exogenous" variables. This surely reveals only part of the story and only a small part at that, since the determinants of employment at a given level of output, while of some independent interest, are hardly germane to an investigator interested in the sources of fluctuations in key macro-economic indicators.[1]

Consequent on the above point, it is essential to consider the labour market in conjunction with the market for output at the very least, on the grounds that the short run exogenous forces driving the economy are likely to originate, in the main, from fluctuations in the supply of labour and the demand for output. The profit maximizing behaviour of firms constrained by a production function then provides the link between the two.

We now construct a formal although not quite complete model along the above lines. There are two basic markets, those for labour and output. There is also a market for money which is made explicit and a market for government bonds which is not. The government budget constraint is omitted although it operates in the background to determine the supply of government debt. Long run effects of the volume of government debt are ignored as is the impact of the future tax payments necessary to service it. The four key segments of the model are the supply and demand for labour and the supply and demand for output. The model is incomplete in the sense that we do not set down explicitly the determinants of the money stock if exchange rates are fixed or of the exchange rate if it is floating. These variables are simply too "far away" from the labour market to make it expositionally worthwhile to model them. Their status as endogenous variables will, however, be noted in our interpretation of the model and taken account of in the empirical work.

Our initial model is one of the simplest classical (Walrasian) type where we assume that all agents are fully informed about all current economic aggregates. We now consider the model explicitly. With an eye to estimation we write the model in log linear form.[2] Furthermore we suppose that the real exogenous variables fluctuate around stationary means. This allows us to define a natural set of "normal" long run equilibrium values for the real variables of the model, these simply being determined by the equilibrium of the model when all the real exogenous variables are set at their stationary means. This makes the model easier to understand and we discuss the adjustments required for empirical implementation at a later stage.

The labour market

(i) Labour supply
The labour supply equation is directly comparable to that specified in Lucas and Rapping (1970). Thus we have

$$n_t^s = d_0 + d_1(w_t - p_t - t_{2t} - t_{3t}) + d_2(w^* - p^*) + d_3(R_t - \dot{p}_t^e) + \sum d_i z_{it} \tag{1}$$

$$d_1 > 0, \qquad d_2 < 0, \qquad d_3 > 0.$$

n_t^s = the supply of labour
w_t = the pre-tax wage rate
p_t = the pre-tax price level
t_{2t} = the tax rate on wages
t_{3t} = the tax rate on goods
$(w^* - p^*)$ = the long run equilibrium "normal" post-tax real wage
R_t = the nominal interest rate
$\dot{p}_t^e$ = the expected rate of inflation
z_{it} = a set of exogenous variables affecting labour supply.

All variables are in logs except t_2, t_3, R_t and we have used the approximation $\log(1 + t_i) \simeq t_i$.

The general form of the equation follows by log linearizing the labour supply function derived from an intertemporal consumption-labour supply model. The key points of such a model are first, the possibility that labour supply is positively related to the real interest rate as future goods/leisure are substituted for current leisure. Second, the possibility of a high degree of intertemporal leisure substitution leading to a high short run labour supply elasticity, d_1, allied to a low or even negative long run elasticity $(d_1 + d_2)$. In a formal analysis of this kind of model the "normal" or long run level of real wages is, in fact, a weighted average of those expected over an individual's lifetime.[3] Our assumption that all the real exogenous variables fluctuate around stationary means ensures that this weighted average will be more or less constant at the long-run equilibrium value $w^* - p^*$ which is the variable we use in the equation. This enables us to avoid the very messy, and in the present context singularly uninformative, analysis of the rational expectations solution of the model if we introduce explicitly the expected real wage terms in our labour supply equation. (Our short cut approximation is, of course, exactly right if we assume that the stochastic processes generating all the exogenous variables are such as to make the real wage in each period equal to $w^* - p^*$ plus a white noise error).

(ii) Labour demand

On the other side of the labour market we first separate the demands for labour by the private and public sector where we may write in levels

$$N_t^d = N_{pt}^d + N_{gt}^d. \tag{2}$$

N_{pt}^d is the private sector demand for labour and N_{gt}^d that of the public sector which we assume is both predetermined (i.e. planned in advance) and always fulfilled (any other assumption is inconsistent with our market clearing approach). We may approximate (2) in log form (lower case) as

$$n_t^d \simeq \lambda_0 + \lambda_1 n_{pt}^d + (1 - \lambda_1) n_{gt}^d$$

and then assuming that private sector labour demand follows from profit maximizing behaviour constrained by a Cobb–Douglas production function, we have

$$n_t^d = a_0 + a_1(w_t - p_t) + a_1 t_1 + a_2(q_t' - p_t) + a_3 k_t + a_4 n_{gt} \tag{3}$$

$$a_1 < 0, \qquad a_2 < 0, \qquad a_3 > 0, \qquad a_4 > 0.$$

n_t^d = the demand for labour
w_t = the pre-tax wage rate
p_t = the pre-tax price level
t_{1t} = the firm's employment tax rate
q_t' = the price of materials and fuel
k_t = the given capital stock.

All variables are in logs except t_1 and we again approximate $\log(1 + t_1)$ by t_1.

The capital stock should be thought of as predetermined in this context and we have assumed that the output effect dominates in our signing of the coefficient a_2 (as it will do in the Cobb–Douglas case). For future expositional convenience we may split the term $a_2(q_t' - p_t)$ into two separate parts, namely $a_2(q_t' - p_{wt}) + a_2(p_{wt} - p_t)$ where p_{wt} is the world output price level in pounds. $(q_t' - p_{wt}) = q_t$ say, may then be thought of as the ratio of the world price of fuel and materials to the world price of output which is clearly exogenous in the British context. $(p_{wt} - p_t)$ is the index of competitiveness of British goods which, under purchasing power parity (ppp), is always zero. In order to illustrate the effect of a ppp assumption on our results it is convenient to specify the coefficient a_2 by two different symbols, thus writing the terms as $a_{21} q_t + a_{22}(p_{wt} - p_t)$. If we then wish to impose ppp on our model we can simply set $a_{22} = 0$. Under floating exchange rates p_{wt}, is, of course, endogenous since it is influenced by the exchange rate. So (3) becomes

$$n_t^d = a_0 + a_1(w_t - p_t - t_{1t}) + a_{21}q_t + a_{22}(p_{wt} - p_t) + a_3k_t + a_4n_{gt} \tag{4}$$

$$a_1 < 0, \qquad a_{21} < 0, \qquad a_{22} < 0, \qquad a_4 > 0.$$

q_t = world price of fuel and material inputs relative to world price of output
p_{wt} = world price of output in pounds.

Note that under constant returns $a_3 = \lambda_1$ and $a_4 = (1 - \lambda_1)$.

The output market

(i) Output supply
In the specification of output supply, some care must be taken concerning that part of output generated by government employees. In 'ine with the national income accounts we suppose that government output is simply equal to the government wage bill where note that this implies that the price of output includes the price of government goods. So, in real terms, we have

$$Y_t^s = Y_{pt}^s + Y_{gt}^s = Y_{pt}^s + \frac{W_t}{P_t} N_{gt}$$

where the variables are not in logs, Y_p^s is private output, Y_g^s is government output, N_g is government employment and W/P is the real wage. This leads to the following approximation in logs (lower case).

$$y_t^s \simeq \mu_0 + \mu_1 y_{pt}^s + (1 - \mu_1)(w_t - p_t) + (1 - \mu_1)n_{gt}. \tag{5}$$

Private sector output supply is determined on the same basis as its labour demand and this leads to

$$y_t^s = b_0 + b_1(w_t - p_t) + b_1 t_{1t} + b_{21}q_t + b_{22}(p_{wt} - p_t) + b_3 k_t + b_2 n_{gt} \tag{6}$$

$$b_1 < 0, \qquad b_{2i} < 0, \qquad b_3 > 0, \qquad b_4 > 0.$$

Here again we have split the materials price term and setting $b_{22} = 0$ allows us to investigate the effects of the ppp assumption. It is also worth noting that under constant returns, the Cobb–Douglas assumption implies that $a_{21} = b_{21}$, $a_{22} = b_{22}$, $b_3 = \mu_1$ and $b_4 = 1 - \mu_1$.

(ii) Output demand

Here we specify the demand side in terms of both an IS and a LM curve since the rate of interest occurs in the labour supply function. Thus we have

$$y_t^d = c_0 + c_1 g_t + c_2(m_t - p_t) + c_3 y_{wt} + c_4(p_{wt} - p_t) + c_5 t_{1t} + c_6 t_{2t}$$

$$+ c_7 t_{3t} + c_8(R_t - \dot{p}_t^e); \qquad c_1, c_2, c_3, c_4 > 0; \qquad c_5, c_6, c_7, c_8 < 0 \tag{7}$$

$$m_t - p_t = A_0 + A_1 y_t + A_2 R_t + A_3 \dot{p}_t^e; \qquad A_1 > 0, \qquad A_2, A_3 < 0. \tag{8}$$

y_t^d = the demand for output
g_t = real government expenditure
m_t = the supply of money
y_{wt} = world income
$\dot{p}_t^e$ = the expected rate of pre-tax output price inflation which we assume, for convenience, to be the same as the post-tax rate
p_t = the post tax price level

t_{1t} = firm's employment tax rate
t_{2t} = the income tax rate
t_{3t} = the tax rate on goods
R_t = the nominal interest rate.

All the variables are in logs except R, t_1, t_2, t_3 and we again use the fact that $\log(1+t_1) \simeq t_i$.

Equation (7) is a standard IS curve solved out for y, leaving output demand as a function of the fiscal parameters, real balances, foreign sector variables and the real interest rate. The LM curve, (8), is standard. Concerning exogeneity assumptions, we take *real* government expenditure as exogenous because the government decides on the quantity of goods to be purchased rather than their value (this is arguably no longer the case but it remained true throughout our sample period). We treat $\dot{p}_t^e$ as exogenous on the grounds that it is of some theoretical interest to consider the short run effects of exogenous shocks *given* expectations of future inflation. In the empirical work $\dot{p}^e$ is, of course, treated as endogenous. Finally, we note that at least under fixed exchange rates, the money stock cannot be thought of as exogenous. (In practice, of course, it is not exogenous under floating rates either, at least as it is normally measured.)

Having set up the model it is of some interest to investigate its comparative static properties. Although we are primarily concerned with the employment equation it is instructive to study first the output equation and only then to consider the determinants of employment and unemployment. In our analysis of the reduced form, the key parameters to watch for are d_3 and the set a_{22}, b_{22}, c_4. If $d_3 = 0$, there is no real interest rate effect on labour supply. If $a_{22} = b_{22} = c_4 = 0$, then we have a "true" classical model in which all prices adjust instantaneously and ppp is a permanent state of affairs. $d_3 = 0$ will be referred to as restriction 1(R1) and $a_{22} = b_{22} = c_4 = 0$ as restriction 2(R2).

If we write the quasi-reduced form output equation as

$$y_t = \omega_0 + \omega_1 g_t + \omega_2 y_{wt} + \omega_3 n_{gt} + \omega_4(m_t - p_{wt}) + \omega_5 q_t + \omega_6 t_{1t}$$
$$+ \omega_7 t_{2t} + \omega_8 t_{3t} + \omega_9 \dot{p}_t^e + \omega_{10}k_t + \sum_{i=11} \omega_i z_{it} \tag{9}$$

then the following points are worth noting (details of the actual coefficients may be found in the Appendix, Section 1). First, the normal real wage $(w^* - p^*)$ has been absorbed into the constant term. Second, $m_t - p_{wt}$, the money stock relative to world prices, is not exogenous and consequently all the other comparative static results are conditional on a particular value of this variable. However, under ppp, $\omega_4 = 0$ and (9) becomes a genuine reduced form. Third, the impact of an increase in either government expenditure or world trade is positive $(\omega_1, \omega_2 > 0)$ unless R1 and R2 both hold. So even under ppp there is not complete crowding out in the short run because of the real interest rate effect on labour supply (cf. Hall 1980). In the long run, of course, there may be a tendency for the nominal interest rate and price expectations to adjust in such a way as to return the real interest rate to its equilibrium level but this is outside the scope of our model. An increase in government employment always raises output $(\omega_3 > 0)$ even if both R1 and R2 hold. This works because real wages rise above their normal level raising labour supply and the consequent fall in private sector labour demand is more than offset by the rise in government labour demand (again cf. Hall 1980). These results are of some independent interest because they emphasise the fact that real wages can move either pro or countercyclically in a competitive model (i.e. the correlation between real wage and employment "innovations" can be anything in an "equilibrium" model). Fourth, the effect of an increase in the relative price of materials is negative $(\omega_5 < 0)$. So even if labour supply is completely inelastic, the input of materials will fall and gross output declines (although what happens to value added is not clear cut). Finally tax effects are all negative $(\omega_6, \omega_7, \omega_8 < 0)$ and the labour supply variables obviously affect output in the same direction as labour supply itself.

Since our aim in this paper is to focus on the labour market and specifically on unemployment we follow Lucas and Rapping and derive a "structural" unemployment equation from the supply side of the labour market. Aside from the "frictional" part of unemployment, fluctuations in labour market activity are reflected in the deviations of labour supply from its "normal" level. Thus when real wages and/or real interest rates are below "normal", workers substitute current leisure for future leisure and goods by prolonging their spells of unemployment. From (1) we may define "normal" labour supply by

$$n^{s*} = d_0 + (d_1 + d_2)(w^* - p^*) + d_3(R - p^e)^* + \sum d_i z_i^* \qquad (10)$$

where $(R - \dot{p}^e)^*$ and z_i^* are suitably chosen levels which are all constant because of the static nature of the long run equilibrium already mentioned. Furthermore, remember that w^* and p^* are post-tax values and so the tax terms in (1) drop out. The *actual* (not log) unemployment rate, u_t, may now be defined by

$$u_t = u_{ft} + n^{*s} - n_t^s \qquad (11)$$

u_{ft} representing frictional unemployment up to some constant. Combining (1), (10), (11) yields our "structural" unemployment equation

$$u_t = -d_1(w_t' - p_t' - (w^* - p^*)) - d_3(R_t - \dot{p}_t^e - (R - \dot{p}^e)^*) - \sum d_1(z_{it} - z_i^*) + u_{ft} \qquad (12)$$

w_t', p_t' are *post tax* wages and prices where the taxes in (1) have simply been incorporated into the pre-tax real wage terms. This equation then reveals that once we control for exogenous labour supply shocks and variations in frictional unemployment, the unemployment rate is negatively related to positive deviations in both real wages and the real interest rate.

We now look at the equivalent reduced form which is simply based on the reduced form version of (12), namely

$$u_t = u_{ft} + n^* - n_t \qquad (13)$$

where n_t is reduced form equilibrium employment which may be written as

$$n_t = \psi_0 + \psi_1 g_t + \psi_2 y_{wt} + \psi_3 n_{gt} + \psi_4(m_t - p_{wt}) + \psi_5 q_t + \psi_6 t_{1t} + \psi_7 t_{2t}$$
$$+ \psi_8 t_3 + \psi_9 \dot{p}_t^e + \psi_{10} k_t + \sum_{i=11} \psi_i z_{it} \qquad (14)$$

where again the normal real wage $(w^* - p^*)$ has been absorbed into the constant and $\psi_4 = 0$ under ppp. The "normal" level of employment n^* corresponds to the long run equilibrium where the exogenous variables take their "normal" values which generate the "normal" values of real wages and the real interest rate specified in (10). Thus we may write the reduced form unemployment equation as

$$u_t = u_{ft} - \psi_1(g_t - g^*) - \psi_2(y_{wt} - y_w^*) - \psi_3(n_{gt} - n_g^*) - \psi_4(m_t - p_{wt} - (m - p_w)^*)$$
$$- \psi_5(q_t - q^*) - \psi_6(t_{1t} - t_1^*) - \psi_7(t_{2t} - t_2^*) - \psi_8(t_{3t} - t_3^*) - \psi_9(\dot{p}_t^e - \dot{p}^{e*})$$
$$- \psi_{10}(k_t - k^*) - \sum \psi_i(z_{it} - z_i^*). \qquad (15)$$

Before discussing the signs attached to these variables, a number of points are worth making. First, as with all the reduced form equations derived from this model, (15) is compatible with most views of how the economy works. As we shall see, none of the signs on the coefficients is particularly startling and most "disequilibrium" theories of the economy would lead to a similar if not identical reduced form. However, the second point is that in the classical model the exogenous shocks will *only* affect unemployment via deviations in the real wage and real interest rates once we allow for exogenous labour supply shocks. This is, of course, a very stringent restriction. Third, even without any deficiencies in current information, all the standard real exogenous shocks will generate fluctuations in output and unemployment. Fourth, we are conscious of the fact that $\dot{p}_t^e$ cannot, in any practical sense, be included in our list of exogenous variables and must be substituted out.[4] Since, under consistent expectations, this term will be a function of observed exogenous shocks plus noise we can simply omit it from (15) without changing the structure of the model. (15) then becomes a genuine reduced form with the exception of the relative money supply term which itself drops out under ppp.

Finally to round off this section we discuss the signs of the ψ coefficients in the employment and unemployment reduced forms. Since they are generally similar to those in the output reduced form we restrict ourselves to a few remarks. As with output $\psi_1 > 0$, $\psi_2 > 0$, so the government expenditure and world trade effects on unemployment are negative even under ppp unless the real interest effect on labour supply is absent in which case there is complete crowding out. Since $\psi_3 > 0$, the government employment effect is negative even under R1 ($d_3 = 0$) and R2 (ppp). Although an increase in the world price of materials relative to manufactures reduces output, there is of course a substitution effect in the opposite direction as far as employment is concerned which makes the unemployment impact indeterminate (i.e. $\psi_5 = ?$). All the tax effects on unemployment are positive as we might expect ($\psi_6 < 0$, $\psi_7 < 0$, $\psi_8 < 0$). Finally $\psi_{10} > 0$, so positive capital stock shocks reduce unemployment. The influence of the labour supply terms on unemployment will be discussed later when the actual variables are considered.

2. A VARIANT OF THE CLASSICAL MODEL WITH LESS THAN FULL INFORMATION

In the previous model, if we assume a floating exchange rate regime with purchasing power parity as our model of exchange rate determination then shifts in an assumed exogenous money stock have no impact on output and employment. Furthermore, if there is no real interest rate effect on labour supply, shifts in world trade and government expenditure also have no real impact. In other words, the inclusion of the *simple* ($d_3 = 0$) intertemporal substitution model of labour supply does not allow fluctuations in response to demand shocks (either nominal or real) unless they involve the demand for labour directly via government employment.

In this section we present a variant of the previous model based on the segmented markets approach introduced by Lucas (1972), which does allow demand shocks to have real effects even under the R1($d_3 = 0$) and R2 (ppp) restrictions. Following Barro (1976), we assume a number of separated markets, labelled x. Agents observe only lagged values of certain aggregate variables although they do possess some current price information at the local level. The mechanics of the model are as follows (cf. Alogoskoufis 1983). Firms observe the local wage $w_t(x)$ and the price at which they can sell their product in the local market $p_t(x)$. There is then some kind of mechanical retailing system operated by non-economic intermediaries which enables workers across all markets to purchase goods at the aggregate price level p_t. At the time of making their supply decisions workers do not observe this price level but they obviously observe the wage $w_t(x)$. The reason for this somewhat artificial arrangement is to capture the fact that workers do not, in reality, buy their firm's product but a bundle of goods produced by many firms. The artificiality arises because we restrict ourselves to a one good world. This kind of problem does not, of course, arise in the Lucas–Barro model because they do not have a labour market.

As well as the local prices, we also assume local variations in some other variables, namely, $q_t(x)$, the local ratio of material prices to that of manufactures; $n_{gt}(x)$, "local" government employment; $g_t(x)$, "local" government expenditure; $y_{wt}(x)$, local foreign demand and $m_t(x)$, the local money stock. These are not observed by agents. In order to make life simple we omit from the previous model all the exogenous variables which are not strictly germane to the present discussion, namely taxes, capital stock and labour supply variables. Furthermore we impose R1($d_3 = 0$) and R2 (ppp), eliminate expected inflation from the money demand function ($A_3 = 0$) and then substitute the nominal interest rate out of the IS–LM system. This leaves us with the following four equation system.

Local Output Demand:

$$y_t^d(x) = C_0 + C_1 g_t(x) + C_2(m_t(x) - p_t(x)) + C_3 y_{wt}(x). \tag{16}$$

Local Output Supply:

$$y_t^s(x) = b_0 + b_1(w_t(x) - p_t(x)) + b_{21} q_t(x) + b_4 n_{gt}(x). \tag{17}$$

Local Labour Demand:

$$n_t^d(x) = a_0 + a_1(w_t(x) - p_t(x)) + a_{21} q_t(x) + a_4 n_{gt}(x). \tag{18}$$

Local Labour Supply

$$n_t^s(x) = d_0 + d_1(w_t(x) - E(p_t|I_t)) + d_2(w^* - p^*). \tag{19}$$

The information set I_t consists of $w_t(x)$ and all lagged variables. Our aim here is then to demonstrate that in this simplified variant of the original model, demand shocks (g, m, y_w) influence output and employment, something they would not do under full information given the R1, R2 restrictions imposed here. Although such a result is clearly a standard extension of the Barro (1976) result on unanticipated money, the details are by no means as straightforward not so much because we have two markets (see Alogoskoufis 1983, for example) but because we have supply shocks in addition $(n_{gt}(x), q_t(x))$.

In order to complete the model we must specify the stochastic processes driving the exogenous variables and here we simply assume

$$m_t(x) = E(m_t|\bar{I}(t-1)) + \varepsilon_{mt} + \varepsilon_m(x) \qquad q_t(x) = E(q_t|\bar{I}(t-1)) + \varepsilon_{qt} + \varepsilon_q(x)$$

$$g_t(x) = E(g_t|\bar{I}(t-1)) + \varepsilon_{gt} + \varepsilon_g(x) \qquad n_{gt}(x) = E(n_{gt}|\bar{I}(t-1)) + \varepsilon_{nt} + \varepsilon_n(x)$$

$$y_{wt}(x) = E(y_{wt}|\bar{I}(t-1)) + \varepsilon_{wt} + \varepsilon_w(x) \tag{20}$$

where $\bar{I}(t-1)$ contains all aggregate variables dated $t-1$ and before and all the ε errors are independently normally distributed with mean zero. We then show, in the Appendix, Section 2, that the model (16)–(20) implies that both aggregate output and employment depend on all the innovations $m_t - Em_t|\bar{I}(t-1)$, $g_t - Eg_t|\bar{I}(t-1)$, $y_{wt} - Ey_{wt}|\bar{I}(t-1)$, $q_t - E(q_t|\bar{I}(t-1))$, $n_{gt} - En_{gt}|\bar{I}(t-1)$ and well as q_t, n_{gt} independently as we would expect. Incomplete information is thus a channel through which the first three of these variables will enter the unemployment reduced form even if the R1, R2 restrictions hold.

3. A NON-COMPETITIVE MODEL

To round off our discussion of the various possibilities, we consider a model where nominal wages are not determined by labour market clearing as normally defined. In this section we follow closely the model constructed by Grubb, Jackman and Layard (1982) but we extend their specification to incorporate certain factors which they have not considered because they investigate all the OECD countries. The debt we owe to their analysis is, however, transparent. In the context of our first model, we shall simply replace the labour supply function (1) by a wage equation of the augmented Phillips curve type. Although such equations appear *ad hoc*, they can easily be derived from an employer-union bargaining model (see for example, Nickell (1982)). Furthermore we may argue that employer-union bargaining is the overwhelming dominant force in the determination of aggregate wages and that any small competitive "rump" is of no consequence.[5]

$$w_t - w_{t-1} = \alpha_0 + \alpha_1(_tp^e_{t+1} - p_t) + \alpha_2(_{t-1}p^e_t - p_{t-1}) + \alpha_3 g^*_t + \alpha_4 u_t + \alpha_5 U_t$$

$$+ \alpha_6 i_2 + \alpha_7 i_3 + \sum \alpha_j z_{jt},$$

$$\alpha_1 > 0, \qquad \alpha_2 > 0, \qquad \alpha_3 > 0, \qquad \alpha_4 < 0, \qquad \alpha_5 > 0, \qquad \alpha_6 > 0, \qquad \alpha_7 > 0. \quad (21)$$

Neutrality implies $\alpha_1 + \alpha_2 = 1$, rates of change of taxes enter naturally in the difference context and the z_{jt} capture shifts in the natural rate of unemployment. U_t is a measure of union power which enters naturally because a more powerful union can impose higher costs on the firm which leads to an increase in the wage bargain. g^*_t is the target rate of growth of real wages at a *fixed* level of unemployment and union power. The two price terms reflect the fact that a part of the wage aggregate includes wages set in the current period with reference to the future while the remainder is made up of wages which have been set in previously determined contracts.

To complete this model we may rewrite the labour demand equation (4) in a manner suggested by Grubb, Jackman and Layard (1982). Assuming that firms are always on their demand functions,[6] and have constant returns to scale, we may write (4) as

$$n^d_t - \bar{n}_t = a_0 + a_1 w_t + a_{22} p_{wt} + a_1 t_1 + a_{21} q_t + \lambda_1 k_t + (1-\lambda_1) n_{gt} - (a_1 + a_{22}) p_t - \bar{n}_t$$

where $\bar{n}_t$ is the labour force. Rewriting the left hand side as $-u_t$ and re-ordering we have a price equation of the form

$$p_t - w_t = \beta_0 + \beta_1(p_{wt} - w_t) + \beta_2 t_1 + \beta_3 q_t + \beta_4(k_t - \bar{n}_t) + \beta_5(n_{gt} - \bar{n}_t) + \beta_6 u_t \quad (22)$$

where

$$\beta_1 = a_{22}/\delta > 0, \qquad \beta_2 = a_1/\delta > 0, \qquad \beta_3 = a_{21}/\delta > 0, \qquad \beta_4 = \lambda_1/\delta < 0,$$

$$\delta_5 = \frac{1-\lambda_1}{\delta} < 0, \qquad \beta_6 = 1/\delta < 0, \qquad \delta = (a_1 + a_{22}) < 0; \qquad \text{note } \beta_1 + \beta_2 = 1.$$

$k_t - \bar{n}_t$ can be viewed as a measure of the "trend" capital-labour ratio.

Equations (21), (22) combined with the output system (6), (7), (8) then generate the complete model which is worth contrasting with the competitive model of the previous section. The key difference is, of course, in the process determining wages. In the non-competitive model, g^*_t, the target level of real wage growth is arbitrary in the sense that it is not entirely circumscribed by competitive forces. Thus, if productivity growth slows down, g_t may not adjust downwards for a variety of reasons. For example, workers may be used to a certain rate of growth of real living standards and bargain to maintain it, or both they and firms may be unaware of the slow down or perhaps workers and their union representatives simply wish to increase their share of value added. Any number of such factors may come into play. An autonomous rise in g^*_t will raise wages and this will, *ceteris paribus*, result in higher real wages, lower output and higher unemployment. Such unemployment may be deemed to be involuntary in the sense that given existing wages and prices, some unemployed individuals are willing to work but are unable to find jobs. Furthermore it may well be the case that these particular individuals have no say in, and little impact on, the wage and price setting process.

A rise in g^*_t in the non-competitive model is, of course, equivalent in its effects to an autonomous reduction in the supply of labour in an equilibrium model. The outcomes are the same but the interpretation is entirely different, the increased unemployment obviously being entirely "voluntary" in the latter context. Thus although the consequences of the wage determining activity of the various groups and institutions in the labour market can be replicated by labour supply shifts in an equilibrium model it is mistaken then to argue that this is the best way of interpreting such activity.

Returning to our analysis of the present model, one particularly fruitful approach is to investigate the level of unemployment which is associated with a stable rate of inflation. As Grubb, Jackman and Layard point out, only equations (21) and (22) need be considered in this regard. Suppose, then, that we define u_t^* to be that unemployment rate consistent with the following conditions: (i) $_tp_{t+1}^e = p_{t+1}$, (ii) $_{t-1}p_t^e = p_t$, (iii) $p_{wt} = p_t$, purchasing power parity, (iv) $p_{t+1} - p_t = p_t - p_{t-1}$. So (21) becomes

$$\dot{w}_t - \dot{p}_t = \alpha_0 + \alpha_3 g_t^* + \alpha_4 u_t^* + \alpha_5 U_t + \alpha_6 \dot{\iota}_{2t} + \alpha_7 \dot{\iota}_{3t} + \sum \alpha_j z_j \qquad (23)$$

and the time derivative of (22) is

$$(1 - \beta_1)(\dot{p}_t - \dot{w}_t) = \beta_2 \dot{\iota}_{1t} + \beta_3 \dot{q}_t + \beta_4(\dot{k}_t - \dot{n}_t) + \beta_5(\dot{n}_{gt} - \dot{n}_t) + \beta_6 \dot{u}_t. \qquad (24)$$

Eliminating $\dot{w}_t - \dot{p}_t$ and solving for u_t^* gives

$$|\alpha_4| u_t^* = \gamma_0 + \gamma_1 g_t^* + \gamma_2 \dot{\iota}_{1t} + \gamma_3 \dot{\iota}_{2t} + \gamma_4 \dot{\iota}_{3t} + \gamma_5 \dot{q}_t$$

$$+ \gamma_6(\dot{n}_{gt} - \dot{n}_t) + \gamma_7(\dot{k}_t - \dot{n}_t) + \gamma_8 U_t + \gamma_9 \dot{u}_t + \sum \gamma_j z_{jt}$$

$$\gamma_1 = \frac{\alpha_3}{1 - \beta_1}, \qquad \gamma_2 = \frac{\beta_2}{1 - \beta_1} > 0, \qquad \gamma_3 = \alpha_6, \qquad \gamma_4 = \alpha_7, \qquad \gamma_5 = \frac{\beta_3}{1 - \beta_1} > 0,$$

$$\gamma_6 = \frac{\beta_5}{1 - \beta_1} < 0, \qquad \gamma_7 = \frac{\beta_4}{1 - \beta_1} < 0, \qquad \gamma_8 = \alpha_5, \qquad \gamma_9 = \frac{\beta_6}{1 - \beta_1}, \qquad \gamma_j = \alpha_{j-2}. \qquad (25)$$

The equation for u_t^* is very useful particularly for the light which it sheds on government policy options. Suppose, for example, that one of the rates of change on the right hand side shifts in such a way that u^* increases.[7] Then g_t^* must adjust downwards to compensate if the economy, as reflected in the level of unemployment and the rate of inflation, is to remain stable. If it does not adjust, then either the rate of inflation must rise or the level of unemployment must rise. Which of these occurs will depend on the government policy response. The more deflationary the policy, the lower the resulting price level, the higher the resulting unemployment and, incidentally, the higher the resulting real wage. Finally it is worth re-emphasizing the contrast with the competitive model. In such a model there is no question of g_t^* not "adjusting". The labour market clears and that is all there is to it.

4. THE EMPIRICAL IMPLEMENTATION OF THE UNEMPLOYMENT MODELS

Although most of the models we have discussed are relatively well defined, there are a number of loose ends which must be tied up before they can be estimated. First, in our theoretical discussion we considered a classical model in which the long run "normal" equilibrium was static. This is, of course, not the case in the post-war British economy so we must discuss how the normal long run levels of the variables are to be specified. Consider first our basic structural equilibrium unemployment equation (12). Here we must define the normal level of real wages $(w^* - p^*)$. In the economy, the "average" supplier of labour is half way through his life-cycle and if the world were certain he would still be on the optimal path computed initially. In this situation, the normal real wage is simply a weighted sum of lifetime real wages. This suggests taking a central moving average of some kind. In an uncertain world, the individual must typically recompute his plan each period, and here the normal real wage is a combination of expected future real wages with past real wages coming through in the initial wealth term. Since estimates of wealth are notoriously unreliable, this again suggests a centred moving average with the past real wages reflecting current wealth. The future real wages will, of course, be expectations. On the basis of these arguments we propose the following definition[8]

$$w_t^* - p_t^* = \tfrac{1}{5}((w'_{t-2} - p'_{t-2}) + (w'_{t-1} - p'_{t-1}) + (w'_t - p'_t) + (w'_{t+1} - p'_{t+1})^e$$
$$+ (w'_{t+2} - p'_{t+2})^e). \tag{26}$$

This represents a five year span which is about as much as we can afford given the length of our data series.

For the rate of interest in (12) we try both the short and the long rate where the latter is, perhaps, theoretically more appropriate. To deal with the real wage and inflation expectation terms we simply substitute in the actual values and use instrumental variables for estimation (see Wickens 1982).

The z variables in equation (12) fall into two groups, those which influence labour supply and those which affect frictional unemployment. In the first group we use (i) the ratio of benefits to post-tax wages (the replacement rate) for the unemployed and (ii) the level of redundancy payments. A third variable, namely the population of working age, enters the labour supply function (1) but we assume that it is the same as its "normal" level. So shifts in aggregate population are assumed not to influence unemployment even in the short run. The "normal" levels of (i) and (ii) are simply defined to be constants and so, for example, "normal" labour supply is defined at some "baseline" replacement rate. The influence of an increase in either of these two variables is clearly to reduce effective labour supply and hence to raise unemployment. Before turning to frictional unemployment it is perhaps worth defending our decision to treat the replacement rate as exogenous when its denominator is clearly determined within the model. We would argue that when the government sets the nominal level of benefits it does not do so *in vacuo* but either explicitly (in some periods) or implicitly uses wages as a yardstick. Thus it effectively chooses a replacement rate and then sets the nominal benefit, uprating it every year except in periods of very low inflation. In any event, we test this hypothesis in our empirical investigations.

The variables which influence frictional unemployment are (iii) the level of mismatching between vacancies and unemployment, (iv) the age composition of the labour force, (v) the degree of variation in the rate of inflation and (vi) the incidence of "employment protection" legislation. The impact of the last of these variables is discussed at some length in Nickell (1979a) and the arguments can be summarized briefly as follows. Any legislation which makes it more difficult and expensive for firms to reduce their workforce tends to reduce the rate at which individuals leave firms to enter unemployment. On the other hand, firms become more cautious in their hiring which tends to reduce the rate at which vacancies are filled and hence increases the average duration of unemployment spells. The net impact of these opposing forces on unemployment is then theoretically indeterminate. The variable we actually use here is the number of unfair dismissal cases decided by Industrial Tribunals. As far as age composition is concerned, the incidence of unemployment is considerably higher for both old and young workers than for those of prime age and thus changes in age composition will influence the rate of frictional unemployment. This will, in fact, be dealt with not by including the relevant variables in the regressions but by constructing a constant age composition unemployment rate which may be used as an alternative dependent variable.

The degree of variation in the inflation rate is a variable which is considered in this context by Attfield, Demery and Duck (1980) who argue that a higher degree of variability leads to more noise in the system with more frequent and relatively uninformative relative price changes. This leads to a lower equilibrium level of economic activity and hence to higher unemployment. (see also Fischer (1981)). Finally it is clear that frictional unemployment will rise if vacancies become less well matched to job seekers in terms of region, occupation and the like. To capture this effect we use the variable which measures the *absolute change* in the proportion of the workforce in production industries on the grounds that mismatching increases with the rate at which workers have to move between two sectors which differ greatly in their occupational structure.

The next equation which we must discuss is the reduced form (15) and here we must specify the normal (starred) levels of all the exogenous variables, other than the z's which we have already considered. There is an element of arbitrariness here but in line with our specification of normal real wages, we propose to use fairly short lagged moving averages. Two possibilities will be considered, namely,

(a)
$$x_t^* = x_{t-1}$$

or

(b)
$$x_t^* = \tfrac{1}{2}(x_{t-1} + \bar{g} + x_{t-2} + 2\bar{g}), \qquad \bar{g} = \text{trend growth rate} \tag{27}$$

The former is a particularly naive model where we suppose that wherever individuals found themselves last year is thought to be normal (i.e. they have short memories). The latter is slightly more sophisticated.[9]

Before discussing the imperfect information model we must comment on the possible dynamics which may enter the estimated versions of (12) and (15). The model we have described is essentially static but partial adjustment of unemployment to shocks may arise from the supply side in the structural equation and from both sides of the labour market in the reduced form. Any form of state dependence in labour supply leads directly to partial adjustment and in this particular context we should expect such state dependence to be particularly strong. Even in the context of a classical equilibrium model, when real wages fall below their normal level, for example, the costs involved in leaving employment may deter all but the most loosely attached individuals from quitting into unemployment. The majority of unemployed individuals do, in fact, enter unemployment via an involuntary separation of one sort or another. These costs of quitting may take the form of loss of specific capital, increased uncertainty concerning future income prospects, loss of rights associated with seniority, drastic falls in consumption due to "imperfections" in the capital market and capital losses on consumer durables due to inability to maintain loan repayments. Thus we should expect to find that the main effect of a fall in real wages below normal would be to prolong the unemployment spells of those who find themselves unemployed rather than to induce an orgy of quitting into unemployment.

So state dependence in labour supply would lead immediately to the incorporation of lagged unemployment in (12) and it should be no surprise if we find it to be significant. In the reduced form model any such effect would be reinforced if we have partial adjustment on the demand side which would arise, for example, if firms faced strictly convex costs associated with labour force adjustment.

Turning now to the imperfect information model discussed in section 2, we need only remark that this implies the addition of a series of "unanticipated" variables to the final model of Section 1 and that these "forecast errors" may be derived directly from models of the processes generating the variables. In order to use them we must, of course, suppose that the rather stringent conditions necessary for identification in such models are satisfied (See Pudney (1982), Nickell (1980a), Buiter (1980) for some discussion of these issues). Finally, before considering the non-competitive model of Section 4, two other topics need to be mentioned. First, in our theoretical model, all taxes are of the simple proportional type whereas, in practice, this is not the case. For firms, the demand for "men" is essentially determined by the tax per man. So whether employers National Insurance contributions are fixed independent of earnings or are earnings related is not important, we need simply consider the total tax paid for each employee, i.e. the average tax rate. For income taxes on workers, the situation is a little more complex.

In the intertemporal model of labour supply it is clearly the marginal tax rate which is important for substitution effects and the average rate for income effects. For the output demand equation, the income effect of taxes is probably dominant and so here we are justified in using the average tax rate (this is, of course, not absolutely exogenous but it is probably close enough to make little odds). Expenditure taxes are also rather difficult to specify precisely because of their changing relative impact on different goods. We see no alternative but to use a simple average tax rate on the expenditure side.

Second we should pay a little attention to how we might expect trade unions to influence our competitive model. In the context of this kind of model one may think of unions as setting wages in their sector at a rather higher level than they otherwise would be, thus disturbing the pattern of relative wages. Unions thus generate a "mark up" in the unionized sector but the base level of earnings is still determined by the competitive process. So on the demand side of the labour market there seems no reason to change anything. Unionized firms may be forced to pay higher wages but there is no particular reason why this should influence the aggregate demand for labour schedule. On the supply side, it can be argued that suppliers of labour are still influenced simply by the average real wage available in the market and nothing changes. Alternatively, however, it might be argued that when suppliers are looking at the margin between unemployment and work, they see their immediate prospects as being in the non-union sector. Thus the benefit levels should be compared to non-union sector earnings in forming the replacement rate variable. This is something we shall consider.

Turning to the non-competitive model of Section 3, the basic empirical problems are the specification of g_t^*, the target rate of growth of real wages and U_t, the measure of union power. In the so called "Sargan" wage equation, g_t^* is assumed to be the difference between a trend and last period's real wage. When such a specification was tried, the relevant real wage term was completely insignificant. An alternative specification is to use a distributed lag of past real wage changes. This seems quite sensible but precise estimation is tricky because of the large Hurwicz biases in small samples. Grubb, Jackman and Layard (1982) have an extensive discussion of ways to deal with this problem but here we simply avoid the issue by forcing g_t^* to be constant. Since it is likely to be slow moving we are probably not doing great violence to the data. To capture union power we utilize one ex-ante measure, namely the percentage of the labour force unionized and one ex-post measure which is an estimate of the *ceteris paribus* mark up of union relative to non-union wages. In conclusion, our estimated non-competitive model should only be viewed as suggestive rather than as the last word on the subject but we feel that it is worth including as a contrast to the more rigorously specified competitive model.

5. RESULTS

In this section we present estimates of the various unemployment models using U.K. annual data from 1950–1979. We use annual data because, for many of the variables of interest, quarterly data is simply not available and too much interpolation is unsatisfactory. Furthermore we can also use data over most of the post-war period rather than restricting ourselves to post 1963 which is the penalty for using quarterly data. The unemployment variable we attempt to explain is the male registered unemployment rate which is the most accurate measure of the aggregate unemployment rate which is available. The measured aggregate registered unemployment rate is rather less accurate because of the large, variable and generally unknown proportion of unemployed women who do not register as such.

In order to set the scene we consider some reduced form equations based on (15) and these are presented in Table I. The first striking feature of these results is the strong showing of the group of variables which reflect either direct labour supply effects such

REVIEW OF ECONOMIC STUDIES

TABLE I

Reduced form unemployment equations (1951–1979)
Dependent variable, male unemployment rate, $u_t(3·15\%)$

Independent variables	1	2	3
u_{t-1}	0·41	0·07	0·31
	(3·8)	(0·4)	(2·7)
(Variance of inflation)$_{(t+(t-1))/2}(3·10)$	0·13	0·155	0·14
	(3·8)	(3·4)	(3·9)
10^{-4} (Unfair dismissal cases)$_t$ (0·45)	0·51	0·86	0·47
	(2·9)	(3·7)	(2·8)
$\lvert\Delta$ per cent employment in production $\rvert_t$ (0·34)	0·80	0·70	0·68
	(4·8)	(3·5)	(4·0)
(Per cent replacement rate)$_t$ (47·2)	0·050	0·073	0·061
	(2·9)	(3·0)	(3·4)
(Redundancy payments (dummy))$_t$			0·31
			(1·27)
(Real government expenditure)$_t$	D −3·87	D' −2·5	U −4·79
	(3·1)	(2·0)	(3·5)
(World trade in manufactures)$_t$	D −2·18	D −1·6	U −3·04
	(1·6)	(1·0)	(2·0)
(Employment tax rate)$_t$	⎱	⎱	D −0·31
	⎰ D 23·4	⎰ D' −23·4	(3·5)
(Income tax rate)$_t$	(4·6)	(3·8)	D −0·20
			(3·6)
(Indirect tax rate)$_t$	D 13·9		D 0·06
	(2·0)		(0·9)
(World materials—manufacturing prices)$_{t-1}$	D −0·82	D' −1·27	U −1·01
	(1·0)	(1·1)	(1·0)
(Capital stock—labour force)$_t$	D 13·5	D' 23·2	D 0·07
	(1·4)	(2·9)	(0·7)
(Government employment—labour force)$_t$	D 12·3		U 2·9
	(2·0)		(0·9)
R^2	0·994	0·990	0·995
S^2	0·041	0·062	0·037
LM (Serial correlation) $(\chi^2(2))$	5·8	3·9	7·2
Durbin's h (squared) $\chi^2(1)$	2·3	3·5	0·16
Parameter stability test (1976–1979)	$F(4, 13) = 0·26$	$F(4, 14) = 0·95$	$F(4, 10) = 1·83$

Notes

1. All variables in the list from government expenditure on are in logs except tax rates. The remainder are not and their means are in brackets.
2. D, D' refer to deviations from the normal levels defined in (27a), (27b) respectively. U refers to unanticipated.
3. The tax rates are all average.
4. t statistics are in brackets below the coefficients.
5. The variables omitted from the equation had both small t ratios and small coefficients. This applies, in particular, to the ratio of money supply to world manufacturing prices in equation (1) and (2) and to unanticipated money shocks in equation (3).
6. The unanticipated variables were generated as residuals from the following equations:
   Real Government Expenditure, 1950–1979

$$\log g_t = -4·74 + 1·03 \log g_{t-1} - 0·32 \log g_{t-2} + 0·74 \log y_{t-1}$$
$$\qquad (5·4) \qquad\qquad (2·0) \qquad\qquad (1·7)$$
$$+ 0·12 \,(x_{t-1} + x_{t-2}) - 0·0095_t$$
$$(0·8) \qquad\qquad\quad (0·8)$$

g = real gov't expenditure, y = real output, x = PSBR/g.
$R^2 = 0·985$,   LM (serial correlation) $\chi^2(2) = 0·049$,   parameter stability (1978–1979) $\chi^2(2) = 0·3$.
World Trade in Manufactures, 1950–1979

$$\log WT_t = 0·49 + 0·81 \log WT_{t-1} - 0·42\Delta \log q_{t-1} + 0·015t$$
$$(5·9) \qquad\qquad (2·8) \qquad\qquad (1·4)$$

WT = world trade, q = world materials-manufactures price ratio.

$R^2 = 0.997$,   LM (serial correlation) $\chi^2(2) = 3.15$,   parameter stability (1978–1979) $\chi^2(2) = 3.7$.

Materials-Manufactures Price Ratio, 1950–1979

$$\log q_t = -0.25 + 0.48 \log q_{t-1} + 0.34 \log q_{t-2} + 0.13 \log WT_{-1} - 0.007_t$$
$$\quad\quad\quad\quad (2.2)\quad\quad\quad (1.8)\quad\quad\quad\quad (0.7)\quad\quad\quad\quad (0.5)$$

$R^2 = 0.718$,   LM (serial correlation)$\chi^2(2) = 3.23$,   parameter stability (1978–1979) $\chi^2(2) = 3.0$.

Government Employment/Labour Force, 1950–1979

$$\log NG_t = -0.49 + 0.84 \log NG_{t-1} + 0.17\Delta \log w_{t-1} - 0.12\, x_{t-1} + 0.0013_t$$
$$\quad\quad\quad\quad\quad (11.2)\quad\quad\quad (1.7)\quad\quad\quad (2.2)\quad\quad (2.4)$$

$$w = \text{wages},\quad x = \text{PSBR}/g.$$

$R^2 = 0.892$,   LM (serial correlation) $\chi^2(2) = 1.43$,   parameter stability (1978–1979) $\chi^2(2) = 1.4$.

Money Supply, 1950–1979

$$\Delta \log M_t = -2.97 + 0.29\Delta \log M_{t-1} - 0.49 \log y_{t-1} + 0.76 \log y_{t-2}$$
$$\quad\quad\quad\quad\quad (1.9)\quad\quad\quad\quad (1.3)\quad\quad\quad\quad (2.0)$$

$$+ 0.27\, (z_{1t-1} + z_{1t-2}) + 0.53\, (z_{2t-1} + z_{2t-2}) - 0.003t$$
$$\quad (1.9)\quad\quad\quad\quad\quad (4.0)\quad\quad\quad\quad\quad (0.3)$$

$$z_1 = \text{PSBR}/M,\quad z_2 = \text{balance of payments}/M.$$

$R^2 = 0.805$,   LM (serial correlation) $\chi^2(2) = 1.28$,   parameter stability (1978–1979) $\chi^2(2) = 5.1$.

as the replacement rate or influences on the level of frictional unemployment such as the variance of inflation. This is perhaps to be expected given that some of these variables are strongly correlated with the broad shifts in unemployment which have taken place over the period. In contrast the relatively weak showing of the exogenous shock variables can be put down to some extent to their collinearity and the relatively small size of the cyclical unemployment changes when compared to the broad shifts. The former results lead to a certain feeling of unease when, for example, we find that around half of the 2% jump in unemployment between 1974 and 1975 is accounted for by the sharp rise in the variance of inflation. In the same vein we find that the impact of unfair dismissal legislation in 1972 has caused a rise in unemployment of over 1 percentage point by 1977.[10] Such results are not, of course, completely out of the question and some may find them appealing. However we feel that they must be treated with some scepticism unless alternative micro evidence points strongly in the same direction. This is the case with the impact of unemployment benefit, for the parameter estimates imply an elasticity of unemployment with respect to the replacement rate between 0.75 and 1.09 which is not completely out of line with the micro evidence for Britain which has accumulated in the last few years (see, for example, Lancaster 1979, Nickell 1979b). With regard to this variable it is also worth noting that when we replace the standard replacement rate by one where the denominator is our estimate of the non-union wage, there is a negligible change in the coefficient. Furthermore a standard Hausman–Wu type test (Hausman (1978)) designed to detect correlation between a variable and the equation error indicated that the hypothesis of zero correlation could not be rejected ($t = 0.56$). This is some justification for assuming it to be (weakly) exogenous. Finally we should note that using an unemployment rate corrected for demographic shifts makes no odds whatever mainly because such a correction has practically no effect on the variable concerned.

Turning to the effect of various types of exogenous shock, we find that those associated with government expenditure and world trade are consistently effective in shifting the unemployment rate in the direction anticipated by theory. This is not the case with taxes on labour which are incorrectly signed and the remaining variables have effects which are generally unrobust. In particular (see note (5) to Table I), money supply variables either relative to world prices or unanticipated do not seem to show up at all. This is presumably because we have already included those truly exogenous forces

68

RES/746 REVIEW OF ECONOMIC STUDIES

which lead to money supply shifts. This is in stark contrast to the results presented in
Attfield, Demery and Duck (1979) where money innovations play a highly significant
role among the determinants of output. Their maintained hypothesis is highly restricted,
however, since most of the variables included here are omitted from their model, so
there is little difficulty in reconciling their result with ours.

With the notable exceptions of world trade and government expenditure, the general
lack of significant and correctly signed coefficients on the exogenous shock variables
leads us back to the question as to whether or not the supply side and frictional variables
are picking up "too much" of the variation in unemployment. The difficulty here is that
unemployment has trended in only one direction since the war and shows little sign of
doing otherwise. Until such time as this trend goes into reverse, time series analysis of
the unemployment rate alone is never going to lead to parameter estimates which are
entirely convincing. On the other hand we should point out that if we exclude the
variance of inflation and unfair dismissals and replace them by a time trend, the resulting
equation is vastly inferior with the exogenous shock variables showing up less strongly
and the time trend not showing up at all.

Comparing the equations, inclusion of the "unanticipated" variables[11] leads to
marginally superior tracking power but equation (1) with the naive difference variables
is vastly more robust in terms of parameter stability. In any event all three equations
tell the same kind of story so the allocation of first prize is not a very important exercise.[12]

Our next step is to consider the estimates of the structural unemployment equation
(12) which will suffer less from the problems imposed by the limited number of degrees
of freedom. The results are presented in Table II. A number of points are worth noting.
First, the significant lagged dependent variable is consistent with a fairly high degree of
supply side state dependence. Second, all the coefficients have the theoretically correct
sign except for that on the real interest rate which is correctly signed only in equation
1 and is effectively zero in the other equations. This remained the case (i) when the
long rate was used instead of the short rate and (ii) when the "normal" level of the real
rate was taken to be a moving average of past real rates. Neither of these changes had
any substantive impact on the equations. The real wage deviations have strong although
not particularly well determined negative effects which comes as rather a surprise in the
light of the results of Altonji and Ashenfelter (1980).[13] Furthermore only equation (1)
passes the test of the overidentifying restrictions which is essentially a test of whether
the instruments are correlated with the equation errors, or equivalently a test of whether
they should be included directly in the equation as exogenous regressors. This implies
that only in the case of equation (1) are we unable to reject (at the 5% level) the
hypothesis that all the impact of the exogenous shocks is transmitted into unemployment
via the endogenous variables once we hold exogenous supply and frictional factors
constant. Furthermore we must in fairness note that if the equations are estimated up
to 1973, the real wage coefficient is very much smaller and the χ^2 test statistic for the
over-identifying restrictions indicates a rejection of the null hypothesis in all cases. So
for the period up to 1973 real wage movements relative to normal do not appear to
have a large enough (partial) correlation with cyclical fluctuations to sustain the equilibrium story and the exogenous shock variables would appear to act via some alternative
channel. However, suppose we take the equations in Table II at face value. They indicate
that a 1% fall in real wages relative to normal is associated with a rise in unemployment
of between 0·14 and 0·28 percentage points in one year with a further 50% rise in the
second year. One might then argue as follows. The one year rise in unemployment
would correspond roughly to a 0·2 to 0·4% fall in employment yielding a short run
labour supply elasticity of about 0·2 to 0·4. Such an elasticity does not seem too
unreasonable. However this argument is not really convincing for the following reason.
Cyclical changes in unemployment may be decomposed into changes in the inflow rate
(mainly involuntary) and changes in duration with the latter contributing at least 60%

TABLE II

Structural unemployment equation (12) 1952–1977
Dependent Variable, Unemployment Rate, u_t

Equation Number	1	2	3	4
Independent variables				
u_{t-1}	0·36	0·43	0·41	0·55
	(2·0)	(3·4)	(3·0)	(4·2)
(Real wage deviations)$_t$	−28·1	−13·9	−18·3	−14·3
	(2·4)	(2·4)	(3·0)	(3·3)
(Real interest rate)$_t$	−0·083	0·015	−0·004	0·006
(short rate)	(1·0)	(0·4)	(0·1)	(0·2)
(Variance of inflation)	0·069	0·079	0·075	0·052
$(t+(t-1))/2$	(0·9)	(1·3)	(1·2)	(0·8)
10^{-4} (Unfair dismissal	0·027	0·037	0·034	0·028
cases)$_t$	(0·8)	(1·5)	(1·3)	(1·1)
$|\Delta$ per cent employment	1·38	1·07	1·18	1·29
in production $|_t$	(3·4)	(4·0)	(4·2)	(4·5)
(Per cent replacement rate)$_t$	0·044	0·029	0·031	0·012
	(1·6)	(1·5)	(1·6)	(0·7)
(Redundancy payments (dummy))$_t$	−0·008	0·45	0·37	0·44
	(0·1)	(1·3)	(1·0)	(1·3)
S^2	0·200	0·107	0·117	0·111
DW	1·94	2·29	2·29	2·22
Box–Pierce ($\chi^2(3)$) (serial correlation)	3·77	3·35	3·24	2·77
$\chi^2_{0.05}(3) = 7·8$				
Test of overidentifying restrictions				
$\chi^2_{0.05}(4) = 9·49, \chi^2_{0.05}(5) = 11·07$	$\chi^2(4) = 6·16$	$\chi^2(4) = 12·8$	$\chi^2(5) = 12·2$	$\chi^2(5) = 10·9$
Parameter stability test (1973–1977)	$F(4, 13) = 1·95$	$F(4, 13) = 1·77$	$F(4, 13) = 1·81$	$F(4, 13) = 2·18$

Notes:
1. Instruments used for real wage deviations and the real interest rate are as follows. Equation 1: regressors of Table 1, equation 1. Equation 2: regressors of Table 1, equation 2. Equations 3 and 4: regressors of Table 1, equation 3. The real interest rate is defined at $R_t - (p^e_{t+1} - p_t)$.
2. Equations 1, 2, 3 define the real wage using the average income tax rate, 4 using the marginal rate.
3. All variables are in logs except for u, real interest rate, tax rates and all the exogenous variables in the equation.
4. t statistics are in brackets below coefficients.

of the total. In other words the majority of the real wage effect translates into a lengthening of the duration of unemployment spells. Taking the 60% figure, a 1% rise in real wages above normal then leads to an increase in duration of between 2·5 and 5% using the mean unemployment rate as the base. This would rise to between 3·75 and 7·5% after two years. So the implied long run duration elasticity of real wage changes is at least 3·75 and probably considerably more. This is completely at variance with the replacement rate studies which we have already mentioned, where a figure of unity would seem to be the upper bound. In other words the labour supply effects required to make the equilibrium model consistent with the data up to 1977 appear to be inconsistent with existing evidence.[14] All in all therefore, we do not feel that this kind of competitive model is consistent with the data.

Let us therefore turn to some estimates of a rather crude version of the non-competitive model discussed in Section III. These are presented in Table III. The wage equations are bereft of any complex expectation terms and have neutrality imposed. There is a significant unemployment term[15] but the other coefficients are rather badly determined although all of the expected sign. The price equation is unremarkable although it is worth noting that the coefficients on capital stock and government employment imply that $1 - \lambda_1 = 0·19$ which should be the average proportion of government

REVIEW OF ECONOMIC STUDIES

TABLE III

Simple wage—price equations 1952–1977

Equation number	Dep. Var. $= \Delta w_t - \Delta w_{t-1}$ 1	Dep. Var. $= p_t - w_t - t_{1t}$ 2
$\Delta w_{t-1} - \Delta p'_{t-1}$	−1·08 (3·3)	
u_t	−0·048 (2·6)	0·021 (3·7)
$(\Delta$ Income tax rate$)_t$	1·22 (1·4)	
$\|\Delta$ per cent employment in production$\|_t$	0·038 (1·3)	
(Per cent replacement rate)$_t$	0·0031 (1·3)	
Union power (i) (Union density)$_t$	0·63 (1·6)	
(ii) (Union mark-up)$_t$	0·69 (1·2)	
Trend	0·0022 (0·6)	
Material prices$_t - w_t - t_{1t}$		0·051 (1·9)
$p_{t-1} - w_{t-1} - t_{1t-1}$		0·38 (2·0)
Capital stock—labour force		0·74 (3·2)
Government employment—labour force		−0·17 (0·6)
Constant	−0·38 (2·9)	−8·48 (3·2)
S	0·028	0·017
DW	1·98	2·36
Box–Pierce $\chi^2(3)$	0·30	6·00

Notes:
1. Instruments used for u_t in equations 1 and 2 are $(D'$ Government expenditure$)_t$, $(D'$ Government investment expenditure), $(D'$ World trade in manufactures), $(D'$ Materials prices—World manufactures prices)$_t$, $(D'$ Capital stock—labour force)$_t$.
2. Instruments used for u_t, (Material prices$_t - w_t - t_{1t}$) in equation 3 are all lagged variables plus $(D'$ World trade in manufactures), $|\Delta$ percentage in production industries$|_t$, (Variance of inflation)$_{(t+(t-1))/2}$, (Unfair dismissal cases)$_t$, (Replacement rate)$_t$, (Redundancy payments dummy)$_t$.
3. t ratios are in brackets below coefficients.
4. All variables are in logs except the tax rates, the replacement rate, the variance of inflation and the per cent of employment in production.
5. As before p' refers to post tax prices, p to pre tax prices, i.e. $p' = p(1 + t_3)$.

employment in total employment (see below (22)). Since it is the same order of magnitude as its correct value (0·16) we shall retain the government employment variable in spite of its insignificance. Using equations 1 and 2 from Table III we may derive the empirical equivalent of the equilibrium unemployment equation (25) as

$$u_t^* = -7.95 + 22.7\dot{t}_{1t} + 25.7\dot{t}_{2t} + 22.7\dot{t}_{3t} + 2.02\dot{q}_t - 6.59(\dot{n}_{gt} - \dot{n}_t)$$
$$- 28.9(\dot{k}_t - \dot{n}_t) + 14.5U_{1t} + 13.2U_{2t} + 1.17\dot{u}_t + 1.53z_{3t}$$
$$+ 0.037z_{1t} + 0.12t. \tag{28}$$

The notation is the same as in (25), $U_{1t} =$ union density, $U_{2t} =$ union mark-up, $z_{3t} =$ the absolute value of the change in the percentage of the workforce employed in production

TABLE IV

Breakdown of the Rise in Unemployment from 1973–1977 (3·8%)
Based on Table I, equation (3)

	Rise in unemployment (percentage points)
Tax shocks	0·48
Government expenditure shocks	0·40
Materials price shocks	0·11
World trade shocks	0·33
Changes in frictional/supply side variables	2·66

TABLE V

Breakdown of the Rise in Unemployment from 1973–1977
Based on Table II, equation (3)

	Rise in unemployment (percentage points)
Fall in real wage below "normal"	1·86
Changes in frictional/supply side variables	1·95

and z_{1t} is the replacement rate. g_t^* in (25) is a constant as we have already noted. The implications of the equation for unemployment are of considerable interest, and in order to bring these out and compare them with the previous model we shall consider the macro-economic events of the period 1973–1977. Unemployment rose during this period by some 3·8 percentage points and we shall first use the reduced form model reported in Table I to provide a breakdown of this increase. The figures in Table IV indicate that about one third of this rise was due to various exogenous shocks with the remainder being due to frictional or supply side variables, mainly increases in the variance of inflation and in employment protection costs. We have already recorded our unease concerning the size of these latter effects but the former ones seem quite sensible. In Table V, we see how the exogenous shocks are translated into unemployment rises on the supply side of the equilibrium model. The decline in real wages below normal during this period (probably due to the highly successful Incomes Policy of the day) led to a massive fall in labour supply mainly in the form of entrants onto the unemployment register extending the duration of their spells. This led to a rise in unemployment of nearly 2 percentage points. Being an equilibrium model there must of course have been a corresponding reduction on the demand side following directly from the exogenous shocks.

In the non-competitive model, the story is rather different. The demand reduction led to a rise in unemployment but with no necessity for the unemployed to remain on their supply functions. What equation (28) reveals are the pressures on the government which led to some of the deflationary exogenous shocks. As we can see from Table VI, around the mid 1970s a number of factors conspired to raise the constant inflation rate of unemployment u^*. Apart from the oil shock, falls in the rate of capital accumulation and hence productivity growth and changes in the trends of taxation led to a 1·00 percentage point rise in the constant inflation rate of unemployment. The large increase in the rate of change of relative material prices could only have served to raise this, if only temporarily. In order to try and stop inflation rising, the government was forced to take a deflationary stance. Of course, in so far as it used tax rates to do so, this worsened the trade off via the tax terms in (28). Finally, of course, it turned to Incomes Policy as a last resort.

REVIEW OF ECONOMIC STUDIES

TABLE VI

Changes in u* in the mid-seventies due to government policy and the oil and productivity shocks

Average $\dot{t}_1$:	1969–1974 = 0·0032,	1974–1979 = 0·014		$\Delta u^* =$	0·25
Average $\dot{t}_2$:	1969–1975 = 0·0085,	1975–1979 = −0·0098		$\Delta u^* =$	−0·47
Average $\dot{t}_3$:	1969–1974 = −0·013,	1974–1979 = 0·0066		$\Delta u^* =$	0·45
Average $\dot{n}_g - \dot{n}$:	1969–1974 = 0·013,	1974–1979 = −0·013		$\Delta u^* =$	0·18
Average $\dot{k} - \dot{n}$:	1965–1974 = 0·038,	1974–1979 = 0·018		$\Delta u^* =$	0·59
Average $\dot{q}_t$:	1965–1972 = −0·01,	1972–1974 = 0·11,	1974–1978 = −0·0068,		

TABLE VII

Contributions to the 3·53 percentage point rise in unemployment between 1953–1957 and 1971–1976

	Table 1 Equation 3		Table 2 Equation 3		Equation (28)
	SR	LR	SR	LR	LR
Variance of inflation	0·55	0·78	0·30	0·51	—
Unfair dismissal cases	0·63	0·91	0·56	0·95	—
|Change in employment in production|	0·47	0·67	0·81	1·37	0·54
Replacement rate	1·07	1·53	0·54	0·92	0·83
Redundancy payments	0·31	0·44	0·55	0·93	—
Union mark-up	—	—	—	—	0·33
Union density	—	—	—	—	0·92
Time trend	—	—	—	—	0·82
Total	3·03	4·33	2·76	4·68	3·44

Note: SR refers to short run, LR to long run. The former are derived directly from the appropriate coefficients in the various equations. The latter then adjusts these using the coefficient on the lagged dependent variable.

Having considered the implications of our models over a short period of rapid economic change, we shall now compare a period in the 50s with the early 70s to see what light we can shed on the secular rise in unemployment over that period. Here we should expect our non-cyclical variables to generate more appealing results than they do for year to year variations in unemployment. In Table VII we present the contribution of the different "secular" variables to the 3·53 percentage point rise in unemployment between 1953–1957 and 1971–1976.

As we might expect, the actual change in unemployment lies between the short run and long run totals presented in the table. Around half the total is consistently accounted for by a combination of the increased generosity of benefits relative to wages and the larger movements of workers between the production and service sectors of the economy. The non-competitive model also indicates that rises in union power have raised unemployment by just over 1 percentage point. Otherwise the numbers require little comment other than to warn again against taking these results too seriously until there is confirmation of these effects from more comprehensive micro-econometric investigations, (as there is in the case of the benefits effect).

CONCLUSIONS

The implications of this investigation are as follows. The equilibrium model of the labour market does not really fit the facts, implying that at least some of the unemployed are off their supply functions. This means that an economic policy which simply relies on regulating those nominal magnitudes over which the government has some control and allows the real economy to adjust as it may, need not generate particularly desirable results. Nominal wage changes appear to be generated by forces other than competitive pressures and we have estimated a very crude empirical model of the consequences of this although we have made little attempt to model the "non-competitive" factors themselves. We have found, in particular, that in the mid 1970s a number of factors conspired together to raise the level of unemployment associated with a constant inflation rate which partly explains the deflationary policy stance taken in the years 1975–1977 in spite of record rises in unemployment.

Turning to the secular rise in unemployment in Britain since the war, we have found a number of tentative explanations, in particular increases in relative price variability associated with larger variations in rates of inflation, increases in the benefit to income ratio, larger shifts in the labour force between different sectors, the introduction of employment protection legislation and the rise in union power. These explanations, although quite appealing, remain somewhat speculative.

APPENDIX

1. The reduced form output equation (9).

The parameters of (9) are as follows. First

$$\pi = \left(c_2 + c_4 + \frac{c_8}{A_2}\right) / \left(1 + \frac{c_8 A_1}{A_2}\right) - \left(\frac{A_2 b_1 a_{22} - b_1 d_3}{A_2(d_1 - a_1)} + b_{22}\right) / \left(1 - \frac{b_1 d_3 A_1}{A_2(d_1 - a_1)}\right)$$

$$= \gamma - \delta = \gamma_1/\pi_1 - \gamma_2/\pi_2 \quad \text{say.}$$

Notice that π_2 must be positive to avoid perverse effects and that $\gamma_1 > 0$, $\pi_1 > 0$, $\gamma_2 \leq 0$, $\gamma > 0$, $\delta \leq 0$, $\pi > 0$. Furthermore $\delta = 0$ under R1 and R2. Turning now to the individual parameters,

$$\omega_1 = -\frac{c_1 \delta}{\pi \pi_1} \geq 0 \quad \text{and} \quad \omega_2 = -\frac{c_3 \delta}{\pi_1 \pi} \geq 0.$$

$\omega_1 = \omega_2 = 0$ under R1 and R2.

$$\omega_3 = \frac{\gamma}{\pi \pi_2}\left(\frac{b_1 a_4}{d_1 - a_1} + b_4\right) > 0$$

since the direct effect of an increase in government employment must dominate the real wage offset.

$$\omega_4 = \frac{1}{A_2 \pi \pi_1 \pi_2}\left(\frac{-c_4 d_3 b_1}{d_1 - a_1} - \left(\frac{b_1 a_{22}}{d_1 - a_1} + b_{22}\right)(A_2 c_2 + c_8)\right) = 0 \quad \text{under R2.}$$

$$\omega_5 = \frac{\gamma}{\pi \pi_2}\left(\frac{b_1 a_{21}}{d_1 - a_1} + b_{21}\right) < 0$$

since the direct effect of an increase in the relative price of materials dominates the real wage offset.

$$\omega_6 = \frac{1}{\pi}\left(\frac{b_1 d_1 \gamma}{(d_1 - a_1)\pi_2} - \frac{c_5 \delta}{\pi_1}\right) < 0,$$

ω_7, ω_8 are similarly negative.

2. The incomplete information model.

The basic model we propose to analyse is that given by equations (16), (17), (18), (19),

(20) in the main text. In labour market equilibrium we have

$$(d_1 - a_1)w_t(x) = \text{constant} + a_{21}q_t(x) + d_1 E(p_t|I_t) - a_1 p_t(x)_t + a_4 n_{gt}(x)$$

or in simpler notation

$$w_t(x) = \beta_0 + \beta_1 q_t(x) + \beta_2 p_t(x) + (1 - \beta_2)E(p_t|I_t) + \beta_3 n_{gt}(x)$$

$$\beta_1 < 0, \qquad \beta_2 > 0, \qquad \beta_3 > 0, \qquad \beta_2 < 1. \tag{A.1}$$

In goods market equilibrium we have

$$(C_2 - b_1)p_t(x) = (C_0 - b_0) + C_1 g_t(x) + C_2 m_t(x) + C_3 y_{wt}(x) - b_1 w_t(x) - b_4 n_{gt}(x) - b_{21}q_t(x).$$

Using (A.1) to eliminate the wage, we obtain an equation of the form

$$p_t(x) = \alpha_0 + \alpha_1 g_t(x) + \alpha_2 q_t(x) + \alpha_3 m_t(x) + (1 - \alpha_3)E(p_t|I_t) + \alpha_4 y_{wt}(x) + \alpha_5 n_{gt}(x)$$

$$\alpha_1 > 0, \qquad \alpha_2 > 0, \qquad 0 < \alpha_3 < 1, \qquad \alpha_4 > 0, \qquad \alpha_5 > 0. \tag{A.2}$$

In order to solve for the rational expectations (RE) equilibrium, we must first note the following points. From (20), the processes generating the exogenous variables satisfy

$$\left. \begin{array}{ll} m_t(x) = m_t^* + \varepsilon_{mt} + \varepsilon_m(x), & m_t^* = E(m_t|\bar{I}(t-1)) \\[4pt] g_t(x) = g_t^* + \varepsilon_{gt} + \varepsilon_g(x), & g_t^* = E(g_t|\bar{I}(t-1)) \\[4pt] q_t(x) = q_t^* + \varepsilon_{qt} + \varepsilon_q(x), & q_t^* = E(q_t|\bar{I}(t-1)) \\[4pt] y_{wt}(x) = y_{wt}^* + \varepsilon_{wt} + \varepsilon_w(x), & y_{wt}^* = E(y_{wt}|\bar{I}(t-1)) \\[4pt] n_{gt}(x) = n_{gt}^* + \varepsilon_{nt} + \varepsilon_n(x), & n_{gt}^* = E(n_{gt}|\bar{I}(t-1)) \end{array} \right\} \tag{A.3}$$

where $\varepsilon_{mt} \sim N(0, \sigma_m^2)$, $\varepsilon_m(x) \sim N(0, \sigma_{mx}^2)$, etc. Furthermore, note that $m_t = m_t^* + \varepsilon_{mt}$ and similarly for the other variables. Remember that $\bar{I}(t-1)$ contains all aggregate variables dated $t-1$ and before, whereas $I_t = (\bar{I}(t-1), w_t(x))$.

To solve for the RE equilibrium we use the method of undetermined coefficients. Thus we let

$$w_t(x) = \bar{\pi}_0 + \bar{\pi}_1 m_t^* + \bar{\pi}_2 g_t^* + \bar{\pi}_3 q_t^* + \bar{\pi}_4 y_{wt}^* + \bar{\pi}_5 n_{gt}^* + \bar{\pi}_6 \varepsilon_{mt} + \bar{\pi}_7 \varepsilon_{gt}$$

$$+ \bar{\pi}_8 \varepsilon_{qt} + \bar{\pi}_9 \varepsilon_{wt} + \bar{\pi}_{10} \varepsilon_{nt} + \bar{\pi}_{11} \varepsilon_m(x) + \bar{\pi}_{12} \varepsilon_g(x) + \bar{\pi}_{13} \varepsilon_q(x)$$

$$+ \bar{\pi}_{14} \varepsilon_w(x) + \bar{\pi}_{15} \varepsilon_n(x) \tag{A.4}$$

$$p_t(x) = \text{as above replacing } \bar{\pi}\text{'s by } \pi\text{'s.} \tag{A.5}$$

I_t obviously contains all starred variables and hence knowledge of $w_t(x)$ is equivalent to knowledge of

$$\nu_t = \bar{\pi}_6 \varepsilon_{mt} + \bar{\pi}_7 \varepsilon_{gt} + \cdots + \bar{\pi}_{15} \varepsilon_n(x) \tag{A.6}$$

From (A.5) we may write

$$E(p_t|I_t) = \pi_0 + \pi_1 m_t^* + \pi_2 g_t^* + \pi_3 q_t^* + \pi_4 y_{wt}^* + \pi_5 n_{gt}^*$$

$$+ E\{\pi_6 \varepsilon_{mt} + \pi_7 \varepsilon_{gt} + \cdots + \pi_{10} \varepsilon_{nt}|\nu_t)$$

Given the normality assumptions, the expectations term is given by

$$E\{\pi_6 \varepsilon_{mt} + \pi_7 \varepsilon_{qt} + \cdots + \pi_{10} \varepsilon_{nt}|\nu_t\} = \theta \nu_t \tag{A.7}$$

where

$$\theta = \frac{\pi_6}{\bar{\pi}_6}\theta_6 + \frac{\pi_7}{\bar{\pi}_7}\theta_7 + \frac{\pi_8}{\bar{\pi}_8}\theta_8 + \frac{\pi_9}{\bar{\pi}_9}\theta_9 + \frac{\pi_{10}}{\bar{\pi}_{10}}\theta_{10}$$

$$\theta_6 = \bar{\pi}_6^2\sigma_m/\Delta, \quad \theta_7 = \bar{\pi}_7^2\sigma_g^2/\Delta, \quad \theta_8 = \bar{\pi}_8^2\sigma_w^2/\Delta, \quad \theta_9 = \bar{\pi}_9^2\sigma_q^2/\Delta, \quad \theta_{10} = \bar{\pi}_{10}^2\sigma_n^2/\Delta$$

$$\Delta = \bar{\pi}_6^2\sigma_m^2 + \bar{\pi}_7^2\sigma_g^2 + \bar{\pi}_8^2\sigma_w^2 + \bar{\pi}_9^2\sigma_q^2 + \bar{\pi}_{10}^2\sigma_n^2 + \bar{\pi}_{11}^2\sigma_{mx}^2 + \bar{\pi}_{12}^2\sigma_{gx}^2 + \bar{\pi}_{13}^2\sigma_{wx}^2$$
$$+ \bar{\pi}_{14}^2\sigma_{qx}^2 + \bar{\pi}_{15}^2\sigma_{nx}^2.$$

We are now in a position to substitute (A.3), (A.4), (A.5), (A.6) into (A.1) and (A.2) and compare coefficients. From (A.2), we obtain

$$\pi_1 = 1, \quad \pi_2 = \frac{\alpha_1}{\alpha_3}, \quad \pi_3 = \frac{\alpha_2}{\alpha_3}, \quad \pi_4 = \frac{\alpha_4}{\alpha_3}, \quad \pi_5 = \frac{\alpha_5}{\alpha_3}, \quad \pi_6 = \alpha_3 + (1-\alpha_3)\theta\bar{\pi}_6,$$

$$\pi_7 = \alpha_1 + (1-\alpha_3)\theta\bar{\pi}_7, \quad \pi_8 = \alpha_2 + (1-\alpha_3)\theta\bar{\pi}_8, \quad \pi_9 = \alpha_4 + (1-\alpha_3)\theta\bar{\pi}_9,$$

$$\pi_{10} = \alpha_5 + (1-\alpha_3)\theta\bar{\pi}_{10}, \quad \pi_{11} \text{ to } \pi_{15} \text{ are similar.}$$

From (A.1) we obtain

$$\bar{\pi}_1 = 1, \quad \bar{\pi}_2 = \pi_2, \quad \bar{\pi}_3 = \beta_1 + \pi_3, \quad \bar{\pi}_4 = \pi_4, \quad \bar{\pi}_5 = \pi_5 + \beta_4,$$

$$\bar{\pi}_6 = \beta_2\pi_6 + (1-\beta_2)\theta\bar{\pi}_6, \quad \bar{\pi}_7 = \beta_2\pi_7 + (1-\beta_2)\theta\bar{\pi}_7, \quad \bar{\pi}_8 = \beta_1 + \beta_2\pi_8 + (1-\beta_2)\theta\bar{\pi}_8,$$

$$\bar{\pi}_9 = \beta_2\pi_9 + (1-\beta_2)\theta\bar{\pi}_9, \quad \bar{\pi}_{10} = \beta_3 + \beta_2\pi_{10} + (1-\beta_2)\theta\bar{\pi}_{10},$$

$$\bar{\pi}_{11} \text{ to } \bar{\pi}_{15} \text{ are similar.}$$

From these we may note first that $\pi_6 = \pi_{11}, \pi_7 = \pi_{12}, \ldots, \pi_{10} = \pi_{15}, \bar{\pi}_6 = \bar{\pi}_{11}, \ldots, \bar{\pi}_{10} = \bar{\pi}_{15}$. We also find that

$$\bar{\pi}_6 = \beta_2\alpha_3/\Delta_1, \qquad \pi_6 = \alpha_3(1-\theta(1-\beta_2))/\Delta_1$$

$$\bar{\pi}_7 = \beta_2\alpha_1/\Delta_1, \qquad \pi_7 = \alpha_1(1-\theta(1-\beta_2))/\Delta_1$$

$$\bar{\pi}_8 = \beta_1 + \beta_2\alpha_2/\Delta_1, \qquad \pi_8 = (\alpha_2(1-\theta(1-\beta_2)) + \beta_1(1-\alpha_3)\theta)/\Delta_1$$

$$\bar{\pi}_9 = \beta_2\alpha_4/\Delta_1, \qquad \pi_9 = \alpha_4(1-\theta(1-\beta_2))/\Delta_1$$

$$\bar{\pi}_{10} = \beta_3 + \beta_2\alpha_5/\Delta_1, \qquad \pi_{10} = (\alpha_5(1-\theta(1-\beta_2)) + \beta_3(1-\alpha_3)\theta)/\Delta_1$$

$$\Delta_1 = 1 - \theta(1-\beta_2\alpha_3).$$

From these we can, of course, solve the implicit equation for θ which turns out to be linear since $\theta_6, \ldots, \theta_{10}$ are independent of θ given the expressions for $\bar{\pi}_6 \cdots \bar{\pi}_{10}$. More importantly, however, we can note that the labour demand equation (18) implies that aggregate employment takes the form

$$n_t = a_0 + a_1(w_t - p_t) + a_{21}q_t + a_4 n_{gt}$$

and using (A.4), (A.5) and the expressions for the π's we have

$$n_t = \bar{a}_0 + a_1\{(\bar{\pi}_6 - \pi_6)\varepsilon_{mt} + (\bar{\pi}_7 - \pi_7)\varepsilon_{gt} + (\bar{\pi}_8 - \pi_8)\varepsilon_{qt} + (\bar{\pi}_9 - \pi_9)\varepsilon_{wt} + (\bar{\pi}_{10} - \pi_{10})\varepsilon_{nt}\}$$

$$+ a_1\beta_1 q_t^* + a_1\beta_3 n_{gt} + a_{21}q_t + a_4 n_{gt}^*$$

$$= a_0 - \frac{\alpha_3 a_1(1-\beta_2)(1-\theta)}{\Delta_1}(m_t - m_t^*) - \frac{\alpha_1 a_1(1-\beta_2)(1-\theta)}{\Delta_1}(g_t - g_t^*)$$

$$- \frac{\alpha_4 a_1(1-\beta_2)(1-\theta)}{\Delta_1}(y_{wt} - y_{wt}^*) + \text{terms in } q_t, n_{gt}, q_t^*, n_{gt}^*.$$

Thus employment and unemployment are influenced by money, government expenditure and world trade innovations in this model.

DATA APPENDIX

All series collected are for years 1948 to 1979 inclusive (32 observations). Where possible labour market variables are for males as the dependent variable for this study is the male unemployment rate. All data refers to the United Kingdom, where possible.

P'_t; post-tax price level

Series used was the "general index of retail prices, all items", 1975 = 100, which is published in ETAS 81.

Q'_t; price of materials and fuel

Series used was the "wholesale price index of materials and fuel purchased by manufacturing industry", 1975 = 100. From 1954–1979 the series is published in ETAS 81. However observations for 1950–1953 were generated by splicing the above with the following series, which is published in various issues of, MDS between December 1954 and August 1958, namely the "price index of basic materials used in broad sectors of industry, excluding fuel used in non-food manufacturing industry", 1949 = 100. No information for 1948 and 1949 is available, so the series was "backcast"[16] from 1950, with suitable attention paid to the outlying (1951) observation generated by the Korean war.

u_t; male unemployment rate

Series used is "males wholly unemployed as a percentage of the number of employees (employed and unemployed) at the appropriate mid-year, for the U.K.". The numbers unemployed exclude "temporarily stopped" but include school-leavers. The data is published in BLSHA, the 8 YB's, and finally DEG Feb. 81. Note that data does not exist for 1948, but can be imputed from the equivalent GB observation in the same table (T.166 BLSHA).

z_{5t}; variance of inflation

Series measures the variance of retail price inflation over the previous 4 quarters, i.e.

$$\text{var}(I_t) = \tfrac{1}{4}\sum_{i=0}^{3}(I_{t-i} - \tfrac{1}{4}\sum_{j=0}^{3}I_{t-j})^2$$

where $I_t = P'_t/P'_{t-1} - 1$. The annual observation is the quarterly average. Note that no 1948 observation exists.

M_t; money supply

Series taken is "money stock, M_3, outstanding at the end of each year", in £ million. The series 1948–1962 is taken directly from Attfield, Demery and Duck (1979), and from 1963 onwards from successive issues of FS.

G_t; real government expenditure

Series is calculated from "general government expenditure on goods and services", in £ million, which is divided by the GDP at factor cost deflator. The constituent components, "final consumption" (G^c_t) and "gross domestic capital formation" (G^i_t), were also calculated. All three series are thus indices at 1975 = 100. The GDP factor cost deflator was used because the equivalent series at constant prices do not exist. All 5 series required are published in ETAS 81.

K_t; capital stock

Series used is "gross capital stock at 1975 replacement cost", in £ thousand million. Data is available yearly from 1958 onward in successive issues of the BB, at various base years (which were easily "spliced" together). Before 1958 only the 1954, 1951 and 1948 observations were published. Data was interpolated using real investment data, namely "total gross domestic fixed capital formation", £ million at 1975 prices, using the usual technique involving the estimation of a decay parameter $\hat{\delta}$ from the postulated relationship,[17]

$$K_n = \sum_{i=1}^{n} (1-\delta)^{n-i} I_i + (1-\delta)^n K_0$$

where K_n, K_0 are end of period and beginning of period capital stocks, I_i is investment. The missing K's are calculated recursively by setting $n = 1$ each time, and using $\hat{\delta}$. The investment series is published in ETAS 81.

Y_{wt}, P_{wt}; world income, world output price level

The series used for Y_{wt} was the "quantum index for world manufacturing exports", $1975 = 100$; and for P_{wt} was the equivalent "world exports, unit value (price) index", $1075 = 100$. The latter series is measured in U.S. dollars, so to convert to pounds sterling we use the pound/dollar exchange rate. The first two series are published in UNB, the latter in ETAS 81.

W_t; pre-tax wage rate

Although data on basic hourly wage rates is published in the BLSHA, the YB's and DEG, the data refers to minimum entitlements determined at national level, and do not pick up rates of wage determined locally or at shop floor level. Thus this series is ignored and we therefore calculate a male hourly wage rate from the following published data:

   E; average weekly earning of full-time male manual workers (21 years and over), at the October in each year, for all industries covered.

   H: average weekly hours of . . . (as E above).

   N^h; average normal weekly hours of male manual workers, for all industries and services.

The overtime premium, π, can be given a value of $0 \cdot 3$, whence

$$E_t = W_t N_t^h + 1 \cdot 3 W_t (H_t - N_t^h)$$

and W_t is easily calculated. We also adjust W_t by a factor that captures the decline of normal hours in total hours, namely $(1 - N^h/45) \, 1 \cdot 3 + N^h/45$, which makes workers relatively better off at lower normal hours for a given hourly wage. W_t is thus the hourly earnings for a 45 hour week.

   All data for E, H, N^h are published in BLSHA, the YB's, and latest issue of DEG (May 81).

$(1 + t_1)_t$; tax on employment born by the firm

Series is calculated by taking the ratio of two indices; "total labour costs per unit of output for the whole economy", $1975 = 100$ and "wages and salaries per unit of output for the whole economy", $1975 = 100$. As the main part of "fixed" labour costs are N.I. contributions this series will reflect the real tax on labour levied on firms. However it is only an index based at $1975 = 100$. Thus the only way to obtain an approximation to

t_{1t} is to take logs

$$\log K(1 + t_{1t}) = \log K + t_{1t}$$

and let $\log K$ "go into" the constant in a regression. The former series is published in BLSHA (T.203), YB 1976 (T.55) and the latest issue of DEG, the latter ETAS 81 (p. 110). Neither series exist for 1948 and 1949, hence a "backcast" of $K(1 + t_s)$ was performed.

$(1 - t_2)_t$; tax rate on wages

Series taken reflects direct tax rate on income, namely "total personal disposable income", £ million, current prices, divided by "total income before taxx', £ million, current prices. In contrast to $(1 + t_1)_t$ and $(1 + t_3)_t$ this series is an actual tax rate, not an index. Both constituent series are published in ETAS 81. We also use a marginal tax rate based on the standard rate of income tax plus an appropriate adjustment for National Insurance contributions.

$(1 + t_3)_t$; tax rate on goods

Series taken was the ratio of the GDP deflator at market prices, 1975 = 100 to the GDP deflator at factor cost, 1975 = 100. The four measures of GDP are all expenditure based. Note that the series is an index, 1975 = 100. All four series taken from ETAS 81.

z_{1t}; replacement ratio

This series roughly measures income whilst unemployed as a proportion of income that would have been received if in employment. The variable is defined as "standard rate of unemployment benefit and/or sickness benefit plus family allowances and/or child benefit plus earnings related supplement (ERS) as a percentage of net income after deducting tax and National Insurance contributions for a married couple with two children". Note that as ERS is not received by everyone the published data has been scaled so that this component of the numerator is $\frac{1}{4}$ its published size. The source is the LBB, 1981 issue, Tables 6.1a and 6.2a.

R_t; the nominal rate of interest

Two series were collected, a "long-rate" and a "short-rate". The latter is "U.K. Treasury Bill Rate" i.e. the average rate of discount for 91-day bills after the weekly tender, and is expressed as a yield (per cent per annum of 365 days). The former is the "yield (i.e. gross redemption yield) on long-dated British Government Stock". Both series are the average over the twelve last working days of each month, and both series are published in BESA 70 (until 1969) then BESA 75 (1970 to 1974) and then in various issues of BEQB.

n_{gt}; public sector employment

Series provided by the Treasury post 1963. Prior to that date we used the series "employees in employment, males and females, in public administration and defence at each mid-year, GB" (BLSHA). This was then adjusted upwards pro-rata to make it of comparable magnitude to the Treasury series.

z_{31t}, z_{32t}; level of mismatching between vacancies and unemployment

Series taken are the one year and two year (respectively) absolute changes in the ratio of "employees in employment, males and females, in index of production industries at each mid-year, GB" to "total employees in employment, males and females at each mid-year, GB." Sources are BLKSHA, YB, DEG.

$K_t/\bar{N}_t$; potential capital/labour ratio

Series was defined as $K_t/(N_t + U_t)$ where K_t, the capital stock, has been described already. U_t is "total unemployed including school-leavers, males and females, U.K.", N_t is "employees in employment, males and females, U.K.". Both variables refer to mid-year, and both are published in ETAS 81. Note that, as before, 1948 observation for U_t does not exist and is imputed from G.B. equivalent observation.

z_{41t}, z_{42t}; age composition variables

Two series are defined as "percentage of male employees (employed and unemployed) who are aged (i) less than or equal to 24 (ii) greater than or equal to 55". The series refers to GB. However the compilation of this series involved a break. Between June 1981 and June 1973 the DEG published age distributions for male employees for the previous year. This series was then curtailed, but in the April 1981 issue age distribution for 1971 to 1980 were published, but for the labour force, not employees. Thus the later series includes employers, self-employed and H.M. Forces, whereas the former does not. A splice was performed to link the two series. In addition 1948 and 1949 observations were generated by "backcasts".

z_{6t}; incidence of "employment protection" legislation

Series used is the number of unfair dismissal cases disposed of during the relevant year by Industrial Tribunals. Further details concerning the legislation can be found in Nickell (1979a). Data is published in various issues of DEG, e.g. 1976–1978 observations are found in September 1979 issue.

z_{2t}: redundancy payments

This is simply a dummy variable which takes the value one from 1967 onwards.

U_{1t}; union density

This variable is defined as union membership as a proportion of employees in employment taken from DEG and YB.

U_{2t}; union mark-up

This series is derived from a series of industry cross-section regressions. There are two versions both described in Layard, Metcalf and Nickell (1978), the first in Table 5 and the second in footnote 24. The second is the one used here. At one point we also require an estimate of the wage in the non-union sector. Noting that the observed average wage = $U_1 W_{nu}(1 + U_2) + (1 - U_1)W_{nu}$, where W_{nu} is the non-union wage, we can thus estimate W_{nu} given time series for U_1 and U_2.

ABBREVIATIONS

BB   "Blue Book", National Income and Expenditure (yearly)
BEQB   Bank of England Quarterly Bulletin.
BESA 70   Bank of England Statistical Abstract, 1970.
BESA 75   As above, 1975 (only published twice).
BLSHA   British Labour Statistics, Historical Abstract, 1886–1968.
DEG   Department of Employment Gazette (monthly)

ETAS 81 Economic Trends Annual Supplement, 1981.
ET   Economic Trends (monthly).
FS   Financial Statistics (Monthly).
LBB 81   "Light Brown Book", "Abstract of Statistics for Index of Retail Prices, Average Earnings, Social Security Benefits and Contributions", published by DHSS, May 1981.
MDS   Monthly Digest of Statistics.
UNB   United Nations Quarterly Bulletin.
YB   British Labour Statistics, Year Book, 1969–1976 (published 8 times, between 1969 and 1976).

We should like to thank Oliver Hart, Mervyn King, Richard Layard, Marcus Miller, and a referee for comments on an earlier draft. The authors also had many illuminating conversations with George Alogoskoufis, Nicos Floros, David Grubb, Richard Jackman, Patrick Minford and others too numerous to mention. Support from the SSRC and the Department of Employment is gratefully acknowledged as well as assistance from Edgar Weissenberger.

NOTES

1. To be fair Lucas and Rapping were perfectly well aware of this point as their discussion at the end of Section III of their paper makes clear. Nevertheless they chose to ignore the problem and treat both output and the price level as exogenous in their empirical model.

2. This is simply an expositional convenience. The model could have been written in a general non-linear form and the comparative statics would have been unaltered.

3. See Sargent (1979) pp. 367–370 for a multiperiod analysis with an explicit solution.

4. There is obviously little to be gained in the present context by leaving the price expectation term in (15) and using a consistent estimation procedure to estimate the equation under some kind of rational expectations assumptions. The relevant structural equation to be estimated is (12) and we only consider the reduced form equation in order to give us some idea of the impact of exogenous shocks on unemployment. In practice it is more revealing to discover their unconditional impact rather than trying, probably unsuccessfully, to net out their effects on inflation expectations.

5. The 1978 New Earnings Survey (Department of Employment 1979), reveals (Table 205) that around 80 per cent of manual employees are covered by collective agreements and at least one third of the remainder are covered by Wages Councils and the like.

6. This is, of course, a contentious assumption since, in the present context, some firms could be constrained by the supply of labour. Taking account of this in a reasonable fashion is very difficult and we therefore stick with our contentious assumption. The straightforward "disequilibrium" alternative exemplified by Rosen and Quandt (1978) seems to us equally contentious and to yield results of little value. For example, the Rosen–Quandt results indicate that the 1930's was a period of excess demand for labour in the U.S!

7. We assume, in our discussion, that if one of the changes refers to a tax variable there is a compensating fiscal change which leaves the general fiscal stance of the government unaltered.

8. We also tried an alternative definition based simply on a past moving average of real wages updated by the trend growth rate. This turned out to be very much inferior, empirically.

9. Again we tried a further alternative, namely $x_t^* = \frac{1}{3}(x_{t-1} + g_t + x_{t-2} + 2g_t + x_{t-3} + 3g_t)$, $g_t = \frac{1}{2}(x_{t-1} - x_{t-3})$, the recent growth rate. This was empirically somewhat inferior to the other two.

10. An extensive analysis of the flows into and out of unemployment reported in Nickell (1980b) indicate that this variable has little net impact although we do find some possible effects in our analysis of vacancies in Nickell (1979a).

11. Starting out with a set of theoretically sensible explanatory variables the equations used to generate the unanticipated variables were selected on the basis of goodness of fit, parameter stability and a flat correlogram. There is, of course, no reason to suppose that the true models for these exogenous variables have remained stable since the war but, with little a priori information, it is an impossible task to elicit such true models from a short data series. The alternative, which we use here, is to try and find a model structure which is stable and hope, thereby, to have included those forces which cause the "true" structure to shift.

12. It is, of course, true that if only unanticipated government expenditure affects unemployment, systematic use of this variable for policy purposes would be impossible under rational expectations. Our equations provide no evidence on the truth or falsity of this proposition.

13. Use of a marginal as opposed to average income tax rate to compute the post-tax real wage leads to a rather smaller coefficient (compare equation (4) with equation (3), for example) but no really significant changes.

14. A glance at the estimates of the labour supply elasticities in Lucas and Rapping (1970) reveal the same sort of problem. They are absolutely enormous because the 1930s were included in the estimation period.

15. This is not a particularly robust coefficient. For example it disappears if the equation is estimated up to 1975. Its absence is not, of course, evidence against a "disequilibrium" model—quite the reverse. It would, however, rule out analysis in terms of an inflation/unemployment trade-off.

16. The estimation of an AR(p) model with time "reversed" (i.e. t becomes $T + 1 - t$ all t), and recursive predictors formed in the usual way.

17. The implied real decay rate was on average $1 \cdot 2\%$ p.a.

REFERENCES

ALOGOSKOUFIS, G. (1983), "The Labour Market in an Equilibrium Business Cycle", *Journal of Monetary Economics* (forthcoming).
ALTONJI, J. and ASHENFELTER, O. (1980), "Wage Movements and the Labour Market Equilibrium Hypothesis", *Economica*.
ATTFIELD, C. L. F., DEMERY, D. and DUCK, N. (1979), "Unanticipated Monetary Growth, Output and the Price Level: U.K. 1946–1977" (mimeo, University of Bristol).
ATTFIELD, C. L. F., DEMERY, D. and DUCK, N. (1980), "A Quarterly Model of Unanticipated Monetary Growth, Output and the Price Level in the U.K. 1963–1978", *Journal of Monetary Economics* (forthcoming).
BARRO, R. J. (1976), "Rational Expectations and the Role of Monetary Policy", *Journal of Monetary Economics*, **2**, 1–32.
BUITER, W. H. (1980), "Real Effects of Anticipated and Unanticipated Money: Some Problems of Estimation and Hypothesis Testing", National Bureau of Economic Research (Working Paper No. 601).
Department of Employment (1979), "New Earnings Survey 1978 (Part F)", HMSO.
FISCHER, S. (1981), "Relative Shocks, Relative Price Variability, and Inflation", *Brookings Papers on Economic Activity*, **2**.
GRUBB, D., JACKMAN, R. and LAYARD, R. (1982), "The Causes of European Stagflation", *Review of Economic Studies*, **49**.
HALL, R. (1980), "Labour Supply and Aggregate Fluctuations", in Brunner, K. and Meltzer, A. (eds.) *Carnegie-Rochester Public Policy Conference Series*. **12** (supplement to the *Journal of Monetary Economics*).
HAUSMAN, J. (1978), "Specification Tests in Econometrics", *Econometrica*.
LANCASTER, T. (1979), "Econometric Methods for the Duration of Unemployment", *Econometrica*.
LAYARD, R., METCALF, D. and NICKELL, S. (1978), "The Effect of Collective Bargaining on Relative and Absolute Wages", *British Journal of Industrial Relations*.
LUCAS, R. E. (1972), "Expectations and the Neutrality of Money", *Journal of Economic Theory*, **4**, 103–124.
LUCAS, R. E. and RAPPING, L. A. (1970), "Real Wages, Employment and Inflation", in Phelps, E. S. *et al. Microeconomic Foundations of Employment and Inflation Theory* (New York, W. W. Norton and Co.).
NICKELL, S. J. (1979*a*), "Unemployment and the Structure of Labour Costs", *Carnegie Rochester Public Policy Conference* **12**. (*Journal of Monetary Economics*, Supplement).
NICKELL, S. J. (1979*b*), "Estimating the Probability of Leaving Unemployment", *Econometrica*.
NICKELL, S. J. (1980*a*), "Some Points on Identification in Unanticipated Money Models". (Working Paper No. 248, Centre for Labour Economics, London School of Economics).
NICKELL, S. J. (1980*b*), "The Determinants of Equilibrium Unemployment in Britain", *Economic Journal* (forthcoming).
NICKELL, S. J. (1982), "A Bargaining Model of the Phillips Curve", (Discusion Paper No. 130, Centre for Labour Economics, London School of Economics).
PUDNEY, S. E. (1982), "The Identification of "Rational Expectations" Models under Structural Neutrality", *Journal of Economic Dynamics and Control*.
ROSEN, H. and QUANDT, R. (1978), "Estimation of a Disequilibrium Aggregate Labour Market", *Review of Economics and Statistics*, **60**.
SARGENT, T. (1979) *Macroeconomic Theory* (New York: Academic Press).
WICKENS, M. (1982), "The Efficient Estimation of Econometric Models with Rational Expectations", *Review of Economic Studies*, 55–67.

Review of Economic Studies (1982) XLIX, 761–782
0034–6527/82/00570761$00.50

Time Series Representations of Economic Variables and Alternative Models of the Labour Market

ORLEY ASHENFELTER
Princeton University

and

DAVID CARD
University of Chicago

Accepting the hypothesis that the time-series "facts" of the aggregate labour market may be summarized by the linear autoregressive and moving average representations of wages, prices, unemployment, and interest rates implies that a useful theory ought to lead to predictions about these representations. Following this approach, this paper first catalogues many of the time-series facts about the aggregate labour market and then compares them against alternative models of the labour market based on the intertemporal substitution and staggered contract hypotheses.

INTRODUCTION

The inability of the empirical models of wage inflation built in the 1960s to predict the simultaneous high inflation and high unemployment of the 1970s led to their virtual demise and to a subsequent rebirth of interest in the theoretical foundations of these models. Both the empirical failure and the spate of theoretical work leave the impression with many economists that virtually any theory is likely to be consistent with the "facts" of the aggregate labour market, and that there simply are not enough facts to discriminate among leading candidates.

At the same time, having learned the hard way from the poor performance of many models in the 1970s, econometric practice has changed so as to emphasize the importance of the dynamic structure of most time series data. In this new view parsimonious descriptions of the data are the autoregressive and moving average (ARMA) characteristics of the various time series that represent the data history of particular markets.[1] Since most of the cyclical characteristics of movements in labour market variables seem to be satisfactorily represented by relatively low order ARMA models, these representations are then taken to be the "facts".[2]

If the ARMA representations of labour market variables are an adequate description of the data, then it seems that a useful theory is one that likewise delivers a linear ARMA representation of the data. Tests of the theory then involve straightforward comparisons of the observed and predicted ARMA representations of the data.[3]

In this paper we employ this research strategy by first summarizing the time series "facts" about the aggregate labour market with which a useful theory must be consistent.

REVIEW OF ECONOMIC STUDIES

Our empirical strategy is to first set out the unrestricted reduced forms from a vector autoregression that contains nominal wages, consumer prices, nominal interest rates, and unemployment. From there we are able to test and catalogue the "exclusion restrictions" that are consistent with the quarterly U.S. time series data. We then compare the facts against the predictions of several elegant and straightforward models due to Lucas (1973), Fischer (1977), and Taylor (1980a) and others that satisfy our methodological criterion for a useful theory. These are also models of considerable practical significance, since the continuing debate over the effectiveness of monetary policy in stabilizing aggregate employment and output has been conducted around them.

Much to our surprise, the facts are not only sufficient to discriminate among these models, they are also sufficient to demonstrate serious problems with at least the simplest specifications of all of them.

1. THE TIME SERIES DATA

Table I(a) provides one elementary description of the basic U.S. quarterly time series on the logarithm of the nominal wage (W), the logarithm of the consumer price index (P), the logarithm of the unemployment rate (U), and the 90 day Treasury Bill rate (R). In this study we have used average hourly straight time earnings in manufacturing as an index of aggregate wages. Precise data definitions and sources are contained in the Appendix. For each of these time series we present in Table I(a) the fourth order univariate autoregressions (AR4) obtained by least squares fit over the period indicated. In all cases here, and in subsequent tables, we have included seasonal dummy variables and linear and quadratic trend terms.

Even the simple data analysis in Table I(a) is revealing because it suggests that these four time series have quite different properties. On the one hand, the nominal wage

TABLE I(a)

Univariate AR 4 representations

| Regressors | Dependent variable[a] (Estimated standard errors in parentheses) | | | |
	W	P	U	R
AR1	0·97	1·54	1·49	1·46
	(0·11)	(0·11)	(0·10)	(0·10)
AR2	−0.02	−0·63	−0·90	−0·90
	(0·15)	(0·21)	(0·18)	(0·18)
AR3	0·09	0·29	0·51	0·63
	(0·15)	(0·20)	(0·18)	(0·19)
AR4	−0·13	−0·26	−0·21	−0·33
	(0·10)	(0·11)	(0·10)	(0·12)
Standard error	0·0046	0·0034	0·0688	0·0054
BP[b]	2·79	7·22	7·58	5·55
(significance)	(0·514)	(0·125)	(0·109)	(0·234)
KS[c]	0·07	0·11	0·12	0·08

Notes:

[a] All regressions cover 1956(1)–1980(1), and include linear and quadratic trends and quarterly dummy variables.

[b] Box Pierce statistic. The statistic is defined as $n \sum_{i=1}^{k} \hat{p}_i^2$, where n is the number of observations, $\hat{p}_i$ is the ith estimated residual correlation, and $k = 8$ in this and subsequent Tables. The statistic has an asymptotic X^2 distribution with $k - p$ degrees of freedom, where p is the number of AR and MA coefficients estimated in the regression. The number in parentheses is the marginal significance of the test statistic.

[c] Kolmogorov Smirnov statistic for estimated residual periodogram. The 5% critical value is 0·13.

rate may apparently be represented as an extremely low order process, perhaps an AR1. The consumer price index, on the other hand, apparently does not have such a low order representation, and significant coefficients appear at three of the four lags present. Higher order autoregressive terms are also important in the representations of unemployment and interest rates.[4] The similarity of the univariate representations of prices, unemployment and interest rates, and the difference between these three and the representation of wages, are remarkable.

As an alternative to these pure AR representations, we give selected low order autoregressive moving average (ARMA) representations of each of the four time series in Table I(b).[5] The similarities and differences of the four series are even more apparent here. The ARMA (1, 2) representation of nominal wages in the first column of the Table

TABLE I(b)

Univariate ARMA representations

| | Dependent variable[a] | | | |
| | (Estimated standard errors in parentheses) | | | |
	W	P	U	R
AR1	0·89	1·79	0·92	0·92
	(0·03)	(0·07)	(0·16)	(0·18)
AR2	—	−0·83	−0·21	−0·04
		(0·07)	(0·16)	(0·18)
MA1	0·05	−0·25	0·39	0·55
	(0·11)	(0·15)	(0·14)	(0·14)
MA2	0·05	−0·10	—	—
	(0·11)	(0·14)		
Standard error	0·0046	0·0035	0·0696	0·0055
BP (significance)	4·04	9·14	10·39	7·02
	(0·544)	(0·58)	(0·065)	(0·220)
KS	0·06	0·14	0·09	0·09

Note:
[a] All regressions cover 1956(I)–1980(I) and include linear and quadratic trends and quarterly dummy variables. Estimates were obtained by numerically minimizing the conditional sum of squared errors of the regression, setting presample errors to zero.

has small and insignificant moving average coefficients at one and two lags. Likewise, the estimated MA coefficients in the ARMA (2, 2) representation of the consumer price index are both insignificant. On the other hand, the first order moving average coefficients estimated for both unemployment and interest rates are sizeable and statistically significant. Furthermore, while the addition of moving average errors to the representation of prices does not alter the estimated AR part of the time series in any appreciable way, the same is not true for either unemployment or interest rates. In fact, while we do not present them here, ARMA (1, 1) representations of unemployment and interest rates appear to be as good descriptions of the two time series as ARMA (2, 1) representations.

On the basis of Tables I(a) and I(b) we can identify a number of preliminary facts about the data in our analysis. First, nominal wages are well represented as an AR1 process. Second, the price level is a higher order AR with complex roots capable of generating business-cycle like responses to innovations. Third, unemployment and interest rates are remarkably similar time series, with each series apparently admitting a parsimonious ARMA (1, 1) representation. Finally, the stochastic parts of each of these time series have largest roots that are not too far from, but always less than, unity.[6] Although it is slightly misleading to say so, rough lower order approximations to these series could accordingly be obtained by first differencing. In the case of nominal wages,

REVIEW OF ECONOMIC STUDIES

first differencing would lead to a (roughly) random series. With prices, first differencing would lead to a first order autoregression with a coefficient of (roughly) 0·7. And, in the case of unemployment and interest rates, first differencing would lead to a first order moving average process with a coefficient or (roughly) 0·50.

In Table II we report the four variable vector autoregression fitted by least squares over the sample period indicated, again including four lags in each variable. Starting

TABLE II

Wages, prices, unemployment and interest rates: vector AR representation

| Regressors | Dependent variable[a] (standard errors in parentheses) | | | |
	W_t	P_t	U_t	R_t
W_{t-1}	0·85 (0·11)	0·09 (0·07)	3·21 (1·55)	−0·21 (0·13)
W_{t-2}	−0·05 (0·15)	−0·11 (0·09)	−0·84 (2·04)	0·08 (0·16)
W_{t-3}	0·13 (0·15)	0·19 (0·09)	−0·46 (2·03)	0·17 (0·16)
W_{t-4}	−0·14 (0·11)	−0·02 (0·07)	0·25 (1·48)	0·12 (0·12)
P_{t-1}	0·60 (0·18)	1·23 (0·11)	2·84 (2·47)	0·04 (0·20)
P_{t-2}	−0·43 (0·29)	−0·52 (0·18)	−4·64 (3·94)	0·28 (0·32)
P_{t-3}	0·12 (0·29)	0·36 (0·18)	1·49 (3·95)	−0·27 (0·32)
P_{t-4}	−0·15 (0·19)	−0·28 (0·11)	−1·05 (2·56)	−0·19 (0·21)
U_{t-1}	−0·003 (0·01)	−0·007 (0·01)	1·16 (0·12)	−0·033 (0·01)
U_{t-2}	0·007 (0·01)	0·011 (0·01)	−0·64 (0·17)	0·029 (0·01)
U_{t-3}	−0·011 (0·01)	−0·003 (0·01)	0·33 (0·17)	−0·018 (0·01)
U_{t-4}	0·008 (0·01)	0·001 (0·01)	0·08 (0·11)	0·010 (0·01)
R_{t-1}	−0·04 (0·11)	0·18 (0·07)	−3·10 (1·50)	1·13 (0·12)
R_{t-2}	−0·2 (0·16)	0·04 (0·10)	1·53 (2·17)	−0·74 (0·18)
R_{t-3}	−0·17 (0·16)	−0·01 (0·10)	0·02 (2·22)	0·41 (0·18)
R_{t-4}	0·00 (0·13)	0·07 (0·08)	4·63 (1·75)	−0·07 (0·14)
Standard error	0·0045	0·0028	0·0612	0·0050
BP (significance)	1·80	4·92	9·58	8·25
	(0·772)	(0·296)	(0·048)	(0·083)
KS	0·06	0·07	0·08	0·09

Note:
[a] See Notes to Table I(a).

with the first column of the Table, there is no indication of effects of lagged unemployment or interest rates on nominal wages, but there is some indication that lagged prices affect nominal wages. A more formal test of each of these hypotheses is contained in Table IV. Here we record the F-ratios to test whether nominal wages are Granger-caused by prices, unemployment, and interest rates, under various maintained hypotheses.[7] In all cases, we find that the test that prices Granger-cause wages is short of statistical significance at the 5% level, but not by a great deal. There is no evidence from this table, however, that either unemployment or interest rates Granger-cause wages.

The second column of Table II indicates statistically significant coefficients of interest rates and wages at one quarter and three quarter lags, respectively, in the regression for prices. The causality tests reported in Table IV provide strong evidence that nominal interest rates cause prices; this fact is robust to the inclusion of lagged wages and/or unemployment in the price equation. A similar conclusion emerges when we test for the significance of lagged wages in determining prices. However, the evidence that unemployment causes prices is weak. When interest rates and wages are excluded, the statistic for the test of causality from unemployment to prices is significant at conventional levels. However, maintaining the presence of lagged interest rates and wage rates, lagged unemployment terms add little to the precision of the forecast for prices.

The third column of Table II provides estimates of the coefficients of lagged prices, wages, and interest rates in the regression for unemployment. Again, the impact of lagged interest rate terms is immediately apparent. There are also relatively large, though imprecisely estimated, effects of lagged wages and prices on current unemployment rates. The test results in Table IV confirm Granger causality from interest rates to unemployment, both with and without lagged wages and prices included in the unemployment regression. The causality tests for wages and prices are more ambiguous. When interest rates are excluded, wages and prices together and separately appear to cause unemployment. However, with interest rates included, the opposite conclusion holds. Finally, it is interesting to observe that there is no strong tendency for lagged wages and prices to enter the unemployment regression with equal and opposite sign.[8] There is however some indication that the sum of the coefficients of lagged wages and prices is zero, confirming the long run homogeneity of unemployment with respect to nominal wages and prices.

The fourth column of Table II gives the estimated regression equation for interest rates. Inspection of the coefficient estimates suggests that lagged unemployment terms have a significant role in the time series representation of interest rates. Indeed, the tests in Table IV indicate that the null hypothesis of no causality from unemployment to interest rates is easily rejected, both in the presence and in the absence of lagged wage and price regressors. By the same token, the test statistic for joint causality from wages, prices, and unemployment to interest rates is highly significant. While taken individually, neither wages nor prices cause interest rates, in combination with unemployment these two series add precision to the forecast of interest rates.[9]

In many applications it is appropriate to consider employment rather than unemployment in the analysis of the aggregate labour market. Although employment and unemployment are not precise mirror images, it is well known that they move in nearly equal, but opposite directions over time. While we do not report the results, our finding is that the substitution of employment for unemployment does not substantially alter any of the properties of the vector autoregression recorded in Table II, or most of the conclusions from the causality tests in Table IV.[10] Similarly, the Treasury Bill rate can be replaced by a longer term interest rate without any important qualitative differences.

In Table III we provide estimates of the correlations among the innovations (residuals) from the regressions reported in Table II. Given information on lagged values of nominal wages, prices, unemployment, and interest rates, these are the contemporaneous correlations among the unpredicted "surprises" in each time series. Surprisingly, none of the correlations between innovations in wages, prices, or unemployment is very large or statistically significant. On the other hand, innovations in all three series are correlated with innovations in interest rates. The strongest correlation exists between innovations in unemployment and interest rates: the unpredicted parts of these two series

TABLE III

Correlation matrix of innovations in vector AR

| | | Innovations in[a] | | | |
		W	P	U	R
Innovations:	W	1·00			
in	P	−0·05	1·00		
	U	0·03	0·05	1·00	
	R	−0·17	0·11	−0·32	1·00

Note:
[a] Residuals obtained from estimated equations reported in Table II. The approximate standard error of each correlation is 0·10.

REVIEW OF ECONOMIC STUDIES

TABLE IV

Causality tests for wages, prices, unemployment and interest rates[a]

Line no.	Test for causality of	By[b]	Maintained lagged regressors[c]	Test statistic	Marginal significance[d]
1	W	P	—	2·09	0·090
2		U	—	0·10	0·992
3		R	—	0·26	0·928
4		P, U, R	—	1·41	0·180
5	P	W	—	4·62	0·002
6		U	—	3·19	0·017
7		R	—	7·65	0·000
8		P, U, R	—	4·41	0·000
9		W	U, R	3·54	0·011
10		U	W, R	0·90	0·469
11		R	W, U	4·35	0·003
12		W	R	3·71	0·008
13		R	W	6·52	0·000
14	U	W	—	3·08	0·021
15		P	—	3·89	0·006
16		R	—	5·70	0·001
17		W, P	—	2·71	0·011
18		W, P, R	—	2·90	0·002
19		W	P, R	1·69	0·161
20		P	W, R	1·12	0·354
21		R	W, P	4·14	0·004
22		W, P	R	1·40	0·211
23	R	W	—	1·25	0·296
24		P	—	0·58	0·688
25		U	—	2·67	0·038
26		W, P	—	1·47	0·182
27		W, P, U	—	2·24	0·018
28		W	U	1·39	0·245
29		P	U	0·93	0·451
30		W	P, U	2·80	0·032
31		P	W, U	2·33	0·063
32		U	P, W	3·42	0·013

Note:

[a] All regressions cover 1956(1)–1980(1) and include linear and quadratic trends and quarterly dummy variables.
[b] The causality test statistic is an F-ratio for the null hypothesis that the coefficients of four lagged values of each of the variables in this column are jointly equal to zero. Four lagged values of the dependent variable are included in both the restricted and unrestricted regressions.
[c] In commputing the F-ratio, four lagged values of each of the variables in this column appear in both the restricted and unrestricted regressions.
[d] Probability of obtaining an F-ratio at least as large as the test statistic under the null hypothesis. A marginal significance level smaller than 0·05 indicates rejection of the null hypothesis at the 5% significance level.

move in opposite directions, just as the level of both series move in opposite directions over the business cycle. As our previous analysis has shown, interest rates and unemployment are closely linked, and this linkage apparently extends to the surprises in each series.

To this point, we have presented our results in terms of nominal wàges and prices. Somewhat different insights are gained by considering real rather than nominal wages. Tables V(a) and V(b) give a brief summary of the data analysis, recast in terms of real wages, prices, unemployment, and interest rates. Table V(a) presents the estimated univariate AR4, AR2 and ARMA (1, 2) representations of real wages. Not surprisingly,

TABLE V(a)

Univariate representations of the real wage

Regressors	Dependent variable: $W - P^a$ (Standard errors in parentheses)		
	(1)	(2)	(3)
AR1	0·99	1·10	0·85
	(0·11)	(0·11)	(0·09)
AR2	0·02	−0·22	—
	(0·15)	(0·12)	
AR3	0·04	—	—
	(0·15)		
AR4	−0·32	—	—
	(0·11)		
MA1	—	—	0·18
			(0·13)
MA2	—	—	0·15
			(0·11)
Standard error	0·0059	0·0063	0·0060
BP (significance)	8·68	12·50	12·41
	(0·070)	(0·052)	(0·047)
KS	0·12	0·15	0·10

Note:
[a] See Notes to Table I(a).

TABLE V(b)

Selected causality tests for real wages[a]

Line no.	Test for causality of real wages by:	Maintained lagged regressors:	Test statistic	Marginal significance
1	P	—	1·26	0·213
2	U	—	0·92	0·456
3	R	—	4·15	0·004
4	P, U	—	1·66	0·122
5	P	R	1·78	0·141
6	U	R	0·95	0·440
7	R	P	5·12	0·001
8	R	P, U	3·13	0·020

Note:
[a] See notes to Table IV.

the representation of real wages is somewhere between the very low order AR for nominal wages and the higher order AR for prices. Neither of the estimated MA coefficients in the ARMA representation of real wages are significant at conventional levels, however, and the first difference of real wages is not far from a white noise process.[11] Table V(b) presents some selected causality tests for real wages. Neither prices nor unemployment cause real wages, alone or in the presence of lagged interest rates. However, the evidence for causality from interest rates to real wages is stronger. As with prices and unemployment, the forecast of real wages can be significantly improved by taking account of past movements in nominal interest rates.

To conclude our empirical analysis, we investigate the appropriate representation of *ex-post* real interest rates in Table VI. The *ex-post* interest rate is defined as the difference between the nominal interest rate and the realized percentage increase in

TABLE VI

Selected prediction tests for ex-post real interest rates[a]

Line no.	Test for prediction of real interest rates by:	Maintained lagged regressors	Test statistic	Marginal significance
1	P	—	6·38	0·000
2	W	—	3·63	0·009
3	U	—	2·42	0·054
4	R	—	1·58	0·187
5	P, W, U, R	—	3·32	0·000
6	P	W, R, U	5·50	0·000
7	W	P, R, U	2·74	0·035
8	U	P, W, R	1·54	0·200
9	R	P, W, U	0·85	0·498
10	U	W, P	1·96	0·109
11	R	W, P	1·22	0·309
12	U, R	W, P	1·40	0·211

Note:

[a] See Notes to Table IV. In computing the tests in this Table, lagged values of the dependnet variable are not included in the regressions.

prices over the relevant holding period. By construction, *ex-post* interest rates differ from their anticipated or *ex-ante* counterparts by the amount of unexpected price increases over the holding period. Under the assumption of rational expectations, the deviation of *ex-post* and *ex-ante* real interest rates is therefore serially uncorrelated and orthogonal to information available at the start of the holding period.[12] It follows that tests of the lagged effects of W, P, U and R on the *ex-post* interest rate are interpretable as tests of the effects of these variables on its *ex-ante* counterpart, under the assumption of rational expectations.[13]

The theoretically useful hypothesis that *ex-ante* real interest rates are constant was supported in early empirical work by Fama (1975). Under the assumption of rational expectations, this implies that *ex-post* real interest rates are composed of a constant term and a serially uncorrelated error. However, as has been reported by Mishkin (1981), we find that this hypothesis may be easily rejected in a sample that includes the post-1972 period. In a regression for *ex-post* real interest rates that uses the 90 day Treasury Bill rate over the sample period 1956–1980, the marginal significance level of a pair of linear and quadratic trend terms is less than 0·1%. Furthermore, the hypothesis that the non-deterministic component of real interest rates is serially uncorrelated is easily rejected.[14]

Prediction tests for *ex-post* real interest rates are reported in Table VI. Taken one variable at a time, lagged wages and prices have a statistically significant impact on the forecast error variance of *ex-post* interest rates. Lagged unemployment terms are not quite significant at the 5% level, while lagged nominal interest rates add very little to the regression for *ex-post* real rates. Similar conclusions emerge when lagged values of all other variables are maintained while computing the tests. However, maintaining the other variables, the marginal significance level of the test for the lagged effects of unemployment is greatly increased. The last three rows of the table report prediction tests for unemployment and nominal interest rates, individually and jointly, maintaining wages and prices in the representation of *ex-post* real rates. Under the assumption of rational expectations, these results indicate that the *ex-ante* real interest rate is a function of lagged nominal wages and lagged prices, but not of lagged unemployment or lagged nominal interest rates.[15]

It it worth indicating that the conclusions from our data analysis of wages, prices, interest rates and unemployment are largely unaffected by considering only the quarterly U.S. time series data to the end of 1972. For the shorter sample, the estimated univariate representations are very similar to those reported in Table I(a) and I(b). Furthermore, most of the conclusions of the causality tests in Tables IV and V(b) are invariant to the choice of the shorter or longer sample period. The only qualitative change from Table IV is that there is much weaker evidence of causality from interest rates to prices and unemployment in the pre-1973 sample. The test results in Table V(b) are also representative of those for the shorter period, although again the evidence for causality from interest rates to real wages is weaker in the pre-1973 data.

On the other hand, the causality tests for *ex-post* real interest rates yield somewhat different results in the two sample periods. In particular, the evidence against the hypothesis that *ex-ante* (and *ex-post*) real interest rates are composed of deterministic components and a serially uncorrelated error is weaker in the earlier data. None of the prediction tests reported in Table VI are significant at the 5% level when the analysis is restricted to pre-1973 data. However, the strongest evidence continues to be that *ex-post* real interest rates are predicted by lagged wages and prices only. With the possible exception of the behaviour of real interest rates, we find that the conclusions from our analysis of 1956–1980 data are fair representations of the data in the early part of the sample.

At this stage it is a straightforward matter to summarize the time series facts at our disposal. First, nominal wages are well represented by an AR1 and there is no evidence that they are Granger caused by unemployment or interest rates, while there is only weak evidence that they are caused by consumer prices. Second, consumer prices are better represented by a higher order AR process *and* there is strong evidence that this series is Granger caused by wages and interest rates. Third, unemployment and interest rates are also better represented as higher order AR processes, or alternatively, as low order mixed autoregressive moving average processes. Fourth, unemployment and interest rates Granger cause each other. Controlling for interest rates, lagged wages and prices do not seem to add to the precision of the forecast of unemployment, although they do have a significant impact on the forecast of interest rates. Fifth, innovations in wages, prices, and unemployment are essentially uncorrelated, while innovations in all three series are correlated with innovations in interest rates. Sixth, the real wage is reasonably described by a low order autoregressive process, or even as a random walk. There is no evidence of causality from prices or unemployment to real wages, but fairly strong evidence of causality from interest rates to real wages. Seventh, *ex-post* real interest rates are predicted by wages and prices but not by nominal interest rates or unemployment. Finally, all of the series we have investigated are characterized by a high degree of serial persistence. In fact, several series, most notably prices and real wages, exhibit largest roots quite close to unity. Innovations introduced into any of these series tend to persist for relatively long periods of time.[16]

2. ALTERNATIVE MODELS OF THE LABOUR MARKET

We next turn to the time series implications of several alternative models of the aggregate labour market. Prior to doing this it is worth observing that there are a number of anomalies in the time series representations set out in Tables I–VI that are going to pose problems for the explanatory power of most simple models of the labour market. First of all, as indicated earlier, nominal wages and prices do not enter the unemployment regression with equal and opposite coefficients at each lag. This characteristic is shared by the (unreported) employment equation in a vector autoregression of wages, prices, employment, and interest rates.[17] One natural interpretation of such an equation is as a reduced form of a dynamic labour demand schedule where nominal wages and prices are allowed separate coefficients.[18] Under this interpretation, however, and abstracting from interest rate effects, the real wage should be driving employment and nominal wages and prices should enter the equation with equal but opposite coefficients. On the other hand, once current and expected future real interest rates are admitted into the labour demand equation, the coefficients of wages and prices are freed. Apparently, any simplified model that ignores the role of interest rates or otherwise fails to distinguish nominal wages and prices in the determination of employment and unemployment will be easily rejected by the data.

Secondly, aggregative models of the labour market typically highlight the role of monetary forces in the explanation of unemployment, wages, and prices. As a consequence, perhaps for simplicity, many such models assume either that the real wage is deterministic, or that it is a serially uncorrelated random variable. It is clear that from our analysis in Table V, and from previous work by Neftci (1978), Sargent (1978), and Altonji and Ashenfelter (1980) that this characterization of the real wage process is simply inadequate. Since these "monetary" models of the business cycle are not intended to address the determination of real as opposed to nominal wage rates, they certainly cannot be faulted for this shortcoming. Nevertheless, this empirical feature of the time series process for real wages may be a clue that suggests that a more appropriate interaction of real and monetary forces will ultimately have to be addressed in a satisfactory model of the labour market and the business cycle.

A. The intertemporal substitution theory of unemployment

In this section we catalogue the implications of Lucas and Rapping's (1970) intertemporal substitution theory of unemployment for the time series representations of wages, prices, unemployment and interest rates. The basic hypothesis of this theory is that differences in the prices of consumption and leisure between the present and future periods induce workers to alter their supply of labour in the current period. The deviation of labour supply from its trend level is interpreted as a measure of individual unemployment. Cyclical movements in labour supply and unemployment are therefore attributed to (potentially misperceived) changes in real interest rates and real wage rates. In the spirit of the approach outlined in the introduction, we ask how this linkage between unemployment and wages, prices and interest rates can be tested against the data as summarized by the unrestricted vector autoregressions presented in the previous section.

The current labour supply decision of a worker can be written as a function of the discounted prices of consumption and leisure in each of the periods in his planning horizon.[19] Adopting a log-linear approximation to this function, we assume that

$$u_{it} = \sum_{j=0} b_j E_{it}(w_{it+j} - p_{t+j}) + \sum_{j=0} a_j E_{it}(R_{t+j} - p_{t+j+1} + p_{t+j}) + v_{it}, \tag{1}$$

where u_{it} is the log of current (measured) individual unemployment, w_{it+j} is the log of the nominal wage rate earned by individual i in period $t+j$, p_{t+j} is the log of the price level in period $t+j$, R_{t+j} is the nominal interest rate in period $t+j$, b_j and a_j are constants, E_{it} is the expectations operator conditional on information available to i at period t, and v_{it} is an error term in individual unemployment.[20] Observe that $(R_{t+j} - p_{t+j+1} + p_{t+j})$ is just the real interest rate between periods $t+j$ and $t+j+1$. According to the intuitive argument given by Lucas and Rapping, the effect of current real wages on unemployment is negative $(b_0 < 0)$, while the effect of expected future real wage rates on current unemployment is positive. The sign pattern of the a_j is unrestricted, although if current leisure is a substitute for leisure and consumption in every future period, then the a_j are positive and non-increasing in absolute value. It is useful as well as traditional, and perhaps empirically harmless in the analysis of business cycle movements in unemployment, to simplify equation (1) by assuming that the elasticity of labour supply with respect to permanent increases in real wage rates is 0. In that case, $\sum_j b_j = 0$, and the first summation in (1) can be replaced by

$$b_0((w_{it}-p_t)-(w^*_{it}-p^*_t)),\qquad(2)$$

where

$$w^*_{it}-p^*_t = -(1/b_0)\sum_{j=1} b_j E_{it}(w_{it+j}-p_{t+j})$$

has the interpretation of a long run average expected future real wage rate. In previous studies by Sargent (1973) and Altonji and Ashenfelter (1980), and in Lucas and Rapping's original empirical work, the effects of current and exected future real interest rates on current unemployment were neglected, and tests of the intertemporal substitution hypothesis involved regressions of current unemployment on expressions like (2).

To explore the empirical implications of the hypothesis described by (1) we need to specify the formation of individual expectations and the nature of the error term in the unemployment function. Throughout, we assume that aggregate nominal wages, prices, and interest rates follow a vector autoregression. Furthermore, we assume that the individual wage rate w_{it} differs from the aggregate by a fixed effect w_i and a serially uncorrelated error z_{it}:

$$w_{it} = w_i + w_t + z_{it}.\qquad(3)$$

Finally, we assume that the individuals' expectations are formed rationally, and that individuals' information sets include w_{it}, w_i, p_t, and R_t, and past values of the relevant aggregate variables.

A simplified basis case

As a basis case, consider a model in which the expected real interest rate is deterministic and the aggregate real wage can be adequately forecast from its own lagged values and lagged values of the nominal interest rate.[21] For the period from the early 1950s to the early 1970s, empirical work by Fama (1975) and Mishkin (1981) suggests that anticipated real interest rates did not depart significantly from a constant.[22] Likewise, at least in systems including only real wages and employment or unemployment, the evidence of previous studies is that real wages are reasonably forecast from their own lagged values (Sargent (1978), Altonji and Ashenfelter (1980)). Our own results in Table V suggest that in fact forecasts of the aggregate real wage can be significantly improved by taking into account the effects of lagged nominal interest rates. However, maintaining interest rates, unemployment and prices add very little to the precision of the forecasts. Consequently, this basis case may be a reasonable framework for initial empirical testing, at least over this particular period.

In this simplified framework, the intertemporal substitution hypothesis can be represented by the set of equations consisting of

$$u_{it} = b_0((w_{it}-p_t)-(w^*_{it}-p^*_t))+v_{it},\qquad(1a)$$

equation (3), and the autoregressive processes generating real wages, interest rates, and prices. By assumption, the deviation of current individual real wages from aggregate real wages is transitory (normalized for fixed effects). An individual's forecast of his own normalized real wage rate in any future period coincides with his forecast of the aggregate real wage rate in that period. If the reduced form for aggregate real wages includes k lags of real wages and interest rates, then

$$(w^*_{it}-p^*_t)=\sum_{j=0}^{k-1} c_j E_{it}(rw_{t-j})+\sum_{j=0}^{k-1} d_j R_{t-j}$$

where $rw_t = w_t - p_t$, and $\{c_j\}$ and $\{d_j\}$ are sets of coefficients. Individuals have three pieces of information with which to update their expectation of the current aggregate real wage: their own wage rate w_{ij}, the aggregate price level p_t, and the current nominal interest rate R_t. Assuming that this information is used to form linear forecasts,

$$E_{it}(rw_t) = E_{t-1}(rw_t) + \phi_1(w_{it} - E_{t-1}(w_t)) + \phi_2(p_t - E_{t-1}(p_t)) + \phi_3(R_t - E_{t-1}(R_t))$$

for a set of coefficients ϕ_1, ϕ_2, and ϕ_3, where E_{t-1} is the expectations operator conditional on information dates $t-1$ and earlier.[23] If the variance of the individual shock to wages is zero, then individuals have complete information on current aggregate real wages and $\phi_1 = -\phi_2 = 1$, while $\phi_3 = 0$. Otherwise, $0 < \phi_1 < 1$. Upon substitution, individual unemployment in the current period is given by:

$$\begin{aligned}
u_{it} = {} & b_0(1 - c_0\phi_1)(z_{it} + z_t) - b_0(1 + c_0\phi_2)e_t - b_0(c_0\phi_3 + d_0)x_t \\
& + b_0(1 - c_0)E_{t-1}rw_t - b_0c_1rw_{t-1} - \cdots - b_0c_{k-1}rw_{t-k+1} \\
& - b_0d_0E_{t-1}R_t - b_0d_1R_{t-1} - \cdots - b_0d_{k-1}R_{t-k+1} + v_{it},
\end{aligned} \tag{4}$$

or, after aggregation,

$$\begin{aligned}
u_t = {} & b_0(1 - c_0\phi_1)z_t - b_0(1 + c_0\phi_2)e_t - b_0(c_0\phi_3 + d_0)x_t \\
& + b_0(1 - c_0)E_{t-1}rw_t - b_0c_1rw_{t-1} - \cdots - b_0c_{k-1}rw_{t-k+1} \\
& - b_0d_0E_{t-1}R_t - b_0d_1R_{t-1} - \cdots - b_0d_{k-1}R_{t-k+1} + v_t,
\end{aligned} \tag{4a}$$

where z_t is the aggregate innovation in wages, e_t is the innovation in prices, x_t is the innovation in nominal interest rates, and v_t is the average of the v_{it}. Individual unemployment is a distributed lag on aggregate real wages and interest rates, plus the sum of the error term v_{it} and linear combinations of the current innovations in individual wages, interest rates, and prices. Aggregate unemployment is a function of k lags of real wages and nominal interest rates, plus an error term composed of combinations of the aggregate innovations in wages, interest rates, and prices.

The implications of the basis case version of the intertemporal substitution hypothesis for the behaviour of real wages, prices and unemployment are summarized in Table T-1. Depending on the error term v_{it} and the real wage forecasting equation, the implications are more or less easily tested against the unrestricted vector autoregressions and causality tests in the previous section. For example, if v_{it} is serially uncorrelated, then we can conclude from (4) that prices do not cause unemployment, maintaining k lags of real

TABLE T-1

Implications of the intertemporal substitution hypothesis: Basis case

Assumptions			Implications	
(1) errors in individual unemployment serially uncorrelated	(a)	real wage forecast by univatiate AR	(i)	prices and interest rates fail to cause unemployment, maintaining real wages.
			(ii)	lagged unemployment does not improve the forecast of unemployment, maintaining lagged real wages.
	(b)	real wages caused by interest rates	(i)	prices fail to cause unemployment, maintaining real wages and interest rates.
			(ii)	lagged unemployment does not improve the forecast of unemployment, maintaining lagged real wages and interest rates.
(2) errors in individual unemployment AR(h)	(a)	real wage caused by interest rates	(i)	unemployment is a distributed lag on real wages, interest rates, prices, and h !ags of unemployment.

wages and interest rates in the unemployment regression, since e_t, z_t, z_t and z_{it} are all uncorrelated with lagged prices.[24] In fact, this implication is consistent with the aggregate time series evidence.[25] More generally, if v_{it} is serially uncorrelated, then the *only* variables in the reduced form for unemployment are those that enter the forecasting equation for real wages. Thus the causality from interest rates to unemployment noted in Table IV is consistent with the theory and the fact that interest rates help to predict real wages. On the other hand, lagged unemployment terms are included in the unemployment equation only the the extent that unemployment Granger causes real wages. Since causality from unemployment to real wages is easily rejected in Table IV, the implication of serially uncorrelated labour supply errors is that lagged unemployment terms should not improve the forecast error of the unemployment regression, maintaining lagged real wages and nominal interest rates. As indicated in Table II, however, three out of four lagged unemployment terms are highly significant in the unrestricted reduced form for unemployment.

On the other hand, if the v_{it} are serially correlated, the implications of the theory are less transparent. If, for example, v_{it} follows an hth order autoregression of the form:

$$H(L)v_{it} = q_{it},$$

for q_{it} serially uncorrelated, and if the parameters of the lag operator $H(L)$ are common to all individuals, then (4) and (4a) can be pre-multiplied by $H(L)$ to give current unemployment as a function of lagged unemployment, lagged real wages, lagged interest rates, lagged prices, and a serially uncorrelated error. While the theory continues to generate cross equation restrictions between the unemployment equation and the reduced form equations for real wages and interest rates, as Table T-1 indicates there are no simple exclusion restrictions on the system that we can verify against the data as summarized in Section 1.

While it is clear that the most restricted versions of the basis case are rejected by the data, the simple addition of serial correlation in the labour supply errors makes it more difficult to test the theory. We conclude that further research effort will be required to assess the empirical support for even this basis case version of the intertemporal substitution hypothesis so long as serial correlation in the labour supply errors is taken to be a reasonable hypothesis for the explanation of persistence in the aggregate unemployment rate.[26] Since the goal of most business cycle theories is to explain this persistence without resort to ad hoc assumptions about microeconomic behaviour, however, we would not count this as a particularly successful feature of the simplified intertemporal substitution model.

The general case

Evidence on both realized and anticipated real interest rates suggest that their levels have not been constant throughout the decade after 1970.[27] The impact of expected real interest rates on current unemployment is therefore a potentially significant factor in tests of the intertemporal substitution hypothesis. Next, we derive from equation (1) the representation of current unemployment assuming that real wages are forecast as part of a vector autoregressive system, and without the assumption that expected real interest rates are constant. Not surprisingly, there are relatively few conclusions that can be drawn from the simple data analysis of the first section for this more general specification of the intertemporal substitution hypothesis.

Suppose that aggregate nominal wages, prices and nominal interest rates are generated by a vector autoregressive system that includes at most k lags of each variable and k lags of the unemployment rate in each equation. Individual unemployment is generated by (1), taking as given the processes for w_t, p_t, and R_t. For simplicity, we assume that the individual specific errors v_{it} are serially uncorrelated. This allows us to postulate a solution for wages, prices, interest rates, and unemployment of the form:

$$y_t = A y_{t-1} + e_t$$

where

$$y_t' = (w_t, w_{t-1}, \ldots, w_{t-k+1}, p_t, \ldots, p_{t-k+1}, R_t, \ldots, R_{t-k+1}, u_t, \ldots, u_{t-k+1}),$$

and

$$e_t' = (e_{1t}, 0, 0, \ldots, e_{2t}, 0, 0, \ldots, e_{3t}, 0, 0, \ldots, e_{4t}, 0, 0, \ldots, 0),$$

is a vector of serially uncorrelated innovations, and A is a $4k \times 4k$ matrix of coefficients. The $4k$ coefficients in the row of A corresponding to u_t are treated as undetermined. Since $E_{it}(w_{it+j}) = E_{it}(w_{t+j})$ for $j > 0$, (1) can be expressed as:

$$u_{it} = b_0(w_{it} - p_t) + \theta' E_{it}(y_t) + v_{it} \tag{5}$$

for a vector of coefficients $\theta = (\theta_1, \ldots, \theta_{4k})$ whose elements are functions of $\{b_j\}$, $\{a_j\}$, and the elements of A. Taking expectations conditional on information available at time $t - 1$, and noting that $E_{t-1}(u_{it}) = E_{t-1}(u_t)$, we obtain:

$$E_{t-1}(u_t) = b_0(E_{t-1}(w_t - p_t)) + \theta' E_{t-1}(y_t). \tag{6}$$

Since $E_{t-1}(u_t)$, $E_{t-1}(w_t)$, $E_{t-1}(p_t)$, and $E_{t-1}(y_t)$ are all functions of $A y_{t-1}$, for (6) to hold identically in y_{t-1} A must satisfy a set of $4k$ restrictions. Given the coefficients of the autoregressive system generating w_t, p_t, and R_t, the coefficients of the unemployment equation are determined by (6).

While the force of the cross equation restrictions imposed by the general model of intertemporal substitution is not transparent, several conclusions are possible with respect to the vector autoregressive system of wages, prices, interest rates and unemployment. First, and fundamentally, Granger causality of unemployment by any variable not directly useful in predicting either real wages or real interest rates is ruled out.[23] Alternatively, assuming that the v_{it} are serially uncorrelated, lagged unemployment terms should enter the regression for unemployment only to the extent that they help to predict real wages or real interest rates. As we have seen in Tables V(b) and VI, there is no evidence that unemployment helps predict either variable. We therefore conclude that the intertemporal substitution hypothesis *by itself* is not capable of describing the aggregate time series data on wages, prices, interest rates and unemployment. On the other hand, by augmenting the model with serial correlation in individual labour supply it may be possible to set out a version of the intertemporal substitution model that is consistent with the data we have presented in the first section of this paper. A definitive assessment of this possibility requires an alternative research strategy that concentrates on the cross equation (rather than the exclusion) restrictions of the model.

B. Long term wage contracts and unemployment

For the purposes of discussing the role of monetary policy in the determination of aggregate employment and unemployment, models with sticky wages or prices appear to be the leading alternative contenders to the intertemporal substitution framework.[29] Models that incorporate what are interpreted to be long term contracts have a plausibility based on the observation of the apparent existence of such contracts, and they have been advanced by Fischer (1977) and Taylor (1980a) among others. The set-up due to Taylor is a remarkably clear example of the kind of testable model that delivers the concise ARMA representations that may be so easily contrasted with the "facts" in Tables I–VI. Although far from identical, Taylor's set-up has many of the same implications for the data as does Fischer's, and so we restrict attention here to the examination of the former.

Taylor assumes that all workers are employed in N-period fixed nominal wage contracts and concentrates on how these wages may be set in the face of a known money supply feedback rule and rational expectations. For the fraction of workers in the labour force whose wages are set in period t, the (logarithm of the) wage is x_t for the next N periods. Assuming a uniform distribution of contract expirations, the average nominal observed wage w_t is a simple moving average of current and past x_t's:

$$w_t = D(L)x_t, \tag{7}$$

where the $N-1$ order lag polynomial has all coefficients equal to $1/N$. Taylor assumes that the nominal wage established in t depends on nominal wages established in the previous $(N-1)$ periods, on expectations of nominal wages to be established in the next $(N-1)$ periods, and on the expected state of aggregate demand over the life of the contract. Let $B(L)$ be a lag polynomial or order $(N-1)$ with $B(1)=\frac{1}{2}$, let e_t represent a measure of aggregate demand in period t, and let $\hat{e}_t = E_{t-1}(e_t)$, and $\hat{x}_t = E_{t-1}(x_t)$. Taylor assumes that x_t is established according to

$$x_t = B(L)x_t + B(L^{-1})\hat{x}_t + hD(L^{-1})\hat{e}_t + z_t, \tag{8}$$

where $h>0$ gives the response of the negotiated wage in t to average expected aggregate demand over the life of the contract, and z_t is a serially uncorrelated error.[30] Note that the weights applied to negotiated wages k periods in the past and expected negotiated wages k periods in the future are equal. The requirement that the coefficients of $B(L)$ sum to $\frac{1}{2}$ implies that the symmetric polynomial $B(L)+B(L^{-1})$ has coefficients that sum to unity.

The model is closed by adding a quantity theoretic aggregate demand equation relating e_t to w_t. A simple formulation is

$$e_t = \gamma w_t + v_t, \tag{9}$$

where v_t is a white noise error and $\gamma < 0$ reflects the fact that in the absence of full accommodation by the monetary authority, higher average nominal wages reduce the level of aggregate demand. Substituting (9) into (8), taking expectations at $t-1$, and noting that $x_{t-k} = \hat{x}_{t-k}$ for $k>0$, we obtain a difference equation in $\hat{x}_t$:

$$\hat{x}_t = B(L)\hat{x}_t + B(L^{-1})\hat{x}_t + \gamma hD(L)D(L^{-1})\hat{x}_t. \tag{10}$$

Now $D(L)D(L^{-1})$ is a symmetric polynomial and can be written as

$$D(L)D(L^{-1}) = 1/N + C(L) + C(L^{-1}), \tag{11}$$

where $C(L)$ is a one sided polynomial or order $N-1$ with a zero constant term. Substituting (11) into (10) and re-arranging, we have:

$$0 = \{B(L) + \gamma hC(L)\}\hat{x}_t + \{B(L^{-1}) + \gamma hC(L^{-1})\}\hat{x}_t + \{\gamma h/N - 1\}\hat{x}_t$$
$$= B^*(L)x_t \tag{12}$$

where $B^*(L)$ is a polynomial with leads and lags to order $N-1$. Since $B^*(L)$ is constructed to be symmetric, there exists $\theta \neq 0$ and a one sided polynomial $A(L)$ or order $N-1$ with a unit constant term and all roots less than or equal to 1 in modulus such that

$$B^*(L) = \theta A(L)A(L^{-1}).$$

Substituting into (12) and dividing by $A(L^{-1})$ gives a solution for $\hat{x}_t$ in terms of past values alone:

$$A(L)\hat{x}_t = 0.$$

From equation (8) it is evident that x_t and $\hat{x}_t$ differ by z_t. Since $x_{t-k} = \hat{x}_{t-k}$ for $k > 0$,

$$A(L)x_t = A(L)\hat{x}_t + x_t - \hat{x}_t$$

$$= z_t, \tag{13}$$

which gives the reduced form solution for the contract wage at time t.

The coefficients of $A(L)$ depend on the coefficients of $B(L)$ and the parameters γ and h. To obtain an expression for the aggregate observed wage, pre-multiply (13) by $D(L)$ to obtain

$$A(L)W_t = D(L)z_t. \tag{14}$$

The time series representation of aggregate demand follows by substituting (14) into (9).

The empirical implications of Taylor's model are summarized in Table T-2. First, as (14) indicates, the nominal aggregate wage has a concise univariate ARMA representation, with the order of both the AR and MA parts equal to the legnth of the underlying

TABLE T-2

Implications of Taylor's overlapping contracts model

Assumptions	Implications
1. N period contracts; errors in wage setting and aggregate demand equations serially uncorrelated.	(i) aggregate nominal wages follow ARMA(N, N). MA part is an unweighted moving average $(1 + L + L^2 + \cdots)$.
	(ii) unemployment follows ARMA(N, N) with same AR part as nominal wages.
	(iii) unit root in AR part of nominal wages if and only if full accommodation or no dampening effect of unemployment on wage demands.
	(iv) unemployment fails to cause current wage settlements.
2. N period contracts; errors in wage setting and aggregate demand equations MA(K).	(i) aggregate nominal wages follows ARMA($N, N+K$).
	(ii) unemployment follows ARMA ($N, N+K$) with same AR part as nominal wages.
	(iii) unit root in AR part of nominal wages if and only if full accommodation or no dampening effect of unemployment on wage demands.
	(iv) unemployment fails to cause current wage settlements.

contracts.[31] Second, by assumption, aggregate demand (or unemployment) has the same basic stochastic structure as nominal wages and prices. Third, the AR coefficients of the nominal wage process are closely linked to the product of the structural parameters γ and h. If neither γ nor h is zero, then all roots of $A(L)$ are less than one in modulus. On the other hand, $\gamma h = 0$ implies and is implied by a unit root in the polynomial $A(L)$.[32] If workers fail to consider the aggregate consequences of their wage demands, or if the monetary authority fully accommodates their wage demands, then the nominal wage process will be non-stationary.

A fourth implication of Taylor's model is that aggregate demand fails to Granger-cause x_t, the level of nominal wages established in currently negotiated contracts. This is a simple consequence of the rational expectations of wage setters: information on past levels of all variables is incorporated into the current decision, and the innovation in x_t is therefore orthogonal to e_{t-k} for $k > 0$. However, since w_t is an average of past x_t, and since x_t is in general correlated with e_t, aggregate wages may be Granger caused by aggregate demand.

At this juncture it is worthwhile pointing out the robustness of most of these implications to the specification of the model. First, as noted by Taylor, the shocks v_t and z_t may be serially correlated. This has the effect of adding a term in the forecasts of v_t and z_t, $\hat{v}_t$ and $\hat{z}_t$ respectively, to the right-hand side of (12). The solution of the model can then be written as:

$$A(L)x_t = \theta^{-1}A(L^{-1})^{-1}\{\gamma D(L^{-1})\hat{v}_t + \hat{z}_t\} + z_t - \hat{z}_t, \tag{13a}$$

which differs from (13) by the addition of a possibly serially correlated error. Clearly none of the basic properties of the simpler model are lost.

A second possible modification is to replace the relative wage setting rule (8) by a purely forward looking real wage setting rule.[33] The average expected price level over the life of the contract is $D(L^{-1})\hat{w}_t$. Suppose that currently negotiated wages are set according to

$$x_t = D(L^{-1})\hat{w}_t + hD(L^{-1})\hat{e}_t + z_t. \tag{8a}$$

This implies that current wages are set to achieve an expected real wage target, modified to the extent that anticipated aggregate demand deviates from trend. Substituting for the definitions of average wages and excess demand, (8a) leads to an expression exactly analogous to (12). The switch from relative to real wage setting leaves the model essentially unchanged.

It will by now be obvious that this model is going to have a hard time explaining the "facts". First, as Table I(b) indicates, we can find no evidence of moving average errors in even an AR1 representation of nominal wages. The presence of such moving average errors is also implied by Fischer's overlapping contracts set-up, and seems to be a fairly broad implication of the presence of overlapping wage contracts of the type that it is usually suggested do exist. Our empirical results imply either that these contracts are not very prevalent, *or* that they take a different form than is usually suggested.[34] Likewise, since the "facts" suggest that an AR1 adequately describes the quarterly wage data, if overlapping contracts of the type suggested by Taylor are actually prevalent, then they must be very short (that is, of two quarters duration or less).

Perhaps a more fundamental difficulty still is our finding that the stochastic structure of the nominal wage process differs strongly from the stochastic structure of both prices and unemployment. Taylor and Fischer set out models in which the real wage is constant and then derive the implication that unemployment has the same basic ARMA structure as wages. A more reasonable empirical statement is that unemployment has the same basic ARMA structure as prices, and that neither of these series have much in common with nominal wages.[35] In fact, in testing the implications of the model represented by (7), (8) and (9), Taylor (1980a) analyses detrended real output and *prices*, rather than nominal wages.

On the other hand, the strict relationship between prices, wages, and unemployment (or output) can be untied by the addition of serially correlated errors to (9) and the price equation, as in Taylor (1979). As a simple example, consider a wage–price and output system composed of (7), (8a), an equation for prices

$$p_t = w_t + \psi_1(L)\xi_t, \tag{15}$$

and a modification of (9):

$$e_t = \gamma_{p_t} + \psi_2(L)v_t. \tag{9a}$$

Here, $\psi_1(L)$ and $\psi_2(L)$ are lag polynomials, and ξ_t and v_t are serially uncorrelated errors. As before, the model can be reduced to a difference equation involving a symmetric polynomial in $\hat{w}_t$ and various combinations of the past shocks as forcing variables. For simplicity, write the solution (after appropriate factorization of the symmetric polynomial) as:

$$A(L)w_t = D_1(L)z_t + D_2(L)\xi_t + D_3(L)v_t. \tag{16}$$

Substituting (16) into (15) and (9a) gives the univariate autoregressive and moving average reduced forms for prices and aggregate demand.

The implications of the model for the reduced forms in Section I depend on the form of the polynomials ψ_1 and ψ_2. For instance, Taylor (1980b) assumes $\psi_1(L) = (1 - \rho_1 L)^{-1}$, which implies that the real wage is an AR1. Our results in Table I(b) suggest $A(L) = (1 - \rho_2 L)$, with a serially uncorrelated error in the right hand side of (16). It is easy to see that these generate an ARMA (2, 1) for prices of potentially the "right shape."[36] While a general specification of the errors in labour supply makes it difficult to test the implications of the intertemporal substitution hypothesis by the simple methods in this paper, a general specification of the price-setting and aggregate demand equations in a long term contracting model has the same effect in that model. It remains to be seen whether a parsimonious version of either model can be made consistent with the aggregate data on wages, prices, and unemployment.[37]

3. CONCLUDING REMARKS

In this paper we have tried to emphasize the usefulness of setting out the unrestricted final forms of the time series data that form the endogenous variables in models of the aggregate labour market *before* proceeding to the elaborate fitting to the data of models that incorporate strong prior information on these final forms. A decade ago this would have been akin to urging that the unrestricted reduced forms of aggregate models of the labour market be fitted to the data and scrutinized before strong prior information in the form of structural exclusion restrictions was imposed.[38] The factual turn of events during the 1970s has finally turned attention to truly dynamic models, and this has likewise turned attention to the dynamic final form representations of time series variables.

Our approach is to first catalogue the "facts", which we take to be the univariate and vector autoregressive and moving average representations of the time series data on unemployment, nominal wages, consumer prices and nominal interest rates, together with the maximal set of exclusion restrictions with which these data are consistent. The next step is to catalogue the implications of the various models that deliver linear ARMA representations of the time series data, and then to compare these implications against the "facts". From the point of view of this research strategy, the regressions reported in Tables I-VI provide the data that challenge any proposed model that purports to explain the time series behaviour of the aggregate labour market.

As we have seen, this challenge is a formidable one. Neither parsimonious models based on intertemporal substitution in labour supply with imperfect information, nor explicit models of wage and price stickiness seem to be consistent with the data. This suggests that there is a large agenda for further research. First, it may be useful to more carefully explore the temporal stability of the results in Tables I-VI. One important message of existing models is that the reduced form representations of various time series variables may not be invariant to changes in public policy. Further data analysis would afford the opportunity to both explore the data and test this proposition. Second, it is important to catalogue and compare in more detail the time series implications of the theoretical models examined here, simple modifications of these models, and other models that exist in the literature or have been suggested.

It is remarkable that the debate over the role of the effectiveness of demand management policies has thus far been carried out in the context of models for which very little in the way of empirical support exists. It is perhaps not very surprising that neither academics nor public officials have thus far listened very carefully to it.

APPENDIX

Data definitions and sources:

Definitions and Sources of the variables in Tables I–IV are as follows:

W = average hourly earnings in manufacturing, excluding overtime and unadjusted for industry composition

Source: Citibase.

P = Consumer price index, wage earners and clerical workers (CPI-W), 1967 = 100.

Source: Citibase.

U = unemployment rate, all civilian workers, not seasonally adjusted.

Source: *Business Statistics: Supplement to the Survey of Current Business*. Washington: Department of Commerce, 1979 and *Survey of Current Business* various issues.

R = yield on U.S. Government 3-month Treasury Bills (rate on new issues).

Source: Citibase.

We are indebted to Willem Buiter for a number of helpful discussions during the preparation of this paper, and to the Editor and two referees for their comments and suggestions.

NOTES

1. See particularly Granger (1969), Sims (1980), Sargent (1976), Hendry (1980) and Wallis (1980).

2. It is worth observing that these are representations for the stochastic parts of the various time series only. Deterministic parts of the time series are typically represented by non-stochastic trends that are removed from the data before or during the analysis.

3. In using this methodology it is important to recognize that theories about the deterministic movement of the variables are not being tested. In effect, what is being offered are tests of explanations for what once was called the Trade Cycle, and they leave open the question of what determines the long run average levels of labour market variables. As a result, much of this research differs sharply in style from the continuing Keynesian tradition of analysing the determinants of long run slack in the labour market. Keynes himself wrote in his Trade Cycle chapter of the *General Theory* that "Since we claim to have shown in the preceding chapters what determines the volume of employment at any time, it follows, if we are right, that our theory must be capable of explaining the phenomenon of the Trade Cycle...", but concludes that "to develop this thesis would occupy a book rather than a chapter, and would require a close examination of the facts." Keynes (1936), p. 313.

4. While we only present data for short (90 day) interest rates, the qualitative properties of time series of longer term bond rates (1 year and 3 year Treasury bonds) are very similar.

5. In Table I(b) we adopt the sign convention that a positive MA (1) coefficient indicates that the lagged white noise error enters positively into the current composite residual.

6. We are aware of the difficulty of testing the null hypothesis of a largest root equal to unity. Fuller (1976) shows that under the null, in a regression that includes constant and trend, the test statistic is biased towards rejection of the null in favour of the alternative of stationarity.

7. We use the (admittedly imprecise) phase "X Granger causes Y" when lagged values of X improve the prediction of Y, maintaining the effects of lagged values of Y as predictors. See Granger (1959). We implement this definition by the usual F-rate for a joint test of the effects of lagged X's on Y.

8. Excluding interest rates, the F-statistic for the null hypothesis that wages and prices have equal and opposite coefficients at each lag has a marginal significance level of 0·01. Maintains interest rates, the marginal significance level of the test statistic is 0·22.

9. Further investigation reveals that causality from prices to interest rates is stronger, the longer the term of the interest rate being considered. For 90 day Treasury Bills, the F-statistic is 0·58. For one year Treasury Bonds, the statistic is 1·30, and for three year Treasury Bonds, the statistic is 2·16.

10. The only difference in the conclusions from the causality tests is that wages and prices (together and separately) Granger-cause employment, controlling for the effects of lagged interest rates.

11. This is consistent with Altonji and Ashenfelter's (1980) conclusion from seasonally adjusted aggregate quarterly data, and also with MaCurdy's (1982) analysis of individual longitudinal data. Tests of the hypothesis that the first difference of real wages is serially uncorrelated (apart from deterministic components) yield a Box–Pierce statistic with a marginal significance level of 0·07, and a Kolmogorov–Smirnov statistic of 0·13, which is just significant at the 5% level. MaCurdy's analysis of microeconomic data suggests that aggregation biases are not the source of this phenomenon. He finds that an ARMA (1, 2) representation of the annual real wage process, with an AR coefficient very close to unity, gives a good fit to the data.

12. This point has been exploited in previous empirical work by Fama (1975) and Mishkin (1981).

13. Let E_t denote expectations conditional on information at t. The *ex-ante* real interest rate is $r_t = R_t - (E_t P_{t+1} - p_t)$ and the *ex-post* real interest rate is $r_t^* = R_t - (p_{t+1} - p_t)$. The deviation of *ex-ante* and *ex-post* rates is $r_t^* - r_t = E_t p_{t+1} - p_{t+1}$. Since

$$E_{t-1} r_t = E_{t-1} R_t - E_{t-1} p_{t+1} + E_{t-1} p_t$$
$$= E_{t-1} r_t^*,$$

the reduced forms for r_t and r_t^* (in terms of variables dated $t-1$ and earlier) are identical. Furthermore, the innovation in r_t is an exact linear combination of innovations in R_t, p_t and the variables used to predict p_t. Finally, the reduced forms for r_t and r_t include only those variables needed to predict R_t and p_t. For our purposes, these include lagged values of p, U, W, and R.

The tests we report are convenient because of the ease of their computation and interpretation. They may not be the most powerful since they ignore the structure of price forecasts implicit in the data under the rational expectations hypothesis.

14. The Box–Pierce and Kolmogorov–Smirnov statistics for this hypothesis are both significant at the 1 percent level. For the sample period 1956–1972, linear and quadratic trend terms are also jointly significant in a regression for *ex-post* real interest rates. However, there is weaker evidence that the non-deterministic component of *ex-post* real rates is serially correlated over this period.

15. These results are not inconsistent with a recent and interesting analysis of real interest rates by Litterman and Weiss (1981). They test and accept the hypothesis that the reduced form for *ex-post* real interest rates is consistent with a univariate representation for *ex-ante* real interest rates. Their tests exploit the implied cross-equation restrictions on the observable vector autoregression implied by the hypothesis.

16. Although we do not give the moving average representations associated with the vector autoregression in Table II, we have found that they tend to exhibit cycles of 16 to 20 quarters, and only fairly weak dampening.

17. The F-statistic for the hypothesis of equal and opposite coefficients has a marginal significance level of $0 \cdot 13$, maintaining lagged nominal interest rates.

18. In fact, this is precisely a generalization of the results reported by Neftci (1978) and the interpretation offered by Sargent (1978) of those results. Geary and Kennan (1979) have observed that Sargent's interpretation has some obvious problems, since the price level should in this case be a measure of the producer price index, rather than the consumer price index. However, we have found that entering both the wholesale and consumer price indexes into the employment equation leads us to reject any causal role for wholesale prices, while retaining the consumer price index.

19. For simplicity we neglect the impact of current wealth, although in principle it is a legitimate argument of the labour supply function.

20. Equation (1) is easily derived by writing the unemployment of i in period t as a function of discounted wages and prices in each of the periods in his planning horizon and then using the homogeneity of the demand function to divide through by the current price level. For example, see Sargent (1979), pp. 366–370.

21. This is formally expressed in the requirement that none of the variables in our system except interest rates Granger cause real wages.

22. Our own results do not reject the hypothesis of a deterministic anticipated real interest rate over this period.

23. Assuming the joint normality of z_{it} and the innovations in aggregate nominal wages, interest rates and prices, the coefficients ϕ, ϕ_2, and ϕ_3 are easily derived from the expression for the conditional mean of the innovation in aggregate wages, given the other three (see for example Dhrymes (1970), pp. 16–18). More generally, E can be interpreted as a linear least squares projection operator, and the ϕ_j as population regression coefficients that minimize the mean square forecast error of the innovation in aggregate real wages, given aggregate prices, interest rates, and individual wages (see Sargent (1979), Chapter X).

24. These implications are very similar to the set of implications tested and rejected in early empirical work by Sargent (1973) and Nelson (1981).

25. The marginal significance level of the test statistic is $0 \cdot 18$.

26. This is an issue that could usefully be studied with longitudinal microeconomic data. This research has just been started in recent years. See, for example, MaCurdy (1981).

27. See for example Mishkin (1981).

28. This conclusion is false if the v_{it} are serially correlated.

29. See for instance, Lucas' discussion of these two competing views in Lucas (1981).

30. $B(L^{-1})$ and $D(L^{-1})$ are polynomials in the lead operator L^{-1}.

31. Note that the MA error $D(L)z_t$ is non-invariable since $D(L)$ has all roots on the unit circle.

32. Recall $B^*(L) = \theta A(L)(L^{-1})$. Note that $B^*(1)$ is the sum of the coefficients of the polynomial B^*. It is easy to show $C(1) = \frac{1}{2}(1 - 1/N)$, and since $B(1) = \frac{1}{2}$, $B(1) = \gamma h$. If $A(L)$ has a unit root then $A(1) = 0$ so $B(1) = \theta A(1) A(1) = 0$, which implies $\gamma h = 0$.

33. This suggestion is pursued in Buiter and Jewitt (1981).

34. See Barro (1977) for a discussion of how optimal overlapping contracts would be constructed and how they contrast with the type of contracts suggested by Taylor and Fischer.

35. Although it is not quite true that unemployment and prices have the same ARMA representations—see Table I(b).

36. Write (15) as:

$$(1 - \rho_1 L)p_t = (1 - \rho_1 L)w_t + \xi_t,$$

and suppose (16) can be written as:

$$(1 - \rho_2 L)w_t = z_t.$$

With appropriate substitutions, we obtain

$$(1 - \rho_1 L)(1 - \rho_2 L)p_t = (1 - \rho_1 L)z_t + (1 - \rho_2 L)\xi_t.$$

37. Taylor (1980b) reports estimation results for an extended specification of his model on quarterly U.S. data. He gives no indication of the fit of the models relative to an unconstrained regression, however.

REFERENCES

ALTONJI, J. and ASHENFELTER, O. (1980), "Wage Movements and the Labour Market Equilibrium Hypothesis", *Economica*, **47**, 217–245.
BARRO, R. J. (1977), "Long-Term Contracting, Sticky Prices, and Monetary Policy", *Journal of Monetary Economics*, **3**, 305–316.
BUITER, W. H. and JEWITT, I. "Staggered Wage Setting without Money Illusion: Variations on a Theme of Taylor" (Discussion Paper 83/80, University of Bristol, Department of Economics).
DHRYMES, P. J. (1970) *Econometrics* (New York: Harper and Row).
FAMA, E. F. (1975), "Short Term Interest Rates as Predictors of Inflation", *American Economic Review*, **65**, 269–282.
FISCHER, S. (1977), "Long-Term Contracts, Rational Expectations, and the Optimal Money Supply Rule", *Journal of Political Economy*, **85**, 191–205.
FULLER, W. A. (1978) *Introduction to Statistical Time Series* (New York: Wiley).
GEARY, P. T. and KENNAN, J. (1979), "The Employment–Real Wage Relationship: An International Study" (Working Paper No. 79-13, McMaster University, Department of Economics).
GRANGER, C. W. J. (1969), "Investigating Causal Relations by Econometric Models and Cross-Spectral Methods", *Econometrica*, **37**, 424–438.
HENDRY, D. F. (1980), "Econometrics—Alchemy or Science?" *Economica*, **47** (188), 387–406.
KEYNES, J. M. (1936) *The General Theory of Employment, Interest and Money* (London: Macmillan).
LITTERMAN, R. and WEISS, L. (1981), Working Paper, Federal Reserve Bank of Minneapolis.
LIU, T. C. (1960), "Underidentification, Structural Estimation, and Forecasting", *Econometrica*, **28**, 855–865.
LUCAS, R. E. and RAPPING, L. A. (1970), "Real Wages, Employment and Inflation", in Phelps, E. S. *et al. Microeconomic Foundations of Employment and Inflation Theory* (New York: W. W. Morton).
LUCAS, R. E. (1973), "Some International Evidence on Output–Inflation Trade-Offs", *American Economic Review*, **63**, 326–334.
LUCAS, R. E. (1981), "Tobin and Monetarism: A Review Article", *Journal of Economic Literature*, **19**, 558–567.
MACURDY, T. E. (1981), "An Empirical Model of Labor Supply in a Life-Cycle Setting", *Journal of Political Economy*, **89**, 1059–1085.
MACURDY, T. E. (1982), "The Use of Time Series Processes to Model the Error Structure of Earnings in a Longitudinal Data Analysis", *Journal of Econometrics*, **18**, 83–114.
MISHKIN, F. (1981), "The Real Interest Rate: An Empirical Investigation". In Brunner, K. and Meltzer, A. (eds.), *The Costs and Consequences of Inflation* (Carnegie Rochester Conference Series on Public Policy). *Journal of Monetary Economics*, **15** (supplement) 151–200.
NEFTCI, S. N. (1978), "A Time Series Analysis of the Real Wages–Employment Relationship", *Journal of Political Economy*, **86**, 281–292.
NELSON, C. R. (1981), "Adjustment Lags Versus Information Lags: A Test of Alternative Explanations of the Phillips Curve Phenomenon", *Journal of Money, Credit and Banking*, **13**, 1–11.
SARGENT, T. J. (1972), "Rational Expectations, the Real Rate of Interest, and the Natural Rate of Unemployment", *Brookings Papers on Economic Activity*, **4**, 429–472.
SARGENT, T. J. (1976), "A classical Macroeconomic Model for the United States", *Journal of Political Economy*, **84**, 207–237.
SARGENT, T. J. (1978), "Estimation of Dynamic Demand Schedules under Rational Expectations", *Journal of Political Economy*, **86**, 1009–1044.
SARGENT, T. J. (1979) *Macroeconomic Theory* (New York: Academic Press).
SIMS, C. A. (1980), "Macroeconomics and Reality", *Econometrica*, **48**, 1–48.
TAYLOR, J. B. (1979), "An Econometric Business Cycle Model with Rational Expectations: Some Estimation Results" (Unpublished Paper, Columbia University).
TAYLOR, J. B. (1980a), "Aggregate Dynamics and Staggered Contracts", *Journal of Political Economy*, **88**, 1–23.
TAYLOR, J. B. (1980b), "Output and Price Stability: An International Comparison", *Journal of Economic Dynamics and Control*, **2**, 109–132.
WALLIS, K. F. (1980), "Econometric Implications of the Rational Expectations Hypothesis", *Econometrica*, **48**, 49–73.

Review of Economic Studies (1982) XLIX, 783–824

0034-6527/82/00580783$00.50

The Intertemporal Substitution Model of Labour Market Fluctuations: An Empirical Analysis

JOSEPH G. ALTONJI

Columbia University

The paper uses two approaches to study whether aggregate fluctuations in employment and unemployment may be explained within a market clearing framework as intertemporal substitution in labour supply. First, log-linear equations for labour supply and unemployment are estimated using a forecasting model to measure wage and price expectations. Second, a utility function is used to derive and estimate an equation for labour supply as a function of the current real wage and consumption. The influence of expected future real wages and interest rates is captured by the consumption variable. The empirical results do not support the intertemporal substitution model.

1. INTRODUCTION

This paper is an empirical analysis of the recent equilibrium explanations of labour market fluctuations based on the intertemporal substitution hypothesis. In essence, the hypothesis explains cyclical fluctuations in employment and unemployment as the response of labour supply to perceived temporary movements in the real wage. The key behavioural postulate is that leisure in the current period is highly substitutable with leisure (and goods) in other periods. Consequently, movements in the current real wage relative to expected discounted future real wage rates elicit a large labour supply response. Households optimally shift consumption of leisure from times when it is (relatively) expensive to times when it is cheap.

The prominence of the intertemporal substitution hypothesis dates from the work of R. E. Lucas and L. A. Rapping (1970). Empirically, Lucas and Rapping (here after, LR) are reasonably successful in explaining labour supply and unemployment from 1930–1965 as functions of the current real wage, the expected future real wage, and the expected real interest rate. Their empirical work is based on the assumption that expectations about future wages and prices are formed adaptively. In particular, after corrections for minor data errors, their work indicates that the elasticity of labour supply with respect to temporary wage changes is around 4·6. Since labour is the dominant input in production, LR have provided a concise theory, with some supporting evidence, as to why aggregate supply is elastic in the short run. This theory is consistent with equilibrium in factor markets and a vertical long run supply curve.

The proliferation of equilibrium business cycle models over the last 10 years has both been stimulated by and added to the importance of LR's work.[1] In these models, intertemporal substitution is the leading explanation for why fluctuations in aggregate demand can result in changes in output, employment, and unemployment rather than simply in price rises. This is clear in Lucas (1977) and is explicitly discussed in recent papers by Hall (1980a) and Brunner et al. (1980).

Until recently, however,[2] the intertemporal substitution hypothesis has not received much attention in empirical work despite its theoretical importance. This is particularly surprising since LR's results are based on the assumption of adaptive expectations rather than on rational expectations. Indeed, Robert Solow (1980) in his recent AEA Presidental Address goes so far as to state:

> It is astonishing that believers [in the intertemporal substitution hypothesis] have made essentially no effort to verify this central hypothesis. I know of no convincing evidence in its favour, and I am not sure why it has any claim to be taken seriously. (p. 7)

The purpose of this paper is to provide a careful investigation of whether the intertemporal substitution model can explain the annual time series data for the U.S. The main obstacle to the analysis is the difficulty associated with measuring expectations of future wages and prices, which play a key role in the model but are not directly observed.

I use two very different approaches. In Sections 2 and 3 I estimate variants of the log-linear labour supply and unemployment equations utilized by LR. Expectations are measured as the forecasts from a system of equations containing (a) an approximation to the reduced form equation for the real wage implied by the rational expectations solution to the labour market model and (b) a set of multivariate and univariate time series models for the exogenous variables in the labour market model. Subject to the qualifications below, this procedure will generate consistent estimates of the expected future wage and price indices. Since the assumption that agents have imperfect information regarding the current real wage, the price level and the money supply plays a key role in the explanation of the links between monetary policy and real economic activity (see e.g. Lucas (1977)), I try several assumptions about the information set on which the forecasts are conditional. In the process, money and price surprises are added to some versions of the model. The parameters of the labour supply and unemployment equations are estimated conditional on the measure of expectations.

The second estimation method (Section 4) uses observed consumption as a proxy in the labour supply equation for expectations of future wages and real interest rates. In the standard life cycle model, both consumption and labour supply are determined as functions of current and expected future wages and prices, interest rates, wealth, and preferences. Using a specific intertemporal utility function, I derive and estimate a log-linear equation for aggregate labour supply as a function of the current real wage and consumption. The influence of wealth, expected future real wages, and expected real interest rates is captured by the consumption variable.

The estimates from the two estimation procedures are similar. The results do not support the intertemporal substitution model. For most specifications, the current real wage, the expected future real wage, and the expected real rate of interest are either insignificantly related to unemployment and labour supply or have the wrong sign.

The paper closes with a summary of the findings, a discussion of some limitations of the analysis, a very brief survey of related research, and some thoughts on the implications of the analysis for future work on the labour market. I turn now to a brief presentation of the LR model.

2. THE LUCAS–RAPPING MODEL

LR's basic equations and notation are summarized below.[3] The labour supply equation (1) is based upon consideration of a two period Fisherian maximization framework in which labour supply is a function of current and expected future real wages (w_t and w_t^*), the real interest rate ($r_t - P_t^* + P_t$), and a wealth variable. It is assumed to be log-linear, with β_1, β_2, β_3', β_3, and β_4 positive.[4] β_3' is the elasticity of labour supply with respect to the expected intertemporal price of goods, holding constant the current real wage

Some basic equations of the LR model with rational expectations

(1) Labour supply

$$N_t - M_t = \beta_0 + \beta_1(w_t) - \beta_2(w_t^*) + \beta_3[r_t - (P_t^* - P_t)] - \beta_4(a_t - M_t) + \varepsilon_{2t}; \qquad \beta_3 = \beta_2 + \beta_3'$$

(2) Aggregate marginal productivity condition for labour

$$Q_t + N_t - y_t = C_0 - C_1(w_t - Q_t) + C_4(Q_{t-1} + N_{t-1} - y_{t-1}) + (C_2 - 1)(y_t - y_{t-1}) + u_{1t}$$

Unemployment equation

(6) $$U_t = g_0 + g_1\beta_1 \cdot (w_t^* - w_t) - g_1\beta_1[r_t - (P_t^* - P_t)] + \varepsilon_{3t}$$

(8) Wage expectations

$$w_t^* = \sum_{i=1}^{k} d_i \hat{w}_{t+i}$$

(9) Price expectations

$$P_t^* = \sum_{i=1}^{k} d_i \hat{P}_{t+i}$$

Notation: (All variables except t and r_t and U_t are in logs)

t = time subscript
w_t = real wage
$\hat{w}_{t+i}$ = rational expectation of w_{t+i}
w_t^* = anticipated future real wage
P_t = current price level
$\hat{P}_{t+i}$ = rational expectation of P_{t+i}
P_t^* = anticipated future price level
r_t = nominal interest rate
a_t = real wealth
M_t = population over 14 years of age with constant age-sex distribution
y_t = real GNP
Q_t = index of labour quality
N_t = labour supply
ε_{2t} = random component of labour supply
u_{1t} = random component, Aggregate Marginal Productivity Condition
ε_{3t} = random component, unemployment equation
U_t = unemployment proportion

and the expected discounted future real wage. The aggregate marginal productivity condition for labour (2) is derived from a CES aggregate production function under the assumption that output is exogenous.[5] I will assume that w_t^* and P_t^* are the rational expectations (RE) of indices of future wages and prices implied by the labour market model and models for P_t and for the other variables taken as exogenous. It is convenient to delay discussion of the solution for w_t^* and the models for the exogenous variables until Section 3.

LR make the key assumption that the labour market clears at the current wage, w_t. They reconcile the assumption that the labour market clears with the large variations in measured employment and unemployment by hypothesizing that unemployment as well as labour supply reflects voluntary substitution between current and future goods and leisure in response to changes in the current wage relative to what is perceived to be its normal level (or trend). LR regard unemployment as a measure of the percentage of workers who do not find work, given search costs, at what they view to be the normal (permanent) wage.[6] The unemployment equation follows directly from this concept of equilibrium unemployment. The level of equilibrium unemployment relative to a base level or normal level of equilibrium unemployment is a function of the amount of labour people wish to supply given current opportunities (indexed by w_t and $w_t^* - (r_t - P_t^* + P_t)$) and the amount they supply when the relationship of w_t and $w_t^* - (r_t - P_t^* + P_t)$ generates the level of intertemporal substitution and labour supply that is consistent with the base level. It is natural to define the base or normal level of unemployment in terms of the unemployment and the labour supply that prevail when the current real wage and the expected discounted future real wage are equal $(w_t = w_t^* - [r_t - P_t^* + P_t])$. When this condition holds, there is no particular incentive to substitute between periods. Evaluation of (1) at $w_t = w_t^* - (r_t - P_t^* + P_t)$ yields equation (3) for normal labour supply N_t^*:

$$(N_t^* - M_t) = \beta_0 + \beta_1(w_t^* - [r_t - P_t^* + P_t]) - \beta_2(w_t^* - [r_t - P_t^* + P_t])$$
$$+ \beta_3'(r_t - P_t^* + P_t) - \beta_4(a_t - M_t) + \varepsilon_{2t}. \tag{3}$$

The amount of equilibrium unemployment will be directly related to $N_t^* - N_t$.

Due to frictional unemployment and other factors, measured unemployment (U_t) will not correspond exactly to equilibrium unemployment even if the market clears. LR argue that the measured unemployment rate is a linear function of $(N_t^* - N_t)$ yielding,

$$U_t = g_0 + g_1 \cdot (N_t^* - N_t) + \varepsilon_{3t}; \qquad g_0, g_1 > 0. \tag{5}$$

Combining of (1), (3) and (5) leads to the unemployment equation (6) above.[7]

3. ESTIMATION USING FORECASTS TO MEASURE WAGE AND PRICE EXPECTATIONS

This section presents estimates of the labour supply and unemployment equations conditional on measures of expected future wages and prices. Section 3.1 discusses the econometric methodology and data. Section 3.2 presents the results.

3.1. *Econometric methods and data*

At the outset, it is useful to state the initial assumptions made in estimating the model:

Assumption 1. $(u_{1t}, u_{2t}, u_{3t})'$ is i.i.d. normal, where $u_{2t} = \varepsilon_{2t} - \theta_2 \varepsilon_{2t-1}$ and $u_{3t} = \varepsilon_{3t} - \theta_3 \varepsilon_{3t-1}$.

Assumption 2. P_t, M_t, Q_t, y_t, D_t and r_t are exogenous with respect to labour supply and unemployment.

Assumption 1 corresponds to LR's error specification but is somewhat more general. This assumption proves to be inadequate. Most of the estimates reported below are for equations with one or two lags of the dependent variables, with or without a correction for serial correlation. If preferences are not additively separable, one would expect lagged labour supply to have a negative partial effect on current labour supply—the population vacations after a period of hard work. On the other hand, fixed costs of arranging employment and human capital accumulation would suggest a positive role for lagged labour supply, although much of the effect of human capital accumulation is to shift the labour demand function rather than the labour supply function.

Assumption 2, also assumed by LR, is made for convenience rather than theoretical appeal, especially in the case of P_t, r_t and y_t. These variables are endogenous to almost any reasonable macro model of the economy, of which the labour market is just one sector. This assumption should be relaxed in future work, but its importance should not be overstated. If one believes (as I do) that fluctuations in the labour supply function (i.e. movement in ε_{2t}) are not a major source of business cycles, then the treatment of P_t, r_t, and y_t as exogenous with respect to the labour supply equation may be a reasonable approximation. Shifts in female labour force participation, changes in social insurance programmes, and changes in the age structure of the population do shift the aggregate labour supply function. But they do so in a gradual way that may be controlled for with trend variables or by dividing the sample. This is done below. The variation in manhours *per capita* is concentrated heavily at business cycle frequencies. Shifts in the labour supply function are not attractive as an explanation for more than a small fraction of these short term movements, especially since such shifts would have to be more important among workers in some industries (e.g. construction and manufacturing) than among those in others. It is worth mentioning that the results of Granger causality tests are consistent for the most part with (Assumption 2), although such tests are not decisive on the issue of simultaneity.[8]

Measuring expectations

To estimate the model, it is necessary to measure the unobserved variables w_t^* and P_t^*. The most elegant approach is to: (1) specify models for the exogenous variables in the labour market equations and for determinants of the exogenous variables, such as the money supply; (2) eliminate w_t^* and P_t^* by solving the complete model for these variables; and (3) estimate the complete model via FIML. This approach has been used by Sargent (1978).[9] The RE solution to the model is presented and discussed in Altonji (1981a). Unfortunately, it is extremely complicated, and the FIML approach was judged to be impractical in the present case.

I have employed a compromise procedure. To summarize briefly, w_t^* is generated as the index of forecasts from a multivariate time series model for w_t consisting of (to a close approximation) the unrestricted reduced form for the wage in terms of the exogenous variables entering the rational expectations solution for w_t^* and equations for the exogenous variables. The latter equations include multivariate equations for P_t and y_t, and univariate models for M_t, Q_t, r_t, and ml_t. P_t^* is also computed from forecasts from these equations.

Data

Before turning to the specification and estimates of the time series models, the data must be discussed. They are essentially the same as those used by LR, updated to 1976 and with revised estimates for the earlier years. The educational quality index (Q_t) is Denison's (1979) series for 1929, 1940–1941 and 1947–1976. Estimates are obtained for the missing years by linking the series to Denison's (1962) series (used by LR) for 1929–1958 via a maximum likelihood procedure under the assumption that they are linearly related with an autocorrelated stochastic term. The same procedure is used to obtain annual hours from Denison's (1979) series for 1929, 1940–1941, 1947–1976, and Christensen and Jorgenson's (1973) series for 1929–1969. The maximum likelihood procedure is described in Altonji (1981a).

Employment (N_t) is the log of man-hours engaged in production in the civilian and government sectors. The price level (P_t) is the log of the 1972 GNP implicit price deflator. The real wage (w_t) is the log of compensation per man-hour (deflated by the implicit price deflator), which includes wages and salaries and public and private fringes. Real output (y_t) is the log of GNP in constant (1972) dollars. Population (M_t) is the log of an index of the number of households corrected for changes in age-sex composition. The nominal interest rate (r_t) is based on Moody's *Aaa* rate. Since this is an annual rate while $P_t^* - P_t$ is an index of i-period inflation rates, an adjustment must be made to the Moody's *Aaa* series. To a first approximation, the i-period interest rate factor is the annual rate times i. The interest rate variable used in the labour supply and unemployment equation is $[\sum_{i=1}^{k} i d_i]$ times Moody's *Aaa* rate.[10] The d_i's are the weights used to construct P_t^* and w_t^*. They are discussed in footnote 14. I used Moody's *Aaa* rate directly in the forecasting models in Table I, although the coefficient on r_t easily could be rescaled. Measured unemployment (U_t) is the fraction of the labour force unemployed, although $-\ln(1 - U_t)$ is the variable actually used in the unemployment equations below.[11] The money supply (ml_t) is the log of currency plus demand deposits.

TABLE I

Forecasting models for the wage and exogenous variables[a,b]

(1) Wage[c]
$$w_t = -34\cdot67 + 0\cdot0238\text{time} + 0\cdot4329w_{t-1} + 0\cdot058w_{t-2} - 1\cdot439Q_t - 0\cdot238P_t$$
$$(4\cdot00)\ (3\cdot88)\qquad (3\cdot29)\qquad (0\cdot445)\qquad (2\cdot03)\quad (4\cdot34)$$
$$+ 0\cdot203P_{t-1} - 0\cdot733r_t + 1\cdot60r_{t-1} + 0\cdot088y_t - 0\cdot359M_t$$
$$(3\cdot88)\qquad (1\cdot28)\quad (2\cdot63)\quad (3\cdot98)\quad (1\cdot67)$$
$$R^2 = 0\cdot999 \qquad DW = 2\cdot40 \qquad SE = 0\cdot0122$$

(2) Price level[c]
$$P_t = 0\cdot791 + 1\cdot032P_{t-1} - 0\cdot762P_{t-2} + 0\cdot302P_{t-3} + 0\cdot228P_{t-4} + 0\cdot468ml_{t-1}$$
$$(4\cdot19)\ (7\cdot00)\qquad (3\cdot55)\qquad (1\cdot38)\qquad (1\cdot63)\qquad (3\cdot55)$$
$$- 0\cdot287ml_{t-2} + 0\cdot249ml_{t-3} - 0\cdot205ml_{t-4} + 1\cdot537r_t + 0\cdot733r_{t-1}$$
$$(1\cdot43)\qquad (1\cdot34)\qquad (1\cdot87)\qquad (1\cdot38)\quad (0\cdot672)$$
$$+ 0\cdot201y_t - 0\cdot372y_{t-1}$$
$$(2\cdot95)\quad (3\cdot81)$$
$$R^2 = 0\cdot998 \qquad DW = 2\cdot213 \qquad SE = 0\cdot0234$$

(3) GNP[c]
$$y_t = -17\cdot05 + 0\cdot0098\text{time} + 0\cdot816y_{t-1} + 0\cdot073y_{t-2} - 0\cdot244y_{t-3} + 0\cdot640ml_{t-1}$$
$$(3\cdot11)\ (3\cdot19)\qquad (4\cdot43)\qquad (0\cdot285)\quad (1\cdot50)\qquad (2\cdot80)$$
$$- 1\cdot009ml_{t-2} + 0\cdot426ml_{t-3}$$
$$(2\cdot49)\qquad (1\cdot96)$$
$$R^2 = 0\cdot992 \qquad DW = 1\cdot791 \qquad SE = 0\cdot0518$$

(4) Population index[d]
$$M_t = 0\cdot0015 + M_{t-1} + 1\cdot487(M_{t-1} - M_{t-2}) - 0\cdot603(M_{t-2} - M_{t-3}) - 1\cdot692u_{M_{t-1}}$$
$$(3\cdot24)\qquad (15\cdot2)\qquad\qquad (6\cdot49)\qquad\qquad (39\cdot6)$$
$$+ 1\cdot030u_{M_{t-2}}$$
$$(43\cdot3)$$
$$R^2 = 0\cdot999 \qquad DW = 2\cdot18 \qquad SE = 0\cdot0048$$

(5) Nominal[c] interest rate
$$r_t = -0\cdot367 + 0\cdot0189\text{time} + 1\cdot0803r_{t-1} - 0\cdot339r_{t-2} - 0\cdot051r_{t-3} + 0\cdot287r_{t-4}$$
$$(3\cdot72)\ (3\cdot71)\qquad (7\cdot07)\qquad (1\cdot50)\qquad (0\cdot213)\quad (1\cdot74)$$
$$R^2 = 0\cdot971 \qquad DW = 1\cdot838 \qquad SE = 0\cdot00327$$

(6) Labour Force[e] quality
$$Q_t = 20\cdot73 + Q_{t-1} - 2\cdot127(\text{time}/100) + 0\cdot0545(\text{time}/100)^2$$
$$(3\cdot28)\quad (3\cdot28)\qquad (3\cdot29)$$
$$R^2 = 0\cdot999 \qquad DW = 1\cdot954 \qquad SE = 0\cdot00187$$

(7) Money supply[c]
$$ml_t = -5\cdot160 + 0\cdot0028\text{time} + 1\cdot916ml_{t-1} - 1\cdot207ml_{t-2} + 0\cdot240ml_{t-3}$$
$$(1\cdot78)\ (1\cdot79)\qquad (12\cdot95)\qquad (4\cdot47)\qquad (1\cdot63)$$
$$R^2 = 0\cdot998 \qquad DW = 1\cdot938 \qquad SE = 0\cdot0428$$

Notes:
[a] In this table r_t refers to Moody's *Aaa* rate.
[b] *t*-ratios in parentheses.
[c] OLS estimate, 1929–1976.
[d] Maximum Likelihood Estimate, 1930–1976.
[e] OLS estimate, 1930–1976.

The sample means, standard deviations, and a correlation matrix for the various series are reported in Table A-I.[12]

The forecasting models

In principle, the RE hypothesis requires that the forecasting equation for the wage be the full reduced form in terms of the RE solution to the model. This equation contains a variety of exogenous variables and their lags, which appear in the reduced form because

TABLE A-I

Sample means and standard deviations of the data: 1930–1976

Variables	Mean	Standard deviation	Variable	Mean	Standard deviation
w_t	8·0372	0·3612	$(N-M)_t$	9·8548	0·0926
$w_t^*/I3_t$	8·1204	0·3573	$(N-M)_{t-1}$	9·8601	0·0946
$w_t^*/I3_t - w_t$	0·0833	0·0270	$-\ln(1-U_t)$	0·0849	0·0721
P_t	3·9846	0·4797	$-\ln(1-U_{t-1})$	0·0839	0·0725
$P_t^*/I3_t$	4·1124	0·5258	Q_t	4·4877	0·0842
$P_t^*/I3_t - P_t$	0·1278	0·0785	y_t	6·3737	0·5193
u_{Pt}	0·0004	0·0202	$y_t - y_{t-1}$	-0·0298	0·0639
u_{mlt}	-0·0003	0·0413	$w_t - Q_t$	3·5495	0·2777
r_t	0·1525	0·0638	$Q_t + N_t - y_t$	12·839	0·286
D_t	0·1064	0·3117	ml_t	4·5697	0·8078
$c_t - M_t$	0·2797	0·2501	N_t	14·725	0·1674
M_t	4·8700	0·1540			

Correlation matrix

COL	Time	w_t	$w_t^*/I3_t$	P_t	$P_t^*/I3_t$	u_{Pt}	u_{mlt}	r_t	D_t	$N_t·M_t$	$(N-M)_{t-1}$	$-\ln(1-U_t)$	$-\ln(1-U_{t-1})$	$c_t-\dot M_t$
ROW	1	2	3	4	5	6	7	8	9	10	11	12	13	14
1	1·0000	0·9968	0·9977	0·9808	0·9862	-0·0090	-0·0114	0·7037	-0·2544	-0·1280	-0·1524	-0·6129	-0·5806	0·9755
2	0·9968	1·0000	0·9972	0·9782	0·9840	-0·0274	-0·0337	0·7168	-0·2666	-0·1353	-0·1383	-0·6030	-0·5891	0·9719
3	0·9977	0·9972	1·0000	0·9799	0·9813	-0·0143	-0·0075	0·6835	-0·2651	-0·1152	-0·1395	-0·6286	-0·5988	0·9787
4	0·9808	0·9782	0·9799	1·0000	0·9920	0·0232	-0·0441	0·6907	-0·3019	-0·0990	-0·0878	-0·6503	-0·6492	0·9658
5	0·9862	0·9840	0·9813	0·9920	1·0000	-0·0176	-0·0792	0·7241	-0·2558	-0·0856	-0·0745	-0·6378	-0·6348	0·9678
6	-0·0090	-0·0274	-0·0143	0·0232	-0·0176	1·0000	0·0589	0·0038	-0·2021	-0·1032	-0·1290	-0·0530	0·0615	0·0051
7	-0·0114	-0·0337	-0·0075	-0·0441	-0·0792	0·0589	1·0000	-0·1971	0·3124	-0·1032	-0·0603	-0·1085	0·1116	-0·0018
8	0·7037	0·7168	0·6835	0·6907	0·7241	0·0038	-0·1971	1·0000	-0·3095	-0·4430	-0·3570	-0·0532	-0·1424	0·5779
9	-0·2544	-0·2666	-0·2651	-0·3019	-0·2558	-0·2021	0·3124	-0·3095	1·0000	0·7186	0·5003	-0·2146	-0·0752	-0·1895
10	-0·1280	-0·1353	-0·1152	-0·0990	-0·0856	-0·1032	-0·1032	-0·4430	0·7186	1·0000	0·8491	-0·6357	-0·5479	0·0383
11	-0·1524	-0·1383	-0·1395	-0·0878	-0·0745	-0·1290	-0·0603	-0·3570	0·5003	0·8491	1·0000	-0·5409	-0·6462	0·0145
12	-0·6129	-0·6030	-0·6286	-0·6503	-0·6378	-0·0530	-0·1085	-0·0532	-0·2146	-0·6357	-0·5409	1·0000	0·9119	-0·7526
13	-0·5806	-0·5891	-0·5988	-0·6492	-0·6348	0·0615	0·1116	-0·1424	-0·0752	-0·5479	-0·6462	0·9119	1·0000	-0·7141
14	0·9755	0·9719	0·9787	0·9658	0·9678	0·0051	-0·0018	0·5779	-0·1895	0·0383	0·0145	-0·7526	-0·7141	1·0000

they are present in the labour supply and demand equations, and/or because they are present in the time series models for P_t, y_t, r_t, Q_t, M_t and ml_t presented in Table I below. Unfortunately, the resulting equation is not estimable due to extreme multicollinearity. After some experimentation in which several insignificant variables were dropped, equation (1) in Table I was selected. The equation contains two lags of the wage rate (only the first of which is significant) and a time trend. N_{t-1} is insignificant with a coefficient very near zero and was dropped.

The wage equation requires forecasts of P_t, Q_t, r_t, y_t and M_t for use in generating forecasts of the wage. To generate these, I have chosen a middle ground between building a full scale macro model of which the labour market equations are just a part at one extreme and specifying univariate ARIMA models for each variable on the other, in an attempt to exploit the most important relationships among the exogenous variables in the labour market model and other variables (namely the money supply) while avoiding the complications of a large model. After some experimentation, multivariate equations for P_t and y_t and univariate models for r_t, ml_t, Q_t and M_t were selected. They are reported in Table I.

The price equation is motivated by the liquidity preference equation in standard macro models, and by the assumption that nominal interest rates reflect expectations of inflation. It loosely resembles the liquidity preference equations in Sargent (1976). A number of alternative equations expressing P_t as a function of current values and 1–4 lags of P_t, ml_t, r_t and y_t were tried, both with and without a time trend. The coefficient on ml_t, the current value of the money supply, is small and statistically insignificant in the equations in which it was included. The choice of the equation (2) in Table I is based on the judgment that the trend and longer lags for r_t and y_t add little, while the third and fourth lags for P_t and ml_t have some importance.

The model for y_t consists of 3 lagged values of y_t and ml_t and a time trend. Price terms were also tried but did not have an important impact. An autoregression with trend is used to describe monetary policy. There is little evidence in the sample of reverse causality from y_t to ml_t. I also tested for but did not find a role for lagged values of P_t in the interest rate equation. In the spirit of Modigliani and Schiller (1973), one might have expected lagged prices to serve as proxies for expected inflation. The Box–Jenkins (1976) procedure was used to guide the specification of the univariate models for r_t, Q_t, ml_t and M_t.[13]

The equations in Table I are used with the chain rule of forecasting to produce forecasts of w_{t+1} and P_{t+1} for each value of t in the sample, conditional on a series of alternative assumptions about the initial conditions or information set on which the forecasts are based. In order of the amount of information, the assumptions are:

$$I1_t = \{P_t, w_t, ml_t, Q_t, r_t, M_t, y_t\}$$
$$I2_t = \{P_{t-1}, w_{t-1}, ml_t, Q_t, r_t, M_t, y_t\}$$
$$I3_t = \{P_{t-1}, w_{t-1}, ml_{t-1}, Q_t, r_t, M_t, y_t\}$$
$$I4_t = \{P_{t-1}, w_{t-1}, ml_{t-1}, Q_{t-1}, r_{t-1}, M_{t-1}, y_{t-1}\}.$$

Use of $I1_t$ amounts to assuming that agents utilize all variables dated t (or earlier) in forming expectations about the future, including w_t and P_t. At the other extreme, under $I4_t$ they use only variables dated $t-1$.

Given the forecasts of w_{t+i} and P_{t+i}, a final assumption about the index weights $d_1 \cdots d_k$ must be made to determine w_t^* and P_t^*. I have assumed that the weights follow a slow exponential decay and terminate after 8 periods.[14] The various series for w_t^* and P_t^* are reported in Altonji (1981a).

The pairwise correlations between the alternative series for w_t^* exceed 0.99978 in all cases. They exceed 0.9955 in all cases for P_t^*. Thus, the choice of information set does not make a great deal of difference in the forecasts.

Estimating the model

Assuming the forecasting models for w_t^* and P_t^* are correctly specified, the estimates of w_t^* and P_t^* are consistent.[15] Fair's (1970) two stage instrumental variables procedure with a correction for first-order serial correlation is used for the labour supply and unemployment equations. This procedure handles the problem presented by the fact that (1) ε_{2t} and ε_{3t}, the error terms in the labour supply and unemployment equations, are autocorrelated, and (2) lagged employment appears in the system through the labour demand equation and (for most of the specifications) the labour supply equation. It also handles the analogous problem presented by the fact that for $I2_t$, $I3_t$, and $I4_t$, w_t^* is correlated with ε_{2t} and possibly ε_{3t}. This correlation is due to the fact that w_t^* is a function of ε_{2t-1} (and may be correlated with ε_{3t-1}), and that these errors are autocorrelated. If the information set includes the current wage, as in $I1_t$, then w_t^* is endogenous since it must be a function of u_{2t}. This presents a special problem that I discuss momentarily.

The Fair procedure is used conditional on the estimates of w_t^* and P_t^*. w_t^* (as well as P_t^*) is predetermined in the model in the case of $I2_t$, $I3_t$ and $I4_t$, which exclude w_t from the information set, and is treated as such in estimation.[16] Under the assumptions above, the model is identified and the coefficient estimates from the instrumental variables procedure are consistent and asymptotically normal.[17] It is important to keep in mind that the model under study is a market clearing model. The procedures used to estimate the labour supply and unemployment equations in both this section and Section 4 assume that the labour market clears, so that manhours are a measure of labour supply. If it does not, biased coefficient estimates are to be expected, since a disequilibrium component will enter both equations as an unobserved error given that the data are for hours worked (as opposed to labour supply) and for total unemployment.

It is natural to generalize the information assumptions listed above by allowing that agents partially observe the innovations in w_t, P_t, and ml_t (u_{wt}, u_{Pt} and u_{mlt} respectively) and that these innovations impact the expectations of w_t, P_t and ml_t (given the information at time t) with coefficients θ_w, θ_P, and θ_{ml} respectively.

One can avoid making an explicit assumption about θ_P and θ_{ml} by adding the estimates of u_{Pt} and u_{mlt} from the forecasting models directly to the labour supply and unemployment equations.[18] However, both the inclusion of u_{wt} in the labour supply equation and the use of w_t^* conditional on w_t under the assumption $I1_t$ introduce simultaneity bias. Altonji (1981a) discusses this problem in detail and concludes that it does not have a satisfactory solution. In any case, I have chosen to use the instrumental variables procedure outlined above even when $I1_t$ is the maintained hypothesis used in generating w_t^*.[19]

3.2. *Results*

In this section I report estimates of a number of versions of the model. The main section deals with instrumental variables estimates for the RE case under alternative assumptions about the information set. I then report results for the perfect foresight case, models with trends, and results for the postwar period. In contrast to LR's results for the adaptive expectations case, the model with RE receives little support.

Before turning to the RE estimates, a few issues must be discussed. Altonji (1981a) reports estimates of the marginal productivity condition (2) over the 1930–1976 sample that are similar to those presented by LR. They are not of major interest here and will not be discussed further.

To maximize the amount of information conveyed by the tables, the WWII dummy D_t is included in the unemployment equation when it appears in labour supply. This is justifiable if D_t captures the effect of the draft in producing negative disequilibrium.

Finally, the tables below present the instrumental variables estimates of several versions of the model under alternative assumptions about the information set. Model

REVIEW OF ECONOMIC STUDIES

1 is the basic model around which LR organize most of their discussion. The labour supply equation contains w_t, w_t^*, and $P_t^* - P_t$. The unemployment equation contains $w_t^* - w_t$ and $P_t^* - P_t$. The other models estimated contain variables plus the following additional regressors.

Model 2: r_t	Model 3: r_t, D_t
Model 4: u_{Pt}, u_{mlt}	Model 5: u_{Pt}, u_{mlt}, D_t
Model 6: $u_{Pt}, u_{mlt}, r_t, D_t$	Model 7: u_{Pt}, r_t
Model 8: u_{Pt}, r_t, D_t.	

The results for models 4, 5, 7, and 8 are basically similar to those for the other models and are omitted here to save space. (See Altonji (1981a).)

The model number is followed by a letter (a, b, or c) that identifies the dynamic specification. The "a" models (1a–6a) are estimated under the assumption of first order serial correlation. The "b" models contain two lags of the dependent variable and no correction for serial correlation. These are estimated using 2SLS with w_t endogenous. The "c" models contain one lag of the dependent variable and the assumption of first order serial correlation.[20] They are estimated using the Fair procedure with a second lag of $N_t - M_t$ added to the instrumental variables list. (See footnote 16.)

Estimates of labour supply and unemployment

Table II presents estimates based on $I3_t$, which excludes the current values of w_t, P_t and ml_t from the information set used to form w_t^* and P_t^*. I will begin with the "b" models. The coefficient on w_t, the estimate of the intertemporal substitution parameter β_1, ranges $-1 \cdot 16$ in model 6b to $-1 \cdot 89$ in model 2b. The estimate of $-\beta_2$, the coefficient on w_t^*, ranges from $1 \cdot 18$ to $1 \cdot 85$. These results contradict the basic premise of the intertemporal substitution framework, which is that labour supply rises in response to increases in the current wage relative to the expected wage. The coefficients are statistically significant at the $0 \cdot 05$ or $0 \cdot 005$ level.

The coefficient on the expected inflation rate, $-\hat{\beta}_3$, ranges from $0 \cdot 20$ to $0 \cdot 32$. It is also of wrong sign, and typically is significant. The coefficient on the nominal interest rate, r_t, ranges from $-0 \cdot 09$ to $0 \cdot 15$ and is not significant. The positive signs are consistent with the model, which states that when r_t rises (holding constant the expected inflation rate and the expected future real wage), workers will substitute future leisure for current leisure and increase labour supply.[21] However, the effect is weak. The coefficient on the price shock u_{pt} is $-0 \cdot 224$ in model 6b. Thus the price shock is weakly negative but insignificant. Note that there is no clear expectation about its sign, which depends upon a variety of unknown factors mentioned above. The presumption, however, is that it would be positive in the labour supply equation and negative in the unemployment equation. The order of magnitude of the coefficient on u_{pt} is too small given the variance of the price shock to play much of a role in explaining labour supply.

There is also no clear expectation about the sign of the money shock u_{mlt}, since money enters both the wage and the price forecasting equations. The presumption, however, is that it should have a positive effect on labour supply and a negative effect on unemployment. As it turns out, u_{mlt} is positive in 6b, with a coefficient of $0 \cdot 20$. Finally, the coefficient on the WWII dummy in 6b is large and highly significant—$(0 \cdot 08)$—as might be expected.

The results for the unemployment equations do not provide much support for the intertemporal substitution theory either. The estimates of $g_1\beta_1$, the effect of an increase in w_t^* relative to w_t, have the wrong sign and are significant in all models. The estimates range from $-1 \cdot 02$ in 6b to $-1 \cdot 3$ in 3b. The coefficient of $P_t^* | I3_t - P_t$ has the wrong sign. It ranges from $-0 \cdot 20$ to $-0 \cdot 26$ and is statistically significant. The nominal interest

TABLE II

Estimates of the Lucas–Rapping model with rational expectations, 1931–1976 information set: ($I3_t$)

	Models with first-order serial correlation[d]							
	Model No.							
Explanatory variable	1a	1a	2a	2a	3a	3a	6a	6a
	Dependent variable							
	$N_t - M_t$	$-\ln(1-U_t)$	$N_t - M_t$	$-\ln(1-U_t)$	$N_t - M_t$	$-\ln(1-U_t)$	$N_t - M_t$	$-\ln(1-U_t)$
Constant	$9\cdot344^a$ (10·1)	0·051 (0·68)	$8\cdot149^a$ (9·72)	0·043 (0·48)	$8\cdot517^a$ (22·5)	0·050 (0·55)	$8\cdot569^a$ (21·6)	0·038 (0·37)
w_t	$-1\cdot264^c$ (1·49)		$-0\cdot913^c$ (1·51)		$-0\cdot909^b$ (1·99)		$-0\cdot954^b$ (2·31)	
$w_t^*\|I3_t$	$1\cdot306^c$ (1·49)		$1\cdot129^h$ (1·807)		$1\cdot075^b$ (2·39)		$1\cdot113^a$ (2·72)	
$w_t^*\|I3_t - w_t$		0·182 (0·43)		$-0\cdot145$ (0·43)		$-0\cdot212$ (0·66)		$-0\cdot289$ (1·05)
$P_t^*\|I3_t - P_t$	$0\cdot256^c$ (1·31)	0·086 (0·84)	$0\cdot334^b$ (1·94)	0·025 (0·26)	$0\cdot380^a$ (2·88)	0·009 (0·10)	$0\cdot582^a$ (3·23)	$-0\cdot44$ (0·36)
u_{Pt}							0·190 (0·76)	$-0\cdot43^a$ (2·69)
u_{mlt}							$0\cdot254^c$ (1·51)	0·058 (0·53)
r_t			$-1\cdot28^a$ (2·80)	0·235 (0·76)	$-1\cdot10^a$ (4·14)	0·25 (0·83)	$-1\cdot18^a$ (4·35)	0·326 (1·13)
D_t					$0\cdot154^a$ (5·97)	$-0\cdot037^b$ (1·80)	$0\cdot141^a$ (5·08)	$-0\cdot052^b$ (2·63)
Lagged residual	$0\cdot804^a$ (9·16)	$0\cdot923^a$ (16·3)	$0\cdot734^a$ (7·32)	$0\cdot932^a$ (17·5)	$0\cdot555^a$ (4·53)	$0\cdot938^a$ (18·3)	$0\cdot577^a$ (4·79)	$0\cdot953^a$ (21·3)
R^2	0·758	0·841	0·799	0·851	0·886	0·862	0·893	0·887
DW	0·920	0·973	1·110	0·960	1·60	1·09	1·46	1·19
SE	0·050	0·030	0·046	0·029	0·035	0·028	0·035	0·026
$\ln(L)$	74·5	97·9	78·7	99·4	91·6	101·2	93·2	105·8

TABLE II (cont.)

Explanatory variable	Model No.					
	2b	2b	3b	3b	6b	6b
	Dependent variable					
	N_t-M_t	$-\ln(1-U_t)$	N_t-M_t	$-\ln(1-U_t)$	N_t-M_t	$-\ln(1-U_t)$
Constant	2·339[a] (2·76)	0·161[a] (3·76)	3·496[a] (5·18)	0·178[a] (4·04)	3·554[a] (5·85)	0·139[a] (3·86)
w_t	−1·888[b] (2·43)		−1·554[a] (2·73)		−1·163[b] (2·49)	
$w_t^*\|I3_t$	1·845[b] (2·48)		1·561[a] (2·86)		1·177[b] (2·61)	
$w_t^*\|I3_t-w_t$		−1·249[a] (3·79)		−1·331[a] (3·99)		−1·020[a] (3·72)
$P_t^*\|I3_t-P_t$	0·324[b] (1·78)	−0·234[b] (2·30)	0·206[c] (1·51)	−0·201[b] (1·94)	0·195[c] (1·65)	−0·255[a] (3·08)
u_{Pt}					−0·224 (0·93)	−0·319[b] (1·73)
u_{mlt}					0·201[c] (1·47)	−0·218[b] (2·28)
r_t	0·151 (0·51)	−0·060 (0·67)	0·017 (0·08)	−0·135[c] (1·33)	−0·088 (0·47)	−0·086 (0·28)
D_t			0·100[a] (4·79)	−0·025[c] (1·68)	0·079[a] (3·40)	−0·013 (0·93)
1st lag of dependent variable	1·086[a] (6·4)	1·036[a] (5·80)	0·734[a] (5·03)	0·955[a] (5·14)	0·831[a] (5·97)	0·962[a] (6·42)
2nd lag of dependent variable	−0·310[b] (1·95)	−0·233[c] (1·43)	−0·113 (0·90)	−0·155 (0·91)	−0·214[b] (1·84)	−0·139 (1·00)
R^2	0·854	0·893	0·921	0·894	0·940	0·936
DW	1·65	1·81	1·738	1·73	1·930	1·70
SE	0·041	0·025	0·030	0·025	0·027	0·020
$\ln(L)$	86·0	107·0	100·1	107·4	106·3	119·1

TABLE II (*cont.*)

Explanatory variable	Models with first-order serial correlation and lagged dependent variable[f]					
	Model No.					
	2c	2c	3c	3c	6c	6c
	Dependent variable					
	N_t-M_t	$-\ln(1-U_t)$	N_t-M_t	$-\ln(1-U_t)$	N_t-M_t	$-\ln(1-U_t)$
Constant	$2\cdot77^b$ $(2\cdot36)$	$0\cdot112^a$ $(3\cdot15)$	$4\cdot04^a$ $(5\cdot81)$	$0\cdot130^a$ $(4\cdot08)$	$4\cdot18^a$ $(5\cdot39)$	$0\cdot108^a$ $(4\cdot43)$
w_t	$-1\cdot41^a$ $(2\cdot90)$		$-1\cdot06^a$ $(3\cdot40)$		$-1\cdot15^a$ $(3\cdot70)$	
$w_t^*\|I3_t$	$1\cdot46^a$ $(3\cdot06)$		$1\cdot11^a$ $(3\cdot71)$		$1\cdot19^a$ $(3\cdot99)$	
$w_t^*\|I3_t-w_t$		$-0\cdot895^a$ $(3\cdot57)$		$-0\cdot958^a$ $(4\cdot29)$		$-0\cdot769^a$ $(4\cdot50)$
$P_t^*\|I3_t-P_t$	$0\cdot191^c$ $(1\cdot33)$	$-0\cdot171^b$ $(2\cdot05)$	$0\cdot182^b$ $(1\cdot78)$	$-0\cdot145^b$ $(1\cdot78)$	$0\cdot345^b$ $(2\cdot71)$	$-0\cdot260^a$ $(3\cdot62)$
u_{P_t}					$-0\cdot021$ $(0\cdot10)$	$-0\cdot452^a$ $(2\cdot99)$
u_{mlt}					$0\cdot263^b$ $(2\cdot02)$	$-0\cdot246^a$ $(2\cdot96)$
r_t	$-0\cdot347$ $(1\cdot05)$	$0\cdot002$ $(0\cdot02)$	$-0\cdot260^c$ $(1\cdot42)$	$-0\cdot080$ $(0\cdot87)$	$-0\cdot365^b$ $(1\cdot83)$	$0\cdot044$ $(0\cdot55)$
D_t			$0\cdot118^a$ $(6\cdot32)$	$-0\cdot030^b$ $(2\cdot23)$	$0\cdot097^a$ $(4\cdot31)$	$-0\cdot012^c$ $(1\cdot32)$
Lagged residual	$0\cdot585^a$ $(4\cdot89)$	$0\cdot224^c$ $(1\cdot56)$	$0\cdot191^c$ $(1\cdot32)$	$0\cdot153$ $(1\cdot05)$	$0\cdot345^b$ $(2\cdot49)$	$0\cdot127$ $(0\cdot87)$
1st lag of dependent variable	$0\cdot664^a$ $(5\cdot41)$	$0\cdot826^a$ $(12\cdot4)$	$0\cdot542^a$ $(7\cdot18)$	$0\cdot817^a$ $(13\cdot6)$	$0\cdot528^a$ $(6\cdot26)$	$0\cdot833^a$ $(17\cdot7)$
R^2	0·859	0·908	0·926	0·917	0·932	0·949
DW	1·70	1·82	1·94	1·82	1·86	1·84
SE	0·037	0·023	0·027	0·022	0·027	0·018
$\ln(L)$	89·4	110·6	104·5	112·9	106·2	124·0

Notes:
[a,b,c] One-tail t test significant at the 0·005 level (a), 0·05 level (b), and 0·10 level (c).
[d] Instrumental variables estimates with w_t endogenous (Fair procedure).
[e] 2SLS estimates with w_t endogenous.
[f] Instrumental variables estimates with w_t endogenous (Fair procedure).

REVIEW OF ECONOMIC STUDIES

rate r_t has the correct sign in all of the equations in which it appears although the estimates are small in absolute value.

u_{Pt} has the expected negative effect on unemployment in 6b with a coefficient of -0.319. The money supply disturbance u_{mlt} also has the expected negative sign with a coefficient of -0.22. Both variables are significant at the 0.05 level.

The third panel of Table II reports the estimates of 2c, 3c, and 6c for the information set $I3_t$. The coefficients on w_t and w_t^* from the "c" specifications of labour supply equations average about -1.2 and 1.2 respectively and are highly significant. $P_t^*|I3_t - P_t$ has the wrong sign in all of the "c" labour supply equations. The point estimates average about 0.24, which is close to the result for the "b" models. The coefficients on r_t are near -0.32.

The results for the "c" unemployment equations are also similar to those for the "b" specification. In 6c, which is typical, the coefficient on $w_t^* - w_t$ is -0.77. This is of the wrong sign and is significant. The coefficient on $P_t^* - P_t$ is -0.26, which is also of the wrong sign and significant. Both the price and money shocks have a significant negative effect on unemployment. The coefficient on r_t is near 0.

The results for models 1a, 2a, 3a, and 6a, which assume first order serial correlation and exclude lagged values of the endogenous variables, are presented in the left panel of Table II. They are reported for the purpose of comparison to LR's results, which are based on a similar stochastic specification. I do not discuss them in detail because they are characterized by low Durbin–Watson statistics and by values of the log likelihood function that are well below the values for the corresponding "b" and "c" model. Suffice to say that the coefficient estimates are qualitatively similar to those for the "b" and "c" specifications. The coefficients on $w^*|I3_t - w_t$ in the unemployment equations are smaller in absolute value and are not significant, while the coefficients on r_t in the labour supply equations are negative, significant, and large in absolute value. The main conclusion to be drawn from Table II is that none of the three sets of models provides much support for the intertemporal substitution hypothesis.

The results for the information set $I4_t$ (which excludes all variables dated t) are also negative with respect to the intertemporal substitution theory. Estimates of 2b, 3b, 6b, 2c, 3c, and 6c are presented in Table III. For 2b, the estimates of β_1 and $-\beta_2$ from the labour supply equation are 0.384 and -0.337 respectively, which are of correct sign. However, neither coefficient is significantly different from 0. The labour supply elasticities have the wrong sign in the other models and are significant in 3c and 6c. Also, $w_t^* - w_t$ has the wrong sign in all of the unemployment equations and is significant in all except 2c. $P_t^* - P_t$ has the wrong sign but is insignificantly different from zero in the labour supply equations. Its sign varies in the unemployment equations. The nominal interest rate r_t has the wrong sign and is significant in the labour supply equations. It is small and variable in sign in the unemployment equations. The price and money shocks u_{Pt} and u_{mlt} generally enter the equations with the correct signs.

In summary, the results for $I4_t$, while less discouraging than those presented above, do not provide much support for the model either. The estimates based on the information sets $I1_t$ and $I2_t$ closely resemble those for $I3_t$ and are not presented to save space.

It should be emphasized that these results are in sharp contrast to the LR model for the adaptive expectations case, in which a Koyck transformation is used to eliminate w_t^* and P_t^* from the model. For LR's sample period and data (corrected for minor errors), the estimates of β_1, $-\beta_2$, and $-\beta_3$ are 4.62, -4.62, and -1.46. The estimates of $-g_1\beta_1$ and $-g_1\beta_3$ are -0.80 and -0.60. The adaptive expectations estimates based on my data and the 1930–1976 sample indicate, if anything, an even greater responsiveness of unemployment to wage and price movements.[22]

Results for the perfect foresight case

As a crude check on whether mismeasurement of wage expectations is responsible for

TABLE III

Estimates of the Lucas–Rapping model with rational expectations, 1931–1976
information set: variables dated $t-1$ or earlier $(I4_t)$

	Models with 2 lags of the dependent variable[e]					
	Model No.					
	2b	2b	3b	3b	6b	6b
	Dependent variable					
Explanatory variable	N_t-M_t	$-\ln(1-U_t)$	N_t-M_t	$-\ln(1-U_t)$	N_t-M_t	$-\ln(1-U_t)$
Constant	3.098[a] (3.52)	0.115[a] (2.90)	3.823[a] (6.06)	0.165[a] (3.55)	3.66[a] (5.79)	0.119[a] (3.22)
w_t	0.384 (0.49)		-0.430 (0.80)		-0.283 (0.57)	
$w_t^*|I4_t$	-0.337 (0.45)		0.488 (0.94)		0.330 (0.68)	
$w_t^*|I4_t-w_t$		-0.906[a] (2.90)		-1.23[a] (3.48)		-0.869[a] (3.06)
$P_t^*|I4_t-P_t$	0.027 (0.17)	-0.158[b] (1.76)	-0.003 (0.029)	-0.127[c] (1.34)	0.047 (0.42)	-0.188[b] (2.49)
u_{pt}					-0.123 (0.47)	-0.314[c] (1.69)
u_{mlt}					0.256[b] (1.82)	-0.249[a] (2.75)
r_t	-0.516[c] (1.67)	-0.044 (0.52)	-0.280 (1.30)	-0.179[c] (1.67)	-0.298[c] (1.48)	-0.060 (0.670)
D_t			0.112[a] (5.30)	-0.039[b] (2.28)	0.082[d] (3.12)	-0.020[c] (1.30)
1st lag of dependent variable	1.220[a] (7.81)	1.175[a] (7.45)	0.790[a] (5.81)	0.999[a] (5.47)	0.904[a] (6.13)	1.05[a] (7.33)
2nd lag of dependent variable	-0.562[a] (3.71)	-0.331[b] (2.20)	-0.226[b] (1.85)	-0.165 (0.95)	-0.314[b] (2.51)	-0.190[c] (1.38)
R^2	0.829	0.897	0.918	0.889	0.923	0.936
DW	1.97	2.22	2.19	2.06	2.17	2.15
SE	0.041	0.025	0.029	0.0261	0.029	0.020
$\ln(L)$	85.1	108.0	102.0	117.9	103.4	119.0

REVIEW OF ECONOMIC STUDIES

TABLE III (*cont.*)

	Models with 1st order serial correlation[f] and lagged dependent variable					
	Model No.					
	2c	2c	3c	3c	6c	6c
	Dependent variable					
Explanatory variable	N_t-M_t	$-\ln(1-U_t)$	N_t-M_t	$-\ln(1-U_t)$	N_t-M_t	$-\ln(1-U_t)$
Constant	3·24[b] (2·67)	-0·000 (0·01)	3·96[a] (5·83)	0·065[b] (1·84)	3·96[a] (5·35)	0·08[a] (3·26)
w_t	-0·306 (0·70)		-0·707[b] (2·37)		-0·617[b] (2·01)	
$w_t^*\|I4_t$	0·362 (0·84)		0·769[b] (2·68)		0·678[b] (2·28)	
$w_t^*\|I4_t-w_t$		-0·091 (0·36)		-0·475[b] (1·98)		-0·564[b] (3·25)
$P_t^*\|I4_t-P_t$	0·039 (0·27)	0·098 (1·22)	0·062 (0·60)	0·030 (0·37)	0·133 (1·10)	-0·191[a] (2·78)
u_{pt}					-0·019 (0·08)	-0·496[a] (3·03)
u_{mlt}					0·179[c] (1·31)	-0·257[a] (3·12)
r_t	-0·472[c] (1·38)	0·025 (0·19)	-0·289[c] (1·60)	-0·090 (0·82)	-0·348[b] (1·82)	0·024 (0·31)
D_t			0·132[a] (6·76)	-0·037[b] (2·32)	0·116[a] (4·91)	-0·023[b] (1·77)
Lagged residual	0·539[a] (4·34)	0·594[a] (5·00)	0·104 (0·15)	0·376[a] (2·75)	0·184 (1·27)	0·046 (0·31)
1st lag of dependent variable	0·629[a] (4·94)	0·871[a] (8·45)	0·542[a] (7·38)	0·860[a] (11·6)	0·545[a] (6·71)	0·880[a] (20·0)
R^2	0·829	0·900	0·912	0·912	0·915	0·943
DW	1·79	1·96	2·00	1·94	1·95	1·95
SE	0·041	0·024	0·030	0·023	0·030	0·019
$\ln(L)$	85·0	108·4	100·4	111·4	101·3	121·7

Note:
[a-f] See Table II.

the findings, I have also estimated models 2b and c and 3b and c under the assumption of perfect foresight. Use of the perfect foresight values of w_t^* and P_t^* (without instrumental variables) when people do not in fact have perfect foresight introduces measurement error into the model. However, as a practical matter future real wages may be predicted with a high degree of accuracy even from a simple autoregression.[23] This suggests that if expectations are rational they cannot be very different from the perfect foresight estimate for w_t^*. Although this argument does not work so well for P_t^*, it is reasonable to expect that if intertemporal substitution plays a primary role in explaining labour supply and unemployment fluctuations and if people have rational expectations, this will show up in the perfect foresight case.[24]

Table IVb reports results for the 1931–1968 sample. To summarize, the results for 2b, 3b, 2c, and 3c resemble closely the RE estimates. Thus, the experiment with perfect foresight provides some evidence that the RE results are not due to errors in the measurement of expectations.

Other results

Table V contains estimates of 2b, 6b, 2c and 6c for the sample 1948–1976 using the information set $I3_t$.[25] Despite small sample problems, the postwar results provide a check on possible biases due to structural shifts or inadequate control for WWII. Also, some economists might take the position that the intertemporal substitution model is appropriate for the postwar years while believing that the Great Depression must in large part be explained by other factors.

For the labour supply equation in model 6c, $\hat{\beta}_1$ and $-\hat{\beta}_2$ are $-1\cdot38$ and $1\cdot36$ for 1948–1976 and $-1\cdot15$ and $1\cdot19$ for 1931–1976. The coefficient on expected inflation is $0\cdot52$ for 1948–1976 and $0\cdot35$ for the whole sample. The price shocks are small and insignificant in both time periods. The coefficient on the money shock is $0\cdot30$ for the postwar period and $0\cdot26$ for the whole sample. The coefficient on r_t is $-0\cdot45$ in the postwar sample and $-0\cdot37$ in the whole sample. It tends to be larger in absolute value in the postwar sample and consistently has the wrong sign.

Turning to the unemployment equation, $w_t^* - w_t$ remains of wrong sign but is less negative in the postwar sample. The expected inflation term also becomes significant and of wrong sign. The price shock, which has the correct sign and is significant in the whole sample, is near zero in the postwar sample. The coefficient on r_t is near $0\cdot25$ in the postwar sample and becomes significant. Finally, the importance of serial correlation and of the lagged dependent variables generally is reduced in the postwar sample. The standard errors of the unemployment equations are only about one half of the standard errors for the 1931–1976 estimates. The smaller postwar residual variances help explain the larger t-values in the postwar sample. If one maintains that variations in tastes in the pre- and postwar periods are roughly comparable, there is evidence that a persistent unobserved term (disequilibrium?) is more prominent in the Great Depression years.

Since the simple autoregressive model of the money supply used in this paper may be criticized, I experimented with Barro's (1978) unanticipated money series in 6b and 6c. This makes little difference. In summary, the estimates for the postwar sample are generally consistent with the findings for the whole sample, and fail to support the intertemporal substitution hypothesis.

I performed a few other experiments which deserve mention. As noted earlier, both w_t and w_t^* are trend dominated. This raises the possibility of bias, since a trend may exist in the error term due to shifts in tastes for labour supply or in demographic changes not controlled for with M_t.

Note that both the adjustment for first order serial correlation and inclusion of lagged dependent variables reduce this possibility. As a stronger check, however, Table IVa presents estimates of models 2, 3, and 6b and c (for $I3_t$) with trend terms added.

TABLE IVa

The Lucas–Rapping model with rational expectations, trend terms added
Information set: $I3_t$, sample: 1931–1976

Explanatory variable	Models with 2 lags of the dependent variable[e]				Models with 1st-order serial correlation and lagged dependent variable[f]			
	Dependent variable				Dependent variable			
Model No.	2b	2b	6b	6b	2c	2c	6c	6c
	$N_t - M_t$	$-\ln(1-U_t)$	$N_t - M_t$	$-\ln(1-U_t)$	$N_t - M_t$	$-\ln(1-U_t)$	$N_t - M_t$	$-\ln(1-U_t)$
Constant	−4·682 (0·37)	3·001[b] (2·27)	4·490 (0·49)	3·215[a] (2·86)	27·7 (1·28)	6·57[a] (3·44)	2·27 (0·17)	4·48[a] (4·92)
w_t	−1·525[b] (2·46)		−1·068[b] (2·37)		−0·576 (1·24)		−0·640[b] (2·04)	
$w_t^*/I3_t$	1·340[b] (2·15)		1·115[b] (2·58)		−0·060 (0·11)		0·662[b] (1·73)	
$w_t^*/I3_t, -w_t$		−0·818[b] (2·52)		−0·711[a] (3·03)		−0·064 (0·28)		−0·393[a] (2·96)
$P_t^*/I3_t, -P_t$	0·240[c] (1·47)	−0·193[b] (2·25)	0·189[c] (1·59)	−0·188[a] (2·73)	0·042 (0·29)	−0·003 (0·04)	0·131 (1·03)	−0·100[b] (1·83)

	(1)	(2)	(3)	(4)	(5)	(6)	(7)	(8)
u_{pt}	0·030 (0·12)		-0·200 (0·77)	-0·313^b (2·26)			-0·031 (0·12)	-0·382^a (2·89)
u_{mlt}		0·215^c (1·54)	0·207^c (1·53)	-0·147^b (1·90)			0·179 (1·29)	-0·119^c (1·68)
r_t			-0·109 (0·60)	0·208^b (1·98)	-0·545^c (1·67)	0·529^a (2·98)	-0·350^b (1·77)	0·298^a (3·73)
D_t			0·080^a (3·38)	-0·028^b (2·39)			0·116^a (4·66)	-0·043^a (4·17)
Time	0·0043 (0·12)	-0·0015^b (2·15)	-0·0008 (0·14)	-0·0016^a (2·74)	0·018^c (1·43)	-0·0034^a (5·19)	0·001 (0·13)	-0·002^a (4·83)
Lagged residual					0·467^a (3·59)	0·405^a (3·01)	0·191^c (1·32)	-0·112 (0·77)
1st lag of dependent variable	1·119^a (7·18)	0·893^a (5·78)	0·834^a (5·98)	0·764^a (5·81)	0·681^a (5·54)	0·585^a (5·19)	0·547^a (6·52)	0·663^a (12·2)
2nd lag of dependent variable	-0·353^b (2·47)	-0·216^c (1·59)	-0·222^b (1·94)	-0·079 (0·73)				
R^2	0·859	0·933	0·934	0·965	0·838	0·922	0·915	0·965
DW	1·84	2·10	1·97	2·13	1·78	1·80	1·96	2·18
SE	0·038	0·020	0·027	0·015	0·040	0·022	0·030	0·015
ln (L)	89·6	118·0	107·2	132·6	86·3	114·4	101·3	133·0

TABLE IVb

The Lucas–Rapping model with perfect foresight, sample: 1931–1968

Explanatory variable	Models with 2 lags of the dependent variable[c]				Models with 1st-order serial correlation and lagged dependent variable[f]			
	2b		3b		2c		3c	
	$N_t - M_t$	$-\ln(1-U_t)$	$N_t - M_t$	$-\ln(1-U_t)$	$N_t - M_t$	$-\ln(1-U_t)$	$N_t - M_t$	$-\ln(1-U_t)$
	Dependent variable				Dependent variable			
Constant	-1·902 (0·54)	0·136[a] (3·69)	0·495 (0·16)	0·154[a] (3·76)	2·32[b] (2·02)	0·081[b] (2·40)	3·55[a] (4·40)	0·087[b] (2·55)
w_t	-5·114[c] (1·62)		-3·392[c] (1·35)		-1·10[b] (2·57)		-0·822[b] (2·53)	
$\sum_{i=1}^{8} d_i w_{t+i}$	4·858[c] (1·64)		3·26[c] (1·39)		1·10[a] (2·74)		0·863[a] (2·84)	
$\sum_{i=1}^{8} d_i w_{t+i} - w_t^g$		-1·052[a] (4·08)		-1·19[a] (4·11)	0·190[c] (1·32)	-0·690[a] (3·64)		-0·710[a] (3·75)
$\sum_{i=1}^{8} d_i P_{t+i} - P_t$	0·102 (0·47)	-0·121[b] (2·00)	-0·025 (0·14)	-0·063 (0·82)		-0·121[b] (1·77)	-0·068 (0·66)	-0·042 (0·50)

u_{pt}

u_{mlt}

r_t	2·582 (1·26)	−0·123 (0·85)	1·45 (0·89)	−0·194 (1·22)	−0·185 (0·39)	0·048 (0·31)	−0·271 (0·86)	−0·024 (0·14)
D_t			0·072 (1·29)	−0·025c (1·33)			0·124a (5·05)	−0·028c (1·60)
Time								
Lagged residual	1·437d (3·96)				0·368b (2·44)	0·227c (1·43)	0·152 (0·95)	0·262c (1·67)
1st lag of dependent variable		1·081a (7·00)	1·100a (3·08)	0·985a (5·66)	0·757a (5·89)	0·855a (13·6)	0·603a (6·58)	0·842a (13·1)
2nd lag of dependent variable	−0·116 (0·33)	−0·238c (1·58)	−0·092 (0·39)	−0·154 (0·92)				
R^2	0·427	0·914	0·725	0·909	0·856	0·921	0·917	0·927
DW	1·316	1·82	1·39	1·66	1·82	1·91	1·87	1·95
SE	0·085	0·025	0·057	0·026	0·040	0·023	0·031	0·023
$\ln(L)$	43·6	89·7	59·2	88·6	71·4	91·3	82·0	92·8

Notes:

a–f See Table II.

g Treated as predetermined in both sets of models. In the models with first order serial correlation, this raises difficulties. See text.

TABLE V

Estimates of the Lucas–Rapping model with rational expectations, postwar (1948–1976)
Information set: $I3_t$

Explanatory variable	Models with 2 lags of the dependent variable[e]				Models with 1st-order serial correlation and a lagged dependent variable[f]			
	Model No.							
	2b	2b	6b	6b	2c	2c	6c	6c
	Dependent variable							
	$N_t - M_t$	$-\ln(1-U_t)$	$N_t - M_t$	$-\ln(1-U_t)$	$N_t - M_t$	$-\ln(1-U_t)$	$N_t - M_t$	$-\ln(1-U_t)$
Constant	6·12[c] (3·37)	0·117[c] (4·84)	6·96[c] (3·84)	0·122[c] (4·84)	8·66[a] (3·37)	0·131[a] (5·33)	8·25[a] (4·55)	0·113[a] (4·96)
w_t	−1·64[a] (4·13)		−1·60[a] (4·11)		−1·64[a] (5·20)		−1·38[a] (4·60)	
$w_t^*/I3_t$	1·68[a] (3·94)		1·63[a] (3·88)		1·83[a] (4·39)		1·36[a] (4·10)	
$w_t^*/I3_t, -w_t$		−0·634[a] (4·52)		−0·651[a] (4·48)		−0·705[a] (4·85)		−0·603[a] (4·49)

	(1)	(2)	(3)	(4)	(5)	(6)	(7)	(8)
$P_t^*/\beta_t - P_t$	0·461ᵇ (2·48)	−0·327ᵃ (4·44)	0·448ᵇ (2·30)	−0·339ᵃ (4·05)	0·486ᵃ (3·15)	−0·349ᵃ (4·76)	0·516ᵇ (2·62)	−0·340ᵃ (4·07)
u_{pt}			−0·514ᶜ (1·35)	0·036 (0·23)			−0·341 (1·04)	0·017 (0·11)
u_{mlt}			0·298 (1·30)	−0·078 (0·73)			0·295ᶜ (1·57)	−0·055 (0·61)
r_t	−0·467ᵇ (2·37)	0·234ᵃ (3·18)	−0·406ᵇ (2·04)	0·237ᵇ (2·80)	−0·855ᵇ (2·57)	0·244ᵃ (3·32)	−0·448ᵇ (2·06)	0·256ᵃ (3·03)
Lagged residual					0·788ᵃ (6·9)	0·126 (0·68)	0·337ᵇ (1·93)	0·140 (0·76)
1st lag of dependent variable	0·149 (0·65)	−0·040 (0·22)	0·225 (0·98)	−0·016 (0·08)	−0·048 (0·29)	−0·209 (1·20)	0·168 (1·11)	−0·114 (0·66)
2nd lag of dependent variable	0·178 (0·90)	−0·050 (0·30)	0·032 (0·16)	−0·119 (0·61)				
R^2	0·857	0·723	0·881	0·731	0·870	0·712	0·894	0·731
DW	1·30	1·86	1·50	1·81	1·66	1·82	1·75	1·84
SE	0·020	0·0083	0·019	0·0086	0·019	0·0083	0·018	0·0084
ln (L)	75·8	101·1	78·5	101·6	77·2	100·6	80·1	101·6

Note:
ᵃ⁻ᶠ See Table II.

Detailed examination of these estimates and comparison with those in Table II indicate that the addition of a trend term does little to change the negative tenor of the results reported earlier. This is also the case for the postwar sample (not shown).

The above experiments were also conducted using $I4_t$ with similar conclusions, although the results are less negative than for $I3_t$. Finally, the estimates are not very sensitive to the use of Darby's (1976) unemployment series for the early years of the sample, which counts participants in the Depression work relief programmes as employed.

4. CONSUMPTION AS A PROXY FOR EXPECTED WAGES AND REAL INTEREST RATES

Despite efforts in the preceding section to provide adequate measures for the wage and price expectations which play a crucial role in the intertemporal substitution theory, doubts remain. In lieu of the unattainable dream of knowing what people's expectations actually were, an alternative approach is to look at other aspects of *observed behaviour* which, with the help of economic theory, indicate what people were expecting. Consumption behaviour is a natural candidate.

To be more specific, suppose that preferences underlying the log-linear labour supply equation are such that, up to a scalar, the log of consumption *per capita* is a function of the same index of expected future wages and real interest rates as labour supply. Furthermore, suppose that the error in the relationship between consumption and these variables does not have a large variance, so that most of the movement in consumption is a response to movement in expected discounted real wages over time. Alternatively, an instrumental variables procedure may be available to correct for the endogeneity of consumption in the labour supply equation given that both variables are determined from the same (unobserved) preferences. One could then use consumption to replace the terms involving w_t^* and $r_t - (P_t^* - P_t)$ in an equation like (1) and estimate the temporary labour supply elasticity β_1. With a few additional assumptions, evidence that labour supply is not responsive to permanent wage shifts would permit inferences to be made about β_2.

Use of consumption data eliminates the need to maintain strong assumptions about the forecasting equations for the exogenous variables, assumptions about the information set, or even the assumption of rational expectations. Problems such as how to model learning in formulating the rational expectations hypothesis if the processes generating the exogenous variables (e.g. the money supply rule) are not stable (an issue ignored in Section 3, and in virtually all of the literature), no longer matter. Consumption as well as labour supply will reflect expectations, regardless of how people form them.[26]

As suggested by the "supposes" in a preceding paragraph, there are a number of difficulties with this approach. As a matter of research strategy, I have chosen to continue to maintain a log-linear form for the labour supply equation. This raises the issue of whether the implicit assumptions about consumer preferences and aggregation over the population underlying the log-linear form for labour supply are such that, to a close approximation, expected future wages and real interest rates affect consumption in the same way that they affect labour supply. Otherwise, consumption is not an appropriate index of these variables for the labour supply equation. A second issue is the problem of simultaneity bias, since consumption and labour supply are also affected over time by unobserved changes in tastes.

It is difficult to address these issues without an explicit specification of consumer preferences and aggregation. Such a specification permits one to compare directly the functional form and error structures of the implied consumption and labour supply equations.

4.1. *An intertemporal model of consumption and labour supply*

A flexible specification of lifetime preferences is most appropriate given that the essence of the intertemporal substitution hypothesis is that goods and leisure in different periods are highly substitutable. Unfortunately, intertemporal utility functions which are not additively separable are difficult to work with, even in the perfect foresight case.

In the absence of a better alternative, I have used an age specific version of the additively separable utility function employed by MaCurdy (1981) in his important work on life cycle labour supply behaviour, along with a simple aggregation story. Assume that individuals who are j years of age at time t seek to maximize the expected value of

$$V_{jt} = \sum_{i=0}^{J-j} \Psi^i [(\beta_c/(\beta_c+1)) \exp (\varepsilon'_{cjt+i} + [(\beta_c+1)/\beta_c] c_{jt+i})$$
$$- \exp (\varepsilon'_{Njt+i} + [(\beta_1+1)/\beta_1] N_{jt+i})] \tag{12}$$

where V_{jt} = utility function of individuals aged j at time t for their remaining life span $(J-j)$: J = life span, Ψ = subjective discount parameter, ε'_{cjt+i}, ε'_{Njt+i}, β_c, β_1 = parameters of the utility function,[27] c_{jt} = log of consumption of an individual aged j, N_{jt} = log of labour supply.

For the utility function to be concave and strictly increasing in consumption and leisure in each period, β_c and β_1 are restricted to $\beta_c < 0$, $\beta_1 > 0$. They are assumed to be constant during the sample period. ε'_{cjt} and ε'_{Njt} are each determined as the sum of 3 components:

$$\varepsilon'_{cjt} = \bar{\varepsilon}_{cj} + t \cdot \varepsilon_c + \varepsilon_{cjt}$$

$$\varepsilon'_{Njt} = \bar{\varepsilon}_{Nj} + t \cdot \varepsilon_N + \varepsilon_{Njt}$$

where $\bar{\varepsilon}_{cj}$ and $\bar{\varepsilon}_{Nj}$ are age specific constants, ε_c and ε_N are trend coefficients, and ε_{cjt} and ε_{Njt} are random disturbances (which may differ among age groups). I make simplifying assumptions about the statistical properties of ε'_{cjt} and ε'_{Njt} below.

Consumers face the budget constraint

$$0 = A_{jt} + \sum_{i=0}^{J-j} \bar{r}_{ti} \exp (N_{jt+i} + w_{jt+i}) - \bar{r}_{ti} \exp (c_{jt+i}), \tag{13}$$

where A_{jt} = wealth of an individual aged j at time t, w_{jt+i} = log of the wage to prevail at $t+i$ for individuals aged j at t, $\bar{r}_{ti}$ = real i-period interest factor at t.

It is not necessary to assume that consumers know the future values of ε'_{cjt+i}, ε'_{Njt+i}, w_{jt+i}, and $\bar{r}_{ti}$ ($i = 1 \cdots J-j$). Instead consumers may re-maximize each period, choosing current labour supply and consumption to maximize expected utility given beliefs about the joint distribution of these variables and the budget constraint. Let λ_{jt} equal the log of the expected value of the marginal utility of period t income for an individual aged j at time t. Assuming an interior solution, it is easy to show that maximization of the expected value of (12) subject to (13) leads to the following equations for current consumption and labour supply:

$$c_{jt} = \beta_c [\lambda_{jt} - \varepsilon'_{cjt}] \tag{14}$$

$$N_{jt} = \beta_1 [\ln (\beta_1/(\beta_1+1)) + \lambda_{jt} + w_{jt} - \varepsilon'_{Njt}]. \tag{15}$$

Note that the log of the expected marginal utility of income in period t for those aged j at t enters both the consumption and labour supply equations in linear form.

To see the relationship between (15) and (1) a solution is needed for λ_{jt}. Unfortunately, even in the perfect foresight case an analytical solution does not exist. λ_{jt} is a non-linear function of initial assets, lifetime wages, real interest rates, the taste parameters and the rate of time preference.[28] One might follow the example of MaCurdy (1981) and simply assume that the solution for λ_{jt} may be approximated as a linear function of current and expected future wages, wealth, and a random disturbance which depends

REVIEW OF ECONOMIC STUDIES

on ε_{cjt+i} and ε_{Njt+i} $(i = 0 \cdots J - j)$. That is,

$$\lambda_{jt} = \text{Const}_j - \sum_{i=0}^{J-j} d_{ji}(\hat{w}_{jt+i} - \bar{r}_{ti}) + \beta_{4j}A_{jt} + \varepsilon_{\lambda jt} \tag{16}$$

where Const_j = age specific constant. d_{ji} = weight given to the expected discounted future wage for period $t + i$ by persons aged j at t. β_{4j} = coefficient on wealth for individuals aged j. $\varepsilon_{\lambda jt}$ = error component which depends on both age and time.

It is necessary to aggregate across age groups. Let s_j equal the (geometric) weight of age group j in the population. For the model to be tractable, it is necessary to assume that the relative weights are constant over time. This assumption is somewhat problematic, especially given that the sample has been extended to 1976. Substituting for λ_{jt} (from (16)) in the consumption equation (14) for each age group, and summing over age groups yields the following relationship for aggregate consumption *per capita*.

$$c_t - M_t = \text{constant} + \beta_c[-\varepsilon'_{ct} - \sum_{i=0}^{J} d_i\hat{w}_{t+i} + \sum_{i=0}^{J} d_i\bar{r}_{ti} + (A_t - M_t) + \varepsilon_{\lambda t}] \tag{17}$$

where $\varepsilon'_{ct} = t \cdot \varepsilon_c + \varepsilon_{ct}$ and $\varepsilon_c, \varepsilon_{ct}, d_i, A_t, \varepsilon_{\lambda t}, \hat{w}_{t+i}$ and c_t are (respectively), weighted averages of $\varepsilon_{cj}, \varepsilon_{cjt}, d_{ji}, \beta_{4j}A_{jt}, \varepsilon_{\lambda jt}, \hat{w}_{jt+i}$ and $c_{jt}(j = 1 \cdots J)$ with the s_j's as weights. The corresponding equation for aggregate labour supply *per capita* is

$$N_t - M_t = \text{constant} + \beta_1[-\varepsilon'_{Nt} + w_t - \sum_{i=0}^{J} d_i\hat{w}_{t+i} + \sum_{i=0}^{J} d_i\bar{r}_{ti} + (A_t - M_t) + \varepsilon_{\lambda t}] \tag{18}$$

where $\varepsilon'_{Nt} = t \cdot \varepsilon_N + \varepsilon_{Nt}$ and $N_t, \varepsilon_N, \varepsilon_{Nt}, w_t, \hat{w}_{t+i}$, and $\varepsilon_{\lambda t}$ are (respectively) weighted averages of $N_{jt}, \varepsilon_{Nj}, \varepsilon_{Njt}, w_{jt}, \hat{w}_{jt+i}$, and $\varepsilon_{\lambda jt}$ with the s_j's as weights.[29] If the linear approximation to λ_{jt} is in fact valid, the equation (18) implied by the utility function (12) is very similar to equation (1). However, the additive separability assumption rules out addition of lagged labour supply to the equation, as is done in the "b" and "c" models above.

In any event, it is not at all clear that the linear approximation to λ_{jt} is justified.[30] While the above analysis is useful in showing the connection between the LR labour supply equation and the utility function and aggregation story presented, there is no need to maintain it in the empirical analysis. Instead, one may work directly with the specifications (14) and (15). This is because λ_{jt} entirely summarizes the effect on labour supply and consumption of wealth, future wages, tastes, and the real interest rate, and because λ_{jt} enters both the labour supply and consumption functions in linear form. The aggregate equations corresponding to (14) and (15) are:

$$c_t - M_t = \text{constant} + \beta_c[-\varepsilon'_{ct} + \lambda_t] \tag{19}$$

$$N_t - M_t = \text{constant} + \beta_1[-\varepsilon'_{Nt} + w_t + \lambda_t] \tag{20}$$

where λ_t is a weighted sum of the λ_{jt}'s, with the s_j's as the weights.

Solving for λ_t in terms of consumption from (19) and substituting the result in (20) yields the labour supply function (21).

$$N_t - M_t = \beta_0 + \beta_1 w_t + \beta_1\beta_c^{-1} \cdot (c_t - M_t) + \beta_1[\varepsilon'_{ct} - \varepsilon'_{Nt}]. \tag{21}$$

The constant terms have been collected in β_0. It is important to note that despite the additivity of preferences, (12) and (21) are consistent with a large short run labour supply elasticity, since β_1 can be any positive number. This is true even if preferences are restricted further to ensure that the long run labour supply curve is vertical (see below). An attractive feature of (21) is that it is less sensitive than (18) or (1) to violation of the assumption that the relative values of the s_j's do not change over time. Changes in the s_j's will affect the relationship between aggregate labour supply and expected future wages (for example) but this change will be captured by c_t. Changes in the s_j's will add trend terms to (21) in addition to the trend terms contained in ε'_{ct} and ε'_{Nt}. In the empirical work below I add a trend term to some of the equations as a control for these factors.[31]

4.2. *Econometric issues*

Several problems must be faced in estimating (21). First, the results of Section 3 suggest that it is unrealistic to maintain that the error term is serially uncorrelated. I report estimates below for the assumption that $\varepsilon_{cjt} - \varepsilon_{Njt}$ is: (i) white noise; (ii) AR(1) with the same parameter for each j; and (iii) AR(2) with the same parameters for each j. Second, w_t is endogenous in the labour supply equation, as it was in the earlier formulation. The presence of $c_t - M_t$ eliminates the severe difficulties associated with measuring w_t^* and P_t^*, but introduces other problems. The use of c_t in (21) amounts to using a proxy for λ_t in (20) that contains the measurement error ε_{ct}. The second problem is that λ_t, and therefore c_t, is a function of the taste parameter ε_{Nt} which appears in the error term of the labour supply equation.

One approach to dealing with these problems is an instrumental variables scheme. Instrumental variables for $c_t - M_t$ are suggested by (17), which expresses $c_t - M_t$ in terms of the current wage, the expected future wage, and the real rate of interest. A WWII dummy and a time trend (for possible taste changes) may also appear in (17) and are used as instrumental variables in some of the estimates below. Since c_t is a function of w_t (through λ_t), the labour demand variables are also used as instrumental variables. Since labour supply N_t is a function of the same set of variables as c_t, I use the same set of instrumental variables for w_t and c_t in estimating (21). As measures of expected future real wages and the real rate of interest I use $w_t^*|I4_t$, $(P_t^*|I4_t - P_t)$, and r_t. $w_t^*|I4_t$ and $P_t^*|I4_t$ will be correlated with the true expectations under any reasonable assumption about expectations, which is all that is required here.

The doubts mentioned earlier about the exogeneity in the labour supply equation of variables such as y_t and P_t provide one source of reservation regarding the instrumental variables procedure just outlined.[32] A second problem is due to the fact that if consumers know their lifetime taste profiles, then the choice of c_{t-1} and N_{t-1} will be influenced by the values for ε_{Nt} and ε_{ct} for the next period. Consequently, the Fair procedure will be inconsistent because c_{t-1} and N_{t-1} will be correlated with the innovation in ε_{ct} and ε_{Nt}. I have not been able to devise a way around this problem, which is a consequence of taking the error term in (21) seriously as an explicit part of the model. It is true that if consumers must predict tastes as they grow older from tastes of older people in the current period,[33] then the usual properties of the Fair procedure hold, since then c_{t-1} and N_{t-1} are uncorrelated with the innovations in ε_{ct} and ε_{Nt}.[34]

As an alternative to the instrumental variables estimates, I also use OLS and GLS to estimate (21) after providing an argument that the attendant biases in the estimate of β_1/β_c, the coefficient on $c_t - M_t$, are minor. To simplify the analysis, assume that β_1 is known and that $\beta_1 w_t$ has been subtracted from both sides of (21). This amounts to assuming that the effect of simultaneity bias on $\hat{\beta}_1$ is small or does not have a large effect on the estimate of $\beta_1 \beta_c^{-1}$. Let $\bar{N}_t = N_t - \beta_1 w_t$. The least squares estimator of β_1/β_c is

$$\widehat{\beta_1/\beta_c} = \frac{\text{cov}(c_t - M_t, \bar{N}_t - M_t)}{\text{var}(c_t - M_t)},$$

where cov ( ) is the covariance and var ( ) is the variance of their respective arguments. From (21), (19) and the formula for OLS, $(\widehat{\beta_1/\beta_c})$ is equal to β_1/β_c multiplied by the following number.

$$\frac{\text{var}(\lambda_t) - \text{cov}(\varepsilon_{ct}, \lambda_t) - \text{cov}(\lambda_t, \varepsilon_{Nt}) + \text{cov}(\varepsilon_{ct}, \varepsilon_{Nt})}{\text{var}(\lambda) - 2\,\text{cov}(\lambda, \varepsilon_{ct}) + \text{var}(\varepsilon_{ct})}. \tag{22}$$

That is, the expectation of $(\widehat{\beta_1/\beta_c})$ is equal to the true value times a scalar. The terms involving ε_{ct} enter because consumption differs from $\beta_c \lambda_t$ by $-\beta_c \varepsilon_{ct}$ (ignoring an irrelevant constant). cov $(\lambda_t, \varepsilon_{Nt})$ enters if ε_{Nt} affects the expected value of the log of the marginal

REVIEW OF ECONOMIC STUDIES

utility of income λ_t. For the perfect foresight case, one can show that λ_{jt} is increasing in both ε'_{cjt} and ε'_{Njt}. Consequently, one may infer that cov $(\varepsilon_{ct}, \lambda_t)$ and cov $(\varepsilon_{Nt}, \lambda_t) > 0$.

It is not reasonable to assume that ε_{ct} and ε_{Nt} are uncorrelated. The marginal utility of consumption in a given period is an increasing function of ε_{ct} and the marginal utility of leisure is an increasing function of ε_{Nt}. Without a detailed analysis, it is difficult to make statements about the behaviour of these taste parameters over time and their stochastic relationship. If the utility from a given amount of consumption relative to the utility from a given amount of leisure is constant over time, then they must be perfectly correlated, with cov $(\varepsilon'_{ct}, \varepsilon'_{Nt}) = $ var (ε'_{ct}). In this case, the numerator and denominator of (22) are equal, and β_1/β_c is unbiased.

Most of Section 3 above assumes implicitly that tastes do not exhibit a trend. (See however, the results with time trends in Table IVa.) If one makes the additional assumption (which I consider to be reasonable) that fluctuations in the stochastic components $\varepsilon_{ct} - \varepsilon_{Nt}$ are not large, one concludes that var (λ_t) will dominate both the numerator and denominator of (22). This is because the large growth in real wages over the sample as well as fluctuations in the value of capital are presumably the main source of variation in λ_t. There is substantial evidence in support of this view. Note first that the variance in the real wage and in consumption per capital which can be "explained" with a trend is large. The sample variances of w_t and $c_t - M_t$ are (0.130) and (0.063) respectively for 1930–1976. A trend explains 99.4 and 95.2% of the variance of these series. In contrast, labour supply *per capita* is not trend dominated. The variance of $N_t - M_t$ is only (0.0086), of which only 2.3% is explained by a trend. The simplest interpretation of these basic facts is that the long run labour supply curve is approximately vertical. In terms of the present model, the growth of wages over time depresses λ_t due to decreasing marginal utility from the consumption of both leisure and goods. Since β_c is negative, consumption *per capita* rises over time (see (19)). Since both λ_t and w_t enter that labour supply equation with the same (positive) sign, the tendency of labour supply to increase with the secular rise of w_t is offset by the fall of λ_t associated with rising expectations about real wages. As noted earlier, there is a large body of evidence from cross-section micro data the labour supply is relatively insensitive to shifts in the lifetime wage profile.

Finally, note that Altonji (1981a) considers and tentatively rejects an alternative explanation of the behaviour of consumption, labour supply, and real wages in which opposite trends in ε_{ct} and ε_{Nt} are held to counteract the effect of w_t on λ_t, and to explain the movements in $c_t - M_t$ and $N_t - M_t$.[35] In summary, there is reason to believe that the bias in estimating β_1/β_c in (21) via least squares is small. Since the preceding argument is stylized and the complication associated with the presence of w_t and the effects of an adjustment for serial correlation have not been considered, it is best to employ both the least squares procedures and the instrumental variables procedure discussed earlier. Given the possibility that a trend is present in tastes over the sample, I estimate the labour supply equation both with and without a trend.

4.3. Results

Table VI reports estimates of several versions of (21), in which $N_t - M_t$ is a function of a constant, w_t, and $c_t - M_t$. Column 1 reports the OLS estimate of the basic model, which excludes a WWII dummy and a trend. Columns 4 and 7 report estimates of the same equation corrected for first order serial correlation and second order serial correlation (respectively). All of the estimates in Table VI are for the sample 1931 to 1976. c_t is the log of real expenditures on non-durables.[36] The estimates in 1, 4, and 7 are similar qualitatively. The estimate of β_1 from column 7 is -0.623. This result is somewhat smaller than but basically comparable to the estimates reported in the previous chapter. It contradicts the intertemporal substitution theory and is highly significant. The estimate of β_1/β_c is 0.872. This is also of wrong sign (and highly significant), since $\hat{\beta}_c$ should be

TABLE VI

Labour supply estimates using consumption to proxy the expected marginal utility of income

Sample: 1931–1976. Dependent variable: $N_t - M_t$. Consumption data: $c_t = $ log of expenditures on consumer non-durables

Explanatory variables	OLS			GLS, 1st-order serial correl.				GLS, 2nd-order serial correl.		Instrumental variables 1st-order serial correlation			Instrumental variables 2nd-order serial correlation		
Column No.	1	2	3	4	5	6	7	8	9	10	11	12	13	14	15
Constant	15·91[a] (18·6)	14·15[a] (7·50)	40·31[a] (4·09)	14·06[a] (11·22)	14·06[a] (18·1)	25·39[b] (2·04)	14·62[b] (1·54)	14·62[a] (20·4)	−5·94[a] (0·54)	19·81[a] (9·11)	16·01[a] (15·8)	33·94[a] (2·07)	17·78[a] (13·6)	16·22[a] (18·8)	7·68 (0·51)
w_t	−0·793[a] (7·08)	−0·567[a] (7·50)	−0·052 (0·25)	−0·55[a] (3·40)	−0·556[a] (5·49)	−0·333 (1·24)	−0·623[a] (5·01)	−0·626[a] (6·68)	−1·015[a] (4·19)	−1·306[a] (4·60)	−0·811[a] (6·13)	−0·410 (1·12)	−1·039[a] (6·04)	−0·836[a] (7·39)	−1·000[a] (3·13)
$c_t - M_t$	1·134[a] (7·03)	0·864[a] (8·09)	0·966[a] (9·03)	0·814[a] (3·63)	0·852[a] (5·92)	0·893[a] (6·26)	0·872[a] (4·83)	0·915[a] (6·78)	0·810[a] (5·51)	1·93[a] (4·74)	1·234[a] (6·50)	1·235[a] (7·05)	1·513[a] (5·82)	1·239[a] (7·39)	1·202[a] (6·82)
D_t	0·172[a] (8·09)	0·172[a] (8·09)	0·172[a] (8·74)		0·151[a] (6·135)	0·153[a] (6·31)		0·096[a] (4·63)	0·086[a] (4·25)		0·140[a] (5·15)	0·141[a] (5·37)		0·089[a] (4·11)	0·087[a] (4·03)
Time			−0·016[b] (2·66)			−0·007 (0·91)			0·012[b] (1·87)			−0·011 (1·11)			0·005 (0·57)
Residual lagged once				0·747[a] (7·62)	0·517[a] (4·10)	0·461[a] (3·53)	1·202	0·981	1·141	0·723[a] (7·09)	0·569[a] (4·69)	0·479[a] (3·70)	1·123	0·982	1·032
Residual lagged twice							−0·619	−0·543	−0·627				−0·628	−0·590	−0·621
R^2	0·592	0·842	0·866	0·805	0·887	0·888	0·881	0·915	0·919	0·693	0·868	0·873	0·854	0·904	0·908
D.W.	0·578	0·998	1·256	1·047	1·534	1·617	2·014	1·945	1·871	1·19	1·50	1·61	2·152	2·04	2·02
SE	0·064	0·041	0·038	0·044	0·034	0·035	0·035	0·030	0·029	0·056	0·038	0·037	0·039	0·032	0·031
$\ln(L)$	62·4	84·3	87·9	79·5	91·9	92·2	90·7	98·4	99·7	68·9	88·4	89·2	87·1	96·8	97·8

Note:
[a]–[c] See Table II.

negative and β_1 should be positive. β_1/β_c does not correspond directly to $-\beta_2$, the coefficient on w_t^* in the labour supply equation (1). To investigate this coefficient, assume that the labour supply does not respond to permanent wage changes. Under this reasonable assumption, the budget constraint implies that consumption must rise in proportion to a permanent increase in the real wage, with $\Delta c_t = \Delta w_t$ given that the variables are in log form. One may use this fact and (21) to show that $\beta_1/\beta_c = -\beta_1$ if the long run labour supply curve is vertical. Thus the coefficients on w_t and c_t should be approximately equal and opposite in sign. The estimates support this, but both coefficients have the wrong sign. The coefficient on c_t is consistent with many of the estimates of β_2 reported in Section 3.

Addition of the WWII variable in columns 2, 5, and 8 does not have much effect on the coefficients of w_t and c_t. Columns 3, 6, and 9 report estimates of the labour supply equation with a time trend as well as a WWII dummy added. The coefficient on c_t agrees closely with the estimates that have already been mentioned. The coefficient on w_t has the wrong sign for all three estimation methods, but the OLS estimate is small and insignificant (-0.051). On the other hand, the GLS estimate in column 9 is -1.02 and significant. Thus, the addition of a time trend does not make a large difference in the results, given that most of the weight should be placed on the GLS estimates. (Note the Durbin Watsons.)

Columns 10–12 and columns 13–15 present instrumental variables estimates of the labour supply equation with corrections for first order and second order serial correlation (respectively). As can be seen, the results are qualitatively similar to the GLS estimates. The instrumental variables estimates of the coefficients on w_t and $c_t - M_t$ are generally a bit larger in absolute value and have larger t-statistics than their GLS counterparts.

In summary, the OLS, GLS, and instrumental variables estimates are remarkably consistent with the estimates of the labour supply equation in Section 3. They do not support the intertemporal substitution theory. These basic findings are not altered by use of consumption expenditures on non-durables net of clothing and shoes. (See Altonji (1981a).) Furthermore, OLS, GLS, and instrumental variables estimates for the 1948–1976 sample period are basically consistent with those for the entire sample. The coefficients on w_t and $c_t - M_t$ are of wrong sign, highly significant, and typically a bit larger in absolute value than the corresponding estimates for the entire sample.[37]

Finally, I tried adding the first lag of the right hand side variables plus two lags of $N_t - M_t$ as an alternative to the assumptions of first and second order serial correlation. This specification is inconsistent with the utility function (12), and the parameters do not have an interpretation in terms of the labour supply-consumption framework of this section. But it does provide an indication of whether the dynamic specifications used in Table VI play a critical role in determining the coefficients on w_t and $c_t - M_t$. Briefly, in the postwar sample the more general lag structure has very little effect on the fit of the equation or on the coefficients of w_t and $c_t - M_t$. In the 1931–1976 sample, the fit is similar to that of the models with second order serial correlation. When the WWII dummy is in the equation, the coefficient on w_t ranges between -0.25 and -0.5 depending on whether a trend is included and on the estimation method. In some cases, the t-statistic is not significant. The coefficient on $c_t - M_t$ falls to 0.7 or 0.8 and remains significant. Thus, the coefficient values are somewhat sensitive to the dynamic specification, but the signs are not.

5. DISCUSSION AND CONCLUSIONS

This section begins with a concise summary of the empirical results and possible explanations for them in terms of alternative views of labour market fluctuations. I then discuss a number of limitations of the study and provide a brief survey of other evidence. The paper closes with a discussion of alternative models of the labour market that combine intertemporal substitution in labour supply with an implicit contracts story about wage adjustment.

Summary of the results

No attempt will be made here to restate in detail the results of Sections 3 and 4. The main findings are the following.

(1) The estimates of β_1, the temporary labour supply elasticity, are concentrated between -0.65 and -1.2 in both Sections 3 and 4. They are statistically significant in many instances.

(2) The estimates of β_2 are concentrated between -0.7 and -1.7 and are statistically significant in many instances.

(3) The estimates of β_3, the coefficient on $P_t^* - P_t$ in Section 3, are typically of wrong sign and are sometimes statistically significant. They centre around 0.3.

(4) The nominal interest rate typically has the wrong sign in the labour supply equation. The estimates from "c" models cluster around -0.3 and are usually significant at the 5% or at the 10% level. In the "b" models the estimates are closer to 0.

(5) The results for the price shocks are mixed. However, the money shocks enter the labour supply equation with the correct sign and are often significant.

(6) $g_1\hat{\beta}_1$, the coefficient of $(w_t^* - w_t)$ in the unemployment equation is almost always of wrong sign and is often statistically significant. A typical estimate is -0.7.

(7) The expected inflation rate has a small and inconsistent effect on unemployment. In the "a" models it is usually very near 0 and insignificant. In the "b" and "c" models $P_t^* - P_t$ has the wrong sign and is significant with a coefficient of -0.2.

(8) The results do not support a role for r_t in the unemployment equation that is in accordance with the intertemporal substitution theory. The coefficients are typically small and insignificant.

(9) Both the price and money shocks enter the unemployment equation with the correct sign. They are usually significant.

(10) The postwar results in both Sections 3 and 4 are basically consistent with the results for the entire sample. If anything, the estimates of β_1 and β_2 are larger in absolute value during the postwar period and remain of wrong sign.

It should be kept in mind that this summary hides considerable variation in the point estimates for the many different experiments reported here or in Altonji (1981a). In several instances the coefficient on w_t has the right sign in the labour supply or the unemployment equation. Nevertheless, the results are basically negative.

As mentioned earlier, the parameter estimates are inconsistent if the labour market is not in equilibrium. One should not be surprised at the negative results if fluctuations in employment and unemployment due to intertemporal substitution are not important and especially if the market clearing assumption is false. But it would be desirable to have a detailed alternative model with which the signs of the various coefficient estimates can be interpreted. I do not provide such a model, but the results based on use of consumption to proxy expectations may be explained if one believes the following.

(i) Intertemporal substitution is of some importance but is not dominant in short term labour market fluctuations. β_1, β_2, and β_3 have the signs assumed by LR but are modest in absolute value.

(ii) Labour demand fluctuates considerably. The underlying sources of the fluctuations are swings in aggregate demand associated with monetary and fiscal policy and changes in investment and consumption resulting from shifts in expectations about the future. Part of the linkage between demand for output and demand for labour is through induced changes in the price level relative to nominal wage levels. Part of the linkage is a direct response under implicit contracts to meet demand for output at pre-set prices. Labour demand also fluctuates in response to supply shocks (e.g. oil and food supply disturbances).

(iii) The labour market does not clear continuously. Short term fluctuations in employment and unemployment are dominated by shifts in labour demand rather than shifts in the labour supply-labour demand equilibrium.

It should be kept in mind that since the dependent variable in the labour supply equation is employment, a disequilibrium component enters the equation as an unobserved error if the labour market does not clear. The positive coefficient on consumption is explained by two factors. First, the response of consumption demand to changes in expectations about future income shifts the labour demand schedule (see ii), which alters the disequilibrium component in the labour supply equation. Furthermore, constraints on finding work in the labour market may affect consumption demand if they are expected to last for several periods (and thus alter permanent income) or if workers are liquidity constrained. Both factors produce a positive relationship between consumption and labour demand, a negative relationship between consumption and the disequilibrium component, and a positive bias on the consumption coefficient in the labour supply equation.

One might expect the bias in the consumption coefficient to produce an offsetting bias in the wage coefficient. This is because $c_t - M_t$ and w_t are trend dominated but $N_t - M_t$ is not. The positive bias in the consumption coefficient would induce an offsetting negative bias in the coefficient on w_t. Unfortunately, the fact that the coefficient on w_t does not rise in all cases when a trend is added to the model indicates that this is not a full explanation. However, when product demand and productivity are controlled for, the real wage is negatively correlated with labour demand, and consequently, with the disequilibrium component in the labour supply equation. Consumption will be related to product demand, and a trend will control for shifts in productivity or labour quality. Thus, the negative sign on w_t is to be expected even in the specifications of the labour supply equation that contain a time trend. If employment fluctuations are dominated by changes in labour demand, the estimates of (21) trace out the marginal productivity condition rather than the labour supply equation.

The implications of disequilibrium in the labour market for the estimates based on use of the forecasting model to measure w_t^* and P_t^* are less clear. None of the variables in (1) and (6) is likely to be as strongly related to product demand as consumption, although w_t^* should be related to consumption demand. Also, reverse causality from disequilibrium to wages, prices, and interest rates may be weaker than from disequilibrium to consumption demand. Thus it is more difficult to interpret the estimated labour supply and unemployment equations as a reflection of the importance of labour demand. Given the lack of movement in w_t relative to w_t^*, one might expect the coefficients of these variables to be small and poorly determined, but not necessarily of incorrect sign. For the "a" models, this is not too far from the truth, especially for the unemployment equation. The coefficients on $P_t^* - P_t$ and r_t are small and variable in sign in the unemployment equation, and $P_t^* - P_t$ is small and somewhat variable in sign in the labour supply equation. With regard to a labour demand interpretation, it is worth mentioning that movements in r_t, given $P_t^* - P_t$ may reflect changes in monetary policy and thus reflect money induced fluctuations in aggregate demand. Under these circumstances, r_t has a negative partial correlation with aggregate demand and has a negative bias in the "labour supply" equation if the labour market does not clear. On the other hand, the positive elasticity of the demand for real balances with respect to income tends to produce a bias in the opposite direction. Note that the positive sign on the money disturbance in the equation for $N_t - M_t$ and the negative sign in the unemployment equation are also consistent with (ii) and (iii) above. Finally, one would expect w_t to be correlated with disequilibrium, providing a source of negative bias in its coefficient. However, this effect does not dominate in the adaptive expectations specification and has less force when product demand and productivity are not controlled for. Altonji (1981a) attributes the RE results to a complicated relationship between shifts in product demand, price changes, and real wage changes, but the discussion is highly speculative. A full understanding of the results for the various specifications requires a full scale model of the labour market and of the relationship between shifts in product demand, price changes, and real wage changes.

Limitations of the analysis

The results are subject to a number of qualifications. Several have already been mentioned, including the possibility that some of the instrumental variables are correlated with the random disturbance in the labour supply equation, and problems with measurement of expectations. In view of the results and discussion surrounding the perfect foresight case and the extent to which the estimates using consumption in the labour supply equation coincide with those in Section 3, I do not believe that mismeasurement of expectations explains the estimates in Section 3. Measurement error in the various data series used is of course a possibility (as in all econometric work). A related possibility is that changes in the skill composition of the labour force over the business cycle may induce a weak negative relationship between manhours and the aggregate wage index. This does not explain the sign on w_t^*, and reference should also be made to the results in Altonji and Ashenfelter for U.S. and U.K. postwar quarterly data, which use less aggregative wage variables.

Recent papers by Hall (1980a) and Barro (1981a) have stressed variation in the real interest rate as a source of variation in the current wage relative to the expected discounted future wage. As noted in footnote 10, the Moody's *Aaa* rate may not be entirely appropriate as a nominal interest rate. Additional estimates should be performed with other interest rate variables, but I doubt if the results will change. In postwar data (1959–1971) Fama (1975) cannot reject the hypothesis that the expected real interest rate on 6 month treasury bills is constant over the sample period. His conclusions are questioned in several papers in the June 1977 *American Economic Review*. In a recent paper Mishkin (1981) presents evidence for several different sample periods and concludes that the expected real interest rate does vary somewhat, although the period Fama examined was fairly quiet. Barro (1981b) presents evidence on the effects of monetary and fiscal policy on real interest rates. At the present time, however, there is little to support the view that real rate is highly variable over the typical business cycle, let alone that it has a strong effect on labour supply. My view is that the real rate and credit availability influence the labour market primarily by shifting product demand in industries such as durable manufacturing, investment goods, and housing, which in turn influences labour demand in these sectors and others.

Taxes are ignored in the empirical work, although variations in tax rates are potentially another source of movement in the intertemporal price of labour. Unfortunately, the addition of tax rates to the model requires a model of expectations of future tax rates; this will be difficult to formulate. Altonji (1981a) argues that a careful treatment of taxes is unlikely to change the results of this paper. To the extent that taxes are progressive, the labour supply response to a temporary wage change is reduced. This is because the labour supply response as well as the wage change raise labour income, which raises the marginal tax rate, offsetting the initial effect of the wage increase on the after tax wage.[38] In addition to this issue, the behaviour of tax rates during the sample period is such that incorporation of tax rates into the model is likely to make the results less rather than more favourable to the intertemporal substitution hypothesis.[39]

138

Finally, one should keep in mind that the results in Section 3 are specific to the log-linear forms used. Perhaps more importantly, the analysis in Section 4 is based on a particular utility function that is additively separable both over time and in the consumption and labour supply arguments for a given period. Work with more general preference structures is needed.[40]

A comparison with other evidence

The findings in this paper are consistent with most of what little aggregate time series evidence is available on the intertemporal substitution hypothesis. Sargent (1973) includes a wage and price surprise in an unemployment equation, with little success. The most closely related study is Altonji and Ashenfelter (1980). We estimate the LR unemployment function (but exclude the real interest rate term) using a univariate time series model to measure expectations about the real wage. We report results for 1929–1976 using the annual time series data prepared for the present paper. We also report results for postwar quarterly U.S. and U.K. data. We find for a variety of specifications that $w_t^* - w_t$ is either insignificantly related to fluctuations in unemployment or has the wrong sign.

Altonji (1981b) tests the market equilibrium assumption in the LR model. In both the RE case and in the adaptive expectations case, there is evidence that the labour market is in disequilibrium. This finding supports the argument that biases in the parameter estimates due to the presence of disequilibrium are responsible for the poor performance of the model.

Hall (1980a) does provide some support for the intertemporal substitution model with RE. He uses detrended data on employee hours and wages that are basically comparable to that used in the present paper. He estimates

$$\exp(N_t) = 7.0 + 0.66(w_t + \bar{r}_{t,1}) \qquad DW = 1.59.$$
$$(1.39) \ (2.36)$$

Here, $\bar{r}_{t,1}$ is the real interest rate 1 year ahead (quarterly data is used) based on the GNP deflator and the rate on one-year commercial paper. He uses the coefficient on $(w_t + \bar{r}_{t,1})$ to calculate on implied elasticity of labour supply with respect to the real wage equal to 0.46. Altonji (1981a) discusses Hall's methods and concludes that his findings are reconcilable with the results reported in this paper and the other aggregate time series evidence. The main point to be made is that since Hall's equation excludes expected future wage rates, the coefficient on $(w_t + \bar{r}_{t,1})$ does not represent the short run labour supply elasticity.

Space does not permit a detailed review of the evidence from microdata studies of intertemporal labour supply. Hall informally summarizes the results from the U.S. negative income tax experiments. These were limited in duration and consequently may be interpreted to measure responses to temporary changes in after tax wages and non-labour income. He also mentions the work of Heckman and MaCurdy (1980) and MaCurdy (1981), who use Michigan Income Dynamics panel data. He concludes that the evidence from the negative income tax experiments suggests a temporary wage elasticity of 0.26 for men and 0.66 for women, for an overall elasticity of 0.40. My reading of the microdata evidence is that the temporary wage elasticity is weakly positive for men and that the possibility that it is large for married women (near 1.0) cannot be ruled out at this time. An aggregate temporary labour supply elasticity in the wide range from 0.1 to 0.6 is consistent with the available evidence.[41]

Concluding remarks

In conclusion, the results of this essay and much of the other evidence cited raise serious doubts about the empirical viability of the intertemporal substitution-market equilibrium view of the labour market. Disequilibrium and the absence of significant short term movements in real wages are suggested as partial explanations for the poor performance of the model. The present study has many limitations, and a variety of avenues for further research should be explored, some of which were mentioned above. Studies of the model using quarterly data, disaggregated by industry and region, and with alternative functional forms would be particularly helpful. Altonji and Ashenfelter's study of the amount of variability in the intertemporal price of leisure should be extended to include interest rates and tax rate changes. Finally, studies of intertemporal labour supply functions using microdata deserve high priority. This is so because an understanding of short run labour supply behaviour is crucial to any model of aggregate supply, and the aggregate data reveals little about such behaviour if the labour market does not clear.

While future research may vindicate the pure intertemporal substitution approach, I believe that replacing the assumption that the wage clears the labour market with an implicit contracts model of wage determination is a more fruitful line of research. One possibility is to stick with a labour supply, labour demand, market clearing framework while assuming that the "wage" that clears the market is not the observed "accounting" wage but rather is a shadow wage. Altonji (1981a) modifies the LR model along these lines. It does not provide a straightforward explanation for the results of this paper.[42] This approach deserves serious investigation, but a variety of factors interfere with the operation of implicit contracts along lines which mimic an auction market. For example, informational asymmetries and enforcement problems undermine arrangements in which firms and workers cooperatively determine employment so that marginal product and the marginal utility of leisure are always equal.[43] My view is that intertemporal substitution, implicit contracts, and disequilibrium all play a role in labour market fluctuations.

An earlier draft of this paper was circulated as Discussion paper No. 107, Dept. of Economics, Columbia University. It is based heavily on Essay 1 of Altonji (1981a). I owe special thanks to my thesis committee, Orley Ashenfelter, Alan Blinder, and James Brown, for their help throughout. I also received valuable comments from Gregory Chow, Angus Deaton, Mark Gersovitz, Stephen Goldfeld, Robert Gordon, Stephen Kealhofer, Christopher Pissarides, Robert Porter, Julio Rotemberg, two anonomous referees, and seminar participants at several universities. I am solely responsible for any remaining errors. My research was supported in part by a grant from the Sloan Foundation to the Department of Economics at Princeton University.

NOTES

1. The paper has also been important in labour economics as a stimulant to research on labour supply and unemployment in a life cycle context, as well as on the nature of unemployment. The best example of the former is the recent work of Heckman and MaCurdy (1980) and MaCurdy (1981) but see also the research on the negative income tax data cited below, and Becker and Ghez (1975). See LR and Heckman and MaCurdy (1980) for references pre-dating LR.

2. See Altonji and Ashenfelter (1980) and Hall (1980a). Altonji (1981b) tests LR's assumption that employment and unemployment fluctuations are an equilibrium phenomenon but is not directly concerned with the parameters of their model. Reference should be made to the comments of Rees (1970), (1972) (and to LR (1972)). Rees is highly critical of LR's theory of unemployment fluctuations, especially for the 1930s. LR appear to admit that the model does not explain the high unemployment rates of the mid to late 30s, but see Darby (1976) and Kesselman and Savin (1978). Hedrick (1973) offers an alternative interpretation of LR's estimates in terms of a Mortenson (1970) type search framework. His results for the extended sample (to 1970) and for the postwar period generally support those of LR. See also Seater (1978).

3. For a detailed discussion of the model and its relationship to the literature, see LR (1970). See also the references in footnote 2 above and the analysis in Section 4, in which the labour supply equation is derived as an approximation from a specific utility function.

4. See LR (1970), pp. 264–266.

5. They include lagged values of Q_t, N_t, and y_t to account for the costs of adjusting labour input. See *Ibid*, pp. 270–271. It would be desirable to explicitly incorporate future expectations about wages, product demand, and worker quality and derive a marginal productivity condition more in keeping with the rational expectations assumption. Sargent (1978) is an important step in this direction. However, his failure to include a product demand variable is a serious drawback for present purposes. As it turns out, the marginal productivity condition performs very well, and it is doubtful that a more sophisticated formulation would have much effect on the other equations in the model, which are of principal interest here.

6. See *Ibid*, pp. 272–279. They comment, "These [LR's] observations suggest strongly that the labour force as measured by the employment survey consists of those who are employed plus those who are unemployed but would accept work at what they regard as their normal wage rates (or, equivalently, their normal occupation)." (p. 273). Essentially the same view is implicit in the highly aggregative equilibrium macro models of Sargent and Wallace (1975) and Barro (1976). It is explicit in Brunner *et al.*, who state, "When the current wage rate is below the rate believed to be permanent, part of the labour force finds it profitable to abstain from accepting employment. These workers appear in the statistics as unemployed until the actual and the permanent real wage rates are equal. Within the context of the model, unemployment is defined as the difference between labour supply when $w_t = w_t^*$ [my notation] and labour supply when actual and permanent wages differ."

7. LR use a slightly different base level for normal labour supply and ignore the nominal interest rate r_t. Their definition leads to (6) with $g_1\beta_1(r_t - (P_t^* - P_t))$ replaced by $-g_1\beta_3(P_t^* - P_t)$. r_t is excluded from some of the specifications used in the empirical work below. One may argue that normal labour supply should be defined at the "normal" real interest rate. If this is a constant, then (6) is unchanged except that the coefficient on $[r_t - (P_t^* - P_t)]$ becomes $-g_1\beta_3$. Finally, normal labour supply may depend on a short moving average of the labour supply error ε_{2t} rather than on ε_{2t} only. In this case, the disturbance in the unemployment equation is a composite error that will depend in part on short term movements in ε_{2t}.

8. The numbers without parentheses in the table below are the marginal significance levels of F-tests of whether the column variables are not Granger caused by the row variables. They are based on the F ratio to test for the significance of 4 lags of the row variable in a regression of the column variable against a trend and 4 lags of the column variable. See Sargent (1979) for a detailed discussion and for references to the econometric literature. The hypothesis that w_t does not cause P_t is accepted at the 5% level but not at the 10% level. A test based on 3 lags of each variable fails to reject no causality from w_t to P_t at the 52% level. There is evidence that N_t is not exogenous with respect to P_t. Also, the test indicates that w_t is not exogenous with respect to ml_t. ml_t is not included in the structural equations but appears as an exogenous variable in the forecasting models of the exogenous variables used below.

Note that the result could be due to the effect of ml_t on variables affecting w_t. In any case, these tests do not rule out a contemporaneous relationship between the variables and so do not rule out simultaneity. As a stronger check, the numbers in parentheses are the marginal significance levels of tests of the null hypothesis that the *current* value and the first four lags of the row variable have 0 coefficients when added to a regression of the column variable on its first 4 lags and a trend. The N_t's are not significant in the equations for w_t and r_t. Rejection of the null hypothesis is likely to result simply from presence of the row variables in the structural equation for N_t and does not contradict the assumption that they are predetermined in that equation. On the other hand, it is possible that w_t has a non zero coefficient and is endogenous in a structural equation such as (1) even though current and lagged N_t's do not play a role in the bivariate representation of w_t, but it is improbable that the various biases would work themselves out in this way.

It should be noted that Sargent (1978) and Neftci (1978) fail to reject no causality from employment to wages. Geary and Kennan (1982) fail to reject no causality from wages to employment as well as from employment to wages. See also Ashenfelter and Card (1982), who examine the relationship among nominal wages, prices, and employment.

	Column Variables				
Row Variables	P_t	r_t	y_t	w_t	ml_t
w_t	0·0888	0·4585	0·4557	—	0·0217
	(0·0059)	(0·5961)	(0·1075)		(0·0406)
N_t	0·0310	0·9723	0·9473	0·2476	0·2862
	(0·0470)	(0·9565)	(0·0000)	(0·3056)	(0·0000)

9. Other references include Hansen and Sargent (1980), Chow (1979), Taylor (1979), and Wallis (1980). Wallis (pp. 64–66) suggests estimating the models for the exogenous variables separately, generating the forecasts of exogenous variables, and then using these forecasts to estimate the labour market equations as a system. The restrictions from the rational expectations solution to the model should be imposed on the way in which the forecasts enter the model through their effects on w_t^*. Note that these effects on w_t^* occur partially through P_t^*. My approach differs from this in that I do not impose the restrictions on the relationship between w_t^* and the exogenous variables. McCallum's (1976) instrumental variables approach was not used, in part because it is inconsistent in the presence of autocorrelated errors. See Flood and Garber (1980).

10. Variations in the term structure of interest rates will cause the i period interest rate factor to vary around the product of i and a long term annual rate such as Moody's *Aaa*. In practice, however, there is sufficient collinearity between interest rates for different lengths of time that I doubt if this makes much difference.

11. LR's use of U_t is based upon the approximation that $N_t^* - N_t \approx [\exp{(N_t^*)} - \exp{(N_t)}]/\exp{(N_t^*)}$. This approximation is accurate only for small values of $[\exp{(N_t^*)} - \exp{(N_t)}]/\exp{(N_t^*)}$ and is substantially in error for the large unemployment rates of the Great Depression. Under the assumption (see LR, pp. 272–273 and the discussion above) that the measured labour force corresponds roughly to the normal labour force and the number employed to actual labour supply, it is easy to show that $-\ln{(1 - U_t)}$ corresponds roughly to $N_t^* - N_t$.

12. The explicit definitions and sources of the variables are as follows. For 1929–1973, employment is the product of number of persons engaged in production [U.S. Dept. of Commerce, (1967), pp. 110–114; (1969), p. 37; (1971), p. 37; (1974), p. 37] and a series on annual hours per worker discussed in detail in Altonji (1981a), p. 126. The series for number of persons engaged was discontinued after 1973. Consequently, for 1974–1976 employment is the generalized least squares prediction based upon a log-linear regression of the employment series for 1948–1973 on a constant and on hours worked by persons engaged in production [U.S. Department of Commerce (1976), pp. 216–217; (1977), p. 48], with a correction for first order serial correlation. The real wage rate equals compensation of employees (U.S. Department of Commerce (1976), pp. 194–197 and (1977), p. 46) divided by the product of full time equivalent employees [U.S. Department of Commerce (1976), pp. 206–209 and (1977), p. 47], the GNP implicit price deflator [U.S. Department of Commerce (1976), pp. 264–265 and (1977), p. 349] and the estimates of annual hours per worker discussed above. Values of the real wage for 1927–1928 are needed to generate the values of w_t^* for 1929 and 1930. They were obtained by joining Lewis' data (1963) p. 202 for these years to the data for 1929–1976 with a ratio link in 1929. Real output is from U.S. Department of Commerce (1976), pp. 2, 7, 327 and (1977), p. 18. Moody's Aaa rate is from U.S. Department of Commerce (1976), p. 1003 and (1978), p. 105. The unemployment rate is from Lebergott (1964) and Council of Economic Advisors (1979), p. 217. The money supply (currency plus demand deposits) which is used in the forecasting equations below, is from U.S. Department of Commerce (1976), p. 992. Data for 1971–1976 is aggregated from the monthly data in various issues of the *Federal Reserve Bulletin*. The age-sex corrected population variable is from LR, p. 286 for 1929–1965. Values for 1966–1976 were computed according to the formula in LR (p. 279, footnote 28) from the data cited therein and the population data for 1966–1976 for males and females aged 14–20, 20–65, and 65 and over which is reported in Bureau of the Census (1974) (series p-25, No. 519) and (1977), p. 25 No. 643. To generate forecasts for 1929 and 1930, values of M_t for 1927 and 1928 are required. These were obtained by a linear extrapolation.

13. For more details, see Altonji (1981a), pp. 131–132.

14. The weights are normalized to sum to 1. The decay parameter is set to 0·8138. The structure and rate of decay chosen for the weights is arbitrary. The assumption is favourable to the equilibrium hypothesis in that it is consistent with a large degree of intertemporal substitutability in the consumption of leisure. Experimentation with different rates of decay made little difference. Indeed, the wage series is so trend dominated and the innovations in the series are so persistent that the wage forecasts for succeeding years are highly collinear. Altonji (1981a), p. 107, documents that indices based on different weighting schemes ranging from a simple average of $\hat{w}_{t+1}$ and $\hat{w}_{t+2}$ to a simple average of the forecasts for the first 8 periods are highly correlated with the index chosen. In summary, the particular forecast weights chosen should have little effect on the results. There is obviously little hope of estimating the weights in the 1930–1976 sample. The scalar used to generate r_t from Moody's Aaa rate, $\sum_{i=1}^{k} id_i$, is equal to 3·465.

15. This statement requires the assumption that agents know (or act as if they know) the true model. If, instead, agents must estimate the forecasting equations using the procedure used in this paper, it would be appropriate to re-estimate the forecasting equations each period using only current and past observations. This method, which is used by Sheffrin (1979), is not feasible here due to data limitations.

16. Due to multicollinearity, it is not always possible to use as instrumental variables all of the variables in the reduced form for w_t along with lagged values of the endogenous variables and the current and lagged values of the predetermined variables in the particular labour supply equation. $(y_t - y_{t-1})$ and $(Q_{t-1} + N_{t-1} - y_{t-1})$, which appear only in the marginal productivity condition, were deleted from the instrumental variables list used to estimate the labour supply and unemployment equations. This does not affect the consistency of the estimates. Results similar to those in the tables below were obtained in instances in which these variables were included in the instrumental variables list. Since w_t is determined between (1) and (2), I used $N_{t-1} - M_{t-1}$ as an instrument in the unemployment equation rather than $-\ln{(1 - U_{t-1})}$. In practice this makes little difference.

17. See Fair (1970). The asymptotic properties of this estimator are not affected by the fact that consistent estimates of w_t^* and P_t^* are used rather than the (unobserved) true values. Altonji (1981a), pp. 51–55, reports estimates of the model using FIML conditional on the estimates of w_t^* and P_t^* obtained from the forecasting equations. The conditional FIML estimates of the labour supply and unemployment equations are very poor and are omitted here. I offer an explanation for these results in terms of an unobserved disequilibrium component which enters both the labour supply and unemployment equations and has a strong impact on the system estimator. In any case the conditional FIML estimates support the conclusion that simultaneous estimation of the labour market equations and the equations for the exogenous variables is not practical.

18. The coefficients on the shocks depend upon the θ's, the parameters of the multivariate and univariate time series models, β_1, β_2, and β_3, and the discount weights. The θ's depend upon the covariance structure of the shocks and "noise". Under very strong assumptions about the covariance structure one can provide

an explicit story about the coefficients on the various shocks by extending Lucas' (1973) framework to the multivariate case. However, the assumptions required are too unreasonable to be worth pursuing here. Note that one conceivably could add "surprises" in the other exogenous variables to the model.

19. Estimation using $w_t^*|I4_t$, which is pre-determined, as an instrument for $w_t^*|I1_t$ is inconsistent in models with serial correlation for the reason discussed in Flood and Garber (1980). This instrumental variables procedure is consistent in the case of the "b" models discussed below, which have serially uncorrelated errors. In practice, use of this alternative estimator made little difference.

20. Since the labour supply equation is treated as a log-linear approximation and is not justified in terms of a preference structure, it is sensible to be open minded about the dynamic specification, especially since mispecified dynamics might result in biases in the parameter estimates. In the spirit of Sargan (1964), I have estimated models 2, 3 and 6 with the first lag of all the right side variables added along with two lags of the dependent variable. This model nests the "a", "b", and "c" specifications. In most cases it does not fit the data as well as the "b" and "c" models, and I omit the results to save space.

21. Inspection of (1) and (6) indicates that the coefficient on $P_t^* - P_t$ and r_t should be equal and opposite in sign in both the labour supply and the unemployment equation. I have not imposed this, in part because of the uncertainty about the consistency of the index for P_t^* and r_t. See footnote 10.

22. See Altonji (1981a). The adaptive expectations specification of the labour supply equation is

$$N_t - M_t = [\beta_0\lambda - \lambda'\beta_2 - \lambda''\beta_3] + (\beta_1 - \lambda\beta_2)w_t - (1 - \lambda)\beta_1 w_{t-1}$$
$$+ (1 - \lambda)\beta_3(P_t - P_{t-1}) + (1 - \lambda)(N_{t-1} - M_{t-1}) + \beta_3 r_t$$
$$- \beta_3(1 - \lambda)r_{t-1} - \beta_4(a_t - M_t) + \beta_4(1 - \lambda)(a_{t-1} - M_{t-1}) + u_{2t}. \quad (10)$$

Here λ is the weight given to w_t and P_t in w_t^* and P_t^* (respectively). The coefficients on the wage variables have a rational expectations interpretation (1) if the real wage is a random walk with drift, (2) people use the random walk model to form expectations, and (3) w_t is not part of the information set used in forming w_t^*. In this case, $(w_t - w_{t-1})$ is proportional to $(w_t - w_t^*)$, and the adaptive results, at least for the wage variables, may be construed as providing some support for the LR model with rational expectations. I do not pursue this, however, because there are many difficulties with such an interpretation of the estimates of (10), not the least of which is that an instrument is used in place of w_t in estimation. For more details, see Altonji (1981a), pp. 45–46.

23. The simple correlations of the perfect foresight value for w_t^* (based on the actual future wage rates and the index weights used to compute w_t^* for the various information sets) with w_t and a trend are 0·9990 and 0·9969 respectively. (The correlation of the perfect foresight index with $w_t^*|I3_t$ is 0·9995.) The within sample mean standard error of the forecast index w_t^* when generated using the chain rule from a first order autoregression for w_t with a trend is only 0·0150. (See Altonji and Ashenfelter (1980), p. 225.) This result is for 1929–1968 based on an autoregression estimated from 1929–1976 with the wage series used in this study. The simple correlations of P_t and time with the perfect foresight value for P_t^* are 0·9782 and 0·9843 respectively.

24. There is an additional problem in the case of an autocorrelated error structure if people do have perfect foresight. This is because the future values of the wage are correlated with u_{2t}. This problem does not afflict the models with white noise errors and lagged endogenous variables. See also the discussion in Section 4.

25. Note that I did not re-estimate the forecasting model using only postwar data. The correlation of $w_t^*|I3_t$ and the perfect foresight values of w_t^* for 1948–68 is 0·9993. The correlation of a trend and the perfect foresight values is 0·9985. The corresponding figures for $P_t^*|I3_t$ and the perfect foresight values for P_t^* are 0·9839 and 0·9871.

26. The basic idea of this section has several antecedents in the literature. At a theoretical level, the idea that consumption and labour supply are jointly determined in a lifecycle setting is of course a very old one in economics. See LR and some of the references in footnote 1, especially Ghez and Becker (1975). At an empirical level, Abbot and Ashenfelter (1976) is a good example of joint estimation of labour supply and commodity demand. Their model is static, however, and the issue of how to measure future expectations does not arise. Hall (1978) suggests that consumption should be treated as an exogenous variable in macro models and is basically an index of unobserved expected future income streams. He does not consider the joint consumption leisure decision and ignores the effects of taste variations on consumption. The latter variations undermine the case that consumption may be treated as an exogenous variable. The most direct antecedent is Metcalf (1974), who uses observed savings behaviour in his study of the extent to which the New Jersey negative income tax experiment measured responses to temporary rather than permanent wage changes.

27. I have used β_1 as the symbol for both the coefficient on the current real wage in the log-linear labour supply equation (1) and as a parameter of the utility function (12) to highlight the connection between Section 4 and the approach of Sections 2 and 3. Although I refer to β_1 as the intertemporal labour supply elasticity in both sections, it is a pure substitution effect in (21) and the substitution effect net of the income effect of a change in w_t (with w_t^* held constant) in (1). This income effect will be small given that it is for a change lasting only one period.

28. In the perfect foresight case, λ_{jt} is implicitly defined by the equation below, which is obtained by substituting the solutions for N_{jt+i}, c_{jt+i} $(i = 0 \cdots J - j)$ into (13)

$$A_{jt} = \sum_{i=0}^{J-j} \{ [\bar{r}_{ti}[\bar{r}_{ti}/\Psi^i]^{\beta_c} \exp{(\beta_c[\lambda_{jt} - \varepsilon'_{cjt+i}])}$$
$$- [\bar{r}_{ti}/\Psi^i]^{\beta_1} \exp{(w_{jt+i} + \beta_1[\ln{(\beta_1/(\beta+1))} + \lambda_{jt} + w_{jt+i} - \varepsilon'_{Njt+i}])} \}.$$

29. In fact, it is necessary to assume that $\hat{w}_{jt+i}$ is equal to the aggregate expectation plus an age specific constant to justify aggregating the d_{ji}'s separately from the $\hat{w}_{jt+i}$'s. The age specific constants then appear in the constant term of the labour supply and consumption equations. Also, note that A_t poses a problem, since the B_{4j}'s are not observed. Data is available only on $\sum s_j A_{jt}$.

30. The constant term and the coefficients in a first order Taylor expansion of λ_{jt} around a particular value of λ_j depend upon the values of the $\hat{w}_{jt+i}$'s r_{ti}'s and A_{jt}. If the variation in these variables over the sample period is large enough, (16) may not be an acceptable approximation. Furthermore, in any given period the d_{jt}'s may vary across individuals in an age group and depend on individual wage expectations. In this case aggregation across individuals in cohort j would not lead to (16).

31. Note that if ε_{cj} and ε_{Nj} are present with $(\varepsilon_{cj} - \varepsilon_{Nj}) \neq 0$, and these differ across age groups, trends in the age distribution introduce what amounts to a quadratic trend into the labour supply equation (21) below. I ignore this possibility.

32. One may argue that the doubts about the exogeneity of y_t (and P_t) are more serious for (21) given that this equation contains ε_{ct}. The results reported below are not very sensitive to exclusion of $y_t - y_{t-1}$, $y_t - M_t$ and $(N + Q - y)_{t-1}$ from the instrumental variables list.

33. By this I mean that a person aged j at time t must predict ε_{jt+i} from $\varepsilon_{j-i,t}$ and knowledge of the process which determines the evolution of tastes for persons at a fixed age.

34. In Section 3, I simply assume that the labour supply error ε_{2t} in (1) obeys an AR(1) process. In this section, the error terms are introduced explicitly as unobserved preference variables for each age group and are then aggregated across age groups. $\varepsilon_{\lambda t}$, which may be regarded as one of the determinants of ε_{2t}, is a function of expectations about future values of ε_{Nt} and ε_{ct}. If consumers know their lifetime taste profiles, they know the future values of these variables. In this case, $\varepsilon_{\lambda t}$ depends on these future values. But then $- \varepsilon_{Nt} + \varepsilon_{\lambda t}$ obeys a complicated higher order process even if $\varepsilon_{ct} - \varepsilon_{Nt}$ is an AR(1). If anticipated taste shifts are important empirically, this would cause a variety of difficulties with the estimator used in Section 3 (and with the estimation procedures used in most of the aggregate time series work on consumption and labour supply). If, however, consumers do not know in advance the shocks to tastes which will occur in the future, and one ignores non-linearity in the relation between $\varepsilon_{\lambda t}$ and the forecasts of future values of ε_{ct} and ε_{Nt}, then $\varepsilon_{\lambda t}$ will be a linear function of ε_{ct} and ε_{Nt}. Under these circumstances, ε_{2t} could obey an AR(1), for the "a" and "c" specifications in Section 3.

35. The utility function (12) does not distinguish between consumption technology (e.g. household production) and "tastes." Consequently, trends in household production technology would show up in part as movements in ε_{cj} relative to ε_{Nj}. It is reasonable to assume that such movements are not cyclical.

36. See Darby (1972) for a discussion of the "appropriate" consumption series. The data is from U.S. Department of Commerce (1976), pp. 92, 93, and 338; (1977), p. 30; and (1978), p. 38.

37. The connection between the analysis of labour supply and consumption and a model of equilibrium unemployment along the lines of LR is not immediate, and I have not performed the analysis necessary to arrive at a carefully specified unemployment equation using consumption as a proxy for unobserved expectations. One can imagine that the theory may be reformulated with equilibrium unemployment depending on the difference between the current real wage and the log of the expected value of the marginal utility of income. I experimented with an unemployment equation in terms of w_t, c_t, and with and without a time trend and WWII dummy. The GLS estimate below is fairly representative. Both c_t and w_t enter significantly with the wrong sign. Taken at face value, the findings for the unemployment equation are basically consistent with the labour supply results.

$$\ln{(1 - U_t)} = -1 \cdot 042 + 0 \cdot 556 w_t - 0 \cdot 645[c_t - M_t] - 0 \cdot 046 D_t + 0 \cdot 806 \varepsilon_{3t-1}$$
$$\quad (2 \cdot 28) \quad (5 \cdot 20) \quad\quad (7 \cdot 02) \quad\quad\quad (3 \cdot 12) \quad\quad (9 \cdot 3)$$

$$\text{SE} = 0 \cdot 020 \quad\quad \text{DW} = 1 \cdot 52 \quad\quad \text{Sample} = 1930\text{--}1976.$$

38. Let e_{tax} be the elasticity with respect to income of 1 minus the marginal tax rate. It is easy to show that

$$d(N_t - M_t)/dw_t = \beta_1[1 + e_{\text{tax}}]/[1 - e_{\text{tax}}\beta_1].$$

Since the variables are in logs, $d(N_t - M_t)/dw_t$ is the total elasticity of labour supply with respect to a temporary change in the wage. If the tax system is progressive, then $e_{\text{tax}} < 0$ and the total elasticity is less than β_1, assuming that β_1 is greater than 0. Thus, the effect of temporary movements in the wage on labour supply is diminished by the response of marginal tax rates. Some rough calculations for the U.S. suggest that this effect may be important.

39. Marginal income tax rates for workers with average annual earnings rose sharply during WWII. The rates were 4·0% in 1939, 10% in 1940, 19% in 1942, and 25% in 1944. At the same time, the personal exemption was lowered in 1942, which increased the number of persons subject to the tax. To the extent that the rise in tax rates was anticipated during the late years of the Great Depression, the high unemployment rates for those years are all the harder to explain in the intertemporal substitution framework. Also, taxes declined somewhat after WWII and one might speculate that an even larger fraction of the taxes during the war years was regarded by the public as temporary. Taxes would depress the current (after tax) real wage relative to the expected discounted future real wage during the war years, when a large increase in labour supply occurred. See Altonji (1981a), Table 17, p. 94. Barro's (1981a) and to a lesser extent Hall's (1981a) analysis of the response of supply to temporary demand disturbances associated with military spending are flawed by the failure to incorporate the effects of tax changes.

40. One may drop the within period additivity assumption by raising the sum of the consumption and labour supply terms to an exponent other than one. Equation (21) remains as one of the first order conditions although β_1 no longer may be interpreted as the short run labour supply elasticity. The exponent may be estimated via the Euler conditions for labour supply and consumption. J. Rotemberg brought this possibility to my attention and currently is pursuing it in collaboration with G. Mankiw and L. Summers. Their preliminary results are consistent with the findings in Section 4. See Mankiw et al. (1982).

41. In a very interesting study Moffit (1979) estimates the compensated labour supply elasticity for males to be 0·12. His estimates are based on the Seattle Negative Income Tax experiment, using data for people who were in programmes of different length. The results of Burtless and Greenberg (1980) also suggest a low estimate. These studies are evidence that intertemporal substitution does take place, but the empirical magnitudes are not large. In the most thorough study to date of intertemporal substitution effects using the Seattle–Denver experiment data, Keeley and Wai (1980) find the own period substitution effect of a change in the wage to be small for husbands and single female heads of household. It is somewhat larger for wives. They find no evidence that cross period substitution effects are important for husbands and single female heads. They do find some weak evidence of such effects for wives. Keeley and Wai conclude that the labour supply reduction resulting from a permanent negative income tax program would be larger than the response to a temporary programme because the response is due primarily to wealth effects. Heckman and MaCurdy (for married women) and MaCurdy (for adult men who worked at least part of the year), use panel data to estimate the elasticity of labour supply with respect to the wage holding constant the marginal utility of lifetime income. The estimates for men range from 0·10 to 0·45. As MaCurdy points out, these estimates are in the same range as those obtained by Ghez and Becker (1975) and Smith (1977) using synthetic cohort data. However, the estimate for married women in Heckman and MaCurdy (1982) is large: (2·2). Smith's estimate for adult white women is 0·56, which is more in line with the results for the negative income experiments.

42. See Azariadis (1979) and Brown (1982) for surveys of the implicit contracts literature. Brown presents time series evidence that real wages fluctuate less than the marginal value product of workers along with other evidence bearing on an implicit contracts interpretation of the labour market. See Barro (1977) for an argument that implicit contracts should not interefere with market equilibrium.

43. See Hall and Lilien (1980). Hall (1980b) stresses the importance of both intertemporal substitution and implicit contracts for models of the labour market.

REFERENCES

ABBOT, M. and ASHENFELTER, O. (1976), "Labour Supply, Commodity Demand, and the Allocation of Time", *The Review of Economic Studies*, **43**, 389–411.
ALTONJI, J. G. (1981a), *Intertemporal Substitution and Labor Market Fluctuations* (unpublished PhD thesis, Department of Economics, Princeton University).
ALTONJI, J. G. (1981b), "Does the Labor Market Clear?" (Discussion Paper No. 110, Department of Economics, Columbia University).
ALTONJI, J. G. and ASHENFELTER, O. (1980), "Wage Movements and the Labor Market Equilibrium Hypothesis", *Economica*, **47**, 217–245.
ASHENFELTER, O. and CARD, D. (1981), "Time Series Representations of Economic Variables and Alternative Models of the Labor Market", Review of Economic Studies, **49**.
AZARIADIS, C. (1979), "Implicit Contracts and Related Topics: A Survey" (CARESS Working Paper No. 79-17).
BARRO, R. J. (1976), "Rational Expectations and the Role of Monetary Policy", *Journal of Monetary Economics*, **2**, 1–34.
BARRO, R. J. (1977), "Long Term Contracting, Sticky Prices, and Monetary Policy", *Journal of Monetary Economics*, **3**, 305–316.
BARRO, R. J. (1978), "Unanticipated Money, Output, and the Price Level in the United States", *Journal of Political Economy*, **86**, 549–580.
BARRO, R. J. (1981a), "Output Effects of Government Purchases", *Journal of Political Economy*, **89**, 1086–1122.

BARRO, R. J. (1981*b*), "Intertemporal Substitution and the Business Cycle", *Carnegie-Rochester Conference Series on Public Policy*, **14**, 237–268.

BOX, G. E. P. and JENKINS, G. M. (1976) *Time Series Analysis: Forecasting and Control* (Holden Day).

BROWN, J. N. (1982), "How Close to an Auction is the Labor Market? Employee Risk Aversion, Income Uncertainty, and Optimal Labor Contracts", *Research in Labor Economics*, **5**.

BRUNNER, K., CUKIERMAN, A. and MELTZER, A. (1980), "Money, Economic Activity and Business Cycles" (unpublished paper).

BURTLESS, G. S. and GREENBERG, D. (1980), "Inferences Concerning Labor Supply Based on Limited-Duration Experiments" (unpublished paper).

CHOW, G. C. (1979), "Estimation of Rational Expectations Models" (Econometric Research Program Memo No. 252).

CHRISTENSEN, L. R. and JORGENSON, D. W. (1973) *Measuring the Performance of the Private Sector of the U.S. Economy, 1929–1969* (Institute for Defense Analysis, Arlington, Va.).

COUNCIL OF ECONOMIC ADVISORS (1979) *Economic Report of the President* (U.S. Government Printing Office).

DARBY, M. R. (1972), "The Allocation of Transitory Income Among Consumer Assets", *American Economic Review*, **62**, 928–941.

DARBY, M. R. (1976), "Three and a Half Million U.S. Employees Have Been Mislaid: Or An Explanation of Unemployment 1930–1941", *Journal of Political Economy*, **84**, 1–16.

DENISON, E. F. (1962) *The Sources of Economic Growth in the United States and the Alternative Before US* (Supplementary Paper No. 13, Council of Economic Development).

DENISON, E. F. (1979) *Accounting for Slower Economic Growth: The United States in the 1970's* (Brookings Institution).

FAIR, R. C. (1970), "The Estimation of Simultaneous Equations Models with Lagged Endogenous Variables and First Order Serially Correlated Errors", *Econometrica*, **38**, 507–516.

FAMA, E. F. (1975), "Short-Term Interest Rates as Predictors of Inflation", *American Economic Reveiw*, **65**, 269–282.

FEDERAL RESERVE BULLETIN, Various issues.

FLOOD, R. P. and GARBER, P. M. (1980), "A Pitfall in Estimation of Models with Rational Expectations", *Journal of Monetary Economics*, **6**, 433–435.

GEARY, P. T. and KENNAN, J. (1982), "The Employment-Real Wage Relation: An International Study", *Journal of Political Economy*.

GHEZ, G. and BECKER, G. (1975) *Allocation of Time and Goods Over the Life Cycle* (NBER).

HALL, R. E. (1978), "Stochastic Implications of the Life Cycle-Permanent Income Hypothesis: Theory and Evidence", *Journal of Political Economy*, **86**, 971–987.

HALL, R. E. (1980*a*), "Labor Supply and Aggregate Fluctuations", *Carnegie-Rochester Conference Series on Public Policy*, **12**, 7–33.

HALL, R. E. (1980*b*), "Employment Fluctuations and Wage Rigidity", *Brookings Papers on Economic Activity*, **11**, 91–124.

HALL, R. E. and LILIEN, D. M. (1980), "Efficient Wage Bargains under Uncertain Supply and Demand", *American Economic Review*, **69**, 868–879.

HANSEN, L. P. and SARGENT, T. J. (1980), "Formulating and Estimating Dynamic Linear Rational Expectations Models", *Journal of Economic Dynamics and Control*, **2**, 7–47.

HECKMAN, J. and MaCURDY, T. E. (1980), "A Life Cycle Model of Female Labor Supply", *Review of Economic Studies*, **47**, 47–74.

HECKMAN, J. and MaCURDY, T. E. (1982), "Corrigendum on A Life Cycle Model of Female Labor Supply" (unpublished paper).

HEDRICK, C. L. (1973), "Expectations and Labor Supply", *American Economic Review*, **63**, 968–997.

KEELEY, M. C. and WAI, H. S. (1980), "Labor Supply Response to a Permanent Negative Income Tax Program" (unpublished paper, SRI International).

KESSELMAN, J. R. and SAVIN, N. E. (1978), "Three-and-a-Half-Million Workers Never Were Lost", *Economic Inquiry*, **16**, 205–225.

LEBERGOTT, S. (1964) *Manpower in Economic Growth: The American Record since 1800* (New York: McGraw-Hill Co.).

LEWIS, H. G. (1963) *Unionism and Relative Wages in the United States: An Empirical Inquiry* (University of Chicago Press).

LUCAS, R. E. Jr. (1973), "Some International Evidence on Output-Inflation Tradeoffs", *American Economic Review*, **63**, 326–334.

LUCAS, R. E. Jr. (1975), "An Equilibrium Model of the Business Cycle", *Journal of Political Economy*, **83**, 1113–44.

LUCAS, R. E. Jr. (1977), "Understanding Business Cycles", in Brunner, K. and Meltzer, A. H. (eds.) *Stabilization of the Domestic and International Economy* (Carnegie-Rochester Series No. 5) 7–29.

LUCAS, R. E. Jr. and RAPPING, L. A. (1970), "Real Wages, Employment, and Inflation", in Phelps, E. *et al.*, *Microeconomic Foundations of Employment and Inflation Theory* (W. W. Norton and Company).

LUCAS, R. E. Jr. and RAPPING, L. A. (1972), "Unemployment in the Great Depression: Is There a Full Explanation?", *Journal of Political Economy*, **80**, 306–310.

McCALLUM, B. T. (1976), "Rational Expectations and the Natural Rate Hypothesis: Some Consistent Estimates", *Econometrica*, **44**, 43–52.

MaCURDY, T. E. (1981), "An Empirical Model of Labor Supply in a Life Cycle Setting", *Journal of Political Economy*, **89**, 1059–1086.

MANKIW, N. G., ROTEMBERG, J., and SUMMERS, L. H. (1982), "Intertemporal Substitution in Macroeconomics" (preliminary draft).

METCALF, C. E. (1974), "Predicting the Effects of Permanent Programs from a Limited Duration Experiment", *Journal of Human Resources*, **9**, 530–555.

MISHKIN, F. S. (1981), "The Real Interest Rate: An Empirical Investigation" (NBER Working Paper No. 656).

MODIGLIANI, F. and SCHILLER, R. (1973), "Inflation, Rational Expectations and the Term Structure of Interest Rates", *Economica*, **40**, 12–43.

MOFFIT, R. (1979), "Estimating a Simple Life-Cycle Model of Labor Supply: The Evolution of a Limited Duration NIT Experiment" (unpublished paper).

MORTENSON, D. T. (1970), "A Theory of Wage and Employment Dynamics" in Phelps, E. S. *et al. Microeconomic Foundations of Employment and Inflation Theory* (W. W. Norton and Company).

NEFTCI, S. N. (1978), "A Time Series Analysis of the Real Wages-Employment Relationship", *Journal of Political Economy*, **86**, 281–292.

REES, A. (1970), "On Equilibrium in Labor Markets", *Journal of Political Economy*, **78**, 306–310.

REES, A. (1972), "Reply", *Journal of Political Economy*, (**80**, 1), 311.

SARGAN, J. D. (1964), "Wages and Prices in the United Kingdom: A Study in Econometric Methodology", in Hart, P. E. *et al. Econometric Analysis for National Economic Planning* (Butterworths Scientific Publications, London).

SARGENT, T. J. (1973a), "Rational Expectations, the Real Rate of Interest, and the Natural Rate of Unemployment", *Brookings Papers on Economic Activity*, **4**, 429–472.

SARGENT, T. J. (1973b), " 'Rational Expectations': A Correction", *Brookings Papers on Economic Activity*, **4**, 779–780.

SARGENT, T. J. (1976), "A Classical Macroeconomic Model for the United States", *Journal of Polical Economy*, **84**, 207–237.

SARGENT, T. J. (1978), "Estimation of Dynamic Demand Schedules Under Rational Expectations", *Journal of Politcal Economy*, **86**, 1009–1044.

SARGENT, T. J. (1979) *Macroeconomic Theory* (Academic Press).

SARGENT, T. J. and WALLACE, N. (1975), "Rational Expectations and the Theory of Economic Policy", *Journal of Monetary Economics*, **2**, 169–183.

SEATER, T. J. (1978), "Utility Maximization, Aggregate Labor Force Behavior and the Phillips Curve", *Journal of Monetary Economics*, **4**, 637–660.

SHEFFRIN, S. M. (1979), "Unanticipated Money Growth and Output Fluctuations", *Economic Inquiry*, **17**, 1–13.

SMITH, J. P. (1977), "Family Labor Supply over the Life Cycle", *Explorations in Economic Research*, **4**, 205–76.

SOLOW, R. M. (1980), "On Theories of Unemployment", *American Economic Review*, **70**, 1–17.

TAYLOR, J. B. (1979), "Estimation and Control of a Macroeconomic Model with Rational Expectations", *Econometrica*, **47**, 1267–1286.

U.S. DEPARTMENT OF COMMERCE, BUREAU OF THE CENSUS (1974, 1977), *Current Population Reports, Series p. 25,* No. 519 and No. 643 (U.S. Government Printing Office).

U.S. DEPARTMENT OF COMMERCE, BUREAU OF THE CENSUS (1976), *Historical Statistics of the U.S., Colonial Times to 1970* (U.S. Government Printing Office).

U.S. DEPARTMENT OF COMMERCE, BUREAU OF ECONOMIC ANALYSIS (1967), *The National Income and Product Accounts 1929–1965* (U.S. Government Printing Office).

U.S. DEPARTMENT OF COMMERCE, BUREAU OF ECONOMIC ANALYSIS (1976), *The National Income and Products Accounts 1929–1974* (U.S. Government Printing Office).

U.S. DEPARTMENT OF COMMERCE, BUREAU OF ECONOMIC ANALYSIS, *Survey of Current Business*, various issues.

WALLIS, K. E. (1980), "Econometric Implications of the Rational Expectations Hypothesis," *Econometrica*, **48**, 49–74.

Review of Economic Studies (1982) XLIX, 825–844
0034-6527/82/00590825$00.50

Labour Force Participation: Timing and Persistence

KIM B. CLARK

Harvard University

and

National Bureau of Economic Research

and

LAWRENCE H. SUMMERS

Massachusetts Institute of Technology

and

National Bureau of Economic Research

This paper examines the relative importance of timing and persistence elements in explaining cyclical fluctuations in labour supply. Data from the natural experiment provided by World War II and cross-sectional data on American local labour markets, as well as aggregate time-series data are used in the empirical work. We find little evidence that timing effects play an important role in labour market dynamics. The evidence suggests that views emphasizing persistence are more accurate, and that previous employment tends to raise the probability of subsequent employment.

1.

Much of the development of applied economic theory within the past 25 years has emphasized the importance of viewing economic decisions in a life cycle context. Consumption decisions are today frequently viewed as being determined by wealth or permanent income. The human capital revolution has brought life cycle considerations to the forefront of modern labour economics. While the life cycle dynamics of labour force participation decisions have important implications for macroeconomic theory and policy, they have received relatively little empirical attention. With the notable exceptions of Lucas and Rapping (1969) and Hall (1980), none of the large body of work on cyclical fluctuations in employment has explicitly relied on a dynamic model of labour supply.[1]

This paper uses several types of data to examine two elements of participation dynamics. The first is the aspect of "timing" which is implicit in the work of Lucas and Rapping, and in Mincer's (1966) early discussion of hidden unemployment. The timing argument, which is presented most explicitly in Ghez and Becker (1975), holds that leisure is easily substitutable across periods. Hence relatively small transitory movements in the perceived real wage or real rate of return can have large effects on the path of labour supply as individuals time their participation to coincide with periods of high transitory wages. On the other hand, permanent changes, because they do not affect the timing decision, are expected to have a much smaller effect on participation.

It is this view of labour supply which underlies new classical macroeconomic models. The dependence is made explicit in Lucas (1975), who claims that "what we do know indicates that leisure in one period is an excellent substitute for leisure in other nearby periods". The ability of classical macroeconomic models to explain fluctuations in employment depends on the presence of strong intertemporal substitution effects. Unless leisure is very substitutable across periods, large observed cyclical variations in employment could not possibly be caused by the response of labour supply to the relatively small fluctuations which are found in real wages and real interest rates.

It is by now clear that models in which only timing elements are present cannot fully account for cyclical fluctuations. The restrictions imposed by rationality imply that the expectational errors which generate business cycles are serially uncorrelated. The serial correlation which is characteristic of business cycles can only be explained in terms of mechanisms which cause shocks to be propagated over several periods. While Lucas (1975), Blinder and Fischer (1980) and Sargent (1980) have considered alternative explanations of persistence in the demand for labour, little attention has been devoted to the question of persistence in labour supply. To a substantial extent, a demonstration of substantial persistence in labour supply decisions undercuts the plausibility of models based on a high elasticity of labour supply with respect to transitory wage movements since it is difficult to see why a long-run decision should be strongly responsive to transitory developments.

The second element of labour force dynamics which we consider is embodied in the "persistence" hypothesis. In this view, past work experience is a key determinant of current employment status. Because of high separation costs and costs of finding new employment, those who are employed tend to remain employed. Persistence of employment might also be rationalized on human capital grounds. Those who are employed longer tend to accumulate more human capital, which raises the return to work in the future relative to leisure. Those out of the labour force may also develop household-specific capital or commitments (i.e. children) which reduce the return to working relative to remaining outside the labour force. There is also some reason to believe that the taste for work may be affected by work experience. Such habit formation effects have been well documented in demand analysis.[2]

This aspect of labour force dynamics appears to be quite important in micro-econometric studies of employment patterns. Freeman (1977) presents extensive evidence indicating that the probability of separation from employment declines with the duration of employment. This result is obtained separately for voluntary separation (quits) in Freeman (1977b) and for voluntary separations (layoffs) in Medoff (1979). Of course it is possible that this pattern results from individual heterogeneity. Those with high withdrawal possibilities are less likely to be observed as employed than those with low probabilities. Heterogeneity has been considered by Heckman (1978) and Yatchew (1977) as an explanation of persistence in labour force participation; both conclude that at least for married women, true state dependence exists. Chamberlain (1978) has devised a methodology for estimating the size of the persistence effect. He finds that, after controlling for individual differences, prior experience raises the odds of participation by a factor of seven. Other researchers have found evidence that persons with employment experience are more likely to be re-employed quickly when unemployed. Persistence effects of this magnitude imply that any measure which affects employment will have important long-run effects.

The differing macroeconomic implications of models in which timing or persistence effects predominate are highlighted by the following example. In an economy which is initially in equilibrium, the government unexpectedly undertakes expansionary policy.[3] Irrespective of whether timing or persistence predominates, the initial impact of the change is an increase in employment and labour force participation. However, timing and persistence effects are opposite in the longer run. An extreme version of the timing hypothesis would hold that individuals desire to spend a fixed proportion of their lives in the labour force which they schedule to coincide with periods of maximum opportunity. If this is the case, labour supply after the shock will be less than it would have been had the shock never occurred, as individuals "schedule" themselves out of the labour force.

Such scheduling effects have been used to counter arguments that the fluctuations in participation that accompany changes in the unemployment rate imply a significant discouraged worker effect.[4] What appears to be discouragement is actually the effect of individuals timing their participation to coincide with periods of maximum opportunity. When timing predominates, output gains from expansionary policy are illusionary. They will be cancelled by a reduction in subsequent output as workers time their withdrawal from the labour force. Thus, models with strong intertemporal substitution effects imply that a transitory increase in the real wage will reduce subsequent labour supply. Morover, a permanent upgrading of opportunities in a timing world imply a much smaller increase in participation than observed in the short run because scheduling effects would no longer occur.

Persistence effects, however, yield a long-run increase in labour supply. Short-run increases in employment will tend to persist as workers remain in the labour force because of habit formation, adjustment costs, or human capital accumulation. Hence, concurrent changes, on this view understate the total increment to output from expansionary policy. The effects of persistence described here potentially complement the process of worker upgrading discussed in Okun (1973), and Thurow (1976).[5]

The relative empirical importance of timing and persistence effects in labour supply is an issue with important implications for macroeconomic theory and policy. Both effects essentially deny the "natural rate" hypothesis as a medium-run proposition. They imply that policy can have an extended impact on the rate of employment without repeatedly fooling economic agents, because in both views labour supply is conditioned by past employment experience.[6] It is this link which translates short-run policy effects into longer-run impacts. As is clear from the preceding discussion, timing and persistence effects have exactly the opposite implications for the long-run direction of expansionary policy. This paper is directed at determining their relative importance in economic fluctuations.

The next section of the paper examines a natural experiment which potentially can shed light on the question at hand. During World War II, the level of female employment and participation rose precipitously. We examine the aftermath of the conflict to see whether the war had a positive or negative impact on subsequent female participation. The third section of the paper lays the groundwork for the econometric analysis, by outlining a simple model of life cycle labour supply which is capable of embodying both timing and persistence effects. The model developed in this section can be examined using several types of data. Section 4 of the paper uses the model to examine the relative importance of timing and persistence effects in accounting for the time-series behaviour of the aggregate labour force participation rate. The fifth section of the paper examines the timing and persistence effects using cross-section data. Essentially, the analysis relies on the observation that differences in unemployment over time are dominated by transitory movements, whereas geographic differences are for the most part permanent. The sixth section of the paper summarizes the empirical results and discusses their implications.

2. THE IMPACT OF WORLD WAR II

Before developing a formal model of life cycle labour supply, it is instructive to examine the one natural experiment which history has provided. The Second World War period and its aftermath offer an ideal testing ground for timing and persistence effects. From 1940 to 1944 real output in the United States increased 46·4% while the unemployment rate fell from 14·6 to 1·2% and averaged 1·3% from 1943–1945. The expansion in real output occurred at a time when large numbers of men were drawn into the Armed Forces increasing the job prospects and potential earnings of women. After 1945, unemployment rose slightly but remained below 4·0% through 1948. In the recession of 1949, the unemployment rate rose 2·1 points to 5·9%. The decade of the 1940s provides a good example of a large spurt in aggregate demand followed by a return to normal growth.

In perhaps the first statement of the timing hypothesis Milton Friedman underscored the instructive quality of the World War II period:

> ... the reaction to a higher wage rate expected to be temporary and then to revert to a lower level will tend to be very different than the reaction to a higher wage rate expected to be permanent. The temporarily higher wage rate would seem more likely to bring forth an increased quantity of labour from a fixed population than a permanently higher one, since there would be strong temptation to take advantage of the opportunity while it lasts and to buy leisure later.

> An interesting case in point is the experience of the United States during World War II, when both the fraction of the population in the labour force and the average number of hours worked per week were substantially higher than during the pre-war period.[7]

Friedman provides no explicit empirical analysis of changes in participation over the period, yet it is implicit in his discussion that World War II marked a period of transitory wage gains which ought to be followed by an increased purchase of leisure in later years. This effect should have been accentuated by the large buildup of wealth which took place during the War. In contrast, if persistence effects were dominant market attachment would have increased with increased work experience, and World War II would have had a long-run positive impact on observed participation.

The issue of long-run versus transitory effects seems particularly important for the female labour force, and particularly for married women. Since almost all able males are always in the labour force, there is little variation in male participation and thus little to be learned about the impact of transitory movements in job opportunities and wages. Females participate much less than men, and their behaviour appears to be much more sensitive to labour market conditions. Moreover, because of the large increase in the Armed Forces and the consequent increase in job opportunities, women were particularly affected by the expansion of demand during World War II.

The impact of World War II on the participation of adult women is documented in Table I.[8] From 1890–1940, the participation rate of adult women 25–64 increased from 13·9 to 25·7%, a compounded annual rate of increase of 1·2% per year. In striking contrast, between 1940 and 1944, the participation rate rose 23·5% (25·7 to 32·5) or 6·0% per year. Among married women, participation increased 2·5% per year from 1890 to 1940 (4·6 to 15·6), but a remarkable 11·3% from 1940 to 1944 (15·6 to 23·9). The marked increase in participation of married women was not confined to a specific age group. After rising very slowly in the twenty-year period before 1940, for example, participation by married women ages 45–64 more than doubled in the early years of the war.

The data in Table I suggest that the war had a major impact on the market behaviour of adult women, particularly those who were married.[9] The data also suggest that the increase in participation was not short-lived. Table II presents projected values of labour force participation, based on trends estimated over the periods 1890–1930 and 1890–1940, for married women and adult women 25–64. Comparison of actual and predicted values confirms the long-term effects of the war. For adult women 25–64, the trend fitted through 1940 predicts the 1940 participation rate, but the actual rate remains above the trend throughout the subsequent decade. The results for married women are even more striking; the actual rate averages 24·7% above the trend for the three time periods noted.[10]

The failure of the participation rate to fall below the trend after the transitory developments of the war had passed seems to be evidence that persistence effects

TABLE I

Participation of adult women by marital status and age 1890–1950

Age marital status		1890	1900	1920	1930	1940	1944	1947	1950
(1)	Adult women 25–64	13·9	16·0	19·6	21·8	25·7	32·5	28·8	31·1
(2)	Married women	4·6	5·6	9·0	11·7	15·6	23·9	20·0	23·0
Marital status by age									
(3)	Women 25–44	15·1	17·5	21·7	24·6	30·5	36·1	31·2	33·3
	Married	—	—	9·0	13·9	16·1	28·8	—	24·3
	Single	—	—	—	75·4	76·8	82·0	—	77·7
(4)	Women 45–64	12·1	13·6	16·5	18·5	20·2	27·1	25·3	28·8
	Married	—	—	6·2	7·3	9·0	21·4	—	19·1
	Single	—	—	—	47·5	56·6	59·1	—	64·8

Source: Line 1 is a weighted average of participation rates for women 25–44 and 45–64 taken from census data in *Historical Statistics of the United States (1975)*, Part 1, Series D38-D39, p. 132. Populations weights were taken from the same source. The values for 1944 and 1947 are based on CPS data and have been *reduced* to make them comparable to the Census definitions. We assumed that the growth rate of participation in the CPS data 1944–1950 was accurate; we thus extrapolated the growth rates back from the 1950 census value. The CPS values are 36·1 for 1944 and 32·0 for 1947.

Line 2 is series D60 from p. 133 of *Historical Statistics*. The data are for women 15 and over from 1890–1930, and 14 and over, 1940–1950. Married refers to all married women whether husband is present or not. As in line 1, the data for 1944 and 1947 were adjusted to accord with Census definitions. The CPS values were 25·6 for 1944 and 21·4 for 1947.

The data in lines 3 and 4 were taken from Census publications as follows:

1920:   U.S. Census, 1920, Vol. 4, p. 694, Table 5—data refer to married women with no distinction based on absence or presence of spouse. The entry for women 45–64 is the rate of participation of women 45 and over.

1930:   U.S. Census, 1930, vol. 5, General Report on Occupation, Chapter 5, Table 5, p. 274—data refer to all married women.

1940:   U.S. Census, 1940, *Employment and Family Characteristics of Women*—Special Report, Table 1, p. 9, and Table 2, p. 10. Data refer to married women, spouse present.

1950:   U.S. Census, 1950, Special Report P-E, No. 1-A, *Employment and Personal Characteristics*, Table 10, p. 1A-101. Data refer to married women, spouse present. Data for 1950 suggest that the category married-spouse present dominates the married-total group. Total married participation rates were 25·8 for women 25–44, and 20·4 for women 45–64.

TABLE II

Predicted trends in participation 1940–1950

	Adult women 25–64			Married women		
	Actual	Predicted 1890–1940 trend	Predicted 1890–1930 trend	Actual	Predicted 1890–1940 trend	Predicted 1890–1930 trend
1930	21·8	22·3	21·9	11·7	11·8	11·5
1940	25·7	25·4	24·4	15·6	15·1	14·6
1944	32·5	26·3	25·5	23·9	16·7	16·0
1947	28·8	27·3	26·4	20·0	17·9	17·2
1950	31·1	28·2	27·3	23·0	19·3	18·4

Source: Table I.

dominated the effects of timing. It is important to note that both effects seem to have been present. The fact that we observe a decline in participation after 1945 suggests that a significant number of women responded to the extraordinary opportunities of that period, and then scheduled themselves out of the labour force in subsequent years. Yet there is little support for a strong version of the timing hypothesis, which would have predicted a fall of labour supply below trend after the war. It seems evident that strong persistence effects were at work. Indeed, the labour force participation rate of women, especially married women, appears to have been permanently increased by World War II. [11]

Two alternative explanations of the apparent positive long-run effect of the war experience deserve further comment. First, it is frequently argued that the war brought changes in social attitudes towards women in the workplace. However, these changes were caused in large part by the increase in the number of women working during the war. Changes in attitudes should be viewed as factors through which the effect of employment experience on long-run increases in participation is mediated. That work experience during the war affected attitudes is evident in a 1944 survey conducted by the United Auto Workers. [10] Half of the women surveyed, who had never worked in a factory before the war, professed a desire to continue in a factory after the war. Over 85% desired to remain employed in some capacity. [11] The view that the increased participation of women was due to a general change in attitudes rather than the conditioning effect of wartime experience is also belied by a comparison of cohort participation rates. The participation rate of women 20–24, who were not directly affected by the war actually fell between 1940 and 1950. If the change in attitudes were general, it would have been expected to rise along with other participation rates.

A second explanation of the long-run increase in female participation following the war relies on the argument that reduced discrimination and increased productivity led to a rise in the permanent relative wage of women following World War II, and thus to an increase in participation. Insofar as this reflected human capital accumulation during the war, it is consistent with persistence effects. However, there is not much evidence that the male–female wage differential fell between the immediate pre- and post-war periods. [12]

The results presented in this section, while quite suggestive, are based on relatively fragmentary data. While there is an indication in the data that persistence effects dominated timing effects, this conclusion deserves much more careful scrutiny. In the next section we develop the model which underlies the more sophisticated econometric analysis of the timing and persistence effects presented in subsequent sections.

3. THE MODEL

This section outlines the model which provides the basis for the empirical work in this study. The model follows closely that of Lucas–Rapping (1969). However, it does differ in several respects, notably the treatment of expectations and our focus on participation rather than aggregate labour supply. Because much of the focus of this study is on how past behaviour as well as expected future developments influence participation, it is necessary to employ a three-period framework, rather than the more common two-period formulation.

Individuals are assumed to maximize an intertemporal utility function of the form:

$$U = U(c_{t-1}, l_{t-1}, c_t, l_t, c_{t+1}, l_{t+1}), \qquad (1)$$

where c represents consumption and l represents leisure, measured as a proportion of total time endowment. The period $t-1$ is assumed to represent the entire past, and the period $t+1$ embodies the whole future. It is assumed that the individual at time t takes consumption and labour supply decisions in period $t-1$ as given.

Individuals maximize the utility function (1), taking as predetermined previous employment experience, and the level of assets A_t, which may be positive or negative. The solution to the maximization problem will depend on their expectations of future nominal wages, w_{t+1}, future prices p_{t+1}, and the interest rate r_t. The budget constraint holds that lifetime consumption cannot exceed lifetime earnings.

Since the focus of this analysis is on the participation decision, the first-order conditions for the maximization of (1) are of little concern. It suffices to observe that an interior maximum with positive participation will occur if the market wage w_t, exceeds the reservation wage w_t^*. The reservation wage, w_t^*, is the minimum wage at which an individual will supply a positive amount of labour, that is, join the labour force.

For the moment we assume, following Lucas and Rapping, that the labour market is in equilibrium, though this assumption will be relaxed subsequently. If the labour market is in equilibrium, the prevailing market wage is potentially available to any possible participants. The reservation wage will depend on tastes, past employment, future opportunities, and assets. This may be written as:

$$w_t^* = f\left((1-l_{t-1}), p_t, \frac{w_{t+1}^e}{(1+r)}, \frac{p_{t+1}^e}{(1+r)}, A_t\right). \tag{2}$$

Notice that we assume here that economic agents know the true price level at each point in time and so rule out misperceptions of the types stressed in some recent macroeconomic models.

The central question of this paper can be posed in terms of the signs of the derivatives of w_t^* with respect to the arguments in (2). The standard assumption that leisure is a normal good yields the unambiguous conclusion that $f_4 > 0$, that is, an increase in wealth, $ceteris\ paribus$, raises the reservation wage. The signs of the effects of the other variables in (2) depend on the form of the utility function (1).

Consider first the sign of f_1, the impact of previous employment experience on current labour supply. With assets held constant, previous employment will affect the reservation wage only insofar as it affects the marginal rate of substitution between current leisure and consumption. The types of arguments usually put forward in discussions of intertemporal substitution suggest that $\partial w_t^* / \partial(1-l_{t-1})$ is negative. Increases in previous work effort raise the marginal disutility of current labour. Formulations adopting this assumption explicitly have been used by Sargent (1980) and Kydland and Prescott (1981). The effect however is theoretically ambiguous. In the presence of adjustment costs, habit formation effects, or accumulation of "leisure capital" the sign can easily be positive.

The effects of changes in the other arguments of (2) can be analyses in a similar fashion. Both expected future wages and prices have uncertain effects. Increases in future wages have a negative income effect on current labour supply. The substitution effect depends on the sign of $U_{l_t l_{t+1}}$. If it is positive, the substitution effect is positive and leisure today and in the future are complements. In the case of an additively separable utility function $\partial w_t^* / \partial w_{t+1}^e$ is unambiguously negative.[13] This illustrates that past experience and future opportunities do not have symmetric effects, since past employment experience has no effect in this case. The difference arises essentially because of the income effects of future wage changes. Increases in expected future prices have a positive income effect on labour supply, and an ambiguous substitution effect depending on $U_{l_t c_{t+1}}$.

So far the theory has been developed for a single individual. People will in general differ in both their tastes and market opportunities as well as in their previous experience and asset accumulation. As a result there will exist a joint distribution of market and reservation wages. The aggregate participation rate L^s is then given by:

$$L^s = \iint\limits_{w>w^*} g(w, w^*)dwdw^*.$$ (3)

It is readily apparent that $\partial L^s/\partial w > 0$: an increase in wages available to all workers will unambiguously raise the participation rate. The so-called "added worker" effect cannot exist in this model. Essentially, this is because at zero labour supply, increases in the wage do not change income. Income effects could be brought in if labour supply was modelled as the result of joint maximization by individuals within a family. They may also arise from changes in non-contemporaneous wages.

It follows from (3) that the participation rate is a function of the wage level, and the determinants of the shadow wage. Recognizing that the labour supply relation is homogeneous of degree zero in wage and the prices leads to the labour supply function:

$$L^s = f\left((1-l_{t-1}), \frac{w_t}{p_t}, \frac{w_{t+1}^e}{p_t(1+r)}, \frac{p_{t+1}^e}{p_t(1+r)}, \frac{A_t}{p_t}\right),$$ (4)

where L^s is the function of the population in the labour force. For convenience we assume a logarithmic functional form. Equation (5) may then be rewritten as:

$$\ln L^s = \beta_0 + \beta_1 \ln(1-l_{t-1}) + \beta_2 \ln\left(\frac{w_t}{p_t}\right) + \beta_3 \ln\left(\frac{w_{t+1}^e}{p_t(1+r)}\right)$$ (5)

$$+ \beta_4 \ln\left(\frac{p_{t+1}^e}{p_t(1+r)}\right) + \beta_5 \ln\frac{A_t}{p_t}.$$

Equation (5) differs from the Lucas–Rapping formulation in that the term $(1-l_{t-1})$ is included, reflecting the assumed dependence of the demand for leisure on leisure enjoyed during the preceding period. While such a dependence would seem to be a clear property of the Lucas–Rapping model, it is lost in the translation into their estimating equation. The term $(1-l_{t-1})$ does appear in their equation but only as a result of a Koyck transformation. While they expect and obtain a positive impact of previous labour supply, it is clear from the above discussion that the effect is actually ambiguous. A strong form of the timing hypothesis would predict a negative effect of lagged labour supply (apart from its role as a distributed lag generator).

At this point, it is useful to consider the expected signs of $\beta_1, \ldots, \beta_5$. The signs depend on the relative importance of persistence and timing elements in fluctuations in labour supply. A key parameter is β_1, the elasticity of current labour supply with respect to past employment experience. Sufficiently large intertemporal substitution effects would insure that $\beta_1 < 0$ so that increases in experience reduce subsequent participation. On the other hand, persistence effects imply $\beta_1 > 0$ so that increases in employment experience raise the participation rate. The coefficient of β_2 is expected to be positive, as increases in comtemporaneous real wages raise the attractiveness of seeking work. The sign of β_3 depends on the relative size of timing and persistence effects. If timing elements predominate, β_3 will be negative as increases in expected wages cause labour supply to decline because of intertemporal substitution effects. In the context of a model like that of Lucas and Rapping, one would expect that $\beta_2 + \beta_3 \approx 0$, since the long-run wage elasticity of labour supply is expected to be small. If adjustment costs or capital accumulation effects cause labour supply decisions to have a permanent character, the sign of β_3 will be positive. The sign of β_4 is ambiguous while β_5 is expected to be negative.

Equation (5) as it stands is a labour supply curve. If the labour market were always in equilibrium, it could be estimated directly using the employment ratio (proportion of the population who are employed) as the dependent variable. If, however, the labour market does not always clear, the level of employment cannot be taken as measure of desired labour supply. However, a measure of supply is provided by the labour force participation rate, the proportion of the population looking for work or working. This variable is the measure of labour supply used in this study. However, estimates using employment as the dependent variable are also discussed.

It is important to be clear about the issues involved in choosing between the employment and participation rate as dependent variables in equation (5). Lucas and Rapping take the position that an equation like (5) characterizes the level of employment, not the participation rate. On their hypothesis, workers who choose not to work because of a transitory decline in wages show up as unemployed and so are counted as labour force participants. Thus their argument implies that studying the labour force participation rate would obscure the important intertemporal substitution effects of wage changes. Although estimates of equation (5) using employment are presented below, we regard the Lucas–Rapping interpretation of the unemployment rate as problematic for several reasons. First, it provides no explanation for the fluctuations in the participation rate which account for a sizeable part of observed employment fluctuations. Second, unemployment is defined as inability to find work at prevailing wages. Individuals who are intertemporally substituting out of employment presumably know the prevailing wage, and do not desire work. They should therefore not report themselves as unemployed. Finally, our previous analysis, Clark and Summers (1979), of individual unemployment experience suggests that the assumption of continuous labour market equilibrium is very problematic.

Once the possibility that the labour market may not clear is recognized, it is necessary to modify equation (5). When involuntary unemployment exists, the assumption that all who want them can get jobs at the prevailing wage is no longer appropriate. Individual decisions regarding labour supply will be affected by the knowledge that search costs are higher when unemployment is higher. Since the mean duration of a completed spell of employment in the United States is only about 20 months (Clark and Summers 1979a), relatively small changes in the duration of pre-employment search can have a large impact on the return to seeking employment. By increasing the duration of search as well as by reducing the pool of good jobs, and increasing the risk of layoff, unemployment discourages labour supply. We thus include the unemployment rate as an additional explanatory variable in some of our empirical work. In the next two sections we estimate alternative forms of (5) using both aggregate time-series and cross-section data for different demographic groups.

4. TIME-SERIES EVIDENCE

This section describes the estimation of (5) using time-series data. Before the model can be estimated, it is necessary to develop operational measures of the variables. Both the proxy for previous employment experience and the measurement of expectations of inflation and the real wage require discussion. In equation (5) previous experience is represented simply by $(1 - l_{t-1})$. This term is supposed to represent the entire past experience of a population group. Using simply the previous year's employment experience would be inappropriate since the logic of both the timing and persistence effects suggests current labour supply is conditioned by a longer history. We therefore follow the work of Houthakker and Taylor (1970) in developing a measure of the "stock" of past employment. We assume that the labour supply of a cohort depends on a set of variables Z (such as those contained in (5)) and on its past employment experience.

Past employment experience is assumed to be represented by:

$$E_t^* = \sum_{i=1}^{\infty} \lambda^{i-1} E_{t-1} = \frac{E_{t-1}}{1-\lambda L},\tag{6}$$

where L is the lag operator. Since participation is a function of this stock and the set of variables Z it is clear that:

$$PR_t = Z_t\beta + \beta_1 E_t^*,\tag{7}$$

where PR_t is the participation rate. Using (6) the model can be expressed in terms of observables as:

$$PR_t = Z_t\beta - Z_{t-1}\lambda\beta + \lambda PR_{t-1} + \beta_1 E_{t-1}.\tag{8}$$

Alternatively, as discussed in the previous section, the employment ratio could be taken as the dependent variable. Using equations (5) and (8), and appropriate measures for participation, employment and Z, the most general specification of our estimating equation can be written

$$PR_t = \beta_0 + \beta_1 E_{t-1} + \beta_2 W_t + \beta_{3t} W_f^e + \beta_{4t} P_f^e + \beta_5 t + \beta_6 UM_t + \lambda PR_{t-1}$$

$$- \lambda [\beta_2 W_{t-1} + \beta_{3_{t-1}} W_f^e + \beta_{4_{t-1}} P_f^e + \beta_5 (t-1) + \beta_6 UM_{t-1}] + v_t,\tag{9}$$

where t indicates times, W_t is the contemporaneous real wage, $_t W_f^e$ and $_t P_f^e$ are expected future discounted wages and prices, E_{t-1} is the ratio of employment to population in the previous period, UM_t is a measure of the unemploymet rate, and v_t is an error term in M.[14] The time trend has been included to reflect the possible influence of slowly changing determinants not captured by other included variables. In this formulation, the coefficient β_1 measures the persistence of labour supply, while λ reflects the lag in formation of the habit stock. The long-run impact of an increase in employment experience is $\beta_1/(1-\lambda)$. This may be interpreted in two different ways. It represents the increase in the participation rate at time t, if employment in all previous periods were raised by one unit. It also can be interpreted as the sum over all future periods of the increases in participation arising from a one-shot increase in employment.

Equation (6) gives us a way of measuring the employment stock and deriving the estimating equation in (9); the second issue which must be considered is the development of measures of expected wages and prices. Most standard econometric procedures seem inappropriate because theory suggests that labour supply should depend on the expected discounted value of wages and prices over a long horizon. Our procedure for modelling expectations begins with an estimate of a set of vector auto-regressions relating wages, prices, and real output.[15] These vector auto-regressions are then simulated using data for each year in the sample to generate forecasts of wages and prices for the succeeding 5 years. These variables, $_t w_{t+i}^e$, are then adjusted to an after-tax basis and discounted back to year t, using year t's municipal bond rate.[16] They are then averaged to form proxies for $w_{t+1}^e/p_t(1+r)$ and $p_{t+1}^e/p_t(1+r)$, which in their logarithmic form we have labelled $_t W_f^e$ and $_t P_f^e$, respectively.

This procedure is somewhat arbitrary in its choice of horizon and in the specification of the vector auto-regressions. However, it seems to be the only computationally feasible way of handling the modelling of expectations which are more than one period ahead. Rational expectations techniques of the sort developed by McCallum (1976) are not applicable in the current example because of the quasi-differencing involved in moving to equation (8).

The data used in the actual estimation cover the period 1951–1981. We have chosen to use annual data because timing and persistence effects are likely to be badly confounded with seasonal fluctuations in higher frequency data. Our measures of the participation rate and employment ratio are age-adjusted rates calculated as fixed weight averages of age-specific rates. This age-adjusted participation rate is used to avoid biases introduced by the changing age structure of the population.

In the results reported below, we have omitted assets from the estimating equation. Like others before us (e.g. Lucas and Rapping (1969)), we found assets to have no significant relationship to participation. This conclusion is based on an assets measure which includes the real value of household financial holdings, excluding equity. A variety of other assets measures which included equity, housing and social security wealth were tried with little change in the results.

Several econometric issues arise in the estimation of equation (9). First, the equation is highly non-linear in the parameters, necessitating non-linear estimation. Second, the error term v_t is likely to be serially correlated. Even if the error term in equation (7) relating participation to Z and E^* were not serially correlated, the transformation of E^* involved in deriving the estimating equation would induce moving average error. Serial correlation in the error term is particularly serious in this case because both lagged participation and employment are included in the regression equation. Since there is no reason to suppose that the error in (8) follows a simple auto-regressive scheme, the usual corrections (e.g. Cochrane–Orcutt) are not appropriate. We have chosen to estimate the equation using two-stage non-linear least squares, treating both lagged participation and employment as endogenous. The instrument list includes a time trend, a squared trend, real Federal government spending, the rate of money growth and the real *per capita* stock of non-residential capital, along with the included exogenous variables. In addition, to allow for simultaneity, the contemporaneous wage is treated as endogenous.

A third econometric difficulty is collinearity, which frequently precludes disentangling estimates of λ, which determines the mean lag of the "past employment" effect, and β_1, the impact effect of changes in employment experience. Frequently, the estimated values of λ lie outside the range $0 \leq \lambda \leq 1$, and so the equations are not meaningful. Therefore, in many of the equations reported below, the value of λ is constrained to the *a priori* plausible value of $0 \cdot 9$. None of the qualitative conclusions were affected by the imposition of this constraint. In particular, all of the conclusions regarding the effects of transitory wage changes are wholly unaffected by the choice of λ.

Table III presents estimates of several variants of Equation (9) using the log of the participation rate as the dependent variable. The results do not suggest that timing effects have an important role to play in explaining cyclical fluctuations. The estimated elasticity of labour supply with respect to a transitory wage change is always small and sometimes negative. Nor is there any clear evidence of a negative relationship between expected future wages and labour supply, as predicted by models which emphasize timing effects. No clear conclusions emerge about the effects of changes in the price of future consumption. It is noteworthy that the increases in the unemployment rate of mature men do appear to reduce the participation rate, as theory predicts.

The data provide weak support for the importance of persistence in explaining fluctuations in labour supply. It is not possible to interpret the estimated effect of employment experience in equations (3)–(5) of Table III because the estimated value of λ lies outside its permissible range. In equation (8), where a time trend is not included, the estimated effect of the "employment stock" variable is both substantively and statistically significant. However, when a time trend is included as in equation (6) and (7), the "employment stock" coefficient remains positive but becomes insignificant. Estimates using the employment-population ratio as a dependent variable are reported in Table IV. The results are qualitatively similar to those obtained using the participation rate as a dependent variable. Here the evidence of persistence effects is very weak. Even when the time trend is omitted as in equation (6) of the table, the employment

REVIEW OF ECONOMIC STUDIES

TABLE III

Timing and persistence effects in time-series participation equations

Equation	CONS	W	W*	P*	UM_t	TIME	E_{t-1}	λ	SEE	D.W.
1	4·975 (0·320)	−0·084 (0·100)	0·009 (0·039)	—	—	—	—	—	0·005	1·48
2	6·620 (0·815)	−0·052 (0·099)	−0·157 (0·122)	0·186 (0·125)	—	—	—	—	0·005	1·72
3	3·814 (0·060)	−0·186 (0·056)	−0·012 (0·041)	—	—	0·007 (0·001)	0·470 (0·234)	−0·501 (0·246)	0·009	1·125
4	3·777 (0·089)	−0·199 (0·060)	−0·030 (0·054)	—	−0·001 (0·003)	0·008 (0·002)	0·326 (0·293)	−0·352 (0·308)	0·008	0·920
5	4·232 (0·052)	0·219 (0·426)	−0·090 (0·454)	0·135 (0·459)	—	—	0·128 (0·444)	−0·127 (0·437)	0·016	0·377
6	0·297 (0·428)	−0·321 (0·179)	0·066 (0·058)	—	—	0·009 (0·005)	0·019 (0·110)	0·9[b]	0·006	1·898
7	0·301 (0·399)	−0·287 (0·181)	0·027 (0·062)	—	−0·002 (0·002)	0·009 (0·004)	0·018 (0·102)	0·9[b]	0·006	1·974
8	−0·584 (0·518)	−0·028 (0·162)	−0·194 (0·466)	0·310 (0·520)	—	—	0·243 (0·123)	0·9[b]	0·006	1·820

Notes:
[a] Number in parentheses are standard errors.
[b] The parameter was set equal to the value indicated.

TABLE IV

Timing and persistence effects in time-series employment equations[a]

Equation	CONS	W	W*	P*	UM_t	TIME	E_{t-1}	λ	SEE	D.W.
1	4·183 (0·041)	0·020 (0·114)	0·158 (0·101)	—	—	—	—	—	0·013	1·94
2	4·197 (0·090)	−0·184 (0·259)	0·434 (0·319)	−0·235 (0·319)	—	—	—	—	0·013	1·91
3	0·128 (2·167)	−0·215 (0·636)	−3·043 (1·966)	3·056 (2·010)	−0·028 (0·010)	0·042 (0·014)	−0·003 (0·497)	0·888 (0·084)	0·021	1·545
4	3·662 (0·387)	0·540 (0·613)	−0·808 (0·922)	0·950 (0·980)	—	0·005 (0·006)	0·261 (0·897)	−0·258 (0·955)	0·018	1·512
5	3·967 (0·021)	−0·051 (0·058)	0·034 (0·057)	−0·169 (0·118)	—	—	−4·121 (2·351)	4·154 (2·346)	0·012	1·801
6	−0·490 (0·994)	−0·564 (0·358)	0·508 (0·457)	−0·166 (0·552)	—	—	0·220 (0·239)	0·9[b]	0·016	2·022
7	0·265 (1·013)	−0·591 (0·422)	0·298 (0·138)	—	—	0·008 (0·011)	0·026 (0·259)	0·9[b]	0·015	2·033
8	1·260 (0·326)	−0·305 (0·096)	−0·009 (0·053)	—	−0·015 (0·001)	0·009 (0·002)	0·05 (0·085)	0·9[b]	0·006	1·490

Notes:
[a] Numbers in parentheses are standard errors.
[b] Parameter has been set equal to indicated value.

stock variable is statistically insignificant. Not surprisingly, the cyclical indicator, UM_t, enters the employment equations in a highly significant way.

The time-series evidence presented here suggests that transitory variations in the perceived real wage have little effect on the rate of labour force participation. We find no indication in the data of the strong intertemporal substitution effects which are the basis of classical macro models. These findings on the effect of transitory wage changes are consistent with the positive impact of lagged employment found in Table III. While the quality of the evidence on lagged employment precludes strong conclusions, the results suggest that work may be habit-forming. Clearly, if experience in employment persists so that the decision to work is a relatively long-term commitment, it is not surprising that transitory wage changes have no discernible effect on labour supply.

These results conflict quite sharply with those of Hall (1980), who finds that the data support the intertemporal substitution hypothesis. Part of the conflict may lie in Hall's inclusion of fluctuations in hours per worker. The most serious problem, however, is Hall's measurement of the "intertemporal substitution parameter". He assumes that labour supply decisions are driven only by the price of future consumption in terms of today's labour. It is difficult to see what utility function would have this property in which the current price of consumption and future price of leisure are irrelevant. Our findings are consistent with the generally negative results obtained by Altonji (1982), and Mankiw, Rotemberg and Summers (1982) regarding the intertemporal substitution hypothesis.

5. CROSS-SECTION EVIDENCE

The comparison of the relationships between labour market variables which are observed in time-series and cross-section data can shed light on the importance of timing and persistence effects. In particular, this section shows that recognizing the distinction between transitory and permanent effects embodied in the two hypotheses provides a frame-work for reconciling the large differences between cross-sectional and time-series estimates of the relationship between unemployment and participation rates. The conflict between these two types of evidence emerged in the early 1960s when several studies found large discouraged worker effects using decennial census data on local participation and unemployment rates, while other studies found very small effects using time-series data (Long (1958), Barth (1968), Bowen and Finnegan (1969)).

Attempts to reconcile the divergent results have generally focused on possible biases in the cross-section evidence. In his often cited review of the evidence Mincer (1966) conjectured that cross-section estimates were biased by omission of migration, seasonal differences across SMSAs in census timing and common errors in the rate of participation and unemployment which give rise to a spurious association. Mincer also noted but did not pursue the permanence of state unemployment differentials. Bowen and Finnegan (1969) have examined each of these possibilities and suggest that none can satisfactorily explain the difference between the two sets of estimates.[17] More recent attempts to resolve the anomaly (e.g. Fleisher and Rhodes (1976)) have also been unpersuasive.[18]

These results suggest that cross-section and time-series estimates cannot be reconciled by pointing to biases in the cross-section data. A potentially more fruitful approach is to recognize the fundamental differences between intertemporal and interspatial variations in unemployment. At any point in time in any labour market the rate of unemployment is composed of both a permanent and a transitory component. In cross-section data, most variation in unemployment is presumably due to variation in the permament component across regions. This is in contrast to the aggregate time-series data where variation in the transitory component is likely to be dominant. Cast in these terms, the cross-section data provide estimates of the long run or permanent effect of unemployment, while transitory effects are captured with time-series data.

At this point, it is important to be clear about the interpretation of the measured unemployment rate. In this section, we adopt the "traditional" interpretation, which holds that the labour market does not clear and that the unempolyment rate affects the attractiveness of seeking work. It is then meaningful to speak of the effect of changes in differences in unemployment rates on labour force participation rates. We prefer the traditional interpretation of the unemployment rate to that of Lucas and Rapping for several reasons. Most important, the substantial permanent component in the differences between local unemployment rates suggest that they are not consequences of transitory wage movement. In addition, the evidence that participation and unemployment rates are negatively correlated is difficult to account for in the classical view. Indeed, in its strong form, it lacks an explanation for fluctuations in the participation rate. Other results described below also incline us towards the "traditional" interpretation of unemployment fluctuations.

In order to reconcile the time-series and cross-section estimates, it is necessary to examine the relationship between transitory and permanent effects, and to establish the conditions under which the permanent effect dominates. This is precisely the issue discussed in Section 3 which distinguishes the timing and persistence effects. There we found that persistence effects imply that employment in previous periods raises current participation. Short-run effects persist. If persistence effects predominate, the response of labour supply to permanent changes in demand should exceed the response to transitory changes. This prediction, which is borne out by the data, is not consistent with strong forms of the timing hypothesis, which imply that the response to transitory fluctuations should exceed the response to permanent changes.

It thus would seem that the predominance of persistence effects receives substantial support in the comparison of cross-section and time-series evidence. Similar support emerges from a comparison of transitory and permanent effects using cross-section data. Use of cross-section data provides a strong test of the relative importance of timing and persistence effects since the two views of labour force dynamics have sharply different implications for the appropriate demand variable in cross-sectional equations. The timing view holds that the important determinant of participation is the deviation of demand from its normal level. When it is above its normal level, workers schedule themselves into the labour force, leaving when it falls below normal. The persistence view, on the other hand, implies that the normal level of demand is the appropriate variable since workers make labour supply decisions on a long-term basis.

The model embodied in this discussion can easily be made explicit. It is assumed that the level of demand may be represented by ER, the proportion of those desiring work who have it ($1 -$ the unemployment rate). We postulate that participation in region i, PR_i, depends on the permanent level of demand, ER_i^p, and the level of transitory demand, ER_i^t, defined as $(ER_i - ER_i^p)$. A simple characterization of the participation equation is given by

$$PR_i = f(ER_i^p, ER_i^t, Z_i) \qquad (10)$$

where Z_i is a vector of variables other than demand conditions which influence the participation rate.

As the discussion in the preceding paragraph makes clear, the persistence view predicts that $f_{ER_i^p}$ will be large while $f_{ER_i^t}$ is not important; the timing hypothesis has the opposite implication. The distinction between the two hypotheses may be drawn more sharply by considering their implications for a change in the normal rate of employment holding constant the current rate. It is apparent from equation (10) that

$$\frac{\partial PR_i}{\partial ER_i^p} = f_{ER_i^p} - f_{ER_i^t}. \qquad (11)$$

The preceding discussion implies that this expression should be positive if persistence dominates and negative under the timing hypothesis. Intuitively, with current opportunities held constant, a decline in future opportunities will increase labour supplied by a worker who can easily substitute leisure across periods. On the other hand, it will make current employment less attractive to a worker for whom leisure is complementary across periods.

These implications of the timing and persistence hypotheses are clearly subject to empirical verification. To test the conditions laid out above we have estimated a basic labour supply model using the data from the 1970 U.S. Census on participation and selected determinants by state. Time-series data (1966–1974) on unemployment by state were taken from the *Manpower Report of the President*. These series are based on a combination of data on unemployment insurance, payrolls and, for some states, the monthly CPS. In addition to variables measuring the permanent and transitory effects of unemployment we have included measures of the permanent or expected real wage as well as structural and demographic variables which affect participation through the shadow wage. As a first approximation we assume that variation in nominal wages across states reflects primarily variation in the permanent component of real wages, so that the level of prices is excluded from the model.[19] For women the basic equation is:

$$\ln PR_{ij} = \alpha_1 + \alpha_2 \ln(WM)_i + \alpha_3 \ln(WW)_i + \alpha_4 EDW_i + \alpha_5 RW_i$$
$$+ \alpha_6 RBW_i + \alpha_7 URB_i + \alpha_8 MIGR_i + \alpha_9 C6_i + \alpha_{10}\ln(ER)_i^p \qquad (12)$$
$$+ \alpha_{11}\ln(ER)_i^t + v_{ij},$$

where the variables are defined as follows:

PR_{ij} = participation rate of the jth demographic group in the ith state
WM = median earnings of men 18 and over
WW = median earnings of females 18 and over
EDW = median years of schooling—females 18 and over
RW = proportion of females in the population 16 and over
RBW = proportion of non-white females in the population 16 and over
URB = proportion of the population residing in Census urban areas
$MIGR$ = total net migration 1960–1970 as a proportion of 1970 population
$C6$ = proportion of families with a child less than six living at home
ER = state aggregate employment rate
$\ln(ER)^p$ = average of $\ln(ER)$ for 1966–1974
$\ln(ER)^t = [\ln(ER) - \ln(ER)^p]$.

Letting EDM_i indicate median years of schooling of males 18 and over, and RBM, the proportion of non-white males in the population, the basic equation for the male group is:

$$\ln PR_{ij} = \beta_1 + \beta_2 \ln(WM)_i + \beta_3 EDM_i + \beta_4 RBM_i + \beta_5 URB_i$$
$$+ \beta_6 MIGR_i + \beta_7 \ln(ER)_i^p + \beta_8 \ln(ER)_i^t + u_{ij}. \qquad (13)$$

The expected effects of the structural and demographic variables included in equations (12) and (13) have been dealt with at length in a variety of places and will receive only brief mention here. Education and degree of urbanization are expected to have a positive effect on participation through their effects on labour force attachment and the costs of transportation. Migration is expected to raise participation in the receiving areas and lower participation in states with net outflow. The proportion of black men (women) in the population is included to control for well-known differences in participation behaviour between blacks and whites. The variable is expected to have a positive sign in the female equation, and a negative sign in the equation for males. The proportion of women in the population is included as a measure of potential competition among women; the expected sign is negative. The proportion of women with a child under six is expected to raise the shadow wage and thus to reduce participation. The expected sign of own-wage variables ($\ln WW_i$ in (12) and $\ln WM_i$ in (13)) is positive. Male earnings have been included in the female equation to allow for the effects of joint decision-making in the family and are expected to reduce female participation. Female earnings on the other hand are specified to have no effect on male participation.

TABLE V

Estimates of the basic cross section model for men and women (standard errors in parentheses)

	Male					Female				
	16–19	20–24	25–44	45–64	65+	16–19	20–24	25–44	45–64	65+
1. Male earnings (WM)	0·19 (0·13)	-0·03 (0·07)	0·06 (0·01)	0·17 (0·04)	0·31 (0·21)	0·42 (0·24)	-0·07 (0·11)	-0·39 (0·11)	-0·17 (0·16)	0·04 (0·24)
2. Female earnings (WW)	—	—	—	—	—	0·34 (0·20)	0·40 (0·09)	0·41 (0·09)	0·53 (0·13)	0·55 (0·20)
3. Education (EDM, EDW)	0·05 (0·04)	-0·0007 (0·02)	0·004 (0·005)	0·03 (0·01)	0·17 (0·07)	0·06 (0·08)	-0·01 (0·04)	0·03 (0·04)	0·06 (0·05)	0·21 (0·08)
4. Proportion female (RW)	—	—	—	—	—	2·28 (3·02)	1·65 (1·41)	-0·04 (1·38)	4·13 (1·99)	0·52 (2·93)
5. Proportion black (RBW, RBM)	-0·44 (0·28)	0·02 (0·14)	-0·05 (0·03)	-0·16 (0·08)	0·53 (0·44)	-1·59 (0·52)	-0·30 (0·24)	0·41 (0·24)	-0·41 (0·34)	0·37 (0·50)
6. Urbanization (URB)	-0·0009 (0·001)	-0·0003 (0·0007)	-0·0004 (0·0001)	-0·0003 (0·0004)	-0·004 (0·002)	-0·0002 (0·002)	0·00003 (0·0009)	-0·0004 (0·0009)	-0·001 (0·001)	-0·005 (0·002)
7. Children under 6 ($C6$)	—	—	—	—	—	0·008 (0·01)	0·004 (0·005)	0·004 (0·005)	0·01 (0·007)	0·02 (0·01)
8. Net migration ($MIGR$)	0·32 (0·11)	0·21 (0·06)	0·02 (0·01)	-0·05 (0·03)	-0·27 (0·18)	-0·08 (0·19)	0·006 (0·09)	0·23 (0·09)	-0·007 (0·12)	-0·33 (0·18)
9. Permanent employment rate (ER^p)	2·56 (1·09)	-0·38 (0·56)	0·63 (0·12)	1·33 (0·30)	3·29 (1·72)	5·97 (1·78)	2·96 (0·83)	2·46 (0·82)	2·31 (1·18)	2·17 (1·73)
10. Transitory employment rate (ER^t)	-3·26 (2·11)	-0·42 (1·08)	-0·05 (0·23)	0·12 (0·58)	4·62 (3·33)	0·85 (3·37)	-0·07 (1·57)	-3·15 (1·55)	-0·29 (2·22)	2·27 (3·27)
11. Full permanent effect (line 9–line 10)	5·82 (2·33)	0·04 (1·19)	0·68 (0·25)	1·21 (0·65)	-1·32 (3·68)	5·12 (3·82)	3·03 (1·78)	5·61 (1·75)	2·60 (2·52)	-0·10 (3·71)
12. Permanent employment rate (ER^p)[a]	2·64 (1·11)	0·37 (0·55)	0·63 (0·12)	1·33 (0·30)	3·18 (1·74)	5·97 (1·76)	2·96 (0·82)	2·45 (0·85)	2·31 (1·16)	2·17 (1·72)
R^2	0·52	0·26	0·65	0·74	0·33	0·71	0·67	0·76	0·60	0·60
SEE	0·09	0·04	0·009	0·02	0·14	0·12	0·06	0·06	0·08	0·12

Note:
[a] Line 12 reports the coefficient of ER^p when ER^t is excluded from the equation.

The differing implications of the timing and persistence views are captured in the coefficients of $\ln (ER)_i^p$ and $\ln (ER)_i^t$. Using the female equation, under the timing hypothesis α_{11} is expected to be positive and to dominate α_{10}, so that $\alpha_{10} - \alpha_{11} < 0$. The persistence hypothesis, on the other hand, implies that permanent effects are dominant so that $\alpha_{10} - \alpha_{11} > 0$. In addition to the basic equations (12) and (13) we also have estimated a specification which allows no role for transitory effects so that $\alpha_{11} = \beta_8 = 0$.

Estimates of the basic model for both men and women are presented in Table V. The principal coefficients of interest, α_{10} and α_{11} (β_7 and β_8 for men) are presented in rows 9 and 10; for convenience we have computed the sum of the coefficients in row 11. The results provide clear support for the importance of persistence effects. The long-run effects of unemployment clearly dominate the transitory effects in virtually all demographic groups. The difference between the permanent and transitory components is less than zero in only three cases, and in no case is the negative coefficient significant. We find the strongest evidence of the persistence effects among women for whom the timing phenomenon was expected to be particularly relevant. In each of the female age groups, except women over 65, the transitory employment rate is totally insignificant, often entering with a negative sign. In contrast, the permanent effects are large and significant. For women 45–64, for example, the permanent effect (α_{10}) is 2·46, which implies that a decline in the permanent rate of unemployment from 0·06 to 0·05 would raise the participation rate by 2·46%. The transitory effect for this group, on the other hand, is $-3\cdot15$, clearly reflecting the dominance of the permanent employment rate which enters negatively in the deviation. The total effect of the permanent rate is thus 5·61. Similar positive effects are found for younger women as for women 45–64. Only among women over 65 does the timing hypothesis find any support and here the estimates are not particularly precise. The sum of the permanent and transitory effects is $-0\cdot10$, which may be marginally important in determining the participation behaviour of women over the age of 65. A somewhat stronger finding for men over 65 leads to the paradoxical conclusion that the timing view, a construct based on life cycle considerations, finds its support only among those nearing the end of their adult lives.

The results in rows 10 and 11 of Table V clearly suggest that changes in the expected rate of unemployment strongly influence the participation decisions of most demographic groups. This conclusion is buttressed in row 12 of Table V, which presents estimates of the effect of unemployment assuming no transitory effects (i.e. $\alpha_{11} = 0$). Among most demographic groups the expected rate of employment enters significantly with a relatively large positive coefficient. Differences in the size of the employment effect within and across demographic groups are consistent with the theoretical role of unemployment laid out in Section 3. We find that unemployment is more important in those groups where employment durations are short. Thus within the male and female categories teenagers are more sensitive to variations in unemployment than are older persons. Similarly, within age groups, women tend to be more responsive than men. It should be noted, however, that the coefficients for the older adult men are far from trivial. We estimate that a 1 point decline in the long-term unemployment rate (0·06 to 0·05) leads to a 0·6% increase in the participation of men 25–44, and a 1·3% increase in the rate of participation of men 45–64.

The evidence on the relative importance of timing and persistence in the cross-section data relies on the use of the unemployment rate to capture market opportunities. We have already discussed some of our reasons for preferring this kind of interpretation in Section 3. But there are two additional issues that need to be addressed. In the first place, classical models would call for the use of permanent and transitory real wages rather than unemployment rates as explanatory variables. The results of including real wages in time-series regressions have been discussed in the preceding section. We have made an attempt to gauge their effect in the cross-section analysis by calculating real wages by state. We used the BLS Standard of Living Estimates for 35 cities to construct state price indices; wages were based on data for manufacturing by state. Both permanent and transitory wage variations had only minor effects on state participation and employment rates. Therefore the unemployment rate has been used as a proxy for the attractiveness of entering and remaining in the labour force. The role of wages and prices in explaining cross-section differences in participation remains an important area for future research.

A second problem concerns the effect of omitted variables. Although we have included a number of structural characteristics of each state in the equation, there is always the possibility that omitted common third factors account for the observed correlations between unemployment and participation rates. We explored this issue by using other variables such as the employment-population ratio in place of the unemployment rate. This had little effect on the qualitative conclusions.[20]

The analysis in this section has shown the predominance of the expected or natural level of demand in explaining participation differences across states. Except for those over 65, there is no evidence for the notion that transitory changes in opportunities play a significant role in decisions about participating in the labour force. These results suggest that a rise in expected opportunities, holding current opportunities constant, will call forth an increase in participation, a response consistent with the implications of persistence in labour supply. The notion that individuals schedule their labour supply according to variations in current opportunities finds little support in these data.

6. CONCLUSIONS

The results in this paper suggest the importance of persistence in labour market decisions. A variety of types of evidence suggest that previous employment experience has an important effect on subsequent labour supply. This implies that labour supply decisions are not very responsive to transitory changes in employment opportunities. While no one of the tests presented in this paper can be regarded as decisive, in conjunction they suggest that persistence elements are more important than timing elements in explaining fluctuations in either the number of persons employed or the number participating in the labour force. Our results leave open the possibility that timing elements are important in explaining cyclical fluctuations in average hours worked and in work effort.

Acceptance of these conclusions has important implications for both macroeconomic theory and policy. These results cast doubt on the medium-run relevance of the natural rate hypothesis. Because policy affects the level of employment in the short run, it has a long-run effect on the position of the labour supply schedule. Workers drawn into the labour force by cyclical upturns tend to remain even after the boom has ended. The converse is true for shocks which reduce employment. At this point, the quantitative importance of these effects is uncertain, although our interpretation of the evidence reported here suggests that they are quite important.

This paper has only begun to touch on the implications of alternative life cycle labour supply models for macroeconomic questions. Both the empirical and theoretical work described in this paper could usefully be extended in several directions. It would be valuable to develop tests which can distinguish different aspects of persistence. In particular, the model developed here completely ignores the accumulation of human capital. The explicit inclusion of human capital in the model would provide a more satisfactory basis for rationalizing the observed persistence in labour supply, and would also suggest relationships between employment experience and subsequent wage levels. It would be valuable to extend the empirical work reported here by attempting direction estimation of utility function parameters using recently developed rational expectations techniques. Unsuccessful estimates of a relatively simple utility function which takes no account of persistence effects are presented in Mankiw, Rotemberg and Summers (1982). While these extensions would be valuable, it is unlikely that they would call into question the main conclusion reached here that a proper theory of labour supply must come to grips with the persistence of participation.

We are grateful for discussions with G. Chamberlain, A. Dammann, R. Freeman, R. Hall, J. Medoff, and C. Sims. Daniel Smith, James Poterba and George Fenn assisted with the computations. This research was supported by ASPER of the U.S. Department of Labour. An earlier version of this paper appeared as an ASPER Working Paper in January 1979.

NOTES

1. At the conference where this paper was presented we became aware of the important paper by Altonji (1982). His work provides a comprehensive set of econometric tests of what this paper calls the timing hypothesis.

2. The most extensive empirical work is reported in Houthakker and Taylor (1970). Theoretical analysis is surveyed by Pollak (1978).

3. In a Keynesian framework, this may be interpreted as temporarily increasing aggregate demand, and increasing employment opportunities. In the context of a classical model, it can be thought of as an unexpected increase in the money stock, leading to a transitory increase in the perceived real wage. In either case the expansionary policy is taken to be temporary in its direct effect.

4. For a recent statement of this argument, see Wachter (1977).

5. It is tempting but inaccurate to regard persistence effects as arguments in support of expansionary policy. If the economy is intially at an optimal Walrasian equilibrium, locking additional workers into employment is not an efficiency gain. Of course this conclusion does not hold if the "natural rate" of unemployment is inefficiently high, as Phelps (1972) suggests is likely to be the case. If, as has been suggested, work is habit-forming, no clear basis exists for welfare judgments.

6. Such hysteresis effects in which the equilibrium level of employment is affected by the transition path have been discussed by Phelps (1972), but have, to our knowledge, received no empirical attention.

7. Milton Friedman, *Price Theory: A Provisional Text*, 1962, p. 200.

8. Ideally one ought to look at the participation of women of different ages rather than different cohorts. Thus, for example, the appropriate way to examine the impact of the war on 50-year-old women is to look at 46-year-olds in 1940 and 56-year olds in 1950. Available data, however, precludes such an analysis.

9. This result was also obtained using employment instead of labour force participation as a measure of labour supply. It should be noted that the participation rates for married women have not been adjusted for differences in fertility. As others have noted, adjusting for fertility would accentuate the divergence between actual rates and extrapolation of 1930–1940 trends (See: Bowen and Finnegan, 1969, pp. 200–201). Fertility in 1940 was exceptionally low, while 1950 was part of the post-war baby boom. It may be that a fertility correction is inappropriate since fertility is jointly determined with labour supply.

10. It might be argued that the purportedly permanent shifts in participation induced by the World War II experience actually reflect the very weak economy of 1940. In order to test this possibility, trends were estimated in 1930. This leads to even greater discrepancies between predicted and actual participation, both during and after the war. As a further check, we estimated trends using data for the whole 1890–1980 period. The results were qualitatively similar, although the estimated effects of the war on subsequent participation were significantly reduced. Of course, this procedure may be inappropriate because the war presumably affected post-war data.

11. *Monthly Labor Review*, May (1944).

12. Both in aggregate and within occupations, there was virtually no change in the ratio of male and female hourly and/or yearly earnings between 1939 and 1950. The data must be interpreted cautiously because of a plethora of selection effects.

13. Strictly speaking, all that is required is that (1) can be represented as $V_1(c_{t-1}, l_{t-1}) + V_2(c_t, l_t c_{t+1}, l_{t+1})$.

14. In the empirical work below, we use the unemployment rate for 35–44 year old men. This avoids problems of demographic adjustment.

15. The estimates were performed using annual data for the period 1949–1981. Two lags on each variable were included. Wages are measured using an index of compensation in the private business sector. Prices are measured using the consumption price deflator, and output is measured as real GNP.

16. The tax rate is the sum of the average marginal tax rate imposed on labour income, Federal income taxes, state and local taxes and Social Security taxes. The municipal bond rate is then used as a crude proxy for the other tax interest rate.

17. In the empirical work reported below, we control for migration so this difficulty does not arise. In results which are not reported, measures of demand were used other than the unemployment rate with very little effect on the results. The problem of seasonality in the census sampling is not dealt with.

18. Fleisher and Rhodes argue that the unemployment rate is properly treated as endogeneous in participation equations. However, the instrumental variables they employ, such as the growth rate of employment are probably at least as likely as unemployment to be correlated with the error term in the participation equation.

19. In the results reported below, earnings are used as a wage proxy. This creates an obvious upwards bias in the estimate of wage effects on labour supply.

REFERENCES

ALTONJI, J. (1982), "The Intertemporal Substitution Model of Labor Market Fluctuations: An Empirical Analysis", *Review of Economic Studies*, **49**.
BARTH, P. (1968), "Unemployment and Labor Force Participation", *Southern Economic Journal*, 375–382.
BLINDER, A. and FISCHER, S. (1980), "Inventories, Rational Expectations, and the Business Cycle" (NBER Working Paper).
BOWEN, W. and FINNEGAN, T. A. (1969) *The Economics of Labor Force Participation* (Princeton University Press).
CHAMBERLAIN, G. (1978), "The Use of Panel Data in Econometrics" (unpublished).
CLARK, K. B. and SUMMERS, L. H. (1979), "Labor Market Dynamics and Unemployment: A Reconsideration", *Brookings Papers on Economic Activity*, 13–61.
FAMA, E. F. (1975), "Short Term Interest Rates as Predictors of Inflation", *American Ecomonomic Review*, 269–282.
FISCHER, S. (1978), "Long Term Contracts: Rational Expectations and the Optimal Money Supply Rule", *Journal of Political Economy*, 111–205.
FLEISHER, B. and RHODES, G. (1976), "Unemployment and the Labor Force Participation of Married Men and Women: A Simultaneous Model", *Review of Economics and Statistics*, 398–406.
FREEMAN, R. (1976), "Individual Mobility and Union Voice in the Labor Market", *American Economic Review*, 361–368.
FREEMAN. R. (1977), "Quits, Separations, and Job Tenure: The Exit-Voice Tradeoff" (unpublished).
FRIEDMAN, M. (1962) *Price Theory: A Provisional Text* (Aldine).
GHEZ, G. and BECKER, G. (1975) *The Allocation of Time and Goods Over the Life Cycle* (National Bureau of Economic Research).
HALL, R. E. (1980), "Labor Supply and Aggregate Fluctuations", *Carnegie Rochester Conference*, **12**, 7–34.
HALL. R. E. (1973), "The Rigidity of Wages and the Persistence of Unemployment", *Brookings Papers on Economic Activity*, 301–350.
HECKMAN, J. (1978), "Statistical Models for Discrete Panel Data Developed and Applied to Test the Hypothesis of True State Dependence Against the Hypothesis of Spurious State Dependence" (unpublished).
HOUTHAKKER, H. and TAYLOR, L. (1970), *Consumer Demand in the U.S.: Analysis and Projections*.
KYDLAND, F. and PRESCOTT, E. (1981), "Time to Build and Aggregate Fluctuations" (mimeo).
LONG, C. (1958) *The Labor Force Under Changing Income and Employment* (Princeton University Press).
LUCAS, R. E. (1975), "An Equilibrium Model of the Business Cycle", *Journal of Political Economy*, 1113–1144.
LUCAS, R. E. (1973), "International Evidence on Output-Inflation Tradeoffs", *American Economic Review*, 316–334.
LUCAS, R. E. and RAPPING, L. (1969), "Real Wages, Employment, and Inflation", *Journal of Political Economy*, 721–754.
MANKIW, N. G., ROTEMBERG, J. and SUMMERS, L. H. (1982), "Intertemporal Substitution in Macroeconomics" (unpublished).
McCALLUM, B. (1976), "Rational Expectations and the Estimation of Economic Models: An Alternative Procedure", *International Economic Review*, 484–490.
MEDOFF, J. L. (1979), "Layoffs and Alternatives Under Trade Unions in U.S. Manufacturing", *American Economic Review*, 380–395.
MINCER, J. (1966), "Labor Force Participation and Unemployment: A Review of Recent Evidence," in Gordon, R. A. (ed) *Prosperity and Unemployment* (Wiley).
OKUN, A. (1973), "Upward Mobility in a High Pressure Economy", *Brooking Papers on Economic Activity*, **1**, 207–252.
PHELPS, E. (1972), *Inflation Policy and Unemployment Theory* (New York).
POLLAK, R. (1978), "Endogenous Tastes in Demand and Welfare Analysis", *American Economic Review*.
SARGENT, T. (1980), *Macroeconomic Theory*.
THUROW, L. C. (1976), *Generating Inequality*.
WATCHER, M. (1977), "Intermediate Swings in Labor Force Participation", *Brookings Paper on Economic Activity*, **2**, 545–574.
YATCHEW, A. (1977), "Heterogeneity and State Dependence in Labor Supply" (unpublished).

Review of Economic Studies (1982) XLIX, 845–859
0034-6527/82/00600845$00.50

Energy and Resource Allocation: A Dynamic Model of the "Dutch Disease"

MICHAEL BRUNO
Hebrew University and NBER

and

JEFFREY SACHS
Harvard University and NBER

It is well known that a domestic resource discovery gives rise to wealth effects that cause a squeeze of the tradeable good sector of an open economy. The decline of the manufacturing sector following an energy discovery has been termed the "Dutch disease", and has been investigated in many recent studies. Our model extends the principally static analyses to date by allowing for: (1) short-run capital specificity and long-run capital mobility; (2) international capital flows; and (3) far-sighted intertemporal optimizing behaviour by households and firms. The model is solved by numerical simulation.

The rise in energy prices in the 1970s caused a significant increase in national wealth in oil-exporting economies. Similar windfalls occurred in economies that enjoyed major resource discoveries. The wealth increases following higher oil prices or resource discoveries have a systematic impact on the sectoral allocation of resources. Booming demand, caused by higher wealth, leads to a shift of an economy's productive resources from tradeable-goods sectors to non-tradeable goods sectors. The squeeze of the tradeables sector in this context has become known as the "Dutch disease", and has been the subject of many recent studies, (*e.g.* Bruno (1982); Buiter and Purvis (1982); Corden and Neary (1980); Forsyth and Kay (1980); and Neary and Purvis (1981)). It is also the subject of a lively policy debate in the U.K.

The analyses of the Dutch disease to date have been incomplete in a number of respects. Most models of the Dutch disease have been static, though the effects of higher wealth on the traded and non-traded goods sectors are inherently dynamic. In our view, a complete theoretical model should allow for: (1) short-run capital specificity, and long-run capital mobility between sectors; (2) capital accumulation in the aggregate; (3) international capital mobility; and (4) far-sighted behaviour by firms and households (in their investment, consumption and savings decisions). Bruno (1982) provides for these factors in a two-period analytical model, and this paper complements that analysis by extending it to the infinite-horizon case. This extension allows for a quantitative assessment of the adjustment path of the economy. This substantial benefit comes at some cost: the model is no longer analytically tractable and must be solved by numerical algorithm, as we describe below.

The model employed here is a direct extension of the framework described by us elsewhere in this volume. In addition to exogenous energy production, firms in the traded and non-traded goods sectors produce output according to two-level CES production functions, combining value-added with intermediate inputs. Capital is assumed to be costly to adjust, so that determinate investment demand equations may be derived. We choose the case in which the investment rate in each sector may be written as a function of the sector's "Tobin's q" (the real price of equity in the sector). Households behave according to a life-cycle consumption model. Domestic and foreign capital markets are fully integrated, so that home assets must earn the world rate of return. At this point there are no monetary assets in the model (the financial assets are equity claims to capital and real bonds), so that monetary policy and exchange rate management are not studied. Unemployment results only from *real* wage rigidities. The model is solved as a perfect foresight, intertemporal equilibrium, in which various policies may be analyzed without being subject to the "Lucas critique."

While some aspects of our model are loosely calibrated to the U.K. economy, the model is *not* equipped at this point to assess the role of the Dutch disease in recent U.K. performance. Thus, we do not seek to add empirical estimates to the British policy debate on this issue. For stimulating contributions to that debate, see Forsyth and Kay (1980) for a view which attributes a large role to the Dutch disease, and Fleming (1981) for an opposing view.

In the next section, the barebones of the "Dutch disease" are set forth, and some of the dynamic issues are described. In Section 2, the full model is detailed, and many of its properties are mentioned. Specific simulation exercises are set forth in the third section, and possible extensions of this analysis are raised in the fourth and concluding section.

I. INTRODUCTION TO THE DUTCH DISEASE

A rise in wealth, e.g. from a resource discovery, leads to a rise in demand for all normal goods, including both traded and non-traded commodities. By assumption, the demand for non-traded goods can only be satisfied domestically, while the demand for tradeables can be satisfied by increased net imports. As demand rises for both types of goods, the relative price of non-traded goods must increase to preserve home-market equilibrium. Factors will be drawn into the non-traded goods sector and away from tradeables. Some of the increased demand for non-tradeables will be satisfied by increased production, and the rest will be eliminated by the rise in the relative price of non-tradeables. The increased demand for tradeables will be met by increased imports, which more than make up for the decline in their domestic production.

Figure 1 illustrates these effects in a simple run static framework, for the case of a resource discovery. There are three sectors: energy (E), non-traded goods (N), and tradeables other than energy (T). Capital is fixed within sectors, while labour is mobile across sectors. Energy production requires no factor inputs. For illustrative purposes, relaxed later, we can assume that all of the domestic energy is exported. Budget balance requires (in the absence of savings, investment, and internation capital flows):

$$P_T Q_T + P_N Q_N + P_E Q_E = P_T C_T + P_N C_N$$

where C denotes consumption by domestic residents and Q denotes domestic production. Market clearing in the non-traded goods market requires $Q_N = C_N$. We will denote the relative price on N in terms of T as π_N $(=P_N/P_T)$, and the relative price of E as π_E $(=P_E/P_T)$.

In an economy without oil $(Q_E = 0)$, equilibrium would be at point A. A discovery of oil in this simple model would shift the consumption possibility frontier vertically in the amount $\pi_E Q_E$. Non-traded good production rises, from Q_N^A to Q_N^B, and the relative price of non-traded goods, π_N, rises (the slope at the point of tangency becomes steeper). Production of tradeables falls absolutely (from Q_T^A to Q_T^B), while net imports of non-oil tradeables rise from zero to $C_T^B - Q_T^B$.

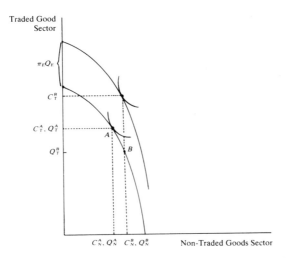

FIGURE 1

The short-run effects of an oil discovery

In general, such a static analysis is inadequate, since the shift from A to B will cause profitability on capital in the two sectors to diverge *and* to differ from the rate of return given on world capital markets. In the long run, these rates of return must equalize, so that a "long-run" analysis might proceed as in Figure 2. Now, we assume that physical capital (with relative price π_k) flows freely between sectors and from abroad so that the marginal value product of capital is always equal to $r^*\pi_k$, where r^* is the fixed world rental rate. By standard results of the Heckschen–Ohlin–Samuelson model (assuming constant-returns-to-scale production technology in N and T), fixing $r^*\pi_k$ also fixes the relative price of non-traded goods to traded goods, π_N, and forces the economy to produce on a Rybczynski line (depicted RR), along which capital in both sectors earns the marginal value product $r^*\pi_k$. In Figure 2, the RR line is drawn according to the assumption that the non-tradeable sector is capital intensive. The line $C(\pi_N)$ in Figure 2 is a consumption-expansion path showing the consumption levels of C_S and C_T for various income levels, at the fixed relative price π_N.

An economy without oil starts at equilibrium at point A. National income in tradeable units is given by the distance OB. An oil discovery, owned by domestic residents, raises GDP by the amount $P_E Q_E$, which is given by BD in the figure. Consumption shifts to point F, at the intersection of $C(\pi_N)$ and the new national budget line.[1] By the assumption of perfect world capital mobility, the relative price π_N remains unchanged, unlike in the short-run model above. Since the new domestic consumption of non-tradeables C_N^F must be satisfied by domestic production of non-tradeables, production must lie on the RR line directly below the point F, at G in Figure 2. At this point, capital and labour inputs have increased absolutely in the N-sector and have decreased absolutely in the T-sector. The basic result of the "Dutch disease" analysis is again confirmed: the (non-oil) tradeable sector is compressed by the discovery of oil. But here, international capital mobility proceeds to the point where the relative price increase of non-traded goods is completely eliminated. Also, once again, net imports of the tradeable good rise sharply.

Figures 1 and 2 provide two faces of the adjustment process, but unfortunately we cannot simply concatenate these two figures to get a truly dynamic analysis. In general,

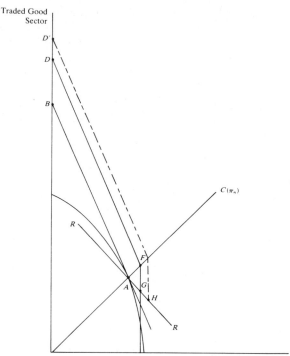

FIGURE 2
Long-run model of oil discovery

the impact effect of the oil discovery will be a shift in investment demands in the two sectors, which will disturb the equilibrium at point B in Figure 1. More importantly, the economy will run current account imbalances as the adjustment proceeds, so that by the time that the long-run of Figure 2 is achieved, national income will have to be adjusted to take into account the economy's net foreign investment position. For example, national income may exceed the level OD (say OD') if the economy runs surpluses along the adjustment path, so that domestic production may occur at H instead of G.

One strong motive for current account surpluses will arise if agents in the economy recognize that the oil is a depleting resource, so that current national income exceeds levels that can be expected in the future. Households may then save, and accumulate foreign assets, in order to maintain consumption levels after the oil is depleted. This is a topic to which we return.

Wealth effects similar to those of an energy discovery arise if the economy is a net energy exporter and π_E increases. However, the analysis is made more difficult in this case if E is not only exported but also used as an *input* to domestic production. In our other study in this volume we discuss the implications of a rise in π_E for production where E is an intermediate input. We simply note two facts here. First, the long-run value of π_N is no longer simply a function of $r^*\pi_k$, but now also of π_E. In our model, the tradeable good sector is the more intensive user of E, so that long-run π_N is a *decreasing* function of π_E. Second, a change in π_E not only affects capital accumulation through demand changes, but also through direct effects on profitability.

Now we turn to the full dynamic model which allows us to find multi-period equilibria in an economy with far-sighted agents.

2. THE SIMULATION MODEL

The complete simulation model is set forth in Table I. It is very similar in structure to the model in Sachs (1982), and detailed justifications of the behavioural relations may be found in that earlier paper. We will briefly outline the structure here, proceeding through the functional blocks of the model. The equation numbers that follow refer to Table I. A list of variables is provided at the end of the table. All variables are written in intensive form, per unit of the full-employment labor force, which grows at rate n.

(a) *Production technology*

The economy is divided into three sectors, including two final goods (N and T) and energy (E). The final-good sectors produce according to two-level CES production functions, which combine value added with intermediate inputs. The intermediate inputs themselves involve a bundle of commodities, including energy, other imported raw materials R, and the output of the other final-good sector. Thus, there is a complete input–output structure for the economy. The production functions for the two final goods may be represented as:

$$Q_T = F^T[V_T(K_T, L_T), M_T(N_T, E_T, R_T)] \tag{1}$$

$$Q_N = F^N[V_N(K_N, L_N), M_N(T_N, E_N, R_N)]. \tag{2}$$

The V and M functions are each CES, with substitution elasticities σ_{1i} and σ_{2i} respectively ($i = N, T$).

The energy sector is assumed not to use other productive inputs.

TABLE I

The simulation model

Production Technology

(1)	$Q_T^{\rho_{1T}} = U_{VT} V_T^{\rho_{1T}} + U_{MT} M_T^{\rho_{1T}}$
(2)	$Q_N^{\rho_{1N}} = U_{VN} V_N^{\rho_{1N}} + U_{MN} M_N^{\rho_{1N}}$
(3)	$Q_E = Q_E$
(4)	$V_T^{\rho_{2T}} = U_{LT} L_T^{\rho_{2T}} + U_{KT} K_T^{\rho_{2T}}$
(5)	$V_N^{\rho_{2N}} = U_{LN} L_N^{\rho_{2N}} + U_{KN} K_N^{\rho_{2N}}$
(6)	$P_T^{\rho_{3T}} = \beta_{VT} P_{VT}^{\rho_{3T}} + \beta_{MT} P_{MT}^{\rho_{3T}}$
(7)	$P_N^{\rho_{3N}} = \beta_{VN} P_{VN}^{\rho_{3N}} + \beta_{MN} P_{MN}^{\rho_{3N}}$
(8)	$P_{VY}(\partial V_T \partial L_T) = w$
(9)	$P_{VN}(\partial V_N \partial L_N) = w$
(10)	$(\partial Q_T/\partial V_T)/(\partial Q_T/\partial M_T) = P_{VT}/P_{MT}$
(11)	$(\partial Q_N/\partial V_N)/(\partial Q_N/\partial M_N) = P_{VN}/P_{MN}$
(12)	$P_{MT}^{\rho_{4T}} = \beta_{NT} P_N^{\rho_{4T}} + \beta_{RT} P_R^{\rho_{4T}} + \beta_{ET} P_E^{\rho_{4T}}$
(13)	$P_{MN}^{\rho_{4N}} = \beta_{TN} P_T^{\rho_{4N}} + \beta_{RN} P_R^{\rho_{4N}} + \beta_{EN} P_E^{\rho_{4N}}$
(14)	$M_T^{\rho_{5T}} = U_{NT} N_T^{\rho_{5T}} + U_{RT} R_T^{\rho_{5T}} + U_{ET} E_T^{\rho_{5T}}$
(15)	$M_N^{\rho_{5N}} = U_{TN} T_N^{\rho_{5N}} + U_{RT} R_T^{\rho_{5N}} + U_{ET} E_T^{\rho_{5N}}$
(16)	$P_{MT}(\partial M_T/\partial N_T) = P_N$
(17)	$P_{MT}(\partial M_T/\partial R_T) = P_R$

TABLE I (*Cont.*)

(18) $P_{MN}(\partial M_N/\partial T_N) = P_T$

(19) $P_{MN}(\partial M_N/\partial R_N) = P_R$

(20) $\dot{K}_T = J_T - (d+n)K_T$

(21) $\dot{K}_N = J_N - (d+n)K_N$

(22) $J_T = K_T \cdot [q_T - P_{JT} + P_T\phi(n+d)/2]/(n+d)$

(23) $J_N = K_N \cdot [q_N - P_{JN} + P_N\phi(n+d)/2](n+d)$

(24) $I_T = J_T \cdot P_{JT} \cdot [1 + \phi/2 \cdot (J_T/K_T - d - n)]$

(25) $I_N = J_N \cdot P_{JN} \cdot [1 + \phi/2 \cdot (J_N/K_N - d - n)]$

(26) $P_{JT} = a_{1T}P_T + a_{2T}P_N + a_{3T}P_F + a4_TP_E$

(27) $P_{JN} = a_{1N}P_T + a_{2N}P_N + a_{3N}P_F + a_{4N}P_E$

Household Sector

(28) $W = H + F$

(29) $F = q_TK_T + q_NK_N + W^E + Z$

(30) $A = \Omega(\delta - n)W + (1 - \Omega)(wL + Tr)$

(31) $(\partial C/\partial C_T)/(\partial C/C_N) = P_T/P_N$

(32) $(\partial C/\partial C_F)/(\partial C/C_N) = P_F/P_N$

(33) $(\partial C/\partial C_E)/(\partial C/C_N) = P_E/P_N$

(34) $C^{\rho_5} = U_{CT}CT^{\rho_5} + U_{CN}C_N^{\rho_5} + U_{CE}C_E^{\rho_5} + U_{CF}C_F^{\rho_5}$

(35) $P_C^{\rho_6} = \beta_{CT}^{\rho_6} + \beta_{CN}P_N^{\rho_6} + \beta_{CE}P_E^{\rho_6} + \beta_{CF}P_F^{\rho_6}$

(36) $A = P_TC_T + P_NC_N + P_EC_E + P_FC_F$

(37) $W^E = \int_0^{\infty} P_EQ_E(1 = \tau_E)e^{-r^*i}dt$

Market Equilibrium Conditions

(38) $\dot{q}_T/q_T = r^* - \text{Div}_T/q_TK_T$

(39) $\dot{q}_N/q_N = r^* - \text{Div}_N/q_NK_N$

(40) $\dot{H}/H = r^* - (w + Tr)/H - n$

(41) $\lim_{t\to\infty} e - r^{*t}q_T = 0$

(42) $\lim_{t\to\infty} e - r^{*t}q_N = 0$

(43) $\lim_{t\to\infty} e - r^{*t}{}_H = 0$

(44) $Q_T = C_T + [a_{1T}J_T + a_{1N}J_N + (I_T/P_{JT} - J_T)] + X_T + T_N$

(45) $Q_N = C_N + [a_{2T}J_T + a_{2N}J_N + (I_N/P_{JN} - J_N)] + N_T$

(46) $\text{Div}_T = P_{VT}V_T - wL_T + q_T[J_T - (d+n)K_T] - I_T$

(47) $\text{Div}_N = P_{VN}V_N - wL_N + q_N[J_N - (d+n)K_N] - I_N$

(48a) $L_T + L_N = \bar{L}$

(48b) $\dot{W}/W = \dot{P}_C/P_C + \rho \log[(L_T + L_N)/\bar{L}]$

Balance of Payments

(49) $\dot{Z} = (P_{VT}V_T + P_{VN}V_N + P_EQ_E + r^*Z) - (A + I_T + I_N) - nZ$

(50) $X_T = \zeta(P_T/P_F)^{-\rho}s \cdot W^*$

Fiscal Policy

(51a) $Tr = \tau_E \cdot P_EQ_E$

(51b) $Tr = r^* \cdot W^E \cdot \tau_E/(1 - \tau_E)$

Notes: 1. Variable and Parameter Definitions

A Total household absorption

C Instantaneous household utility

C_E Household consumption of energy

C_F Household consumption of foreign final goods

C_N	Household consumption of N
C_T	Household consumption of T
E_N	Energy input into N
E_T	Energy input into T
F	Financial wealth of households
H	Human wealth of households
I_T	Total investment expenditure in T
I_N	Total investment expenditure in N
J_T	Gross fixed capital formation in T
J_N	Gross fixed capital formation in N
K_T	Capital stock in T
K_N	Capital stock in N
L_T	Labour input in T
L_N	Labour input in N
M_T	Intermediate input bundle in T
M_N	Intermediate input bundle in N
N_T	Non-traded input into T
P_C	Consumer price index
P_E	Price of energy input
P_F	Price of foreign final good
P_{JN}	Price of investment good in N
P_{JT}	Price of investment good in T
P_N	Price of non-traded good
P_R	Price of imported, non-energy raw material input
P_T	Price of tradeable good
P_{VN}	Value-added deflator in N
P_{VT}	Value-added deflator in T
Q_E	Production of energy
Q_N	Production of traded good
q_N	Tobin's q in non-tradeable sector
q_T	Tobin's q in tradeable sector
r^*	World interest rate
R_T	Raw material (non-energy) input into T
R_N	Raw material (non-energy) input into N
T_N	Traded-good input in N
Tr	Transfer payments from government (net)
τ_E	Tax rate on energy revenue
V_N	Value-added in N
V_T	Value-added in T
w	Nominal wage rate
W	Household sector wealth (for life-cycle households)
W^E	Wealth from energy production
W^*	World wealth
X_T	Exports of domestic traded-good
Z	Domestic holdings of foreign bonds

2. Other parameters

d	Rate of depreciation
n	Rate of population growth
δ	Rate of time preference for life-cycle savers
ϕ	Cost-of-adjustment parameter in investment functions
Ω	Proportion of life-cycle households in total

3. At any moment, K_T, K_N, and Z are predetermined. W^*, r^*, Q_E, P_F, P_R, P_E, and the parameter values of the model are exogenous. Thus, the 51 equations determine: Q_T, V_T, M_T, Q_N, M_N, Q_E, L_T, L_N, P_T, P_{VT}, P_N, P_{VN}, P_{MN}, N_T, R_T, E_T, T_N, R_N, E_N, J_T, J_N, I_T, I_N, K_T, $\dot{K}_N$, q_T, q_N, P_{JT}, P_{JN}, W, H, F, W^E, A, C_T, C_N, C_E, C_F, C, P_C, $\dot{q}_T$, $\dot{q}_N$, H, Div_T, Div_N, Z, X_T, Tr, and w or $\dot{w}$ (depending on (48a) or (48b)). In the case of (48b), w_c (w/P_c) is predetermined. Note that current the values of H, q_T, Q_N are determined implicitly by the transversality conditions (41), (42), and (43).

4. Equation pairs (4), (6); (5), (7); (12), (14); (13), (15); (34), (35) are linked by duality relationships, as spelled out in our study Bruno and Sachs (1982). The parameters in these equations are therfore subject to cross-equation restrictions.

Indeed, in this model, the issue of time pattern of oil production and "optimal depletion policy" is ignored, as the cash flow from energy production is treated as exogenous.

The production functions (1) and (2) imply dual relationships linking the prices of the final outputs with the prices of the various inputs. As we described in Bruno and Sachs (1981), these relationships are also of the CES type, since the CES function is "self-dual". Thus, we have:

$$P_T = Q_T[P_{VT}, P_{MT}(P_N, P_E, P_R)] \qquad (6)$$

$$P_N = Q_N[P_{VN}, P_{MN}(P_T, P_E, P_R)]. \qquad (7)$$

Note that these equations implicitly define the true value-added deflators P_{VT} and P_{VN} in terms of the other prices.

At any moment, the capital stocks in the final-good sectors are predetermined. Output supply functions conditional on K_T and K_N may then be derived, as was shown in detail in our other essay in this volume. Specifically, we impose the first-order conditions that $\partial V_i / \partial L_i = W/P_{Vi}$, $\partial Q_i / \partial V_i = P_{Vi}/P_i$, $\partial Q_i / \partial M_i = P_{Mi}/P_i$, $(i = T, N)$, etc., as in equations (8) to (11) in Table 1.

The optimal investment policy for the firm makes the rate of gross physical capital formation an increasing function of the sectoral Tobin's q (see Bruno and Sachs (1982)) for an extended discussion). For each sector, a unit of physical capital is a composite good, involving a fixed proportion of four commodities, so that P_I is a weighted average of P_N, P_T, P_E, and P_R. The investment equations are shown in Table 1 as (22) and (23).

(b) Household sector

Households supply labour, hold asset portfolios, and make consumption choices among traded, non-traded, energy, and imported final goods. We assume that a portion Ω of all households are perfect life-cycle savers, optimizing consumption expenditure over an infinite horizon. The remaining proportion $(1 - \Omega)$ of households are myopic or credit-constrained, and these households merely consume their labour income, without accumulating or holding financial assets. This division in households is made in recognition of the empirical evidence on consumption expenditure that shows current consumption to be more closely tied to current income than is predicted by a pure life-cycle model. (See Hayashi (1982), and Hall and Mishkin (1982) for example).

For a given class of intertemporal utility functions, life-cycle households choose total consumption expenditure $p_C C$ as a fixed fraction δ of contemporaneous wealth: $p_C C = \delta W$. A rigorous justification for this equation may be found in Sachs (1982). Non-life cycle households simple spend $(w + Tr)L$, where Tr are net *per capita* transfers from the government. Total private absorption is the sum of spending of these two groups:

$$A = \Omega \cdot \delta W + (1 - \Omega) \cdot (w + Tr) \cdot L. \qquad (30)$$

Once total spending is chosen, households divide expenditures among the variety of available goods, including N, T, E, and F (the foreign final good). Thus, $A = P_E C_E + P_T C_T + P_N C_N + P_F C_F$, with the consumption levels selected to maximize an instantaneous CES utility function. The consumption equations are given in the model as (31) through (33).

Next, consider wealth (W) held by the life-cycle households. This is comprised of human wealth and financial wealth. Human wealth is the discounted value of future labour income (inclusive of net transfers from the government) as implied by (40). Financial wealth is the sum of equity and bond holdings and oil wealth, where the latter is the post-tax discounted value of the future stream of oil revenues. (See (29) and (37) in Table I.)

(c) *Market equilibrium conditions*

There are three types of market equilibrium conditions: for assets, commodities and factor inputs. For assets, we assume that the foreign bond, and domestic equity claims to capital in the N and T sectors are all perfect substitutes, so that the ex ante expected yields must be identical. The foreign bond has a fixed instantaneous yield r^*. The yield on domestic equity is the sum of the dividend yield (Div_i/q_iK_i) and capital gains $(\dot{q}_i/q_i)$, so that

$$r^* = (\mathrm{Div}_i/q_iK_i) + (\dot{q}_i/q_i), \qquad i = T, N. \tag{38}$$

The expression for dividends is given in (46), and is based on the assumption of all-equity firms with no retained earnings (see Sachs (1982) for a more complete discussion).

There are market equilibrium conditions for the final goods sectors, that require:

$$Q_T = C_T + C_T + [a_{1T}J_T + a_{1N}J_N + (I_T/P_{JT})] + X_T + T_N \tag{44}$$

$$Q_N = C_N + G_N + [a_{2N}J_N + (I_N/P_{JN} - J_N)] + N_T. \tag{45}$$

The bracketed expressions represent the inputs of each sector into investment demand. Note that one element of final demand for the tradeable commodity is export demand X_T (which is of course not present in the non-traded sector). X_T is written as a function of exogenous foreign wealth W^*, and the relative price of the foreign final good:

$$X_T = \zeta(P_T/P_F)^{-\rho_x}W^*. \tag{50}$$

We do not need market clearing equations for energy, raw materials, or the foreign final good, since we assume that these commodities are in perfectly elastic supply on the world market.

The model is solved under two alternative assumptions for the labour market, either (a) full employment, with flexible real wages; or (b) less-than-full-employment, with sluggish real wage adjustment as a function of the rate of unemployment. Under assumption (a)

$$\bar{L} = L_T + L_N \tag{48a}$$

and under (b)

$$\dot{W}/W - \dot{P}_C/P_C = \rho \log[(L_T + L_N)/\bar{L}] \tag{48b}$$

Finally, there are the balance of payment accounting relationships, according to which the accumulation of foreign bonds by domestic residents equals the current account surplus: $(\dot{Z})_t = CA_t$. The current account is given as the difference of national income and national absorption, in (49).

3. SIMULATION RESULTS

The model parameters used in the simulations (Table II) are "guesstimates" rather than econometric estimates. Mr. Louis Dicks-Mireaux of Harvard University is now engaged in a careful econometric specification of the model. Thus, the estimates here are meant to provide a plausible order of magnitude for various effects, rather than precise measures.

To choose parameters for the production block of the model, the 1973 input–output table of the United Kingdom was used as a benchmark for factor shares. The elasticity of substitution between V_i and M_i, and between K_i and L_i, is set at $0\cdot8$. The value is probably too high for short-run substitutability, but perhaps more acceptable for the intermediate-run analysis carried out here. The elasticity of substitution among the components of M_i is set at $0\cdot5$. The remaining parameters of the production function are then selected to yield the 1973 factor shares as shown in the input–output table.

REVIEW OF ECONOMIC STUDIES

TABLE II

Key parameter values for simulation

ρ_{1T}, ρ_{1N}	$-0\cdot3$	U_{LN}	$0\cdot05$
ρ_{2T}, ρ_{2N}	$-0\cdot25$	U_{NT}	$2\cdot5$
ρ_{3T}, ρ_{3N}	$0\cdot2$	U_{RT}	$1\cdot6$
ρ_{4T}, ρ_{4N}	$0\cdot5$	U_{ET}	$0\cdot09$
ρ_{5T}, ρ_{5N}	$-0\cdot25$	U_{TN}	$0\cdot41$
d	0	U_{RN}	$0\cdot07$
n	$0\cdot02$	U_{EN}	$0\cdot79$
ϕ	10	a_{1T}	$0\cdot3$
δ	$0\cdot02$	a_{2T}	$0\cdot6$
r^*	$0\cdot04$	a_{3T}	$0\cdot1$
Ω	$0\cdot50$	a_{4T}	$0\cdot014$
ρ_S	$-0\cdot5$	a_{1N}	$0\cdot3$
σ_F	$1\cdot25$	a_{2N}	$0\cdot6$
τ_E	$0\cdot9$	a_{3N}	$0\cdot1$
U_{VT}	$0\cdot43$	a_{4N}	$0\cdot014$
U_{MT}	$0\cdot41$	β_{CT}	$0\cdot333$
U_{VN}	$0\cdot68$	β_{CN}	$0\cdot486$
U_{MN}	$0\cdot16$	β_{CE}	$0\cdot059$
U_{LT}	$0\cdot11$	β_{CF}	$0\cdot132$
U_{KT}	$0\cdot02$		

The procedure yielded the following production relations:

$$Q_T = [0\cdot43 V_T^{-0\cdot25} + 0\cdot41 M_T^{-0\cdot25}]^{-4}$$

$$Q_N = [0\cdot68 V_N^{-0\cdot25} + 0\cdot19 M_N^{-0\cdot25}]^{-4}$$

$$V_T = [0\cdot72 L_T^{-0\cdot25} + 0\cdot16 K_T^{-0\cdot25}]^{-4} \cdot (0\cdot62)$$

$$V_N = [0\cdot52 L_N^{-0\cdot25} + 0\cdot26 K_N^{-0\cdot25}]^{-4} \cdot (0\cdot55)$$

$$M_T = [2\cdot5 N_T^{-1} + 0\cdot09 E_T^{-1} + 11\cdot65 R_T^{-1}]^{-1}$$

$$M_N = [0\cdot41 T_N^{-1} + 0\cdot07 E_N^{-1} + 0\cdot79 R_N^{-1}]^{-1}.$$

Three simulation exercises were undertaken to illuminate the links of North Sea oil to the rest of the U.K. economy. First, we consider alternative budgetary methods of redistributing the proceeds of oil revenue taxes to the public, under the assumption of continuous full employment.

Second, we analyse the effects of a rise in energy prices, under the contrasting assumptions of flexible and fixed real wages. Third, we study the dynamic responses to a domestic oil discovery, again assuming full employment conditions. It is important to stress that the simulation results provide qualitative rather than quantitative measures of the effects of the various disturbances, since the model is only loosely calibrated to the U.K. economy.

All results are stated as percentage deviations from a base case, in which the economy is on an equilibrium growth trajectory. In the base case, the economy is characterized by a declining stream of domestic energy production, very similar to that assumed by Forsyth and Kay (1980). For the first 15 years, domestic energy production exceeds energy consumption by about ten percent; energy production then falls by 50% for the following 15 years, and falls again by half (to 25% of original production) for the remaining horizon of the economy. With an assumed world real interest rate of four percent, these assumptions make the country a net energy *importer* in present value terms (but presumably much less of one than the U.K.'s competitors).

Simulation 1: Budget policy and oil revenues

Under current projections, over 80% of North Sea oil earnings will be collected in taxes in the next decade. An important issue of public policy is how to manage the government budget in light of the oil revenues, both in terms of expenditure and debt policy. In this first exercise, we focus on debt management for a given trajectory of expenditure on goods and services.

Increased revenue from oil taxes can be used to reduce public debt (or equivalently, accumulate official reserves) or to make increased transfer payments to the private sector. As is well known, this choice is irrelevant under assumptions of perfect foresight, competitive capital markets, and infinitely-lived households (i.e. households with an operative bequest motive between generations). However, for finite-lived or capital-constrained households, the budget decision has an important bearing on the intertemporal distribution of consumption expenditure, and thus on prices, output, and capital accumulation as well. As described earlier, $(1 - \Omega)$ percent of the households in this model are "capital constrained", so that the budget choices will affect the growth path of the economy. In the simulations we set Ω equal to 0·5.

As a simple illustration, consider two alternative policies. In the base case, the government simply returns current tax revenue in transfers according to (51a) in Table 1 (we label this the "current-transfer" policy); in the second case, the government pays out in each period the constant, perpetuity-equivalent of its oil revenues according to (51b) (we label this the "constant-transfer" policy). Since oil revenues decline over time with the diminution of production, the current transfer is initially greater, and then later less, than the perpetuity-equivalent transfer. In the constant-transfer case, the government initially runs a budget surplus to build up reserves, the income of which is then used to sustain transfers after oil production subsides.

In sum, a switch from a current to a constant transfer policy shifts consumption to a *later* date, and smooths the intertemporal path of consumption expenditure and presumably the intertemporal distribution of utility across generations. In terms of the equilibrium in Figure 2, production is farther out along the RR line in equilibrium (e.g. at point H rather than G), so that there is greater non-tradeable production and less tradeable sector production than under a current-transfer regime. The analogy to Figure 2 is close but not perfect, though, since in the simulation model, P_N/P_T (π_N) may change slightly in equilibrium, and the relative price of domestic tradeable to foreign tradeable final goods, P_T/P_F, may also vary. (The movement of π_N apparently results from the fact that the real price of investment goods P_{JN}/P_T and P_{JT}/P_T vary in the long run.)

The specific quantitative results of the policy shift are shown in Table III. Under the constant-transfer policy, consumption and the terms of trade P_T/P_F are reduced in the early years, as is the relative price of non-traded goods to traded goods P_N/P_T.

TABLE III

Effects of a shift to a constant-transfer policy

	1980	1985	1990	Steady-state
K_T	0·0	0·2	0·4	−0·3
K_N	0·0	0·0	0·2	0·6
P_T/P_F	−0·6	−0·5	0·2	0·3
P_N/P_T	−0·6	−0·2	−0·2	0·2
Q_T/L_T	−0·2	−0·2	−0·1	0·1
Q_N/L_N	0·0	0·0	0·0	0·1
W/CPI	−0·2	−0·2	−0·2	0·2

Note: All variables are measured by their percentage change over base-case values, where in the base case all oil tax revenues are redistributed in the period of their collection.

Pecause of the terms-of-trade effect, real wages fall by 0·2%. Since P_N/P_T falls, production in the traded goods sector is stimulated, and K_T is higher in the short run, relative to the current-transfer case. Over time, the consumption expenditure in the constant-transfer policy rises relative to consumption in the base case, so that short-run effects are essentially reversed in the long-run. By sustaining consumption in the long-run, the constant-transfer policy results in higher steady-state P_T/P_F and P_N/P_T. The higher long-run consumption level means a larger non-traded goods sector, and a reduced traded-goods sector. Thus, K_N is 0·6% higher in equilibrium and K_T is 0·3% lower than under the current transfer policy.

Simulation 2: A 5% increase in world energy prices

Next, we study a small increase in the world price of energy, first under the assumption of continuous full-employment, and then with sluggishness in real wages. We assume a constant-transfer policy for government revenues. The specific shock is a permanent, unanticipated, one-shot rise in the world energy price of 5% in 1980. The effects are shown in Table IV. Details for a single sector's adjustment to higher P_E may be found in our other study in this volume.

TABLE IV

Energy price increase (5%): flexible wages

	1980	1985	1990	Steady-state
K_T	0·0	−0·2	−0·3	−0·5
K_N	0·0	0·0	0·1	0·1
P_T/P_F	0·3	0·3	0·3	0·3
P_N/P_T	0·0	0·0	−0·1	−0·1
Q_T/L_T	−0·2	−0·2	−0·2	−0·2
Q_N/L_N	−0·2	−0·2	−0·2	−0·2
W/CPI	−0·4	−0·4	−0·4	−0·5

Note: All variables are measured by their percentage change over base-case values. For this set of simulations, the government pursues a constant-transfer policy.

The novel effect here is the differential behaviour of the final goods sectors, which results from the higher energy-intensity of production in traded goods (again, see Bruno (1982) for details). When energy prices rise, full employment requires a 0·4% drop in real wages, as shown in Table IV. Substitution away from energy inputs reduces labour productivity in the tradeable sector. Q_N/L_N is also reduced as labour shifts from the traded to the non-traded goods sector. Because of the shift of labour into non-tradeables, the marginal product of capital in N actually *rises* when energy prices increase and that sector's capital accumulation increases very slightly. Profitability in T, on the other hand, is hard hit, and investment in T is sharply negative. In the steady state, K_N rises by 0·1% while K_T falls by 0·3%.

With temporary real wage rigidity, as shown in Table V, the unemployment rate jumps one percentage point upon impact of the oil shock, falling over time at a rate of about 0·2 percentage points per year. Note that the 1970 real wage stays 0·4% above the full employment level (cf. Table IV). It is easy to show that an excess real wage of 0·4% corresponds roughly to 1% unemployment under the elasticity assumptions of the model.[2] The unemployment depresses investment, but only slightly, since rational entrepreneurs know that the unemployment (and resulting low profits) are temporary. In 1985, K_T and K_N are a mere one-tenth of one percent lower than in the full employment

TABLE V

Energy price increase (5%): Sluggish real wages

	1980	1985	1990	Steady-state
K_T	0·0	−0·3	−0·4	−0·5
K_N	0·0	−0·1	0·0	0·1
P_T/P_F	0·7	0·4	0·3	0·3
P_N/P_T	0·0	0·0	0·0	−0·1
Q_T/L_T	0·1	−0·1	−0·2	−0·2
Q_N/L_N	0·1	0·2	−0·2	−0·2
W/CPI	0·0	−0·4	−0·5	−0·5
Unemployment Rate (percent)	1·0	0·2	0·0	0·0

Note: All variables except rate of unemployment are measured by their percentage change over base-case values. For this set of simulations, the government pursues a constant-transfer policy.

case. Finally, note that the real wage rigidity worsens the economy's international competitiveness after the oil shock, with P_T/P_F about 0·4% higher during 1980 than in the full-employment case.

Simulation 3: Evaluating the effects of the North Sea oil sector: The Dutch disease

The present model is well-suited to study the effects of North Sea oil production on resource allocation, though it is not yet calibrated on the demand side. To get a feel for the qualitative effects of the North Sea oil boom, we compare simulations of the economy with and without domestic energy production. The effects of a one-shot move from no production to self-sufficiency are illustrated in Table VI. We assume that energy production immediately, costlessly, and unexpectedly comes on line in 1980, and then follows the declining production profile outlined earlier.

The domestic oil wealth improves the country's terms of trade (P_T/P_F) by 0·2% initially, and raises the relative price of home to traded goods by 1·1%. There is substantial shift of labour to the non-traded goods sector, and production Q_N rises by 2·7%, while Q_T falls by 1·9%. Average labour productivity in non-traded goods accordingly falls by −0·1% initially. The terms-of-trade improvement also raises real wages by 0·8 percentage points.

TABLE VI

Energy sector windfall: Estimated effects

	1980	1985	1990	Steady-state
K_T	0·0	−0·7	−1·1	−1·3
K_N	0·0	1·2	2·0	−3·2
P_T/P_F	2·0	2·0	2·1	1·8
P_N/P_T	1·1	0·8	0·6	0·3
Q_T/L_T	0·8	0·8	0·8	0·7
Q_N/L_N	−0·1	0·2	0·4	0·5
W/CPI	0·8	0·9	1·0	1·1
Q_T	−1·9	−1·9	−1·8	−1·6
Q_N	2·7	2·9	3·0	2·9

Note: All variables are measured by their percentage change over base-case values, where in the base case, there is *no* domestic energy production. These estimates treat the emergence of the energy sector as a one-shot, unanticipated phenomonum in 1980.

The oil discovery prompts a boom in investment in N, and a squeeze in investment and profits in T. By 1985, K_N rises by $1 \cdot 2\%$ and K_T falls by $0 \cdot 7\%$. Importantly, the continued expansion of the non-traded goods sector and decline of the traded goods sector substantially reverses the relative price increase P_N/P_T. In the long run, P_N/P_T falls back to $0 \cdot 3\%$ above its initial value.

An important point not often stressed in the discussion on the Dutch disease is that optimizing, far-sighted households (and government) will not consume all current oil revenues, but will rather save in anticipation of the future decline in energy production. Thus, much of the current energy revenues should show up in current account surpluses. To the extent that the revenues are saved in the short run, the sectoral reallocation of production is postponed for the future. And to the extent that the current revenues overstate the "perpetuity equivalent" of oil earnings (i.e. to the extent that current production exceeds "permanent production"), a focus on current production levels overstates the resource allocational consequences of the oil sector.

4. CONCLUSIONS AND EXTENSIONS

Our model of a dynamic perfect foresight equilibrium in a multi-sector open economy elaborates earlier findings concerning the Dutch disease. For instance, in the third simulation we see clearly that the net effect of the energy sector is to reduce long-run production of other tradeables, and to improve the economy's terms of trade on final goods. The first simulation demonstrates that the size of this effect depends on government budget policies concerning the redistribution of oil-tax revenues to the private sector.

There are three extensions to this work that seem very fruitful at this point. Most importantly, the model must be more accurately parameterized to depict the behavioural relationships in the U.K. economy. As indicated earlier, this work is now being undertaken at Harvard by Mr. Louis Dicks-Mireaux. Second, a monetary sector and nominal and real price rigidities can be built into the present framework, along the lines of Buiter and Purvis (1982). Important aspects of the U.K. adjustment process in recent years have involved the interaction of monetary and real phenomena. For example, the strong appreciation of the pound sterling in the late 1970s has often been attributed to its role as a "petro-currency", and this appreciation has had a profound effect on the real economy.

Finally, a one-country model can be usefully embedded in a multi-country context allowing us to endogenize the world rate of interest, foreign prices, and foreign wealth. As pointed out in Sachs (1982), the overall effects of higher oil prices are importantly determined by shifts in these "world" parameters, which have been held fixed in this study.

This paper was presented under the original title "Input Price Shocks and the Slowdown in Economic Growth, Part II". The paper is part of a joint study of the authors on the macroeconmic effects of supply shocks. We thank Mr. Louis Dicks-Mireaux for very able research assistance, and an anonymous referee for valuable comments. Support from the National Science Foundation is gratefully acknowledged.

NOTES

1. There is a subtle point in determining the country's new budget line after the oil discovery. The discovery induces a capital inflow, and the economy moves down the Rybczynski line from A to G. The initial capital stock is K, and after the shock the stock is $K + \Delta K$. Initially, $GDP = r^* \pi_k K + wL$; now $GDP = r^* \pi_k (K + \Delta K) + wL + P_E Q_E$. Whether the foreign capital comes in the form of rentals from abroad, or foreign direct investment, or domestic investment financed from abroad, there will be a service income outflow (each period) in the amount $r^* \pi_k \Delta K$. Thus, GNP rises exactly by the value of oil production. The budget line, through AB, shifts to DF.

2. As a rough approximation, $d \log L \simeq -[S_L/(1-S_L)] \cdot \sigma_{KL} \cdot d \log (W/P_V)$ where S_L is the share of labour in value added, and σ_{KL} is the elasticity of substitution between K and L in value added (see Bruno and Sachs (1982)). With $S_L = 0.75$, $\sigma_{KL} = 0.8$, we find $d \log L \simeq -[0.75/0.25] \cdot 0.8d \log (W/P_V)$, or $d \log L \simeq 2.4d \log (W/P_V)$. Thus, with W/P_V about 0.4% above its equilibrium value, employment is reduced by about 1.0%.

As an empirical matter, it is quite likely that $\sigma_{KL} = 0.8$ is too high for a year-to-year calculation. While some authors have assumed Cobb–Douglas technology, our own estimates in Bruno and Sachs (1982) tend to show lower magnitudes (between 0.2 and 0.4). With a lower σ_{KL}, the short-run movements in unemployment would be scaled down (approximately in the same proportion as the reduction in σ_{KL} itself).

REFERENCES

BRUNO, M. (1982);, "Adjustment and Structural Change under Supply Shocks", *Scandanavian Journal of Economics* (forthcoming).

BRUNO, M., and SACHS, J. (1982), "Input Price Shocks and the Slowdown in Economic Growth: Estimates for U.K. Manufacturing", *Review of Economic Studies*, **49**.

BUITER, W. H. and PURVIS, D. D. (1981), "Oil, Disinflation, and Export Competitiveness: A Model of the 'Dutch Disease' ", forthcoming in Bhandari, J. and Putnam, B. (eds.) *The International Transmission of Economic Disturbances under Flexible Exchange Rates* (MIT Press).

CORDEN, W. M., and NEARY, J. P. (1980), "Booming Sector and De-industrialization in a Small Open Economy" (mimeo).

FLEMING, J. S. (1982), "U.K. Macro-Policy Response to Oil Price Shocks of 1974–75 and 1979–80", *European Economic Review* (forthcoming).

FORSYTH, P. J., and KAY, J. A. (1980), "The Economic Implications of North Sea Oil Revenues," *Journal of Fiscal Studies*, **1**, 1–28.

HAYASHI, F. (1982), "The Effect of Liquidity Constraints on Consumption: A Cross-Sectional Analysis" (mimeo, Department of Economics, Northwestern University).

HALL, R. E. and MISHKIN, F. (1982), "The Sensitivity of Consumption to Transitory Income: Estimates from Panel Data on Households", *Econometrica*, **50**.

NEARY, J. P., and PURVIS, D. D. (1981), "Real Adjustment and Exchange Rate Dynamics", presented at the NBER Conference on Exchange Rates and International Macro-economics, Cambridge, Mass.

SACHS, J. (1982), "Energy Growth under Flexible Exchange Rates", forthcoming in Bhandari, J. and PUTNAM, B. (eds.) *The International Transmission of Economic Disturbances under Flexible Exchange Rates* (MIT Press).

VAN WIJNBERGEN, S. (1981), "Optimal Investment and Exchange Rate Management in Oil Exporting Countries: A Normative Analysis of the Dutch Disease" (mimeo, Development Research Center, World Bank).

PART II

UNIONS, REAL WAGES AND EMPLOYMENT IN BRITAIN 1951–79

By S. J. NICKELL *and* M. ANDREWS*

Introduction

IT is now commonplace for Trade Unions to be allotted a large share of the blame for the parlous state of the British economy although precise estimates of how much of the blame are rather harder to come by. It is our present purpose to shed more light on this issue by investigating in some detail the relationship between Trade Unions, real wages and employment. There are two key issues here. First, what is the impact, if any, of Trade Unions on the level of real wages and second, what is the effect of real wages on employment? In spite of the obvious importance of this subject very little empirical work has even been attempted in this field. Honourable exceptions are to be found in the work of Jim Symons on labour demand in manufacturing and Patrick Minford on the impact of trade unions in the labour market.[1] Minford (1983) is the work which is most closely related to that presented here although our analysis differs from his in many respects which will become clear as we proceed. However it is the work of Patrick Minford in this area plus our dissatisfaction with the current state of the art in relation to the Phillips Curve which prompted us to undertake this investigation.

The basic idea lying behind our work is straightforward. Collective bargaining is the primary mode of wage determination in Britain. Nearly 80 per cent of manual and 50 per cent of non-manual workers are covered by collective agreements. (New Earnings Survey, 1978, HMSO). In addition a considerable proportion of the remaining non-manual workers are covered by Wages Councils and similar "quasi" collective agreements. Furthermore, in the non-manual sector, earnings in the non-union sector are also *de facto* determined collectively in certain areas, notably in some professions (solicitors, for example). We therefore suppose that we can safely model aggregate wage determination in Britain as arising from a large number of union-firm wage bargains[2] disregarding the small contribution of the "competitive" sector.[3]

* We are most grateful to Paul Kong for his admirable assistance, and to the SSRC and the Department of Employment for financial help. We would also like to thank Oliver Hart, Richard Layard, Andrew Oswald, Alan Walters and participants in the Unemployment Seminar at the London School of Economics for their comments on an earlier draft.

[1] See Symons (1981), (1982) and Minford (1983), for example.

[2] There is a problem with the view that wage bargains are effectively struck at firm level. While it is true that the role of national agreements in actually determining wages at firm or plant level has declined a great deal since the War, it remains true that in the Public Sector, national bargaining is still the norm. Nevertheless, it seems not unreasonable to treat the National Coal Board, for example, as a firm whose wage bargaining behaviour is similar to that of the firms in the private sector. We also ignore the problems which may arise if a firm deals with number of unions. We simply treat the union side as a single entity.

[3] It is also woth noting that the inclusion of a competitive sector in the theoretical framework seems to have little impact on the form of the final model to be estimated (see Minford, 1983).

We next suppose that collective bargaining proceeds in the following stylised fashion. Firms and unions bargain about the nominal wage to rule over a particular period but firms retain the "right to manage" and set employment unilaterally. This is, in fact, a generalisation of the popular model discussed in Oswald (1982), for example, where unions set the wage unilaterally given the firm's demand function. Here we suppose that although unions are aware of the demand curve, they and the employers actually *bargain* about the wage. Thus we suppose that the intensive wage bargaining which we observe in practice is something more than a process by which firms spell out the demand function and unions choose the wage. The model we use also differs from that where firms and unions bargain about both employment and the wage equally. This model we find unappealing *a priori*, on the basis of the observation that firms are continuously adjusting the size of their labour force without any intensive bargaining with unions except in the rare cases where the adjustment involves compulsory redundancy.[4]

Our model generates a labour demand relation and a nominal wage function. The latter is easily transformed into a real wage function and this then forms the basis of a two equation model determining real wages and employment. In the next section we set out the model in detail and then in Sections 2 and 3 we present our empirical model. This enables us to compute the employment effects of a number of factors including trade unions. The paper concludes with a summary and some general remarks.

1. A model of unions and wage determination

In this section we present a simple static model of employment and wage determination. In practice, because of adjustment costs and the like, the future profits of the firm will not, in fact, be independent of decisions taken in the current period. However we shall suppose that firms bargain on the basis of a single period profit function which could be viewed as a long run relationship with complete adjustment of employment to the wage. Similarly unions suppose that the demand for labour is based on this single period profit function although again this could be looked at as the long run demand. In stylised form, the bargain proceeds as follows. Suppose that the union has a utility function over wages and employment, $u(w, n)$ and the firm has a utility function over profit $U(\pi(w, n))$ where w is the wage, n is employment and π is profit. Given the wage, the employer sets employment $n^*(w)$ to solve

$$\max_n \pi(w, n).$$

[4] It has been suggested that "overmanning", which is supposed to be commonplace in Britain, is an example of the consequences of unions negotiating about employment. This is not quite the same, however. Even if the union insists on "too many" men per machine, the employer still has the power to determine the total numbers of men employed. The union is not, in fact, arguing about total employment but essentially about the conditions and intensity of work.

The firm and union then have a utility over wages of the form $U(\pi(w, n^*(w)))$ and $u(w, n^*(w))$ respectively. They bargain and the outcome we suppose to be a flexible variant of the well known Nash solution. de Menil (1971) and McDonald and Solow (1981) both have extensive discussions of alternatives in this context and the objections to the axioms underlying the Nash solution are set out in detail in Luce and Raiffa (1967) pp. 128–134. However, in spite of these objections, we feel that this solution is no less arbitrary than any others and does yield "common sense" comparative static results. Indeed it is unlikely that the comparative statics for alternative bargaining solutions would be very different. To implement the Nash solution we must define "fall back" levels of profits and union utility, $\bar{\pi}$, $\bar{u}$ say, and then the wage outcome solves

$$\max_{w} [U(\pi(w, n^*(w))) - U(\bar{\pi})]^{\beta} [u(w, n^*(w)) - \bar{u}].$$

The "fall back" levels of firm profit and union utility represent those levels which can be attained by the firm and the union in complete isolation. A point worth noting is that if we set $\beta = 0$, we have the situation where the union sets the wage given the demand curve. This model is thus a special case of that used here.

Before we proceed to impose some structure on the general functions π and u, it is worth briefly giving some further consideration to the alternative model where the firm and the union bargain over both wages and employment. Using the same notation, the outcome of the bargain is given by

$$\max_{w,n} [U(\pi(w, n)) - U(\bar{\pi})]^{\beta} [u(w, n) - \bar{u}].$$

As is well known (see McDonald and Solow 1981), the outcome of this bargain is Pareto Efficient in the sense that no adjustment of employment or wages can make the firm better off without making the union worse off. Since the previous model does not have this rather appealing property, it is worth considering why firms might wish to impose the negotiating rule that they will only talk about wages when the outcome is such that further discussion about employment could yield higher profits without impairing the union's welfare. One powerful argument is that, as we have already noted, firms find it desirable to make continuous adjustments to their total level of employment. They would, presumably, find the idea of continual negotiation on this issue, with possible discussion of wages thrown in, as simply too costly an interference with their managerial function.

As far as the consequences of the two models are concerned, they are more or less identical in their implications for wages (see Nickell 1982) but different in their implications for employment. In our chosen model, if a shift in some exogenous factor, union power for example, leads to an increase in wages, the consequence is clearly a reduction in employment as the firm moves up its demand curve. In the Pareto Efficient wage/employment bargain the consequence is different in the sense that wages and employment both move up. The union uses its increased power to raise both wages *and* employment (for a proof of this latter fact, see the Appendix). This model thus has the strong implication that a rise in union power will raise employment. Since we know of no evidence either in our results or elsewhere, to support this contention, this is an additional reason for not pursuing this particular model any further.

Our next step is to impose some structure on the general functions π and u. Here we follow closely Nickell (1982). The nominal wage bargain, W_t, is struck at t for the interval t to $t+1$. Both firm and union have identical point expectations of prices during this period, namely P_{ft}^e for producer prices and P_{rt}^e for consumer prices. The firm has a production function $A_t g(n_t)$, $g' > 0$, $g'' < 0$ where A_t is a predetermined productivity factor. Real profits π_t may thus be written

$$\pi_t = p_t A_t g(n_t) - w_t(1 + t_{1t})n_t - C_t \tag{1}$$

where $p_t = P_{ft}^e/P_{rt}^e$, $w_t = W_t/P_{rt}^e$, $t_1 = $ the employment tax rate and $C = $ fixed costs. "Fall back" profits $\bar{\pi}$ are constant for the purposes of the bargaining model but they may be a function of exogenous variables such as union power which will subsequently be important.

Turning now to the union's objective, we start by assuming that the union "takes account of" a fixed pool of workers of size l.[5] These include existing employees $n_{t-1}(1-\delta)$ where δ is the separation rate. We next suppose that the utility of the n_t workers who are employed by the firm in the coming period is v_t and of the $l - n_t$ who are not is $\tilde{v}_t$. For those staying with the firm we specify utility as

$$v_t = v(w_t(1 - t_{2t}) - \bar{w}_t) \tag{2}$$

where t_2 is the income tax rate and $\bar{w}_t$ is a "baseline" level of real wages. So we assume that utility is a function of post-tax real wages relative to some changing baseline which captures the fact that the "subsistence" real wage rises over time with the general level of well-being. Thus, in order to obtain the same degree of utility in 1975 as in 1955, an individual requires a higher real wage reflecting the fact that wellbeing is not simply an absolute concept but also contains a relative element.

For those workers who do not find employment within the firm in the next period, utility is specified as

$$\tilde{v}_t = \omega_t v \left[\frac{B_t}{P_{rt}^e} - \bar{w}_t \right] + (1 - \omega_t) v \left[\frac{W_t^*(1 - t_{2t})}{P_{rt}^e} - \bar{w}_t \right]. \tag{3}$$

ω_t is the proportion of the next period spent unemployed receiving benefits B_t and $(1 - \omega_t)$ is the proportion spent employed receiving an expected alternative wage W_t^*. We naturally suppose ω_t to be increasing in the

[5] The union may not be aware of the identity of all the workers in this pool and they may not even be union members. There is thus an element of "social responsibility" involved here and l is simply a number which reflects this.

aggregate unemployment rate but it may be a function of other exogenous variables which we shall consider at a later stage. Following Jackman and Layard (1981), we write the expected alternative real W_t^*/P_{rt}^e as

$$\frac{W_t^*}{P_{rt}^e} = w_{t-1}(1+g_t), \qquad w_{t-1} = W_{t-1}/P_{rt-1}$$

where g_t is the expected level of real wage growth in the economy as a whole. If we treat the replacement ratio $R_t = B_t/W_t^*(1-t_{2t})$ as exogenous, (3) can be rewritten as

$$\tilde{v}_t = \omega_t v(R_t w_{t-1}(1-t_{2t})(1+g_t) - w_t) + (1-\omega_t)v(w_{t-1}(1-t_{2t})(1+g_t) - \bar{w}_t) \tag{4}$$

Now we must consider the utility function of the union. This we take to be a weighted sum of the utilities of all the l workers where existing employees in the firm may be accorded a higher weight than those from outside. Union utility u_t is thus given by

$$u_t = n_{t-1}(1-\delta)v_t + \alpha(n_t - n_{t-1}(1-\delta))v_t + \alpha(l-n_t)\tilde{v}_t$$
$$= ((1-\alpha)(1-\delta)n_{t-1} + \alpha n_t)v_t + \alpha(l-n_t)\tilde{v}_t \text{ if } n_t \geq n_{t-1}(1-\delta) \tag{5a}$$

$$u_t = n_t v_t + (n_{t-1}(1-\delta) - n_t)\tilde{v}_t + \alpha(l - n_{t-1}(1-\delta))\tilde{v}_t$$
$$= n_t v_t + (\alpha l + (1-\alpha)(1-\delta)n_{t-1} - n_t)\tilde{v}_t \text{ if } n_t < n_{t-1}(1-\delta) \tag{5b}$$

α is the weight accorded to those not currently employed within the firm where we would expect $0 \leq \alpha \leq 1$. We treat (5a) as the typical case with (5b) only coming into operation in periods of very rapid contraction. The union "fall-back" position is simply taken to be the utility obtained if all workers leave the firm and obtain $\tilde{v}_t$. Thus $\bar{u}_t$ is given by

$$\bar{u}_t = n_{t-1}(1-\delta)\tilde{v}_t + \alpha(l - n_{t-1}(1-\delta))\tilde{v}_t$$

So if $n_t \geq n_{t-1}(1-\delta)$
$$u_t - \bar{u}_t = ((1-\alpha)(1-\delta)n_{t-1} + \alpha n_t)(v_t - \tilde{v}_t) \tag{6a}$$

and if $n_t < n_{t-1}(1-\delta)$
$$u_t - \bar{u}_t = n_t(v_t - \tilde{v}_t). \tag{6b}$$

Note that (6b) is simply equivalent to (6a) with $\alpha = 1$.

We are now in a position to consider the firm, union bargain. First we must specify the demand for labour which is derived from

$$\max_{n_t} p_t A_t g(n_t) - w_t(1+t_{1t})n_t - C_t$$

which yields $n^*(p_t A_t, w_t(1+t_{1t}))$ as the solution to

$$p_t A_t g'(n_t) - w_t(1+t_{1t}) = 0. \tag{7}$$

Firm and union bargain about w_t and the outcome solves[6]

$$\max_{w_t} G(w_t) = \beta \log (U(\pi_t) - \bar{U}_t) + \log (u_t - \bar{u}_t)$$

where

$$\pi_t = p_t A_t g(n^*(w_t)) - w_t(1 + t_{1t})n^*(w_t)$$
$$\bar{U}_t = U(\bar{\pi}_t)$$
$$u_t - \bar{u}_t = ((1 - \alpha)(1 - \delta)n_{t-1} + \alpha n^*(w_t))(v_t - \bar{v}_t)$$

with $\alpha = 1$ if employment falls below $n_{t-1}(1 - \delta)$. The first order condition is

$$G_w = \frac{\beta U' \pi_w}{U - \bar{U}} + \frac{u_w}{u - \bar{u}} = 0 \tag{8}$$

with $G_{ww} < 0$ as the second order condition.

We now present comparative static results under the assumption that $n_t \geqslant (1 - \delta)n_{t-1}$. The following notation is useful.

$r = -v''w(1 - t_2)/v'$, individual relative risk aversion.

$r_f = -U''\pi/U'$, firm's relative risk aversion.

$\varepsilon_v = v'w(1 - t_2)/(v - \tilde{v})$, elasticity of worker's utility increment w.r.t. income.

$\varepsilon_u = U'\pi/(U - \bar{U})$, elasticity of firm's utility increment w.r.t. profit.

$c = wn(1 + t_1)/\pi$, $s_n = -(pnAg' - wn(1 + t_1))/\pi$, $s_{nn} = -n^2 pAg''/\pi$, $s_R = pAg/\pi$

$s_\alpha = \alpha/(\alpha + (1 - \alpha)(1 - \delta))$, $n = -g'/g''n$, the elasticity of labour demand which is assumed constant, at least in the locality of the equilibrium.

All these are positive and $s_\alpha < 1$. The following is also worth noting:

$$w^2 G_{ww} = -\{\beta^2(r_f \varepsilon_u + \varepsilon_u^2)c^2 + r\varepsilon_v + \varepsilon_v^2 + s_\alpha^2 \eta^2\} < 0.$$

Let $\Delta = -w^2 G_{ww} > 0$.

Starting with those variables which influence wages via "outside" utility $\tilde{v}$, we have

(i) lagged real wages, w_{t-1}. $\partial \log w_t / \partial \log w_{t-1} = b_1 = \varepsilon_v^2/\Delta > 0$
(ii) expected real wage growth, g_t. $\partial \log w_t / \partial g_t = b_1 > 0$
(iii) replacement ratio, R_t. $\partial \log w_t / \partial \log R_t = \omega b_1 > 0$
(iv) proportion of period spent unemployed, ω_t. $\partial \log w_t / \partial \omega_t = b_2 =$

$$\varepsilon_v \frac{(v(Rw) - v(w))}{\Delta(v - \tilde{v})} < 0$$

These results are all clear cut. A rise in last period's real wage, in expected real wage growth, in the replacement rate or a fall in the proportion of the period spent unemployed all raise opportunities outside the firm. This raises the bargaining power of the union and leads to a higher wage outcome.

(v) baseline real wage, $\bar{w}_t$. $\partial \log w_t / \partial \log \bar{w}_t = b_3 = \dfrac{r\varepsilon_v}{\Delta} - \dfrac{\omega\varepsilon_v(v'(Rw) - v'(w))}{\Delta(v - \tilde{v})}$

[6] It is convenient to take logs of the Nash solution objective function.

This cannot, in general, be signed but we feel that the second term is likely to be small because the factor ω is small. This negative term arises because a rise in the baseline real wage leads to a greater loss in utility for the unemployed relative to the employed because of diminishing marginal utility. This lowers utility opportunities outside the firm relative to those inside leading to a fall in the wage bargain. The other probably larger effect is positive.

(vi) income tax rate, t_{2t}. $\partial \log w_t/\partial t_{2t} = b_4 = b_3 - \varepsilon v/\Delta = ?$

There are two important offsetting effects here. The positive impact on wages is essentially a compensation effect arising from diminishing marginal utility. On the other hand a rise in income taxes acts as a tax on wage increases and shifts the union's employment-wage trade-off in favour of the former. We expect this effect to be smaller.

Remaining with the union side, we have the following effects via the union utility function.

(vii) past employment, n_{t-1}. $\partial \log w_t/\partial \log n_{t-1} = b_5 = s_\alpha(1-s_\alpha)\eta/\Delta > 0$
(viii) weight attached to outsiders, α. $\partial \log w_t/\partial \log \alpha = b_6 =$

$$-\frac{s_\alpha(1-s_\alpha)}{\alpha(1-\alpha)}\eta/\Delta < 0$$

Higher past employment in the firm gives the union greater bargaining power leading to a higher wage. On the other hand, the more weight the union attaches to "outside" workers, the lower the wage bargain since it puts more effort into employment at the margin.

Finally on the employer's side we have the following.

(ix) relative producer prices, p_t. $\partial \log w_t/\partial \log p_t = b_7 =$
$\{\beta^2(r_f\varepsilon_u + \varepsilon_u^2)cs_R - (\varepsilon_u c\beta + s_\alpha(1-s_\alpha)\eta)\eta\}/\Delta = ?$
(x) productivity index, A_t. $\partial \log w_t/\partial \log A_t = b_7$
(xi) employment taxes, t_{1t}. $\partial \log w_t/\partial t_{1t} = b_8 =$
$\{b_1 + b_4 - (1+(b_3/r)\eta) - s_\alpha\eta\}/\Delta = ?$
(xii) fall back brofits, $\bar{\pi}$. $\partial \log w_t/\partial \log \bar{\pi} = b_9 = -\beta^2\varepsilon_u^2 c/\Delta < 0$

For the first three of these there are two opposing forces at work which can loosely be thought of as income and substitution effects. For example, if the relative producer price or productivity is higher, the firm can simply afford both to pay more and employ more workers. On the other hand the higher level of employment ·associated with this means that wage increases are more expensive at the margin than employment increases. We should expect the income effects to dominate leading to a positive impact on wages for producer prices and productivity and a negative effect for employment taxes. Higher fall back profits, on the other hand, provide the employer with greater bargaining power and lead unambiguously to a fall in the wage bargain.

This completes the list of comparative static results concerning the wage bargain when the resulting change in the labour force is not too large in the downward direction. If, on the other hand, the resulting employment level is such that $n_t < n_{t-1}(1-\delta)$ we have essentially the same results with $\alpha = 1$. Nothing changes sign under these circumstances but because s_α becomes one the impact of n_{t-1} is zero. The other derivatives will however change size since α influences G_{ww}. If only affects one term here so these changes should not be large and hence we feel justified in supposing our resulting equation to have constant coefficients.

The outcome of this model is a pair of equations determining w_t and n_t. Linearising, we may write the labour demand function as

$$\log \dot{n}_t = a_0' + a_1 \log p_t A_t - a_1 \log w_t (1+t_{1t})$$

and the wage equation as

$$\log w_t = b_0' + b_1 \log w_{t-1} + b_1 g_t + \omega b_1 \log R_t + b_2 \omega_t + b_3 \log \bar{w}_t$$
$$+ b_4 t_{2t} + b_5 \log n_{t-1} + b_6 \log \alpha_t + b_7 \log p_t + b_7 \log A_t$$
$$+ b_8 t_{1t} + b_g \log \bar{\pi}_t.$$

If we suppose that the economy consists of N identical firms, then the aggregate equations will have the same form as those above with shifted constant terms since $\log n_t N = \log n_t + \log N$. So if we redefine n_t, n_{t-1} as measures of aggregate employment we have an identical structure. Furthermore, if we have a fixed total labour force equal to L, we may write $\log n_{t-1}$ as

$$\log n_{t-1} = \log L + \log (n_{t-1}/L) = \log L + \log (1 - u_{t-1}) = \text{constant} - u_{t-1}.$$

Using this and rewriting in more explicit nominal terms we have the following employment and real wage equations.

$$\log n_t = a_0 - a_1 \log \frac{W_t}{P_{ft}^e}(1+t_{1t}) + a_1 \log A_t. \tag{9}$$

$$\log (W_t/P_{rt}) = b_0 + \log (P_{rt}^e/P_{rt}) + b_1 \log (W_{t-1}/P_{rt-1}) + b_1 g_t$$
$$+ \omega b_1 \log R_t + b_2 \omega_t + b_3 \log \bar{w}_t + b_4 t_{2t} - b_5 \log u_{t-1}$$
$$+ b_6 \log \alpha_t + b_7 \log (P_{ft}^e/P_{rt}^e) + b_7 \log A_t + b_8 t_{1t}$$
$$+ b_9 \log \bar{\pi}_t. \tag{10}$$

Our previous results indicate the following signs. $a_1 > 0$, $b_1 > 0$, $b_2 < 0$, $b_3 > 0$ probably, $b_4 > 0$ probably, $b_5 > 0$, $b_6 < 0$, $b_7 > 0$ probably, $b_8 < 0$ probably, $b_9 < 0$. In the next section we consider how these equations can be estimated and present some results.

2. The empirical model and the data

As they stand, equations (9) and (10) cannot be estimated directly since many of the variables are not observable. Starting with the labour demand equation we first consider the variable A_t which refers to the general level of productivity. More specifically we assumed a (value added) production relation of the form $A_t g(n_t)$. Suppose the basic gross output production function is of the form

$$y_g = f(n, k, m)$$

where y_g is gross output, k is capital stock and m is the input of raw materials and fuel. Suppose that P_m is the price of the latter input. Then value added in terms of consumer goods is

$$\frac{P_f}{P_r} f(n, k, m) - \frac{P_m}{P_r} m.$$

Suppose that capital stock is predetermined but the material/fuel input is adjusted optimally in the current period. Then we may write value added as

$$y = \max_m \left(\frac{P_f}{P_r} f(n, k, m) - \frac{P_m}{P_r} m \right). \tag{11}$$

Suppose optimal material/fuel input is given by $m^*(n, k, P_m/P_f)$. Then (11) can be rewritten as

$$y = \frac{P_f}{P_r} \left\{ f\left(n, k, m^*\left(n, k, \frac{P_m}{P_f}\right)\right) - \frac{P_m}{P_f} m^*\left(n, k, \frac{P_m}{P_f}\right) \right\} = \frac{P_f}{P_r} h\left(n, k, \frac{P_m}{P_f}\right)$$

This suggests that A_t should be specified as some function of k_t and $(P_m/P_f)_t$ and this is indeed how we proceed.[7] Furthermore we would expect A to be increasing in k and decreasing in P_m/P_f and so we shall take a log linear approximation of the form

$$\log A_t = c_0 + c_1 \log k_t + c_2 \log P_m/P_f, \qquad c_1 > 0, \qquad c_2 < 0. \tag{12}$$

The real wage term in the labour demand equation (9) is specified with expected producer prices in the denominator. This we shall simply replace with actual producer prices. In reality employment is not fixed on a period by period basis as assumed in the model but may be adjusted rather more frequently. This seems to us a strong enough reason to dispense with the expectation. However this leads us to the more serious problem of translating the static model of (9) into a dynamic model which will undoubtedly be required in the empirical work. The combination of adjustment costs and aggregation leads to a labour demand relation in which employment adjusts slowly towards a target which depends on both current and future expected values of relative prices (see Sargent (1978) or Nickell (1981), for example). Here we choose to keep things simple by replacing the future expectations by distributed lags thereby compounding adjustment lags with expectational

---

[7] If, for example, $f = n^\alpha k^\beta m^\gamma$ then $h = (1-\gamma)\gamma^{\gamma/1-\gamma} \left(\frac{P_m}{P_f}\right)^{-\gamma/1-\gamma} k^{\beta/1-\gamma} n^{\alpha/1-\gamma}$.

ones. We recognise the dangers involved, particularly that of parameter instability which can arise simply because of changes in the expectations formation mechanism caused perhaps by shifts in the processes driving the relative price series. However we feel that as a first step it is best to see if we can detect anything in the data which corresponds to our perhaps naive formulation of labour demand. So the static version of our final model has the form

$$\log n_t = (a_0 + a_1 c_0) - a_1 \log \frac{W_t(1 + t_{1t})}{P_{ft}} + a_1 c_1 \log k_t + a_1 c_2 \log \frac{P_{mt}}{P_{ft}} \quad (13)$$

and the dynamic version to be estimated would include distributed lags of $\log n$ and the relative price terms. In the aggregate context, the current relative prices are, of course, endogenous.[8]

Turning to the more complex real wage equation, many of the variables require some discussion. Starting with the term in the expected price ratio $\log (P_{rt}^e/P_{rt})$, we shall try two possibilities, $(\log P_r(t, t+1) - \log P_{rt})$ and $(\log P_r(t-1, t) - \log P_{rt})$ where $p(s, t)$ refers to the expectation formed at time s about time t. We may need both because, working with annual data, the wage index contains wage bargains which are set more or less contemporaneously to which the first term is relevant and wage bargains which were set up to a year ago and for these the second term seems more appropriate. Both these terms are endogenous and for the price expectation variables we use the fitted values from a subsidiary regression. In addition, although we prefer the real wage formulation of equation (10), we shall also consider the equivalent version with $\log (W_t/P_{rt}^e)$ as the dependent variable for reasons which will become apparent.

The variables g_t and $\log \bar{w}_t$ refer to the expected growth in real wages in the economy as a whole and the baseline level of real wages. These we attempt to capture by using a distributed lag on real wages and some measure of trend productivity. $\log A_t$ is also, of course, related to this latter variable. In the context of the employment equation we took A_t to be related to the absolute level of the capital stock. In this equation, however, this must clearly be normalised[9] and we use the labour force as the normalising factor to smooth out the cyclical variations in productivity. The relative price of materials enters as before and this discussion suggests that

---

[8] This simple "neoclassical" labour demand function has been estimated for U.K. manufacturing by Jim Symons (with results presented in Symons, 1981) but surprisingly has never, to our knowledge, previously been applied to aggregate U.K. employment prior to the work of one of the authors of this paper which is set out in Andrews (1983). The equations presented here are taken more or less directly from this work.

[9] Our theoretical model has a fixed labour force and so there is no problem. If the total labour force changes over time, however, it is clear that real wages cannot depend simply on the level of capital stock but on its size relative to some measure of the working population.

we replace the terms in g_t, $\log \bar{w}_t$, $\log A_t$ as follows:

$$b_1 g_t + b_3 \log \bar{w}_t + b_7 \log A_t = \sum_{j=1} \alpha_j \log (W_{t-j}/P_{rt-j}) + \beta_3 \log (k_t/L_t)$$
$$+ \beta_4 \log P_{mt}/P_{ft} + \text{constant}$$

with $\beta_3 > 0$. $\beta_4 < 0$. L_t is a measure of the total labour force.

In our theoretical section we took the replacement ration R_t as exogenous on the grounds that benefits are set relative to some wage norm by policy makers. An alternative possibility, favoured by Patrick Minford, is to assume that policy makers set real benefits for the unemployed which suggest the use of benefits normalised on retail prices as the relevant variable. Here we shall look at both possibilities as well as a number of different measures of the benefit level (unemployment benefit, supplementary benefit etc.). The variable ω_t measures the proportion of the relevant period which an individual who loses his job can expect to remain unemployed. This immediately suggests writing it as an increasing function of the unemployment rate. There is, however, at least one other relevant factor here. In reality there are wide variations in unemployment and in labour demand in different sectors of the labour market, regional, occupational and industrial and these to some extent indicate a degree of mismatch between supply and demand. For a variety of reasons which may loosely be collected under the heading "comparability", wages tend to move together across different labour markets and wages in sectors exemplified by high demand and low unemployment tend to tow along wages in sectors where the labour market has some degree of slack. This leads to some problems of aggregation and suggests that aggregate wage rises will be less influenced by any particular average level of unemployment, the more this is due to mismatch across the different sectors. So if we can find some measure of mismatch, we should expect it to exert a positive impact on wages for any given level of unemployment.[10] So we may write

$$\omega_t = \text{constant} + \beta_5 u_t + \beta_6 mm_t, \qquad \beta_5 > 0, \qquad \beta_6 < 0 \qquad (15)$$

where mm is the level of mismatch. The variable we use as an indicator of mismatch is the *absolute* annual *change* in the proportion of employees in the production sector. The idea here is that the greater the *absolute* shift in employment between sectors with disparate occupational structures, the greater the resulting level of mismatching.

The term $\log \alpha_t$ measures the weight which the union attaches to "outsiders". It might be argued that unions devote less attention to outsiders when unemployment is high and they are deeply concerned with preventing job losses and/or wage cuts among their existing employees. This suggests that we specify $\log \alpha_t$ as

$$\log \alpha_t = \text{constant} + \beta_7 u_{t-1}, \qquad \beta_7 < 0. \qquad (16)$$

[10] This argument is, in fact, closely related to the ingenious discussion of aggregation in Lipsey (1960).

The term $\log(P^e_{ft}/P^e_{rt})$ is the expected ratio of producer to consumer prices and this we take to be simply the inverse of the current rate of indirect tax t_{3t}. Thus

$$\log(P^e_{ft}/P^e_{rt}) = \log[(1+t_{3t})^{-1}] \simeq -t_{3t}. \tag{17}$$

Finally in this sequence we have $\log \bar{\pi}_t$, the level of "fall back" profit available to the firm. This is directly influenced by "union power" in the sense that a strong union can impose very high costs on a firm if it refuses to strike a bargain. So if U_p is union power, we may write

$$\log \bar{\pi}_t = \text{constant} + \beta_8 U_{pt}, \qquad \beta_8 < 0. \tag{18}$$

In the empirical work we use two estimates of union strength, one based on the proportion of employees in unions, the so called union density and the other based on a measure of the union/non-union wage "mark-up" for which a time series is now available. This is based on an extension of the series presented in Layard, Metcalf and Nickell (1978), Table 5. It is important to note that these proxy measures of union power are somewhat deficient for our purposes. The union density is clearly rather a crude measure and given the possibility of reverse causation, that is high wage rises leading to higher recruitment, we must treat this variable as endogenous. The "mark-up" is, in some sense, an *ex post* measure which also has endogenous elements. Thus an increase in union power leads to both higher union wage rises and a higher "mark-up".[11] It is important, therefore, to purge these variables of their endogenous elements by appropriate use of instruments in order to capture only the exogenous impact.

The upshot o this discussion is a real wage equation of the form

$$\log(W_t/P_{rt}) = \beta_0 + \beta_1(\log P_r(t, t+1) - \log P_{rt}) + \beta_2(\log P_r(t-1, t) - \log P_{rt})$$
$$+ (\alpha_1 + b_1)\log(W_{t-1}/P_{rt-1}) + \sum_{j=2} \alpha_j \log(W_{t-j}/P_{rt-j})$$
$$+ \beta_3 \log(k_t/L_t) + \beta_4 \log(P_{nt}/P_{ft}) + \omega b_1 \log R_t + b_2\beta_5 u_t$$
$$+ b_2\beta_6 mm_t + b_4 t_{2t} + (b_6\beta_7 - b_5)u_{t-1} - b_7 t_{3t} + b_8 t_{1t} + b_9\beta_8 U_{pt}. \tag{19}$$

$$\beta_1 > 0, \quad \beta_2 > 0, \quad (\alpha_1+b_1), \alpha_j = ?, \quad \beta_3 > 0, \quad \beta_4 < 0, \quad \omega b_1 > 0, \quad b_2\beta_5 < 0,$$
$$b_2\beta_6 > 0, \quad b_4 > 0, \quad (b_6\beta_7 - b_5) = ?, \quad b_7 > 0, \quad b_8 < 0, \quad b_9\beta_8 > 0.$$

The signs are the ones which we expect but as the listing following equation (10) indicates some of these are merely probable. The endogenous variables

[11] It is also worth remarking that the fact that we can estimate the mark-up for manual workers in the covered relative to the uncovered sector is rather opposed to the spirit of this paper where we suppose that the uncovered sector is of negligible importance in wage determination. We would simply reiterate that the uncovered manual sector is very small but not so small as to make estimates of the time series variation in the mark-up entirely meaningless.

are price expectations, P_{mt}/P_{ft}, u_t, the measures of union power and possibly the replacement ratio, R.

The data used are annual for the U.K. from 1951–79. We use annual data because many of the variables are not available quarterly and we are also able to cover nearly all the post-war period which is, of itself, of some considerable interest. Details, definitions and a listing of each variable are to be found in the data appendix.

The two equation model is not, of course, a complete structural model in the sense that there are a number of endogenous variables not explained within it. These are unanticipated inflation, the real price of materials and energy and the union power variables (note that the unemployment rate is one minus the employment rate and is thus determined by the model). It is also worth noting that although the capital stock is predetermined, it is, of course, an endogenous variable in the long run and thus our explanation of the path of real wages, for example, is conditional on the path of the capital stock. Another point worth considering is precisely how aggregate demand shocks influence employment. The answer is that they come through via the forecast error in prices. For example, a contractionary fiscal and monetary policy leads to lower prices than expected (both directly and via rises in the exchange rate) and this results in higher real wages and lower employment, with the lags in the employment equation ensuring that the impact is spread over several years. The period 1979–81 is a classic example of this process in operation.

Given the plethora of endogenous variables, we must consider the choice of instruments. We can choose from the complete list of exogenous variables in the implicit economy wide model lying behind our labour market sector. Since there are rather more such instruments available than degrees of freedom we have to be selective, choosing those which are particularly relevant in the light of the endogenous variables included in the equations. A list of instruments used for each equation is presented in the notes to Table 1 but it is worth remarking that the estimated equations exhibit a considerable degree of stability in response to rather wide variations in the chosen instruments.

3. The results

Final estimates of equations (13) and (19) are given in Table 1 and we comment first on the labour demand function. Generally it seems fairly robust with sensible coefficients particularly in terms of the crucial long run effects. The size of the χ^2 associated with instrument validity suggests the possibility that some of the instruments, particularly those on the demand side, should actually appear in the equation. We are, of course, particularly keen to try and obtain some picture of the real wage effect on employment including "output effects" and hence we do not want to corrupt this by holding constant demand elements. However it is worth noting that the inclusion of our demand side instruments, in particular government expenditure and world trade variables, in the equation has no impact whatever. Their coefficients and t statistics are negligible and the other coefficients remain unchanged. In any event the χ^2 test, uncorrected as it is for degrees of freedom, is liable to reject the null too frequently in small samples and it is clear, given our relatively small sample, that adjustment for degrees of freedom will put it down well into the region of non-rejection. Turning to the coefficients themselves, the lagged employment coefficients indicate a fairly rapid response to price changes with most of the long run adjustment to real wage changes being completed in 2 years. As the current real wage effect is negligible there is no response for a year but in the long run the elasticity of employment with respect to the real wage is -0.51. This may be compared with Jim Symon's estimate of rather more than unity for the manufacturing sector (Symons 1981). The fact that the aggregate elasticity is considerably lower is only to be expected, given the far higher degree of openness of the manufacturing sector in comparison with the rest of the economy. The consequently larger output demand elasticities in this sector lead immediately to higher factor demand elasticities via the Marshallian Rules. The long run elasticity of material prices with respect to employment is around -0.08 although in the short run there is a small positive effect suggesting perhaps some fairly rapid substitution of employment for materials and fuel which is dominated by the output effect over the long period.

The real wage equation (the first real wage column, Table 1) also appears quite satisfactory although, in comparison with the specification set out in equation (19), a number of terms are notably absent. We had no success whatever with the expected price deviations, their incllusion resulting in coefficients which were small, incorrectly signed and poorly determined ($t < 1.0$ in all cases). Furthermore, there was little impact on the other coefficients. These results are rather worrying and we feel that errors in our measurement of price expectations are largely to blame (the same difficulty is mentioned in Minford 1983). This inability to capture the unanticipated inflation term is, in fact, a more serious problem that would appear at first sight. As we have already noted, it is this term which captures demand shocks. If we cannot pick these up adequately in the equation they will be relegated to the error thereby invalidating nearly all of our current dated instruments. They will also render our current tax variables endogenous. In practical terms this means that the coefficients on all the current dated variables except the capital stock will be picking up demand shocks and the estimated equation will no longer represent the structural wage bargaining equation. Thus, for example, a rise in taxation leads to a contraction which leads to an increase in expected prices relative to actual prices. The fact that this term is in the equation error induces an upward bias in the tax effects. In order to deal with this problem, we utilise two strategies. The first is to use only lagged instruments and endogenise all the current dated variables except the capital stock. The second is to use the nominal wage relative to

TABLE 1

Labour demand and real wage equations for the U.K. 1951–79

Employment equation

Dependent variable — Independent variables	Employment (log n_t)
log n_{t-1}	1.127 (8.3)
log n_{t-2}	-0.492 (3.1)
*log $\left(\dfrac{W_t(1+t_{1t})}{P_{ft}}\right)$	0.00678 (0.1)
log $\left(\dfrac{W_{t-1}(1+t_{1t-1})}{P_{ft-1}}\right)$	-0.194 (3.0)
*log (P_{mt}/P_{ft})	0.0359 (1.7)
log (P_{mt-1}/P_{ft-1})	-0.0673 (3.8)
log k_t	0.217 (3.3)
Constant	4.225 (4.1)

Wage equations (Lagged instruments only)

Independent variables	Real wage (log W_t/P_{rt})	Expected real wage (log W_t/P_{rt}^e)
*u_t	-4.10 (6.3)	-3.62 (3.6)
mm_t	0.035 (4.0)	0.0374 (2.6)
*log R_t (real benefits)	0.060 (0.9) $\}$ +	0.031 (0.3) $\}$ +
log R_{t-1}	0.060 (0.9)	0.031 (0.3)
*log (P_{mt}/P_{ft})	-0.074 (2.4) $\}$ +	-0.029 (0.6) $\}$ +
log (P_{mt-1}/P_{ft-1})	-0.074 (2.4)	-0.029 (0.6)
log (k_t/L_t)	0.68 (1.8)	1.18 (1.9)
*U_{p1t} (union density)	0.65 (1.6)	0.115 (0.2)
*U_{p2t} (mark up)	0.044 (1.9)	0.068 (2.3)
log $(1+t_{1t-1})$	0.47 (0.6)	-0.45 (0.4)
t_{2t}	0.97 (1.7)	0.64 (0.9)

		$\log(1+t_{3t})$	−1.48	−1.31	−1.40
			(7.3)	(5.4)	(4.3)
		Constant	6.00	6.64	14.0
			(1.2)	(1.3)	(1.7)
S	0.00675		0.0112	0.0119	0.0182
DW	2.05		2.41	2.33	1.46
Parameter stability test (1976–79)	$F(4, 18) = 0.56$ (5% = 2.90)		$F(4, 14) = 2.15$ (5% = 3.11)	$F(4,14) = 1.49$	$F(4, 14) = 5.3$
Instrument validity test	$\chi^2(8) = 18.8$ (5% = 15.5)		$\chi^2(6) = 7.32$ (10% = 10.6)	$\chi^2(7) = 10.5$	$\chi^2(6) = 10.6$

[1] ≠ Constrained equal.

[2] Some variables require more precise definition. mm_t, the mismatch variable refers to the absolute annual change in the proportion of the employed labour force in production industries. R_t is benefits normalised on retail prices. Benefits refer to the unemployment benefit received by a two child family plus $\frac{1}{4}$ of Earnings Related Supplement. U_{p2t} is the log of the union/non-union mark up. U_{p1t} is the union density.

[3] * Refers to endogenous variable. Instruments are as follows: *Labour demand*: replacement rate (unemployment benefits/post-tax wages), current and lagged; population of working age, current and lagged; real government expenditure, current and lagged; world raw material prices relative to world manufacturer prices; current and lagged; the sum of all the taxes $(t_1 + t_2 + t_3)$. *Real wage* (columns 1 and 3): log world trade in manufactures (WTM) current and lagged; log real government expenditure (G) current and lagged; log world raw material prices relative to world manufacturing prices (QPW), current and lagged; union density lagged; union mark-up lagged; log real wages lagged. *Real wage* (column 2): log world trade in manufactures, first and second lags; log real government expenditure, first and second lags; log world raw material prices relative to world manufacturing prices, first and second lags; union density lagged; union mark up lagged; log real wages lagged; mismatch lagged; tax rates lagged. (Note in this equation t_{2t}, $\log(1+t_{3t})$, mm_t are treated as endogenous).

[4] t ratios are in brackets.

expected prices as the dependent variable. The first strategy is valid so long
as inflation innovations are orthogonal to lagged variables. This will be true
under rational expectations, for example. The second strategy is valid so
long as the measurement error in expected prices is orthogonal to our
instruments. The relevant equations are reported in the second and third
real wage columns of Table 1.

The crucial points to report about these three equations are as follows.
Unlike the results in Minford (1983), there are no lagged real wage effects.
This is presumably explained by our inclusion of trend productivity which
effectively captures the persistence in real wages. Second, we were unable to
detect any strong replacement ratio effects (the "best" is given in the table).
Third, the impact of unemployment is very well determined and robust
across all three equations. Furthermore, this is not simply an artefact of the
rise in unemployment and fall in real wages at the time of the
Healey/Callaghan incomes policy. The coefficient is, in fact, marginally
larger if the sample is terminated at 1975. This is rather reassuring par-
ticulrly as the reported equations contain no incomes policy dummies. We in
fact performed many experiments with such dummies and on no occasion
were we able to find them making a contribution which was other than
negligible in terms of size or significance. Fourth, the union power variables
show up reasonably well although union density is not very robust across the
three equations. However, the last equation explaining the expected real
wage is itself somewhat unrobust and we feel that the second provides a
better representation of the structural wage equation. Unfortunately, because of the weakness of the instruments, the parameters are not well
determined but the differences between this equation and the first real wage
equation are not large. Note, however, that the tax effects are attenuated
which is precisely what we expected. We would, therefore, consider the tax
effects of the second equation to be the more reliable. Finally a word about
trends. In the labour demand equation, a trend is highly collinear with the
capital stock and is thus not required. In the real wage equations, if a trend
is included its coefficient is not significantly different from zero although its
inclusion does have some marginal effects, notably to attenuate the coefficient on union density and to reinforce that on the union mark-up. The
ultimate employment effect on unions is hardly altered.

The next stage in our analysis is to use the two estimated equations to
generate results concerning the impact of unions and other matters. In order
to do this we must solve for the "quasi-reduced form" equation by substituting out the real wage. In order to do this we may first note that

$$u_t = \gamma \frac{(L_t - n_t)}{L_t} \simeq -\gamma \log \left(1 - \frac{(L_t - n_t)}{L_t}\right) = \gamma(\log L_t - \log n_t) \qquad (20)$$

where L_t is the potential labour force and γ is the factor that translates the
"true" total unemployment rate into the registered male unemployment

rate, u_t. We chose to use the male rate because we feel that this more closely approximates the true unemployment rate (for men and women) than the aggregate registered rate. γ is, of course, not known precisely but a reasonable estimate would be between 1 and 0.9. Substituting (20) into the real wage equation, taking long run solutions and solving for $\log n$ yields the following equations based on the first and second estimated real wage equations respectively.

$$\log n = (1 + 2.10\gamma)^{-1}\{\text{constant} + 0.27 \log k - 0.92t_1 - 0.64t_2$$
$$+ 0.25t_3 - 0.047 \log R - 0.018mm - 0.36U_{p1} - 0.024U_{p2}$$
$$+ 0.003 \log P_m/P_f + (2.10\gamma + 0.35) \log L\}. \tag{21a}$$

or

$$\log n = (1 + 1.80\gamma)^{-1}\{\text{constant} + 0.25 \log k - 0.75t_1 - 0.50t_2 + 0.16t_3$$
$$- 0.062 \log R - 0.017mm - 0.33U_{P1} - 0.022U_{p2} + 0.010 \log P_m/P_f$$
$$+ (1.80\gamma + 0.35) \log L\} \tag{21b}$$

These equations may be thought of as long run quasi-reduced forms. They are long run in two senses. First, complete adjustment to shifts in the exogenous variables has occurred and second, price expectations are fulfilled and thus demand shocks are absent. These are only quasi-reduced forms because $\log n$ is not written entirely in terms of exogenous variables. However since the coefficient on the materials price ratio is negligible, conditioning on a given level of this variable will not distort the implications which we shall draw to any significant extent. Even so, some care must be taken with the interpretation of this equation. Although we quite reasonably take the capital stock, k, as predetermined in our estimation we must bear in mind that the following kind of argument is not completely legitimate: equation (21) reveals that employment would have been x per cent higher in the long run if employment taxes, for example, had risen by y per cent less in the post-war period. The problem with this kind of argument is, of course, that in the long run, the level of capital stock is also influenced by taxes. Nevertheless, since the capital stock effect on employment is very small (as it should be), this is not a serious problem.

Concerning the two equations (21a) and (21b), they are gratifyingly similar with the second having somewhat smaller tax effects as expected. Turning to the key question of union effects, our union power measures rose by $\Delta U_{p1} = 0.11$ and $\Delta U_{p2} = 0.92$ between 1954–8 and 1974–9. The two equations give the corresponding impact on log employment (for given capital stock and potential labour supply changes) as $-0.061/(1 + 2.1\gamma)$ and $-0.055/(1 + 1.8\gamma)$ respectively which represent a decline of between 1.95 and 2.1 per cent. This yields a union employment effect since the immediate post-war period of around 400,000 for an unchanged capital stock path. Given that employment is currently about four million below potential labour supply this suggests that the union effect, although substantial, is hardly overwhelming.[12] Furthermore it is worth noting that the measures of union power which we have used are only proxies and may be picking up other effects. Also their coefficients are not very well determined so the estimate we have produced is subject to a fairly high degree of uncertainty. It is also worth noting that if we use the third real wage equation in Table 1 where the expected real wage is the dependent variable our estimates of the union effect are very much the same although the mark-up effect is rather more powerful relative to the density effect in this formulation.

Aside from the union effects which are the main focus of this paper, the following further points based on equations (21a) and (21b) are worth noting. First, even with the more reliable equation (21b), the employment effects of taxes on labour falling either on the firm or the worker are surprisingly large (and quite similar as would be expected). As with the union effects however, a glance at the estimates in Table 1 reveal these to be rather badly determined. Second, the impact of unemployment benefit levels on employment is weak and poorly determined. This contrasts markedly with the powerful effect noted in Minford (1983) but is further evidence of the lack of robustness displayed by this variable in time series investigations (see, for example, the discussion in Atkinson (1981) and the results of Beenstock and Warburton (1982)). Third, the impact of indirect taxes on employment is positive although it is not, in fact, significantly greater than zero. This suggests that unions have not been able to compensate employees for indirect tax changes although this result is only tentative and requires further investigation. Finally there is a well determined although small effect associated with our somewhat crude measure of mismatching (absolute change in proportion of employment in production). This variable increased between 1954–8 and 1974–9 by an amount which yields an employment fall of around 0.25 per cent.

In conclusion we should note a few caveats. First these results are based on a particular model which has been imposed on the data. The strongly neoclassical labour demand function, although apparently quite robust does not allow for any direct effect of aggregate demand on employment, as would arise in a model where firms are output constrained. Nevertheless we were unable to detect any such direct effects when we included the variables at our disposal. Second some of the key coefficients are rather badly determined. This is worth emphasising because the use of the estimated coefficients to derive equations (21a, b) allied to the absence of standard errors in this equation[13] gives it an air of precision which is somewhat spurious. In practice this implies that the same kind of model estimated over a different period with different instruments, for example, could very well give a rather different impression although it may not be any different in the statistical sense from that presented here.

---

[12] Note that the effects to which we refer are long run. Thus the level of union power in 1974–9 would only have its full long run impact in the early 80's.

[13] Since the coefficients in (21) are highly non-linear functions of those we have estimated we feel that it is not worth attempting to approximate their standard errors.

Summary and conclusions

We have derived a two equation model determining real wages and employment from an explicit firm-union bargaining procedure. This has been estimated and on the basis of our point estimates we have noted (i) that the impact of unions on employment via their effect on real wages has been of the order of 400,000 since the War, (ii) that taxes on labour have a strong impact on employment, (iii) that the level of unemployment benefits has only a marginal impact on employment.

What conclusions should we draw from the fact that unions appear to have some impact on employment? First, it is worth pointing out that this should hardly come as a surprise. Indeed it would be more surprising if the introduction of unions in a decentralised economy did not have any employment effects. However, we believe that it would be a mistake to conclude that the sensible response to this fact would be to attempt to weaken the power of unions. One of the important roles of unions is to protect the interests of relatively weaker groups of employees in the economy. To weaken their ability to do this does not seem particularly desirable. Of course, it is commonplace to argue that the real incomes of these weaker groups can be protected by appropriate fiscal policies. Although this is undoubtedly correct, the evidence suggests that such protection cannot, in fact, be relied upon and that for many groups trade union power represents their main source of protection. How then can unions perform this role without undesirable employment consequences? A possible answer is suggested by the fact that if unions and employers bargain equally about employment and wages, the consequences would be beneficial to both parties and would lead to a higher level of employment than simply bargaining about wages (see Section 1). This indicates that a greater degree of involvement of employees' representatives in firm and indeed in economy wide decision making might lead to a more desirable outcome than that attained by legislative force.

Centre for Labour Economics, London School of Economics and Political Science

APPENDIX

We are concerned here with the properties of the solution to

$$\max_{n,w} (U(\pi(w, n)) - U(\bar{\pi}))^{\beta}(u(w, n) - \bar{u}).$$

It is simple to show that a necessary condition for the solution to this problem is

$$\pi_n/\pi_w = u_n/u_w \tag{A1}$$

which is, in fact, the condition for a Pareto Optimal point in w, n space. From the expressions for π and u in the main text (equations (1) and (6)), we have

$$\pi_n = pAg' - w, \qquad \pi_w = -n, \qquad u_n = (v - \tilde{v}), \qquad u_w = v',$$

ignoring taxes and setting $\alpha = 1$ for simplicity of exposition. So (A1) becomes

$$pAg' - w = -\frac{(v - \bar{v})}{v'} \qquad (A2)$$

In the main text we suppose that union power only influences $\bar{\pi}$ and so does not enter (A2). Taking total derivatives of (A2) yields

$$pAg'' \, dn = \frac{v - \bar{v}}{v'^2} v'' \, dw. \qquad (A3)$$

Since $g'' < 0$, $v'' < 0$ and all the other terms are positive, (A3) implies that sign $(dn) =$ sign (dw). As a consequence a change in union power moves wages and employment in the same direction.

DATA APPENDIX

Variable	$\log n$	$\log \dfrac{W(1+t_1)}{P_f}$	$\log (P_m/P_f)$	$\log k$	$\log (W/P_r)$	u_t	$\log (k/L)$	U_{p1}	U_{p2}
Column no.	1	2	3	4	5	6	7	8	9
1949	9.90	8.66	—	5.34	—	—	—	—	—
1950	9.91	8.67	4.83	5.36	—	—	—	—	—
1951	9.92	8.66	5.03	5.38	−0.472	1.2	−4.55	0.450	−2.53
1952	9.92	8.67	4.79	5.40	−0.474	1.6	−4.54	0.451	−2.21
1953	9.93	8.69	4.67	5.43	−0.451	1.7	−4.52	0.446	−2.41
1954	9.94	8.72	4.64	5.45	−0.412	1.4	−4.50	0.442	−2.66
1955	9.96	8.76	4.63	5.48	−0.379	1.1	−4.49	0.445	−2.41
1956	9.97	8.79	4.62	5.50	−0.347	1.2	−4.48	0.441	−1.97
1957	9.97	8.80	4.58	5.53	−0.335	1.6	−4.46	0.440	−1.83
1958	9.97	8.82	4.48	5.55	−0.320	2.2	−4.43	0.432	−1.90
1959	9.97	8.84	4.48	5.58	−0.292	2.4	−4.41	0.429	−2.04
1960	9.99	8.90	4.46	5.62	−0.229	1.8	−4.39	0.431	−1.83
1961	10.01	8.93	4.42	5.65	−0.198	1.7	−4.37	0.429	−1.77
1962	10.02	8.94	4.39	5.68	−0.193	2.3	−4.35	0.427	−1.66
1963	10.02	8.96	4.39	5.72	−0.172	2.8	−4.33	0.427	−1.90
1964	10.04	9.00	4.40	5.75	−0.137	2.0	−4.30	0.431	−1.83
1965	10.05	9.05	4.38	5.79	−0.101	1.7	−4.27	0.432	−1.66
1966	10.05	9.12	4.37	5.83	−0.064	1.8	−4.24	0.426	−1.77
1967	10.04	9.14	4.34	5.87	−0.053	3.0	−4.19	0.428	−1.77
1968	10.03	9.18	4.39	5.91	−0.028	3.3	−4.14	0.431	−1.61
1969	10.03	9.22	4.39	5.95	−0.011	3.3	−4.10	0.473	−1.56
1970	10.02	9.32	4.38	5.99	0.088	3.6	−4.06	0.509	−1.35
1971	10.00	9.34	4.32	6.03	0.124	4.7	−4.01	0.514	−1.35
1972	10.00	9.39	4.27	6.06	0.192	5.1	−3.98	0.514	−1.17
1973	10.03	9.43	4.46	6.10	0.221	3.6	−3.96	0.505	−1.17
1974	10.03	9.44	4.68	6.13	0.258	3.6	−3.93	0.516	−1.39
1975	10.03	9.50	4.61	6.16	0.287	5.5	−3.91	0.537	−1.17
1976	10.02	9.47	4.70	6.19	0.240	7.1	−3.89	0.549	−1.20
1977	10.03	9.43	4.70	6.22	0.172	7.4	−3.87	0.567	−1.14
1978	10.03	9.49	4.61	6.24	0.228	7.2	−3.85	0.577	−1.27
1979	10.04	9.54	4.65	6.27	0.257	6.8	−3.83	0.590	−1.24

[1] $\log n$. Employees in employment, males and females, mid-year GB. ETAS 81.

[2] $\log \{W(1+t_1)/P_f\}$. W is the pre-tax wage rate. This is calculated as follows. We first take the following data: $E =$ average weekly earnings of full-time male manual workers (21 years and over), at the October in each year, for all industries covered; $H =$ average weekly hours of ... (as E above); $N^h =$ average normal weekly hours of male manual workers, for all industries and services. The overtime premium, π, can be given a value of 0.3, whence

$$E = WN^h + 1.3W(H - N^h)$$

and W is easily calculated. We also adjust W by a factor that captures the decline of normal hours in total hours, namely $(1 - N^h/45)*1.3 + N^h/45$, which makes workers relatively better off at lower normal hours for a given hourly wage.

Variable Column no.	log(1+t₁) 10	t₂ 11	log(1+t₃) 12	log R 13	DPROD 14	log WTM 15	log G 16	log QPW 17	RR 18	Tax 19
1949	—	—	—	—	—	—	—	—	38.3	9.28
1950	4.50	—	—	3.13	—	2.64	9.32	0.817	36.5	9.28
1951	4.50	0.134	4.64	2.97	0.564	2.83	9.50	0.922	36.0	9.28
1952	4.51	0.129	4.63	3.11	0.118	2.83	9.54	0.768	41.5	9.28
1953	4.50	0.121	4.63	3.09	0.107	2.94	9.56	0.712	39.3	9.27
1954	4.51	0.122	4.63	3.06	0.161	3.00	9.51	0.726	36.7	9.27
1955	4.51	0.123	4.63	3.16	0.487	3.04	9.49	0.749	39.4	9.27
1956	4.51	0.126	4.63	3.13	0.161	3.14	9.52	0.718	37.1	9.28
1957	4.50	0.129	4.63	3.10	0.275	3.22	9.52	0.701	35.5	9.27
1958	4.51	0.136	4.62	3.32	0.244	3.18	9.49	0.642	44.0	9.28
1959	4.51	0.134	4.62	3.30	0.535	3.26	9.53	0.651	41.9	9.28
1960	4.51	0.135	4.62	3.30	0.359	3.40	9.57	0.651	39.5	9.27
1961	4.51	0.143	4.62	3.44	0.065	3.43	9.61	0.639	44.3	9.28
1962	4.51	0.150	4.62	3.41	0.729	3.50	9.66	0.641	43.0	9.30
1963	4.52	0.148	4.62	3.53	0.668	3.56	9.69	0.639	47.4	9.30
1964	4.51	0.152	4.63	3.50	0.159	3.69	9.76	0.677	44.6	9.30
1965	4.52	0.165	4.63	3.62	0.061	3.78	9.80	0.672	49.3	9.33
1966	4.54	0.170	4.64	3.62	0.181	3.85	9.86	0.653	53.2	9.37
1967	4.55	0.178	4.64	3.70	0.586	3.91	9.94	0.660	57.1	9.39
1968	4.56	0.185	4.65	3.69	0.534	4.04	9.98	0.577	56.1	9.41
1969	4.56	0.190	4.67	3.64	0.031	4.19	9.99	0.576	53.5	9.44
1970	4.57	0.193	4.67	3.75	0.487	4.26	10.02	0.573	54.3	9.45
1971	4.57	0.194	4.65	3.86	0.999	4.34	10.03	0.583	58.3	9.44
1972	4.57	0.183	4.63	3.91	1.270	4.43	10.05	0.583	56.2	9.41
1973	4.58	0.184	4.62	3.92	0.603	4.55	10.14	0.681	54.8	9.41
1974	4.58	0.205	4.61	3.94	0.311	4.64	10.20	0.825	55.2	9.42
1975	4.61	0.229	4.61	3.90	1.542	4.61	10.24	0.798	53.0	9.47
1976	4.62	0.233	4.61	3.85	0.793	4.72	10.25	0.820	53.1	9.50
1977	4.63	0.223	4.63	3.84	0.095	4.76	10.19	0.847	55.5	9.51
1978	4.64	0.207	4.62	3.88	0.432	4.81	10.18	0.798	53.1	9.49
1979	—	0.196	4.64	3.81	0.518	4.87	10.20	0.911	47.3	9.50

All data for E, H, N^h are published in BLSHA, the YB's, and latest issue of DEG (May 81).

$(1+t_1)$ is the tax on employment borne by the firm.

Series is calculated by taking the ratio of two indices; 'total labour costs per unit of output for the whole economy', 1975 = 100 and 'wages and salaries per unit of output for the whole economy', 1975 = 100. As the main part of 'fixed' labour costs are N.I. contributions this series will reflect the real tax on labour levied on firms. However it is only an index based at 1975 = 100. Thus the only way to obtain an approximation to t_{1t} is to take logs

$$\log K(1+t_{1t}) \simeq \log K + t_{1t}$$

and let $\log K$ 'go into' the constant in a regression. The former series is published in BLSHA (T. 203), YB 1976 (T. 55) and the latest issue of DEG, the latter in ETAS 81 (p. 110).

P_f is the firm's output price index. This we define as the retail price index (all items, ETAS 81) ÷ $(1+t_3)$. t_3 is the tax rate on goods. This is the ratio of the GDP deflator at market prices, 1975 = 100 to the GDP deflator at factor cost, 1975 = 100. The measures of GDP are all expenditure based. Note that the series is an index, 1975 = 100. All series taken from ETAS 81.

[3] $\log(P_m/P_f)$. P_f as above, P_m is the price of materials and fuels. The series used was the 'wholesale price index of materials and fuel purchased by manufacturing industry', 1975 = 100. From 1954–1979 the series is published in ETAS 81. However observations for 1950–53 were generated by splicing the above with the following series, which is published in various issues of MDS between December 1954 and August 1958, namely the 'price index of basic materials used in broad sectors of industry, excluding fuel used in non-food manufacturing industry', 1949 = 100.

[4] $\log k$. k is the capital stock. The series used is 'gross capital stock at 1975 replacement cost', in £ thousand million. Data are available yearly from 1958 onward in successive issues of the BB, at various base years (which were easily 'spliced' together). Before 1958 only the 1954, 1951 and 1948 observations were published. Data were interpolated using real investment data, namely 'total gross domestic fixed capital formation', £ million at 1975 prices, using the usual technique involving the estimation of a decay parameter $\hat{\delta}$ from the postulated relationship,

$$K_n = \sum_{i=1}^{n} (1-\delta)^{n-i} I_i^{\cdot} + (1-\delta)^n K_0$$

ABBREVIATIONS

BB	'Blue Book', National Income and Expenditure (yearly)
BEQB	Bank of England Quarterly Bulletin
BESA 70	Bank of England Statistical Abstract, 1970
BESA 75	As above, 1975 (only published twice)
BLSHA	British Labour Statistics, Historical Abstract, 1886–1968
DEG	Department of Employment Gazette (monthly)
ETAS 81	Economic Trends Annual Supplement, 1981
ET	Economic Trends (monthly)
FS	Financial Statistics (monthly)
LBB 81	'Light Brown Book', 'Abstract of Statistics for Index of Retail Prices, Average Earnings, Social Security Benefits and Contributions', published by DHSS, May 1981
MDS	Monthly Digest of Statistics
UNB	United Nations Quarterly Bulletin
YB	British Labour Statistics, Year Book, 1969–1976, (published 8 times, between 1969 and 1976).

where K_n, K_0 are end of period and beginning of period capital stocks, I_i is investment. The missing K's are calculated recursively by setting $n = 1$ each time, and using δ. The investment series is published in ETAS 81.

[5] $\log (W/P_r)$. W as above. P_r is the retail price index (all items, ETAS 81).

[6] u. Male unemployment rate. The series used is 'males wholly unemployed as a percentage of the number of employees (employed and unemployed) at the appropriate mid-year, for the U.K.'. The numbers unemployed exclude 'temporarily stopped' but include school-leavers. The data are published in BLSHA, the 8 YB's, and finally DEG Feb. 81.

[7] $\log (k/L)$. L is the sum of employees in employment as described above but referring to the UK and unemployment in the UK, males and females, mid-year. ETAS 81, DEG.

[8] U_{p1}. Union density. The proportion of employees unionised. DEG.

[9] U_{p2}. log of the union/non-union mark-up. The procedure by which this variable was estimated is described in Layard, Metcalf and Nickell (1978), Table 5.

[10] $\log (1+t_1)$. Employment tax on firms described above.

[11] t_2. Average rate of income tax. The series taken reflects the direct tax rate on income, namely 'total personal disposable income', £ million, current prices, divided by 'total income before tax', £ million, current prices. In contrast to $(1+t_1)_t$ and $(1+t_3)_t$ this series is an actual tax rate, not an index. Both constituent series are published in ETAS 81.

[12] $\log (1+t_3)$. The tax rate on goods described above.

[13] $\log R$. R is the level of real benefits. The variable R is the product of the replacement ratio and $W(1-t_2)/P_r$, which has already been described. The replacement ratio roughly measures income whilst unemployed as a ratio of income that would have been received if in employment. The variable is defined as 'standard rate of unemployment benefit and/or sickness benefit plus family allowances and/or child benefit plus earnings related supplement (ERS) as a percentage of net income after deducting tax and National Insurance contributions for a married couple with two children'. Note that as ERS is not received by everyone the published data have been scaled so that this component of the numerator is $\frac{1}{4}$ its published size. The source is the LBB, 1981 issue, tables 6.1a and 6.2a.

[14] DPROD. This is the absolute change in the proportion of employees in production industries. It is the one year absolute change in the per cent ratio of 'employees in employment, males and females, in index of production industries at each mid-year, GB' to 'total employees in employment, males and females at each mid-year, GB'. BLSHA, YB, DEG.

[15] $\log$ WTM. WTM is world trade in manufactures. The series used is the 'quantum index for world manufacturing exports', 1975 = 100. UNB.

[16] $\log G$. G is real government expenditure. Series is calculated from 'general government expenditure on goods and services', in £ million, which is divided by the GDP at factor cost deflator. The GDP factor cost deflator was used because the equivalent series at constant prices do not exist. ETAS 81.

[17] $\log QPW$. QPW is the pound price of material/fuels (P_m) divided by the world export unit value index converted from dollars to pounds using the current exchange rate. UNB, ETAS 81.

[18] RR. Replacement rate as described under 13.

[19] Tax. $\log (1+t_1)+t_2+\log (1+t_3)$. Variables described above.

REFERENCES

ANDREWS, M. (1983), "The Aggregate Labour Market—An Empirical Investigation into Market-Clearing", London School of Economics, Centre for Labour Economics, Discussion Paper No. 154.

ATKINSON, A. B. (1981), "Unemployment Benefits and Incentives", in J. Creedy ed. *The Economics of Unemployment in Britain*, Butterworths, London.

BEENSTOCK, M. and WARBURTON, P. (1981), "An Aggregate Economic Model of the U.K. Labour Market", *Oxford Economic Papers*, July.

DE MENIL, G. (1971), *Bargaining: Monopoly Power Versus Union Power*, Cambridge Mass. M.I.T. Press.

JACKMAN, R. and LAYARD R. (1981), "Trade Unions, the NAIRU and a Wage-Inflation Tax", London School of Economics, Centre for Labour Economics, Discussion Paper No. 100.

LAYARD, R., METCALF, D. and NICKELL, S. (1978), "The Effects of Collective Bargaining on Relative Wages and Absolute Wages", *British Journal of Industrial Relations*, November.

LIPSEY, R. (1960), "The Relation between Unemployment and the Rate of Change of Money Wage Rates in the U.K. A Further Analysis", *Economica*, February.

LUCE, R. D. and RAIFFA, H. (1967). *Games and Decisions*, New York, John Wiley.

McDONALD, I. M. and SOLOW, R. M. (1981), "Wage Bargaining and Employment", *American Economic Review*, December.

MINFORD, P. (1983), "Labour Market Equilibrium in an Open Economy", *Oxford Economic Papers* (this issue).

NICKELL, S. J. (1981), "An Investigation of the Determinants of Manufactuaring Employment in the U.K.", London School of Economics, Centre for Labour Economics, Discussion Paper No. 105.

NICKELL, S. J. (1982), "A Bargaining Model of the Phillips Curve", London School of Economics, Centre for Labour Economics, Discussion Paper No. 130.

OSWALD, A. (1982), "Wages, Trade Unions and Unemployment: What can Simple Models tell us", *Oxford Economic Papers*, November.

SARGENT, T. (1978), "Estimation of Dynamic Labour Demand Schedules under Rational Expedctations", *Journal of Political Economy*, pp. 1009–45.

SYMONS, J. S. V. (1981), "The Demand for Labour in British Manufacturing", London School of Economics, Centre for Labour Economics, Discussion Paper No. 91.

SYMONS, J. S. V. (1982), "Relative Prices and the Demand for Labour in British Manufacturing", London School of Economics, Centre for Labour Economics, Discussion Paper No. 137.

LABOUR MARKET EQUILIBRIUM IN AN OPEN ECONOMY*

By PATRICK MINFORD

THE object of this paper is to describe and estimate (on UK data) a model of the 'natural' rate of unemployment and the 'natural' levels of all those other real variables associated with it—such as real wages, the real exchange rate, and the level of output. The argument briefly will be that the labour market in an open economy clears at a real wage substantially influenced by government or government-permitted intervention in that market, especially the tax/benefit structure and the unionisation rate.

Section 1 outlines a stylised version of the open economy model to be used. Sections 2 and 3 deal with the labour market in detail, this being the major focus of the paper. In the final section we present our estimates for the UK labour market equations and using them as part of the macroeconomic model draw out the implications for the UK natural rate.

1. The model in outline

It is assumed that industry is competitive and distributed into two sectors, unionized and non-unionized (or 'competitive') in a way that is outside firms' control. Firms are able to buy capital goods on an international market at a world real rental cost which is enforced domestically by perfect capital mobility. Each firm enjoys constant returns to scale but is limited by a fixed factor ('entrepreneurship'), so that marginal product declines as the industry expands. It buys imported inputs at a given world price. Accordingly, we write the demand for labour in each sector by profit-maximizing firms as:

$$L_u^d = (\overset{-}{w_u}, \overset{-}{T_F}, \overset{+}{e}, \overset{+}{k}) \tag{1}$$

$$L_c^d = (\overset{-}{w_c}, \overset{-}{T_F}, \overset{+}{e}, \overset{+}{k}) \tag{2}$$

where u, c subscripts stand for union and competitive sectors respectively, L^d = labour demand, w = real wage, T_F = labour tax rate (as fraction of wage) paid by employer, e = real exchange rate (price of domestic goods relative to price of imported goods, in common currency), k = aggregate (positive) effect of technological progress, real rental on capital, and fixed factor supplies. The expected signs are indicated over the variables.

* I am grateful to George Brennan for his assistance on all aspects of this research. Latterly Christos Ioannidis and Alison Sprague assisted me substantially in the revision of this paper. I have benefited from comments by Orley Ashenfelter, Daniel Benjamin, Willem Buiter, David Forrest, Oliver Hart, Roger Latham, Richard Layard, Mervyn King, Steve Nickell, David Peel, the editors of this issue and anonymous referees, as well as from many helpful seminar discussions. George Bain kindly provided data from his unpublished research on union density by industry. This work forms part of the SSRC funded Liverpool Research Project on the International Transmission Mechanism.

We complete the description of firms' activities by writing down their production function (we only need the economy's aggregate) as a supply of output equation:

$$Q = (\overset{+}{L_u^d} + \overset{+}{L_c^d}, k) \tag{3}$$

where Q = total output of the economy. To avoid aggregation problems we assume the production functions of union and non-unionized industry are identical.[1]

We now turn to the behaviour of workers and unions. Unions maximize the present value of their potential members' aggregated real incomes by setting the union wage. This gives rise to a variable mark-up equation of the form (to be derived below):

$$w_u = m(\overset{+}{UNR}, \overset{-}{P^{ue}}, \overset{+}{k})w_c \tag{4}$$

where m (= one plus the mark up) is a function of UNR (= the unionization rate), k, and P^{ue} (= unanticipated inflation). UNR enters as a proxy for the elasticity of demand for union labour, it being argued that the more unionised an industry, the greater the difficulty of substitution of non-union for union labour in that industry, whether in union firms or by the expansion of non-union firms. P^{ue} enters because unions find it convenient—in order to minimize the transactions costs of controlling work conditions—to draw up nominal wage contracts with only partially contingent price clauses; hence a surprise in prices will reduce the real union wage.

It is assumed that firms choose workers' hours given the union-set wage rates. Therefore unionised workers are rationed in their labour supply. We assume that total labour supply of hours in the economy is such that the marginal rate of substitution of leisure for goods equals the *marginal* net real wage available. This is, for union and non-union workers alike, the real wage in the competitive market (which is assumed to be continuously cleared), minus benefits lost and taxes paid through working extra. Because of the wide differences in individual tax/benefit circumstances tight restrictions across the parameters of benefit, tax, and real wage variables are unlikely to hold and we write labour supply, L^s, generally as:

$$L^s = (\overset{+}{w_c}, \overset{-}{b}, \overset{-}{T_L}, POP) \tag{5}$$

where b = real unemployment benefit, T_L = tax rate (fraction of wage) paid by employee, POP = size of (registered) working age population (because this also acts as a proxy for demographic trends, the sign is left ambiguous).

---

[1] (3) is derived from the production function (29) below by substituting for capital (from the marginal productivity condition for capital) in terms of the cost of capital, labour, and the fixed factor.

The labour market equations are completed by the equilibrium condition in the competitive sector:

$$L^s - L_u^d = L_c^d \tag{6}$$

and by the unemployment relation:

$$U = POP - L^s. \tag{7}$$

where U = unemployment. (7) states that those registered as potential workers will draw unemployment benefits if not working and still therefore under UK practice be counted as unemployed (this is of course an oversimplification).

(6) taken with (1), (2), (4) and (5) yields a solution for w_c, w_u, L_u^d, L_c^d, L^s, in terms of e, T_F, T_L, UNR, k, and POP. Using (3) we can then solve for Q, and from (7) for U. The set-up, the economy's 'supply side', is illustrated in Fig. 1.

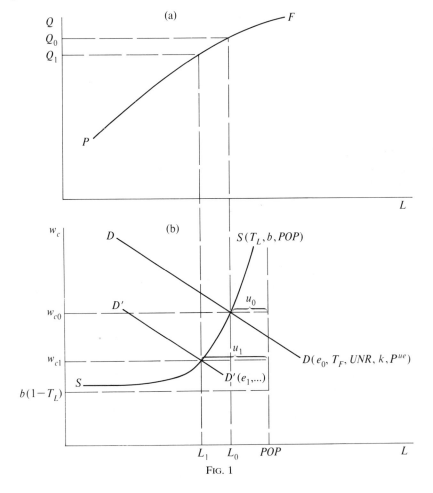

Fig. 1

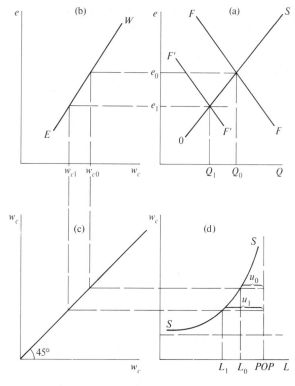

FIG. 2

Quadrant (a) shows the equation of the production function (3); quadrant (b) shows SS, the equation of labour supply (5), and DD, total labour demand $L_c^d + L_u^a$ in terms of w_c from (1), (2), and (4) the mark up relation.

We may now conveniently extract from this an open economy supply curve, relating output supply to the real exchange rate, holding the other variables constant. Thus as we lower e, shifting DD to the left, we trace out a falling output path along the PF curve corresponding to the DD/SS intersection; this is illustrated by the points (w_{c_1}, Q_1, L_1) corresponding to $D'D'$. This is shown in Fig. 2, quadrant (a), as OS. We trace through in quadrants (b)–(d) the correspondence between real exchange rate, real wages, employment and unemployment, for given other variables. (Note that changes in all these other variables will shift both the OS and EW curves, and changes in T_L, b, POP will shift the SS curve. Also note that the shift in OS due to P^{ue} is the 'Phillips curve' effect.)

We now introduce the last relationship, required to close the open economy model in equilibrium. It will have been observed that the open economy aspect has added e, the real exchange rate, as a supply side determinant; were this a closed economy, e would be absent, and there would be a unique equilibrium supply, corresponding to that which can be

produced given labour market equilibrium. This is the usual vertical aggregate supply curve set up. However the addition of e has produced an
upward sloping supply curve; the reason being that as e rises, the terms of
trade improve and with them profits, enabling firms to induce a higher
labour supply profitably.

To close the model we specify a current account balance (x) equation and
set it to equilibrium:

$$0 = x = (\overset{+}{WT}, \overset{-}{e}, \overset{-}{Q}) \tag{8}$$

where WT = the volume of world trade (or output). (8) simply states that the
demand for imports by UK residents must be equal to the demand for UK
exports by foreign residents, equilibrium occurring through e, our index of
relative home to foreign prices. We can if we wish generalise (8) to allow for
an equilibrium net transfer (e.g. inwards and a current account deficit for an
LDC, outwards and a surplus for a mature capital exporting country). The FF
curve in Fig. 2, quadrant (a), illustrates (8). If this was a 'small' open
economy, then the FF curve would be horizontal. But in this model this is
not an appropriate assumption. Full equilibrium of the economy—with
corresponding 'natural rates'—occurs at the intersection of the FF and OS
curves. So one may think of OS as describing the short run supply *curve* of
the economy, the intersection FF/OS as determining the *point* of equilibrium.

To determine the short run behaviour of the economy requires the
addition of an IS, or short run aggregate demand curve. This we do not
specify here as it raises short run macroeconomic issues of impact effects and
dynamics that are not our primary concern here. (Full model simulations of
these aspects using the 'Liverpool model'—Minford, 1980—of which the
supply equations described in this paper are now a part, are available on
request from the author; broad findings about lags are mentioned briefly
below.)

In the rest of this paper we focus in detail on the determination of the OS
curve by (1)–(7). We take (8), the FF curve, from earlier work (Minford,
1980).

2. The labour market in detail

(a) *Labour market structure*

We distinguish a non-union and union sector for a given industry. The
non-union sector we suppose to be competitive with atomistic suppliers of
labour facing atomistic firms. In Britain, this sector consists primarily of the
small business sector of private industry. Examples are the numerous small
road haulage firms in the highly unionised (approx. 95%) Transport and
Communication sector dominated by British Rail, British Road Services and

the National Bus Company; and the large numbers of family engineering firms in the Metal Goods sector (approx. 69% unionised). Additionally the major parts of certain sectors are non-unionised; this applies notably to agriculture (only 22% unionised), construction (27%), and timber and furniture (35%).

The extent of formal unionisation is not necessarily a good guide to the extent of union dominance over wages because wage agreements for non-union employees are frequently linked automatically to union agreements (under 'agency shop' arrangements), and on the other hand wage agreements nationally negotiated by unions in highly unionised sectors (such as vehicles or engineering) are merely reference points for shop floor negotiation in individual firms in which the union may be powerless. Mulvey (1976) for example found in a study of 77 MLH manufacturing industries in 1976 that the union/non-union wage differential was 0 for industries covered only by national agreements, against 46 to 48% for industries covered by company, district or local government and 41 to 46% for those covered by national with supplementary agreements. Unfortunately coverage data is only available from the early 1970s; and even this is not free of interpretational problems. Unionisation is the only reasonably long time-series, and it seems likely to be reasonably well correlated with the extent of union dominance in wage agreements. As a measure of the absolute extent of the non-union sector at a point of time, it is unreliable; but the coverage data confirm the view that there is a significant part of the British economy where unions have no direct influence on wages. For example, in April 1973, as against an average unionisation rate of 49%, the extent of coverage by national-with-supplementary or by company, district and local agreements was 43% for manual men, 35% for manual women and much less for non-manual workers. Given that the public sector has very high unionisation rates and effective coverage is probably close to 100%, the extent of the non-union sector in Britain's private sector should not be underestimated.

(b) *The theory of labour supply*

The theory of unemployment that is currently most popular among labour economists is 'search' theory. Suppose that a man has been made redundant. He then searches for a new job for his particular skill. Extra time spent searching costs him extra; this cost includes the outlays on search net of any utility derived from leisure (which of course could be negative). He gets job offers at regular intervals with a wage attached to it which is taken randomly from a distribution (which he knows) of potential wages for the job type. He accepts an offer when it is equal to or greater than the expected wage from the next offer minus the extra cost of search involved in waiting for another period.

This theory is undoubtedly suitable for individuals in certain labour markets; notably, where the individual has a clearly defined job preference and jobs of that type become available periodically, and have a wage distribution attached to them. For example, professional people, such as an economics lecturer, may be well described by it. However, the vast mass of jobs are manual or semi-skilled non-manual; within these jobs some are restricted by union entry conditions, others are in industries with little union intervention. There would seem to be for such jobs a 'going rate', one in the union sector where jobs are rationed, and one in the non-union sector (if there is one for that job type) where jobs are freely available at the rate. Take taxi-drivers for example; there are areas such as Newcastle where there is close regulation of rates and attempted control of entry, and areas such as Liverpool which are effectively deregulated. An unskilled man could become a taxi-driver in Liverpool at will (he simply joins a 'taxi garage', which leases a cab to him); or he could try to get a more profitable regulated job in Newcastle. But it is by no means clear that he will 'search' and remain unemployed. Rather, he may well decide whether it is worth his while to do either job. If he concludes that the deregulated one is good enough, but the regulated one would be better if it came up, he may take the deregulated one and be ready to drop it and shift when and if the other comes up. It seems unlikely that he would remain unemployed, 'searching' the union or regulated sectors, unless he decided that the non-union rates were just not attractive at all; if he did so, he would lose income without necessarily enhancing his chances of a union job.

These considerations suggest an alternative model of the work decision, which is 'new classical' in spirit. The worker has knowledge of 'going rates' in unregulated, or non-union sectors in which he has the necessary skills to work; he does not need to 'search' for this knowledge. He decides when to enter and when to withdraw from these sectors in a standard 'optimising' manner; i.e. he maximises the present value of his expected welfare, given these wage rates and other relevant prices, including benefits out of work and taxes etc. in work. Though all workers would like to have a union job, it is assumed that the chances of getting one are not affected by taking a non-union job, so that the union wage does not affect his work decision.

It turns out in this model that the number of people willing to work at *union* wages is irrelevant to the determination of wages or jobs in either the union or the non-union sectors. The reason is straightforward; the union's mark-up over the non-union real wage is determined by its monopoly power interacting with technology and demand conditions; this monopoly power is precisely the power to ignore the desires of non-union members for better wages within the controlled sector. In practice of course this ability would be eroded substantially, the larger the non-union sector; but this erosion depends not so much on the non-union members' frustration as on the enhanced ability of firms to hire non-union members beyond the reach of the union (as in the USA, with firms hiring in the South rather than the unionised North East).

The model therefore implies that the total supply of labour will be dependent on the level of current real wages in the non-union sector ('free market wages'), net of tax and expenses, relative to on the one hand net out of work benefits and on the other expected future net real non-union wages. In other words, the people who are 'on the margin' of supply in the labour market are in the non-union sector (in 'unprotected jobs'), typically on low wages and 'unattractive' jobs; hence the importance in labour supply of replacement ratios for low income households, for these are the ones most likely to withdraw under additional pressure. (By implication, replacement ratios for average workers—who will be unionised typically—are likely to be of no relevance).

There are various ways in which the supply of labour could contract as real wages fell. Workers could decide to quit more frequently, taking longer periods between work; for manual men for whom explicit part-time work is awkward, this would approximate to part-time working over the year as a whole. Workers could take spells of work abroad, and spells on benefits at home. Workers could decide not to work at all until real wages picked up again; for example, they could withdraw from the labour market in recessions and return in boom periods. Most drastically, they could withdraw indefinitely and change their life-style to one of living on benefits and casual, possibly undeclared, earnings, on the assumption that real wages are never likely to be sufficiently attractive. To those accustomed to the ways of prosperous Southern areas of the country, such ideas may seem unfamiliar, even outrageous; but it has to be said that they are part of the everyday gossip and casual empiricism of an area such as Liverpool.

Viewed in this way, the distinctions between decisions on 'duration' of unemployment and those on 'participation in work' become blurred; there is in essence a continuous decision on more or less or no participation in work.

This decision is naturally viewed as taken for the fiscal year. For example, someone wanting to work half the time would be best advised to work half the year and be unemployed for the other half (in either order); that way he uses up his tax allowances. Were he to work for one year and be unemployed for the whole of the next year, he would fail to use and subsequently lose his tax allowances in the second year under the UK tax system operating over our sample period.

Let us define π_{it} as the proportion of the current fiscal year's hours the worker i currently plans to devote to work rather than leisure on which we assume he obtains a real benefit payment, b_{it}; for his work he obtains the real non-union wage, $w_{ict} \times (1 - T_{Lt}) = w'_{ict}$ where T_L is the direct tax rate. We assume the worker's adjustment costs are low for non union employment and can be neglected; this assumption may work rather well for low-paid manual work which constitutes the bulk of non-union employment close to the poverty line where unemployment is heavily concentrated. It also conveniently avoids introducing lags until later in the analysis. We therefore write quite simply that worker i maximises in each time period his (quadratic) utility,

$$U_{it} = \left(\gamma_i I_{it} - \frac{\beta_i}{2} \pi_{it}^2 + \pi_{it}\{\alpha_i + v_{it} + D_t\} \right) \tag{9}$$

subject to

$$I_{it} = (1 - \pi_{it})w'_{ict} + \pi_{it}b_{it}; \tag{10}$$

I_{it} = his real net income rate; α_i = personal characteristics (e.g. family size) dummies, v_{it} = random factors, and D_t = seasonal factors affecting preferences. The solution from the 1st order condition is:

$$\pi_{it} = \frac{\gamma_i}{\beta_i}(b_{it} - w'_{ict}) + \frac{1}{\beta_i}(\alpha_i + v_{it} + D_t) \tag{11}$$

In a cross section analysis taken at a point in time, π_{it} can be interpreted as the chances of a person being unemployed. In a cohort study of a cross-section over a period of time, π_{it} can be interpreted as the fraction of this whole time period worker i is unemployed.

We could treat all individuals as having the same γ_i, β_i. This would be defensible under the crude quadratic assumption if they all faced similarly sloped budget constraints; for then similar substitution effects in response to benefit changes could be expected. However, in the UK we can distinguish three major groups in the bulk of our sample period, according to their benefit status as illustrated in Fig. 3. There are 'flat rate' benefits—i.e. effectively the minimum paid, shown as point A. People on net incomes to the left of A^2 will face a budget line with no slope. They are likely to be at a corner solution, where they do no work at all, and be unresponsive to benefit or wage changes.

Then there was an earnings related supplement (ERS, abolished December 1981) which raised the benefit/wage ratio to $\frac{2}{3}$ for those whose incomes relative to flat rate benefits put them below this ratio otherwise. Their budget line will have a slope of 33% therefore; they accordingly may be at a tangency point with some substitution effect. The group to the right of A includes these people as well as those with benefit/income ratios between $\frac{2}{3}$ and 1.

Finally, there was a ceiling on ERS, i.e. an income above which ERS became a flat rate supplement, shown as point B. Those to the right of B will have benefit/wage ratios progressively less than $\frac{2}{3}$ as income rises, and their budget lines will slope more steeply; so that their tangency point will be where the substitution effect may be smaller. (At very high incomes budget lines become shallow again with the higher rate of tax; however this is not of much concern for unemployment).

---

[2] The point A is properly the wage at which the flat rate benefit level is just attractive enough to make 100% leisure preferable. This point could occur at a replacement ratio lower than 100% (for some possibly higher).

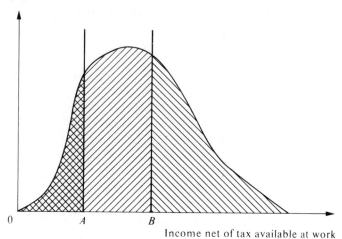

Income net of tax available at work

FIG. 3. Distribution of income and benefit status for a typical household type.

A = Flat rate benefit 'cut off' point
B = Earnings related benefit 'cut off' point } see text

If we were carrying out a cross section analysis, it would pay us to use a utility function which spanned these possibilities. However, we are proposing a time-series analysis for which this gives no particular gain. Instead, we note that for our population at t,

$$\pi_t = \sum_{j=2}^{3} q_{jt}\left\{\frac{\gamma_j}{\beta_j}(b_{jt} - w'_{jct}) + \frac{1}{\beta_j}(\alpha_j + v_{jt} + D_t)\right\} + q_{lt} \tag{12}$$

where q_{jt} = proportion of population in category j (j ranging over the 3 groups just described), and j-subscripted parameters and variables are the averages in each group. q_{lt} is the group to the left of A who are assumed to prefer 100% leisure.

The q_{jt} are themselves functions of the general non-union wage, (w_{ct}), the flat rate benefit, (b_f), the ERS(b_{ers}), and the upper limit (b_{max}), as well as of the income distribution. Most importantly, as flat rate benefits rise, more people will be drawn into the area to the left of A where they may decide not to work at all. Since someone who does not work at all will be unemployed 12 times as long as someone who takes a 2 month spell every two years, these people dominate the unemployment stock. In a time-series analysis, we may expect the elasticity of unemployment (under the UK system) to the benefit/income ratio to be very low for a low aggregate ratio (e.g. around 0.5), to rise as the ratio rises, reaching a peak, and dropping again towards zero as the population becomes concentrated around or to the left of A. Such a supply curve is illustrated in Fig. 4.

This illustrates the important general point that while cross-section studies of populations are undoubtedly of great value, they do not necessarily provide ready answers to questions about reactions of populations over

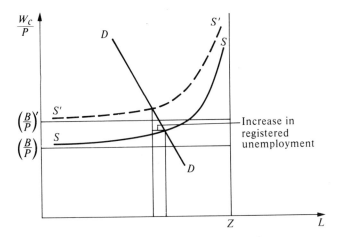

FIG. 4. Increase in benefits.

time. In this case to translate cross-section findings into time-series predictions of the effect of benefit changes one requires to know the income distribution, the location of points A and B, the reservation wage levels, and the elasticity between A and B. Such a translation is likely to be hazardous at best; a time-series relationship, for all its faults, provides a useful direct estimate of the reactions under investigation.

It is extraordinarily hard to think of tractable set ups for estimating exactly this time series model. So far it has eluded us. The discussion must suffice as underpinning for a quite orthodox linear time-series representation. We write unemployment, $U_t = (1 - \pi_t)POP_t$ as a linear function of benefits, real non-union wages, the direct tax rate, POP (the size of the labour force), and q (a measure of the toughness with which benefit disqualification provisions are enforced).

We set competitive wages as the dependent variable. Later we will do the same when we estimate the labour supply reaction to average wages (i.e. over both union and non-union sectors), on which alone we have data. The decision to normalise on wages is in principle arbitrary and unsubstantive. However, there is a potential practical advantage, which appears to be highly relevant. If the economy has been operating over the sample period in the elastic portion of the supply curve shown in Fig. 4, i.e. where benefit wage ratios are rather high and there is a high degree of 'real wage rigidity', α_3 in (13) will be rather low, possibly insignificant; normalising on unemployment would then give poorly determined results, whereas normalising on real wages will give well determined ones (this is the same argument as used under conditions of high capital mobility for estimating interest rate rather than capital flows equations). That this is the case is borne out by what we know about benefit/wage ratios for unskilled workers, by the well-known UK facts of real wage rigidity, and indeed by our results which show a low, marginally insignificant, and far from robust unemployment coefficient in the wage equation (also a fairly common finding in standard Phillips curve wage equations). Our equation is therefore:

$$w_{ct} = \alpha_0 + \alpha_1 q_t + \alpha_2 POP_t + \alpha_3 U_t + \alpha_4 T_{Lt} + \alpha_5 b_t \tag{13}$$

where $b = vb_{ers} + (1-v)b_f$, v being the weight for those drawing earnings related benefit.

We now turn to the union sector, where we suppose the union to maximise the expected real incomes of its potential members, M (assumed to be exogenous and defined as for example in Bain and Price (1980):

$$\sum_{i=0}^{\infty} d^i \mathbf{E}_{t-1} Y_{t+i} \tag{14}$$

subject to

$$Y_{t+i} = w_{ct+i}(M - L_{ut+i}) + w_{ut+i}L_{ut+i} \tag{15}$$

and

$$L_{ut+i} = \beta_0 + \beta_1 k_t - \beta_2 w_{ut} + \lambda L_{ut*i-1} \tag{16}^3$$

The latter demand for labour function is the linear analogue of equation (30) below (but with lagged adjustment); k_t represents the effects on labour productivity of capital costs, technological progress and other factors, $L_{ut} =$ labour demand in union firms, $w_{ut} =$ union real wages, $0 < b < 1$ is the union discount factor. (The real exchange rate, e_t, is substituted out in terms of that part which responds directly to w_{ut}, included in β_2, and the rest, included in β_1).

This is a standard treatment in which members are assumed to be risk-neutral and those who lose their jobs are treated as having the same

---

[3] (16), which is the reduced form demand by firms with rational expectations, is written for simplicity in terms of w_{ut}, k_t only, on the assumption that these follow an ARI process. Generalisation to higher order and moving average processes complicates (21) but does not alter its nature, i.e. planned real union wages remain a function of lagged (possibly more than once) real wages and of expected future competitive real wages and technology. β_2 also depends on the union's preferences because these influence the process driving w_{ut}. However, allowing for this also makes no essential difference to (21), as can be seen by rewriting (16) as

$$L_{ut+i} = \beta_0 + \mathbf{E}_{t+i} \sum_{j=0}^{\infty} \beta_3^j(\beta_1 k_{t+i+j} - \beta_2 w_{ut+i+j}) + \lambda L_{ut+i-1},$$

where β_3 is the inverse of the unstable root in firms' Euler equation, treating w_{ut} as exogenous. The equivalent of (20), for large i, then becomes

$$\mathbf{E}_{t-1}\left[\left\{1 - \left(2\frac{(1+\lambda\beta_3)}{\beta_3 + d\lambda}\right)B + \left(\frac{\lambda + d^{-1}\beta_3}{\beta_3 + d\lambda}\right)B^2\right\}w_{ut+i+1} = \frac{-1}{\beta_3 + d\lambda}[(1 - \beta_3 B^{-1})(1 - \lambda B)W_{ct+i}\right.$$

$$\left. + \beta_2^{-1}(1 - d\lambda B^{-1})(1 - d^{-1}\beta_3 B)\beta_1 k_{t+i} + \beta_2^{-1}\beta_0(1 - \beta_3)(1 - d\lambda)(1 - d^{-1}\beta_3)]\right]$$

Factorisation of { } yields the equivalent of (21) for w_{ut+i}(large i); w_{ut+i} tends towards this process, because the importance of β_3 is less the smaller i.

marginal utility of income as those who obtain higher wages; but see Oswald (1982) for a discussion of the theoretical underpinnings of the union decision, including this set up forced on us here for practical reasons.

The first order conditions yield:

$$\underset{t-1}{\mathrm{E}}\left[w_{ut+i}-w_{ct+i}=\frac{L_{ut+i}}{\beta_2}-\frac{d\lambda(w_{ut+i+1}-w_{ct+i+1})}{1-d\lambda B^{-1}}\right] \qquad (17)$$

or

$$\underset{t-1}{\mathrm{E}}\left[w_{ut+i}-w_{ct+i}=(1-d\lambda B^{-1})\beta_2^{-1}L_{ut+i})\right] \qquad i\geq0 \qquad (18)$$

where B is the lag operator instructing us to lag variables but *not* the expectations operator, and the $\underset{t-1}{\mathrm{E}}$ outside the square brackets indicates that all variables are expected values conditional on information at $t-1$.

Hence using (17):

$$\underset{t-1}{\mathrm{E}}\left[w_{ut+i}-w_{ct+i}=\beta_2^{-1}\frac{(1-d\lambda B^{-1})}{(1-\lambda B)}(\beta_0+\beta_1 k_{t+i}-\beta_2 w_{ut+i})\right] \qquad i\geq0$$

$$(19)$$

so that:

$$\underset{t-1}{\mathrm{E}}\left\{\left[1-\frac{2}{d\lambda}B+\frac{1}{d}B^2\right]w_{ut+i+1}=-\frac{1}{d\lambda}(1-\lambda B)w_{ct+i}-\frac{\beta_1}{\beta_2 d\lambda}(1-d\lambda B^{-1})k_{t+i}\right.$$

$$\left.-\frac{\beta_0(1-d\lambda)}{\beta_2 d\lambda}\right\} \qquad (i\geq0) \quad (20)$$

The transversality condition for the union is that the rate of increase of real wages as given by (20) converges in infinite time to the constant rate determined by the trends of w_{ct} and k_t; any other solution is suboptimal (in fact 'a road to ruin' leading to the extinction of the union either by pricing its members totally out of the union industry market or by pricing them so far below the non-union industry market as to cause them all to leave the union). This condition is met, following the operator method of Sargent (1979), e.g. pp. 333–8) by factoring

$$\left(1-\frac{2}{d\lambda}B+\frac{1}{d}B^2\right) \quad \text{as} \quad (1-\rho_1 B)\left(\frac{1-(\rho_2 B)^{-1}}{-(\rho_2 B)^{-1}}\right)$$

where ρ_1 is the stable root and ρ_2, the unstable root, is used forwards. For a unique stable solution we require that one root is stable, the other unstable (i.e. there is a saddlepath solution), which is satisfied here since

$$\rho_2=(d\lambda)^{-1}(1+\sqrt{1-d\lambda^2})>1, \qquad \rho_1=(d\rho_2)^{-1}=\frac{\lambda}{1+\sqrt{1-d\lambda^2}}<1.$$

The solution for w_{ut} is then:

$$\mathop{E}_{t-1} w_{ut} = \rho_1 w_{ut-1} + \frac{1}{\rho_2 \, d\lambda} \sum_{i=0}^{\infty} \rho_2^{-i} \mathop{E}_{t-1} \left[(1 - \lambda B) w_{ct+i} \right.$$

$$\left. + \frac{\beta_1}{\beta_2} (1 - d\lambda B^{-1}) k_{t+i} + \frac{\beta_0}{\beta_2} (1 - d\lambda) \right] \quad (21)$$

In other words, the planned real union wage depends upon initial levels and the expected path of non-union real wages and other cost factors. We shall rewrite (21), using the F^* prefix to denote the summed and discounted forward values of w_{ct} and k.

We also note that β_2 will fall as expected union power increases, measured by UNR (the unionisation rate). The larger the union sector as a proportion of any given industry, the greater the difficulty of substituting non-union for union labour (a) by unionised firms (directly), (b) by the non-unionised firms (indirectly) through their own expansion. This difficulty is due to 'primary' strike action against (a) and union firms, which would be breaching implicit or explicit 'closed shop' arrangements, and 'secondary' strike action against (b) and non-union firms, because they would be interfering with unions' industrial purposes. Thus at any given real union wage, higher union density in an industry (and so greater strike power) lowers the elasticity of demand for union labour; this is true also in the long run, because the strike threat operates against free entry into the non-union sector. For these reasons, using an expansion of the terms in k and the constant, we add an argument in UNR to (21). So we write (dropping hereafter the t-subscripts throughout):

$$\mathop{E}_{-1} w_u = v_0 + v_1 F_w^* w_c + v_2 F_k^* k + v_3 F_u^* UNR + \rho_1 w_{u-1} \quad (22)$$

We wish to incorporate the observed facts of nominal wage contracting by a proportion of unions. The typical settlement length in our sample period has been one year, and we suppose that the proportion with 1 year contracts is c, the rest implicitly recontracting continuously via shop floor alterations of piece-rates, overtime etc.

For the latter, w_u is given by (22); they will succeed in setting w_u at the planned level. The former however set *nominal* wages, W_u, consistently with (22), given the information set at the settlement date and the expected price level over the coming year so that:

$$W_u = 0.25 \left(\mathop{E}_{-1} \sum_{j=0}^{3} P_{+j} \right) \mathop{E}_{-1} w_u \quad (23)$$

Given that a constant proportion settle each quarter, the change in contracted nominal wages in any quarter will reflect (apart from planned real change) 0.25 times the average inflation rate expected at $t-1$ for the coming year ($PEXP_{-1}$). Real wages however will change by this deflated by the actual change in prices since the last quarter. Hence actual real wages will be approximately:

$$W_u = \frac{W_u}{P} \approx \mathbf{E}_{-1} w_u - (\Delta \log P - 0.25 PEXP_{-1}) \tag{24}$$

for values of $\mathbf{E}_{-1} w_u$ close to a (normalised) unity.

Putting contracts and non-contracts together yields:

$$w_u = v_0 - cP^{ue} + v_1 F_w^* w_c + v_2 F_k^* k + v_3 F_u^* UNR + \rho_1 w_{u,-1} \tag{25}$$

where $P^{ue} = (\Delta \log P - 0.25 PEXP_{-1})$ is 'unanticipated inflation'.

Our (only) observable series for wages is the total:

$$w = uw_u + (1-u)w_c \tag{26}$$

Substituting from (25) we get:

$$w = uv_0 - ucP^{ue} + uv_2 F_k^* k + uv_3 F_u^* UNR + \{uv_1 F_w^* + (1-u)(1-\rho_1 L)\}w_c + \rho_1 w_{-1} \tag{27}$$

Referring back to (13) we may observe that the arguments of w_c consist of tax and benefit rates, demographic trends, benefit disqualifications, and the unemployment rate. In (13) and (22) it is natural to assume—and is not broadly violated by the data—that the tax and benefit rates follow a random walk, and that the demographic trends, UNR, q, and k are random walks with a time trend. This allows us to transform these variables into their current and lagged values, constants, and time trends. This leaves the expected unemployment rate and we shall write $\{uv_1 F_w^* + (1-u)(1-\rho_1 L)\}U$ as a function of the lagged and current unemployment rate and of the *natural* rate, U^*, at t; the latter at this stage we have forced to proxy by a time trend.

Finally we obtain our wage equation as:

$$\log w = c_0 - ucP^{ue} + c_1 q + c_2 UNR + c_3 \log POP + c_4 T_L + c_5 \log b + c_6 \log U + \rho_1 \log w_{-1} \tag{28}$$

We have adopted a loglinear formulation and have dropped lagged values for certain variables. Forced to choose between a time trend and log POP because of their high collinearity, we omitted the (generally quite insignificant) time trend. Nothing serious appears to hang on these approximations.

We choose to enter log U rather than U into this supply curve because our theory suggests that, at high unemployment levels, a 1% change in benefits will have a larger absolute effect on unemployment than at low unemployment levels because the slope of the supply curve will be flatter (more 'wage rigidity'). A log formulation has this property.

The relation between (28), our 'supply' equation, and the equilibrium model of Lucas and Rapping (1969) can be seen by rewriting (28) as:

$$U = (\overset{-}{P^{ue}}; \overset{+}{UNR, POP, T_L, b, w_{-1}}; \overset{-}{w}) \tag{28}'$$

(28)' indicates that unanticipated inflation, P^{ue}, reduces unemployment. The role of 'expected normal real wages' is taken by the variables between semi-colons; these depress labour supply (raise registered unemployment). Finally current real wages raise labour supply and depress unemployment. Of course the derivation and true meaning of (28)' is quite different from that in the Lucas equilibrium model. But the family resemblance is striking; were someone to use the Lucas model on an 'as if' basis for the UK, he should obtain reasonable results (e.g. Batchelor and Sherriff, 1980).

(28) also has a family relationship with the wage equation suggested by Hines (1964), who first stressed the role of union power in wage-setting, in our view quite correctly. Nevertheless, as might be expected from the twenty year gap in formulations, ours is different in important ways. The most important one is that the Hines wage equation was intended as a 'cost-push' theory of *nominal* wages and so of inflation; this formulation was effectively rebutted by Purdy and Zis (1973). (28) however has no implications for inflation, other than temporary, and relates to *real* wages.

3. The demand for labour

Individual firms are regarded as competitive and atomistic each with a fixed endowment of entrepreneurship which gives them decreasing returns to scale. They therefore determine an optimal supply of output and demand for labour given the actual and expected prices and wages facing them.

We write the ith firm's production function in the form

$$Q_i(1 - \mu) = f(K_i, L_i, \bar{T}_i) \tag{29}$$

where μ is the (assumed inflexible) share of imports in production and $\bar{T}$ is the stock of the exogenous factor ('entrepreneurship') which is assumed to be growing steadily over time. Using the cost-minimising conditions and the production function, we can write down a labour demand function in terms of output as:

$$L_i^d = \phi(w_i(1 + T_F), r_i, Q_i, \bar{T}_i) \tag{30}$$

We can also substitute in this for output, from the profit-maximising condition that marginal cost = price, and so obtain the reduced form demand function for labour as:

$$L = \psi(w_i(1 + T_F), e, r_i, \bar{T}_i) \tag{31}$$

which corresponds to (1) and (2) above; e is the relative price of imported inputs (the real exchange rate as before), r_i the real cost of capital.

It is convenient to base estimation on (30) treating Q as planned (or 'desired') output; (33) below is its form in implementation. We then use an estimate of the marginal cost curve below, (38) (taken from Minford (1980)) to complete the supply model; from (33), (38), and the labour supply equation (28), we then derive the 'OS' curve relating e to Q as explained in the introduction.

Writing (29) more generally, also in an adjustment formulation and aggregating over the i firms gives familiarly:

$$\Delta \log L^D = \mu (\log L^* - \log L_{-1}) \qquad (32)$$

where $L^* = \phi[(1 + \overset{-}{T_F})w^*, \overset{+}{Q^*}, t]$ and t picks up the trend in T and r.

This formulation, though *ad hoc*, corresponds approximately to the final form of an optimal plan by individual firms (e.g. see Nickell, 1981). The starred variables are the desired or expected future outcomes, as appropriate. Since we use unemployment as the quantity measure, our operational demand equation becomes:

$$\log U = \mu\gamma_1(\log w^* + T_F) + \mu\gamma_2 \log Q^* - \mu\gamma_3 t + (1 - \mu) \log U_{-1} \qquad (33)$$

(Note that any residual effect of *POP* is captured here by the time trend). We continue to use $\log U$ for convenience given its use in (28); we test later whether this choice causes empirical difficulties.

Equations (28) and (33) define a sub-model of the labour market which is conditional on planned output. Planned output depends upon the rest of the model interacting with this sub-model. The sub-model aggregates over *all* sectors of the economy, including nationalised industries and public services. We therefore treat a rise in unit labour costs in the public sector (due say to increased public sector unionisation) in the same way as one in the private sector. The reason is that the government budget constraint compels the government to spend the resources generated by given levels of taxation and borrowing; *given* these levels a rise in public sector labour costs forces substitution and contraction effects on labour demand just as in the private sector.

It is true that there is an aggregation problem since these levels will be changing over time and, because labour intensity may differ between public and private sectors, so changing labour demand. We treat any such drift as exogenously determined by political choice (on tax burdens and, for borrowing, on inflation targets); but it is included in the 'productivity' time trend along with other sources of trend such as the efficiency of taxation, relative raw material costs and real capital costs, none of which we could in practice identify separately. (This applies also to rising unionisation which would in principle lower γ_1 over time as discussed above, and contribute a compensating time-dependent alteration to the constant term.)

Empirical work on U.K. labour market

Our labour demand and supply equations have been deliberately kept to the simplest form in order to economise on degrees of freedom. Possibly intensive searching would yield some insights into nuances of dynamic structure; but we doubt if much could be gained, because the major exogenous variables in the labour subsector are benefit and tax variables, for which the best predictor turns out to be close to the current value. The only exogenous variable to show significant autocorrelation is UNR; this both displays a strong upward time trend and positive first order autocorrelation which could form the basis for a better predictor. Planned/expected output creates more of a problem; Nickell (1981) reports encouraging results for a labour demand function in which quite complicated patterns of coefficients on future expected values are generated. At this stage, we have merely looked at expected values up to a year ahead using instrumental variables for the quarterly version and the model predictions for the annual.

Our study relates to most of the post-war time series data conveniently available from the CSO's data bank; namely quarterly data for the whole economy, for manufacturing and for individual industries and for annual data for the whole economy only. The Liverpool model is annual; but the other work serves as a further check and is possibly more informative because quarterly.

Whole economy time series: Quarterly data

The results that follow are based on benefits and average net direct taxes paid by a married man with two children whose wife is not working. Clearly this is not properly representative of those on the margin of employment and unemployment. We have also therefore checked the sensitivity of our results for a variety of weighting procedures; a full set of results for benefits and tax series weighted according to unemployment shares for six household-types (single, married $+0$ up to $+4$ children) is available on request but is not different in any important way from those shown here.

The disqualification variable turned out to be generally insignificant in the quarterly analysis (e.g. Table 5). An annual series was also not available for our full annual sample. We therefore dropped this variable altogether from the main reported results.

Our quarterly results for the whole economy are shown in Table 3. All variables have the correct sign and are significant. In the 'supply' or 'wage' equation we tested the following restrictions: that the coefficient on benefits (b) and tax rates (T_L) were (a) equal to each other and (b) also both equal to unity in the long run. (a) would come about if $\alpha_4 = \alpha_5 = 1$ in (13), i.e. if the benefit/net non-union wage *ratio* affected the supply of labour, an assumption that is widely made in the literature. (b) would occur if additionally in (27) $\{uv_1 F_w^* + (1-u)(1-\rho_1 L)\}w_c \approx (1-\rho_1)w_c$, a condition that in general seems unlikely to be met. In general we find that (a) is met but (b) is not and report the results for (a) accordingly.

The fact that benefits and direct taxes have an equal coefficient in the supply or wage equation, but one that is significantly less than unity in the long run, suggests that versions of this equation with unemployment as the dependent variable and the benefit/income *ratio* as a regressor are mis-specified (unless the level of real wages is also included); the reason as already discussed lies in the way w_c enters the supply equation which is as a complex dynamic term.

In so far as one is interested in the long run partial elasticity of unemployment to the replacement ratio, this equation provides an estimate of $4\frac{1}{2}$, well above previous time series of the UK. Maki and Spindler (1975) found a partial elasticity for the postwar period of 0.6. This estimate is flawed by the use of the ERS benefit ratio which only applied to a minority of unemployed, and by the ambiguous status of the estimating equation, which is neither a structural equation nor a reduced form. Also, the most recent re-working of their data by Junankar (1981) reveals that the equation is fairly vulnerable to shifts in estimation period. Holden and Peel (1981) have estimated reduced form equations on UK postwar time series using benefits paid to a married man on average earnings with 2 children which find an elasticity of around 0.4 to the replacement ratio; however since other exogenous variables, such as world trade and unionisation, have been omitted and rolled into the error process, the coefficient estimate may be biased. Similar problems and comments arise in the context of the work on inter-war data by Benjamin and Kochin (1979) and others (see Benjamin and Kochin *et al.* 1982). This type of time-series work has been stimulating and suggestive; but it would appear that it has established only that benefits probably matter for unemployment, to an *undetermined* degree.

Unionisation enters the supply equation strongly. The long run elasticity of real wages to *UNR* (at its mean value of 0.48) is about unity.

It is tempting to attempt to derive an estimate of the union mark-up from this coefficient. In so far as any tentative estimate of this union mark-up emerges from our work, it is of the order of 60%.[4] Other estimates have

[4] An estimate of the *increase* in the union mark-up due to increased unionisation can be obtained from the model as follows. Reduced form effects give

$$\frac{d \log U}{dUNR} = 11.5; \quad \frac{d \log w}{dUNR} = 0.8; \quad \frac{d \log U}{d \log w_c} = -10.0$$

(partial elasticity from supply equation); $d \log w = \alpha d \log w_u + (1-\alpha)d \log w_c$ where α is the proportion of workers covered by union agreements (according to New Earnings Survey 1978 this was 0.71 for men and 0.68 for women, if *all* agreements are included). Hence

$$\frac{d \log w_u - d \log w_c}{dUNR} = \frac{1}{\alpha}\left(\frac{d \log w}{dUNR} - \frac{d \log w_c}{dUNR}\right) = \frac{1}{0.7}\left(0.8 + \frac{11.5}{10.0}\right) = 2.79$$

The change in *UNR* over our sample period 1955–79 was 0.14, hence the change in $\log (w_u/w_c)$ is put at 0.39 implying a rise in the mark-up of 48 percentage points. Assuming that the mark-up was quite low in 1955 (say 10% as in some early studies such as Pencavel (1974) on 1964 data), we could take 60% as an appropriate estimate with 50% as lower bound. This is subject to the qualification that *other* factors than *UNR* could have affected the mark-up.

varied substantially, and have given rise to substantial controversy. Most recently, Treble (1982) has pointed out the tenuous basis for the majority of these estimates which use a methodology originated by Lewis (1963). If one averages available estimates of this type for the UK mark-up (Parsley, 1980), it comes out around 25%, with a high variance. Treble (1982), used a random coefficients estimator to rework the data of Mulvey (1976), who gave estimates for the UK around 30%, and obtained an estimate of about 40%. This is closer to our implicit figure; however there is still reason to believe it is downward biased.[5]

Another issue on which these results throw some light is the prevalence of one-year non-contingent contracts. The term, P^{ue}, will have a coefficient of minus unity if such contracts are universal in the sector under investigation; its absolute size below unity indicates the proportion of workers governed by such contracts. It is normally regarded as a 'stylised fact' about the UK that most wages are governed by such contracts. Indeed this is confirmed by evidence from wage *rates*. Yet in Italy where inflation rates have been similar over the past decade, indexation is virtually universal, and this of course is equivalent to a shortening of contract length. Belgium and the Netherlands also have widespread indexation in spite of a lower inflation experience. It is also the case that recorded labour contract lengths (on wage rates) declined in the UK from about 2 years in the early 1950s to around 1 year by the mid 1970s (Minford and Hilliard 1978). There is therefore some

---

[5] Treble's criticism and proposal can be simply reproduced. Lewis proposed to use the identity

$$\log W_i = \log W_{Ni} + \mu_i \alpha_i$$

where W_i = average wage, W_{Ni} = non-union wage, μ_i = union mark-up, α_i = proportion unionised (all in industry i at a point in time); letting $\mu_i = \mu$ and $\log W_{Ni} = f(\chi_i) + \varepsilon_i$ where χ_i is a vector of industry characteristics, estimate

$$\log W_i = f(\chi_i) + \mu \alpha_i + \varepsilon_i$$

Treble points out that μ is not constant and that the χ_i have been chosen in *ad hoc* manner; consequently he argues that estimates of μ have varied widely because of omitted variable bias (χ_i) and because the error contains the error in μ, θ_i, in the form $\theta_i \alpha_i$ and so is correlated with α_i. He proposes that since the χ_i are arbitrary, they be dropped and that μ be written $\delta + \theta_i$, and the equation be estimated by the random coefficients method as

$$\log W_i = \delta \alpha_i + (\varepsilon_i + \theta_i \alpha_i).$$

The problems however go deeper than Treble suggests. Clearly micro theory would lead us to expect $\log W_{Ni}$ to depend negatively, and μ_i to depend positively, on α_i; it also should suggest an appropriate list of χ_i apart from α_i. Thus the relation should be:

$$\log W_i = f(\chi_i, \overset{-}{\alpha_i}) + \mu(\overset{+}{\alpha_i})\alpha_i + \varepsilon_i$$

Therefore in addition to the problems Treble mentions there is the bias from omitting α_i from the model for $\log W_{Ni}$. The coefficient on α_i estimated by Mulvey *et al.* includes the negative effect on $\log W_{Ni}$ and is hence downward biased. This downward bias of course persists in Treble's own reworking. Furthermore, Treble's removal of all χ_i from the regression increases the likelihood of omitted variable bias.

evidence both that UK contract behaviour is sensitive to the inflation rate
and yet that it is out of line with some continental behaviour.

Our results which relate to earnings suggest that one year contracts are far
from universal. In fact the coefficient on P^{ue} was ultimately dropped in the
aggregate economy equation because it had the wrong sign, besides being
insignificant. It is possible to reconcile this finding with the prevalence of 1
year contracts for wage *rates* by appealing to wage drift. Presumably matters
are arranged on the shop floor so that earnings are indexed to some degree
to the inflation rate. Variation in overtime and piece rates or clocking on/off
conventions, could well be used to achieve this effect. On this basis the UK
contract behaviour is seen to be roughly in line with the continental
practices cited. At the same time there seems no reason to believe that the
change in contract lengths evidenced by wage rate data would be seriously
misleading (indeed, Minford and Hilliard found it to reflect the predictions
obtained from a transactions–cost minimisation approach).

Other features of the real wage equation are the (on the whole) significant
role of unemployment, the fairly speedy adjustment rate (90% in 2 years),
and the modest negative effect on real wages of the rising workforce. The
unemployment term implies that the supply curve of labour is not infinitely
elastic ('real wage rigidity') over the *whole* sample period; the (partial) long
run elasticity of unemployment to real wages is around $-9\frac{1}{2}$, probably
implying (Table 1) an elasticity of *labour supply* to real wages of over unity
and to real benefits of about -0.5. Nevertheless, prior to 1973 the unemployment term is insignificant (Table 4) indicating a much higher elasticity
(and so greater real wage rigidity).

The negative effect of the rise in workforce presumably reflects its bias
towards married women and juveniles, who have it would seem generated
some lowering of the real supply price of labour.

The speed of adjustment should reflect approximately that of unionised
firms in their labour demand decisions (i.e. in the U equation). No cross-
equation constraint was applied but the free estimates are encouragingly
close.

The demand for labour (here the unemployment) equation shows strong
effects of output, real wages grossed up for employees taxes paid by
employers, and productivity. The restriction that real wages and taxes have
the same coefficient is rejected; this odd result does however not occur for
manufacturing (results not reported) and suggests it may be due to unusual
behaviour in the non-manufacturing sector (especially perhaps the public
sector). The unrestricted equation (Table 5) gives a much higher coefficient
on taxes than on wages which is hard to rationalise (and requires more
research, probably on expectational aspects). We therefore prefer and have
reported the restricted estimate.

We may use the quarterly results to estimate the partial elasticity of
supply and demand for labour approximately, if we assume some relation
$\partial \log L/\partial \log U$. Supposing that changes in employment are exactly equal,

though oppositely signed, to changes in unemployment, then

$$\frac{\partial \log L}{\partial \log U} = \frac{\partial L/L}{\partial U/U} = \frac{-\partial U/L}{\partial U/U} = \frac{-U}{L} = -(\text{unemployment rate})$$

However, owing to failure to register by a proportion (for fear of disqualification, partly), this will be an underestimate. If we impose $\partial \log L/\partial \log Q = 1$ (assuming that fixed entrepreneurship does not introduce significant diseconomies of scale within the region of our sample) in our demand equation, we obtain the following elasticities for the rest:

TABLE 1
Elasticities

Demand for labour	to real wages	-0.5
	(plus N.I. contributions)	
	Output	1.0 (imposed)
Supply of Labour	to real wages	1.2
	Real Benefits	-0.6
	(grossed up for employees' taxes)	

(The implied $\partial \log L/\partial \log U = -0.118$ implying $\partial L = -2.4\partial U$ at the mean unemployment rate of 0.05. This implication that the unemployment rate would rise by about 1 percentage point for every $2\frac{1}{2}\%$ drop in output, is roughly consistent with Okun's Law).

Various issues can be raised with these equations.

As far as specification tests are concerned, the equations are reasonably invariant both to changes in time period and to relatively obvious specification changes. Tables 4 and 5 illustrate. Stability over time periods is fairly impressive; both equations pass the Chow test and an F-test for equality of coefficients.[6] The key parameter values do not move much; the only exception is the real wage cost coefficient in the unemployment equation, which drops away if experience from the mid-sixties is not included. The reason for this is that much of the rise in T_F, employers' taxes, occurred between 1964 and 1967 (Fig. 8); excluding this data therefore both removes interesting variation and alters the trend in this variable.

The unemployment equation is free of autocorrelation, as indicated by the X_4^2 test. The wage equation suffers from 3rd order autocorrelation; the X_4^2 test is just significant at the 5% level, and it turns out that the residual at the 3rd lag is also just significant in the regression for that test. However, the autocrorelation is modest; correction for it makes no difference to the point estimates, though it makes them better determined (Table 5, Col. 1).

Inclusion of a time trend in the wage equation and the labour force in the

---

[6] The Chow test give F-values for the wage equation of 1.1 (truncated at 76.4), 0.6 (truncated at 67.1), for the unemployment equation of 1.04 and 1.0 respectively. The F-tests for constancy of coefficients (with the sample split in 1973) were 0.68 for real wages and 0.11 for unemployment.

unemployment equation leaves parameter values unchanged; and both additional variables are insignificant.

Various other variables have been suggested as potential candidates for inclusion in the wage equation, within its overall specification. These include: the age structure of the population (those less than 20, A20, those more than 55, A55), the degree of toughness in denying benefit (TOUGH), inflows (INF) and outflows (OUT) from the unemployment register. Table 5 shows results with a variety of these. They are uniformly disappointing however. Table 5 also shows that, if benefits and direct tax are split up, the coefficients are not significantly different, though that on tax is less well-determined and the higher of the two.

Our choice of $\log U$ rather than U in the demand function was made for convenience and could perhaps cause a loss of definition in the estimates. Table 5 shows (last column) however, that it does not. Significance levels are broadly unchanged as are the elasticity estimates at the mean; there is a slight rise in the coefficient on output, a slight fall in that on labour costs. We therefore maintained the log form.

Is there reverse causation from real wages to real benefits and if so is it such as to bias our results? The vast proportion of benefits paid out (i.e. excluding the earnings related supplement which applied to under 20% of the unemployed) have been determined by reference to flat rate entitlements and not by a ratio to earnings, and these entitlements are fixed about 6 months in advance of the year to which they apply. Furthermore, the entitlements have been mainly governed by political considerations (e.g. the Wilson government's decision to raise benefits substantially in the late 60's) and the ratio to real wages has been permitted to vary considerably, as real wages have varied; this suggests that politicians have had in their minds varying 'poverty base lines' which have borne little systematic relationship since the mid 60s with real wages. It is however possible that current price changes affect both real wages and real benefits jointly. We used a version of the Wu test of exogeneity (Smith, 1983) to check this; this regresses real wages on an Instrumental Variable estimate of real benefits, the other variables, and the residual of benefits from this I.V. estimate. Exogeneity is tested by the significance of this residual. As Table 6 shows, there is some evidence of endogeneity, but it does not bias the coefficients seriously as the equation with the I.V. estimate of benefits above reveals.

To test more specifically whether the common price deflator itself was generating the relationship between real wages and real benefits, we included it (on an I.V. basis) in the regression (Table 6, column 5). It can be seen that it is entirely insignificant.

We also found (Table 6) no significant relationship from *lagged* real wages to real benefits, which suggests that whatever is determining benefits it is probably not real wages. In fact, real benefits follow a random walk according to this work. This is not too surprising a result with such a highly politicised variable.

Unionisation itself may respond to real wages and unemployment, and hence may bias the coefficients. We also carried out the Smith/Wu test for this, with a clearly negative result (Table 6).

It may be asked; how far can the equilibrium relationships (28) and (33) estimated here be distinguished from disequilibrium relationships of a standard form? In the first place, our (33) is regarded as reflecting the demand for labour; it is also common in disequilibrium models to assume that employment is 'on the demand curve' (e.g. because wages are set by noncontingent contracts where firms choose quantity), and if so to use equations amounting to (33).

The distinction lies in (28), a 'supply price' equation, as compared with the 'sticky wage change' equations used in disequilibrium models. A multiplicity of these 'Phillips curves' exist in the literature; these take the form:

$$\Delta \log W = f(\Delta \log P^E_{-1}, U, \log w^*, \log w_{-1}) \tag{34}$$

where $\Delta \log P^E$ = expected inflation, $\log w^*$ = equilibrium real wage. If (a) the arguments of $\log w^*$ are chosen in the same way as by us, (b) rational expectations are used for $\Delta \log P^E$ and (c) a unit coefficient were imposed on it then indeed the resulting equation will be indistinguishable from (28).[7] But by the same token there would be little dispute about the causes and natural rate of unemployment!

This manifestly is not the case because the Phillips curve form typically used in disequilibrium models has none of the properties (a)–(c). Such a typical Phillips curve in UK models is that due originally to Sargan (1964) and since widely used (e.g. in the NIESR model, Brookes and Henry (1983)). It is of interest therefore to compare this form with (28).

We therefore carried out a non-nested test. We estimated a Sargan-type (S) equation over our quarterly data, obtaining a prediction series $\log \hat{W}_S$. To obtain a prediction series, $\log \hat{W}_{(28)}$, for our equation we took the predictions for $\log w$ from (28) and added to them our I.V. estimate of $\log P$. (S) and (28) were then reestimated with respectively $\log \hat{W}_{28}$ and $\log \hat{W}_S$ as additional arguments; the significance of these indicates the extent to which the alternative model rejects the equation being estimated. The results (Table 7) show that $\log \hat{W}_S$ is totally insignificant in (28), while $\log \hat{W}_{28}$ has a t-value of 1.5 in (S), just short of significance. While (28) cannot quite reject S, S certainly cannot reject (28).

The test is handicapped by the failure to compare like with like; (28) is a *real* wage equation and to compare it with S, a nominal equation, $\log \hat{P}$ has to be added, in principle from the Liverpool model as a whole but in practice here from an I.V. estimate. The properties of the test with I.V. estimates as arguments are also not known. Nevertheless, there is certainly no prima facie evidence here against (28).

---

[7] Our model, as an equilibrium model, implies that unemployment is voluntary whereas such a disequilibrium model would imply involuntary unemployment. For this reason it is unlikely that the arguments of w^* would be the same, even if (b) and (c) were adopted.

This conclusion is strengthened by the following consideration: the Sargan equation can be regarded as an unrestricted multivariate time series representation of our model. Fitted to the same data, such a representation is therefore likely to be reasonably good, and any rejection by a properly restricted model could be expected to be marginal on a fairly small sample. (For issues raised in this type of comparison, see Wallis, 1980).

Annual data

A word is necessary about the annual results for 1955–79, Table 2. These were estimated using *expected* output and inflation from the Liverpool Model. As in the quarterly equations the contract (unanticipated inflation) term is either zero or the wrong sign; nevertheless, this is surprising because the data are for wage *rates* where contracts are unambiguously important. This may be the result of aggregation over the calendar year. However, the long run coefficients are similar to the quarterly ones for 1964–79. Such differences as there are (i.e. rather higher coefficients on *UNR* and *POP*) are presumably the result of the rather longer time period covered.

Empirically, therefore, the whole economy equations give a reasonably robust performance. Nevertheless, they are based on a limited number of observations and one would wish to corroborate the coefficient estimates from other evidence.

Other evidence

The model we described earlier can be used at the industry level as a 'micro' model. In our unemployment registration system people register for particular jobs so that they can be classified by industry; we interpret the unemployment figures by industry as mirroring the original activities of the unemployed and so as closely reflecting changes in employment in that industry. Besides unemployment, we have real wages and output by industry, and unionisation rates in 13 of the industries; where we do not have them, we have used some closely matching rates and failing that the aggregate unionisation rate. The other variables do not vary across industries and remain our aggregate figures.

Our full industry results are set out in Minford *et al.* (1983, pp. 129–30). Table 8 (row 5) gives a summary. In all industries bar one, the benefit variable has a highly significant effect on real wages, while unionisation in the industry is significant in 8 of the industries and has t-values over 1.5 in another 2. In the unemployment equations, in 15 of the industries real wage costs are significant, often highly so, and in the other two they have the appropriate sign and are merely not so well-determined.

Hence for our key coefficients, for benefits, union power, and wage costs, there is widespread evidence in the industry level data. This represents strong and striking confirmation of our model of wages and unemployment at the most detailed level; there are over 1000 observations in these industry samples.

Further evidence on these relationships is available both from regional UK data for 1978 and on time series for Belgium, whose system of benefits and degree of union power show close parallels with that of the UK. Analogous relationships with variations of this model reflecting institutional differences in each country have also been detected for Germany, France, and Italy—see Minford *et al.* (1983).

Sources and definitions—Tables 2–7

Sources

U	Unemployment	D of E Gazette
Q	Total output of all industries	CSO
w	Real average earnings	CSO
T_F	Employers NI contributions as percentage of gross (national) average earnings, male manual workers national figures.	Ann. Abst. Stats. D of E
UNR	National unionisation rate	D of E Gazette
POP	National Working population	Economic Trends
P_{ue}	$\Delta \log P - (PEXP_{-1}/4)$	
$PEXP_{-1}$	Expected average change of price level in coming year, i.e.	

$$\log\left[E_{-1}(P_0 + P_1 + P_2 + P_4)/4\right] - \log\left(P_{-1} + P_{-2} + P_{-3} + P_{-4}\right)/4$$

The expected value in this expression $E_{-1}(\ )$ was derived by an instrumental regression on lagged values and on rates of change of output and money supply.

$b =$ A weighted average of real benefits (national figures)

$$\left[\frac{(B + ERS) \times 0.3 + (B + R + M) \times 0.7}{P}\right]$$

B	Flat rate benefits, man with wife and second child	DHSS
ERS	Earnings related supplement based on gross average earnings	Holden and Peel (1979)
R	Local authority rents	Dept. Environ.
M	School meals	DES
T_L	Percentage of national gross average earnings lost in taxes and national insurance contributions (national figures) (man with wife and second child)	Holden and Peel (1979)
P	Retail price index (all items)	Economic Trends
$\char"005E$	denotes use of instrumental variable estimate	

TABLE 2

3SLS estimates of supply and demand equations on annual data (t-values)*

1955–1979	$\bar{R}^2$	DW	BP(4)	See

$\log U_t = 40.72 + 1.89(\log \hat{w} + T_F)_t - 2.63 \log Q_t^{\text{EXP}}$ 0.87   1.51   13.1   0.184
    (2.03) (1.10)   (1.30)

$\qquad\qquad\qquad + 0.058t + 0.52 \log U_{t-1}$
$\qquad\qquad\qquad$ (0.84)   (2.85)

$\log w_t = 6.26 - 0.062 \log \hat{U}_t + 0.12(\log b + T_L)_t$ 0.96   2.51   6.3   0.026
    (1.16) (1.53)   (2.90)

$\qquad\qquad + 0.92 UNR_t - 0.70 \log POP_t + 0.80 \log w_{t-1}$
$\qquad\qquad$ (2.66)   (1.43)   (4.72)

Notes

Unexpected inflation failed to enter with the right sign. w = wage rates.

Q_t^{EXP} = prediction from Liverpool Model of next year's output, based on this year's exogenous variables (and last year's endogenous).

Instruments used for variables with $\hat{\ }$: T_{Ft}, T_{Lt}, Q_t^{EXP}, $\log U_{t-1}$, t, $\log b_t$, UNR_t, $\log POP_t$, $\log w_{t-1}$.

TABLE 3

Real wage and unemployment equations for whole economy

(t-values bracketed)   Quarterly: 1964.2 to 1979.2

$\log w_t = 0.34 - 0.00162\text{D}1 + 0.0024\text{D}2 + 0.0044\text{D}3 - 0.024 \log \hat{U}_t + 0.11\{(\log b) + T_{Lt}\}$
    (1.5)(2.75)   (0.41)   (0.77)   (2.1)   (3.1)

$\qquad + 0.45 UNR_t - 0.016 \log POP_t + 0.77 \log w_{t-1}$
$\qquad$ (2.4)   (0.1)   (12.0)

$\bar{R}^2 = 0.47$;   S.e.e. $= 0.0125$; $\chi_4^2 = 10.3^*$;   D.W. $= 1.719$

$\log U_t = 13.3 + 0.000419 \text{D}1 - 0.125 \text{D}2 + 0.0047 \text{D}3 - 2.17 \log \hat{Q}_t + 1.04\{(\log \hat{w}_t) + T_{Ft}\}$
    (5.2) (0.01)   (3.52)   (0.13)   (4.5)   (2.7)

$\qquad + 0.008t + 0.744 \log U_{t-1}$
$\qquad$ (2.6)   (11.3)

$\bar{R}^2 = 0.96$;   S.e.e. $= 0.4986$; $\chi_4^2 = 2.9^*$;   D.W. $= 2.008$

Instrumental estimates shown by $\hat{\ }$.

Instruments used: (Lagged) inflation, output, real wages, real benefits, unemployment; (current) change in log £M3, T_F, UNR, T_L, D1, D2, D3.

* This is the Lagrange Multiplier test for residual independence (the regression residuals are regressed on the right hand side variables and their lagged values, up to 4 in this case; $T \times R^2$ where T is the sample size is distributed as χ^2). The critical value of χ_4^2 is 9.5 at the 5% level (11.1 at the $2\frac{1}{2}$% level). See Godfrey (1978).

TABLE 4

Real wage and unemployment equations for different sample (whole economy) (constant and seasonal dummies included but not reported)

Dependent variable = log w_t

Sample =	64.2–79.2	64.2–73.1	73.2–79.2	64.2–76.4	67.1–79.2
log $\hat{U}_t$	-0.024	0.010	-0.033	-0.022	-0.027
	(2.1)	(0.5)	(1.6)	(1.8)	(1.7)
$(\log b_t) + T_{Lt}$	0.12	0.06	0.126	0.13	0.11
	(3.2)	(0.7)	(1.4)	(2.9)	(2.0)
UNR_t	0.45	0.63	0.48	0.65	0.47
	(2.4)	(1.8)	(0.9)	(2.3)	(1.8)
log POP_t	-0.02	0.21	0.09	0.2	0.006
	(0.07)	(0.4)	(0.1)	(0.7)	(0.02)
log w_{t-1}	0.77	0.72	0.77	0.68	0.78
	(12.2)	(3.7)	(7.4)	(6.3)	(11.0)
$\bar{R}^2$	0.98	0.95	0.86	0.98	0.97
S.e.e.	0.0155	0.0103	0.0183	0.0152	0.0161
R.S.S.	0.0.1242	0.00181	0.00875	0.00975	0.010912
D.W.	1.72	1.95	1.62	1.74	1.67

Dependent variable = log U_t

Sample =	64.2–79.2	64.2–73.1	73.2–79.2	64.2–76.4	67.1–79.2
log $\hat{Q}_t$	-2.17	-3.36	-2.2	-2.48	-2.2
	(4.5)	(3.4)	(3.3)	(4.7)	(4.6)
$(\log \hat{w}_t) + T_{Ft}$	1.04	1.69	0.07	1.7	0.18
	(2.7)	(1.3)	(0.1)	(3.2)	(0.3)
t	0.008	0.010	0.013	0.005	0.013
	(2.6)	(0.7)	(2.2)	(1.3)	(3.4)
log U_{t-1}	0.74	0.78	0.71	0.70	0.68
	(11.3)	(8.7)	(7.0)	(9.5)	(9.0)
$\bar{R}^2$	0.96	0.94	0.90	0.94	0.94
S.e.e.	0.097	0.062	0.116	0.096	0.097
R.S.S.	0.4987	0.0693	0.3624	0.3985	0.4035
D.W.	2.0	1.56	2.16	2.12	2.05

Instruments as in Table 3

TABLE 5

Some alternative specifications. Quarterly 1964.2 to 1979.2 (constants and seasonal dummies included but not reported)

Dependent variable = log w_t

Columns (5)–(8): sample **1964.2 to 1978.4**; column (9): sample **64.2 to 77.4**. Columns (1)–(4): full sample.

Regressor	(1)	(2)	(3)	(4)	(5)	(6)	(7)	(8)	(9)
$\hat{p}_t^{ue}$	0.58 (1.3)	0.3 (0.4)	0.29 (0.5)	0.4 (0.7)	—	—	—	—	—
log $\hat{U}_t$	−0.030 (8.1)	−0.023 (1.7)	−0.028 (1.8)	−0.023 (1.8)	−0.029 (1.7)	−0.02 (1.6)	−0.02 (1.3)	−0.02 (2.0)	−0.02 (1.7)
$\hat{U}_t$ (millions)	—	—	—	—	—	—	—	—	—
log b_t	—	0.11 (1.9)	—	—	—	—	—	—	—
$(\log b_t) + T_{Lt}$	0.14 (4.5)	—	0.125 (3.4)	0.11 (1.9)	0.12 (3.1)	0.13 (3.3)	0.14 (2.6)	0.12 (2.0)	0.13 (2.7)
T_{Lt}	—	0.16 (1.0)	—	—	—	—	—	—	—
UNR_t	0.48 (5.6)	0.44 (2.3)	0.50 (2.6)	0.40 (1.5)	0.47 (2.2)	0.43 (2.2)	0.37 (1.5)	0.44 (2.2)	0.35 (1.6)
t	—	—	—	0.003 (0.2)	—	—	—	—	—
log POP_t	−0.004 (0.8)	−0.002 (0.01)	0.035 (0.2)	−0.05 (0.2)	0.04 (0.3)	−0.08 (0.3)	−0.07 (0.3)	−0.02 (0.1)	−0.2 (0.6)
log w_{t-1}	0.75 (14.1)	0.76 (11.1)	0.73 (10.8)	0.74 (8.6)	0.78 (12.1)	0.76 (11.3)	0.76 (11.6)	0.77 (11.8)	0.76 (8.2)
log (INF)	—	—	—	—	0.01 (0.5)	—	—	—	—
log (OUT)	—	—	—	—	—	−0.02 (0.8)	—	—	−0.007 (0.6)
TOUGH	—	—	—	—	—	—	—	0.0001 (0.5)	—
A55	—	—	—	—	—	—	−0.04 (0.5)	—	—
A20	—	—	—	—	—	—	—	—	—
ρ_{-3}	−0.35	—	—	—	—	—	—	—	—

Dependent variable = log U_t and U_t (million)

Regressor	log U_t	log U_t	U_t (million)
log $\hat{Q}_t$	−2.43 (5.6)	−2.13 (4.3)	−2.02 (6.1)
log $\hat{w}_t$	−0.04 (0.1)	—	0.56 (1.8)
$(\log \hat{w}_t) + T_{Ft}$	—	1.23 (2.5)	—
T_{Ft}	2.0 (4.7)	—	—
t	0.019 (4.6)	0.006 (1.3)	0.009 (3.6)
log U_{t-1}	0.59 (8.1)	0.75 (11.2)	—
U_{t-1}	—	—	0.79 (12.8)
log N_t	—	0.78 (0.5)	—

TABLE 6

Tests of Exogeneity for b and UNR. Quarterly: 1964.2 to 1979.2 (constants and seasonal dummies included but not reported)

Dependent variable	$\log w_t$					$\log b_t$	
$\hat{p}^{ue}$	0.42 (0.7)	−0.04 (0.1)	0.14 (0.3)	—	—	$\log b_{t-1}$	0.96 (18.4)
$\log \hat{U}_t$	−0.022 (1.8)	−0.023 (1.8)	−0.023 (2.0)	−0.020 (1.8)	−0.018 (1.4)	$\log U_{t-1}$	0.009 (0.5)
$(\log \hat{b}_t)+T_{Lt}$	0.12 (3.0)	0.09 (2.2)	—	—	—	$\hat{p}^{ue}_t$	−0.15 (0.3)
$(\log b_t)+T_{Lt}$	—	—	0.12 (3.1)	0.11 (2.8)	0.13 (3.5)	$\log w_{t-1}$	−0.06 (0.5)
UNR_t	0.45 (2.2)	0.49 (2.4)	—	—	0.59 (1.7)	T_{Ft}	0.05 (0.4)
$\log POP_t$	0.005 (0.02)	−0.16 (0.7)	0.03 (0.1)	−0.03 (0.1)	0.19 (0.4)	t	−0.0001 (0.1)
$\log w_{t-1}$	0.76 (11.1)	0.84 (14.2)	0.77 (11.4)	0.79 (12.4)	0.76 (11.9)	$\bar{R}^2$	0.93
$\log b_t - \log \hat{b}_t$	0.13 (1.85)	—	—	—	—	D.W.	1.76
$U\hat{N}R_t$	—	—	0.42 (2.0)	0.40 (1.9)	—	Box–Pierce (χ^2_{16})	11.0
$UNR_t - U\hat{N}R_t$	—	—	0.63 (1.4)	—	—		
$\log \hat{P}$	—	—	—	—	−0.28 (0.6)		

Instruments as in Table 3.

(e) *The natural rate—estimates and policy effects*

An idea of how sensitive the long run unemployment effects are to the different data examined here can be obtained from Table 8.

By comparison, Nickell (1979a,b), Lancaster (1979) and Mackay and Reid (1972) have found elasticities of unemployment duration to the replacement ratio of around 0.6 in cross-section studies of samples of the unemployed. Lancaster went as far as to conclude that 'an elasticity of this order could now be regarded as established beyond reasonable doubt'. These studies employ a totally different methodology and data set from that used here; until our methodology has been tried out properly on such cross-section data, it would be inappropriate to comment on these estimates in detail.

Nevertheless, there is one major issue to be raised with all these studies. They all assume, within a search model framework, that intended (or desired) duration is never long term (or 'infinite'), or in terms of the search model that the offer–acceptance rate never tends to zero. We have suggested above that a person's optimal level of unemployment per fiscal year will

TABLE 7

Tests of wage equation ((28) in nominal terms) against Sargan equation (S)

	S equation		Quarterly 1964.2 to 1979.2 (28) = Wage equation (nominal)	
Dependent variable	$\log W_t$		$\log W_t$	
$\log W_{t-1}$	1.0	1.0	$\log \hat{P}_t$	1.0
C	0.25	0.32	C	1.14
	(2.1)	(2.5)		(0.3)
$\Delta \log P_{t-1}$	0.33	0.38	$\hat{p}^{ue}$	0.22
	(2.1)	(2.4)		(0.6)
$\log U_{t-1}$	−0.019	−0.020	$\log \hat{U}_t$	−0.015
	(1.9)	(1.9)		(1.4)
$\log W_{t-1} - \log P_{t-1}$	0.001	−0.041	$(\log b_t) + T_{Lt}$	0.11
	(0.02)	(0.6)		(3.4)
t	0.0008	0.0019	UNR_t	0.42
	(1.5)	(2.1)		(1.4)
$\log \hat{W}_{t(28)}$	—	−0.31	$\log POP_t$	−0.10
		(1.5)		(0.3)
D1	−0.001	−0.002	$\log W_{t-1} - \log P_{t-1}$	0.78
	(0.2)	(0.3)		(11.0)
D2	0.012	0.012	$\log \hat{W}_{t(S)}$	−0.004
	(2.3)	(2.3)		(0.1)
D3	−0.010	−0.011	D1	−0.005
	(1.8)	(2.0)		(0.9)
S.e.e.	0.01443	0.01427	D2	−0.001
DW	1.58	1.55		(0.1)
			D3	0.004
				(0.8)

Instruments as in Table 3. $\log \hat{W}_{t(28)}$ is prediction of $(28) + \log \hat{P}_t$. $\log \hat{W}_{t(S)}$ is prediction of S equation.

TABLE 8

% change* of unemployment with respect to		Percentage point changes in:		
	% change in benefits	Unionisation rate	Personal tax rates	Employer tax rates
From aggregate model				
(Annual data)	1.5	11.3	1.5	2.5
(Quarterly data)	2.8	11.5	2.8	5.9
From average of industry models	4.0	9.3	4.0	8.4
Liverpool Model	2.8	11.5	2.8	5.9

* *not* percentage point change. Calculations assume that each set of equations for w and U is combined with rest of Liverpool Model (i.e. (37) and (38) below).

depend sensitively on the slope of his budget constraint (as roughly measured by the replacement ratio). For high ratios (very shallow slopes) he may
go to a 'corner solution' and decide to work not at all, or only for brief spells
when market wages are exceptionally favourable. Such people are likely to
exhibit a very low elasticity to changes in the ratio; this is Nickell's finding
for those on long durations (six months or more). Yet the implication, if our
suggestion is correct, is precisely the opposite to that which he draws (that
there is little effect of the ratio on long term unemployment); it is that at
some ratio these people would cease to have a corner solution and would
participate 'properly' again in employment, having therefore at this ratio a
very high ('switching') elasticity to it.

We now proceed to evaluate the properties of the equations for the whole
economy. These are based on the quarterly estimates of the long run
coefficients, being the better-determined, except for the productivity growth
time trend which comes from the annual unemployment equation (fitted
over the full sample period, it appears more reliable). The lagged dependent
variable coefficients are taken from the annual equations. The long run
coefficients of equations (28) and (33) in the Liverpool Model are accordingly:

$$\log U^* = -8.48(\log Q^* - 0.022 \text{ time [years]}) + 4.06(\log w^* + T_F) \quad (35)$$

$$\log w^* = -0.10 \log U^* + 0.48(\log b + T_L) - 0.07 \log POP + 1.96 UNR \quad (36)$$

The coefficients of $\log U_{t-1}$ and $\log w_{t-1}$ are respectively 0.52 and 0.80.

In the rest of the model the long run relationship between real wages and
output, when absorption is constrained by the condition that the current
account is in balance is:

$$\log Q^* = -0.65e^* + 0.46 \log WT \quad (37)$$

and the long run relationship between the real exchange rate and real
wages (given by the pricing equation) is:

$$e^* = 1.86(\log w^* + T_F) - 0.033t \text{ (years)} \quad (38)$$

where WT = index of world trade volume, e = real exchange rate.

We can use these four equilibrium equations to compute the effects on the
natural rate of unemployment, real wages and output of various permanent
changes in taxation, benefits and unionisation—see Table 9. (All tax and
benefit changes are offset notionally by lump sum transfers, leaving net
government revenues unchanged; these, which include the effect of changes
in output, are noted in Column 5).

It can be seen that per unit of revenue cost cuts in National Insurance
charges paid by firms are more effective in reducing unemployment than
cuts in the standard rate while to equal the effect on unemployment of a
10% cut in real benefits it would require cuts in N.I. charges costing the

TABLE 9
Effects of regime changes[3]

Fall of	Unemployment[1] ('000)	Real (%)[1] Wages	Output[1] (%)	Available[2] for lump sum transfers (£billion p.a., 1982 prices)
10% in benefits	−500	−2.1	+2.5	+3.4
0.01 in T_F	−90	+0.6	+0.5	−0.6
0.01 in T_L	−55	−0.2	+0.25	−0.9
0.01 in UNR	−170	−0.8	+1.0	+1.1

[1] Computed on 1980 values.

[2] Includes extra revenue from rise in output. Negative figure denotes net drain on Exchequer. Assumes marginal overall tax rate of 0.4.

[3] *Source:* Simulations of Liverpool Model.

Exchequer a net £6 billion p.a. more. However, the effectiveness of a cut in taxes on employees in reducing unemployment would presumably be increased the more it was concentrated on the lower paid; one may presume that if totally concentrated on those at the bottom end each £ of tax cut would have an effect on unemployment comparable with that of a £ of benefit cut. At present most of those in the 'unemployment trap' would pay significant tax if they were working (Minford *et al.*, 1983).

The lags before these policy effects come through depend upon the dynamics of the policy variables. For benefits, unionisation, and income taxes one third of the full effect comes in year 1, $\frac{2}{3}$ by year 2, 80% by year 3, and all by year 5. For employers' taxes the lags are much shorter (since the direct effects on labour costs are large and immediate): $\frac{2}{3}$ of the full effect comes in year 1, and all by year 2.

Finally, we may use these equations to compute the natural rate in 1980. The Charts that follow show the model's 'prediction' for this from 1956–80, as well as the behaviour of the exogenous variables. The natural rate of unemployment is estimated at about $1\frac{3}{4}$ million ($7\frac{1}{4}$%) in 1980; roughly this figure also emerges from both quarterly and annual wage/unemployment equations run on their own over their respective samples treating actual output exogenously as y^*. The date at which it began its dizzying rise can be set fairly precisely at 1965, i.e. the beginning of Labour government after 13 years of Tory government. This led to a sharp rise in union power, in benefits and in taxation.

In 1970 taxes were cut, and the rise in real benefits halted, by Mr. Heath's Tory government; however, the cut in taxes was unsustainable because it led to very large budget deficits and has subsequently been more than reversed, while real benefits began to climb again in the mid-1970s as Labour rule resumed. Union power rose steadily during the 1970s and finally world trade growth collapsed in the second half of the 1970s. So the upward trend was resumed from 1973.

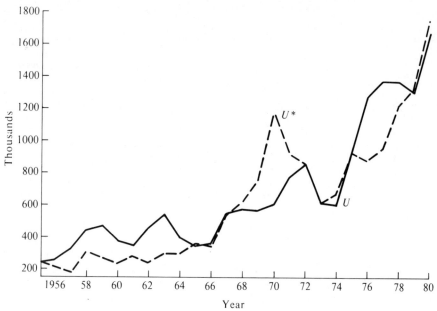

FIG. 5. *U* (unemployment) and *U** (equilibrium unemployment).

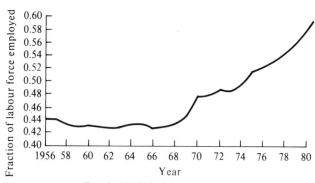

FIG. 6. *UNR* (unionization rate).

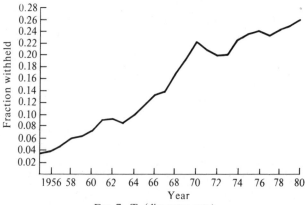

FIG. 7. T_L (direct tax rate).

P. MINFORD

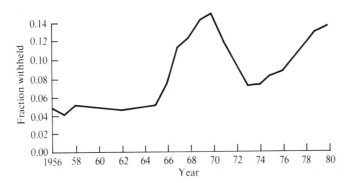

FIG. 8. T_F (employers' tax rate on labour).

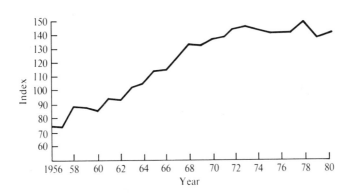

FIG. 9. b (real benefits).

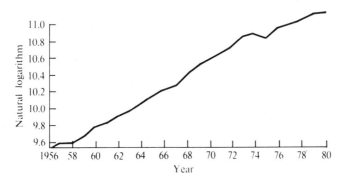

FIG. 10. log WT (world trade volume).

Conclusions

This paper has attempted to produce a theory of the 'natural rate' for the open economy. The interaction with the balance of payments on current account via a stock flow mechanism has been argued to reinforce the direct effects of labour market intervention on unemployment and output. This interaction parallels the feedback onto the labour market through the budget constraint (output = spending) in a closed economy subject to the same intervention.

On annual data, expected output and inflation derived from the model were used in estimation; this was not possible with the quarterly data, though we hope to go this further step once a quarterly version of the full model is estimated. It may also be possible to improve on the 'expected values' used for the exogenous variables; in this paper actual values are used.

Nevertheless, these future changes seem unlikely to alter our major findings, judging from the similarity of the annual results (where some are already incorporated) to the quarterly. These findings were that there is a significant and powerful total elasticity of real benefits on unemployment (operating through higher real wages) of nearly 3; this is substantially higher than other post war estimates in so far as these are comparable. Tax rates on employers and employees have analogous impacts, though the elasticities are much lower. Finally, and perhaps most strikingly, we find that in the past two decades union monopoly power has increased significantly and caused a substantial rise in real wages, with corresponding unemployment. The total elasticity of unemployment to the unionisation rate (our index of union monopoly power) is no less than $5\frac{1}{2}$.

The natural rate of unemployment in the UK in 1980 is estimated to be of the order of $7\frac{1}{4}\%$ or around $1\frac{3}{4}$ million. The analysis of this paper suggests that it can be lowered substantially by measures (such as those discussed in Minford *et al.*, 1983) to reduce real benefits, labour tax rates and union monopoly power.

University of Liverpool

REFERENCES

BAIN, G. and PRICE, R. (1980), *Profiles of Union Growth: A Comparative Statistical Portrait of 8 Countries*. Oxford: Blackwell.

BATCHELOR, R. A. and SHERIFF, T. D. (1980), 'Unemployment and Unanticipated Inflation in Post War Britain'. *Economica*, 47, 179–92.

BENJAMIN, D. and KOCHIN, L. (1979), 'Searching for an Explanation of Unemployment in Inter War Britain'. *JPE 87*, No. 3, 441–470.

BENJAMIN, D. and KOCHIN, L. and Critics (1982), 'Unemployment and Unemployment Benefits in Twentieth Century Britain: A reply to Our Critics', and Preceding Critics' Comments, *Journal of Political Economy*, 90, 369–436.

BROOKES, S. and HENRY, S. G. B. (1983), 'Reestimation of the National Institute Model', *National Institute Economic Review*, 103, 62–70.

GODFREY, L. G. (1978), 'Testing for Higher Order Serial Correlations in Regression Equations when the Regressors include Lagged Dependent Variables', *Econometrica*, 46, 1303–10.

HINES, A. G. (1964), 'Trade Unions and Wage Inflation in the United Kingdom, 1893–1961', *Rev. Econ. Stud.*, 31, 221–52.

HOLDEN, K. and PEEL, D. A. (1979), 'The Determinants of the Unemployment Rate: Some Empirical Evidence', *The Statistician*, Vol. 20, No. 2, 101–7.

HOLDEN, K. and PEEL, D. A. (1981), 'Unemployment and the Replacement Ratio—Some Reduced Form Estimates for the UK', *Economics Letters*, 8, 349–354.

JUNANKAR, P. N. (1981), 'An Econometric Analysis of Unemployment in Great Britain, 1952–75', *Oxford Economic Papers*, 33, 387–400.

LANCASTER, T. (1979), 'Econometric Methods for the Duration of Unemployment', *Econometrica*, 47, 939–956.

LAYARD, R., METCALF, D. and NICKELL, S. (1978), 'The Effect of Collective Bargaining on Relative and Absolute Wages', *British Journal of Industrial Relations*, 287–302.

LEWIS, H. G. (1963), *Unionism and Relative Wages in the United States*, University of Chicago Press.

LUCAS, R. E. and RAPPING, L. S. (1969), 'Real Wages, Employment and Inflation', *Journal of Political Economy*, 77, 721–54.

MAKI, D. and SPINDLER, A. (1975), 'The Effect of Unemployment Compensation on the Rate of Unemployment in Great Britain', *Oxford Economic Papers* 27, 440–54.

MACKAY, D. E. and REID, G. L. (1972), 'Redundancy, Unemployment and Manpower Policy', *Economic Journal*, 82, 1256–72.

MINFORD, A. P. L. and HILLIARD, G. (1978), 'The Cost of Variable Inflation', *in Contemporary Economic Analysis*, (M. J. Artis and A. R. Nobay, eds) London, Croom Helm.

MINFORD, A. P. L. (1980), 'A Rational Expectations Model of the UK under Fixed and Floating Exchange Rates' in *The State of Macroeconomics*, Carnegie Rochester Conference Series on Public Policy 12, 293–355.

MINFORD, A. P. L., DAVIES, D. H., PEEL, M. J. and SPRAGUE, A. S. (1983), *Unemployment— Cause and Cure*, Oxford, Martin Robertson.

MULVEY, C. (1976), 'Collective Agreements and Related Earnings in UK Manufacturing in 1973', *Economica*, 43 (172) 419–27, *November*.

MUTH, J. F. (1961), 'Rational Expectations and the Theory of Price Movements', *Econometrica*, 29, 315–35.

NICKELL, S. (1981), 'The Demand for Labour Function in UK Manufacturing'. Paper presented to Treasury Academic Panel, Centre for Labour Economics, LSE.

NICKELL, S. (1979a), 'The Effects of Unemployment and Related Benefits on the Duration of Unemployment'. *Economic Journal*, 89, March, 34–49.

NICKELL, S. (1979b), 'Estimating the Probability of Leaving Unemployment', *Econometrica*, 47, 1249–1266.

OSWALD, A. J. (1982), 'The Microeconomic Theory of the Trade Union', *Economic Journal*, 92, 576–595.

PARSLEY, C. J. (1980), 'Labour Union Effects on Wage Gains: A Survey of Recent Literature', *Journal of Economic Literature*, 18, pp. 1–31.

PENCAVEL, J. H. (1974), 'Relative Wages and Trade Unions in the United Kingdom', *Economica*, 4, 194–210.

PURDY, D. L. and ZIS, G. (1973), 'Trade Unions and Wage Inflation in the UK: A Reappraisal', in *Essays in Modern Economics*, M. Parkin (ed.) Longman, 1973, 294–327. Reprinted in *Inflation and Labour Markets* (D. Laidler and D. Purdy, eds.), Manchester University Press, 1974.

SARGAN, J. D. (1964), 'Wages and Prices in the United Kingdom', in *Econometric Analysis for National Economic Planning*, (P. E. Hart, G. Mills and J. K. Whittaker, eds.), Butterworth.

SARGENT, THOMAS J. (1979), *Macroeconomic Theory*, Academic Press.

SMITH, R. (1983), 'On the Classical Nature of the Wu–Hausman Statistics for the Independence of Stochastic Regressors and Disturbance', *Economics Letters*, Vol. 11, No. 4, 357–364.

TREBLE, J. G. (1982), 'Does the Union/Non-Union Wage Differential Exist?' Paper given to 1982 AUTE Conference at Surrey University, mimeo, University of Hull.
WALLIS, K. F. (1980), 'Econometric Implications of the Rational Expectations Hypothesis', *Econometrica*, 48, 49–72.

IMPERFECT COMPETITION, UNDEREMPLOYMENT AND CROWDING-OUT*

By DENNIS J. SNOWER

1. Introduction

THE microfoundations of the conventional macroeconomic models characteristically assume that the economy is prefectly competitive. This assumption has been incorporated in both market-clearing and non-market-clearing models. By contrast, this paper develops a macroeconomic model which rests on imperfectly competitive micro-foundations and explores the implications of imperfect competition for the effectiveness of government policy with regard to wages, prices, and employment.

There are a number of reasons why such an approach appears worthwhile. First, whereas the distinctiveness and practical significance of imperfectly competitive behavior has long been acknowledged in microeconomic analysis, the repercussions of this behavior in macroeconomic activity remain largely unexplored. Second, the division of market power among agents in the private sector has important implications for the effectiveness of government policy. Third, the assumption of imperfect competition provides a way out of logical difficulties generated by the conventional non-market-clearing macroeconomic models.

These non-clearing models (e.g. Benassy (1975), Barro–Grossman (1976), Malinvaud (1977), Muellbauer–Portes (1978)) presuppose (a) perfect competition, so that all agents are price takers, and (b) that prices are set at levels which do not clear their respective markets. However, perfect competition requires that agents are able to buy and sell all that they wish to demand and supply at the going prices (given tastes, technologies, and endowments), while non-clearing markets imply that agents are not able to do so. As Arrow (1959) noted, the assumption of perfect competition breaks down when agents are rationed.

In general, by changing the prices, agents could manipulate the rations they face. For example, a firm which is rationed in the product market (i.e. which would be willing to sell more than it does at the going prices) may be able to manipulate the product demand it faces by varying the product price. Thus, in the absence of institutional restrictions on price change, when markets do not clear, agents have no incentive to remain price takers. To say that a firm faces a price-manipulable product demand ration simply means that it faces a non-vertical product demand curve. The rations which agents face under non-market-clearing conditions may be interpreted quite

* I am indebted to Andrew Oswald for his many stimulating insights. I am also very grateful for all the helpful reactions I have received from my colleagues at the Stockholm Institute for International Economic Studies (especially Lars Calmfors, Gene Grossman, Thor Gylfason, and Assar Lindbeck) and at Birkbeck College (especially Gerry Kennally and John Moore). The support of the Leverhulme Trust and the Social Science Research Council is gratefully acknowledged.

simply as the demand and supply curves which agents with market power take into account when making their decisions.

Of course, there are special circumstances in which markets do not clear and agents nevertheless remain price takers. For example, the government may institute wage-price controls and the prescribed wages and prices may not clear their respective markets. Here the government preempts the market power which the agents of the private sector would otherwise have made use of. Besides, there may be administrative costs of price change (see, for example, Barro (1972), Sheshinski and Weiss (1977))—such as the cost of replacing price tags and printing new catalogues—which may induce agents to accept their existing rations. Yet it appears quite doubtful that these costs are of major practical significance in explaining price stickiness in the face of large variations in production and employment.

So let us assume that there is imperfect competition and that prices are flexible. In other words, there are no legal or administrative restraints on price change and the price makers may set their prices freely in accordance with their objectives.

The macroeconomic model under consideration here is based on micro-foundations in the spirit of Chamberlain's (1933) monopolistic competition. These microfoundations have three salient features. First, both products and labor services are assumed to be differentiated. There are a fixed number of product markets (one for each type of product) and a fixed number of labor markets (one for each type of labor).

Second, the price setters are assumed to have monopoly power in the markets in which they operate, but none in any of the other markets. Each price setter in a particular market recognizes that his activity has no significant influence on the activity of agents in all other markets. In particular, sellers are assumed to be price setters in their markets. Firms have monopoly power in their respective product markets and households (through the vehicle of their unions) have monopoly power in their respective labor markets. Firms set their product prices in accordance with their profit-maximizing objectives; households (through their unions) set their wages in accordance with their utility-maximizing objectives.

Third, there is free entry of firms into each product market and this drives the profits of all firms to zero. Thus, households earn wage income, but no profit income.

This paper is akin to Hart's (1982) macroeconomic model of imperfectly competitive activity. However, in Hart's analysis, (i) firms and unions behave as Cournot–Nash oligopolists in the product and labor markets, respectively (rather than as Chamberlainian monopolistic competitors), (ii) there is no free entry of firms which drives profits to zero (as is the case here), and (iii) certain agents are assigned to certain markets and this assignment is given no choice-theoretic rationale.

Within this analytical framework, it will be shown that:

(A) *Every imperfectly competitive equilibrium (ICE) generates under-*

employment, i.e. the ICE level of employment falls short of the socially optimal level. This result is explained by showing that the division of responsibility for price and quantity decisions among imperfectly competitive agents invariably give rise to allocatively inefficient trades.

(B) *An increase in government expenditure invariably crowds out private-sector expenditure.*

(C) *An increase in government expenditure gives rise to a wage–price spiral.* The magnitude of the wage–price spiral is related to the size of the crowding-out effect.

Result (A) is concerned with the nature of unemployment under ICE. The explanation of unemployment in terms of allocative inefficiency of imperfectly competitive trades has already been examined in a partial-equilibrium framework by McDonald and Solow (1981) and provides an alternative to the quantity rationing of the conventional Keynesian models as well as the argument based on increasing returns (Weitzmann (1982)). Result (B) is rather surprising. It stands in contrast to the "Keynesian features" of Hart's (1982) analysis. Result (C) contributes to the well-known controversy about how government expenditure changes "split" between price effects and quantity effects.

The paper is organized as follows. Section 2 concerned with the interrelations among the various agents and discusses the salient assumptions underlying the imperfectly competitive structure of our model. Section 3 describes the behavior of the agents and portrays the imperfectly competitive general equilibrium. Section 4 shows how government expenditure changes generate wage–price spirals and crowd out private sector expenditures. Section 5 deals with the nature of under-employment and trading inefficiency under imperfect competition. Finally Section 6 summarizes the main conclusions of our analysis.

2. Structure of the model

2a. *The interrelations among agents*

The economy under consideration contains three types of agents: firms, households, and government. There are two types of markets: product and labor markets. The households supply labor to the firms and the firms supply produced goods to the households and the government. In the hands of the households, the produced goods are nondurable consumption goods; in the hands of the government, they are nondurable public goods, which are imposed (without price) on the household.

The households pay for their consumption purchases by means of their wage income; the firms pay for their labor purchases from their sales revenue; and the government finances its expenditures by imposing an identical lump-sum tax on each household and (depending on the interpretation below of firms' fixed costs) possibly also on each firm (but the government budget constraint is not important for the analysis below).

As noted, we allow the products to be differentiated. There are a fixed

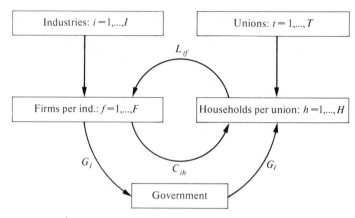

FIG. 1. Grouping of economic agents.

number (I) of products, each produced by one "industry". Each industry contains F identical firms. (F is a variable, since the number of firms per industry is such as to ensure zero profits.) No industry produces more than one type of product.

Labor services are also differentiated. There are a fixed number (T) of labor types. Each household can provide labor of only one type. All households of a single type group together to form a trade union. There are a fixed number (H) of households per union. No union offers more than one type of labor service.

This configuration of labor and product markets is pictured in Fig. 1. L_{tf} is the amount of type-t labour demanded by firm f; C_{ih} is the amount of type-i product demanded by household h; and G_i is the amount of type-i product demanded by the government (and imposed on the households).

2b. *The division of price and quantity decisions*

The next step in setting up our model is to specify which agents are to be assigned control over which price and quantity variables. Each of the product and labor markets is assumed to consist of a "heavily populated" and a "lightly populated" side. On the former side, each agent is sufficiently small relative to the market so that his activity has no influence on the activity of the other market participants. On the latter side, each agent is sufficiently large relative to the market to have some monopoly power (see Hart (1978)). Let us adopt the usual convention that the lightly populated side of the market makes the price decisions, while the heavily populated side makes the quantity decisions.

In particular, each firm faces a large number of buyers (viz. the households and the government) in its product market. The firm has some monopoly power in this market, whereas the buyers do not. Consequently, the firm sets the price of its product and each of the buyers decides how much to purchase at that price.

Each union faces a large number of buyers (viz. the firms in its labor market). Once again, the union has some monopoly power in this market, but the buyers have none. Thus, the union sets the wage at which its members are willing to work and each of the firms decides how much labor to hire at the offered wage.

The usual justification for this division of price-quantity decisions among agents is that it economizes on transactions costs. The reason why department stores, airlines, supermarkets, etc. do not make price–quantity bargains with each of their customers is that the cost of negotiating these bargains is prohibitive. Letting a small number of sellers decide the price and a relatively large number of buyers decide individually what amounts to purchase at this price economizes on the informational prerequisites for satisfying the demands and supplies in a market.

To make the price decision, each seller needs to know the demand curve he faces, which means that he needs information on the supply behavior of his few competitors (if any) and the aggregate demand forthcoming in response. To make the quantity decision, each buyer only needs to know the announced price. The reverse set-up—numerous households making the price decision and few firms making their individual quantity decisions—would entail greater transactions costs. For now the numerous buyers would require information on each other's demand behavior and on the aggregate supply and the few sellers would require information on each other's supply behavior. Alternatively, bilateral price–quantity bargains between each buyer and seller would imply even greater information requirements.

These matters have not been spelled out rigorously in the literature on imperfect competition. Authors in this area have simply made the plausible assumption (supported by casual observation) that the above-mentioned division of decision-making obtains in markets with heavily and lightly populated sides. This practice is followed here.

2c. *Microfoundations of the macromodel*

The set-up has a Keynesian flavor since the *sellers* in the product and labor markets are the ones who are being "rationed". This circumstance is due to the assumption that the sellers are on the lightly populated sides of their markets and thus they become price setters, facing demand curves for their commodities. (The buyers in all markets are perfect competitors.) The firm's product demand curve (which depends, among other things, on its product price) takes the place of its nonmanipulable product demand constraint in the conventional "reappraisal-of-Keynes" models, and the union's labor demand curve (which depends, among other things, on the wage) takes the place of the household's nonmanipulable labor demand constraint.

The standard Keynisian macro model which has emerged from the literature on the "reappraisal of Keynes" is constructed from microfoundations in which groups of identical agents face rigid wages and prices. All firms are commonly assumed to be alike, each producing a homogenous output by means of a homogenous labor input, and all households are also assumed to be alike, each consuming a homogenous product and supplying a homogenous labor service. Consequently, the aggregate supplies and demands in the labor and product markets are simply equal to an individual agent's supply and demand in these markets multiplied by the number of agents of that type in the economy.

By contrast, this paper constructs a macroeconomic model from microfoundations in which agents are imperfectly competitive on account of product and labor–service differentiation. These microfoundations must be erected on different principles from those underlying the reappraisal-of-Keynes models, since products and labor services are not homogenous. Thus, the demands for and supplies of products of different types cannot be added to one another to yield economy-wide product demands and supplies. Similarly, the economy-wide labor demands and supplies cannot be derived by summing over different labor markets.

Instead of assuming that all firms and all households are alike—which they are not, since different firms may produce products of different types and different households may supply labor of different types—we assume that all firms' production functions and all households' utility functions are "identical" and "symmetric". All production functions are identical in the sense that they have the same functional forms (for example, in the case of two products, Q_1 and Q_2, and two types of labor L_1 and L_2, $Q_1 = f(L_1, L_2)$ and $Q_2 = f(L_1, L_2)$). They are symmetric in that the various types of labor needed to produce a particular output enter the production function in the same way (for example, $f(L_1, L_2) = f(L_2, L_1)$). Similarly, all utility functions are identical by virtue of their identical functional forms (for example, for two households with utility functions U_1 and U_2, supplying labor of types L_1 and L_2, $U_1 = U(Q_1, Q_2, L_1)$ and $U_2 = U(Q_1, Q_2, L_2)$); they are symmetric since the products consumed by each household enter the utility function in the same way (for example, $U(Q_1, Q_2, L_1) = U(Q_2, Q_1, L_2)$).

The upshot of these assumptions is to make the demand functions alike and the supply functions alike in all labor and all product markets. The identity and symmetry of all production functions implies that the aggregate demand for labor of type t—the sum of the (identical) demands by all firms bidding for this labor—has the same functional form as the aggregate demand for any other labor type. Also, the identity and symmetry of all utility functions implies that the aggregate supply of type-t labor—the sum of the (identical) supplies by all households offering this labor—has the same functional form as any other aggregate labor supply. Consequently, the type-t labor market serves as a microcosm of the economy-wide labor market.

The same may be said of the type-i product market. The identity and symmetry of all utility functions and all production functions means that the aggregate demand for and supply of product i have the same functional forms as any other product demand and supply, respectively. Thus, the type-i product market is a small version of its economy-wide counterpart.

2d. *Monopolistic competition*

As an imperfectly competitive general equilibrium model, the model presented here falls within the tradition established by Benassy (1976, 1978), Grandmont–Laroque (1976), Negishi (1978), Hahn (1978), Hart (1982), and others. We will assume that, in equilibrium, the price setters know the true demand curves facing them and, in this respect, our model has particular affinity to the last two references.

As noted, the imperfect competition of the model here is akin to Chamberlain's monopolistic competition in three respects: (i) products and labor services are differentiated; (ii) each price setter in a particular market recognizes that his actions, by themselves, have no effect on the behavior of agents in other markets, and (iii) free entry of firms into each product market reduces all firms' profits to zero.

Whereas (i) specifies the "monopolistic" element in monopolistic competition, (ii) and (iii) describe the "competitive" elements. On account of (iii), we obviously must allow for the possibility of more than one firm in each product market. Yet whereas the number of firms in each product market is sufficiently large to eliminate all profits, it is not large enough (as stipulated below) to eliminate firms' monopoly power in their product markets (i.e. not large enough to make the product demand curves they face perfectly elastic.)

Characteristics (i) and (iii) are straightforward; characteristic (ii) needs further motivation. Each firm assumes that variations in its product price have no effect on the price–quantity decisions of agents in the labor markets and the other product markets, and each union assumes that variations in its wage have no repercussions on the product markets and the other labor markets.

This assumption is justified if each seller has some monopoly power in the particular market in which he sells, but none in any other market. Hart's (1978) analysis implies that this condition holds whenever each seller is of significant size relative to his market, but of negligible size relative to every other. Loosely speaking, a seller is of negligible size in his market whenever the expenditure on his product occupies a negligible proportion of each buyer's total budget; otherwise the seller is of significant size.

In order for each union t to have monopoly power in the type-t labor market and the buyers in that market to have none, we assume the following:

(A1) Each industry uses a sufficiently small subset of all the labor types so that each union t is of significant size relative to the type-t labor market.

(A2) Each labor type is demanded by a sufficiently large number of industries so that each industry demands a negligible proportion of each labor type.[1]

Similarly, in order for each firm f in industry i to have monopoly power in the type-i product market and the buyers in that market to have none, we make the following assumptions:

(A3) Each household consumes a sufficiently small subset of all firms' products so that each firm f is of significant size relative to its type-i product market.

(A4) The product of each firm is demanded by a sufficiently large number of households so that all the households belonging to a particular union demand a negligible proportion of each firm's output.[2,3]

Furthermore, the activity of each union t in its labor market has a negligible effect on all other markets whenever assumption (A4) holds and

(A5) The distribution of labor types among firms is such that all the firms which demand labor of type t, taken together, demand a negligible proportion of the aggregate demand for any other labor type.

Similarly, the activity of each firm f in industry i has a negligible effect on all other markets whenever assumption (A2) holds and

(A6) The distribution of firms' outputs among households is such that all the households which demand one firm's product, taken together, demand a negligible proportion of the aggregate demand for any other firm's product.

Finally, in order for each labor market and each product market to be a small version of economy-wide labor and product markets, respectively, we assume the following:

(A7) Each firm uses the same number of labor types.

(A8) Each labor type is demanded by the same number of firms.

(A9) Each household consumes the same number of products.

(A10) Each firm's output is demanded by the same number of households.

(A11) Each firm faces the same, exogenously given, government demand for its product.

---

[1] If each firm acts independently of all other firms, then it is sufficient to make the less stringent assumptions that (a1) each *firm* uses a "small" subset of all labor types and (a2) each labor type is demanded by a "large" number of *firms*. However, given the behavioral assumptions of Section 3, the firms in each industry do not act in isolation, and consequently the assumptions (A1) and (A2) are required.

[2] To ensure that the buyers in the type-i product market have no market power, it is sufficient to make the less stringent assumption that each household demands a negligible proportion of each firm's output. The assumption (A4) is required to ensure that the activity of each union t has a negligible effect on every product market (as noted below).

[3] Assumptions (A1) and (A2) imply that there are more industries than trade unions in the economy. Assumptions (A3) and (A4) imply that there are more households than firms. In sum, $I > T$ and $T \cdot H > F \cdot I$. Assumption (A4) does not imply that $T > F \cdot I$ (which is impossible, since $T < I$) as long as we do not require that all households belonging to one union consume the same set of products.

3. Behavior of the imperfectly competitive agents

3a. *The firms*

Each firm sets its product price and makes its employment decision so as to maximize its profit subject to its product demand functions and its production function. Since it has monopoly power in its product market but none in any other market, it takes the prices of all other products and the wages of all labor types as given.

All firms in an industry are identical in that (a) they produce identical outputs, (b) they hire identical sets of labor types, (c) they use identical technologies, (d) they face the same wages, and (e) they face the same demand functions for their products.[4]

When examining the effects of government employment policy on production–employment and wage–price decisions in Section 4, it will be convenient to rule out those effects which operate via induced changes in the number of firms per industry. To do so, we make two simplifying assumptions:

(i) Each firm in an industry recognizes that it is the same as all other firms in that industry. Thus, its price setting and employment decisions are made under the presumption that all other firms in the industry make the same decisions.

(ii) Each firm's production function exhibits constant returns to scale.

Recall that each firm in an industry uses a "small" subset of all the labor types.[5] For expository implicity (but without substantial loss of generality), we assume that each firm requires just one type of labor. Thus, the firm's production function may be expressed as $L_{tf}^D = J(Q_{if}^s)$, where L_{tf}^D is the demand for type-t labor by firm f and Q_{if}^s is the supply of type-i product by firm f. (Since all production functions are assumed to have the same functional form, J is not subscripted by firm or industry.) The production function satisfies $J' > 0$ and $J'' = 0$.

Let P_i and W_t be the price of product i and the wage of labor t, respectively. (Since each firm in an industry knows that it sets the same price as all other firms in that industry, P_i is not subscripted by firm. Since all firms face the same wages, W_t is not subscripted by firm either.) The firm's

---

[4] This is ensured by the forces of competition on the buyers' side of each product market and by the assumption that each firm faces the same, exogenously fixed government demand for its product. Assume an initial state in which the demands for a particular product i are not distributed equally among the firms in industry i. Each firm's product demand curve (with price and quantity on the vertical and horizontal axes, respectively) is the horizontal sum of the government demand and the downward-sloping demand curve of each of its household customers. The greater the share of aggregate product demand which a firm attracts, the higher its profit maximizing price (given non-decreasing marginal costs). The forces of competition tend to equalize the prices which different firms charge for a particular product and thereby also the demands which these firms face.

[5] This is implied by assumption (A1) together with the assumption that all firms in an industry hire identical sets of labor types.

IMPERFECT COMPETITION

profit may be expressed as $\pi_{if} = P_i \cdot Q_{if}^s - W_t \cdot L_{if}^D - A$. "$A$" may be interpreted either as a fixed cost of production (paid as a lump sum to the households) or as a lump-sum tax (levied by the government).

The aggregate demand for product i is the sum of the government and household demands for this product (G_i and C_i, respectively). C_i may be derived from the households' optimization programs, to be considered below. According to these programs, $C_i = C_i(P_i, G_i)$.[6] Since each firm in industry i has an equal share of the demand for product i and since each firm perceives its product demand correctly, its perceived product demand function may be expressed as $Q_{if}^D = (1/F) \cdot [C_i(P_i, G_i) + G_i]$, where F is the number of firms per industry.

Thus, the behavior of firm f in industry i may be summarized by the following optimization program:

Maximize

$$\pi_{if} = P_i \cdot Q_{if}^s - W_t \cdot L_{if}^D - A \qquad (1)$$

subject to

$$Q_{if}^s = (1/F) \cdot [C_i(P_i, G_i) + G_i]$$
$$L_{if}^D = J(Q_{if}^s),$$

where the endogenous variables are P_i, Q_{if}^s, and L_{if}^D; W_t, F, and G_i are exogenous to the firm's decision making.

Solving the firm's problem yields an equation for the profit-maximizing value of P_i:

$$\frac{d\pi_{if}}{dP_i} = [C_i(P_i, G_i) + G_i] + [P_i - W_t \cdot J'] \cdot C_i^P = 0, \qquad (2)$$

where $C_i^P = (\partial C_i / \partial P_i) < 0$. (The second-order condition for profit maximization is assumed satisfied.)[7]

Equation (2) shows that, for a given production function and product demand function, the firm's product price depends on the wage W_t and the level of government expenditure G_i. Letting $(d\pi_{if}/dP_i) = \psi$, equation (2) may be rewritten in shorthand form:

$$\psi(P_i, W_t, G_i) = 0, \qquad (2')$$

[6] As noted below, this consumption function emerges under the simplifying assumption that each household consumes just one type of product. In the absence of this assumption, the consumption function must be expressed differently. Given our assumptions concerning the identity and symmetry of all production functions and all utility functions in the economy, all product prices must be equal in the imperfectly competitive equilibrium (which is assumed unique). Let all prices, except that of product i, be set at their equilibrium level, $\tilde{P}$. Then the aggregate private-sector demand for product i may be written as $C_i = C_i(P_i, \tilde{P}, G_j)$. This function enters the firm's optimization program, with $\tilde{P}$ exogenous to the firm. In the ICE, $P_i = \tilde{P}$ for all i.

[7] In equation (2), the first term of the middle expression is unambiguously positive. In order for the second term to be unambiguously negative, $P_i > W_t \cdot J'$, i.e. the real wage falls short of the marginal product of labor.

where

$$\left.\frac{\partial P_i}{\partial W_t}\right|_{\psi=0} = \tfrac{1}{2} \cdot J' = a > 0 \tag{2a}$$

("a" is a constant) and

$$\left.\frac{\partial P_i}{\partial G_i}\right|_{\psi=0} = -\frac{1+C_i^G}{2 \cdot C_i^P} > 0, \tag{2b}$$

where $C_i^G = (\partial C_i/\partial G_i) > 0$ and (for simplicity[8]) we have used the first-order approximation of the consumption function: $C_i^P < 0$ and $C_i^{PP}, C_i^{PG} = 0$. In other words, the firm reacts to an increase in the union t's wage offer and to an increase in the government expenditure i by raising its product price.

The firm's product supply function and labor demand function may be derived from the reaction function above:

$$Q_{if}^s = Q_{if}^s(W_t, G_i) \tag{3a}$$
$$\phantom{Q_{if}^s = Q_{if}^s(}{\scriptstyle(-)}{\scriptstyle(+)}$$

where

$$\frac{\partial Q_{if}^s}{\partial W_t} = \left(\frac{1}{2 \cdot F}\right) \cdot C_i^P \cdot J' < 0$$

and

$$\frac{\partial Q_{if}^s}{\partial G_i} = \frac{1+C_i^G}{2 \cdot F} > 0;$$

$$L_{tf}^D = L_{tf}(W_t, G_i) \tag{3b}$$
$$\phantom{L_{tf}^D = L_{tf}(}{\scriptstyle(-)}{\scriptstyle(+)}$$

where

$$\frac{\partial L_{tf}}{\partial W_t} = \left(\frac{1}{2 \cdot F}\right) \cdot C_i^P \cdot (J')^2 = L_{tf}^W < 0$$

$$\frac{\partial L_{tf}}{\partial G_i} = \frac{J' \cdot (1+C_i^G)}{2 \cdot F} = L_{tf}^G > 0.$$

Recall that each labor type is demanded by a "large" number of industries. Let I_t be the number of industries requiring labor of type t. Then the aggregate demand for this type of labor is

$$L_t = I_t \cdot F \cdot L_{tf}(W_t, G_i).$$

3b. *The unions*

As mentioned above, the households which supply a particular type of labor (say, type t) join a single trade union (union t). All households in a particular union are alike in that (a) their utility functions have the same functional forms and (b) they receive the same wage incomes.

---

[8] Provided that the uniqueness and stability of the ICE are preserved, this approximation does not affect the qualitative conclusions of our analysis.

Each union is assumed to represent the interests of its member households, in the sense that its objective function and budget constraints are the sum of its members' utility functions and budget constraints, respectively.

Each union t sets the wage W_t, thereby determining the total amount of employment available to its members. It divides this employment equally among them. Each member household uses its labor income to buy consumption goods. (Recall that profits are driven to zero and thus households earn no profit income.)

Each union maximizes its utility function subject to its labor demand function and its budget constraint. Since it has monopoly power in its labor market but none in any other market, it takes the wages set by all other unions and the prices of all products as given.

As noted, each household consumes a "small" subset of all product types. For simplicity (but once again without any substantial loss of generality), we assume that it consumes only one type of product. However, all the households belonging to a single union consume several products (as implied by footnote 3). For simplicity, let us assume that no product is consumed by the members of more than one union.[9] Then our microfoundations require that, since each type-t labor is demanded by I_t different industries, the members of each union consume I_t different products.

The behavior of union t may be summarized by the following optimization program:

Maximize

$$U = U(\underset{i \in S_t}{C_i^D}, L_t^S, \underline{G_i}) \tag{4}$$

subject to

$$L_t^S = I_t \cdot F \cdot L_{tf}(W_t, G_i)$$

$$\sum_{i \in S_t} P_i \cdot C_i^D = W_t \cdot L_t^S - P_i \cdot R_t,$$

where S_t is the set of all product types consumed by the members of union t, the first argument of the utility function is a vector of all these product types, L_t^S is the aggregate type-t labor supply, the third argument of the utility function is a vector of all public goods, and $P_i \cdot R_t$ is the value of the lump-sum taxes paid by the member households.[10] (Since the utility functions of all unions have the same functional form, U is not subscripted by union.) Note that each union correctly perceives its labor demand function. Let $U_C = (\partial U/\partial C_i^D) > 0$ for all $i \in S_t$ (by symmetry), $U_L = (\partial U/\partial L_t^S) < 0$, $U_G = (\partial U/\partial G_i) > 0$ or all i; $U_{CC}, U_{LL} < 0$ and all cross partial derivatives are equal to zero. The endogenous variables are W_t, C_i^D, and L_t^S; P_i, I_t, F, and G_i are exogenous.

[9] Since products can be classified in countless ways (by physical characteristics, location, recipients, etc.) no matter of principle is at stake here.
[10] P_i is the price of any product i. Since all product prices are equal in equilibrium and since our analysis is confined to equilibrium conditions, the choice of this product is immaterial.

Solving the union's problem yields an equation for the utility-maximizing value of W_t:

$$\left[U_L + U_C \cdot \left(\frac{W_t}{P_i} \right) \right] \cdot L_{tf}^W + U_C \cdot \left(\frac{1}{P_i} \right) \cdot L_{tf} = 0. \tag{5}$$

(The second-order condition for utility maximization is assumed satisfied.)[11]

Equation (5) indicates that, given the union's preferences and labor demand function, the union's wage offer depends on the product price P_i and the level of government expenditure G_i. Equation (5) may be rewritten as

$$\phi(W_t, P_i, G_i) = 0, \tag{5'}$$

where

$$\left. \frac{\partial W_t}{\partial P_i} \right|_{\phi=0} = -\left(\frac{1}{2} \right) \cdot \left(\frac{U_L}{U_C} \right) = b > 0 \tag{5a}$$

("b" is a constant) and

$$\left. \frac{\partial W_t}{\partial G_i} \right|_{\phi=0} = -\left(\frac{1}{2} \right) \cdot \left(\frac{L_{tf}^G}{L_{tf}^W} \right) > 0,$$

where (for simplicity[12]) we have assumed that U_{CC} and U_{LL} are negligibly close to zero and used the first-order approximation: $L_{tf}^W < 0$ and $L_{tf}^{WW}, L_{tf}^{WG} = 0$. In other words, the union reacts to an increase in the price of product i and to an increase in government expenditure i by raising its wage offer.

The union's labor supply function and consumption demand function may be derived from the reaction function above:

$$L_t^s = L_t^s(P_i, G_i) \tag{6a}$$
$$\quad\quad {\scriptstyle(-)\ \ (+)}$$

where

$$\frac{\partial L_t^s}{\partial P_i} = I_t \cdot F \cdot L_{tf}^W \cdot b < 0,$$

---

[11] The second term of the left-hand expression is unambiguously positive. In order for the first term to be unambiguously negative, $U_c \cdot (W_t/P_i) > -U_L$, i.e. the real wage must exceed the marginal rate of substitution of consumption for leisure.

[12] Once again, our qualitative conclusions are not affected by this assumption, provided that the uniqueness and stability of the ICE are preserved.

and

$$\frac{\partial L_t^s}{\partial G_i} = (\tfrac{1}{2}) \cdot I_t \cdot F \cdot L_{tf}^G > 0;$$

$$C_i^D = C_i(\underset{(-)}{P_i}, \underset{(+)}{G_i}) \tag{6b}$$

$$\frac{\partial C_i}{\partial P_i} = -\frac{W_t}{(P_i)^2} \cdot L_t + \frac{b}{P_i} \cdot [L_t + W_t \cdot I_t \cdot F \cdot L_{tf}^W] = C_i^P < 0,^{13,14}$$

$$\frac{\partial C_i}{\partial G_i} = \left(\frac{1}{2 \cdot P_i}\right) \cdot I_t \cdot F \cdot L_{tf}^G \cdot \left[W_t - \left(\frac{L_{tf}}{L_{tf}^W}\right)\right] = C_i^G > 0.$$

C_i^G may be interpreted as a Keynesian marginal propensity to consume. It is the rise in consumption demand due to a rise in wage income, generated by a rise in government expenditure.

3c. The imperfectly competitive equilibrium

Thus far, we have examined the price-setting behavior of the firms given the wages determined by the unions and the wage-setting behavior of the unions given the prices determined by the firms. For a given set of government expenditures, equation (2') represents each firm's reaction function and equation (5') represents each union's reaction function. In the imperfectly competitive equilibrium (ICE), these two stories are interrelated.

At the ICE, the following three conditions are satisfied: (i) the wages faced by the firms are those which maximize the utilities of the unions, (ii) the prices faced by the unions are those which maximize the profits of the firms, and (iii) the number of firms per industry (F) is such that the profit of each firm is zero.

In Fig. 2, the reaction functions of a representative firm and a representative union are labelled θ_F and θ_H, respectively. (Equations (2a) and (5a) indicate that both are straight lines.) The wage–price combination (W_t^*, P_i^*) which characterizes the ICE is given by the intersection of these two reaction functions.[15] Thereby conditions (i) and (ii) above are satisfied. Note that neither reaction function depends on F. Thus, the equilibrium wage–price combination does not depend on the number of firms per industry, which is set to satisfy condition (iii).

---

[13] Recall that all prices are equal in equilibrium and hence and P_i may be chosen for $i \in S_t$.

[14] Rewriting the union's reaction function:

$$\phi = U_c \cdot [W_t \cdot L_{tf}^W + L_{tf}] + P_i \cdot U_L \cdot [L_{tf}^W] = 0$$

The second term of the middle expression is unambiguously positive. In order for the first term to be unambiguously negative,

$$[L_{tf} + W_t \cdot L_{tf}^W] < 0.$$

[15] In Figure 1, it is clearly not necessary for the firms in the particular industry i to employ the households in the particular union t. Nor is it necessary for the households in union t to purchase product i. The reason is that in the ICE the prices of all product types and the wages of all labor types are equal.

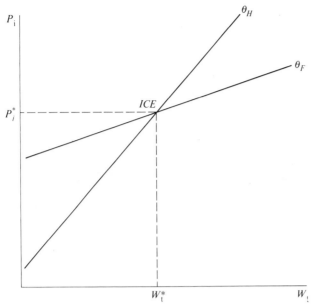

FIG. 2. The imperfectly competitive equilibrium.

4. The effectiveness of government policy

Suppose that the economy is initially at an imperfectly competitive equilibrium, associated with a given level of government expenditures (falling equally on all firms). Thereupon these government expenditures rise (by equal amounts for every firm). What are the implications of this policy for wages, prices, production, and employment?

In the model outlined above, government expenditures are financed through lump-sum taxation of the households and firms. Yet since the aim of this section is to explore how strong the case for crowding-out is under imperfectly competitive equilibrium conditions, let us break the government's balanced budget constraint in this policy exercise. Two things should be noted about the resulting "helicopter drop" of government expenditures. First, if it can be shown that a rise in government expenditures crowds out private-sector expenditures, then it is trivial to show that this government expenditure increase matched by a lump-sum tax increase crowds out private expenditure even more. Second, the proposed policy exercise could be performed without breaking the government's budget constraint if we were to include fiat money in our economy and let the government expenditure increase be financed through it. For example, we could assume (as is commonly done in the microfoundations of monetary macroeconomic models) that households demand money as a store of value, whereas firms have no net demand for money since their revenues always cover their costs. In that case, real money balances would enter the households' utility functions and their budget constraints would set consumption plus money balance

accumulation equal to wage income net of household taxes. Then a government expenditure increase financed through money creation leads, via
Walras' Law, to a rise in money-balance accumulation by the households.[16]
These complications have no effect on the qualitative conclusions of this
section, and so, for simplicity, we let government expenditures rise by
themselves.

The policy change gives rise to multipliers in wage–price levels and
production–employment levels. Let us investigate the wage–price multiplier
first. The relation between the levels of wages and prices (on the one hand)
and the level of government expenditures (on the other) is given by
equations (2′) and (5′) (the firm's and the union's reaction functions, respectively). Totally differentiating these equations,

$$\frac{dP_i}{dG_i} + \frac{\psi_W}{\psi_P} \cdot \frac{dW_t}{dG_i} + \frac{\psi_G}{\psi_P} = 0$$

$$\frac{dW_t}{dG_i} + \frac{\phi_P}{\phi_W} \cdot \frac{dP_i}{dG_i} + \frac{\phi_G}{\phi_W} = 0.$$

Using the properties of the reaction functions (derived above),

$$\frac{dP_i}{dG_i} - a \cdot \frac{dW_t}{dG_i} = -\left(\frac{1 + C_i^G}{2 \cdot C_i^P}\right) \tag{7a}$$

$$\frac{dW_t}{dG_i} - b \cdot \frac{dP_i}{dG_i} = -\left(\frac{1 + C_i^G}{2 \cdot C_i^P}\right) \cdot \frac{1}{J'}. \tag{7b}$$

Solving the system (7a−b), we obtain the effect of a change in government
expenditures on prices

$$\frac{dP_i}{dG_i} = -\left(\frac{1}{1 - a \cdot b}\right) \cdot \left(\frac{1 + C_i^G}{2 \cdot C_i^P}\right) \cdot \left(1 + \frac{a}{J'}\right), \tag{8a}$$

and on wages

$$\frac{dW_t}{dG_i} = -\left(\frac{1}{1 - a \cdot b}\right) \cdot \left(\frac{1 + C_i^G}{2 \cdot C_i^P}\right) \cdot \left(\frac{1}{J'} + b\right). \tag{8b}$$

Note that the effect on the real wage is ambiguous.[17]

---

[16] The fiat money would also serve as a unit of account (numeraire) whereby the values of the
produced goods and labor services are measured. Such a unit of account has been implicitly
presupported in the analysis above, although for simplicity it has not been explicitly included in
our model as a treadable commodity.

[17] $\dfrac{d(W_t/P_i)}{dG_i} = \left(\dfrac{1}{P_i}\right) \cdot \left[\dfrac{dW_t}{dG_i} - \dfrac{W_t}{P_i} \cdot \dfrac{dP_i}{dG_i}\right]$

$\qquad = -\left(\dfrac{1}{P_i}\right) \cdot \left[\left(\dfrac{1}{1 - a \cdot b}\right) \cdot \left(\dfrac{1 + C_i^G}{2 \cdot C_i^P}\right)\right] \cdot \left[\left(\dfrac{1}{J'} + b\right) - \dfrac{W_t}{P_i} \cdot \left(1 + \dfrac{a}{J'}\right)\right]$

given that $(a \cdot b) < 1$ (see below),

$$\frac{d(W_t/P_i)}{dG_i} \gtreqless 0 \Leftrightarrow \frac{W_t}{P_i} \lesseqgtr \frac{2}{3} - \frac{1}{3} \cdot \frac{1}{J'} \cdot \frac{U_L}{U_c}.$$

Given these price and wage effects, the associated effect on the production of each output type may be derived. Recall that $Q_i = C_i(P_i, G_i) + G_i$. Thus, using equation (8a),

$$\frac{dQ_i}{dG_i} = (1 + C_i^G) - \frac{1}{2} \cdot \left(\frac{1 + C_i^G}{1 - a \cdot b}\right) \cdot \left(1 + \frac{a}{J'}\right). \tag{9a}$$

The effect on the employment of each labor type may be derived as well. Recall that $Q_i = F \cdot Q_{if}$, $L_t = I_t \cdot F \cdot L_{tf}$, and $L_{tf} = J(Q_f)$. Thus, $L_t = I_t \cdot F \cdot J(Q_i/F)$. Given constant returns to labor, $L_t = I_t \cdot J(Q_i)$. Thus,

$$\frac{dL_t}{dG_i} = I_t \cdot J' \cdot (1 + C_i^G) - \frac{1}{2} \cdot I_t \cdot J' \cdot \left(\frac{1 + C_i^G}{1 - a \cdot b}\right) \cdot \left(1 + \frac{a}{J'}\right). \tag{9b}$$

These multipliers may be interpreted in the same way as the standard Keynesian multipliers. According to the Keynesian story, a rise in government expenditures on the output of firms leads these firms to hire more labor; the resulting rise in income leads households to purchase more output of the firms, which in turn leads to more employment, and so on. The Keynesian production and employment multipliers may be portrayed as the resultants of this sequence of events. Analogously, the effect of fiscal policy in our model may also be interpreted in terms of a sequence of reactions by myopic agents.

Suppose that when the government increases its expenditures, each firm believes that the expansion of product demand is specific to its own industry. It does not realize that the boom is an economy-wide phenomenon. Each industry is an "island"; information about product demand on other islands is not instantaneously available. In particular, each firm in industry i perceives the rise in government expenditure on product i (dG_i) and the concomitant rise in private-sector expenditure ($C_i^P \cdot dG_i$), but it assumes that the demand for all other products remains unchanged at its initial ICE level.

Consequently, each firm of the industry reacts by raising its product price as well as its production and employment. Yet since each industry is small relative to the labor market in which it participates, the firms in each industry expect their price–quantity decisions to have no effect on the wages they pay. Given this presumption, the profit-maximizing rise in the price of the ith product is

$$d_1 P_i = \left(\frac{\partial P_i}{\partial G_i}\bigg|_{\psi=0}\right) \cdot dG_i = -\left(\frac{1 + C_i^G}{2 \cdot C_i^P}\right) \cdot dG_i > 0, \tag{10a}$$

where $d_1, d_2, d_3, \ldots$ are the changes taking place in the first, second, third, etc. rounds of the multiplier process.

The associated changes in production and employment are

$$d_1 Q_i = C_i^P \cdot d_1 P_i + (1 + C_i^G) \cdot dG_i$$
$$= \tfrac{1}{2}(1 + C_i^G) \cdot dG_i > 0 \tag{10b}$$

$$d_1 L_t = \tfrac{1}{2} \cdot I_t \cdot J' \cdot (1 + C_i^G) \cdot dG_i > 0 \tag{10c}$$

The wages set by the unions are initially at their original ICE level. Now each union finds that, at its initial wage, the prices of the products its members consume have each risen by an amount given in (10a) and the labor demand curve it faces (relating its labor demand to its wage) has shifted by an amount given in (10c). Each union believes that both the price and employment changes are specific to its members. Thus, it raises its wage offer. However, since each union is small relative to the product markets in which it participates, it expects its wage change, as well as the associated change in its members' consumption, to have no effect on the product prices its members pay. Thus, each union's optimal wage increase is

$$d_1 W_t = \left(\frac{\partial W_t}{\partial P_i}\bigg|_{\phi=0}\right) \cdot d_1 P_i + \left(\frac{\partial W_t}{\partial G_i}\bigg|_{\phi=0}\right) \cdot dG_i$$

$$= -\left(\frac{1+C_i^G}{2 \cdot C_i^P}\right) \cdot \left(b+\frac{1}{J'}\right) \cdot dG_i > 0. \qquad (10d)$$

In the second round of the multiplier process, each firm faces a situation different from that in the first round: government expenditure on its product remains unchanged at its first-round level, but the cost of its labor has risen. Each firm believes that the wage rise is specific to its own industry. Thus, each firm's optimal price adjustment is

$$d_2 P_i = a \cdot d_1 W_t = -a \cdot \left(\frac{1+C_i^G}{2 \cdot C_i^P}\right) \cdot \left(b+\frac{1}{J'}\right) \cdot dG_i > 0 \qquad (11a)$$

and the associated adjustments in production and employment are

$$d_2 Q_i = C_i^P \cdot d_2 P = -a \cdot \left(\frac{1+C_i^G}{2}\right) \cdot \left(b+\frac{1}{J'}\right) \cdot dG_i \qquad (11b)$$

$$d_2 L_t = -I_t \cdot J' \cdot a \cdot \left(\frac{1+C_i^G}{2}\right) \cdot \left(b+\frac{1}{J'}\right) \cdot dG_i. \qquad (11c)$$

Each union also faces a different situation from that in the first round of the multiplier process: its labor demand curve has not shifted (since government expenditures remain at their first-round level), but the product prices which its members face have risen. Thus, it adjusts its wage accordingly:

$$d_2 W_t = b \cdot d_2 P_i = -b \cdot a \cdot \left(\frac{1+C_i^G}{2 \cdot C_i^P}\right) \cdot \left(b+\frac{1}{J'}\right) \cdot dG_i > 0 \qquad (11d)$$

The third round of the multiplier is analogous to the second. The price and wage changes are

$$d_3 P_i = a \cdot d_2 W_t$$

$$d_3 W_t = b \cdot d_3 P_i.$$

In order for the multiplier process to be stable, $a \cdot b < 1$. We assume this to be the case (making the standard use of the correspondence principle).

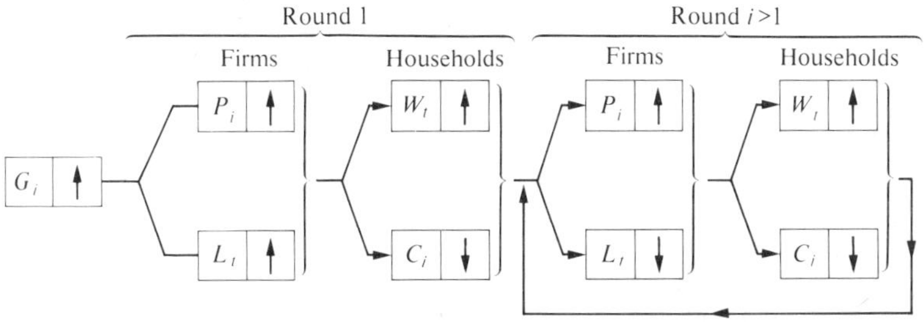

FIG. 3. The interaction of the wage–price multiplier and the employment multiplier.

Summing the entire sequence of price effects (equations (10a), (11a), etc.) yields the price multiplier of equation (8a). Similarly, the sum of the wage effects (equations (10d), (11d), etc.) yields the wage multiplier of equation (8b) and the sum of the production and employment effects yields the production and employment multipliers of equations (9a) and (9b), respectively.[18]

It is interesting to note that in this imperfectly competitive economy, government expenditure crowds out private-sector expenditure. The immediate impacts of a rise in government expenditure on production (before firms and unions begin to change their prices and wages, respectively) is

$$\left(\frac{dQ_i}{dG_i}\right)_{initial} = (1 + C_i^G).$$

The production multiplier (9a) is the sum of this term plus another which is unambiguously negative. Thus,

$$\left(\frac{dQ_i}{dG_i}\right)_{initial} > \left(\frac{dQ_i}{dG_i}\right).$$

In other words, the initial fiscal policy impact is invariably greater than the final impact (after the private sector has reacted fully).

Proposition. In the imperfectly competitive economy above, government expenditure invariably crowds out private-sector expenditure. If $(1 - a \cdot b) \gtreqqless \frac{1}{2} \cdot (1 + a/J')$, then $dQ_i/dG_i \gtreqqless 0$ and thus there is partial, perfect, and multiple crowding-out, respectively.

In sum, a rise in government expenditure conjointly elicits a wage-price spiral and a crowding-out of production and employment. The mechanism whereby this happens is illustrated in Fig. 3. The price and quantity effects are interrelated because the firms and the households each make a price

---

[18] In general, the number of firms per industry changes in the course of this multiplier process and affects the values of C_i^P and C_i^G. These second-order influences are ignored here. C_i^P and C_i^G may be interpreted as linear approximations of the consumption function in the neighborhood of the initial equilibrium.

decision together with a quantity decision. As shown, in response to a government expenditure increase, firms raise the price level and the employment level; households react by raising the wage level and reducing consumption. In all subsequent rounds, firms respond to household activity by raising the price level and reducing employment, whereupon households raise the wage level and reduce consumption. In this manner, the crowding-out effect of government expenditures may be explained.

5. Under-employment and trading efficiency

The imperfectly competitive equilibrium is invariably characterized by under-employment, in the sense that the ICE level of employment always falls short of the socially optimal level. To demonstrate this proposition, let us compare the first-order conditions for social optimality (on the one hand) with those for profit-maximization and utility-maximization under ICE (on the other).

The socially optimal levels of employment, consumption, and government expenditure may be determined by solving the following optimization problem:

Maximize

$$\sum_{t=1}^{T} U\left(\underset{i \in S_t}{C_i}, L_t, \underline{G_i} \right) \tag{12}$$

subject to <

$$L_t = \sum_{j \in E_t} J(Q_j) \quad \text{for} \quad t = 1, \ldots, T$$

$$Q_i = C_i + G_i \quad \text{for} \quad i = 1, \ldots, I$$

where E_t is the set of all industries j requiring labor of type t.

The first-order conditions for social optimality may be reduced to

$$U_C + U_L \cdot J' = 0 = \xi^{SO} \tag{13a}$$

$$U_C - U_G = 0 = \xi^{SO} \tag{13b}$$

("SO" stands for "social optimum".) These two conditions are pictured in Fig. 4, where C_i^{SO} and G_i^{SO} denote the socially optimal levels of consumption and government expenditure on product i, respectively.

This social optimum cannot be attained through the ICE. The reaction function of the imperfectly competitive firm (2′) implies that

$$\frac{W_t}{P_i} < \frac{1}{J'} . \tag{14a}$$

Moreover, the reaction function of the imperfectly competitive union (5′) implies that

$$-\left(\frac{U_L}{U_C} \right) < \frac{W_t}{P_i} \tag{14b}$$

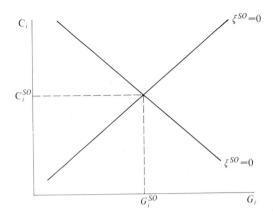

FIG. 4. The social optimum.

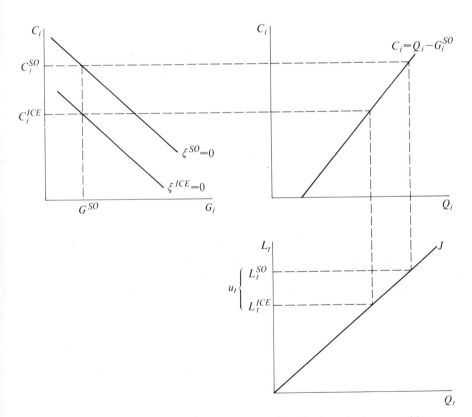

FIG. 5. The level of under-employment generated by the imperfectly competitive
equilibrium.

Consequently, at the ICE,

$$-\left(\frac{U_L}{U_C}\right) < \frac{1}{J'}. \tag{15}$$

However, the social optimality condition (13a) may be rewritten as

$$-\left(\frac{U_L}{U_C}\right) = \frac{1}{J'}. \tag{13a'}$$

Thus, in Fig. 5, the imperfectly competitive relation between consumption and government expenditure ($\xi^{ICE} = 0$) lies everywhere beneath the socially optimal relation between these variables ($\xi^{SO} = 0$). Suppose that government expenditure is set at its socially optimal level, G_i^{SO}. Then consumption under imperfect competition falls short of its socially optimal level by ($C_i^{SO} - C_i^{ICE}$) and employment under imperfect competition falls short of its socially optimal level by $u_t = (L_t^{SO} - L_t^{ICE})$. u_t is our measure of under-employment generated through the imperfectly competitive equilibrium.

An interesting rationale for the existence of under-employment under imperfect competition is that imperfectly competitive trades are always allocatively inefficient. This may be demonstrated quite simply by considering the firms' iso-profit loci and the unions' iso-utility loci. The former family of loci (for a representative firm)

$$\frac{dW_t}{dP_i}\bigg|_{\pi_{if} = \text{constant}} = -\frac{\partial \pi_{if}/P_i}{\partial \pi_{if}/W_t}$$

is depicted in Fig. 6. Clearly, the higher loci are associated with lower profits. Thus, for any given W_t, the firms choose that price which permits the lowest possible iso-profit locus to be attained. In other words, the wage–price combination which the firms select are given by the set of points at

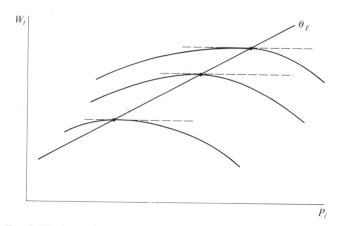

FIG. 6. The iso-profit loci and the firm's selected wage–price combinations.

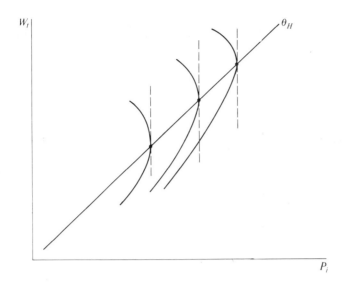

FIG. 7. The iso-utility loci and the union's selected wage–price combinations.

which the iso-profit loci are horizontal. In this manner we trace out the θ_F curve (of Fig. 2).

The family of iso-utility loci (for a representative union) is pictured in Fig. 7. The rightward loci are associated with lower utility. Thus, for any given P_i, the union chooses that wage which allows the leftmost possible iso-utility locus to be reached. Consequently, the wage–price combinations which the unions select are given by the set of points at which the iso-utility loci are vertical. This exercise yields the θ_H curve (of Fig. 2).

As noted above, the imperfectly competitive equilibrium lies at the intersection of the θ_F and θ_H curves. Since the iso-profit locus is horizontal and the iso-utility locus is vertical at this intersection point, the two loci (which are everywhere continuously differentiable) must cross one another. Yet in that event, the trades of consumption and labor which takes place between the firms and the unions cannot be allocatively efficient. Efficient trades occur when, for any given iso-profit locus, the unions attain the leftmost possible iso-utility locus (or, equivalently, for any given iso-utility locus, the firms attain the lowest possible iso-profit locus). In other words, efficient trades occur at the points of tangency between the iso-profit and iso-utility loci. These trades are depicted by the ET curve in Fig. 8. As shown the ET curve passes to the left of the imperfectly competitive equilibrium point (ICE in Fig. 8).

In order to compare the employment implications of efficient versus imperfectly competitive trades, it is convenient to characterize these trades in terms of consumption and government expenditure. The set of all efficient

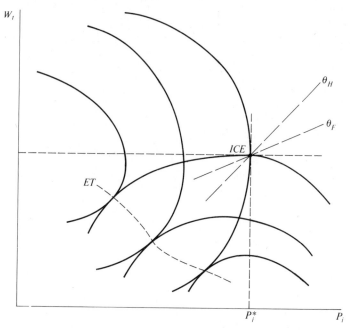

FIG. 8. Efficient trades and the imperfectly competitive equilibrium.

trades may be generated by the following optimization problem:
Maximize

$$V = \sum_{i=1}^{I} \sum_{f=1}^{F} \left(\frac{\pi_{if}}{P_i}\right) + \sum_{t=1}^{T} U\left(\underline{C_i}_{i \in S_t}, L_t, \underline{G_i}\right) \tag{16}$$

subject to

$$\sum_{f=1}^{F} \left(\frac{\pi_{if}}{P_i}\right) = k_i \cdot Q_i \quad \text{for} \quad i = 1,\ldots, I$$

$$Q_i = C_i + G_i \quad \text{for} \quad i = 1,\ldots, I,$$

$$L_t = \sum_{j \in E_t} J(Q_j) \quad \text{for} \quad t = 1,\ldots, T$$

where G_i and k_i ($i = 1,\ldots, I$) are exogenously given and $0 \leq k_i \leq 1$. Here the allocation of resources is not governed by imperfectly competitive agents, but rather by a hypothetical dictator who enforces allocative efficiency. Maximizing the sum of all real profits and utilities ensures that the iso-profit loci are tangent to the iso-utility loci (viz., that it is impossible to raise profit without reducing utility). The parameters k_i determine which point of tangency is to be selected. As the k_i's span the interval between zero and unity, the entire set of feasible trades is covered.

The first-order conditions for efficient trades are

$$k_i + U_c + U_L \cdot J' = 0 = \xi^{ET}, \quad \text{for} \quad i = 1,\ldots, I. \tag{17}$$

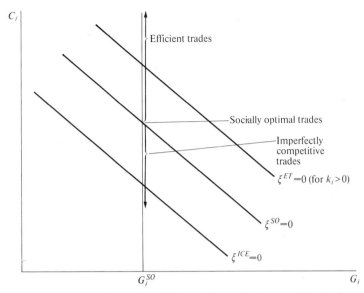

FIG. 9. Consumption under efficient and imperfectly competitive trades.

This condition implies that $-(U_c/U_L) \leqslant J'$. Recall that social optimality requires that $-(U_c/U_l) = J'$, whereas under imperfect competition $-(U_c/U_L) > J'$. In Fig. 9, $\xi^{SO} = 0$ and $\xi^{ICE} = 0$ depict the $C_i - G_i$ combinations under social optimality and imperfect competition, respectively, while $\xi^{ET} = 0$ depicts these combinations under efficient trades for $k_i > 0$. (When $k_i = 0$, the $\xi^{SO} = 0$ and $\xi^{ET} = 0$ curves coincide.) Set government expenditure at some exogenously given level, say G_i^{SO}. It is evident from the figure that consumption—and therefore also employment—is always greater under efficient trades than under imperfectly competitive trades. In this way, the under-employment generated through imperfect competition may be explained in terms of the allocative inefficiency of imperfectly competitive trades.

The previous section showed how government expenditure crowds out private-sector expenditure under imperfect competition. It may now be asked whether the same is true for efficient trades. The answer is affirmative. Totally differentiating condition (17), we find that

$$\frac{dC_i}{dG_i} = -\frac{(J')^2 \cdot U_{LL}}{U_{cc} + (J')^2 \cdot U_{LL}},$$

which lies between -1 and 0. Thus, there is partial crowding out when trades are allocatively efficient.

6. Conclusion

In conclusion, this paper shows that moving from a standard Keynesian model in which agents face non-manipulable demand constraints to an imperfectly competitive model in which their demand constraints are price-manipulable means taking a very big step indeed. The former model—which rests on weaker choice-theoretic foundations since it does not explain price-setting behavior—does not mimic the workings of the latter. The nature of unemployment is radically different in the two models: in the former, there is involuntary unemployment due to wage rigidity; in the latter, there is voluntary under-employment due to trading inefficiency. Correspondingly, the effectiveness of government policy is also different in these models: a rise in government expenditure stimulates private-sector expenditure (through inter-market spillovers emerging when wages and prices are fixed) in the Keynesian model, but it reduces private-sector expenditure (via induced changes in wages and prices) in the imperfectly competitive model.

Birkbeck College, University of London

REFERENCES

ARROW, K. (1959), "Towards a Theory of Price Adjustment" in *The Allocation of Economic Resources*, ed. M. Abramovitz, Stanford: Stanford University Press.
BARRO, R. J. (1972), "The Theory of Monopolistic Price Adjustment", *Review of Economic Studies*, 39, 17–26.
—— and GROSSMAN, H. (1976), *Money, Employment and Inflation*, Cambridge, Cambridge University Press.
BENASSY, J.-P. (1975), "Neo-Keynesian Disequilibrium Theory in a Monetary Economy", *Review of Economic Studies*, 42, 503–24.
—— (1976), "The Disequilibrium Approach to Monopolistic Price Setting and General Monopolistic Equilibrium", *Review of Economic Studies*, 43, 69–81.
—— (1978), "A Neo-Keynesian Model of Price and Quantity Determination in Disequilibrium" in *Equilibrium and Disequilibrium in Economic Theory*, ed. by G. Schwodiauer, Riedel.
CHAMBERLAIN, E. H. (1933), *The Theory of Monopolistic Competition*, Massachusetts: Harvard University Press.
GRANDMONT, J. M. and LAROQUE, G. (1976), "On Keynesian Temporary Equilibria", *Review of Economic Studies*, 43, 53–67.
HAHN, F. (1978), "On Non-Walrasian Equilibria", *Reviews of Economic Studies*, 45, 1–18.
HART, O. (1982), "A Model of Imperfect Competition with Keynesian Features", *Quarterly Journal of Economics*, XCVII, 109–138.
—— (1978), "Monopolistic Competition in a Large Economy with Differentiated Commodities", *Review of Economic Studies*, 46, 1–30.
MALINVAUD, E. (1977), *The Theory of Unemployment Reconsidered*, Oxford, Blackwell.
McDONALD, I. M. and SOLOW, R. M. (1981), "Wage Bargaining and Employment", *American Economic Review*, 71 (5), 896–908.
MUELLBAUER, J. and PORTES, R. (1978), "Macroeconomic Models with Quantity Rationing", *Economic Journal*, 88, 788–821.
NEGISHI, T. (1978), "Existence of an Underemployment Equilibrium", in *Equilibrium and Disequilibrium in Economic Theory*, ed. by J. Schwodiauer, Reidel.
SHESKINSKI, E. and WEISS, Y. (1977), "Inflation and Costs of Price Adjustment", *Review of Economic Studies*, 44, 287–303.
WEITZMAN, M. L. (1982), "Increasing Returns and the Foundations of Unemployment Theory", *Economic Journal*, 92, 787–804.

JOB SEARCH AND YOUTH UNEMPLOYMENT

By LISA M. LYNCH*

In recent years there has been a marked increase in youth unemployment in Great Britain. Not only has the incidence of unemployment risen but the duration has increased as well. Even within the context of generally worsening economic conditions, this rise in the incidence and duration of youth unemployment has received particular attention by policy makers. There is concern that if young people have an early discouraging labour market experience, this will have long term consequences on their attitudes towards work and their assimilation into the labour market. In this paper we attempt to determine those factors which cause some young people to experience longer spells of unemployment than others. In particular, we examine the influence of unemployment benefits on the duration of unemployment. We take advantage of the theoretical developments of search theory and link this directly with data on the duration of youth unemployment.

In Section 1 of this paper we briefly review attempts to link formal models of optimal search behavior to data on the duration of unemployment. In particular, we utilize an approach developed by T. Lancaster and A. Chesher (1984) to derive analytically a set of interesting elasticities related to the duration of unemployment. In Section 2, we describe the data set used and characteristics of the unemployed in this sample. Since the approach mentioned above depends upon the ability to observe an individual's reservation and expected wage we discuss the reliability of our measures of these variables. In Section 3 we present our empirical findings, discuss their limitations and possible sources of bias, and compare the estimates with those obtained in other studies. Finally, in Section 4 we summarize the results and examine possible policy implications. Specifically, we discuss whether or not the supposed relationship between unemployment benefits and the duration of unemployment holds for young workers.

1. The model

Studies of the determinants of the duration of unemployment could be divided until now into two categories. The search theorists of the 60's and the 70's concentrated on the development of theoretical models to explain the search process of rational agents, but there was little concern with linking these theoretical developments with actual data. On the other hand, empirically oriented work reflected little of the theoretical developments and tended to rely upon ad hoc models to describe the duration of unemployment. Only recently have there been attempts to apply the theoretical

* I would like to thank Steve Nickell, Chris Pissarides, Ray Richardson, and the participants of the SSRC Labour Study Group conference on Applied Micro Labour Economics at the University of Warwick for their many valuable comments on an earlier draft.

developments of search theory to data on the duration of unemployment. Specifically, studies by Kiefer and Neumann (1981), Nickell (1979), Lancaster (1979), and Salant (1977) have drawn together search theory with data on the duration of unemployment to make inferences about the behavior of unemployed job seekers. In particular, Lancaster and Nickell have estimated re-employment probabilities of unemployed British adults within the search theory framework. While their approach is not ad hoc and they are able to explore issues such as state dependency, their work suffers from a problem common to all cross section analysis—the bias which results from the omission of unobserved variables such as motivation (uncontrolled heterogeneity). Attempts to control for heterogeneity and true state dependency prove to be difficult.

Lancaster and Chesher (1984), however, have developed an approach which overcomes some of the statistical problems encountered in previous studies and deduce structural parameters rather than estimate them. They derive from a search model equations for the re-employment probability, the expected wage, and the optimal reservation wage. Under specific assumptions it can be shown that it is possible to use this system of equations to measure the response of the reservation wage and the re-employment probability to changes in unemployment income and the arrival rate of job offers.

Lancaster and Chesher construct a model of the behavior of an individual who wishes to maximize the present value of his income stream discounting in continuous time. More general results, however, can be obtained using a search model in discrete time.[1] Let us assume that utility is a function only of income, that the time horizon is infinite, and that an unemployed young person knows the distribution of wage offers, $f(w)$,[2] available in the labour market, but does not know where the job offers are located. In each period the probability of receiving a job offer is λ. The probability of accepting this job offer will be determined by an optimal reservation wage, ζ, which is chosen to maximize the expected returns from search. Therefore, the probability of re-entering employment is composed of two elements—the probability of receiving a job offer, and the probability of accepting the offer. This re-employment probability can be expressed as:

$$\theta = \lambda\{1 - F(\zeta)\} \qquad (1)$$

where $1 - F(\zeta)$ is the probability that the offer, w, is greater than the reservation wage, ζ (i.e. that the individual accepts the offer). Assume that in each period s percentage of jobs dissolve for unknown reasons, and that the probability of receiving a job offer, λ, the distribution of wage offers, $f(w)$, and s are all time independent.

[1] The following is a standard search model such as that proposed by Mortenson (1970). For a review of search models see Lippman and McCall (1976).

[2] The density function of the cumulative distribution of wage offers, $F(w)$.

Applying a model developed by Pissarides (1983) to examine efficiency aspects of financing unemployment insurance, we let U be the net worth of an unemployed worker and $V(w)$ be the net worth of earning w income per period. The net worth of an employed worker can be expressed as:

$$V(w) = \frac{w}{1+r} + s\frac{U}{1+r} + (1-s)\frac{V(w)}{1+r} \qquad (2)$$

where earned income, w, is received at the end of the period, $V(w)$ is calculated at the beginning of the period, s is the probability of becoming unemployed, $1-s$ is the probability of remaining employed, and r is the discount rate. Solving for $V(w)$ we obtain:

$$V(w) = \frac{1}{r+s}(w+sU) \qquad (3)$$

The expected conditional earnings from an accepted job offer are:

$$E(w \mid w \geq \zeta) = x = \frac{\lambda}{\theta} \int_{\zeta}^{\infty} wf(w)\,\mathrm{d}w; \qquad (4)$$

which, after simplification and integration by parts, becomes:

$$x = \zeta + \frac{\int_{\zeta}^{\infty}(1-F(w))\,\mathrm{d}w}{1-F(\zeta)} \qquad (5)$$

The expected net worth then from accepting a job offer is:

$$V(x) = \frac{1}{r+s}(x+sU) \qquad (6)$$

Unemployed workers may receive income while unemployed, b. At the same time they incur costs of search, c, so that their net income is $b-c$. This implies that their net worth while unemployed is:

$$U = \frac{b-c}{1+r} + \theta\frac{V(x)}{1+r} + (1-\theta)\frac{U}{1+r} \qquad (7)$$

Solving U and substituting for $V(x)$ we have:

$$U = \frac{1}{r(r+s+\theta)}\{(r+s)(b-c)+\theta x\} \qquad (8)$$

Since we have defined the reservation wage as that wage which equates the marginal benefit of accepting a job with the marginal benefit of continuing search

$$V(\zeta) = U \qquad (9)$$

Substituting for $V(\zeta)$ and U we find that

$$\zeta - (b - c) = \frac{\theta}{r+s}(x - \zeta) \qquad (10)$$

Using equations (5) and (10) we can define the optimal reservation wage function as:

$$\zeta = (b - c) + \frac{\lambda}{r+s}\int_{\zeta}^{\infty}(1 - F(w))\,\mathrm{d}w \qquad (11)$$

Differentiating equation (11) with respect to $(b-c)$ and λ, and then differentiating θ with respect to $(b-c)$ and λ, will give the response of the reservation wage and the re-employment probability to changes in unemployment income and in the rate of arrival of job offers.

If we have data on x, ζ, b and c and we assume, as Lancaster and Chesher have shown, that the relevant portion of the wage offer distribution for any individual is either Pareto or Exponential, we can obtain the formulae and solutions presented in Table 1 for the elasticities in terms of the observed variables x, ζ, b and c.[3]

2. The data

The data we use in this paper came from a longitudinal survey of young people living in London.[4] The sample originally contained 1,922 boys and girls from both inner and outer boroughs who were planning to leave school in the summer of 1979. They were subsequently interviewed approximately every six months about their labour market experience. For our analysis we use data on those who were unemployed in April of 1980 and November 1980. In April the respondents had been out of school for almost one year and in November they had been out of school for one year and a half.

In the November 1980 interview the average duration of an interrupted spell of unemployment was approximately seven months. The unemployment rate was 7% for the boys and 10% for the girls. Seventy nine percent of the unemployed young people came from the inner city boroughs while the percentage of survey participants who lived in the inner city was only 57%. Non-whites had a disproportionately higher level of unemployment as they represented almost 30% of the unemployed, but only 15% of those in the survey.

Our definition of unemployment includes all those who stated that they were looking for work regardless of whether they were registered as unemployed. We have used this definition of unemployment since we found a substantial amount of non-registration especially, among girls (48% not

---

[3] See Lancaster and Chesher.

[4] See Ray Richardson, "Unemployment and the Inner City—a Study of School Leavers", L.S.E. mimeo, June 1980 for a complete descriptive analysis of this data set.

Table 1

Elasticity	Formula	Solution
$\dfrac{\partial \log \zeta}{\partial \log (b-c)}$	$=\dfrac{(b-c)}{\zeta}\dfrac{1}{1+\theta/(r+s)}$	$\dfrac{(b-c)}{\zeta}\dfrac{(x-\zeta)}{x-(b-c)}$
$\dfrac{\partial \log \zeta}{\partial \log \lambda}$	$=\dfrac{1}{\zeta}\dfrac{\zeta-(b-c)}{1+\theta/(r+s)}$	$\dfrac{\zeta-(b-c)}{\zeta}\dfrac{(x-\zeta)}{x-(b-c)}$
$\dfrac{\partial \log \theta}{\partial \log (b-c)}$ (Pareto assumption)	$=\dfrac{-f(\zeta)}{1-F(\zeta)}\dfrac{(b-c)}{1+\theta/(r+s)}$	$-\dfrac{1}{(1-\zeta/x)}\dfrac{(b-c)}{\zeta}\dfrac{(x-\zeta)}{x-(b-c)}$
$\dfrac{\partial \log \theta}{\partial \log (b-c)}$ (Exponential assumpition)	$=\dfrac{f(\zeta)}{1-F(\zeta)}\dfrac{(b-c)}{1+\theta/(r+s)}$	$-\dfrac{(b-c)}{x-(b-c)}$
$\dfrac{\partial \log \theta}{\partial \log \lambda}$ (Pareto assumption)	$=1-\dfrac{f(\zeta)}{1-F(\zeta)}\dfrac{\zeta-(b-c)}{1+\theta/(r+s)}$	$1-\dfrac{1}{(1-\zeta/x)}\dfrac{\zeta-(b-c)}{\zeta}\dfrac{(x-\zeta)}{x-(b-c)}$
$\dfrac{\partial \log \theta}{\partial \log \lambda}$ (Exponential assumption)	$=1-\dfrac{f(\zeta)}{1-F(\zeta)}\dfrac{\zeta-(b-c)}{1+\theta/(r+s)}$	$1-\dfrac{\zeta-(b-c)}{x-(b-c)}$

registered) and non-whites (39% not registered). If we only counted those who were registered as unemployed we could have obtained misleading results.

As it can be seen in Table 1 the solutions to the model require measures of the reservation wage, expected wage, unemployment income and costs of search of those who are unemployed. Given difficulties with obtaining accurate estimates of the weekly costs of search in this survey we assume for the moment that costs are zero. The implications of this assumption will be discussed in the next section. Each young person who did not already have a job arranged was asked the following questions: (1) "What is the lowest weekly wage you would accept before tax and other deductions?"; (2) "How much do you expect to earn before tax and other deductions?"; and (3) "How do you manage for money while you are out of work and how much does that amount to each week?". We interpret the answer to question one as the reservation wage, ζ, the answer to question two as the expected wage, x, and the answer to question three as unemployment income, b. The model implies that $b \leq \zeta$ and $\zeta \leq x$. We tested these restrictions and found that only two cases failed the $\zeta \leq x$ test while all the cases had $b \leq \zeta$.

The following table reports mean, maximum, and minimum values for these variables along with the mean of earnings for those employed at the time of the interview. As can be seen below, the income expectations of the unemployed seem sensible given the earnings of their contemporaries who are employed.

TABLE 2
Sample characteristics of workers November 1980

	Mean	Maximum	Minimum
Reservation Wage	£39.65	60.00	20.00
Expected Wage	48.92	80.00	25.00
Unemployment Income	15.49	28.00	0.00
Gross Earnings of the Employed	54.05	—	—

3. The results

The results using the solutions in Table 1 are reported in Tables 3 and 4. The data are from the November 1980 interview with results from April reported in Appendix A. The elasticities were calculated, not estimated, for each individual using the individual's own values of x, ζ, and b. We present here the mean values of the elasticities of the reservation wage with respect to unemployment income and the arrival rate of job offers, disaggregated by race and sex. Since we have found ethnicity a significant determinant of the duration of unemployment in other work,[5] we decided to check whether a possible reason for this was a different response of the reservation wage of non-whites to changes in benefits. We report elasticities by sex as well to see if the additional responsibility of household work that many of the girls may have affects their responses. We also disaggregated these elasticities by length of unemployment spell but these results are not reported here since the elasticities remained constant across the duration groups.

These results suggest that the elasticity of the reservation wage with respect to unemployment income is low. Overall there is little variation across race or sex. The responsiveness of the reservation wage to the probability of receiving a job offer is low as well. This suggests that even if a particular individual is more likely to receive a job offer than another, he or she does not vary his or her reservation wage accordingly. Non-whites are the most responsive to changes in the arrival rate of job offers and girls the least. Finally, there is little difference between the two interviews when the results of Table 3 and 4 are compared with those in Appendix A.

In the following two tables, 5 and 6, we report mean values of the elasticities of the re-employment probability with respect to unemployment income and the arrival rate of job offers. To test the sensitivity of our results to the assumption made concerning the shape of the wage offer distribution we report results for both the Pareto and Exponential distributions.

There have been a number of studies that have estimated the elasticity of the re-employment probability with respect to unemployment income for adult workers. The studies of Nickell (1979), Lancaster (1979), and Lancaster and Chesher (1984) found the value of this elasticity to lie in the range of 0.6 to 1.00. The study of Atkinson, Gomulka, Micklewright and Rau (1982)

[5] See Lynch (1983).

TABLE 3
Elasticity of reservation wage w.r.t. unemployment income[6]

Characteristic	Elasticity
Race: White (41)	0.108
Non-White (11)	0.099
Sex: Male (29)	0.109
Female (23)	0.102
All Total cases = 52	0.106

TABLE 4
Elasticity of reservation wage w.r.t. offer probability

Characteristic	Elasticity
Race: White	0.141
Non-White	0.168
Sex: Male	0.161
Female	0.128
All	0.146

TABLE 5
Elasticity of re-employment probability w.r.t. unemployment income

Characteristic	Pareto	Exponential
Race: White	−0.493	−0.578
Non-White	−0.439	−0.489
Sex: Male	−0.488	−0.519
Female	−0.473	−0.619
All	−0.483	−0.559

TABLE 6
Elasticity of re-employment probability w.r.t. offer probability

Characteristic	Pareto	Exponential
Race: White	0.303	0.248
Non-White	0.281	0.267
Sex: Male	0.282	0.270
Female	0.319	0.230
All	0.298	0.252

[6] Although there were 87 people unemployed, 35 cases were omitted because they had already arranged a job. This meant that they were not questioned about their reservation wage or expected wage.

however, found it to have values between zero and 0.6 depending upon the specification of the replacement ratio. The elasticities reported in Table 5 are somewhat smaller than most elasticities reported in earlier studies suggesting that while an increase in benefits will increase the duration of youth unemployment, this increase will be less than for adult workers. The average elasticity increases between the two interviews but there appears to be little difference across race or sex.

It is not possible to determine a priori the sign on the elasticity of the re-employment probability with respect to the probability of receiving a job offer. As the probability of receiving a job increases there are two conflicting effects. On the one hand, the more likely an individual is to receive a job offer the more likely it is that he or she becomes employed. But on the other hand, as the individual perceives that there are more job offers available, he or she may increase his or her reservation wage, which results in a decreased probability of accepting a job offer. Since the elasticity on the reservation wage with respect to the arrival rate of jobs is small it is not surprising that the elasticities reported here have a positive sign indicating that the first effect outweights the second. There is little difference in the elasticities for the various groups and the values do not alter greatly between the two interviews. Moreover, for both re-employment probability elasticities the assumption of Pareto or Exponential distribution seems inconsequential.

Since these reported elasticities are not particularly intuitive the following table is devised to show the impact of changes in unemployment income or the arrival rate of job offers on the reservation wage and the expected duration of unemployment of a "representative" unemployed young person. This "representative" individual has a reservation wage of £39.65 per week with an expected duration of unemployment equal to 24 weeks. ("+" and "−" indicate increase or decrease)

TABLE 7

Policy change	Reservation wage	Duration*
10% increase in unemployment income (i.e. by £1.55 per week)	+£0.42	+1.15 weeks
50% increase in the arrival rate of job offers	+£1.13	−3.58 weeks
* Under Pareto assumption		

Although a fifty per cent increase in the arrival rate of job offers might appear high, this is not the case. If there is proportionality between the arrival rate of job offers and the vacancies series this figure is consistent with fluctuations of vacancies over the cycle. These results suggest that it might be more effective for policy makers to operate through the demand side rather than the supply side of the economy to obtain a reduction in the duration of youth unemployment.

Given the assumption of the shape of the offer distribution, it is possible to obtain the coefficient of variation of wage offers, $\sigma = 1 - \zeta/x$.[7] Lancaster and Chesher (1984) find $\sigma = 0.13$ for adult workers which is almost identical to that estimated by Kiefer and Neumann (1981) where $\sigma = 0.14$. Our estimate is larger with $\sigma = 0.19$ which may suggest greater returns for young workers who wait for a better job offer. Since the sample used here is very homogeneous it was expected that the value of σ would have been smaller than that found in previous studies.

Until now we have assumed that weekly costs of search are zero. To obtain some idea of the implications of this assumption we assumed that for the average youth weekly costs equalled £5.00. With this assumption the elasticity of the reservation wage with respect to unemployment income decreased from 0.106 to 0.057 and the elasticity of the re-employment probability with respect to benefits declined from -0.483 to -0.301. Therefore, the assumption of zero costs leads to an upward bias in these elasticities.

In addition to zero costs our results are sensitive to other assumptions made in the model. For example, Lancaster and Chesher show that the assumption of a Pareto vs. a Lognormal wage offer distribution causes an upward bias in the elasticity of the re-employment probability with respect to benefits. At the same time, the assumptions of risk neutrality and no leisure cause a downward bias in this elasticity.

A crucial assumption of our model is the constancy of the reservation wage over a spell of unemployment. However, studies by Kasper (1967) and Kiefer and Neumann (1981) have found that the reservation wage declined over time. To see how accurate this assumption is for our sample we estimated by OLS the determinants of the reservation wage including the duration of unemployment. The results are reported in the following table:

TABLE 8

OLS of log of reservation wages in November 1980

Variable[2]	Coefficient	Standard error
Constant	3.672	0.174
Log of unemployment income	0.013	0.044
Ethnicity (White)	0.174	0.097
Sex (Male)	0.087	0.104
Exams (Taken)	-0.147	0.897
Borough of residence:[1]		
Outer I	-0.106	0.132
Outer II	-0.262	0.152
Inner I	0.049	0.132
Inner III	0.061	0.161
Turnover	-0.017	0.099
Job status in April	-0.032	0.116
Duration of current spell of unemployment	-0.002	0.002

No. of cases = 52.
R squared = 0.48.
[1] Inner II borough has been retained in the estimation.
[2] See Appendix B for description of the variables.

[7] Under the Pareto assumption.

As it can be seen, duration has no significant influence on the reservation wage. This is similar to results obtained by Stephenson (1976) who found the reservation wage for young workers in the U.S. declining extremely slowly. We were also able to observe the reservation wage of those unemployed at both the April and November interviews. Only 29% of those decreased their reservation wage between the two interviews. While these results appear to contradict those of Kiefer and Neumann they are consistent. The data set used by Kiefer and Neumann consisted of older men approaching the end of their working life. Search theory predicts that a finite time horizon leads to a decreasing reservation wage. Since young workers are at the beginning of their work experience the assumption of an infinite time horizon and constant reservation wage is perhaps not so inappropriate. It is interesting to note that unemployment income is insignificant here as a determinant of reservation wages.

4. Conclusions and policy implications

The above results indicate that demand factors appear to be at least as important as supply factors as an explanation of youth unemployment. This is supported by other work[8] in which re-employment probabilities for young workers were estimated using maximum likelihood. In this work unemployment income was an insignificant determinant of the probability of becoming re-employed with ethnicity and state dependency the most important variables. All of these results suggest that young workers are affected by the probability of receiving a job offer at least as much as by the probability of accepting a job offer. The image of young workers choosing "a life on the dole" and turning down numerous job offers is not supported by the data. At the April interview of the survey those who were unemployed were asked whether or not they had turned down any job offers. Only 15% had received any job offers with the majority of those receiving only one offer.

An additional interesting result is the significance of ethnicity in estimates of the duration of unemployment and reservation wages. As Table 8 shows, non-whites have significantly lower reservation wages than whites. At the same time, we have seen that there is little difference in the elasticities reported between whites and non-whites. This suggests that their higher proportion of unemployment is not necessarily supply determined.

The approach we have used in this paper, of deducing rather than estimating elasticities, has the advantage of depending upon economic theory and avoiding the difficulties of heterogeneity and other statistical problems associated with maximum likelihood and ordinary least squares estimation. However, this procedure carries the disadvantage of not testing whether search theory is the appropriate framework for the study of the duration of unemployment. We have also had to make several assumptions that may bias final estimates. It would seem, however, that the restrictions

[8] See Lynch (1983).

imposed by the model are not as extreme for young workers as they may be for other groups.

University of Bristol

APPENDIX A

April results

	Elasticity	
Reservation Wage w.r.t. unemployment income	0.080	
Reservation wage w.r.t. offer probability	0.148	
	Pareto	Exponential
Re-employment probability w.r.t. unemployment income	−0.336	−0.306
Re-employment probability w.r.t. offer probability	0.323	0.357
Total cases = 70		

APPENDIX B

Variables:
- Net income = gross income calculated using an earnings equation estimated for those employed in November 1980. Reductions were then made for tax and national insurance contributions assuming no dependents.
- Ethnicity 1 = white; 0 = non-white.
- Sex 1 = male; 0 = female
- Exams 1 = taken; 0 = no exams taken
- Turnover 1 = change of jobs; 0 = no job changes
- Job status in
- April 1 = employed; 0 = unemployed
- Duration = number of weeks unemployed in current spell of unemployment.
- Boroughs: Inner I = Lambeth
  Inner II = Hammersmith
  Inner III = Tower Hamlets
  Outer I = Hounslow
  Outer II = Bromley

REFERENCES

ATKINSON, A. B., GOMULKA, J., MICKLEWRIGHT, J. and RAU, N. (1982), "Unemployment Duration, Social Security and Incentives", L.S.E. mimeo. June.

KIEFER, N. M. and NEUMANN, G. R. (1981), "Individual Effects in a Non-Linear Model: Explicit Treatment of Heterogeneity in the Empirical Job-Search Model". *Econometrica*, July, pp. 965–980.

KASPER, H. (1967), "The Asking Price of Labor and the Duration of Unemployment". *The Review of Economics and Statistics*, Vol. 49, pp. 165–172.

LANCASTER, T. (1979), "Econometric Methods for the Duration of Unemployment". *Econometrica*, pp. 939–956.

LANCASTER, T. and CHESHER, A. (1984), "An Econometric Analysis of Reservation Wages". *Econometrica*, forthcoming.

LANCASTER, T. and NICKELL, S. (1980), "The Analysis of Re-employment Probabilities for the Unemployed". *Journal of the Royal Statistical Society*, A143.

LIPPMAN, S. and McCALL, J. (1976), "The Economics of Job Search: A Survey", *Economic Inquiry*, June and Sept., pp. 155–89, 347–67.

LYNCH, L. M. (1983), "Determinants of Unemployment and Earnings Behavior of Young Workers in Britain: 1950–1980". Ph.D. thesis, L.S.E.

MORTENSON, D. T. (1970), "Job Search, the Duration of Unemployment and the Phillips Curve", *American Economic Review*, pp. 847–862.

NICKELL, S. J. (1979), "Estimating the Probability of Leaving Unemployment", *Econometrica*, pp. 1249–1266.

PISSARIDES, C. (1983), "Efficiency Aspects of the Financing of Unemployment Insurance and Other Government Expenditures", *Review of Economic Studies*, January.

PISSARIDES, C. (1982), "From School to University: The Demand for Post-Compulsory Education in Britain", *Economic Journal*, Sept.

RICHARDSON, R. (1982), "Unemployment and the Inner City—A Study of School Leavers", L.S.E. mimeo. June.

STEPHENSON, S. P. JR. (1976), "The Economics of Youth Job Search Behavior", *Review of Economics and Statistics*, pp. 104–111.

SALANT, C. W. (1977), "Search Theory and Duration Data: A Theory of Sorts", *Quarterly Journal of Economics*, pp. 39–57.

HOUSING AND UNEMPLOYMENT IN GREAT BRITAIN*

By BARRY McCORMICK

I. Introduction

IT has long been suspected that U.K. housing policy inhibits the movement of labour to growth areas, but recent evidence suggests that the council housing programme may also have influenced either the total level of unemployment, or its location. The least ambiguous evidence of such a linkage is provided in a cross-section survey of unemployment—Nickell (1980)—in which council tenants are found to be about 60% more likely to be unemployed than the average worker in other tenures holding constant various personal and occupational characteristics. The robustness of this finding remains unexplored, but in view of the accumulating evidence that council housing has substantially reduced labour mobility between areas (see e.g. Hughes and McCormick (1981)) it is perhaps unsurprising that various authors including Nickell have asked how far the higher unemployment amongst council tenants, ceteris paribus, can be explained in this way. In view of the important issues connected with this problem, further consideration of the relationship between unemployment and housing circumstance maybe helpful, and this is the purpose of the paper.

Section II examines the reasons why house tenure may exert a separate influence on unemployment. Section III describes the empirical analysis. Unraveling the relationship between housing circumstance and the various aspects of unemployment is complicated by the diversity of arguments that appear a priori plausible. First, the empirical section considers how far the reported correlation between house tenure and unemployment arises incidentally because the occupations pursued by council tenants are quite different to those of owner-occupiers, with the shift dummies in Nickell's study not fully allowing for the implications of this upon unemployment. Secondly, for the housing markets in many countries it is natural to assume that job-mobile workers will prefer rental accommodation. Whereas the length of queues in Britain for unfurnished rental accommodation—which is "controlled" in the economic sense, and comprises over 90% of rental accommodation—suggest that this effect may be weaker, it remains important to ask how far higher unemployment amongst tenants reflects higher job turnover. A related point is the possibility that certain workers are more

* I am grateful to John Aldrich, Peter Asch, Saul Estrin, Paul Geroski, Christopher Gilbert, Christine Greenhalgh, Nick Kiefer, Mervyn King, and David Laidler for helpful comments on earlier drafts. I am also grateful to Alan Holmans of the Department of the Environment and Gordon Hughes, my co-author of related work, for numerous helpful conversations. None of the above should bear responsibility for errors of any kind in the final product. Financial support was provided by the Department of the Environment and the University of Southampton. Finally, able research assistance from Craig Alexander and Platon Tinios is acknowledged.

likely to become unemployed—perhaps due to being alienated or work-shy—and such workers are more likely to either choose rental accommodation or be refused a mortgage. This constitutes a considerable barrier to overcome but an attempt to separate out his influence by combining aggregate census and individual cross-section data is discussed. Thirdly, council tenants might be thought to have higher unemployment, ceteris paribus, as a consequence of the concentration of council housing into particular labour market areas, for example, (a) the North and Scotland, and (b) urban areas. In the process of considering these various explanations, certain facts are uncovered concerning unemployment amongst manual workers, which complement Nickell's survey.

There remains the possibility that house tenure is correlated with unemployment because tenure exerts an independent influence on the cross-section distribution of unemployment. The final part of the empirical section discusses this in the light of the hypotheses advanced in Section II. Conclusions and caveats are summarized in Section IV.

II. Hypotheses

A great deal of the empirical work in the next section is concerned with examining the robustness of the view that tenure does exert a separate influence on unemployment, and does not simply reflect occupational choices, non-observed personal characteristics such as not "fitting well" into society, or locational considerations. When constructing and evaluating these experiments it will be valuable to bear in mind the possible reasons why tenure might exercise an independent influence on unemployment after these other factors have been accounted for. These reasons may be grouped into two quite different "transmission mechanisms" by which housing policy might alter the pattern of unemployment.

Hypothesis A: Certain housing policies—perhaps especially council house construction and/or private sector rent controls—may have had an important influence on the distribution of workers between labour market areas. Thus, if wages are not locally flexible and the Government does not adopt an offsetting regional policy to increase labour demands, these policies may influence *the location of disequilibrium (excess supply) unemployment.*

Hypothesis B: A properly specified model of individual unemployment would include variables which are influenced directly by house tenure, such as the ratio of benefits while unemployed to earnings; and variables affected indirectly by house tenure, such as household wealth. Because the opportunity cost of becoming unemployed may therefore be affected by house tenure it follows that policies towards house tenure mix may also influence *the zero-inflation (natural) rate of unemployment.*

Hypothesis A: Council housing and the spatial distribution of labour supply

This section describes two ways in which housing policies—particularly in the rental sector—may have altered the spatial distribution of workers. The consequences of this for local unemployment are discussed at the end of the Section.

(i) The construction of council housing in an area is likely to prompt certain households to substitute public for local private housing which either reduces the price of private housing, and/or shortens the queues for "controlled" private rental housing. A less tight local private housing market—and perhaps especially rental housing—may encourage migration into the area, particularly by young persons, thereby increasing the supply of labour in areas with heavy council building programmes.

There are two significant objections to this argument. First, the construction of council housing has to a certain extent been accompanied by the demolition of old housing so that the effect of council construction on slackness in local housing markets is smaller than would otherwise have been the case. Secondly, an increased availability of council housing leads to a chain reaction of households moving between tenures. The most significant final consequence of this may be to reduce the number of households in furnished rental accommodation, which in 1973–4—the period to which my data relates—was not controlled in the economic sense. If the supply of furnished rental housing of any given quality was highly price elastic, then migrants may have received little additional incentive to migrate to the area. I now turn to a second reason why housing policy may alter the location of labour supply.

(ii) Housing subsidies vary in kind according to their specificity to the local area. For *owners-occupiers* the subsidy occurs in the form of tax concessions which are not location-specific. Nor are there location-specific gains for the small groups of households in *furnished rental accommodation*; for the years of my data—1973 and 1974—and in the decades prior, this accommodation was not controlled. In contrast, for tenants in *unfurnished rental accommodation*—both council and privately owned—the housing subsidy may be substantial[1] and is specific to a local area. Because this location specific subsidy will reduce the propensity to migrate we may expect that if two towns have identical labour markets, but unequal amounts of unfurnished rental accommodation, there will occur a net inflow of labour into the town with more location-specific housing subsidies until labour market conditions in that town sufficiently deteriorate to redress the balance of incentives. In this way labour accumulates in towns with large proportions of unfurnished rental housing.

The preceding argument resembles a description of the net migration flows accompanying the familiar "wage-compensating" principle, in which

[1] See Hughes (1979).

spatial unemployment differentials may arise because workers in certain areas receive non-marketable location-specific benefits (e.g. beaches, county cricket grounds). However, usual applications of this principle assume that *all* workers in a town receive a location-specific benefit (see for example Hall (1972)). Where workers in certain house tenures (or in certain industries) receive a location-specific benefit, different *fractions* of the workforce in each town are affected. This distinction is important because it might be thought that those not receiving the location-specific housing benefit will gradually migrate until spatial differences in wages or unemployment are eliminated. Thus the plausible intuition that workers accumulate in areas where a large proportion of housing subsidies occur in a non-transferable form requires a different formulation to the familiar wage-compensating principle. Such an intuition may, however, be confirmed by extending the wage-compensating idea to allow individuals to attach a value to living in a particular town—possibly changing from period to period—as well as to labour and housing market benefits. This allows *all* workers to have a probability of migrating even if they receive a non-transferable housing subsidy. It is not within the scope of this paper to present an exposition of this model but its basic features may be readily summarized. (A full description of this model is available from the author upon request). The gross migration rate from a town becomes a weighted average of the migration rates of the workers with and without the housing subsidy. A large proportion of non-transferable housing subsidies in a town increase the weight on the low migration rate workers, and induces net immigration which either forces down wages or increases unemployment until net immigration ends. Applying this argument suggests that between say 1960, when $\frac{2}{3}$ of the 1971 council house stock was in place, and the early 1970's the period to which the findings refer, labour was gradually pulled, ceteris paribus, to areas in which council construction had been greatest.

Two ways have been described by which excess labour supplies may accumulate in those areas where unfurnished rental housing is most common. However, even if housing policy has redistributed the labour supply, it need not also have affected the pattern of unemployment if either (a) wages are locally flexible, or if (b) regional policy is successfully used to alter the location of labour demand.

Hypothesis B: The influence of policies towards house tenure on the zero-inflation (natural) rate of unemployment

Although it is unlikely that house tenure per se will affect an individual's willingness to become unemployed, it may be an important determinant of other variables which are hard in practice to measure accurately, and would be expected to influence unemployment.

First, house tenure may affect unemployment propensity because it has a substantial influence on the ratio of income while unemployed to earnings while employed. If income whilst unemployed is *less* than the relevant threshold on the supplementary benefit scale, an applicant for social security will receive the difference between income and this threshold, together with a top-up equal to housing expenditure: this comprises rent for tenants, and rates, mortage interest payments and maintenance for those purchasing. The treatment of tenure groups also differs, perhaps in a more significant way, if income while unemployed exceeds the supplementary benefit threshold. (A more likely occurrence on the 1970's when unemployment pay included an earnings-related supplement). This is because tenants with incomes above the supplementary benefit threshold remain eligible for rent rebate, but owners are ineligible for a subsidy towards interest payments on mortgages, and maintenance. The net effect of these arguments is to suggest that the opportunity cost of unemployment could differ substantially between (a) tenure categories, and (b) those owning, according to the size of debt.

A second argument concerns neighbourhood effects. It is widely held that the failure of many workers to take-up the supplementary benefit to which they are entitled may, in part, be due to lack of information. The concentration of low income families into Council estates may increase the availability of such information and reduce both uncertainty and the probability that the benefits available to the unemployed will be understated. For example, it is widely known that an unemployed tenant with liquid assets of less than £2,000 would receive a top-up above the supplementary benefit scale to cover the rent, but it is perhaps less known that a similar worker purchasing a house is also entitled to a top-up to cover the mortgage interest payments, rates and maintenance. This information asymmetry may be reinforced by the existence of a greater stigma being attached to unemployment for those living in owner-occuped housing areas,—a stigma which may be declining over time. To summarize, even if actual benefits while unemployed are equal across tenures, workers in rental estates may either be less uncertain concerning the value of benefits or subjectively perceive them to be greater.

A third argument concerns the role of wealth in labour supply decisions. A worker who owns his house outright will, ceteris paribus, have more wealth than a similar one with a mortgage, and this may reduce the labour supply in the form of taking a longer spell of unemployment when searching for a new job. A worker in controlled rental property—private or council— enjoys the income from the capitalized value of his housing subsidy which, if he is content to remain in the rental sector, may be regarded as personal wealth. Such a tenant may consider himself more wealthy than many owner-occupiers with realizable capital. These interesting issues deserve more detailed attention, but this would be of limited appreciability here in the absence of comprehensive wealth data on the G.H.S. tapes.

I now turn from this outline discussion of why housing circumstance might significantly influence variables such as the replacement ratio and wealth, and thus the perceived utility loss from becoming unemployed, to describe the empirical analysis.

III. The empirical analysis

The analysis in this section begins by using individual data to consider the relationship between house tenure and unemployment. The possibility that the higher individual unemployment amongst council tenants reported by Nickell reflects a failure to properly control for the very different jobs pursued by council tenants is approached in the first instance by focussing upon manual workers, of whom 56.7% in the sample studied were renting accommodation. To also try to safeguard against the possibility of simul-

TABLE 1

Job turnover and unemployment amongst British manual workers[1]

Category	Sample size	Percentage changed job in past year	Percentage unemployed
All	6825	13.51	3.15
House tenure			
Own mortgage	1986	12.08	1.16
Own outright	968	9.61	2.89
Private unfurnished tenant	617	16.86	4.38
Council tenant	3254	14.90	4.21
Region			
Depressed region[2]	2623	14.64	4.54
Yorks–Humbs, East Anglia	918	12.96	2.83
Elsewhere	3284	12.76	2.13
Age			
<25	220	35.00	3.18
$25 \leq$ age ≤ 43	2759	18.81	3.08
$44 \leq$ age ≤ 53	1804	9.31	2.61
$54 \leq$ age ≤ 60	1155	6.41	3.64
$61 \leq$ age	887	9.47	3.83
Skill			
Skilled	4234	12.19	2.46
Semi-skilled	1704	13.97	4.58
Unskilled	887	18.94	3.72
Number of children			
<3	5842	12.41	2.67
3 or 4	848	19.69	5.19
>4	135	22.22	11.11
Sex			
Female	557	13.08	2.51
Male	6268	13.37	3.21

[1] The sources of the data are the 1973 and 1974 General Household Surveys. The data concerns male and female manual heads of household.

[2] "Depressed" regions are Scotland, Wales, North and North West. These regions have distinctly larger coefficients when included as explanatory dummy variables together with other regional dummy variables, in models of individual unemployment.

taneity bias arising because current unemployment may have influenced the success of mortgage applications and thereby tenure, all workers who have lived in their present accommodation for less than one year are dropped from the sample. Since workers in *furnished* rental accommodation are a small, highly atypical group, for whom current tenure is likely to be both temporary and a function of job mobility, these data are also excluded from the analysis. Finally, since the arguments relating to the influence of house tenure on labour market activity are largely concerned with the incentives of heads of household, we shall focus upon these data. For the remaining sample of 6825 workers the unemployment and job turnover pattern for various categories of manual worker is given in Table 1. (The basis of the sample is more fully described in the Appendix). On a simple comparison basis, private and council tenants are over $3\frac{1}{2}$ times more likely to be unemployed than workers with mortgages.

Estimates for logit equations of the probability of being unemployed are reported in Table 2. For each equation, the intercept describes the unemployment rate of a head of household living in mortgaged owner-occupied accommodation in the South East, GLC, South West, and West/East Midlands; who is single, unskilled, male, aged 25–44 and with two children or less. Equations were estimated with various other independent variables—including educational qualifications—but none of these proved significant or altered in an important way the results reported here.

Model 1 implies that the probability of being unemployed is significantly greater for workers who either own outright or are in unfurnished rental accommodation—council or private—than for equivalent ones in mortgaged accommodation. Further, the size of the coefficients, in comparison with those for more familiar economic variables such as living in a depressed area, or being skilled, suggests that housing circumstance is of considerable economic importance. The results for the other variables are largely consistent with a priori expectation, but attention might be drawn to the heavily negative coefficient on being female. A likelihood ratio test that the coefficients on the three tenure dummies are equal cannot be rejected at the 5% level. It would therefore appear that the most appropriate distinction to draw when characterising the relationship between house tenure and individual unemployment is between workers with mortgages and other workers, rather than between council tenants and other workers: workers with mortgages have substantially lower unemployment rates.

In order to try to meet the criticism that the results from Model 1 may reflect a tendency for the less able or more myopic manual workers to rent accommodation, Model 2 describes estimates using only skilled manual workers. As in Model 1, the results confirm that the most plausible distinction is between workers with a mortgage and those in other housing circumstances, rather than between council tenants and the remainder. It is also of some interest to note that regional differences play a more pronounced role in explaining unemployment amongst skilled manual workers.

TABLE 2
Parameter estimates of a logit model of unemployment incidence[1,3]

	Model		
	1	*2*	*3*
Independent variables	*All manual workers*	*Skilled manual workers*	*Manual workers not in "depressed" regions*
Intercept	−3.38	−4.09	−3.57
	(9.13)	(9.67)	(7.22)
Married	−1.15	−1.50	−1.12
	(5.75)	(5.34)	(3.84)
Female	−1.47	−0.19	−1.53
	(4.46)	(0.32)	(3.25)
3 or 4 dependent children	0.89	0.96	1.05
	(4.45)	(3.38)	(3.37)
⩾5 dependent children	1.68	1.75	1.50
	(5.42)	(3.93)	(2.95)
Depressed regions[2]	0.65	1.14	—
	(4.17)	(4.71)	
Yorks–Humberside, East Anglia	0.31	0.68	0.33
	(1.35)	(1.99)	(1.39)
Age < 25	0.25	0.55	0.58
	(0.41)	(1.09)	(0.92)
44 ⩽ age ⩽ 53	0.10	−0.23	0.24
	(0.50)	(0.81)	(0.80)
54 ⩽ age ⩽ 60	0.26	0.37	0.56
	(1.18)	(1.19)	(1.70)
61 ⩽ age	0.315	0.30	0.44
	(1.29)	(0.83)	(1.24)
Own outright	0.80	0.90	0.61
	(2.67)	(2.29)	(1.57)
Council tenant	1.06	0.97	0.65
	(3.97)	(3.14)	(2.16)
Private unfurnished tenant	1.19	1.16	0.95
	(4.51)	(2.80)	(2.49)
Unearned income	0.0012	0.00024	−0.00013
	(0.84)	(0.21)	(0.12)
Skilled	−0.24	—	−0.61
	(1.09)		(1.85)
Semi-skilled	0.26	—	0.32
	(1.14)		(1.00)
λ^2	148.1	99.6	66.3
DF	16	14	15

[1] Asymptotic "*t*" ratios are given in parentheses.
[2] "Depressed" Regions are Scotland, Wales, North and North West. (See Table 1).
[3] Sample sizes are 6825, 4234 and 4202 for Models 1, 2, 3 respectively.

Thus far it has been assumed that it is appropriate to allow for different regional conditions with shift dummies. Model 3 allows for interactions between region of residence and the other explanatory variables, and provides a check that the results do not hinge on rental housing being more common in depressed areas. The results for Model 3 confirm that the findings also hold in the more "prosperous" regions, although workers without mortgages are now estimated to have unemployment rates, ceteris paribus, only about 100% greater on average. The results for Model 3, together with the city-level evidence which follows below, strongly undermine the view that linkages between unemployment and tenure arise simply because of locational factors. In passing, it is also worth noting that either being skilled or not being aged 25–43 would appear a more important influence on unemployment in the prosperous areas.

We may now consider whether the findings in Table 2 arise from tenants being more job-mobile. An analysis of the probability of job-mobility and the role of house tenure is summarized in Table 3. Both council and private tenants—but not those owning outright—have higher job turnover rates than workers with mortgages. These results hold with striking consistency for Models 2 and 3, which are again limited to just skilled workers, and those living in more prosperous regions, respectively. Concerning the variables other than tenure, it is worth noting that age and skill have such a well defined role in the turnover equation in comparison with the unemployment equation. However, regional factors, which help explain unemployment, have only a minor role to play in determining job turnover.

The contrasting effects of tenure on the probabilities of unemployment and turnover are found using the parameters described in Model 1 of Tables 2 and 3. In the first two rows of Table 4 the predicted unemployment and turnover rates for a representative worker are described according to tenure group: whereas council tenants are about 30% more likely than those with mortgages to change job in any given year, council tenants are about 180% more likely to be unemployed. Similar arguments may be used for both those owning outright and renting privately, relative to having a mortgage. Putting the same point differently, only a fraction of the lower unemployment amongst workers with mortgages can be explained by lower job turnover. Even adopting Model 3 in Tables 2 and 3, which only considers workers living in relatively prosperous areas, a similar qualitative conclusion emerges: workers without mortgages are substantially more likely to be unemployed-tenants by about 105%, owners-outright by 90%—whereas tenants have job turnover rates about 40% higher than mortgagees, and owners-outright have similar turnover rates to mortgagees.

It is now appropriate to consider how far the findings can be explained by a tendency for work-shy or alienated workers to be more likely to become rental tenants. It appears possible that there is *something* in this proposition, the question is how much, and whether the higher job turnover rate approximately captures it. Interestingly there is an empirical way of answering this question, without knowing which workers are work-shy or alienated under a quite reasonable assumption.

Assume that workers differ according to two characteristics (r, ψ) where ψ measures an inherent unobserved disposition to be out of work because of either being work-shy or alienated, and r reflects another characteristic, such as "rental tenant", which may independently influence unemployment probabilities. If workers with high ψ are more inclined to enter rental

TABLE 3
Parameter estimates of a logit model of the annual probability of moving job[1,3]

Independent variables	Model		
	1 All manual workers	*2* Skilled manual workers	*3* Manual workers not in "depressed" regions
Intercept	−0.93	−1.41	−0.81
	(4.23)	(5.23)	(2.80)
Married	0.40	0.25	0.32
	(2.31)	(1.00)	(1.33)
Female	0.06	−0.36	0.10
	(0.31)	(0.67)	(0.34)
3 or 4 dependent children	0.10	0.01	0.05
	(0.98)	(0.04)	(0.34)
⩾5 dependent children	0.11	−0.12	0.17
	(0.48)	(0.36)	(0.58)
Depressed regions	0.06	0.10	—
	(0.79)	(1.01)	
Age<25	0.73	0.80	0.43
	(4.54)	(4.02)	(1.92)
44⩽age⩽53	−0.80	−0.94	−0.84
	(7.85)	(6.73)	(6.42)
54⩽age⩽60	−1.27	−1.28	−1.36
	(9.05)	(6.31)	(7.27)
61⩽age	−1.12	−1.20	−1.21
	(7.78)	(5.01)	(6.61)
Own outright	0.14	−0.03	−0.05
	(0.98)	(0.17)	(0.24)
Council tenant	0.33	0.40	0.37
	(3.48)	(3.38)	(3.11)
Private unfurnished tenant	0.50	0.58	0.54
	(3.56)	(3.10)	(3.09)
Skilled	−0.68	—	−0.74
	(5.68)		(4.63)
Semi-skilled	−0.44	—	0.47
	(3.51)		(2.80)
Occupational pension[2]	−1.49	−1.67	−1.34
	(17.51)	(14.77)	(12.48)
λ^2	693.8	468.1	371.3
DF	15	13	14

[1] Asymptotic "t" ratios are given in parentheses.
[2] This variable takes the value 1 if the individual held an occupational pension in their job one year prior to interview.
[3] Sample sizes are 6825, 4234 and 4202 for Models 1, 2, 3 respectively.

accommodation—whether by choice, or because building societies can observe ψ and screen on the basis of it—then in an individual level cross-section study of unemployment, the parameter on r will be biased upwards.[2]

[2] In defense of the estimates in Table 2 it might be argued that building societies are more likely to allow the size of mortgage, rather than the decision to offer a mortgage, to be influenced by the individual's work-history, or outlook on life.

TABLE 4
Predicted rates of unemployment and turnover[1,2]

	Mortgage holder	Own outright	Council tenant	Private unfurnished tenant
Percentage unemployed	0.70	1.55	2.00	2.28
Percentage leaving job per annum	12.30	13.88	16.30	18.79
Percentage with <50 weeks worked in a year with job change	21.04	28.78	34.28	25.41
Percentage with <50 weeks worked in any year	2.59	3.99	5.59	4.77

[1] The figures refer to a representative worker with the following characteristics: married, male, skilled manual worker, aged 25–43 with <3 children, annual unearned income of £35, an occupational pension, living outside Scotland, Wales, North and North West.
[2] Rows, 1, 2, and 3 are computed from Column 1 in Tables 2, 3, 7 respectively. Row 4 is computed from rows 2 and 3.

However, if the distribution of ψ across a town's workforce is the same for all large towns then in an aggregate cross-section study explaining the town's unemployment rate, the parameter on "the proportion of workers in rental accommodation" will provide an unbiased estimate of the effect of tenancy on individual unemployment. To see this, assume equation (1) is the correct model of the probability of unemployment for individual type i, U_i,

$$U_i = u_0 + \sum_j u_j x_{ij} + \beta r_i \tag{1}$$

where $x_{ij} = 1$ if individual type i has characteristic j, and 0 otherwise;
 u_j is the incremental unemployment associated with characteristic j;
 $r_i = 1$ if individual type i is a rental tenant, and 0 otherwise and
 β is a parameter describing the influence of tenancy.
Assume characteristic m is not observed, and x_{im} takes the value 1 if an individual of type i is unemployment prone. By Theil's misspecification theorem, omitting x_{im} will result in the estimated parameter on r_i being equal to $\beta + \gamma u_m$, where γ is the slope coefficient on r_i when x_{im} is regressed on r_i and the other x_{ij} variables ($j \neq m$). If workers with an inherent tendency to become unemployed are inclined to enter rental accommodation, then $\gamma > 0$, and the estimated parameter on r_i in (1) is upward biased.
Now suppose there are n_{it} workers of type i, and a work force of N_t in town t. The unemployment rate of town t, $\bar{U}_t$, is

$$\bar{U}_t = \frac{1}{N_t} \sum_i n_{it} U_i = u_0 + \frac{1}{N_t} \left[\sum_j u_j \sum_i n_{it} x_{ij} + \beta \sum_i r_i n_{it} \right]$$

$$= u_0 + \sum_j u_j f_{jt} + \beta f_{rt} \quad \text{where} \quad f_{jt} = \sum_i \frac{n_{it} x_{ij}}{N_t} \tag{2}$$

f_{jt}, f_{rt} are fractions of workers with characteristics j and r in town t. If the fraction of workers with characteristic m is the same in each town ($f_{mt} =$

$f_m, \forall t$) then we have

$$\bar{U}_t = (u_0 + f_m u_j) + \sum_{j \neq m} u_j f_{jt} + \beta f_{rt} \tag{3}$$

The parameter on f_{rt}, the fraction of workers in rental accommodation, is an unbiased estimate of β, and less than the estimated coefficient on being a rental tenant using individual data by γu_m. Intuitively, the reason for this is that if tenure does not exert a separate influence on unemployment, building more rental housing in a town does not alter the town's unemployment rate, even though alienated or workshy people in each town may tend to live in rental housing, and be more frequently unemployed.

Another reason for studying cross-section city-level data is to check further that the relationship between house tenure and unemployment does not arise simply from unfurnished rental housing being more common in certain locations. Initially, this was examined in Model 3, Table 2, by focussing on workers in more prosperous areas; we now consider whether the significance of the council variable reflects the location of council housing in urban areas where unemployment is generally higher. One way of approaching this is to consider only the urban sector, and study whether unemployment is greatest where rental housing is most common.

A cross-section analysis of large towns (county boroughs) in England and Wales

Unemployment is assumed to be determined by the local labour force characteristics, including the hose-tenure mix, and the recent change in the demand for labour. To ensure the predicted unemployment rate for each town is bounded by zero and one, a logit transformation is used. Thus, assuming U^h is the proportion of adult male unemployed in town h and x_i^h is the proportion of workers with characteristic i in town h

$$U^h = \left[1 + \exp - \left(\alpha_0 + \sum_1 \alpha_i x_i^h \right) \right]^{-1}$$

where $\alpha_i (i = 1 \dots k)$ are parameters to be estimated.

This equation can be rewritten in a "log odds ratio" form where the dependent variable may be interpreted as the log of the odds that a randomly selected male member of the town's working population will be unemployed.

$$\log_e \left(\frac{U^h}{1 - U^h} \right) = \alpha_0 + \sum_1^k \alpha_i x_i^h \tag{1'}$$

Since frequencies are used to construct the dependent variable, (1') will have heteroscedastic residuals. Assuming these frequencies are based on independent samples from binomial populations, the asymptotic variance of the estimator of the log odds ratio will be approximately equal to λ^h where

$\lambda^h = (U^h(1-U^h))^{-1}$. To achieve efficient parameter estimates and confidence intervals of the appropriate length, the equations were estimated using weighted least squares. Each equation was first estimated using ordinary least squares and from the predicted value of U^h an estimate of $\sqrt{\lambda^h}$ was found. (2′) was then estimated

$$\frac{\log_e (U^h/1-U^h)}{\sqrt{\lambda^h}} = \frac{\alpha_0}{\sqrt{\lambda^h}} + \sum_1^k \alpha_i \frac{x_i^h}{\sqrt{\lambda^h}} \tag{2′}$$

The variables capturing the composition of the local labour supply—age, marital status, occupation—are listed in Table 1 and are self-explanatory. Because it might be thought that council housing is greatest in towns with declining demand for labour, and this might explain the correlation between local unemployment and council housing, some care is taken with the specification of the local demand for labour. It is assumed that the supply of labour to the county borough is unchanging between 1966 and 1971, and the change in employment (ΔE), is used to proxy the change in the demand for labour. Further it is plausible to consider the possibility that the effects of an increase in the demand for labour on unemployment, differ from the effects of a *substantial* decrease, and so the interaction $\Delta E \times Z$ is included, where $Z = 1$ if the decline in employment in a city exceeds the sample average of 2.9%.

The results are described in Table 5. Column 1 contains the results of the basic model. The proportion of council tenants has a positive coefficient estimate, but the "t" statistic is 1.44 which is only significant on a one tailed test at the 10% level. The proportion of tenants in unfurnished private rental also has a positive coefficient of similar size, but it also is not significantly different from zero. Since the hypothesis that the coefficients on these two variables ae equal cannot be rejected at the 5% level (using an F test)—an important finding since it mirrors the results in Table 2—the equation is re-estimated using the proportion of workers living in unfurnished rental accommodation (either council or private) as the explanatory variable. In all regressions calcuated using tenure in this form, the parameter for the combined variable is positive and significant, generally at the 1% level. The shorter confidence intervals associated with unfurnished rental can be explained by a positive simple correlation ($r^2 = 0.34$) between the percentage of council tenants in a town and the percentage of tenants in unfurnished rental housing. In equation (3) the skill composition of the town is controlled for in more detail, but the results do not change the role of tenure and confirm a priori intuition concerning the rank correlation between each skill group and the size of its parameter estimate. In equation (4) the proportion in furnished rental is included. This has an insignificant negative coefficient.

Two basic points follow from this. First, provided each town has the same proportion of workers with unobserved characteristics that lead them to be

TABLE 5

Unemployment in large towns in England and Wales with dependent variable $\log(U/1-U)$

Variable	Summary statistics mean (std devtn)	weighted least squares estimates[1]			
		1	2	3	4
Proportion of workers in council housing (A)	0.25 (0.15)	0.560 (0.389)			
Proportion in unfurnished private rental (B)	0.10 (0.06)	0.628 (0.992)			
Proportion unfurnished tenants (A+B)	0.35 (0.19)	—	0.578 (0.210)	0.494 (0.209)	0.548 (0.230)
Proportion married	0.52 (0.03)	−1.840 (1.647)	−1.858 (1.589)	−1.230 (1.567)	−1.883 (1.669)
Proportion older than 54	0.21 (0.02)	−0.056 (1.710)	−0.030 (1.627)	−1.367 (1.667)	−0.950 (1.715)
Proportion younger than 25	0.20 (0.02)	5.567 (2.437)	5.565 (2.418)	2.693 (2.623)	3.999 (2.598)
Proportion unskilled	0.10 (0.03)	—	—	2.710 (1.72)	1.923 (1.180)
Proportion semi-skilled	0.26 (0.06)	—	—	2.530 (1.26)	—
Proportion skilled	0.35 (0.05)	−2.212 (0.991)	−2.217 (0.812)	−2.314 (0.820)	−2.508 (0.823)
Proportionate change in employment from 1966 to 1971 (ΔE)	−0.029 (0.082)	0.749 (0.812)	0.787 (0.795)	1.005 (0.775)	0.765 (0.791)
ΔE×Z	−0.044 (0.047)	−2.710 (1.174)	−2.710 (1.165)	−2.691 (1.128)	−2.550 (1.162)
Proportion in furnished private rental accommodation	−0.022 (0.016)	—	—	—	−2.959 (3.018)
Mean value of dependent variable	−3.005				
Standard error of estimate[1]		0.312	0.312	0.295	0.305

[1] Standard errors are given in parentheses. These were calculated as $[\sum(e_i-\bar{e})^2/T-K]^{-\frac{1}{2}}$ where the e_i are residuals from equations using the WLS parameter estimates but with the unweighted values of variables. T is the number of observations and K is the number of variables.

[2] The definition of Z is given by: $Z=1$ if $\Delta E < -2.9\%$ and $Z=0$, otherwise.

Source: The 1971 Census. For a similar study not concerned with housing, see Metcalf (1975).

unemployment-prone, holding constant observable characteristics such as skill level etc., then the economic and statistical significance of controlled rental tenure in Table 2 suggests that not all the effect of tenure on unemployment in individual data can be explained by the tendency of such unemployment-prone individuals to enter rental accommodation either by choice or because of being denied a mortgage. Secondly, we may compare the results in Table 5 with those in Models 1 and 2 of Table 2, which share with the data of Table 5 the common property of being drawn from both depressed and prosperous regions of the country. Comparing the two sets of coefficients on unfurnished tenancy indicates that, as expected, the coefficients found using individual data are larger—and by a factor of two—than those found from aggregate data. Part of this difference arises because in Table 2 those owning-outright are not included in the norm group. After correcting for this, unfurnished tenancy carries a coefficient of 0.74 using individual data, which remains greater than that of about 0.52 from aggregate data. A comparison of these two figures suggests that part of the estimated higher unemployment found using individual data—perhaps about one third—may be explained by tenants having non-observed personal characteristics which increase individual unemployment.

In view of this we may mark-down by one-third our estimate of unexplained higher unemployment amongst tenants in Models 1 and 2 of Table 2 from around 180% to 120%. Assuming the influence of non-observed personal characteristics on (a) tenure choice—the value of γ; and on (b) unemployment—the value of u_m—is broadly similar in prosperous regions to that in the country as a whole, ceteris paribus, we may assume that the bias in individual data, γu_m, is similar for Model 3, and mark-down the estimate for higher unemployment amongst tenants in Model 3, Table 2, by one-third from about 105% to 70%. Thus by controlling for (a) various observed characteristics, and in particular interactions between tenure and region, as well as (b) non-observed personal characteristics, the unexplained unemployment differential between tenants and mortgagees is reduced from 250% to 70%. At this point it is perhaps worth noting that the adjustment made for non-observed personal characteristics is, perhaps appropriately, about the same as that consequent upon higher job turnover amongst tenants.

Before continuing with the analysis, it is worth noting that changes in employment over the previous five years, ΔE, do have a substantial effect on local unemployment, although there would appear evidence of an asymmetry between increases and reductions in employment: a large decline in city employment $(Z = 1)$ leads to large and statistically significant increase in local unemployment, but an increase or small decline in employment has a statistically insignificant effect on unemployment.

It is reasonable to ask how far the correlation between council housing and unemployment in Table 5 is the consequence of targeting council housing at historically depressed areas. (This hypothesis cannot readily explain the similar coefficients on council and private unfurnished accommodation in Table 5). The labour demand variables, which might be thought to deal with this objection, refer to a five year period prior to 1971, and although this is sensible to explain current structural problems, it may be thought not to reflect long-term features of the local labour market. Estimates of council house stocks below regional level are not available before 1961, and so to examine the immediate post-war years, county borough council house building levels per head during the council housing boom period 1945–56 were regressed on the borough unemployment rate in

1951.[3] This relationship is not significant $(F = 0.20)$. It is also noteworthy that during the period 1945–1967, when about $\frac{2}{3}$ of the 1971 council housing stock was built, the aggregate unemployment rate did not exceed 3% and in particular, during the period 1948–1956, when about $\frac{1}{4}$ of the 1971 stock was constructed, unemployment was virtually absent, averaging about 1%. Even in the Northern region, unemployment did not exceed 2.8% until 1959, and for much of this period was less than 2.4%. Thus, in the post-war period to 1967, unemployed workers were sufficiently scarce relative to the high level of council house applicants, for it to be plausible to assume that variations in their numbers across towns probably had little influence on where council housing was built; instead variables such as the quality of the housing stock and the level of slum clearance, the proportion of manual workers in an area, and local political tendencies appear more appropriate explanatory variables.

Finally, we may consider how far council housing was targeted on high unemployment areas in the inter-war period. If the regional council house construction rates per head of population for 1919–1945 are compared with average regional unemployment rates, no correlation is found to exist.[4] Similarly no correlation exists between the regional *stock* of council dwellings in 1960 per head of population and the mean regional unemployment rate, 1947–60. Thus as recently as 1960, when $\frac{2}{3}$ of the 1971 council house stock was in place, it would have been hard to make a case that council construction had been concentrated into depressed areas: heavy building in the Midlands and North West, together with relatively little in Wales being the upsetting features.

Towards an understanding of unemployment differentials between house tenures

The analysis so far has examined the extent to which the higher unemployment amongst tenants and those owning-outright described in Table 1 can be explained by various characteristics including occupational structure, locational considerations, job turnover, or non-observed personal characteristics. If compared with a mortgagee, the probability of being unemployed for a tenant has been found to be about 70% greater, and that of an outright owner about 100% greater, ceteris paribus. How are these remaining differences to be explained? There is no compelling reason why the same argument will explain the higher unexplained unemployment amongst both tenants and owners-outright—and indeed, the data below suggests a different pattern of unemployment for the two groups—thus each of the tenure categories is considered in turn. Unfortunately the data do not allow a

[3] The unemployment data was drawn from the 1951 Census and the building figures from *Housing Return* (command 65), 1956.
[4] Further details are available from the author.

comprehensive analysis, including a suitably nested comparison of Hypotheses A and B, for renters. Nevertheless, certain indicative points can be made.

First, considering the unexplained higher unemployment of those owning-outright, there appear to be two remaining possibilities: (a) owning-outright may exert a wealth/incentive effect, along the lines described in Hypothesis B, or (b) appropriate explanatory variables have not been included or properly specified. To take this further, two experiments are described using a sample constructed as before, except that since our focus is no longer upon the influence of tenancy, both manual and non-manual workers are studied. Also a finer grid of age-dummies is added in order to check that the correlation between own-outright and unemployment does not arise from a correlation between age and owning-outright.

The results are described in Model 1 of Table 6. As can be seen, own-outright remains highly statistically significant, and in economic terms the increase in unemployment that is predicted to accompany changing from owning outright to a mortgage is equivalent to that of switching from being an unskilled manual worker to being a managerial/professional worker, all else equal. Secondly, to allow for possible interactions between the housing dummies, only workers who were buying or who owned-outright were considered in Model 2. This sharply reduces the number of unemployed from 273 to 88, and the size of the sample, so that the level of significance is reduced on several variables. However, own-outright has the expected sign, is significant at the 5% level on a one-tailed test, and in economic terms its importance for incremental unemployment is about as great as in the previous model. In terms of probabilities, owners-outright in Model 2, Table 6, are predicted to have a 70% higher probability of being unemployed than mortgagees; larger differentials have usually been found in other models.

In view of this it is perhaps reasonable to suppose that the arguments raised under hypothesis B may help explain the high unemployment of owners-outright relative to mortgagees. Furthermore, because mortgagees eventually own-outright, and have unemployment rates similar to tenants, ceteris paribus, the result also casts further doubt on the view that the remaining unexplained difference in unemployment between mortgagees and tenants is simply the consequence of an unobserved factor, such as alienation, influencing on a greater scale than has been allowed for, the likelihood of both becoming unemployed and purchasing accommodation.

Finally, we may consider the unexplained higher unemployment amongst tenants relative to mortgagees, and the extent to which a large proportion of it can be attributed to Hypothesis A. First, let us proceed under the assumption that Hypothesis A is valid: unemployment amongst tenants is a consequence of excess labour supply accumulating in localities where council housing is concentrated, rather as it is ordinarily supposed that excess labour supply explains higher unemployment in certain regions, holding constant the characteristics of the local labour force. The results in Model 1, Table 2

HOUSING AND UNEMPLOYMENT IN GREAT BRITAIN

TABLE 6
Parameter estimates of a logit model of unemployment incidence[1]

Independent variables	All manual and non-manual 1	Owner-occupied sector 2
Intercept	−4.52	−4.57
	(14.42)	(10.09)
Married	−1.06	−1.09
	(5.90)	(3.60)
Female	−1.15	−1.26
	(4.29)	(2.63)
3 or 4 dependent children	0.94	0.33
	(5.12)	(0.82)
⩾5 dependent children	1.65	*
	(5.47)	
Depressed regions[3]	0.61	0.29
	(4.52)	(1.26)
Yorks–Humberside, East Anglia	0.33	−0.27
	(1.64)	(0.68)
Age ⩽ 25	0.41	−0.08
	(1.25)	(0.10)
40 ⩽ age ⩽ 44	0.05	0.02
	(0.22)	(0.00)
45 ⩽ age ⩽ 49	0.15	−0.04
	(0.68)	(0.10)
50 ⩽ age ⩽ 54	0.06	0.26
	(0.24)	(0.64)
54 ⩽ age ⩽ 58	0.45	0.81
	(1.99)	(2.13)
59 ⩽ age ⩽ 62	0.39	0.75
	(1.59)	(1.78)
63 ⩽ age	0.60	1.31
	(2.26)	(3.06)
Own outright	0.64	0.49
	(3.00)	(1.80)
Council tenant	0.91	—
	(4.74)	
Private unfurnished tenant	0.81	—
	(3.30)	
Unearned income	5.4×10^{-5}	—
	(0.92)	
Clerical worker	0.45	0.70
	(1.63)	(2.01)
Skilled manual worker	0.45	0.78
	(1.78)	(2.39)
Semi-skilled manual worker	0.95	1.09
	(3.58)	(2.92)
Unskilled manual worker	0.63	0.45
	(2.05)	(0.81)
λ^2	206.9	64.1
DF	21	17

imply that moving from a prosperous to a depressed region, ceteris paribus, will increase the probability of being unemployed by about 85–90%; in comparison, the finding of the previous section assuming Hypothesis A, is that switching from being a mortgagee to tenancy, ceteris paribus, *within* a region moves the representative worker to a locality where the labour market is sufficiently more slack to increase the probability of being unemployed by about 70% (and as much as 100% if Model 1 of Table 2 is used). The point this raises is that it is unusual to suppose that labour market conditions vary intra-regionally for a worker with standardized characteristics, by such a great extent relative to the inter-regional variation.

The relative contribution of Hypotheses A and B may also be considered by comparing not just the level, but the pattern of higher employment amongst tenants with that of workers in depressed areas. It has already been determined that various personal considerations may increase tenants' job turnover rates, thus the comparison focusses upon the pattern of unemployment following a job separation, which may be analysed by distinguishing the probability that a job leaver moves more or less directly to a new job, q; and the duration of unemployment for those entering unemployment. Concerning the latter, both Hypotheses A and B predict that tenants will have longer unemployment durations: Hypothesis A proposes that tenants tend to live in slack labour market areas, which makes it harder to leave unemployment; Hypothesis B proposes that unemployment is perceived by tenants as less costly. However the hypotheses carry potentially conflicting implications for q: Hypothesis B suggests that tenancy encourages unemployment and reduces q; Hypothesis A suggests that tenancy is a proxy for living in a slack labour market, and thus will have a similar effect on q as living in a "depressed region". Workers in a depressed area are less likely to quit one position without first finding a new job, but an involuntary job move is less likely to result in a direct move to a new job. Thus the net effect on q of living in an area of excess labour supply is ambiguous.

Table 7 describes an analysis of whether job changers move directly to a new job. Workers who have at least 50 weeks of employment income in a year with a job change are assumed to move directly to the new job (the conclusions are not sensitive to this threshold) and the dependent variable is the logit of the probability of working at least 50 weeks conditional upon having changed employer. The coefficient on council tenancy is negative,

---

[1] Clerical: non-manual ancillary/non-manual supervisory/junior non-manual.

[2] * Indicates that there exist insufficient observations in this category for the programme to converge. Thus, the parameter for 3 or 4 dependent children represents at least 3 dependent children.

[3] Depressed regions comprise Scotland, North-West, North and Wales (see Table 1).

[4] As in the previous Tables the data is drawn from the 1973 and 1974 General Household Surveys and concerns heads of household.

[5] Assymptotic "t" ratios are given in parentheses.

[6] The sample sizes are 11,546 for Model 1 and 6550 for Model 2.

TABLE 7

Parameter estimates of a logit model of the conditional probability of working $\geqslant 50$ weeks in a year with a job change

Independent variables	Model		
	1 All manual workers	2 Skilled manual workers	3 Manual workers not in "depressed" regions
Intercept	−0.18	0.53	−0.70
	(0.42)	(1.01)	(1.17)
Married	0.57	0.49	0.93
	(1.67)	(1.01)	(1.84)
Female	0.30	0.51	0.78
	(0.74)	(0.48)	(1.33)
3 or 4 dependent children	−0.30	−0.12	−0.29
	(1.60)	(0.48)	(1.11)
$\geqslant 5$ dependent children	−1.94	−1.81	−1.27
	(3.51)	(2.30)	(2.16)
Depressed regions	−0.18	−0.27	—
	(1.17)	(1.34)	
Yorks–Humberside, East Anglia	−0.13	−0.44	−0.13
	(0.58)	(1.54)	(0.59)
Age < 25	0.26	0.50	0.17
	(0.99)	(1.48)	(0.45)
$44 \leqslant \text{age} \leqslant 53$	−0.10	−0.11	−0.14
	(0.51)	(0.42)	(0.54)
$54 \leqslant \text{age} \leqslant 60$	−0.28	−0.16	−0.54
	(1.03)	(0.40)	(1.43)
$61 \leqslant \text{age}$	−0.89	−0.61	−1.13
	(2.99)	(1.25)	(2.97)
Own outright	−0.42	−0.34	−0.046
	(1.48)	(0.84)	(0.12)
Council tenant	−0.67	−0.93	−0.76
	(3.86)	(4.22)	(3.42)
Private unfurnished tenant	−0.24	−0.36	−0.042
	(0.96)	(1.03)	(0.13)
Unearned income	−0.0086	−0.0034	−0.0013
	(0.65)	(1.71)	(0.85)
Skilled	0.44	—	0.54
	(2.01)		(1.83)
Semi-skilled	0.30	—	0.42
	(1.32)		(1.36)
Occupational pension[2]	0.27	0.17	0.68
	(1.58)	(0.72)	(3.08)
λ^2	83.2	44.2	65.37
DF	17	15	16

[1] Asymptotic "t" ratios are given in parentheses.
[2] This variable takes the value 1 if the individual held an occupational pension in their job one year prior to interview.
[3] Sample sizes are 922, 516 and 538 for Models 1, 2, 3 respectively.

large and significant in all three models, indicating that council tenants, on leaving a job, are much less likely to move directly to a new job. In contrast, the coefficient on being in a "depressed region" is rather small in size and not significantly different from zero. If these two observations are to be reconciled with the proposition that most of the higher unemployment amongst council tenants is to be explained by Hypothesis A, it must be assumed that intra-regional variations in labour market slack are substantially greater than inter-regional variations.

The implications of Model 1 for the probability, q, are given in row 3 of Table 4: amongst workers with mortgages who change jobs, one in five become unemployed; amongst council tenants, one in three do so. The evidence summarized in rows 2 and 3 of Table 4 may be combined to describe the probability that in any given year a worker will be employed for less than 50 weeks (row 4). This probability is 5.6% for council tenants, which is about twice as great as for those with mortgages.[5]

Finally, a further problem with Hypothesis A is that although the effects of council and unfurnished private tenancy on unemployment are very similar, the actual and planned regional migration activity of the two tenure groups is distinctly different (see Hughes and McCormick (1981) (1983)): whereas council tenants are less likely to migrate than owner-occupiers, as required by Hypothesis A, those renting privately have higher actual and planned migration rates than those owning houses, ceteris paribus. Local house moves are also more frequent amongst private renters than council tenants. One possible explanation for these results may be that the value of the rent subsidy to private tenants is typically less than for council tenants, whose accommodation is generally more modern and maintained to a higher standard.

IV. Conclusions

This paper has examined the relationship between the four major house tenure categories in Great Britain and the probability of being unemployed. A simple comparison of unemployment rates between tenures, for head of household manual workers who had lived in their accommodation for over one year, shows that relative to mortgagees, tenants of unfurnished accommodation—both council and private—are 250% more likely to be unemployed, and those owning outright 150% more likely to be unemployed. After allowing for various conventional characteristics, these differentials are reduced to 105% for tenants, and to 70% for those owning outright.

---

[5] There are two other features of Table 7 that are of incidental interest. First, skilled, and married workers are more likely to move directly to a new job, as are those leaving jobs with occupational pensions. Secondly, the only age category of consequence is old-workers, over 60, who are highly likely to work less than 50 weeks if they change job.

An attempt was made to check how far non-observed personal characteristics might influence both the probability of entering rental accommodation and that of becoming unemployed. Evidence from city-level data suggests that to allow for this, the differential for tenants over mortgagees might reasonably be marked down to 70%.

Why do tenants and those owning outright have about 70% higher unemployment rates than mortgagees, ceteris paribus? In the case of those owning outright, the sole remaining arguments are those under Hypothesis B, suggesting that these workers have a 70% higher "natural rate" of unemployment than mortgagees. Perhaps the especially important influences are the role of wealth, and the absence for those owning outright of short term liquidity pressures provoked by the need to meet mortgage payments.

In the case of renters, who comprise over half the sample, it has been argued that Hypothesis A—labour markets become more slack in those parts of a region where council housing is concentrated—may not plausibly explain a large proportion of the residual effect of tenancy on unemployment, nevertheless it is hard to dispute that a fraction—tentatively in a range of one tenth to one half—of the higher unemployment of tenants might be accounted for in this way. Thus after allowing for the intraregional slack reflected in the tenancy variable, the unexplained higher unemployment of tenants, relative to mortgagees (35–63%) is somewhat less than that of owners-outright (70%); with the remaining differentials in both instances being tentatively attributed to differences in the "natural rate" of unemployment for the various groups, Hypothesis B.

What do these findings suggest concerning the social security system towards unemployment? Any system which provided extreme incentives to certain classes of workers to become unemployed—especially one based on tenure, which is only loosely linked to life-cycle income—would be undesirable. If social security policy is to have effects on unemployment over the life-cycle which are neutral between workers entering the rental and owner-occupied sectors, then concomitantly, the effect of tenancy on unemployment, holding constant personal characteristics and labour market slack, must lie between the effect of having a mortgage and that of owning outright. The evidence here suggests that we can be reasonably sure this is the case, even if some of the more contestable judgements are moderately relaxed. Although it is important for policy purposes to recognise the concentration of unemployment into rental estates—for example, in improving the location of "Job Centres", and eliminating artificial barriers to mobility—it is plausible to tentatively conclude that the higher unemployment amongst tenants simply reflects a combination of locational and demographic characteristics together with a public policy towards unemployment incentives which is reasonably neutral between workers entering the rental or owner-occupied sector. Comparisons such as those in Table 1 are critical for motivating certain policy developments, but on closer inspection cannot be interpreted as evidence that social security policy towards renters is patently generous.

University of Southampton

APPENDIX

Sample

The sample consists of heads of households interviewed in the General Household Survey of 1973–74 who were members of the labour force but excluding those sick without jobs who were not searching for a new job. These respondents were all manual workers who have lived in their present accommodation for at least one year. The small percentage of workers in furnished rental accommodation were excluded. This leaves 6825 observations.

BIBLIOGRAPHY

HALL, R. E. (1972), "Turnover in the Labour Force", Brookings Papers on Economic Activity, pp. 709–762.

HUGHES, G. (1979), "Housing Income and Subsidies", *Fiscal Studies*, pp. 20–38.

HUGHES, G., and McCORMICK, B. (1981), "Do Council Housing Policies reduce migration between regions?" *Economic Journal*, December, pp. 919–937.

HUGHES, G. and McCORMICK, B. (1983), "Actual and potential migration in Great Britain", Southampton University Discussion Paper No. 8310.

METCALF, D. (1975), "Urban Unemployment in England", *Economic Journal*, September, pp. 578–89.

NICKELL, S. (1980), "A picture of male unemployment in Britain", *Economic Journal*, December, pp. 776–794.

THE REAPPEARING PHILLIPS CURVE

By M. T. SUMNER *and* R. WARD*

Introduction

THE object of this paper is to test the hypothesis that the process of wage inflation in the UK has been generated by a stable structure over the period 1958–80. The model used for this purpose is the operational version of the expectations-augmented excess demand hypothesis formulated and tested by Parkin, Sumner and Ward (1976), hereafter PSW. Their fitting period terminated in 1971. Since then both inflation and their excess demand proxy, the unemployment rate, have risen to levels that were scarcely imaginable in the quarter century following World War II. The collapse of the Bretton Woods system which conditioned earlier behaviour has been followed by a decade of unprecedented and unpredictable volatility of exchange rates. Successive governments have made repeated attempts to influence wage determination through persuasion or direct controls. Supply shocks, virtually ignored since Jevons' failure to relate the business cycle to sun-spots, have re-entered the vocabulary of macroeconomics after an unusually painful episode of learning by losing. Other behavioural functions, though subject to only some sub-set of these changes in the economic environment, have proved to be extremely unreliable guides to conditions in the 1970s, however distinguished their intellectual parentage and their in-sample performance.

In general the model performs rather better when fitted to the extended sample, which permits more precise determination of the parameters, than in the original estimation period. The qualitative conclusions are identical: the trade-off between wage inflation and unemployment is negatively sloped in the short run but vanishes in the long run; and it remains extremely difficult to identify successful attempts to moderate the pace of wage inflation by government edict. The stability tests are, however, ambiguous. Post-sample forecasting performance is satisfactory, but the results suggest that a shift took place during the estimation period in either the structure of the wage equation itself, or in the subsidiary relation between employees' expectations and their observable proxies. Either interpretation leaves little or no scope for a shift in the relation between unemployment and excess demand for labour.

An expectations-augmented excess demand model

The distinguishing feature of the PSW model is its range of expectational variables which derives from the difference between the product wage paid by employers and the real wage received by employees. The product wage

*We are grateful to A. J. Buxton, L. N. Christofides, S. G. B. Henry, M. Parkin, R. L. Thomas, G. Zis, the editors and referees for comments on earlier drafts. Remaining errors and omissions are our own responsibility.

includes employers' social security contributions paid at rate t_e on the
nominal wage W, and is deflated by the wholesale price which firms receive
for their output, P_e. Employees pay income tax and social security contributions at the effective rate t_c, and their real wage is defined in terms of the
retail price index, P_c. Demand for and supply of labour are most conveniently assumed to be log-linear functions of the product wage and real
wage respectively,

$$D = D\left[\frac{W(1+t_e)}{P_e}\right]^{-\alpha}$$

$$S = S\left[\frac{W(1-t_c)}{P_c}\right]^{\beta}$$

When wage rates are under negotiation, the tax rates and price levels which
will obtain during the currency of the agreement are not known but must be
predicted; their expected values are denoted by the superscript e.

The behavioural assumption of the model is that wages are fixed so as to
reduce any existing excess demand for labour, and to offset any predicted
changes in economic conditions which would disequilibrate the labour
market in the foreseeable future. Using the approximation

$$\log(1+X) \simeq X,$$

proportionate excess demand is represented as

$$X = (D-S)/S$$
$$= \log D - \log S.$$

The expected change in excess demand is therefore given by

$$\Delta X^e = -\alpha(w + T_e^e - p_e^e) - \beta(w + R_c^e - p_c^e)$$

where lower-case letters denote the proportionate rates of change of wages
or prices, T_e^e is the anticipated change in employers' social security contributions, and

$$R_c^e = \log((1-t_c^e)/(1-t_c))$$

is the anticipated rate of change of the retention ratio.[1] After substituting
the behavioural assumption

$$\Delta X^e = -\theta X,$$

rearrangement yields

$$w = \frac{\theta}{\alpha+\beta} X + \frac{\alpha}{\alpha+\beta} p_e^e + \frac{\beta}{\alpha+\beta} p_c^e - \frac{\alpha}{\alpha+\beta} T_e^e - \frac{\beta}{\alpha+\beta} R_c^e$$

The rate of change of wages depends on excess demand for labour, the
inflation rates anticipated by firms and households with coefficients that sum

[1] $T_e^e = \log(1+t_e^e) - \log(1+t_e) \simeq \Delta t_e^e$, and $R_c^e \simeq -\Delta t_c^e$.
In the absence of anticipated changes in statutory tax rates and allowances, the expected change
in the average tax rate (Δt_c^e) is the difference between marginal and average tax rates, weighted
by the expected growth of income.

to unity, and a similarly weighted average of the tax changes anticipated by employers and employees.

In the original application of the model wage inflation was measured as the annualised quarter-on-quarter change in weekly wage rates.[2] Excess demand for labour was proxied by a moving average of the unemployment rate, U, and tax change anticipations by actual tax changes. The anticipated inflation rates were constructed from qualitative survey data using the method suggested by Carlson and Parkin (1975). This procedure allows the relation between actual and expected magnitudes to be determined by the data rather than assumption.

The unrestricted estimate of this equation, reproduced in the first column of Table 1, yielded two important conclusions. First, the distinction between actual and anticipated magnitudes was critical: the properly measured price expectations performed much better than actual tax changes, which were insignificant and in the employees' case incorrectly signed; and the substitution of actual for anticipated inflation produced markedly inferior results. Secondly, the coefficient restrictions directly implied by the model could not be rejected. In the long run when expectations are fully adjusted, there is no trade-off between inflation and unemployment. Furthermore, when the restrictions were imposed the coefficient on unemployment became significant.

With the exception of Henry (1981) most criticism has focused on the statistical results, particularly the high standard error of the unemployment coefficient in the unrestricted estimates; and it has been suggested that this partial relation would collapse if the fitting period were extended beyond 1971. The remainder of the paper is devoted to these issues.

The extended sample

The fitting period used in the experiments reported below runs from the third quarter of 1958, when CBI (then FBI) survey data on firms' price expectations first became available,[3] to the end of 1980. Gallup data on household price expectations are not available in a consistent form for the whole of this period;[4] instead the inflation anticipated by employees is proxied by the actual rate of change of retail prices, denoted by p, with a one-quarter delay to minimise simultaneity problems. Two other small changes were made to the PSW specifications: their distinction between firms' price expectations in home and export markets, which was initially

---

[2] Precise definitions and sources are given in the Data Appendix.

[3] PSW extended their sample by 'backcasting' with their fitted expectations functions.

[4] The subject of the Gallup question was changed from the level of prices to the inflation rate during the sample period. Apart from the splicing problem, which is being examined by R. A. Batchelor, the proportion of survey respondents who expected prices to fall was frequently negligible during the 1970s, with consequent difficulties for applying the Carlson–Parkin method.

TABLE 1
Wage inflation

Equation estimation period	1 1956(2)–1971(4)	2 1958(3)–	3 1980(4)	4 1958(3)–1970(4)	5 1971(1)–1980(4)	6 1958(3)–	7 1980(4)
Intercept	3.98 (2.00)	3.20 (2.50)	4.00 (3.72)	5.46 (2.74)	11.56 (2.22)	4.64 (4.63)	5.68 (5.73)
U	−0.64 (0.70)	−0.40 (0.81)	−0.99 (2.37)	−1.03 (0.93)	−1.90 (2.66)	−1.09 (2.74)	−1.29 (3.30)
p_e^e	0.40+0.13 (2.06) (0.55)	0.72 (5.03)	0.74 (6.17)	0.71 (5.92)	0.56 (2.04)	0.76 (6.71)	0.65 (5.63)
p_c^e	0.33 (1.06)						
p		0.19 (1.55)	0.24 (2.42)	−0.14 (1.26)	0.20 (1.32)	0.20 (2.04)	
p^*							0.31 (3.25)
T_e	−0.30 (0.59)	−0.25 (1.50)	−0.25 (1.75)	−0.01 (0.12)	−0.29 (1.06)	−0.23 (1.69)	−0.23 (1.78)
R_c	0.11 (0.44)	−0.38 (1.98)	−0.41 (2.52)	0.31 (1.65)	−0.61 (2.66)		
R_c^*						−0.68 (3.93)	−0.65 (3.86)
D			29.00 (6.09)		29.29 (4.87)	29.09 (6.42)	29.69 (6.78)
$\bar{R}^2$	0.48	0.51	0.68	0.50	0.51	0.69	0.71
DW	1.64	1.42	1.15	1.54	1.15	1.16	1.30
$F_1(7,76)$			3.40				1.30
$F_2(6,83)$			0.48				0.58

[1] *t*-ratios in parentheses.
[2] In equation (1) the two p_e^e coefficients refer to expected price changes in home and export markets respectively. The two insignificant dummy variables used by PSW to represent incomes policies in 1961–62 and 1966–67 have been omitted.
[3] F_1 tests for stability between 1958(3)–70(4) and 1971(1)–80(4), F_2 between 1958(3)–80(4) and 1981(1)–82(2). The 5% critical values are 2.13 and 2.21 respectively.

incorporated but turned out to be insignificant, was dropped; and a one-quarter lag on T_e was found to produce a marginal improvement in its performance. As in the original study seasonal dummies were insignificant both individually and in combination, and were therefore eliminated.

The results reported in the second column of Table 1 are very similar to those of PSW. The sum of the price coefficients remains close to unity, though the weights have shifted towards employers. Both fiscal variables perform better in the extended sample, with correct signs and higher *t*-ratios, though their sum is still less than expected. The coefficient on unemployment is rather lower than before, and it remains insignificant. The most notable feature of the extended period, however, is not the regression results but the behaviour of the data, particularly on the dependent variable. Almost 30% of the residual sum of squares is accounted for by the second

THE REAPPEARING PHILLIPS CURVE

quarter of 1978, when the annualised rate of wage inflation jumped from an average of 6.3% in the preceding four quarters to 36.8%, then fell to an average of 11.5% in the following four quarters. Although the remainder of the wage change series is noisy, there is no remotely comparable episode.

Reasons for this eccentric behaviour will be suggested at a later stage. For the present the outlier is simply neutralised by including a dummy variable,

$$D = \begin{cases} 1 \text{ in } 1978(2) \\ 0 \text{ elsewhere} \end{cases}$$

in the estimating equation. The results of removing this distorting influence are shown in equation (3) of Table 1. All the variables are now significant, and the sum of the inflation coefficients is almost exactly unity. The use of the actual rates of change of retail prices and taxes as proxies for the corresponding expectations does not appear to bias their coefficients to anything like the extent found by PSW; this contrast is sufficiently striking, particularly for employees' taxes and inflation, to warrant further examination.

In a series of experiments on various sub-periods, illustrated by equations (4) and (5), the employees' tax change variable R_c never appeared with the correct sign or attained significance in periods ending as late as 1970, and never failed to appear with the correct sign and a significant coefficient in periods starting in 1971 or later. Accordingly zero values were imposed on R_c until end-1970 and the equation was re-estimated for the full period, with the results shown in equation (6). The coefficient on the truncated variable, denoted by R_c^*, and its t-ratio are raised; the sum of the tax coefficients is now very close to unity; the effect on the remaining variables and on the overall goodness of fit is minor. If the deleted values of R_c are added as a separate variable its coefficient remains incorrectly signed and insignificant.

Similar but more extensive experiments were carried out on the entry of the retail price inflation rate, p. It was split at four-quarter intervals ranging from end-1963 to end-1971, and included as two separate variables in regressions on the full sample. In terms of overall fit, the insignificance of the earlier values, the significance of the later ones, and the stability of their coefficient, the best dating of the split was at end-1969. This conclusion was confirmed by entering p at alternative dates in regressions terminating at end-1970: permitting only the last four values of p to be non-zero improved the fit, and yielded a correctly signed and significant coefficient on p itself, whereas it was perversely signed when introduced at any earlier date. Attempts to phase p in gradually were unsuccessful.[5] The results for the full

---

[5] During the revision of this paper our attention was drawn to a study by Patterson (1982), who models the breakdown of money illusion as a Markov process and infers that the transition to 'rational' wage determination was concentrated in the period 1969–72. For reasons discussed later, the results of the truncation exercise seem to us more plausibly interpeted as a change in the expectations variable than as a change in its coefficient.

period with retail price inflation truncated at end-1969, denoted by p^*, are reported as equation (7) in Table 1. The unemployment coefficient is now noticeably higher in absolute value than in equation (3), and the relative coefficients on the two price expectations are closer to those found by PSW.

Equations (3) and (7) both yield satisfactory post-sample predictions, as indicated by the F-tests recorded in the last row of Table 1; but their performance within the estimation period, tested in the penultimate row, differs markedly. In view of the contrast between the two sub-periods shown by equations (4) and (5), it is scarcely surprising that equation (3) fails the stability test; whereas the F-value becomes insignificant when the insignificant employees' price and tax change anticipations are suppressed in the first sub-period. The intriguing question that then arises is whether the belated emergence of the predicted relationship between these variables and wage inflation reflected a jump in their coefficients, signifying the breakdown of fiscal and money illusions and of the wage equation itself, or shifts in the mechanisms of expectations formation towards closer conformity with actual tax and price changes.

This question has a direct bearing on the calculation of the natural unemployment rate, discussed in a later section, and on its variations over time. Equation (7) clearly indicates that there was no long-run trade-off after 1970, but its implications for the earlier part of the period hinge on the interpretation of p^* and R_c^*. If their irrelevance to wage determination in the 1960s is ascribed to a zero coefficient or to employees' failure to form non-zero expectations, there was simply no natural unemployment rate; but if it merely reflects a weak association between actual and anticipated magnitudes the interpretation of the results becomes more complicated, for if employees' expectations were in fact influencing wage changes throughout, their omission in the earlier part of the period must be disguising some other unfavourable shift in the equation.

A zero coefficient on employees' anticipations during the first sub-period seems the least satisfactory interpretation of equation (7), for it would merely transform the problem to that of explaining why expectations were formed for the purpose of being ignored in wage negotiations. To discriminate between the remaining possibilities, zero (or more generally, constant) expectations and mismeasurement of expected by actual magnitudes, requires direct evidence on household anticipations during the 1960s, which for inflation is available in the form of the Carlson–Parkin series.

They themselves concluded that

'when inflation is rapid, expectations approximate a second-order error-learning process, whilst when inflation is mild [i.e. until mid-1967], expectations approximate an autoregressive scheme' (Carlson and Parkin, 1975).

The weak association which this statement implies between actual and expected inflation for the 1960s as a whole is confirmed by an insignificant correlation of 0.2 between their series, extended by 'backcasting', and p

during 1958–69. The evident inaccuracy of employees' anticipations does not, however, exclude the possibility that they exerted an influence on wage fixing. The Carlson–Parkin series was therefore included orthogonally with p^* in further regressions over the full sample period and as a replacement for p over the sub-period ending in 1970, in an attempt to smooth out the abrupt change in employees' behaviour suggested by equation (7). In neither experiment did it attract even a weakly significant coefficient.

Constancy of employees' inflation expectations up to 1970 therefore emerges as the least implausible explanation of the results in Table 1, at least when the first two, relatively turbulent years of the PSW sample are eliminated. Whether anticipations were effectively constant at zero, as assumed so far, or at some higher level is a question considered in a later section.

Other influences on wage inflation

It will not have escaped the reader's attention that the Durbin–Watson statistics of all the equations for the full period lie below the lower bound. The serial correlation of the residuals has clearly not been induced by truncating p and R_c, for equations (2) and (3) are also contaminated; nor is it a consequence of combining two fundamentally different processes of wage determination before and after 1971, for, as equations (4) and (5) indicate, the problem appears in both sub-periods. It can be eliminated by applying a first-order Cochrane–Orcutt transformation without producing drastic changes in the parameter estimates of their significance; for example, when estimated by GLS equation (7) becomes

$$w = 5.11 - 1.10U + 0.76p_e^e + 0.18p_c^* - 0.20T_e - 0.58R_c^* + 29.01D$$
$$\quad\;(2.15)\quad (5.54)\quad (1.82)\quad (1.62)\quad (3.95)\quad\;\;(7.71)$$
$$\bar{R}^2 = 0.75 \qquad \text{DW} = 1.75 \qquad\qquad\qquad (8)$$

It would be preferable, however, to remove the serial correlation by explanation rather than elimination.

A search for an explanation in terms of the form and content of the excess demand mapping proved fruitless. An exhaustive attempt to detect non-linearities in the response of wage inflation to unemployment produced inferior results to those of the linear version presented above. No remotely significant role for the rate of change of unemployment could be isolated. Finally, extensive trials incorporating the lagged real wage failed to produce results of any consequence. Whether deflated by the wholesale or retail price index, measured gross or net of tax, and entered alone or in combination with a time trend, the real wage remained stubbornly insignificant, was incorrectly signed much more often than not, made little difference to the other parameters and none to their significance.

An alternative possibility that requires examination is that the low Durbin–Watson statistics in Table 1 reflect the successive imposition and relaxation of incomes policies. No econometric support has been advanced for the hypothesis that direct controls can have a lasting effect on the wage inflation rate or even the wage level; but several investigators have reported some success for incomes policies in rephasing wage inflation. Wages sometimes, though by no means always, rise less rapidly than they otherwise would have done while controls are in operation, but catch up the lost ground when the controls are relaxed. Failure to allow for such a rephasing effect need not bias the parameter estimates, but it could induce serial correlation of the residuals.

Previous studies give little guidance as to which particular policy episodes are worth considering, for the dating of 'successes' appears to move forward with the estimation period. For example, in a sequence of investigations into the real wage bargaining model, the single success identified changes from the Freeze and Severe Restraint of 1966–67 in 1948–74 (Henry, Sawyer and Smith, 1976), through the Phase 1 Freeze of 1972–73 in 1961–77 (Henry and Ormerod, 1978), to the Social Contract (Phases 1 and 2) of 1975–77 in 1963–78 (Henry, 1981). The absence of consistent results is unfortunate, for the only gap in the chronology of incomes policies between July 1961 and March 1979 occurred from August 1971 to September 1972 (Fallick and Elliott, 1981, Appendix); it is therefore impossible to investigate all the possibilities. Instead a separate dummy was specified for any policy episode which had been identified as successful in any recent study, or which had not been investigated previously. The (no doubt impressionistic) list which emerged consisted of 1966(3)–67(2), 1972(4)–73(1), 1975(3)–76(2), 1976(3)–77(2), 1977(3)–78(2), and 1978(3)–79(1). For obvious reasons no allowance was made for catch-up.[6]

Many of the coefficients were incorrectly signed, and only one, on the 1976(3)–77(2) dummy, was significantly negative. How much of its success is attributable to Phase 2 of the Social Contract *per se*, and how much to an expectational jolt, administered by the fiscal and monetary package that earned the IMF's seal of approval but unrecorded in p_c^*, must remain a matter for conjecture. Whatever its source, the timing of this success accounts for the otherwise inexplicable jump in the rate of wage inflation in 1978(2), when catch-up proved too strong a force to be contained by Phase 3.

Table 2 repeats the full-period regression with the inclusion of an incomes policy dummy for 1976(3)–77(2), denoted by *I*. The earlier conclusions

---

[6] Even when attention is confined to a smaller number of policy episodes, the inclusion of catch-up dummies, each conventionally as long as the policy dummy which preceded it, can lead to unintentional overlap and consequential problems of interpretation. For example, in one of his experiments Henry (1981, Table 2.5) found that the policy operating in 1967(3)–69(2), usually dismissed as a weak successor to Freeze and Severe Restraint, was correctly signed, marginally significant and not wiped out by catch-up. This favourable impression is, however, heavily qualified when allowance is made for the highly significant catch-up from the Freeze and Severe Restraint in 1967(3)–68(2). Over the whole interval 1966(3)–71(2), the two policies and associated catch-up are credited with an *increase* in wage rates of 95 per cent!

TABLE 2
Effect of incomes policy

Equation	9	10	11	12
Intercept	2.47	3.30	3.82	4.86
	(2.11)	(3.40)	(4.21)	(5.44)
U	−0.14	−0.73	−0.82	−1.02
	(0.33)	(1.94)	(2.28)	(2.90)
p_e^e	0.81	0.82	0.83	0.73
	(6.16)	(7.59)	(8.16)	(7.03)
p	0.18	0.24	0.20	
	(1.66)	(2.62)	(2.29)	
p^*				0.30
				(3.57)
T_e	−0.26	−0.26	−0.24	−0.24
	(1.71).	(2.03)	(1.98)	(2.09)
R_c	−0.28	−0.31		
	(1.57)	(2.14)		
R_c^*			−0.57	−0.55
			(3.69)	(3.64)
I	−11.97	−10.74	−10.28	−10.13
	(4.37)	(4.76)	(4.78)	(4.91)
D		27.28	27.45	28.03
		(6.41)	(6.78)	(7.21)
$\bar{R}^2$	0.59	0.73	0.75	0.77
DW	1.83	1.54	1.53	1.72

Note: the estimation period is 1958(3)–80(4) throughout.

regarding the truncation of employees' price and tax change variables are unaffected, there are no dramatic changes in the other parameters, and the Durbin–Watson statistic reaches the top of the inconclusive range. Three-quarters of the reduction in the level of wages effected by Phase 2 was restored during a single quarter.

No doubt there are more elaborate patterns of dummy variable which would improve the statistical results still further. There is no reason to suppose that intervention has a uniform impact on wage inflation throughout the formal life of an incomes policy; and a more thorough search would identify other periods in which otherwise inexplicable jumps in the inflation rate could be construed as evidence of catch-up. Further elaboration could not, however, change the results substantially, and it would inevitably arouse disputes on points of insignificant detail. Most incomes policies have failed to make any detectable impact; one episode disrupted the pattern of wage inflation that would otherwise have been observed, but its net effects are small and uncertain.

The natural rate of unemployment

The sum of the cofficients on anticipated inflation is close to unity in all the regressions estimated on the full sample. The same is true of the

TABLE 3
Homogeneity tests

Equation	13	14	15
Estimation method	OLS	GLS	OLS
Intercept	5.74	5.19	4.89
	(5.87)		(5.50)
U	−1.41	−1.29	−0.96
	(4.82)	(3.23)	(3.49)
p_e^e	0.68	0.81	0.71
	(7.37)	(8.50)	(8.59)
p^*	0.32	0.19	0.29
	—	—	—
T_e	−0.28	−0.29	−0.32
	(2.67)	(3.10)	(3.38)
R_c^*	−0.72	−0.71	−0.68
	—	—	—
I			−9.79
			(4.85)
D	29.96	29.27	28.00
	(6.95)	(7.78)	7.27)
$\bar{R}^2$	0.71	0.75	0.77
DW	1.32	1.77	1.71
F	0.28	0.94	0.72
U^*	3.1	3.0	3.7

Notes:
[1] The estimation period is 1958(3)–80(4) throughout.
[2] F tests the dual homogeneity restrictions on the expected inflation and tax change coefficients. The 5% critical value is (approximately) 3.10.
[3] U^* is the estimated natural rate of unemployment; see text for discussion.

tax-change coefficients when the employees' series is truncated. Table 3 shows the results of imposing the price and tax constraints separately on the preferred specifications. Whether the distorting effects of incomes policy are ignored, eliminated by transformation or included makes no difference: in no case can the homogeneity constraints be rejected. Whatever interpretation is put on the truncation procedure, the results constitute strong evidence that there was no long-run trade-off in the 1970s.

Assuming that prices are set as if by a mark-up on unit labour costs, that there are no changes in any tax rates and no other sources of divergence between p_e^e and p^*, and that output per person employed grows at its post-1970 average rate of 1.32 per cent per annum, the natural rate of unemployment lies between 3 and 4 per cent depending on the precise specification, as shown in the last row of Table 3. With employers' and employees' tax rates both rising at their post-1970 average rates, the rate of wage change rises by about 0.7 percentage points, *ceteris paribus*; the corresponding estimates of the natural unemployment rate are clustered around 4 per cent.

If the results of the truncation experiments are interpreted as evidence of money illusion or of a persistent belief in price (and tax-rate) stability during the first half of the period, there was no natural rate before 1970 but rather a negatively sloped long-run trade-off. Suppose, however, that employees' inflation and tax-change expectations were constant but not zero up to 1970; the imposition of zero values in the truncation experiments would then be concealing a rise in the natural rate between 1969 and 1971, when employees' expectations entered explicitly. An upper bound on the implied increase in the natural rate can be set by assuming that expectations were correct on average during 1958–69. Using the coefficients of Table 3 and the mean values of p and R_c to end-1969, employees' expectations would have contributed about 1.5 percentage points, incorporated in the intercept, to the rate of wage inflation. The 'true' intercept therefore shifted upwards by the same amount between the sixties and seventies, raising the natural unemployment rate in the process by an amount ranging between 1.1 (equation (14)) and 1.8 (equation (15)) percentage points.

These estimates, though far smaller than some of the alternatives currently available,[7] are maxima derived from extreme and implausible assumptions. In particular, the supposition that employees' expectations were correct on average, during a period when the rate of change of retail prices rose fom 0.8 per cent per annum in the first two years to 5.2 per cent in the last two, is not easy to accept. Any more moderate assumption would, of course, scale down the implicit rise in the natural unemployment rate *pari passu*.

The factors which forced expectations into line with a changed reality, or alternatively which dissipated the remnants of money illusion, are a matter for speculation. Our failure to detect any evidence that p and R_c attained their full influence on wage determination only gradually suggests some kind of shock to the bargaining process, or to the expectations of half the participants in that process. One possible candidate is a change in the rate of inflation itself. Carlson and Parkin attribute the break they detected in the expectations–formation mechanism to a shift from 'low' to 'high' inflation; but in a longer perspective it was not until 1969, rather than 1967, that inflation moved above the range experienced since the end of the Korean War and conceivably stimulated a 'change of gear' in Flemming's (1976) terminology. Alternatively the collapse of the Bretton Woods system might reasonably be held, for reasons surveyed by Sumner and Zis (1982), to have changed the relation betwen expectations and experience. The final collapse occurred after the appearance of employees' inflation expectations in our

---

[7] See especially Minford (1983), but also Sumner (1978). Note that both impose homogeneity throughout their sample.

wage equation; but by the end of the 1960s evidence was already accumulating that the devaluation of sterling was only the first in a series of
disturbances to the postwar structure of fixed exchange rates, which by
limiting the scope for and duration of variations in national inflation rates
had served as an anchor for expectations. Whether it is possible to discriminate between these potential explanations, which are not of course independent, is far from clear.

The reasons for the change in the performance of employees' tax changes
are even less apparent; but two developments during the period are at least
suggestive. First, personal allowances were seldom adjusted, despite the
acceleration of price change; and the adjustments that were made, in 1965
and 1969, did not compensate for even the current year's inflation. In
consequence the real tax threshold facing a representative family had fallen
14 per cent from its 1963 peak by 1979. Thereafter nominal adjustments
were larger and more frequent, but by then awareness of the tax system may
have been built into employees' negotiating stance. Secondly the reduced
rates of tax were abolished in 1969 and 1970, thus increasing the significance of the (then) standard rate of income tax. The consequence of these
two developments was that half of the increase in effective tax rates which
took place during 1958(3)–70(4) was concentrated in the last three years of
the period.

It would not be surprising if these changes in the fiscal environment and in
the experience of and prospects for inflation altered the process of wage
determination. If they are as important as our results suggest they certainly
warrant more systematic investigation than is feasible within the confines of
the present paper.

Conclusions

There is a well determined short-run trade-off between wage inflation and
unemployment which appears to have been stable over the period examined
in this paper. At the mean of unemployment its slope is close to the value of
-1.05 implicit in Phillips' (1958) original estimate, though there is no
evidence of the non-linearity which he reported. This partial Phillips curve is
augmented by tax and price change expectations which dominate the behaviour of wage inflation in the long run. The evidence against a long-run
trade-off during the last decade is overwhelming, but in the earlier part of
the period the results do not permit sharp discrimination between the
'money illusion' and 'inaccurate expectations' hypotheses. The former would
imply a shift in the structure of wage determination, but one associated with
the expectational augmentation of the Phillips curve rather than the relation
between unemployment and excess demand for labour. The latter would
imply a shift in the auxiliary relation between actual and expected magnitudes which, depending on the degree of inaccuracy assumed in the first
sub-period, could conceal a shift in the short-run Phillips curve itself.

The resolution of this ambiguity is one of the outstanding questions posed by this investigation. The other is the relative importance of the two sides of the labour market in the wage inflation process. The price coefficients accord employers a weight of two-thirds or more and employees one-third or less, while the tax coefficients reverse these proportions; in the PSW formulation they should be identical. Obvious possibilities for examination include differences in the distribution of tax and price change expectations around their means, different responses to legislated and automatic increases in tax rates, alternative assumptions regarding the income bracket of the representative tax payer, and constraints on the rapidity with which employers can pass higher social security charges backwards without reducing wage levels. Alternatively, the discrepancy may simply reflect data deficiencies, for if employees' inflation expectations are more closely related to employers' anticipations than to actual inflation, the coefficients on p_e^e and p^* would assign too little weight to employees. That possibility has obvious implications for the pre-1970 period, for any suspicion of money illusion would not then be confined to employees.

It is sometimes alleged that the inclusion of employers' price expectations raises a more fundamental problem than that of determining the relative importance of the two sides of the labour market. CBI respondents are presumably well aware of wage changes taking place currently and of those likely to be negotiated in the near future; if they determine their prices by adding a mark-up to labour costs, the model is bound to fit well even if wages are determined by a quite different process than that postulated, perhaps by the

'numbers trade union leaders pick out of the air when they make wage claims' (Wiles, 1973)

The general point that any set of results can be interpreted in many different ways is incontestable. The difficulty with this particular version is that it leaves nothing for the other variables of the model to explain, but they consistently make significant contributions to the results. Employers' price expectations are certainly a powerful influence on wage inflation, but they do not dominate the estimating equation.

From the standpoint of the policy maker the only agreeable features of the results are that the natural unemployment rate is not as high as some other recent estimates suggest, and the response of wage inflation to unemployment does not appear to diminish as unemployment increases. On the other hand, the response is already slow enough to make the reduction of inflation a painfully protracted process. There is no evidence that the pace of wage change responds to short-run changes in the rate of productivity growth, so the initial effects of deflation may be perverse. Apart from their indirect effects operating through the excess demand for labour, tax increases exert a direct impact on wage changes which severely limits their usefulness as a weapon of anti-inflationary policy. Finally, the only incomes policy which achieved a significant impact on the rate of wage increase was accompanied by a highly publicised and externally sanctioned deflationary package; their concurrence makes it impossible to disentangle their separate contributions to moderating wage inflation, but the restraint was in any case short-lived and subsequently offset by catch-up.

University of Sussex
University of Salford

DATA APPENDIX

The data used is quarterly, 1958 quarter (3) to 1982 quarter (2).

Abbreviations:

BLS: *British Labour Statistics, Historical Abstract*, HMSO, 1971.
DEG: Department of Employment *Gazette* (monthly).
AAS: *Annual Abstract of Statistics.*

Definitions:

$w = \log [W_t/W_{t-1}] \times 400$, where W is the quarterly average of the monthly observations of the UK index of weekly wage rates of all workers, all industries. (*Source*: BLS and DEG).

$U =$ four-quarter moving average, lagged two quarters, of the quarterly average of monthly observations of the registered total wholly unemployed in Great Britain, expressed as a percentage of the total number of employees, employed and unemployed, in Great Britain. (*Source*: BL and DEG).

$p_c = \log [P_{t-1}/P_{t-2}] \times 400$, where P is the quarterly average of the monthly UK general index of retail prices (all items). (*Source*: BLS and DEG).

$p_e^e =$ firms' average expectation of the future rate of change of their own wholesale domestic prices, expressed at an annual percentage rate. (*Source*: this series was derived from responses to the CBI Industrial Trends Survey according to the method described in Carlson and Parkin (1975); for (1972(1) to 1980(4) the series is contemporaneous with the surveys, but from June 1958 to September 1971 the survey was tri-annual and quarterly observations over this period were obtained by linear interpolation).

$T_e = \log [(1+t_e)/(1+t_e)_{-1}] \times 400$ where T_e is the total national insurance contribution (flat rate plus graduated) paid by employers with respect to each adult male worker, not contracted out of the scheme, earning the average adult male manual worker's wage, expressed as a proportion of that wage. (*Sources*: contribution rates from AAS. Quarterly average wage derived by interpolation from April and October figures for average weekly earnings of all adult male manual workers obtained from BLS and DEG. From 1958(3) to 1962(4) simple linear interpolation was used. From 1963(1) use was made of the monthly index of average earnings of all workers from BLS and DEG to estimate the movements of average weekly earnings between the bi-annual figures. From 1970 onwards the April observation is taken from the New Earnings Survey and refers to the earnings of all male adult manual workers).

$R_e = \log [(1-t_e)/(1-t_e)_{-1}] \times 400$, where t_e is the total national insurance contribution (flat rate plus graduated) paid by each male adult employee, not contracted out of the scheme, plus the total income tax payable by a married man with two children (one aged under 11 years and the other aged between 11 and 16 years) claiming no other allowances and earning the average adult male manual worker's wage, expressed as a proportion of that wage. (*Source*: as for T_e).

REFERENCES

CARLSON, J. A. and PARKIN, M. (1975), Inflation Expectations, *Economica*, N.S. *42*, 123–38.

FALLICK, J. L. and ELLIOTT, R. F. (eds.) (1981), *Incomes Policies, Inflation and Relative Pay*, Allen and Unwin, London.

FLEMMING, J. (1976), *Inflation*, Oxford University Press.

HENRY, S. G. B. (1981), Incomes Policy and Aggregate Pay, in Fallick and Elliott.

HENRY, S. G. B. and ORMEROD, P. A. (1978), Incomes Policy and Wage Inflation: Empirical Evidence for the UK 1961–1977, *National Institute Economic Review*, 85, 31–9.

HENRY, S. G. B., SAWYER, M. C. and SMITH, P. (1976), Models of Inflation in the UK: An Evaluation, *National Institute Economic Review* 77, 60–71.

MINFORD, A. P. L. (1983). Labour Market Equilibrium in an Open Economy, *Oxford Economic Papers*, this issue.

PARKIN, M., SUMNER, M. T. and WARD, R. (1976), The Effects of Excess Demand, Generalized Expectations and Wage-Price Controls on Wage Inflation in the UK, 1956–71, in Brunner, K. and Meltzer, A. H. (eds.), *The Economics of Price & Wage Controls*, Carnegie-Rochester Conference Series on Public Policy, 2, North-Holland, Amsterdam.

PATTERSON, K. D. (1982), A Simple Non-Stationary Markov Model of the Transition between Mutually Exclusive Groups: Modelling the End of the Money Illusion, *Oxford Bulletin of Economics and Statistics* 44, 305–20.

PHILLIPS, A. W. (1958), The Relationship between Unemployment and the Rate of Change of Money Wage Rates in the UK, 1861–1957, *Economica*, N.S. *25*, 283–99.

SUMNER, M. T. (1978), Wage Determination, in Parkin, M. and Sumner M. T. (eds.), *Inflation in the United Kingdom*, Manchester University Press and University of Toronto Press.

SUMNER, M. T. and ZIS, G. (1982), On the Relative Bias of Flexible Exchange Rates, in Sumner, M. T. and Zis, G. (eds.), *European Monetary Union: Progress and Prospects*, Macmillan, London.

WILES, P. J. D. (1973), Cost Inflation and the State of Economic Theory, *Economic Journal* 83, 377–98.

PRIVATE COSTS AND BENEFITS OF UNEMPLOYMENT: MEASURING REPLACEMENT RATES

By A. W. DILNOT and C. N. MORRIS*

I

RECENT years have seen rapid rises in levels of unemployment in the UK and elsewhere, and a growing interest in the relationship between benefit levels and income in work. On the policy front, fears that incentives to seek or retain work were being blunted by an over-generous benefit system have contributed to decisions to abolish earnings related supplements to Unemployment Benefit, to cut the real value of Unemployment Benefit, and, most recently, to tax it. In the academic literature, the development of models of the determinants of unemployment duration employs a search theory technique in which the key element is the individual's choice of 'reservation wage'. Recent examples are studies by Maki and Spindler (1975), Nickell (1979), Lancaster (1979), Burdett (1979), Atkinson *et al.* (1982), and Feldstein and Poterba (1982). A major factor in the individual's choice of reservation wage in these studies is the ratio of net income if unemployed to that in work. Some commentators (for example, Minford (1983)) have used calculations of these 'replacement rates' for specific individuals to claim that excessive benefit levels are a major cause of the current high levels of unemployment.

Although in this paper we focus on replacement rates as an essential element in the unemployment duration literature, it is clear that their correct specification is also necessary for the more general problem of intertemporal labour supply. Ever since Lucas and Rapping (1970), models in this area have regarded labour supply as that supply of labour which is forthcoming at a given set of wages and prices, but few explicitly recognise the role of the changing tax and benefit system.

The importance of benefit incomes to work incentives, and the number of people who would be nearly as well off if unemployed is a subject of continuing controversy. The debate centres on the measurement of 'replacement rates', which compare net incomes in and out of work for a given individual. Because the benefit system is complex, and because it interacts with the tax system, the calculation of replacement rates is complicated, and can vary significantly between individuals with the same income.

This complexity has led to a wide variety of replacement rates, which we consider in Section II, and has led some commentators to observe[1] that

* The work described in this paper forms part of the IFS project on the Distributional Effects of Fiscal Policy, financed by the Gatsby Foundation. The authors are very grateful to John Kay, Richard Disney, and two anonymous referees for helpful comments; any errors remain our own.
[1] See, for example, Atkinson and Rau (1982) and Davies *et al.* (1982).

there are a large number of possible ways of measuring them, each suited to answering a different question.

We consider that this view is mistaken. The effect on family incomes of a given length spell of unemployment is a question which has, in principle, a well-defined and unambiguous answer. At any point in time, each individual has an expected income stream if employed and an expected income stream if unemployed. The actual estimation of the two streams may cause problems (not least for the individual concerned), because of the complexity of the calculations necessary and the uncertainty of future events, but the principle of what such an estimation should be is clear. The theoretical basis for replacement rates is developed in Section III.

The second controversy over replacement rates is not about what such a rate should measure, but over the number of individuals with sufficiently high replacement rates to affect work incentives significantly. The net income which an individual can expect if unemployed varies with his housing costs, the position in the tax year, any previous unemployment history, the number of his children, and so on. Much of the debate is carried on by comparing replacement rates for specific individuals. The problem with this is that one can 'prove' virtually anything by such a method, depending on the specific case chosen. The only way to get a clear picture of the importance of replacement rates is to estimate them for a large and representative sample of individuals.

In Section IV we present the results of such an estimation, whereby individual replacement rates are calculated for all family units in the Family Expenditure Survey. Both the absolute levels of replacement rates, and the ways in which these have changed over the period are of interest; we have estimated distributions of replacement rates for households interviewed in the years 1968, 1975, 1978 and 1980 (the latest year's data available). Changes in level of replacement rate are caused not only by changes to the tax and benefit system, but also by changes in the demographic, income and expenditure structure of the population. We have therefore simulated the effect of the changing tax and benefit system on a constant population base; this includes simulating recent changes such as the taxation of unemployment benefit and the abolition of Earnings Related Supplements.

We conclude that average replacement rates rose between 1968 and 1978, partly because incomes in work were depressed by increased direct taxation and partly because of changes to the benefit system, but that much of the rise was due to population changes. They have fallen since 1978, and short-term rates have fallen steeply in the last two years.

Various terms referring to replacement rates have been used in the literature. Here we define an average replacement rate as referring to the average financial penalty from a completed spell of s weeks of unemployment, a marginal replacement rate as referring to the financial penalty resulting from an additional period of unemployment, a short-term rate as referring to a short period of unemployment (where s is 4 or 13 weeks, say) and long term to periods of a year or more. The choice of replacement rate when considering an individual's decision to retain or leave employment depends on the expected frequency of wage offers; this is discussed further in Section III.

In 1980, a combination of Earnings Related Supplements (ERS) and tax rebates meant that short-term average rates were considerably higher than long-term; some 12% of family heads faced average short-term replacement rates in excess of 90%. Because the benefit system is geared to providing for needs, such as children, it is families with children that face the highest rates; many fewer single people have replacement rates in excess of 90% than do families. The policy changes of abolition of ERS and taxation of Unemployment Benefit, combined with further cuts in the real level of Unemployment Benefit have significantly reduced average replacement rates in the short-term.

However, these calculations of average rates may underestimate the effect at the margin, as they contain low benefit receipt in the first weeks of unemployment. Once an individual is unemployed, it is the marginal rate which is relevant to his employment decision. This examines the financial penalty from an additional week of unemployment. Marginal rates are higher than average rates for a four week period and considerably lower for a 52 week period. In 1980, over 15% of the employed population had marginal rates in excess of 90% for the fifth week, although this has been significantly reduced by recent policy changes. In contrast, very few (some 2%) had long-term marginal rates in excess of 90%.

II

Over the last eight years, interest in the concept and measurement of replacement rates has grown steadily. Measures comparing incomes in and out of work have been used for policy purposes and in econometric models examining the determinants of unemployment. In many cases the measures present simple calculations for specific households; these can be seriously misleading for they can only represent a particular case and not the myriad of circumstances which individuals actually face. In fewer cases attempts have been made to base estimates on actual households as represented in the Family Expenditure Survey or, more recently, in the DHSS Cohort Study of the Unemployed.

In the academic literature, replacement rates have been modelled mainly as variables in models of unemployment duration. The majority of such models have as their theoretical basis the 'search theory' of unemployment. The key assumptions of this theory are that the individual maximises the expected present value of his income, over an infinite horizon, that while unemployed he receives a constant rate of benefit b, that he has other income y, whether in or out of work. Job offers arrive randomly; these job offers, for jobs which are assumed to last for ever, are described by a constant wage w, giving a total income in work of $w + y$.

The individual accepts a job if the wage offered exceeds his reservation wage, w^*, at that point in time, chosen to maximise the present value of expected income, $V(w^*)$. If the individual becomes employed s periods hence, expected lifetime income is:

$$v(w^*, s) = b \int_0^s e^{-\rho u}\, du + \left. \bar{w} \right|_{w^*} \int_s^\infty e^{-\rho u}\, du \qquad (1)$$

where ρ is the individual's discount rate and $\left.\bar{w}\right|_{w^*}$ is the expected value of the wage offer conditional on its exceeding w^*. Nickell (1979) then uses (1) and assumes that benefits and the mean of the wage offer distribution move proportionately for different individuals, to show that the re-employment probability becomes a function of $b/\bar{w}$, where $\bar{w}$ is the mean of the complete wage offer distribution. Nickell recognises the inadequacy of assuming b and $\bar{w}$ are constant throughout the spell and tries various alternative empirical specifications in response to this.

Since Nickell, a number of authors have experimented with alternative specifications of b and w, usually by manipulating the basic algebra in (1) or introducing new factors. One (Atkinson et al. (1982)) introduces a term c for cost of search while unemployed, and re-employment probability becomes a function of $w - b$. Another extension (Burdett (1979)) introduces leisure; here the individual maximises the expected discounted sum of utility. In this formulation the choice of job search depends on the ratio $(b + y)/(w + y)$. The introduction of income tax into the expression generates (Atkinson et al. (1982)) still more possible forms. In the USA, a large number of studies of a similar nature have been carried out (see Hammermesh (1981)). Econometric evidence from the United States suggests that the main effect of unemployment insurance has been to influence the temporary lay-off decision of firms (Topel and Welch (1980)).

Search theory has been used, in general, to provide a justification for a particular form of the replacement rate, but the models are of necessity highly simplified, the assumptions required to justify each form are generally strong and the link between theory and subsequent empirical work weak. This has led many people to conclude that there is no such thing as the replacement rate for an individual and that a variety of possible candidates should be experimented with. Although it is clear that what should be included is the individual's expectation of the financial loss from unemployment, none of the measures reported in the literature include either expectations of changes to wages, benefits and taxes or attempt to discount the resulting income streams.[2]

The majority of the modelling that is reported in the academic literature focusses on the replacement rates of the unemployed population, a group

---

[2] King (1980) pointed out the importance of the discount rate in replacement rate measures and noted that 'in the conventional replacement ratio ... it is assumed to be infinite; in the Atkinson–Flemming (1978) marginal replacement ratio it is assumed to be zero!'

which has lower income in work than the average of the population. In order to get a picture of the overall effect of the tax and benefit system on work incentives, it is necessary to model replacement rates for both the employed and unemployed populations. The only study of which we are aware which attempts to do this systematically is that of Kay, Morris and Warren (1980). This considered replacement rates for households in the Family Expenditure Survey, as in the present paper, principally in order to examine the effects of the policy options of taxing benefits and cutting their real value. The major defect of this study was that it did not recognise that replacement rates involved a comparison between expected income streams. Individuals were treated as if their unemployment spell started at the beginning of a tax year and no discounting procedure was used, so that replacement rates were unaffected by the timing of net income receipts. Individuals were assumed to expect their current income if in work throughout the period, and that the tax and benefit systems would remain constant.

Perhaps the most widely quoted replacement rates are those calculated by the Department of Health and Social Security (DHSS) and reported twice a year in written parliamentary answers. These compare net weekly spending power (NWSP) when in work with NWSP out of work for specific individuals. They assume all benefit entitlements are taken up (including free school meals and welfare milk). They do not include income tax refunds, on the grounds that their receipt is not automatic;[3] this somewhat inconsistent approach has the effect of lowering replacement rates. However the main objection to these calculations is that they are specific and only cover a small number of cases, whereas those which, as in this paper, use large sample surveys recognise the heterogeneity of individual tax and benefit experience.

Recently DHSS have published[4] estimates of the replacement rates of households represented in the Cohort Study of the Unemployed. The individuals considered had been unemployed for at least three months, but had been employed at some time during the previous year; thus limiting the sample to 38% of the original cohort sample. The calculations were based on actual receipts and not estimated entitlements, and in neither case were tax rebates included. There are, however, a large number of factors which, when combined with the exclusion of income tax effects, mean that the estimates are somewhat misleading. The first is that the particular time period chosen—comparing incomes out of work immediately after a benefit uprating with incomes in work before—causes a significant upward bias to the replacement rates. This choice of time period also means that the sample

---

[3] The official explanation of this approach is that:
'It is not realistic to regard tax refunds as part of the regular weekly income of an unemployed person, since he does not automatically receive these refunds, and when payments are made, they usually occur at monthly intervals. Moreover, the payment of tax refunds will depend not only on the point of time in a tax year but also on the number of weeks employment during the tax year.' (HC, OR Vol 917 col 246) We do not understand this reasoning. In fact, tax refunds are automatic while benefits have to be claimed.

[4] Davies et al. (1982).

is not representative of the 'average' sample over a year—it contains relatively few school leavers, for example. The comparisons reported compare incomes during the second and third months of unemployment with incomes in work, thus giving a fairly rosy picture of replacement rates (they omit lower receipts during the earlier weeks, but choose a period during which ERS is being received). No account is taken of the possibility that the individual would have had a wage rise if he had remained employed. The estimates answer questions about the employment position of the currently unemployed. They also answer an ex post question, because other adjustments (such as the wife earning more in response to her husband's unemployment) have been made by the households. The timing of receipts is not taken into account; no attempt is made to discount the net income streams.

In a recent contribution, Narendranathan, Nickell and Stern (1982) have attempted to use the Cohort Study information to provide more robust estimates of unemployment duration. While this is a significant advance on the previous literature, the replacement rate variable (essentially the one described above) is still fairly naive; although the improved data provides better ex post information, their model is essentially forward looking, so a backward looking variable is mis-specified. A second problem is that the exclusion of subsequent expected tax refunds must cause a significant (downward) bias.

III

Consider an individual facing a choice between unemployment for a given spell or remaining in work. His expected income if continually in work will consist of his wages (plus any other income), any Family Income Supplement, Child Benefit, or Rent and Rate rebates to which he is entitled, less his tax, National Insurance and superannuation payments. The net income received in this spell will change if his income changes or if the spell crosses a tax year end or a benefit uprating. Denote this net income in any period t by $f(t)$. If instead he is unemployed for s weeks, his expected income will then consist of Unemployment Benefit (UB), and/or Supplementary Benefit (SB) plus any other income (including his wife's earnings, if any), plus Child Benefit and possibly rent and rate rebates. This income will change during the spell of unemployment.[5] The spell may cross a benefit uprating. Denote the net income during unemployment and on subsequent return to work by $g(t)$.

Some of the financial implications of a spell of unemployment extend beyond the period of unemployment itself. The most important of these in practice is its effect on future tax liabilities. We assume that all these factors have worked themselves out x weeks after unemployment ends.

---

[5] Benefit receipt follows the pattern of two 'waiting weeks', followed by 26 weeks with ERS, followed by 24 weeks of flat-rate UB (if he has had a previous spell of unemployment this pattern may start in the middle), followed by dependence on SB.

Then the financial loss caused by a spell of unemployment of s weeks, beginning in period $T+1$ will be

$$L = \int_{T}^{T+s+x} f(t)e^{-\rho t}\, dt - \int_{T}^{T+s+x} g(t)e^{-\rho t}\, dt \qquad (2)$$

where ρ is the individual's discount rate.

The higher is L, the less likely the individual is to choose unemployment. An exactly analogous calculation occurs for those unemployed at time T, here the higher is L, the more likely the individual is to choose re-employment.

Conventionally, the financial loss from unemployment is expressed as a replacement rate—the ratio of income out of work, g, to income in work, f. However f and g are functions of time. The average replacement rate for a spell of s weeks is R_s, where the financial loss from s weeks unemployment is equivalent in present value terms to a reduction in income from f to $R_s f$ for a period of s weeks. Thus R_s is defined by

$$R_s \int_{T}^{T+s} f(t)e^{-\rho t}\, dt + \int_{T+s}^{T+s+x} f(t)e^{-\rho t}\, dt = \int_{T}^{T+s+x} g(t)e^{-\rho t}\, dt \qquad (3)$$

solving for R_s gives:

$$R_s = \frac{\int_{T}^{T+s} g(t)e^{-\rho t}\, dt - \int_{T+s}^{T+s+x} (g(t)-f(t))e^{-\rho t}\, dt}{\int_{T}^{T+s} f(t)e^{-\rho t}\, dt} \qquad (4)$$

Although the actual form of the income streams $f(t)$ and $g(t)$ is somewhat complex and difficult to estimate, the replacement rate relevant to the employment choice is given unambiguously by (4). This measures the average replacement rate for a spell of s weeks beginning in period $T+1$, for an individual interviewed at time T.

As well as the average cost of a spell of unemployment, we are also interested in the marginal cost of an additional weeks unemployment. Suppose the income stream of someone unemployed for s weeks is $g(t)$ and that of someone unemployed for $s+1$ weeks is $g(t)$. Then the present value of the financial penalty from an additional week's unemployment (as seen from the individual's current position) on top of an existing spell of s weeks is:

$$L' = \int_{T}^{T+s+x} g(t)e^{-\rho t}\, dt - \int_{T}^{T+s+x} g'(t)e^{-\rho t}\, dt \qquad (5)$$

In the marginal case, the first s weeks are the same in both income streams, and the weeks from $T+s+2$ vary only in that tax refunds are different.

The principle followed for the average replacement rate was to compare the present value of the income derived from a spell of s weeks unemployment (including the value of any subsequent tax refunds) with the present value of the income derived from s weeks employment. In this case we cannot merely compare income in week $T+s+1$ under the two states; the previous spell of unemployment will have generated tax refunds which will artificially raise net income in that week in stream g. We therefore define $\bar{w}$ to be the constant real net income which generates the same present value as $g(t)$ from $T+s+1$ for ever, so that R', the marginal (one week) replacement rate conditional on a previous spell of s weeks unemployment becomes:

$$R' = 1 - \frac{\int_{T+s}^{T+s+x} g'(t)e^{-\rho t}\,dt - \int_{T+s}^{T+s+x} g(t)e^{-\rho t}\,dt}{\bar{w}} \tag{6}$$

or one minus the ratio of the financial penalty from an additional week's unemployment and $\bar{w}$.

Average and marginal replacement rates answer very different questions; for example it may be the case that, on average, spells of 12 and 13 weeks of unemployment produce high replacement rates while the 13th week on its own does not. The average replacement rate describes the incentive which an individual has to take, or retain, a job rather than contemplate an s week spell of unemployment. The marginal replacement rate describes the incentive which he will have, after s weeks of unemployment, to take work rather than remain unemployed for an additional week.

In fact, the average and marginal rates defined above are two special cases of a matrix of replacement rates for each individual, $R(s, m)$, where s is the spell of unemployment preceding that considered and m the extra period considered. Average rates in this notation are then the special case $R(0, m)$ and marginal rates $R(s, 1)$. $R(26, 52)$, for example, would reflect the financial penalty from 52 weeks of unemployment following a 26 week spell.

We believe that the definition of replacement rates offered in this section is that which should be included in the models of unemployment duration considered in Section II. In particular, if the individual expects job offers to arrive with an average frequency of once every m weeks, then the 'marginal' replacement rate $R(s, m)$ is the relevant measure governing his choice of taking a job now or waiting for the next offer. The marginal replacement rate $R(s, 1)$ reported in Section IV is the relevant measure if job offers arrive frequently.

IV

We now turn to the empirical estimation of average and marginal replacement rates as defined in (4) and (6). This hinges on the calculation of expected net income if in work, $f(t)$, and if out of work, $g(t)$, for the full sample of family units where the head is in full time employment in each year's Family Expenditure Survey.[6] The replacement rates reported assume full take-up of benefit entitlement[7] (we explore the relaxation of this and other assumptions later in this section), and that the individual expects all benefits to be uprated by the year-on-year change in the Retail Prices Index (RPI) in November, and the tax system to be indexed, again by year-on-year RPI, in April. We have no direct information on the date of the individual's annual pay award. so the distributions reported here calculate four replacement rates, each assuming the pay rise occurs in one of the four quarters of the year for each individual and assign a probability[8] to each dependent on the individuals' industry group. Similarly, we have no information as to whether an individual is contracted-in or -out of the State Earnings Related Pension Scheme (SERPS), so for those years where contracting out was possible we calculate two replacement rates and assign a probability to each dependent on the individual's occupation and industry group.

The replacement rates calculated refer to the ratio of net incomes; no account is taken of work expenses (which would raise replacement rates but about which we have little information) or of discretionary benefits, although the main passport benefits (free school meals and welfare milk) are included. In the absence of information about individuals' personal discount rates,[9] we employ a net real rate of return of zero to discount the income streams. Appendix D of Dilnot and Morris (1982) contains a stylised example of the calculation of a replacement rate for an individual.

The replacement rates calculated here refer to the position of the family head. Although existing spouses earnings are taken into account in all the calculations the implicit assumption is that he/she will not alter earnings etc. during a period of unemployment of the head.

We begin by examining the position of employed family heads in 1980, in Table 1. At that time Earnings Related Supplement (ERS) was still in existence, and tax refunds were payable during spells of unemployment, although the real value of unemployment benefit was cut by 5% in November 1980. On average, family heads in the working population could expect 71% of their discounted net income if unemployed for 4 weeks, and 66% if unemployed for 52 weeks beginning the week after interview. The 52 week replacement rates do in general contain 26 weeks of ERS, which means they are higher than estimates relating to the very long term, for which the 53rd week marginal rate is a better indicator.

---

[6] Details of the sample used and the calculations described in this section are given in the Appendix.

[7] The calculation of benefit entitlement is somewhat complex (and described in the Appendix); in particular it may depend on the previous employment history of the individual concerned.

[8] This probability reflects the timing pattern of wage settlements in each industry and is based on the Incomes Data Services '1978 Review of Settlements'. The actual matrices used are reproduced in Appendix C of the Working Paper.

[9] We report results assuming work expenses are a uniform 5% of net income later in the section. In fact, this is a high figure. For further discussion see Atkinson and Micklewright (1982).

PRIVATE COSTS AND BENEFITS OF UNEMPLOYMENT

TABLE 1
Distributions of average replacement rates in 1980

% with RR	length of unemployment spell (weeks)		
	4	13	52
Up to 0.4	2.5	1.4	4.7
0.4 –0.5	8.3	6.6	11.9
0.51–0.6	15.6	13.7	19.3
0.61–0.7	21.6	20.5	24.9
0.71–0.8	23.9	25.4	22.0
0.81–0.9	16.9	20.4	12.3
0.91–1.0	7.5	9.1	3.9
Over 1.0	3.7	2.9	1.0
Average RR	0.708	0.727	0.657

TABLE 2
The variation average of replacement rates by the type of family in 1980; 13 week unemployment spell

	Average RR	% with RR >0.9	% with RR <0.5
Single	0.661	8.5	19.2
One-parent families	0.750	13.6	3.8
Couples	0.746	9.6	3.4
Couples +1 child	0.755	14.1	1.7
Couples +2 children	0.773	17.2	1.0
Couples +3+ children	0.822	30.2	0.6
Overall	0.727	12.0	8.0

TABLE 3
The variation of replacement rates by range of earnings in 1980: 13 week unemployment spell

	Average RR	% with RR >0.9	% with RR <0.5
Up to 75% average	0.813	28.0	0.2
76%–150% average	0.721	7.4	9.5
Over 150% average	0.596	0.7	20.7

TABLE 4
Distributions of 'marginal' replacement rates in 1980

	5th week	14th week	53rd week
Under 0.5	6.9	5.8	47.8
0.51–0.7	29.6	33.4	40.2
0.71–0.9	48.1	48.7	10.1
Over 0.9	15.4	12.1	1.9
Average RR	0.746	0.740	0.503

Just under 4% of individuals had replacement rates in excess of 100% for a four week period, and 1% for a 52 week period. The distributions present a different picture from previous estimates. Among other reasons this is because individuals whose unemployment spell includes a benefit uprating but not a pay rise will have higher replacement rates, and those whose spell includes a pay rise but not a benefit uprating lower replacement rates; there will be a wider dispersion of replacement rates than in estimates that do not include the expectation of tax, benefit, and wage increases.

The distribution of replacement rates varies widely between family units, largely because benefits are related to number of children and housing costs, while wages are not. Table 2 shows, for a 13 week unemployment spell, the average for different family types, and the number with replacement rates over 90%, and below 50%. Single people, who stand to receive smaller benefits, have lower average replacement rates, and large familes higher. Some 30% of couples with 3 or more children have replacement rates above 90%, compared with 8.5% of single people, and a very small proportion of large families have replacement rates below 50%.

This variation by family size has a corollary in that those with low earnings do not necessarily have high replacement rates. In Table 3 we examine how replacement rates vary by range of head earnings. Because many of our family heads are single people, over 70% of the group with earnings below 75% of average male manual earnings have replacement rates below 90%. This has important policy implications; high replacement rates are a function of family circumstances as well as earnings, so that policy changes aimed at reducing them need either to concentrate on increasing the income of families with children in work or reducing the incomes of these families out of work. Policy changes which affect all workers, such as changes to the tax system, are thus blunt instruments for this purpose.

The replacement rates so far examined are 'average rates'; that is they refer to the overall financial loss from an s week spell of unemployment. To individuals who have already been unemployed for a period, or who are considering how long such a period should be, it is the 'marginal' replacement rate which is relevant. This reflects the financial loss from an additional week's unemployment. In Table 4 we examine the distribution of marginal rates in 1980. The 'marginal' 53rd week rate is the limit to which average spells in excess of a year will tend; on average the working population has a 53rd week marginal rate of 0.5, and less than 2% have rates over 0.9. Short-term marginal rates tend to be higher than average rates, because benefit receipt is lower in the first four weeks of a spell.

We have also examined the development of replacement rates since 1968. To do this we have applied the tax and benefit systems in force during the relevant year to the FES sample for that year. Table 5 shows how average 13 week replacement rates, marginal 53rd week rates, and the proportions with high and low rates have moved over the period. The latest data available refers to 1980.

PRIVATE COSTS AND BENEFITS OF UNEMPLOYMENT

TABLE 5
The development of replacement rates over time

	13 week average			53rd week marginal		
	Average	% with >0.9	% with <0.5	Average	% with >0.9	% with <0.5
1968	0.751	15.1	3.6	0.457	5.0	56.8
1975	0.752	18.9	6.7	0.577	3.3	33.4
1978	0.808	27.3	3.6	0.623	4.7	22.5
1980	0.727	12.0	8.0	0.503	1.9	47.8

TABLE 6
The development of replacement rates over time with constant population (1980)

	13 week average			53rd week marginal		
	Average	% with >0.9	% with <0.5	Average	% with >0.9	% with <0.5
1968	0.870	35.2	0.5	0.537	2.8	30.7
1975	0.751	17.2	5.9	0.498	2.5	50.5
1978	0.790	21.0	2.3	0.519	2.2	44.0
1980	0.727	12.0	8.0	0.503	1.9	47.8
1982	0.597	3.2	28.0	0.510	2.2	52.3
1983	0.600	2.9	21.0	0.504	1.9	53.2

TABLE 7
The effects on replacement rates of various policy changes

	13 week average			53rd week marginal		
	Average	% with >0.9	% with >0.5	Average	% with >0.9	% with <0.5
1983 base	0.600	2.9	21.0	0.504	1.9	53.2
Allowance rise 6%	0.602	2.9	20.4	0.506	1.8	50.9
Base rate cut 1%	0.595	2.8	21.9	0.499	1.9	54.4
NI cut 1%	0.594	2.6	22.0	0.490	1.8	54.3
Child Ben. +£1.65	0.598	2.5	20.9	0.501	1.4	53.4

Over the period the benefit system became a little more generous relative to earnings, but the major change was the increased taxation of income in work both through income tax increases, and through increased National Insurance contributions. Benefits paid to those in work have also changed significantly with the development of housing benefits. The overall result was an increase in average and marginal replacement rates until 1978,[10] and a fall in 1980.

These changes in average and marginal rates over the period are partly a product of changes to the tax and benefit system and partly the result of

[10] Note that this is at variance with Nickell (1979) who states that replacement rates (according to Taylor's data) fall over the period. We see later that with a constant population base this statement would hold; however, demographic and other movements have led to an increase. The rise between 1975 and 1978 is partly due to the lower real value of ERS in 1975; because ERS is based on 'reckonable earnings' in a period before the current year, high inflation in preceding years erodes its real value.

changes to the income and demographic structure of the population and macroeconomic changes which affect previous employment history. In Table 6, we present the results of applying tax and benefit systems (in 1980 prices) for each year to the 1980 population. This provides an, albeit approximate, method of decomposing the change into system and population elements. In contrast to Table 5, it shows a fall in replacement rates between 1968 and 1978. If the population in 1968 had been the same as it was in 1980, replacement rates then would have been very much higher. The population changes, which have tended to increase replacement rates include significant increases in the proportion of net income spent on housing and an increase in the number of single person households. Alternatively, if the changes to the tax and benefit system which have occurred over the period had been faced by a constant (1968) population, then replacement rates would be lower than they now are.

The recent policy changes have continued the downward trend; although tax allowances have fallen in real terms, and National Insurance contributions increased, the combined effect of abolition of Earnings Related Supplement, the taxation of Unemployment Benefit and the cut in its real value more than offset this. In 1983, assuming the structure of the population to be that of 1980, the average 13 week replacement rate is 0.60 compared with 0.73 in 1980, and only 3% of individuals have replacement rates in excess of 90%. Marginal replacement rates rose slightly to 1982 (because of increases in direct taxation), but are now at a similar level to 1980.

There has been much recent debate on appropriate policy changes designed to lower replacement rates. In Table 7, we examine the effect, on the 1983 estimates, of various changes to the system, all of which cost around £1 billion per year to implement. The most effective method of reducing the average replacement rates is to cut the rate of National Insurance contributions. This is because these are paid only by those in work. A more effective way of reducing the numbers with high replacement rates is to increase Child Benefit (because this is taken into account for SB purposes it mainly benefits those in work). By far the least effective—and the most often suggested—is a rise in income tax allowances, which actually increases replacement rates. This is because, as benefits are now taxed, a rise in the allowance benefits, broadly, those working and those unemployed by the same money amount. It will thus raise the replacement rate of an individual who has lower income out of work.

The results reported so far have been based on a particular set of assumptions; individuals are assumed to expect receipt of all benefits to which they are entitled, to discount at the prevailing rate of inflation, to obtain the tax refunds due to them during spells of unemployment (received after six weeks at the beginning, then every four weeks), to expect indexation of the tax and benefit system and to expect pay rises. In Table 8 we report the results of sensitivity tests of the estimates, based on a 13 week period of unemployment.

TABLE 8
Sensitivity of replacement rate estimates to particular assumptions: 1980 13 week unemployment spell

	Average RR	% with RR >0.9	% with RR <0.5
Main Estimate.	0.727	12.0	8.0
No receipt of FIS or R+R. rebates at work	0.729	12.7	8.0
Personal discount rate 5% above inflation	0.717	9.1	16.7
No tax/wage/benefit rises expected.	0.734	13.3	13.2
Work expenses 5% gross wage.	0.814	35.3	8.7

   The exclusion of FIS and Rent and Rate rebates from the calculation of incomes in work has a small upward effect on replacement rates. There are not in fact many households in the employed population with large entitlements to either. Assuming a higher discount rate for the individual has the effect of lowering replacement rates; the value of subsequent tax refunds is smaller. Removing the assumption of tax, wage or benefit changes has ambiguous effects on replacement rates—benefit rises raise replacement rates while wage rises and tax system indexation lower it. Overall, the average replacement rate rises slightly, as does the proportion with RR's above 0.9. Excluding work expenses at 5% of gross income (a high figure) from net income in work, raises the average 13-week replacement rate, and the proportion with rates over 0.9 considerably.

   These observations allow us to make some comment on the likely bias, both in terms of direction and size, of the inadequate measures surveyed in Section II. Our major objections to these measures were that they failed to take account of expected future changes (these increase the dispersion of replacement rates and raise them slightly), that no discounting procedure was adopted (if the discount rate is zero, then replacement rates are biased upwards, if infinity then downwards) and that tax rebates are either ignored or inadequately treated (ignoring tax refunds unambiguously biases replacement rates downwards). They also allow us to compare our results with those using other assumptions; less-than-100% take-up of benefits in work has a small downward effect on the results, while including work expenses would increase the estimates.

   So far we have been considering the effect of unemployment on individuals who are currently employed. In Table 9, we report the results of analogous calculations for those who are unemployed at interview date. These individuals have on average lower wages in work than the average of the working population, leading to higher replacement rates. However, the existence of a previous unemployment spell means that entitlement to ERS or Unemployment Benefit is exhausted earlier, and tax refunds are lower.

TABLE 9
Replacement rates for the unemployed 1980

	Average RR	% with RR above 0.9	% with RR below 0.5
13 week average	0.660	12.9	35.7
53rd week marginal	0.556	6.1	54.0

The distribution of replacement rates for the unemployed population is more dispersed than that for the employed; those unemployed short-term have fairly high replacement rates, while the long-term unemployed, (who are dependent on SB and receive no ERS) have low ones. If the family has other income—for example if the spouse works—little or no benefit may be payable after a year's unemployment. The final result of all these effects is that the unemployed sample in 1980 had, on average, lower average replacement rates than those in the working population. The marginal replacement rate for the unemployed is, in contrast, somewhat higher. This is because the effects described above will be equally true of the working population after 52 weeks, and so the lower basic incomes of the unemployed swell the ratio.

V

What we have tried to do in this paper is specify and measure precisely the replacement rates that are relevant to individuals' employment decisions. Since we have found this exercise difficult, and have used a large amount of computer time to do so, it is doubtful that the unemployed have actually performed the same calculations; but this does not mean that popular perceptions of these relationships are not substantially influenced by what they really are.

We have estimated, over a large sample of employed and unemployed households, replacement rates on such a base. Over the period from 1968 to 1978, increases in direct taxation of income in work, changes in the benefit system, increases in housing costs, and demographic changes led, on balance, to an upward trend in replacement rates. In 1980, some 12% of individuals had 13 week average rates in excess of 0.9. Replacement rates for long periods of unemployment, both average and marginal, were much lower.

The recent policy changes of abolition of ERS and the taxation of Unemployment Benefit have significantly lowered short-term replacement rates, both average and marginal, but had little effect on long-term rates. Although short-term rates were high until these changes, long term rates never have been, and the percentage with replacement rates over 0.9 is now very low.

Institute for Fiscal Studies, London

APPENDIX

In this Appendix, we summarise the modelling of the tax and benefit system and the development of replacement rates. A fuller exposition is given in Dilnot and Morris (1982).

Our data source is the full Family Expenditure Survey for the years 1968, 1975, 1978 and 1980. This is a survey, carried out by the Office of Population Censuses and Surveys, of the income and expenditure of around 7000 households each year. Interviews are conducted throughout the year, with the interview period for any given household lasting two weeks. Income and Expenditure variables are thus those current at a particular date, although some retrospective information—such as benefit history—is also collected. Both income and expenditure information is available in a highly disaggregated form by source and commodity. The main results from the Family Expenditure Survey are published each year (e.g. HMSO (1980)); a full description of the survey is given in Kemsley, Redpath and Holmes (1980) and in the annual information packs available from the Department of Employment.

Considerable manipulation of the household data was performed by the authors before the commencement of the current exercise. Information on individuals within each household are used to divide the individuals into families for tax and benefit purposes. Retrospective information, particularly on employment history, is examined to create an estimate of taxable income so far this tax year.

The replacement rates calculated in this paper refer to the financial position of the head of the family unit; they are essentially static in nature and implicitly assume no response on the part of a spouse. Replacement rates for secondary earners are not considered. The base sample used is, for the 'working population' those family heads who are labelled 'in full-time employment' and aged less than the state pension age. For operational reasons, those with no information as to industry or employment status are also excluded. The definition excludes the self-employed. The exclusion of pensioners and other groups limits the sample to 50% of all family heads in 1980. The 'unemployed' population are those who are labelled 'out of employment but seeking work', and exclude those 'temporarily away' and those labelled 'unoccupied'.

For each family unit in the base sample we then derive the following magnitudes at time t, the date of interview.

w	'normal' wage for currently unemployed/current for working
u	previous weeks off work in last 52
m	mortgage interest
c	total number of children
c_i	number of children in 4 age groups, $i = 1, 4$
r	rent
ra	rates
wi	existence of wife = 1 if yes, 0 if no
we	wifes earnings
y	other income
o	one parent status = 1 if yes, 0 if no
fis	current receipt of FIS, if any
$r + r$	current receipt of rent and rate rebates, if any
sb	current receipt of supplementary benefit, if any
ub	current receipt of unemployment benefit, if any
d	other deductible items (life insurance etc) for tax
i	contracted in/out indicator for SERPS (calculated by IFS) (1 if contracted in, 0 if out)
wa	allowance accumulated this tax year
ta	implied tax paid so far this tax year

At the date of interview, the parameters of the tax and benefit system are (all evaluated in weekly terms).

Income Tax

MA_t	Married Allowance
SA_t	Single Allowance
CTA_t	Child Tax Allowances
r_t	Basic Rate
$r_{t2}...r_{tr}$	Higher Rates
$b_{t2} ... b_{tm}$	Higher Rate Thresholds

(plus other parameters such as investment income ceiling and surcharge).

National Insurance

LEL_t	Lower earnings limit
UEL_t	Upper earnings limit
$niin_t$	NI contracted-in rate
$niou_t$	NI contracted-out rate

Family Income Supplement

IL_t	Income limit for one child
IL_{tpc}	Income limit per additional child
MAX_t	Maximum receipt permitted for one child
MAX_{tpc}	Additional maximum receipt per additional child

Rent & Rate Rebates

NA_{ts}	Needs allowance—single
NA_{tm}	Needs allowance—married
NA_{tpc}	Needs allowance per child
D_{th}	Disregard—head
D_{tw}	Disregard—wife
MAX_{tr}	Maximum receipt of rent rebate permitted (varies by region)
MAX_{tra}	Maximum receipt of rate rebate permitted (varies by region)

Unemployment Benefit

UB_{ts}	Single UB rate
UB_{tm}	Married UB rate
UB_{tpci}	($i = 1, 4$) child addition depending on age

Earnings Related Supplement (ERS)

ERS_{tb}	ERS floor
ERS_{tc1}	First ERS ceiling
ERS_{tc2}	Second ERS ceiling
ERS_{tr2}	First ERS rate
$ERSMX$	Maximum ERS as % flat rate

Free School Meals + Free Welfare Milk

FSM	Weekly value per child
FW^tM_t	Weekly value per child

Child Benefit

CB_t	Child Benefit per child
OCB_t	One parent addition to Child Benefit

Supplementary Benefit

SB_{ts}	Single SB rate
SB_{tm}	Married SB rate
SB_{tci}	Child addition depending ($i = 1, 4$) on age

Family Allowance

FAM_{tci} ($i = 1, 3$)	Allowance per child, depending on whether 1st, second, or third or subsequent child
FAM_{tD}	Clawback of tax allowance per child

At time t, given these rules and assuming no previous spell of unemployment; we calculate

i) *Weekly Income Tax* if A_t is allowance (dependent on marital status, age, age of spouse, age of children pre-1979)

let $TY = w + y - A_t - m - d + \max((we - SA_t, 0), 0)$

so income tax is $TY * r_t$ for $TY \leqslant b_{t2}$

$$b_{t2} * r_t + (TY + b_{t2}) * r_{t2} \quad \text{for} \quad b_{t2} < TY \leqslant b_{t2}$$

and so on.

The cumulative tax system operates as follows:

1. If, during the tax year, the individual has either not worked or received less income than he has accumulated allowances (ua) then he pays no tax until his cumulative liability (cl) exceeds $ua * r_t$
2. If he reaches the end of the tax year before $cl = ua * r_t$, any remaining ua is lost

3. If the individual has paid tax so far this tax year, but now becomes unemployed, he is entitled to a tax refund of $A_t * r_t$ for each week until $A_t * r_t > ta$ where ta is tax paid so far in the tax year. In practice, this refund is paid, on average, every four weeks and for short spells of unemployment is not paid until re-employment, when if the correct forms are exchanged etc, the refund will be paid (either directly or as a reduction in tax liability for the next period) in the next pay period. In empirical modelling for $A_t * r_t > ta$ we assume a full refund one week after return to work. During a long period of unemployment, we assume the first refund is paid after six weeks, followed by payments every four weeks.

National Insurance contributions are

$$i * w * niin_t + (1-i) * ((w - LEL_t) * niout_t + LEL_t * niin_t) \quad \text{for} \quad LEL_t < w \le UEL_t$$

$$0 \quad \text{for} \quad w \le LEL_t$$

$$i * UEI_t * niin_t + (1-i) * ((UEL_t - LEL_t) * niout_t + LEL_t * niin_t) \quad \text{for} \quad w > UEL_t$$

Benefits in Work
Family income supplement

$$IL = IL_t + IL_{tpc}$$

$$MAX = MAX_t + MAX_{tpc}(c-1)$$

$$FIS = \max(0, \min(MAX, ((IL - w - we \div y) \times 0.5)))$$

Child Benefit

$$cb = CB_t \times c + OCB_t \times o$$

Rent and Rate Rebates

$$NA = NA_{ts} + wi(NA_{tm} - NA_{ts}) + cNA_{tpc}$$

$$Y = \max((w - D_{th}), 0) + \max((we - D_{tw}), 0) + y + cb + F1)$$

$$\text{Rent rebate} = \min(MAX_{tr}, \min(r, 0.6r + (NA - Y) \times 0.25)) \quad \text{if} \quad NA > Y$$

$$= \min(MAX_{tr}, \min(r, 0.6r + (NA - Y) \times 0.17)) \quad \text{if} \quad NA \le Y$$

$$\text{Rate rebate} = \min(MAX_{tra}, \min(ra, 0.6ra + (MA - Y) \times 0.08)) \quad \text{if} \quad NA > Y$$

$$= \min(MAX_{tra}, \min(ra, 0.6ra + (NA - Y) \times 0.06)) \quad \text{if} \quad MA \le Y$$

Free School Meals + Free Welfare Milk

$$\text{If} \quad FIS > 0 \qquad FSM = FSM_t \times \text{number of children aged} > 5$$

$$FWM = FWM_t \times \text{number of children aged} < 5$$

Benefits while unemployed

SB_t supplementary benefit scale rate applicable to family
UB_t Unemployment benefit flat rate applicable to family
$R + R_t$ Rent and rate rebates (see below) given $UB + ERS + y$
ERS_t Earnings related supplement applicable to family

$$SB_t = SB_{ts} + wi(SB_{tm} - SB_{ts}) + \sum_{i=1}^{4} C_i \times SB_{tpc_i} + r + ra - y - we - cb$$

$$UB_t = UB_{ts} + wi(UB_{tm} - UB_{ts}) + \sum_{i=1}^{4} C_i \times UB_{tpc_i}$$

$ERS_t = 0 \quad$ (if $w < ERS_{tb}$)

$\quad = (w - ERS_{tb}) \times ERS_{tr1} \quad$ (if $ERS_{tb} \leqslant w < ERS_{tc1}$)

$\quad = (ERS_{tc1} - ERS_{tb}) \times ERS_{tr1} + \min(((w - ERS_{tc1}) \times ERS_{tr2}), (ERS_{tc2} - ERS_{tc1}) \times ERS_{trs})$

(otherwise)

1. If the individual has a short previous unemployment record and is currently receiving *SB*, but not *UB*, we assume he has an incomplete contribution record and that he claims *SB* in future.
2. If the individual has a long previous unemployment record and is currently receiving *SB* but not *UB* we assume he has exhausted his *UB* entitlement in this spell and is therefore entitled to *SB*.
3. If the individual is currently receiving *UB*, we wish to know his position in the benefit cycle and entitlement to *ERS*. For the currently unemployed we assume that all weeks unemployment in the last 52 weeks are one spell or two or more linked spells, so that previous weeks of unemployment position us in the cycle.

He may be entitled to rent and rate rebates or supplementary benefit.

$$\text{BENEFIT} = UB + ERS_t + \max(SB, R + R)$$

For those currently working, with less than 39 weeks in the past 52 unemployed, we assume any period of unemployment is not linked with the period considered.

The above gives us a full picture of net income at time *t*, given complete adherence to the tax and benefit rules:

Net income for those working $= w + y + we + cb + FIS + R + R + FSM + FWm - TAX - NIC = NY_w$

Net income for those unemployed $= \text{BENEFIT} + y + cb + we = NY_u$

Similar calculations are performed for every week from time *t* for the family unit under two states, one with an unemployment spell of *s* weeks followed by employment, the other continuously working. At any point, the parameters for this evaluation may change. In the week beginning April 6th, the tax and NI system is assumed to be indexed from its state at time *t* by the annual increase in the RPI at that date, and to continue like this until the subsequent April. In the week the uprating occurred last year the benefit system is also assumed to be indexed and to remain so until the following October/November. A pay rise may also occur, although we do not know when.

The procedure adopted is to calculate four replacement rates, each assuming the pay rise occurs in the first week of each quarter and use these, weighted by the proportion of settlements occurring in that quarter for industry of the head in examining the final distribution.

BIBLIOGRAPHY

ATKINSON, A. B. and FLEMMING, J. S. (1978), "Unemployment, Social Security and Incentives", *Midland Bank Review*, Autumn pp. 6–16.
ATKINSON, A. B. (1980), "Unemployment Benefits and Incentives". Taxation, Incentives and Distribution of Income Project. Paper 11, July.
ATKINSON, A. B. and MICKLEWRIGHT, J. (1981), "Unemployment and 'Replacement Rates'", Unemployment Project, Working Note No. 8.
ATKINSON, A. B. and MICKLEWRIGHT, J. (1982), "Work expenses and replacement rate calculations", Unemployment Project, Working Note 13.
ATKINSON, A. B., GOMULKA, J., MICKLEWRIGHT, J. and RAU, N. (1982), "Unemployment Duration, Social Security and Incentives" (forthcoming *J. Pub. Econ*).

ATKINSON, A. B. and RAU, N. (1981), "The Specification of Income Taxation and Benefits in Models of Unemployment", Duration Unemployment Project Note No. 9.

BECK, J. H. (1982), "Perverse Effects of Partial Taxation of Unemployment Benefits", *National Tax Journal*, Vol. 35, No. 2 June.

BOADWAY, R. W. and OSWALD, A. J. (1983), "Unemployment Insurance and Redistributive Taxation", *Journal of Public Economics*.

BURDETT, K. (1979), "Search, Leisure and Individual Labour Supply", in Lippman & McCall, *Studies in the Economics of Search*. North Holland, Amsterdam.

DAVIES, R., HAMILL, L., MOYLAN, S. and SMEE, C. H. (1982), "Incomes in and out of work", *Employment Gazette*, June 1982 Vol. 90, No. 6.

DILNOT, A. W. and MORRIS, C. N. (1982), "Modelling Replacement Rates", Institute for Fiscal Studies Working Paper 39.

FELDSTEIN, M. and POTERBA, J. (1982), "Unemployment Insurance and Reservation Wages", (forthcoming *J. Pub. Econ.*).

HAMMERMESH, D. S. (1981), "Transfers, Taxes and the NAIRU", in Meyer, L. H. ed., *The Supply Side Effects of Economic Policy*.

HECKMAN, J. J., KILLINGSWORTH, M. R. and MACURDY, T. (1981), "Empirical Evidence on Static Labour Supply Models: A Survey of Recent Developments", in Hunskin *et al.*, *Economics of the Labour Market*, HMSO.

HMSO (1980), Family Expenditure Survey 1980.

KAY, J. A., MORRIS, C. N. and WARREN, N. A. (1980), "Tax, Benefits and the Incentive to Seek Work", *Fiscal Studies*, Vol. 1, No. 4 November 1980.

KEMSLEY, REDPATH, R. and HOLMES, (1980), "Family Expenditure Survey: A handbook of Fieldwork and Coding Procedures", HMSO.

KING, J. (1980), Replacement Ratios, "Inland Revenue Central Division", (unpublished note).

LANCASTER, T. (1979), "Econometric Methods for the Duration of Unemployment", *Econometrica*, Vol. 47, pp. 939–956.

MAKI, D. and SPINDLER, B. A. (1975), "The Effect of Unemployment Compensation of the rate of Unemployment in Great Britain", Oxford Economic Papers, Vol. 27, (November) pp. 40–54.

MINFORD, P. (1982), "The Development of Monetary Strategy in 'The 1982 Budget' ", ed. J. A. Kay, IFS/Blackwells.

MINFORD, P. (1983), "Unemployment Cause and Cure", Martin Robertson, Oxford.

NARENDRANATHAN, W., NICKELLS, S., and STERN, J. (1982), "Unemployment Benefits Revisited," Centre for Labour Economics LSE, Working Paper 462.

NICKELL, S. J. (1979), "The Effect of Unemployment and Related Benefits on the Duration of Unemployment", *Economic Journal*, Vol. 89 (March).

NICKELL, S. J. (1979a), "Estimating the Probability of Leaving Unemployment", *Econometrica*, Vol. 47, pp. 1249–1266.

TOPEL, R. and WELCH, F. (1980), "Unemployment Insurance: Survey and Extensions", *Economica*, **47,** 351–379.

WARREN, N. A. (1980), "Unemployment Compensation and Work incentives", IFS Working Paper No. 17.

LIST OF CONTRIBUTORS

C. A. GREENHALGH, University of Oxford

P. R. G. LAYARD, Centre for Labour Economics, London School of Economics

A. J. OSWALD, University of Oxford

MICHAEL BRUNO, Hebrew University and National Bureau of Economic Research

JEFFREY SACHS, Harvard University and National Bureau of Economic Research

D. GRUBB, Centre for Labour Economics, London School of Economics

R. JACKMAN, Centre for Labour Economics, London School of Economics

MARTIN ANDREWS, London School of Economics

STEPHEN NICKELL, London School of Economics

ORLEY ASHENFELTER, Princeton University

DAVID CARD, University of Chicago

JOSEPH G. ALTONJI, Columbia University

KIM B. CLARK, Harvard University and National Bureau of Economic Research

LAWRENCE H. SUMMERS, Massachusetts Institute of Technology and National Bureau of Economic Research

P. MINFORD, Liverpool University

D. SNOWER, Birkbeck College, London

L. LYNCH, Bristol University

B. McCORMICK, Southampton University

M. T. SUMNER, University of Salford

R. WARD, University of Salford

C. N. MORRIS, Institute for Fiscal Studies

A. W. DILNOT, Institute for Fiscal Studies